Preparing to Teach Texas Content Areas

The TExES EC-6 Generalist and the ESL Supplement

SECOND EDITION

Janice L. Nath
University of Houston—Downtown

John M. Ramsey
University of Houston

Boston   Columbus   Indianapolis   New York   San Francisco   Upper Saddle River
Amsterdam   Cape Town   Dubai   London   Madrid   Milan   Munich   Paris   Montreal   Toronto
Delhi   Mexico City   Sao Paulo   Sydney   Hong Kong   Seoul   Singapore   Taipei   Tokyo

Vice President and Editor in Chief: Jeffery W. Johnston
Publisher: Kavin M. Davis
Editorial Assistant: Lauren Carlson
Vice President, Director of Marketing: Margaret Waples
Senior Marketing Manager: Christopher Barry
Senior Managing Editor: Pamela D. Bennett
Senior Operations Supervisor: Matt Ottenweller
Senior Project Manager: Mary M. Irvin
Senior Art Director: Diane Lorenzo
Cover Designer: Candace Rowley
Cover Art: Foto Search
Full-Service Vendor: Niraj Bhatt, Aptara®, Inc.
Composition: Aptara®, Inc.
Printer/Binder: RR Donnelley
Cover Printer: RR Donnelley
Text Font: Stone Serif

Credits and acknowledgments borrowed from other sources and reproduced, with permission, in this textbook appear on appropriate page within text.

Every effort has been made to provide accurate and current Internet information in this book. However, the Internet and information posted on it are constantly changing, so it is inevitable that some of the Internet addresses listed in this textbook will change.

Library of Congress Cataloging-in-Publication Data

Nath, Janice L.
 Preparing to teach Texas content areas: the TExES ED-6 *Generalist* and the ESL supplement / Janice L. Nath, John M. Ramsey. — 2nd ed.
  p. cm.
 ISBN-13: 978-0-13-704028-5
 ISBN-10: 0-13-704028-8
  1. Elementary school teachers—Certification—Texas—Study guides.   2. Elementary school teachers—Texas—Examinations—Study guides.   3. English language–Study and teaching—Foreign speakers.
I. Ramsey, John M. II. Title.
 LB1763.T4P755 2011
 372.11209764—dc22

2010021780

www.pearsonhighered.com

ISBN 13: 978-0-13-704028-5
ISBN 10:   0-13-704028-8

This book is dedicated to the memory of one of our authors and friends, Dr. W. Joe Kortz. Joe was an incredible educator whose energy and love of education has touched many lives and will continue to do so through his words.

Preface

History

The Texas State Board for Educator Certification (SBEC) implemented a new teacher examination testing program in 2002 that supplanted the ExCETs (Examination for the Certification of Educators in Texas), the testing program that had been in place for Texas educators since 1986. These new tests were named the Texas Examinations for Educator Standards (TExES). The main purpose for change was a more seamless and cohesive alignment between educator certification and the mandated student curriculum (the Texas Essential Knowledge and Skills [TEKS]). A special P-16 Initiative brought together SBEC, the Texas Education Agency (which regulates elementary and secondary public education), and the Texas Higher Education Coordinating Board (which oversees higher education) to initiate these new tests for many content areas and for the *Pedagogy and Professional Responsibilities (PPR)*.

National Evaluation Systems (a private educational testing corporation) developed the TExES under contract from SBEC, but the state awarded its testing contract to Educational Testing Service (ETS) in 2006 with the understanding that, for the time, the testing framework would not change. ETS continues to provide testing sites (both for paper-and-pencil and computer exams) and scoring of these examinations.

The redesigned testing program was based on educator standards that defined the rigorous content and professional knowledge and skills that an entry-level educator should possess. This book is focused on preparing prospective teachers for one of the certification examinations, the EC-6 *Generalist* examination for content areas in each of the five domains: English language arts and reading; mathematics; social studies; science; and the fine arts, health, and physical education. This book also offers a chapter to help in obtaining a supplemental certificate to teach ESL. Many districts in Texas now require this certificate within a stipulated time after being hired or even prior to being hired.

The Audience: The Prospective Teacher for EC-6 Children

This book is intended for those who are seeking certification to teach younger children (EC-6) in Texas. These prospective teachers must meet an array of quality and preparation criteria, including at least two state-administered examinations (the PPR and the *Generalist*) and, perhaps, the ESL supplemental. This book addresses the standards, competencies, and associated content of the *Generalist* and the ESL examinations. The *Generalist* standards and competencies require knowledge and skills associated with early childhood and elementary curricular content developed directly from the TEKS (for children) and appropriate learning and assessment practices. The second examination that is specifically required for EC-6 certification is the *Pedagogy and Professional Responsibilities* (PPR) examination, which focuses specifically on the knowledge and skills associated with classroom pedagogy and professional ethics. If you are also studying for the PPR test, we recommend *Becoming an EC-6 Teacher in Texas,* edited by J. Nath and M. Cohen (2011).

Content: *Generalist* Subject Areas

This book is a preparation resource that can be used as either a primary source text or a supplemental review guide for this examination. Note that this book is not a TEA (Texas Education Agency) publication; rather, it is an effort by experienced and dedicated educators to contribute to the certification process for the benefit of the state's prospective teachers and their students. These educators are fully aware that passing this examination is not all that is needed to make a good teacher. Each of these authors has seen a number of wonderful teacher candidates who may not have passed the state examinations easily, but who teach outstanding lessons with children. However, we do submit that this is excellent information for any teacher of children to know.

Seven areas of content knowledge align solidly with the TEKS (the basic mandated student curriculum of the state of Texas): reading/language arts, mathematics, science, social studies, art, music, and health/physical education. Three additional chapters—one on teaching theatre arts, one on preparing for the English as a second language (ESL) exam, and a study skills chapter—assist examination takers in the preparation process.

Each chapter is organized around the standards for that subject area. The chapter presents the standards, a list or summary of the competencies with discussion, an overview of the related knowledge base (i.e., the facts, concepts, skills, and appropriate practices), practice examination questions and discussion, an example lesson plan, a blank form for writing your own lesson plan, and an observation form for the classroom. However, due to the nature of each content area's standards and competencies, each chapter also has its own unique organization. For example, some subject areas have more standards than competencies, whereas others have more competencies than standards. In some chapters these will be summarized, and in others, they are listed precisely. Thus, the length and organization of each chapter varies.

Standards refers to broad, general goal statements related to each content area. They serve as an inclusive "umbrella" for that particular subject. **Competencies** are akin to objectives, operationalizing each standard into a number of more specific sub-components of knowledge, skills, and appropriate practices. In some chapters, these competencies are paraphrased from the official text published by SBEC due to the length or redundancy of the competencies.

The examination questions that are included both within chapters and at the end of each chapter use a multiple-choice format and are written at the comprehension, application, and analysis levels of Bloom's taxonomy. The content areas are not necessarily treated equally in terms of the number of questions for each. For example, the reading/language arts component of the examination represents about 40 percent of all examination questions. The mathematics, social studies, science, and combined fine arts, physical education, and health components, however, represent 15 percent each of all examination questions. Because there is no separate section for theatre arts on this examination, these questions are integrated with other content areas. The ESL questions are exclusively for the ESL examination rather than for the *Generalist* examination.

Rationale for This Book

Prospective Texas teachers currently come from all over the United States and the world. The quality and quantity of their educational experiences and cultural backgrounds vary to a significant extent. Their prior knowledge about the U.S. public school curricula also varies. However, Texas mandates its own statewide curricula and requirements for all teachers who seek certification in Texas. Texas history under the content area of social studies, for example, is a mandated curricular requirement, and Texas requires its teachers to have appropriate knowledge of that subject, regardless of other educational preparation and background. This book provides a resource tool for prospective Texas teachers to identify, review, or remediate the knowledge, skills, and appropriate practice required for the *Generalist* in all content areas covered by this examination. In addition and as mentioned, many districts are requiring their teachers to have completed an ESL certification prior to being hired or to obtain this supplemental certification as soon as they are able to do so. The ESL chapter provides a basic review for passing the ESL TExES—an area crucial for teachers who will increasingly find children in their classrooms from many countries and who speak languages other than English.

New to This Edition

- To align to the new Texas certification levels, fifth- and sixth-grade content has been added in every chapter.
  - New vocabulary
  - Concepts
  - Teaching skills
  - Questions
- Texas Essential Knowledge and Skills (TEKS) for children have been consulted for every chapter
- Texas Assessment of Knowledge and Skills (TAKS) information for fifth- and sixth-grade levels, the new *Generalist* standards and competencies, and new content area knowledge and research are now included in all chapters
- More technology coverage has been added throughout. Web site examples of concepts are included to strengthen author discussions
- Coverage of U.S. and world history has been increased and is more substantial
- Science and social studies coverage has been increased and is more substantial

The major addition to these chapters focuses on the added grades for the new Texas certification levels. Because some elementary schools include grades five and six in their buildings, the state believes that the new overlap in certification levels (EC-6 and 4–8) provide better coverage for Texas schools. Although the EC-6 level requires a *generalist* background (teaching all content areas), the 4–8 certification still requires specialization in a content area(s) and so is more suited to middle schools with subject area specializations. To add these two levels (fifth and sixth grade) to the book, authors reviewed the TEKS for children, TAKS information for these grade levels, the new *Generalist* standards and competencies, and new content area knowledge and research, after which they revised their chapters to include all these areas. Thus, considerable new vocabulary, concepts, teaching skills, and questions for these added grade levels are part of the additions. Technology has also been incorporated more in various chapters. For instance in the chapter on music, Web site examples of many concepts and types of music are given so that the reader may hear an example of what the author is discussing. In the art chapter, Web sites are provided for examples as well.

After you have read each chapter, we urge you to go back and read all the standards and the competencies and, as you do, question yourself to see if you know the information presented there as a check of your learning. In addition, read all the questions and the rationales for their answers, because many of them include information important to the content area chapters. New information is presented throughout the chapters, including the questions and in their answers.

Organization of This Book

This book is divided into 10 chapters. Chapter 1 presents generic study skills as well as study skills specific to this exam, along with examination preparation guidelines. Chapter 2 begins the content areas with language arts and reading, perhaps the most important chapter in this book, due to its emphasis of 40 percent on the *Generalist*. Chapter 3 offers information on mathematics; Chapter 4 covers social studies; Chapter 5 presents science; art is found in Chapter 6 and music in Chapter 7; Chapter 8 provides information on health and physical education; Chapter 9 imparts guidelines on theatre arts; and Chapter 10 discusses the ESL supplemental certification. Authors were tasked with offering as much content and other teaching information as possible, but all were restricted by length limitations. We hope that you continue to seek more content information, theories, and ideas for good teaching. Each chapter concludes with a lesson plan (demonstrating how to implement the content area in the classroom), a blank form to complete for your own lesson plan, a classroom observation instrument to help focus on best practices for that subject, and a number of questions to retest your knowledge and test-taking skills.

SBEC: Additional Background

If you have ever wondered who makes up the rules for certifying teachers, counselors, principals, superintendents, or any of the other professional roles in public schools, the answer is the State Board for Educator Certification (SBEC) in Texas, currently a part of the Texas Education Agency (TEA). Because education is one of the powers reserved to the states under the Tenth Amendment to the U.S. Constitution, each state is really responsible for much in its own system of public education, including decisions about who is licensed to teach in that state.

SBEC is the result of a 1995 action by the Texas Legislature. Its purpose is "to recognize public school educators as professionals and grant educators the authority to govern the standards of their profession" (TEA, 1995). This board is responsible to TEA and the Texas Legislature for overseeing all aspects of the preparation, assessment, certification, and standards of professional conduct of educators in the state's public schools and, in addition, for accountability of teacher preparation entities. SBEC was reorganized under TEA several years ago, and many changes may continue to take place regarding this restructuring.

In the past several years, SBEC brought about great change in Texas teacher certification. It implemented an accountability system for entities that prepare educators (institutions of higher learning, as well as numerous alternative certification programs). It also phased out the historic practice of issuing lifetime certificates in favor of certificates that are renewable every 5 years. A renewal currently requires documentation of professional development during the 5-year life of the certificate to ensure that educators stay current in their professional knowledge. SBEC also changed (and will continue to change) the certification levels to better meet the emerging needs of schools in the state.

Structure

SBEC is currently composed of 11 voting members appointed by the governor to 6-year terms. These members are:

- four classroom teachers
- one counselor
- two school administrators
- four citizens of the state not employed in public schools.

There are also currently three nonvoting members:

- one dean of a Texas college of education, appointed by the governor
- one staff member of Texas Education Agency, appointed by the commissioner of education
- one staff member of the Texas Higher Education Coordinating Board, appointed by the commissioner of higher education.

Members

Although members are appointed for 6-year terms, as is usual with a group this size, individuals sometimes move or change positions so that they can no longer hold a certain seat (e.g., a classroom teacher becomes an assistant principal). To get the most up-to-date information on the current membership of the State Board for Educator Certification, the best source is their Web site (http://www.sbec.state.tx.us). This Web site contains a wealth of information on the SBEC Board, its current membership, scheduled meetings, agendas, minutes, and information on requirements and standards that apply to various types of certificates. It also provides press releases and reports generated by the board and its staff, as well as information on investigations and enforcement of certification standards and the Code of Ethics. You may download the standards and a practice booklet (with all of the competencies listed) for your tests from this site or from http://texes.ets.org. Go to the "Preparation Manuals" and then to the EC-6 *Generalist* site. Besides helping Texas educators become more familiar with many areas of education in Texas, it is also an excellent source of information for individuals who are certified in another state or country and who wish to become certified in Texas.

A Note from the Editors

Good luck to all prospective teachers on this test and in your classrooms! We hope that this book will help you pass the examination and will also help you become an excellent and knowledgeable teacher. May you give your best to children each and every day!

Acknowledgments

We thank Esther Huff, who continues to be an excellent teacher in all ways . . . even at 86.

We would like to thank the reviewers of our manuscript for their comments and insights: Lin Moore, Texas Women's University; and Patricia Leek, University of Texas at Dallas.

Reference

Texas Education Agency. (1995). Board member information. Retrieved May 11, 2010, from http://www.tea.state.tx.us/index4.aspx?id=416

About the Editors

Janice L. Nath, Ed.D., is an associate professor in the Department of Urban Education and recently served as Associate Dean at the University of Houston—Downtown in the College of Public Service. Dr. Nath is the co-editor of a number of books on teacher preparation and certification, including *Becoming a Teacher in Texas: A Course of Study for the Elementary and Secondary Professional Development ExCET; Becoming an EC-4 Teacher in Texas: A Course of Study for the Pedagogy and Professional Responsibilities (PPR) TExES; Becoming an EC-6 Teacher in Texas; Becoming a Middle or High School Teacher in Texas;* and *Preparing for the Texas PreK–4 Teacher Certification: A Guide to the Comprehensive TExES Content Areas Exam.* Teacher education is her main area of interest, along with technology in teacher education, action research, and others. She has been actively involved in field-based teacher education for many years and served as the chair of AERA's (American Educational Research Association) Professional Development School Research SIG, chair of the Texas Coordinators for Teacher Certification Testing (formerly, the ExCET Coordinators Association), and chair and treasurer of CSOTTE (Consortium for State Organizations for Texas Teacher Education). In 2004, she was awarded her university's Scholarship/Creativity Award for research, and more recently, the Howsam Award from the Texas Association of Colleges for Teacher Education and the Booker Award from the Texas Association of Teacher Educators in recognition of significant contributions to the educator preparation process in Texas. Her other co-edited books investigate professional development school research and include *Forging Alliances in Community and Thought: Research in Professional Development Schools* and *Professional Development Schools: Advances in Community Thought and Research,* and she is currently working on Volume IV of this PDS series.

John Ramsey, Ph.D., is Associate Professor of science education at the University of Houston. Dr. Ramsey has served as department chair, director of teacher education, doctoral and masters advisor, and principal investigator for numerous funded projects. His professional experience includes more than 30 years in middle, secondary, and higher education. He is co-author or co-editor of 9 books and published 25 referenced research articles. He received the highest university teaching award granted at the University of Houston and was honored with the 2001 Research Excellence Award from the North American Association of Environmental Education. He conducted more than 300 international and national professional development workshops and presentations and has served as a consultant to the United Nations, national and state agencies, international governments, non-government organizations, and businesses.

About the Authors

Michael L. Connell, Ph.D., is an associate professor in the Department of Urban Education and Director of the Center for the Professional Development of Teachers at University of Houston–Downtown. Dr. Connell has more than 25 years of mathematics education experience at both graduate and undergraduate levels, working with students in field-based teacher certification programs. His research interests lie at the intersection between educational technology, learning theory, and mathematics education, and he has written, presented, and published extensively in these areas.

Joyce M. Dutcher, Ed.D., is a retired assistant professor in the Department of Urban Education at the University of Houston–Downtown. Her passion has been to make a difference in the lives of young children, as seen in the early childhood courses that she taught at the university and in outreach initiatives like those at the House of Tiny Treasures, a preschool for Houston's homeless children. Prior to coming to UHD, Dr. Dutcher was an early childhood teacher curriculum coordinator, as well as administrator in two of Texas' largest school districts. She presented regularly at conferences on topics related to early childhood, science education, and systemic educational reform, and she continues to be active in education.

Diana J. Everett, Ph.D., CAE, is the Executive Director for the Texas Association for Health, Physical Education, Recreation, and Dance (TAHPERD). Currently, she is Chair for the Society of Association Managers, board member for the Texas Society for Association Executives, and on various committees for the American Alliance for Health, Physical Education, Recreation, and Dance. Prior to joining TAHPERD in November 1999, Dr. Everett was the Executive Director for the National Association for Girls and Women in Sport (NAGWS). While at NAGWS, Dr. Everett served on committees with the U.S. Department of Health and Human Services, was a liaison with Congressional members, and coordinated national committees for NAGWS/AAHPERD. A lifelong Texan, Everett received a Ph.D. in physical education with a specialization in sport administration from Texas Woman's University, a master's in physical education from Baylor University, and a bachelor's in physical education from The University of Texas–Arlington. Prior to moving into association management in 1995, she taught physical education, health, and biology and coached for 11 years at various high schools in Texas.

Mel E. Finkenberg, Ed.D., currently serves as Interim Dean of the College of Education and was a Regents Professor and Chair of the Department of Kinesiology and Health Science at Stephen F. Austin State University in Nacogdoches, Texas. Prior to his appointment at SFA, he served as Professor and Chair of the Department of Physical

Education and Recreation/Leisure Studies at California State University, Los Angeles. Dr. Finkenberg has also been an exercise physiologist at NASA's Johnson Space Center and has taught elementary physical education. Dr. Finkenberg has been President of the Texas Association of Health, Physical Education, Recreation and Dance, and was selected as the Association Scholar for 1999. He was awarded the Honor Award by this group as well. He served as Vice President for Physical Education of the Southern District American Alliance for Health, Physical Education, Recreation and Dance. He recently received this association's Honor Award. At SFA, he was named Distinguished Professor and selected as the Phi Delta Kappa Educator of the Year. Dr. Finkenberg served as Vice President of the National Association for Physical Education in Higher Education. In 2001, he received that Association's Distinguished Administrator Award.

Lynn S. Freeman, Ed.D., is an assistant professor at the University of Houston–Victoria who serves as coordinator for the post-baccalaureate teacher certification program at University of Houston–Cinco Ranch. Prior to joining UHV, Dr. Freeman was a clinical associate professor at University of Houston–Main Campus, where she taught elementary science methods and served as a Field Coordinator of professional development sites. A science teacher prior to teaching in higher education, her research interests include teaching at-risk students and distance learning. In 2003, she was named Teacher of the Year by the West Houston Chamber of Commerce.

Cynthia G. Henry, Ed.D., was formerly a clinical associate professor in the Department of Curriculum and Instruction at the University of Houston and served as the Coordinator for the Teacher Internship Program. She was also actively involved in field-based teacher education there. Dr. Henry currently works with gifted and talented students and ESL students near Atlanta, Georgia. She is co-editor of *Becoming a Teacher in Texas: A Course of Study for the Elementary and Secondary Professional Development ExCET.* Her research interests include teacher education, gifted and talented education, and parent involvement.

Laveria F. Hutchison, Ed.D., has served as Assistant/Associate Professor of Curriculum and Instruction (1974–present), Language Arts/Literature/Reading coordinator (1992–1998), Middle/Secondary Education coordinator (1998–2006), and department chair (2006–present). After receiving a B.A. degree from Livingstone College, she served as a teacher in several school districts in South Carolina. After receiving her Ed.D. from Ball State University, she joined the faculty at Alabama State University before joining the faculty at the University of Houston. Her research has focused on comprehension instruction, vocabulary development, and content-area teacher research. She has presented research papers at the American Education Research Association, the National Reading Conference, the International Reading Association, the World Congress on Reading, and the European Conference on Reading. Her role in literacy research has allowed her to be a member of the editorial review board of *The Journal of Literacy Research*, to chair committees at the international level, and to serve on the reading standards committee for the International Reading Association. She is currently the Principal Investigator for a grant funded by the National Science Foundation and the U.S. Department of Education. Dr. Hutchison has published more than 30 articles in national journals, written book chapters, and served as a reviewer for research organizations, textbook companies, and federal granting agencies. She has assisted with establishing STEM partnerships with Houston school districts and has consulted with school districts in Indiana, Mississippi, Minnesota, and Texas as an invited educator to assist with "closing the achievement gap" among underserved children.

Kathryn Lilie Jenkins, Ed.D., is an Assistant Professor of Early Childhood Education in the Department of Urban Education at the University of Houston–Downtown. Her area of interest and expertise is developmental education with a focus on play, organization of the physical and emotional environments, authentic assessment, and integrated instructional strategies. Outside the collegiate-level classroom, her research conducted at the House of Tiny Treasures, a preschool for Houston's homeless children, focuses on both the students' and faculty's growth and development. There, she has explored the developmental levels of play, oral language, effective professional development models, effects of music and movement on socialization, and process-oriented art's effects on storytelling. In the past, Dr. Jenkins was also part of a collaborative research project investigating the enhancement of observation skills of preservice teachers using art, in collaboration with the Museum of Fine Arts, Houston. Currently, she is co-investigating the emotional and cognitive effects of collaborative partnerships between university students, HTTs students, and teachers and faculty. Dr. Jenkins currently serves as Vice President of Programs for the Houston Area Association for the Education of Young Children; is a consulting editor for *Young Children,* the journal for the National Association for the Education of Young Children; and is a children's literature editor for the Southern Early Childhood Association. She also serves on the Collaborative for Children Partners Council and on the appointed commission of "Teaching the Whole Child" for the Association of Teacher Educators.

William J. Kortz, Jr., Ed.D. (deceased), served as a University of Houston–Downtown faculty member in the Department of Urban Education teaching bilingual, ESL, and technology curriculum up until 2009–2010. He was the recipient of the Manchester Who's Who of Professionals and Business Executives (2005), the TExES Teacher Award at Sam Houston State University (2004), and the Positively Pasadena Award (1995) for teaching innovation. In addition, he was an active member of the National Association of Bilingual Education (NABE), the Texas Association of Bilingual Education (TABE), the Texas Alternative Certification Association (TACA), the Association for the Advancement of Computers in Education (AACE), Toastmasters International, and the National American Council for Online Learning (NACOL). He was previously a technology director for a distance learning initiative, The Texas Center for Academic Excellence (TXCAE) at Sam Houston State University. He designed online programs for upper-level courses in educational leadership and ESL certification at Texas A&M and Sam Houston State University. He served as a public school bilingual teacher in grades 3–5 and an ESL teacher/coordinator in grades K–12. He published eight Texas teacher certification guides, including *Pass the TExES Bilingual EC-4* and *Pass the TExES ESL EC-12.* Dr. Kortz also taught more than 150 TExES teacher certification seminars in districts, state educational region centers, and universities across Texas.

Charles E. Lamb, Ed.D., was a faculty member at the University of Texas at Austin from 1979 to 1994. He served as a faculty member at Texas A&M University from 1994 to 2001. As Professor Emeritus, he continued to teach part-time as well as serve on graduate committees. He frequently spoke at conferences and served as an educational consultant.

Norene Vail Lowery, Ph.D., is an assistant professor at Houston Baptist University. Dr. Lowery previously taught mathematics education for graduate and undergraduate students at the University of Houston. Current research interests include grant writing, assessment, curriculum, pedagogical content knowledge, the integration of literature and mathematics, and the preparation of preservice teachers. She has served as an adjunct professor with other local universities, as well as teacher, district mathematics specialist, and administrator in the public school system. Dr. Lowery has presented at professional conferences, written and directed grants, and published a variety of journal articles and book chapters.

Carrie Markello, Ed.D., is a Visiting Assistant Professor at the University of Houston, where she teaches art education classes to preservice *generalist* teachers and art educators. She is an active member of the Houston art community and founding member of Grassroots: Art in Action, a nonprofit organization promoting connections between artists and educators. In addition to her teaching, Markello creates mixed media artworks and has an extensive exhibition history.

D. Rozena McCabe, Ph.D., is Professor of Kinesiology at Huston-Tillotson University. She earned her Bachelor of Science degree from Trinity University and Masters of Education degree from Stephen F. Austin University. She earned her Ph.D. in physical education with a specialization in motor learning and control from Texas Woman's University. Since arriving at Huston-Tillotson in 2000, she has served as Department Head of Physical Education and Recreation, Acting Chair for the Division of Professional Studies, and Athletic Director. Dr. McCabe is currently Department Head for Teacher Education and Kinesiology and Chair of the QEP (Quality Enhancement Plan) for HT. She has presented at professional conferences and published articles on such topics as active learning strategies, empowering female athletes, and issues related to the acquisition of motor skills.

Sara Wilson McKay, Ph.D., is currently an Associate Professor of Art Education at Virginia Commonwealth University. Her research on the politics of vision explores the ways that works of art create new seeing, how looking can be a dialogic process, and the possibilities of seeing more of the educational process in and through art. In her many publications in the leading journals of art education, Dr. Wilson McKay examines how the arts encourage democratic participation toward social justice. She was previously a faculty member at the University of Houston.

Janice L. Nath is a co-editor. Her information is found in "About the Editors."

John Ramsey is a co-editor. His information is found in "About the Editors."

Rena M. Shull, Ph.D., is currently an assistant professor in the Department of Education at Rockhurst University in Kansas City, Missouri. Dr. Shull had previously taught mathematics methods as a visiting and clinical professor at the University of Houston, where she also served as a field coordinator for professional development school sites. From 1979 to 1993, she taught high school mathematics. Dr. Shull maintains an interest in number sense, research on lesson plan design, and the use of technology in the mathematics classroom.

Eleanore S. Tyson, Ed.D., is a clinical professor at the University of Houston–Central Campus. She teaches undergraduate and graduate literacy courses in the UH teacher preparation program. Among her favorite courses to teach are those in children's literature. She has also worked with Web-based lessons related to children's trade books. She currently serves on the board of the Greater Houston Area Reading Council, and was recently appointed to a committee for the UH Library. Dr. Tyson received her doctoral degree from the University of Houston.

Trenia L. Walker, Ed.D., is an associate professor at Texas Tech University, and prior to that, Washington State University–Vancouver in the Department of Teaching and Learning. Dr. Walker also taught social studies methods at the University of Houston for several years, in addition to being a classroom history teacher in Houston ISD. Her current research explores transformative learning theories and the implications for technology, popular culture, and globalization in social studies teaching and learning.

Mary E. Wingfield, Ed.D., has been a science methods professor for preservice elementary teachers in the teacher preparation program at the University of Houston–Downtown and the University of Houston–Main for many years. She served on State Board of Educator Certification Oversight Teams to assist in review of certification performance at entities throughout the state. As a former science teacher, she is interested in helping enhance the efficacy of new science teachers and in promoting scientific literacy in Texas elementary school children.

Brief Contents

Contents

Chapter 3 Preparing to Teach Mathematics in Texas   97

Michael L. Connell
Norene Vail Lowery
Rena M. Shull
Charles E. Lamb

Chapter 4 Preparing to Teach Social Studies in Texas 164

Trenia L. Walker
Janice L. Nath

Chapter 5 Preparing to Teach Science in Texas 290

Mary E. Wingfield
Lynn S. Freeman

Chapter 6 Preparing to Teach Art in Texas 336

Sara Wilson McKay
Carrie Markello
Janice L. Nath

Chapter 7 Preparing to Teach Music in Texas 374

Janice L. Nath

Chapter 8 Preparing to Teach Health and Physical Education in Texas   439

D. Rozena McCabe
Diana J. Everett
Mel E. Finkenberg
Janice L. Nath
John M. Ramsey

Chapter 9 Preparing to Teach Theatre Arts in Texas 486

Kathryn L. Jenkins
Janice L. Nath
Joyce M. Dutcher

Chapter 10 Teaching English as a Second Language (ESL) in Texas   521

William J. Kortz, Jr.
Janice L. Nath

1 Preparing to Pass the TExES *Generalist*

Janice L. Nath
University of Houston—Downtown

Cynthia G. Henry

Intuitively, we know that studying early and studying smart for the *Generalist* pays off with a higher test score, but research also concludes that good things happen for those who work to improve their studying and test-taking skills—in addition to simply knowing the content so that you can teach it better. Students with strong study skills find it easier to study, consistently earn better grades and higher test scores, and become more successful in life. Therefore, we begin with this chapter by giving you some general and specific strategies and hints to help you study for and complete this examination with success. Chapter 1 is designed along a timeline and written in a question-and-answer format to facilitate your learning.

Let's Talk About the Test

Standards, Domains, and Competencies

The state of Texas provides guidelines that tell teachers exactly what knowledge and skills Texas children need to possess, how they should go about their professional lives, and what knowledge teachers need for Texas classrooms. This information is found in three places: (1) the *Texas Essential Knowledge and Skills* (TEKS) for children, (2) the TExES *Standards* (Texas Examinations of Educator Standards), and (3) the TExES *Competencies* developed for teachers in both pedagogy and content. All three of these areas are important for teachers to learn, understand, and use. Because much of our knowledge about children, teaching, and content is in a constant state of change, it is important information for teachers to learn now but also to understand that they must continuously update their learning throughout their careers as teachers as well.

Because you are entering a career in which professionalism is important, you may be interested in how this exam, which controls entrance to the profession, has been developed. The TEKS for teaching children specific content are developed first (and are updated periodically), followed by the standards for teachers, which are solidly based on the TEKS. Committees for teacher standards, made up of Texas educators, parents, and business and community members, also consider current educational research, as well as national standards that are set by content-area specialists within their specialized organizations (e.g., the National Council of Teachers of Mathematics [NCTM]). Standards are established to cover all of the major content areas taught to children in Texas, and for the *Generalist*, these content areas have been divided into five *domains*. Each of these domains is an *umbrella* for one of the five tested areas. The following table shows these five domains with the percentage for each domain currently on the test.

Domain I	English, Language Arts, and Reading	32%
Domain II	Mathematics	19%
Domain III	Social Studies	19%
Domain IV	Science	19%
Domain V	Fine Arts, Health, and Physical Education	12%

After development of the teaching standards, committees turn to establishing a framework for testing. This framework provides the *competencies*, which are specific knowledge and skills for testing each domain. As you read these competencies under each domain, note that there are two parts. The first is a *competency statement*, which is a general beginning statement about an area of knowledge under one of the domains. For example, in language arts, one such *competency statement* about oral language reads, "The teacher understands the importance of oral language, knows the developmental processes of oral language, and provides children with varied opportunities to develop listening and speaking skills" (Texas Education Agency [TEA], 2009, p. 18). Directly following each of these broad statements, there is a list of descriptive statements that delineates or defines what Texas specifically wants teachers to know and be able to do with these concepts. You can be expected to be tested directly on the competency statements and the specific details and vocabulary of these descriptive statements. For example, one of the many descriptive statements under the oral language competency statement reads: "The beginning teacher knows basic linguistic concepts (e.g., phonemes, segmentation) and the developmental stages in the acquisition of oral language—including phonology, semantics, syntax, and pragmatics—and recognizes that individual variations occur within and across languages" (TEA, p. 18). Therefore, before testing, you should ensure that you not only know the general statements but also the specific definition of terms listed and those terms inside the parentheses. By reading the TEKS, the standards, the competency statements, and the descriptive statements, you will know exactly what will appear on the test. The sequence of development is shown next.

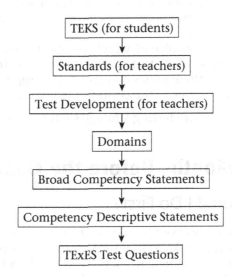

To continue the process, committees then design test questions in a multiple-choice format to assess knowledge of the teaching skills and content knowledge stated in these standards and competencies. After the questions are piloted, they finally become part of the test bank. These questions come in several formats, as discussed next.

Item Formats

All items are in multiple-choice format. However, they are arranged as single items, stimulus material items, and clustered items. Each of these formats is described next.

- *Single item format:* A single problem or question is presented with four answer choices. You are required to choose the correct response or ending statement and mark this on your answer sheet.
- *Stimulus material item format:* Following some type of stimulus material, a question is asked that may require you to analyze a given chart, graph, map, table, and so on. The stimulus could also be a real-world classroom situation, a dialogue between a teacher and student, or an example(s) of a student's or students' work. When answering this type of question, be sure to read the stimulus very carefully.
- *Clustered item format:* A group of questions or problems is related to each other in some way. There may be only two or three related questions— or there can be many questions, as you will see in a *Teacher Decision Set*, which requires you to follow a long scenario, answering questions as the scene unfolds over several pages.

Currently, there are 140 questions on the *Generalist* examination. Following are a few initial helpful hints for this examination:

- When answering any of the questions, always make sure that you are answering from the point of view of the Texas standards and competencies (both for the *Generalist* and the PPR [*Pedagogy and Professional Responsibilities*]). No correct answer on the test ever contradicts the philosophies of these standards and competencies. It pays to learn them very well.

- The test has the same biases that the PPR TExES contains, such as student choice and responsibility, authentic assessment, self-assessment and reflection, relevant instruction, age-appropriate instruction, use of technology and the community as resources, use of cooperative groups, and higher-level thinking.

- If you have a choice of which of the two required tests you take first, it may be worthwhile to take the PPR first so that you have a clear understanding of these issues and can better apply the desired Texas pedagogy and philosophies to the content-area questions.

We discuss more testing strategies later in the chapter.

 ## Several Months Before the *Generalist*

What Should I Do First?

Begin by thinking about the registration process for this exam well in advance so that you can make a plan for studying over the length of time you have and can select the time and method that is best for you. It can be difficult to obtain a testing space at some locations if you do not register early, so consider getting this underway as soon as you begin to think about testing.

There are currently two options for taking this test—a paper-and-pencil version or a computer-administered test (CAT). Think about which of these options might be best for you. For example, as a testing strategy, it may help you to be able to underline or otherwise mark in your test booklet, so the paper-and-pencil route may be most advantageous. If you do a great deal of work on the computer and feel more comfortable in a technological format, you may want to choose the electronic version (CAT). Use the Web site listed at the end of this chapter to find the schedule for paper-and-pencil testing and to see when and where the nearest CAT is offered. Most locations that offer the CAT are at Texas universities or colleges. The CAT is offered quite often, so this method can be more versatile. If you want to take the examination on the computer, you are currently allowed to retake it after 90 days (should you do not do well), rather than waiting until a specific day for the paper-and-pencil test.

If you are in a teacher preparation/certification program, you may be required to take the *Generalist* during a particular phase of your program. If so, determine exactly when that is, but also be sure to check with your program about what your responsibilities are in the registration process. Most programs have a certification officer or TExES coordinator. Find out who this is and check in with him or her often.

If you are not required to adhere to a particular time for the Generalist, you should think carefully about your test date and take the proper steps to register for the date and time that is most beneficial to your situation. This is important, because testing sites can fill up early, forcing you to drive further or to be assigned to a test at a time other than what may be your best. For instance, if you are a morning person, you definitely want the morning session; if you do not "get going" until later in the day, you probably want to start your test after lunch. If your prime choice of sites is already closed, search for other sites in proximity on your own. The testing company, ETS (Educational Testing Service), is currently working to automatically show you sites that are still open nearby if your first choice is full.

Make sure that you have decided on the best time and method to take the *Generalist* and have begun the registration process properly (either through the state or through your teacher preparation entity). Registration is available online, but you may still need an approval to test if you are being recommended for certification through a university or alternative certification program (ACP). Your university or teacher preparation program may also have its own deadlines or other requirements prior to the state deadline to obtain approval, so pay close attention to these dates as well.

There are several other items that you must also take care of prior to registration. You must have a *TEA account* to register, so this should be taken care of in advance at https://secure.sbec.state.tx.us/SBECOnline/login.asp?. All registration for testing is currently online, and you must have also created a *testing account* on the ETS TExES Web site (www.texes.ets.org) before you may test. All information for ETS registration is matched against your TEA profile, so be sure that the two match exactly. If you have name changes or other changes in information previously given to the Texas educational databank, be sure to take care of those changes first to avoid confusion and possibly losing a test date. As a note, you also must go through the fingerprinting process to become certified in Texas, so be sure to allow time for that as well (instructions are on the TEA Web site given at the end of the chapter).

When you register, be very careful to sign up for the correct test. The test that you request is the only one that will be brought to the site or loaded at a CAT site for you. If you request the wrong test, you will be out of luck that day. You must also print out your admission ticket—they are no longer sent in the mail. All of this information is found in the registration booklet (http://www.texes.ets.org/assets/pdf/texes/registration_bulletin_texes_excet_feb_09_update.pdf). If there are any problems, you may currently contact ETS Customer Service at 1-800-205-2626.

Be aware of registration cutoff dates. Late registration and changes in registration cost you more money and can cost you a delayed test day. Early registration and close attention to filling out the correct information help ensure that you are assigned your preference. Again, Web site addresses and phone numbers for registration and information can be found at the end of this chapter.

How Should I Begin Preparing for the *Generalist*?

Begin as soon as possible. Studying for this important exam can seem to be overwhelming when you first begin to look at all that you should know. There are so many questions that could be asked! The good news is that much of it will probably be a review of what you already know.

For the most benefit, break your task into smaller, more manageable steps. The key is to get organized by developing time management skills and material management skills. Start early to review and learn new information!

How Should I Manage My Time?

You must set both manageable time goals and workload goals for each study session. For example, if you

Helpful Hint:

To become a certified teacher, you must also take the PPR *(Pedagogy and Professional Responsibilities)* TExES. We highly suggest, however, that you do not plan to take more than one of these tests per testing day. Many people do not do well taking more than one test because they become tired and lose concentration as the day passes. Some teacher preparation entities prohibit you from taking more than one test per day because of this concern. Plan your testing schedule carefully so you have plenty of time to get a passing score on both examinations prior to obtaining a teaching position or, if you already have a teaching position, to keep your job.

begin studying for the exam 4 months before your test date, plan to study about 3 days a week for approximately 30 to 60 minutes per session. This is a manageable and reasonable study schedule for most. However, if you begin preparing for the *Generalist* 1 or 2 months before the test date, you must study more days during the week and spend more time in each study session to ensure that you cover the materials on the test sufficiently.

Helpful Hint:
Download the EC-6 Preparation Manual at www.texes.ets.org/assets/pdf/testprep_manuals/191_*generalist*_ec_6.pdf for some practice questions and other information.

You may be taking classes, student teaching, or holding a teaching position or another job at the same time you are studying for this exam. If so, you will be juggling many dates and assignments. This is the time to purchase and use a daily planner (if you have not already) that allows you to write down all the dates that you need to remember. This not only helps set aside your study time, but it also alerts you to the many deadlines and dates for the registration process. A good idea is to back up deadlines on your calendar at least by a day (e.g., if there is a due date on Nov. 3, back it up to Nov. 2) so that you are sure to meet the deadline. Scheduling your study sessions by writing them on your calendar (as you would an appointment with your doctor or dentist) emphasizes the importance of this time for you. Also, try to schedule your study sessions for the same time of the day or evening. This helps you develop and stick to a study routine.

Helpful Hint:
Schedule your study sessions when you feel the most energetic and motivated. Understanding your patterns of mental energy and fatigue help you get the most out of your study time.

Did you know that our brains more easily remember the first and last items we read as compared to items in the middle of a passage or list? This is important if you want to maximize the amount of material you can remember. Do not study continuously during your study sessions. It is better to take frequent study breaks to create as many beginnings and endings as possible without forfeiting any of those minutes you have set aside for your entire session. For example (as noted earlier), each chapter of this book is divided into sections to deal with separate domains, then further into smaller sections of separate standards. Several concepts are often covered in each of these subdivisions. Try to concentrate on one of these smaller sections for a bit, and then go on to another. When you take your breaks, however, they should not be too long. A brief 2- to 5-minute mental vacation is all that it takes to give your mind a rest as it absorbs material you have just read. Some suggestions for brief study breaks include listening to a favorite song, stretching your muscles by doing a few exercises, getting a drink or snack, or simply closing your eyes for a few moments. With that said, try not to let others interrupt your shorter study sessions too much. Thirty minutes of good time can be more effective than 2 hours of study time that is constantly interrupted by others. Close the door and use your time to focus.

For each of your study sessions, you must also set a workload goal that can be accomplished within the time allotted for your study session. For example, a reasonable workload goal would be to read five to ten pages of content material from a textbook or study guide or to work through several practice questions and their correct answers.

Helpful Hint:
If you are taking the PPR or another test, try to schedule at least several weeks (if not longer) in between exams to mentally rest before gearing up to study for the next one. This allows you to better focus for the next exam.

Setting small time goals and workload goals is a powerful and effective way to overcome most study blocks that can often make a longer study session seem overwhelming. As Henry Ford once said, "Nothing is particularly hard if you divide it into small jobs" (www.brainyquote.com/quotes/quotes/h/henryford125392.html).

What Material Management Skills Do I Need, and How Do I Develop Them?

You may have many materials that help you study for this test besides this book. The material management skills you need include keeping your study materials organized and accessible. If your study materials are scattered throughout your house, apartment, dorm room, or other locations, you waste valuable time locating and organizing them before you can begin your study session. A procrastinator often subconsciously uses this excuse to put off studying. Find an easily accessible place, such as a desk, bookcase, or filing cabinet, and return all of your study materials to this location when you have finished using them. Using different-color file folders, manila file folders with colored labels for each content area, or a binder with tabs for each area is an effective method of organizing a large body of study material. For example, if you place all of your mathematics materials in a red file folder or binder section, you will be able to locate them quickly when you are ready to study that content area. Further organization of your materials may be necessary if the content contains multiple areas that you must study and review separately. Because some domains contain many subsections, several file folders of the same color should be labeled separately with each content title—but stored together in a box, desk drawer, or binder for easy access.

As well as material management skills, there are other methods for creating an optimal study environment. These methods include

- keeping your study environment at approximately 68 degrees, as cooler temperatures normally help improve concentration and memory
- studying while facing a blank or neutral wall; looking at a wall of eye-catching posters or pictures can be distracting
- ensuring your study environment is well lit with high-watt, soft-light bulbs, because fluorescent or insufficient lighting can increase mental fatigue.

Keeping Up the Momentum

How Should I Spend My Study Time, and on What Should I Concentrate When I Only Have a Few Weeks Before Taking the *Generalist*?

If you have been preparing on your own for a while, now is the time, if possible, to organize a study group for review sessions. However, make sure that it is a group that is serious about studying and providing positive support. Many times, other students or teachers who are also preparing for this examination can offer fresh insight into the content and can help maintain motivation for your study sessions. Discussing terms and concepts with others requires you to become actively involved with the material, and one of the best ways to learn something new is to explain it or teach it to someone else. Learning theory tells us that retention is greatest when we teach others—use that to your advantage. Generating your own practice questions and

Helpful Hint:

Plan to do something fun after a study session. Studying for this examination requires hard work, commitment, and dedication on your part. Therefore, it is important to schedule an enjoyable activity with which to reward yourself after a study session.

answers and reviewing content material with a partner or a small group of other test takers is one of the most effective means of preparing for an important examination.

At this point, you should feel confident that you are covering new material and reviewing old material in an effective manner. Select those main subject areas in which you feel you are still struggling, and concentrate on those areas first. The Language Arts/Reading Domain is weighted more heavily (followed by mathematics, science, social studies, etc.), so when you do not have much time left, focus on where you need it most with your group or individually.

USE YOUR SENSES. Successfully completing the *Generalist* requires you to know and remember a considerable amount of information. Using numerous sensory channels to store information is a powerful way to remember and recall what you have learned. Try to use your senses of sight, hearing, and touch during each study session. Learning theory tells us to use all modalities with children in teaching lessons. Try to make that work for you as well. Make it a habit to visualize, discuss, draw, diagram, or create flashcards for what you are studying. These strategies help you make connections with the content material and, in turn, help you recall the information you need when you take the examination. Specific memory models help as well. For example, you may have heard sayings such as, "Please Excuse My Dear Aunt Sally," in mathematics to help you remember the order of operations, but you can create your own models to help you remember some of the information needed for this test, too. For example, "**K**now **C**hildren **A**nd **A**lways **S**hare **E**verything" (or Always Eagerly Share in new Bloom's) may help you remember the elements of Bloom's taxonomy (**k**nowledge, **c**omprehension, **a**pplication, **a**nalysis, **s**ynthesis, and **e**valuation). Finding or creating little songs, rhymes, or funny pictures also help you retain the wealth of material required for this exam.

Helpful Hint:

In addition to studying with this guide, you may benefit by attending a university, district, regional, school-sponsored, or commercial review seminar. A specially prepared review can be a worthwhile investment and can offer additional insights and guidance in your preparation process. Take advantage of these opportunities, particularly if you have previously not done well on this examination.

USE YOUR TIME WISELY. Using your time wisely is a critical component in getting the most out of each study session. If you focus your attention and concentration powers on the materials you are studying, you are more likely to stay motivated to accomplish your goals. To help, try the following suggestions:

- **Buy in!** If you are going to teach young children in Texas, you really must know all of this content information! It will be good for students and good for you as a professional. It is expected as a part of your professional knowledge. Buying into this idea helps keep you motivated to learn it all and helps you become a more knowledgeable teacher!
- **Alternate your activities.** Use each study session to review two or more content areas. For example, do not spend an entire study session focusing only on basic science concepts. Switch over to history after a time. Changing topics within a content area or studying two completely different content areas during one session helps keep your mind fresh.

- **Use index cards for notes, Post-its®, and selectively underline or highlight as you read.** Using these strategies help you focus on the most critical ideas and concepts in the material. You may want to use Post-it® notes on pages that are critical, or write information that you believe you might forget easily on index cards. This forces you to think about the information being presented and what it means to you, and you can take the cards with you to study when you are standing in line, grabbing a bite to eat, or have a few free minutes. Selectively underlining stops you from getting to the end of a page or section and wondering what you have just read.

- **Download the TEKS and released TAKS (or STAAR in the near future) for students** and check to see if you know each term and concept listed through sixth grade (http://ritter.tea.state.tx.us/teks/). Although the authors of these chapters have addressed the TEKS (Texas Essential Knowledge and Skills), going through the list is a good way to review. In addition, old TAKS (Texas Assessment of Knowledge and Skills) tests are currently released every 3 years. As the STAAR (State of Texas Assessment of Academic Readiness) replaces the TAKS, these exams with no doubt be available after a time as well. Downloading and actually taking these tests is also an excellent way to see if you have the same content and skills that are required by children who you will be teaching. The best way to access the current released tests is to go http://www.tea.state.tx.us/index3.aspx?id=3850&menu_id3=793, or simply type "released TAKS tests" into a search engine.

- **Begin and end on a positive note.** Incorporating this strategy is a simple way to maintain your focus and motivation for studying. If you are not a person who enjoys studying for long and difficult examinations, end your study session at a point where it is easy and logical for you to pick up and begin again. Beginning and ending on a positive note go a long way toward keeping you motivated and helping you concentrate and focus.

As a reminder, the number of indicators within each domain or content area reflects the coverage of the content area on the *Generalist*. Therefore, those domains or content areas with more indicators have more questions on the exam. You should spend a greater percentage of your study time reviewing the material in those areas—for example, as shown earlier, language arts has (in the past) taken up to 32% of the test questions. You may see any current changes on these percentages by going to the Web site listed earlier or at the end of the chapter in the preparation manual.

 ## Two Weeks Before the *Generalist*

How Can I Best Spend My Time Two Weeks Before the *Generalist*?

PLAYING GAMES. Continue to review your study materials both individually and with your study partner or study group, if possible. You should have a good review schedule in place by now that meets your study needs. Now is also the time to test yourself before you are tested, and one way to test yourself is to construct a final set of flashcards, as mentioned previously. These should include important terms, concepts, definitions, and key concepts for the standards and competencies that still seem hard to remember. Carry these cards with you at all times so that you can review a few minutes here and there. Use them as traditional flashcards, or use them in a matching game.

Another idea is to use the content material and practice questions throughout this book to help you make up additional questions. Creating your own questions helps you begin thinking like the test developers. You may be surprised how closely your questions actually match the real test questions!

What Strategies Should I Use for This Multiple-Choice Exam?

TEST HINTS FOR MULTIPLE-CHOICE ITEMS ON THIS EXAM. The *Generalist,* as you may remember, is written in a multiple-choice format. The Preparation Manual for this exam (download at www.texes.ets.org/assets/pdf/testprep_manuals/191_*generalist*_ec_6.pdf) should be read carefully. This test is designed to make you think by recalling factual information, analyzing information, comparing it with other knowledge you have, or making decisions about information. You will be asked to answer each question by choosing one of several answers. Then you mark your answer choice on a separate answer sheet (a Scantron) or click on your choice on the computer. One of the best ways to answer multiple-choice questions is to narrow your answer options by using the process of elimination. Following are several helpful suggestions for narrowing your answer.

- **Focus on exactly what is being asked.** Examine the question or question stem and try to determine what the question is *really* asking. After selecting an answer, go back to check if your choice is an exact match for the question. For example, if the question is asking you about the most effective focus activity for a science lesson, you should select an answer that talks about a focus activity rather than another part of the lesson plan. Many test takers miss answers because they fail to give this step proper attention. The test writers have deliberately designed many of these questions to be sure you have the ability to analyze carefully—so be very sure that you do!
- **Test your answer.** By filling in the blank with your choice and reading it back, you can see if the answer you selected makes sense.
- **Watch the grammar.** If the question demands a noun, look for an answer that is a noun; if a verb is required to complete a question stem, be sure to select an answer that is a verb.
- **Analyze verbs.** Related to the hint above, you should look closely at the verbs to analyze what the question requires. This can also be a good indicator of the correct answer. For example, if a question contains the word *prepare*, the answer should indicate something to do with preparation; that is, something the teacher would do prior to teaching. If the question deals with managing students, the answer must have some aspect of classroom management. Some of these can be tricky, so analyze, analyze, analyze!
- **Read all answer choices before choosing an answer.**
- **Eliminate incorrect answers first.** Place an X next to the answer choices you know are incorrect (if you are taking the paper-and-pencil version). You will probably be able to eliminate one or two choices immediately after using this strategy. Be sure to eliminate an answer that has any hint of negativity toward children or their parents or does not agree with the PPR or *Generalist* standards in any manner at all.
- **Read the question and the related paragraphs and other material carefully.** As you read, underline key information and circle key words or phrases—or note them carefully if you are taking the computer version. These definitely should include words that would change the answer (*first, last, next, best, least, not,* etc.). If you feel that three of the answers are similar, go back to the paragraph to make sure you did not miss one of these types of words that could change the meaning.
- **Remember that when two choices are similar, one of them is usually the correct answer.**
- **Look for an umbrella situation.** If an answer can cover another answer, the umbrella is probably the correct answer. For example, if choice *A* reads, "A teacher should establish time allotments ahead of time for

each student to practice his or her PowerPoints," and choice *B* reads, "A teacher should give students a rubric, time to plan, and time for practicing PowerPoints," choice *B* is a better umbrella answer because choice *B* would undoubtedly cover time allotments in the rubric and in the planning stage, and it is more detailed.

- **Go with your first hunch.** Our first choice is correct more often than not. Mark this first choice on every question as you go. If you have a concern about a particular question and answer, place a small question mark beside the number or note it on the computer and come back if there is time. If there is no time left, at least you have given it your best shot. Unanswered questions are counted as wrong. This is a long examination with considerable reading. If you have to come back to many unanswered questions, you may run out of time. Go ahead and mark your gut reaction on every first pass.

STRATEGIES THAT ARE PARTICULAR TO THIS EXAMINATION.

- **Remember your pedagogy.** Do not answer in ways that go against good educational theory or your PPR (*Pedagogy and Professional Responsibilities* TExES test) competencies. Never, ever answer contrary to any of these competencies or standards, even if you have seen practices in your school experiences as a child or an adult that do not match them. Always go with the state-given competencies or standards—not with your own experiences (unless they match the state given information).
- **Know the standards and the vocabulary.** Knowing the TEKS, standards, and competencies well for this exam give you an edge. Pay close attention to the vocabulary in the competencies; know what every word means. It is difficult to apply the vocabulary in real-life situations if you do not know what particular terms mean.
- **Think TEXASLAND!** Like at Disneyland, assume that everything good for children is available and select that answer. If you discard a choice because you think that it offers something not available or not seen in your experiences or in real live schools, you will get it wrong. Put yourself in the place of children in the scenario. Ask yourself what would be best or most exciting for me (as a child), and choose that answer. Think roses and rainbows, field trips and technology, parents who are eager to participate, and so forth. If an answer indicates that something would be less work or easier for the teacher—that is usually *not* the right answer. Texas expects that you, as a teacher, will work hard to offer the ultimate experiences for children.
- **Answer shorter items first.** Go through the exam and answer the shorter items first (unless they are part of a cluster group of questions or fall into a Teacher Decision Set; then do not do those during the first pass). This strategy may be particularly useful if you are a slower reader. After answering these single items, go back to others that have longer paragraphs or other more complicated stimulus data to analyze, along with the cluster items and the Teacher Decision Sets. (Note: This strategy is *not* suggested for the PPR exam, because there is so much that you would have to reread in that test.)
- **Do not forget the TExES biases.** We mentioned this earlier, but it is important. These include looking carefully for right answers that have the following: encouraging student choice and responsibility,

*H*elpful Hint:

If the question is a scenario-based question, try to visualize the classroom and what is happening. Try to see the teacher acting in ways that reflect the *Generalist* and the PPR competencies and standards. Cut to the chase of what it is you believe the question is asking by ignoring superfluous information. Select your answer, and again, go back to the question to double-check if your selection answers that *particular* question.

higher-level thinking, authentic assessment, self-assessment, providing relevant instruction, age-appropriate instruction, use of technology and using the community as resources, using cooperative groups, and so forth.

- **Isolate the grade level on which the question is centered.** It can make a big difference in your answer. Your answer about instruction is different for each grade level, especially because the levels now stretch from Pre-K to up to sixth grade, so be sure to look for this information in pedagogy questions. An answer for fifth graders may be very different than an answer for kindergarten students.

Remember that a blank answer is wrong on the *Generalist*. Even if you do not know the answer to a question, it is to your advantage to guess rather than to not answer at all. If you run out of time, quickly mark the same letter answer for all items you did not have a chance to answer before you turn in your test.

- **Watch for trial items.** Remember that a number of the questions on this exam are *trial items* (piloted questions) and are not graded as a part of your score. If a question seems not quite right, select an answer and go on rather than fixating on it. The test makers may simply be trying out a question for validity.

- **If you are taking the paper-and-pencil version, mark all your answers first in the test booklet as well as on your Scantron.** That way, should you discover that you are not on the correct number on your Scantron, you can come back to your booklet where you have clearly marked the answers without wasting time rereading to find out where you went wrong.

One Week Before the *Generalist*

With Only One Week to Go, What Can I Do to Best Prepare for the *Generalist*?

There are several important issues to consider in the week before you take the *Generalist*. First, continue to review your study materials both individually and with a study partner or group (if possible). If you have been following a well-designed study schedule, this last week before the exam should be a review week. This is not the time to begin learning new content. At this point, you should feel confident with your knowledge base in almost all of the competencies, so spend your study time on the few competencies, terms, or formulas that you need to further practice and review. Remember to study the most heavily weighted items (language arts/reading) very well.

HOUSEKEEPING. You also have a few housekeeping chores to complete this week. First, read your test admission ticket carefully. Your admission ticket provides you with important information, such as the exam date, the exam administration site, the time of the exam, the exam for which you are registered, and what to bring to the exam. Remember that the testing company and the state do not guarantee either the time or the site that you originally requested. If your request for a site is already filled, they will assign you to the next closest site or another time. You should reprint your admission ticket to be sure that nothing has changed (and do so again on the day of the exam, if possible). If you arrive at a different site or a different time from what is on your ticket, you will not be allowed to test. Mistakes are sometimes made for the actual test itself, so check carefully to make sure ETS has the exact test listed that you requested. Again, there are no extra tests brought to a site, so if your requested test was incorrectly recorded and you did not catch it in time, you will not be allowed to test. If you are taking more than one exam on the same day (and we hope you are not), you will receive a separate admission ticket for each. Remember to take your admission ticket(s) with you to the exam site. You will not be allowed to enter a testing session without your ticket.

Make sure you know how to get to the test administration site. Although the address is printed on your test admission ticket, you may want to consult a road map or MapQuest, or make a dry run to the site a few days before your exam. This helps you figure out how long it takes you to drive to the site on your exam day and what traffic, road construction, or parking problems you may encounter along the way. Arriving in a rush of anxiety over getting there on time can cause you to begin the exam flustered and not at your best. Remember that if you arrive late to the site for registration, you may be refused admission to the test that day and refused a refund for missing your exam. If you are driving to a testing site from out of town, you may want to request an afternoon testing time or make a hotel reservation to avoid driving in the early morning hours. Be sure to book early—others may have the same idea.

Additional information about testing requirements, registration, test results, and obtaining a teaching certificate can be found in the Registration Bulletin on the ETS Web site. It is always suggested to check this site several times prior to your test to find out the very latest information and possible changes. ETS is working to ensure that moved sites or cancelled testing due to weather or other problems are posted on their Web site as soon as they know about it. This type of information could appear as late as the morning of a test, so check before you go.

TEST ANXIETY. This week you may be feeling some test anxiety about taking the *Generalist*. Test anxiety is a psychological response to a perceived threatening situation. Most of your fellow test takers are also feeling a little anxious and nervous. In fact, feeling this way before an important exam is perfectly normal and can be beneficial, as it helps increase your alertness and improves your attention to the task at hand. However, many test takers who are too calm are not motivated to do their best work. Having an edge can be good, but feeling a great deal of anxiety and nervousness can interfere with your performance on the *Generalist*. Test takers who experience a high level of test anxiety can lose their concentration, feel their hearts pounding, experience lightheadedness, break out in a cold sweat, or be unable to recall simple information when completing the exam. Highly anxious test takers tend to score lower on tests than less anxious test takers. Try the following strategies to help you control test anxiety on this examination:

- **Register for only one test at a time.** We state this several times because it is so important. Some people put these tests off and then reach their time limit when they must pass on a particular testing date or be ineligible to apply in time for the new school year, or they may even lose their jobs if they do not pass. This anxiety can be extremely detrimental to test taking. Research continues to show that some who attempt to take more than one test do not do well on one or both tests. Because these tests are such long reading tests, at a certain point, anxiety or a loss of concentration can cause you to not be at your best.
- **Ensure that you are thoroughly prepared for the exam.** Many times test takers use test anxiety as an excuse for lack of studying for the exam. Overpreparation may be the best way to prevent test anxiety; the better you know the material, the more confident you are about taking the test. However, remember that you do not have to make an "A" on this test to pass, so you do not have to answer every single question correctly. If you come across information you do not know, just go on and try to answer those items that you do know correctly.
- **Simulate the testing situation multiple times so that it is as close as possible to the real experience.** This includes taking timed practice

tests, working with other test takers (as mentioned earlier), and completing chapter exercises that help you visualize and experience what the *Generalist* is like. After completing the practice questions and exercises in this book, use them as a guide to help you generate additional questions for each competency. Remember that the test can ask questions selected from thousands of bits of information from all of the content areas. Practice tests can hit only a limited number of these items. Study for many details, even though you may not see them on the practice tests. Do not forget to download and take released TAKS (or STAAR) tests.

- **Reserve this day for this examination alone.** Trying to catch a plane, be a member of a wedding party, or even having a big date later that day or evening can cause you to lose concentration during the test. This is an expensive test, and the hard copy version is not offered often, so reserve this day for testing and focus on the test alone, especially if you are taking the paper-and-pencil exam.

- **Arrive early.** Many test takers who must drive a considerable distance can begin to panic if they think they may not arrive in time for registration. Some sites have parking a considerable distance away, so those who arrive late may be rushing to get seated in time to begin. Both of these situations set up a negative beginning for the hours of testing to come.

Helpful Hint:

Do not answer questions based on your own personal classroom observations and teaching experiences *unless* these experiences match the same actions and philosophies found in the materials for this examination and other tests involving professional development philosophies (the PPR).

- **Do relaxation exercises and practice positive self-talk before and during the exam.** Take several slow, deep breaths before beginning the exam and visualize yourself successfully completing the test. Throughout the exam, say to yourself, "I have studied hard," "I know this material," or "I am confident that I am doing well."

- **Eliminate distractions.** If another test taker causes you to begin to lose your concentration or creates anxiety for any reason (tapping or making other noises, causing the table to move, etc.), ask the proctor to move you. Do not address the other person directly, as the proctor could view it as cheating (which could cause you to lose your test score for that day).

The Night Before the *Generalist*

What Should I Do the Night Before the *Generalist*?

Spend the night before the *Generalist* organizing for the exam the next day and doing a relaxing activity to take your mind off the task ahead. Reprint and read your admission ticket again to confirm you know where you are going and exactly what time you are expected to be there and in your seat. It is usually 30 minutes prior to the actual posted starting time. Also, collect all of the supplies you need for the following day, including your valid admission ticket, two pieces of acceptable identification that match *exactly* the name on your admission ticket, several sharpened No. 2 pencils with erasers, an accurate watch that does not beep, a snack, and a lunch if you are taking more than one exam on the same day (and, again, we hope you are not). Although you cannot eat or drink (perhaps other than water) inside the actual room, you may step outside for a break. Computer rooms may have other restrictions. Therefore, you may want to put an energy bar or a drink in your pocket or purse to give you a mid-test boost, as there may be no snack machines available at the test site. At the time of publication, only water bottles with screw-on tops are being allowed inside the actual room where people are testing on paper, but check the current registration information to insure that no changes in this requirement have been made.

You are required to bring identification with you to get into the site. The two pieces of identification you must bring (always check for changes) are:

- One government issued photo ID, in the name in which you are registered
- One secondary ID with a signature

In the Registration Bulletin you will find examples of acceptable forms of identification, what to do if you forget your required forms of identification, or what to do if you do not have photo identification with your current name, and so on, as well as a complete list of prohibited items. Many personal items are prohibited at the exam site, and you will be asked to store them at your own risk in a designated area if you should bring any of these with you. Following is current list of prohibited items:

Briefcases	Electronic pagers	Watches that beep	Calculators
Backpacks	Audiotapes	Highlighters	Calculator watches
Packages	Dictionaries	Notebooks	Any written or
Textbooks	Photographic or	Scratch paper	unauthorized
Spell checkers	recording devices	Slide rules	materials
Cellular phones			

Talking on a cell phone or using a cell photo phone may be interpreted as cheating and could cost you a test score. Leave your phone and other communication devices at home or in your car so you do not have to worry about them during the test. The proctors are not responsible for making sure that these items are safe while you are testing. Visitors, including friends and relatives, must remain outside the test site. Remember to read the most current Registration Bulletin carefully to ensure that you understand the most recent requirements for this examination.

After organizing your supplies for the following day, you should plan to do something enjoyable so that you will not begin to fret about the day ahead of you. If you do plan to review this evening, spend only about an hour going over your notes or flipping through your flashcards. Do not use this time as a long study session to cram for tomorrow's exam.

Most important, you should go to bed early and get a good night's sleep. If you wake up all night worrying if the alarm will go off, set two. Waking up feeling refreshed goes a long way in helping you to feel confident about the task ahead. Sleeping is not a waste of time with a huge day in front of you.

 ## The Day of the *Generalist*

What Should I Do on the Day of the *Generalist*?

BEFORE THE EXAM. When the big day is finally here, there are several things you can do to help yourself be as successful as possible. First, eat a nutritious breakfast if you are scheduled to take the exam in the morning, or eat a healthy lunch if you are scheduled to take the exam in the afternoon. Nutritionists suggest that foods high in protein and low in carbohydrates can produce mental alertness. Based on this suggestion, you should eat "brain foods," such as lean meats and fish, leafy green vegetables, and peanuts, while avoiding cereals, pastas, potatoes, and breads. Also, do not overload on caffeine before taking the examination; this can impair your ability to concentrate and focus. You want to be as calm and relaxed as possible, and this is very difficult to do if you have infused your body with too much coffee or cola. An added distraction is that you may find your concentration broken by having to leave the test for too many restroom breaks.

Dress in loose, comfortable clothing, and do not forget any lucky charms if they are a psychological boost to you. You should dress in layers so that you can take off or put on a jacket or sweater if the room temperature feels too hot or cold during the test. Feeling comfortable and relaxed goes a long way in helping you focus on the exam during the many hours of testing.

A third rule of thumb to follow on test day is to arrive early at the test site and sit by yourself in the testing room. By arriving early (as discussed earlier), you do not feel rushed and have time to relax and become comfortable with the testing environment. If you can separate yourself from your fellow test takers, you will be able to tune out their chatter about how difficult they think this test is going to be and how worried they are about failing. If you cannot choose your seat and other test takers are talking around you, use this time to focus on all of the hard work you have put into studying for this exam and how that effort will pay off for you. Practice your positive self-talk and deep breathing exercises, if needed. When testing begins, however, be sure to be in your assigned seat, if applicable. You may not receive credit if you are not seated where you were assigned.

Sometimes the test may not begin on time, and there may be long lines. Do not let this delay bother you, as the monitors must give you the correct amount of time as soon as the test begins. If you have a major complaint about the site or the monitors, you may put this into writing and send it to ETS within 7 days at their Web site (www.ets.org). They may set up a retest with no charge if the conditions at your testing site made it difficult to deliver a fair test.

DURING THE EXAM. After the examination has been distributed, read the test directions very carefully. This is especially important when taking a multiple-choice test like the *Generalist* because of the various types of item formats described earlier in this chapter. Hard-copy test takers can also make serious mistakes when answers are required to be recorded on a separate Scantron and scored by a test-scoring machine. Be sure to stop and check about every 10 questions to make sure your Scantron number matches the question number you are answering. If you do mismatch your answer sheet, it is much better to catch this early and correct it rather than realizing what you have done at the end of the test—or not catching it at all. Do not forget to circle the number in your test booklet, too, as a precaution.

Helpful Hint:

Because the Generalist is very long and demanding, you may find it easier to take several short breaks during the testing session rather than working continuously through the exam. Try closing your eyes or putting your head on your desk or table for 15 seconds (being sure not to nod off). If you feel yourself becoming tense, take a few deep breaths and practice positive self-talk, reminding yourself that you do know this material. Step outside for a moment and walk around briskly, or have that energy bar that you brought in your purse or pocket.

TIME MANAGEMENT. Time management is a big factor in the successful completion of this examination. Remember that if you do not control your time, it will control you. Because the room in which you are testing may not have a clock, you may not be able to see a clock from where you are sitting, or the clock may not be accurate, make sure to bring with you an accurate watch that does not beep. Because the *Generalist* is a timed test, keeping track of the time you have left helps you budget your remaining time during the test session. Use all of the time allotted for the testing session by pacing yourself through the exam. There are difficult questions on this test, so do not spend too much time on any one question. Mark your first inclination and put a question mark beside it if you are uncertain, and then go on—with the aim to come back if you have time.

When you are first given your test booklet or see your computer test, note how many questions your particular exam has and divide your time by the number of questions. Also, factor in the number of minutes that you think that you will need to schedule for breaks. This gives you an idea of how many questions you must answer per hour to finish—including brief breaks. Move at a consistent pace through the exam and monitor yourself to keep track of how much time you have left. Allow at least 5 minutes at the end of the test to thoroughly check your answer sheet, making sure that you have marked an answer for each question—even if you have to quickly just guess. If you guess correctly, you are ahead. If you leave the item blank, it is wrong. Also, it would be a shame to lose a point for an incomplete erasure or a mark made outside the guidelines. Clean up your Scantron very thoroughly. If you believe that you may have some stray marks and if you are within a point or two of passing, you can request a Scantron recheck. Having your test rechecked is probably not worth it unless you have a very close to passing score. If your circumstances are such that you are out of time for keeping your job and you believe that your Scantron was a bit messy, directions for having your answer sheet rechecked are found in the Registration Bulletin.

SUMMARY

In conclusion, studying for and passing the *Generalist* is an important component in your becoming an effective Texas teacher. By following this schedule, organizing your time and materials, and using good study skills, you have an excellent chance of being successful on this examination and entering the classroom as a competent and confident educator. Teachers who know their content well are miles ahead when it comes time to planning good lessons for children. This advantage is compounded by those who also understand how to teach the content well. We hope that you find information about both of these areas in the chapters that follow and that you take the time and effort to thoroughly learn about both—for yourself (in passing the exam), but even more than that, for your children. Each chapter has numerous questions at the end that help you practice your knowledge and testing strategies. Be sure to work through each question and its rationale.

If you have questions about the Registration Bulletin, completing forms, test dates and registration deadlines, test cancellation, score reports, or other information regarding the *Generalist,* please write, call, or e-mail the following company:

ETS Web site: http://texes.ets.org/
   1-800-205-2626
   Email: texes-excet_inquires@ets.org

More contact information is available on the ETS Web site.

For disability information: www.ets.org/disability, or call 866-387-8602

If you have certification questions or questions about which tests you need, you may want to call or write the State Board of Educator Certification (SBEC). Information and Support Center are currently located at the Texas Education Agency (TEA):

Texas Education Agency

Educator Certification & Standards

1701 North Congress Ave.

WBT 5-100

Austin, TX 78701-1494

Telephone: (888) 863-5880 (toll free) Local
   Number: 512-936-8400

E-mail address: sbec@tea.state.tx.us

Web site: http://www.sbec.state.tx.us
   (certification information)

Check for new Web sites and phone numbers if those listed above are no longer current. The information listed here was current at the time of publication. However, the state changes its organizational structure, its testing structure, and so on, more often than you think. If you are in a teacher preparation program, stay in touch with a university advisor or certification officer to regularly review your program of study and any changes made in the state's testing requirements.

We wish you the best of luck on your examination!

REFERENCES

Texas Education Agency. (2009). *Preparation Manual: 191 Generalist*. Retrieved on April 4, 2010, from http://www.texes.ets.org/assets/pdf/ testprep_manuals/191_generalist_ec_6.pdf

2 Preparing to Teach Language Arts and Reading in Texas

Laveria F. Hutchison
University of Houston—Central Campus

Eleanore S. Tyson
University of Houston—Central Campus

This chapter discusses the English Language Arts and Reading (Early Childhood–Grade 6) section of the *EC-6 Generalist*. It includes standards for knowledge and classroom applications in literacy instruction and related areas such as oral language, phonemic awareness, spelling, comprehension, developmental writing, and assessment. This is, perhaps, one of the most important chapters to learn. No matter what subject you are teaching, you will *always* be working with children on reading skills.

The authors of this chapter would like first to stress the importance of under-standing each element of these standards as a test taker. As an example, let's consider *Standard VIII: Development of Written Communication*. First, the test taker must know each stage of the writing process and its relationship to the other English Language Arts and Reading standards and assessment proce-dures, including the vocabulary and related best practices. The test taker must then understand the purpose of each test item, and connections should be made back to the standard's key terms and concepts. In this way, a test taker determines the best answer that relates to the standard. It is a circular process that goes from the standard to the purpose of the question and to the con-nection of response choices. As you study this chapter, you must also connect this information with the *Pedagogy and Professional Responsibilities (PPR)* TExES. There are questions in this exam that test not only content knowledge but also your knowledge of best teaching practices and pedagogy. It takes practice in order to become a successful TExES question analyzer, but you can acquire this skill.

The English Language Arts and Reading section of the *Generalist* consists of 12 standards and accounts for more than 30 percent of the total TExES *Generalist* test items. What becomes readily apparent as you begin to study is that each of the Standards in the chapter is tightly interwoven with the others. It is impossible to separate one from another, and so you see many overlaps. This should encourage you to see that all that is presented in the standards and competencies must be learned in concert. In addition, these standards correlate with the Texas Essential Knowledge and Skills (TEKS) for English Language Arts and Reading that tell teachers what knowledge and skills *children* should gain at each grade level. Of course, that means that teachers must not only know the content listed in the TEKS in order to teach these skills, but they must also be able to use the best methods to teach this information. Table 2.1 summarizes the instructional components of the TEKS for language arts and reading for Pre-K through 6th grade.

Table 2.1 Summary of Pre-K–Grade 6 TEKS for Language Arts and Reading

Pre-K	Students interact with responsive adults and peers in a language and print-rich instructional environment that provides opportunities for development in the following areas: **1.** Listening comprehension **3.** Functions of print **2.** Phonological awareness **4.** Letter knowledge
Kindergarten	Students engage in instructional activities that promote development of oral language usage, conceptual knowledge, narrative and expository print forms, alphabet usage, and letter formation.
Grade 1	Students engage in instructional activities that promote development of independent readers and writers by using various print forms, by providing reading materials that promote fluency and understanding, and by demonstrating the conventions of writing and spelling.
Grade 2	Students engage in instructional activities that promote development of independent readers by providing instruction that promotes sight vocabulary development, teaching and demon-strating a variety of word identification strategies, teaching comprehension skills, demonstrat-ing graphic presentations, teaching note-taking procedures, and teaching conventions of writing and spelling.
Grade 3	Students engage in instructional activities that promote structural analysis skills, glossary skills, elements of the writing process, independent reading activities, and activities that provide a transition from manuscript writing to cursive writing.
Grade 4	Students engage in instructional activities that demonstrate story structure analysis, produce narrative and expository writing products, practice the parts of speech in a variety of written forms, emphasize awareness of correct spelling and grammar, and demonstrate application of the elements of writing.

(continued)

Table 2.1	Continued
Grade 5	Students engage in instructional activities that promote critical listening, reading, writing, and understanding of a speaker's or writer's message while incorporating such elements into their own writing and production of projects and reports that are based on research and supported by visual graphics.
Grade 6	Students engage in instructional activities that enable them to master previously learned skills: note taking, researching, reading a variety of literature genres, understanding and using literary devices, applying grammar and usage skills, applying spelling and punctuation functions, and creating and evaluating film, technology and other viewing products and presentations.

As you read the information about each standard, you should try to capture the relationship between the TEKS for children in grades EC-6 and this *Generalist* examination. You can find a listing of these TEKS on the following Web site: http://ritter.tea.state.tx.us/rules/tac/chapter110/ch110a.pdf.

 # Standard I: Oral Language

Competency 001: Teachers understand the importance of oral language, know the developmental processes of oral language, and provide students with a variety of instructional opportunities to develop listening and speaking skills.

The teacher knows the basic linguistic concepts and knows developmental stages in acquiring oral language. He or she plans oral language instruction based on informal and formal assessment, recognizes speech delays or differences requiring thorough evaluation and intervention, and designs instructional practices that promote purposeful listening activities. The EC-6 teacher provides various instructional activities that allow children to have opportunities to engage in oral language activities that involve adult and peer participation and provides opportunities for children to evaluate the effectiveness of their own spoken language. There is an instructional environment provided by the teacher that promotes discussions about books, objects, experiences, pictures, and other print and nonprint sources. Remember that the TEKS actively promote oral language development and instruction.

Try this practice question:

Mr. Jones teaches a kindergarten class comprised of a diverse population of children with varying language proficiency levels. Which activity from the following list would be the least effective in encouraging language development for all his students?

A. Mr. Jones facilitates a story writing activity in which all children contribute to the story as he writes the class story on chart paper. Class members then act out the story they created.

B. Children memorize and chorally present a poem selected by the teacher to be shared with parents in a class presentation.

C. Mr. Jones creates language centers, such as a listening center, a puppet center, and a grocery store center, where children can work during different times of the day.

D. Mr. Jones arranges children in "Think, Pair, Share" cooperative groups to discuss the experiment as it progresses.

Remember that the question asks for the least effective activity. Choice *A* incorporates and includes the language and voice of all students in the classroom. Because students also see the teacher writing down what they say, children can understand how reading and writing are associated. Additional language use and oral expression are reinforced through the retelling and acting out of the story at the end. Choice *B* does not promote language proficiency unless children understand the words in the poem. There is an indication that, because it is a teacher-selected poem, the message of the poem may have more meaning for the teacher and parents than for the students. Choice *C* is well rounded in the teacher's attempt to meet the language needs of all students, whether they can or cannot recognize rhyming words or whether their language proficiency level is highly communicative or weak. The activities described in the centers would promote the language development of all children at any level of proficiency. Choice *D* encourages communication through one of many types of cooperative groupings. Children have time to think about an answer, share it with a partner, and, finally, share it with the group so that they have the opportunity to test it out with others and reflect on it before sharing with a large group. Therefore, choice *B* is correct as the least effective activity.

Children come to school with a myriad of backgrounds and with varying degrees of language proficiency, and these differences in language development have been strongly shaped and influenced by language used in the home. Children fortunate enough to have had a rich literacy background at home are often confident and articulate. Their oral language is frequently quite advanced for their age. However, there are those children who, for a variety of reasons, are shy or reluctant to speak or have not had the advantages of language development offered by some homes (including some where English is not the first language). Teachers must be aware of individual experiences with language to best meet the learning needs of their students. These children must feel comfortable speaking with another person at a personal and informal level before they will contribute to class discussions, speak out in a cooperative group, volunteer to take part in a skit, or give an oral report. When responding to questions about this standard, be aware that questions about students' language development will most likely focus on teacher awareness of individual students' background experiences with language and current language proficiency. The teacher's ability to meet students' learning needs with an appropriate instructional strategy (by considering individual students' learning and instructional levels, learning styles, personal backgrounds, and so forth) will build on each student's present ability levels.

As the novice teacher begins to investigate the conceptual development of oral language (speaking and listening), it is a good idea for him or her to review the features and stages of language development. A well-developed oral language base in young readers is important in learning to read. Although learning theories that explain the processes children follow in learning language are sometimes controversial, educators usually accept the following sequence (Jewell & Zintz, 1986):

1. Vocalizing sounds (crying or babbling) to obtain a response from a parent or caregiver.
2. Recognizing a stimulus-producing sound (hears a barking sound and looks at the family's dog).
3. Generalizing a word to identify an object (parent asks for the ball, and child responds by identifying the ball in a variety of ways, such as looking at or touching the ball).
4. Speaking by age 3 years in phrases and sentences containing approximately four words, understanding the concept of "yes" and "no," asking and answering simple questions, and following directions, such as, "Pick up the ball and give it to Mommy."

5. Developing language skills in preschoolers through focusing on using four to five words in a sentence, using a limited number of grammar rules, creating and orally presenting personal stories (about going to the zoo or to McDonald's), asking and answering questions, and describing objects and personal events.
6. Acquiring a speaking vocabulary of 2,000 to 3,000 words by kindergarten age and continuing to develop oral language competencies.
7. Developing a continuous ability to produce words that includes the use of social talk, correct grammar, and construction of oral and written complex sentences.

There are many ways to encourage the development of age-appropriate oral language skills. Early childhood teachers should foster a language-rich environment by displaying charts showing labelled pictures of objects or actually displaying concrete objects, using picture books to enhance oral language development, providing technology, using word walls that display high-frequency sight words or new vocabulary (such as an "adjective wall," displaying items that identify colors, introducing symbols that explain directions, and so forth). Instructional practices that integrate language development should provide expanded time-chunks for incorporating many or all of the entire *language development components* (speaking, reading, spelling, writing, and listening) that engage children in literacy as a whole. This type of intradisciplinary approach allows children to listen to or orally read a variety of cognitive resources, such as predictable books, literature-based basal readers, trade books, computers, newsprint, and visual media from peers, librarians, teachers, and other adults.

One element for beginning teachers to consider is that classroom instruction needs to relate to students from culturally and linguistically diverse backgrounds. Linguistic considerations also include the various **dialects** and languages present in classrooms, so diverse backgrounds include those students who speak Standard English, who speak nonstandard English, who are bilingual, who are emerging English speakers, and who speak no English at all. Let us investigate some strategies and terms that connect with these young learners.

The **language experience approach (LEA)** is an instructional method that incorporates the various components of language arts by using children's experiences and backgrounds as a structure for developing stories—individually or in a heterogeneous group. These group or individually generated stories can encourage discussion on ideas about school activities, field trips, a trade book, observations, structured words, personal experiences, creative stories, or a variety of other topics. LEA is connected to Piaget's schema theory (building on the known) by using students' experiences, backgrounds, and prior knowledge as a starting point for developing stories as the teacher writes down children's orally told stories and responses. LEA allows children to observe the organization and mechanical functions of written language by watching the teacher print directionally from left to right and from top to bottom. Children also see printed word organization and spacing, punctuation, letter formation, and sentence structure. In addition, children with limited English proficiency (LEP) and with limited background experiences can benefit from LEA because they are better able to comprehend reading material that they themselves have dictated to the teacher.

Because the connection between LEA and children with limited English proficiency is mentioned, there is the need to discuss **nonstandard dialects**. These are dialects used by children who are bilingual, multilingual, and who speak only English. It is important to note that Standard English is a dialect that is effectively used by many members of society (we might call it *business English dialect*). Nonstandard English is often connected to the usage of grammatical variations in language production. A dialect may belong to a cultural group, and usage within that group requires certain language rules just as with Standard English. In relationship to LEA and how to most effectively deal with nonstandard English in classroom situations, consider the following conversational example between a student and a teacher:

Teacher: Have you decided on a title for your story?

Student: Yup. Me go write bout my cat are going to have kittens.

Teacher: Oh! I think that is a great idea. *You are going to write about how your cat* is going to have kittens. Let's get started.

The teacher accepts the child's idea that is stated in nonstandard English and models another way to restate the child's sentence using Standard English. Note that the teacher focuses on the ideas the child offers. The teacher is accepting of the statement and not critical of the child's language used to give the idea in this conversation. It is important to note that a child's personal usage of oral and written language has an important multicultural aspect, because not being accepting of a child's language production, especially when the language includes nonstandard English, could deter learning risks and language growth. However, teachers should also do the following: (1) always model many examples of correct and effective speech structures and writing examples in classroom situations, (2) ask children to clarify their responses, and (3) provide feedback that encourages Standard English. Many teachers feel that a goal for children with dialects is *bidialectism*, meaning that children can feel less pressure using their home dialect as they learn to be successful in using Standard English in school and later in the business world.

It is important to state again that children enter school with oral and listening vocabularies that have been developing since they were born. These vocabularies have been shaped by children's cognitive, linguistic, cultural, and experiential backgrounds. A teacher's goal should be to promote children's development of reading and writing vocabularies that closely parallel these oral and listening vocabularies. As mentioned, Piaget's word *schema* reminds us that it is easier to learn if we can attach new knowledge to something already known (1973). Unless they are very young children, students have also had differing language arts and reading instruction. Kari, for example, had Mrs. Morrison in first grade, who is a very traditional reading teacher, whereas Jack had Mr. Keller, a new teacher who was not well trained in language arts/reading. Brittani, however, had Mrs. Gleason, a new teacher from an excellent university program with many new innovations. All of these children will arrive in second grade with different reading backgrounds that are not necessarily based on their intelligences, so their new second-grade teacher must take these differences into consideration in designing instruction for each child's success. By the time a child has arrived in the sixth grade, he or she has a wealth of different experiences that may affect how well a child can read and use the components of language arts at that point.

Language interference is the use of sounds, syntax, and vocabulary of two languages simultaneously as a child participates in literacy activities. **Bilingual education** involves presenting reading and other subject area materials in the child's native language, while gradually introducing English. **English as a Second Language (ESL)** teachers may work with children from a variety of countries and who speak a number of languages who are all placed together in one class. As the beginning teacher instructs children who are in the process of learning English (English Language Learners, or ELLs), it is important to explain the common meanings of English words before beginning instruction and to use strategies such as LEA. Many ESL techniques and much more information on ELLs are listed in Chapter 10.

In a language arts classroom, *listening* is a significant part of oral language learning. Students who become active listeners can remember important parts of a story, follow directions, respond to purpose-setting questions set by the teacher, participate in cooperative groups, and improve their vocabulary development. As children learn to listen critically, the teacher should provide learners with practice in building on prior knowledge, in learning to synthesize information from more than one source, and in solving problems. As students learn to listen for appreciation, the teacher should emphasize the understanding of mood and of the use of **figurative language**. Although there are a variety of instructional components that can be used, note taking and questioning are two that are important in this area. Books on tape (or CDs) in listening centers can also provide experiences for EC-6 children in a variety of different voices.

Note taking is a selective listening activity that allows children to organize ideas, identify main ideas, and provide study points. Teachers can model developmentally appropriate note taking for students by presenting a graphic organizer, such as a graphic mapping activity or an outline of the content (which may be partially filled in), and modelling in oral presentations. As children learn the developmental appropriate process of identifying and recording important information, they can engage in cooperative groups to compare ideas. Additional information about note taking is included in the discussion of Standard VII of this chapter.

Questioning is another area that can promote effective listening and higher-level thinking. Teacher questioning should promote responses from children that help them comprehend literal, inferential, and evaluative areas of ideas and meanings. Additional information about comprehension is included in the discussion of Standard VII later in this chapter.

Learning a language involves understanding how to analyze words—often through sound. The discussion of this standard highlights several components of linguistic concepts, and then proceeds to discuss those that beginning teachers should recognize as part of the decoding process. EC-6 teachers should understand the concept of **decoding**, or unlocking the meaning of a word, very well. Numerous studies by educational researchers have provided information on the processes young children use in decoding words (Rupley & Willson, 2000). As children attempt to pronounce a word, they gain information from the way a word is spelled (**orthography**), the way a word is pronounced (**phonology**), the way a word is defined (**semantics**), the recognition of the sounds heard in a word (**segmentation**), the sentence structure (**syntax**), and the meaning of a word in its **contextual** setting. This is a challenging process for teachers to convey to children and for children to apply to listening and the many **text forms** (or printed materials) encountered in classrooms.

Word analysis is a strategy that includes three cueing systems that good readers develop and learn to use: (1) **graphophonic** (sound/symbol relationships), (2) **syntactic** (patterns of phrases, clauses, and sentences), and (3) **semantics** (meaning of words and combinations of words). To become proficient in word analysis, children must develop an effective *sight vocabulary* (instantly recognizable words) and know how to use contextual and structural analysis, as well as **phonics** skills. All these are considered **facilitative** skills and are not considered reading. The actual *understanding*, or comprehension, of what has been read is the **functional** part of reading.

There are many strategies for developing and expanding vocabulary. Aside from using glossaries that are located in the back of textbooks, dictionaries, and thesauruses, students can use word walls, examine homophones and homographs, study idioms, metaphors, and similes, explore riddles and other word plays, engage in word sorts, and create *semantic maps* (word clusters) and **semantic feature analysis** grids. Teachers may also label concrete items in the classroom with the words. Following are descriptions of some of the important terms in this paragraph:

1. **Homographs.** Words spelled the same but have different pronunciations and meanings: for example, "She is wearing a red *bow*." "She will *bow* to the queen."
2. **Homophones.** Words that sound the same but have different spellings and meanings: for example, "He is wearing a *red* shirt," "He *read* the book."
3. **Idioms.** Figurative sayings that have special meanings in a particular language or dialect: as an example, "*Keep your shirt on!*" basically means "Don't get angry."
4. **Metaphors.** Comparison of two unlike things without using *as* or *like*; an example is "*The moon was a silver dollar against the night sky.*"
5. **Semantic map** *(word cluster)*. Writing a word or concept in the center circle (or bubble) of a cluster, drawing rays, writing information about the word or concept, and making connections between the word or concept and the related unit of study.

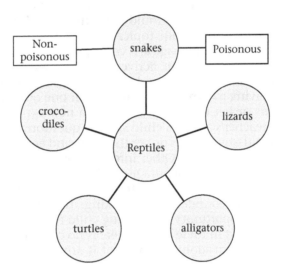

6. **Semantic feature analysis.** Comparisons between things using a chart.

Animal	Size	Habitat
Cow	Large	Domestic
Squirrel	Small	Wild
Dog	Medium	Domestic

7. **Similes.** Comparisons between two things of a different kind or quality using *like* or *as*. An example is "*The rain came down like transparent sheets.*"
8. **Word sorts.** Sorting a collection of words taken from a word wall or other source into two or more categories.
9. **Word wall.** A list of words children are learning or know posted on a poster (or an actual wall in a classroom) in a highly visible location.

A discussion of integrated language arts should include thematic learning units. **Thematic units** are used to connect the various *components of language arts* (speaking, reading, spelling, writing, and listening) with other content areas. Thematic units may have a focus in any content area (science, health, mathematics, history, etc.). Children enjoy units on, for example, butterflies, apples, shapes, cultures of other lands, and so forth. A first-grade thematic learning unit in social studies, for instance, could focus on "The Pilgrims Celebrating Thanksgiving at Plymouth." In this unit, children might read (or their teacher can read to them) textbook information and **trade books**. Trade books are children's literature that teachers can sometimes use in instructional settings instead of basal readers or textbooks about the topic. In addition, in this example of a thematic unit, children could **research** this period of history by investigating lifestyles, tasting foods the Pilgrims found in America, focusing on significant people, and so forth. Children could examine a variety of sources, including computer-generated resources, to collect information about the topic. It is important for teachers to consider instructional activities that address children's interests. As an example, the teacher might encourage children to participate in writing or performing a short play that highlights this significant period. The unit might focus on games that children played during those times (both Pilgrim and Native American) compared to games children play now. Mathematics elements might compare the difference between how much things cost during that period with the present, or they may measure to determine how large the houses were in Plymouth colony. Counting songs (with lyrics on a Thanksgiving theme) combine mathematics, reading, and music. Thematic units should contain a number of subject areas and skills under the umbrella of one topic.

An important language arts concept to be considered is **oral expression**. In a language arts classroom, active speaking is recognized as a critical element of learning. It takes practice and feedback to become adept in expressing oneself orally. Having a **conversation** with even one other person who is not a member of his or her own family may be a new experience for some young children. A teacher's asking a child specific questions about his or her interests can help a child organize his or her thoughts and encourage the communication of information and ideas. Other informal speaking activities, such as role-playing using a telephone, encourage a child to adjust voice volume and wait for the other person's response. In this way, a child learns telephone etiquette while gaining confidence in speaking. **Textless** (or **wordless**) **picture books** provide an opportunity for a young child to tell a story to the teacher. Because there is no text in these books, there is no correct way to relate the story, so the child has the freedom to interpret it any way he or she chooses. From this "reading," the teacher can assess a child's *sense of story* (a term used to describe a child's understanding of how a story begins, unfolds, and concludes), as well as vocabulary development and communication skills. **Show-and-tell** builds speaker's confidence and stimulates conversation. It also provides an important link between home and school because the child brings something from home that is special to him or her. Children are more articulate when they are talking about something that is well known and important to them. **Discussions** about special events or favorite books can also afford opportunities for oral language development. **Puppets** are confidence builders for many children. Children who refrain from speaking in class will frequently feel comfortable talking to (or through) a puppet. The puppet becomes the center of attention, so the child feels less self-conscious and can therefore be more articulate. Other strategies for encouraging oral language development include **interviews, oral reports, debates**, and dramatic presentations.

An extremely profitable way to encourage oral expression is through the use of cooperative groups. Productive noise levels vary when students are encouraged to work in pairs or in larger cooperative groups. These groups encourage discussions, reactions, and negotiations with a partner or in a small group before speaking before many. In using cooperative groups, teachers structure instruction so children use discussion purposefully. Teachers can promote active speaking in classroom situations by implementing activities such as:

1. **Rereading stories.** Asking children to talk about their favorite parts of the story and their favorite characters in the story.
2. **Retelling stories.** Teachers may have children use props, puppets, dolls, and so on in the retelling process to encourage comprehension and fluency. (See discussion of story retelling under Standard VII.)
3. **Choral reading** and speaking that allow children to orally share written words. Choral delivery can also be used in a thematic unit as children orally read a poem or, in a science class, read a section of print together. Singing songs from music books or other sources has this effect as well.
4. **Readers' theater**, which involves children's reading from a prepared script or from a script that children have written. Children learn to project the voice of characters, bring characters to life, and have eye contact with their audience. This activity incorporates reading and oral fluency skills by student performances and listening skills by the audience.
5. Social classroom talk, or **conversation**, that encourages informal discussions about characters in books or formal discussions about how to solve a problem.

Although this particular standard and competency focuses on oral language learning (speaking and listening), reading and writing cannot be separated. Students should have the opportunity to actively and orally read from a variety of sources such as books, poems, magazines, computer screens, and other types of print. Students are encouraged to actively write and read aloud such products as poems, creative stories, journal entries, drafts and edited works, records of science experiments, and many other types of writing products. Very young children may begin to develop products (such as shape books, picture books that show familiar objects, and letter books) and be encouraged to read or explain them to others.

As teachers plan instruction for oral language skills, effective assessment practices are important to collect for making decisions about further instructional practices. Teachers of young children usually collect instructional information on oral and listening skills by the use of observations, from parents during conferences, from informal conversations, from various types of assignments, and from formal and informal tests. Observational data can be recorded on checklists, in field notes, in notebooks, or in any form that will allow the teacher to organize and summarize collected data. Technology currently allows recordings or other artifacts to be scanned and stored for evaluation over time. This can enhance portfolio assessment of children. Recordings of oral skills can be particularly helpful in showing progress or lack thereof. Parental input is important because parents can provide information about the child's home environment. In addition, parents can be encouraged to promote literacy activities in the home by (1) asking a variety of questions about favorite topics such as pets and toys; (2) placing labels on objects/things that are in the home such as *light, door, window,* or *bed;* (3) rereading books or other materials that children seem to love and enjoy or having children read to them; (4) helping children place cut-out magazine pictures into categories such as "animals that bark," "things that people eat," "things that are green," and so on; (5) playing developmentally and age-appropriate games; (6) providing many opportunities for conversation; (7) reading predictable books; (8) going to the community library to select books to read and reread at home; (9) encouraging and showcasing schoolwork and other beginning attempts of literacy activities in the home; and in many other ways. Astute teachers prepare take-home kits for parents to work with their children on relevant skills. Formal assessments used in early literacy settings usually measure knowledge of letters, oral vocabulary development, recognition of words, and visual and auditory discrimination ability (Barrett, 1965). The informal and formal assessment procedures that highlight different instructional practices will be discussed again in Standard X.

Try these practice questions:

Mrs. Ruiz has several Pre-K children who are reluctant to speak in class. What activity might be *least* effective in stimulating the development of their oral language?

   A. Have students use puppets to tell a familiar story.
   B. Have students role-play telephone conversations.
   C. Have students "read" aloud textless, or wordless, books.
   D. Have each child bring a show-and-tell item to class and allow each child the option of describing it or not.

Consider what activity might encourage a shy or reluctant child to speak in a class setting. With regard to choice *A*, young children will often speak using a puppet, even though they may be too shy to speak face-to-face to an adult. Choice *B*, role-play conversations using a play telephone, offers a familiar and comfortable way for a young child to express himself or herself. Choice *C*, read aloud textless, or wordless, picture books affords a framework for oral story-telling. Because each of the these choices could be used effectively to promote oral language development, we can assume the correct answer is *D*. Show-and-tell is often used with young children because it permits them to talk about a topic or item that is important to them in a relaxed and accepting atmosphere. However, the activity is normally conducted in a whole class circle, so shy children may still find this intimidating. Also, if they choose not to describe their item, it does not stimulate their oral language development. The answer is *D*.

Mr. Cate, a fourth-grade teacher, has invited a guest speaker to discuss the important events related to the upcoming rodeo. Realizing that the speaker's main objective is to present a wide range of information over a 30-minute time period, which of the following would be the best listening practice for Mr. Cate to implement for the children to use as they listen to the speaker?

   A. Provide a list of purpose-setting questions.
   B. Arrange the children into cooperative groups.
   C. Provide a summary of the speaker's discussion.
   D. Provide the children with an open note-taking sheet.

Remember that Mr. Cate wants to provide activities to support effective listening practices that allow his children to identify purposes for listening to the speaker. The use of cooperative grouping, recommended in choice *B*, could be an effective practice for peer engagement to discuss aspects of the speaker's ideas *after* the speaker has finished. Providing the children with either a written or an oral summary of the speaker's ideas, recommended in choice *C*, could provide ideas about the speaker's presentation *afterward*. The note-taking sheet, recommended in choice *D*, does not provide a purpose for listening to the speaker. Having a purpose to listen to the speaker assists children in focusing on the content of the speaker's ideas, and this knowledge allows them to have the information necessary to engage in other activities. Choice *A* is the best response because good questions give children an effective method for gaining information by providing a rationale for collecting information during the speech. The answer is *A*.

Students in Miss Lucio's urban kindergarten class dictated a story about their field trip to the fire station. What should she not expect in the content of their oral delivery?

   A. Standard English
   B. Inconsistent grammar structure
   C. Details about the field trip
   D. Events highlighting the field trip

Choices *B*, *C*, and *D* are components of the Language Experience Approach (LEA) that are frequently found in dictated stories and that are discussed in Standard I. Each of these elements should be expected; therefore, choice *A*, Standard English, is what the teacher should not expect in a dictated story at this time in the young child's development. However, Standard English, or "business" English, is the target teachers try to reach with students. The answer is *A*.

Miss Chavez, a Pre-K teacher, plans to provide a list of at-home activities for parents to use. Which parental activities should she not suggest?

   A. Allow your child to assist in planning family activities.
   B. Read books to your child and allow your child to discuss the pictures.
   C. Use a scripted conversation developed by professional reading teachers to help reinforce vocabulary.
   D. Clip pictures from magazines that represent the "color of the week."

In this situation, Miss Chavez could appropriately recommend choices *A*, *B*, and *D* to parents as activities that could foster literacy concepts. The teacher could provide suggestions for vocabulary to be used at home but should not ask for scripted parent/child conversations. Scripted conversations might not match the parent/child normal patterns of talk, thereby appearing unnatural, stilted, and contrived, making both parent and child uncomfortable and unmotivated. The answer is *C*.

Standard II: Phonological and Phonemic Awareness

Competency 002: **Teachers understand the components of phonological and phonemic awareness and utilize a variety of approaches to help students develop this awareness and its relationship to written language. (See note after Standard I.)**

The teacher understands the significance of phonological and phonemic awareness instruction to the reading process, adjusts instruction to meet the developmental needs of children, uses assessment practices to plan instruction, designs a variety of age-appropriate instructional activities, and is able to enlist the collaboration of families and of other professionals to promote each child's phonological and phonemic awareness. Remember that beginning in Pre-K and continuing through grade 6, TEKS objectives require using a variety of print and nonprint language activities that expose children to phonemic awareness instruction.

Use this kindergarten teacher's instructional activity to answer the practice question that follows the activity:

Miss Fuentes, a kindergarten teacher, asks Alex, Mario, Mac, Armando, and Kasi to come to the literacy table. Miss Fuentes plans to use an oral activity to practice rhyming words. Following is the activity she uses with the children:

I am going to say two words together. After I say the words, I will call on one of you to tell me if the words rhyme. If the words rhyme, say "yes." If the words do not rhyme, say "no."

She uses the following list:

1. top/pop	**5.** sun/man
2. rag/big	**6.** make/take
3. sack/bat	**7.** pig/peg
4. look/book	**8.** could/should

Identify the prereading skill the kindergarten teacher is using.

A. Segmenting of rhyming sounds
B. Auditory discrimination of rhyming pairs of words
C. Visual discrimination of rhyming pairs of words
D. Blending

Choice *B* is the correct response because the teacher is presenting pairs of words orally to the group of students for the purpose of having them identify rhyming pairs. A description of segmenting and blending is presented later in this section. The answer is *B*.

This standard highlights the concept of **phonological awareness** (the ability to use *letter-sound knowledge* to identify an unknown word) and **phonemic awareness** (the ability to recognize that spoken words are made up of a sequence of individual sounds that contributes to the young reader's ability to recognize and pronounce unknown words) (Rubin, 2000). When first approaching sound awareness and word analysis, children must first realize that sentences are composed of separate words. One can already see how easily the concepts of oral literacy discussed in Competency 1 (speaking and listening) overlap with the concepts within this competency. As a teacher begins to develop instructional activities that demonstrate to the young reader that words are made up of a series of sounds, it is important to realize that several reading researchers have found that phonemic awareness abilities are strong indicators and predictors of successful reading development (Cunningham, Cunningham, Hoffman, & Yopp, 1998; Juel, 1988; Stanovich, 1994). When young learners cannot recognize certain sounds in words, the teacher must begin to isolate these problems and design instruction that addresses the particular area of difficulty in phonemic awareness. Phonemic awareness is a necessary skill for the young reader to acquire in learning to read and spell. According to Adams (1990), young readers should be able to perform the following phonemic awareness tasks that relate to learning to read and to spell.

1. **Rhyming and Alliteration. Rhyming** requires the young reader to recognize rhymes or to produce patterns of rhyming words. Rhyming is believed to be the least difficult phonemic awareness task to develop because young children have usually been exposed to oral productions of rhyming word patterns from books that were read to them, singing songs, adults' oral play language, and other auditory media sources. Initially, rhyming is developed through listening. Later, the young reader learns to identify rhyming patterns in various types of printed materials. The following sentence is an example of rhyming: The girl who wore a *hat* was sitting next to her *cat*. **Alliteration** requires the young reader to recognize words in a sentence or phrase that mostly begin with the same letter sound. The following sentence is an example of alliteration: T̲all T̲anya took t̲iny t̲ots t̲o t̲own.

2. **Blending.** This task requires the young reader to blend a series of orally produced sounds to form a word. As an example, the teacher would produce the separate sounds of /t/, /o/, /p/ to the reader and expect the reader to say *top*.

3. **Segmenting beginning and ending sounds in words.** The young reader who has the ability to hear sounds in words should be able to hear and identify sounds at the beginning or end of a word. The teacher could ask the reader to identify the sound heard at the beginning of the word top (the /t/) and also the sound heard at the end (the /p/).

4. **Phoneme substitution.** This refers to the manipulation of sounds to create new words (changing an /m/ to a /b/ in *mat* to make *bat*) (Gipe, 2010).

As the young child develops phonemic awareness, he or she can recognize that words rhyme, that words can begin and end with either the same sound or a different sound, and that words are made of **phonemes** (the smallest unit of sound in a language that distinguishes one word from another word) that can be blended to form words. For example, when a child knows the phonemes /b/ /a/ /t/ represent the sounds "buh," "a," "tuh," he or she can blend them together to say the word "bat."

It is important to mention again that parents can play a significant role in the development of children's progress in their phonemic awareness development by reading, saying, or singing rhymes together, playing oral language games, and encouraging early written expression by using scribbles and forms of invented spelling. **Invented spelling** is a written approximation based on how a child determines the spelling of a word. As an example, a kindergarten student might write the following sentence to describe his new puppy: M PUE ES QT AN VRE TNE (My puppy is cute and very tiny.). The discussion of *Standard VIII: Development of Written Communication* provides additional information related to invented spelling. Within send-home packets, as mentioned earlier, early childhood teachers and early elementary school teachers can also provide examples of reading materials and language activities that parents can use in the home to promote phonemic awareness. The home reinforces the work that teachers do at school. Young children need to be able to (1) associate sounds with letters in words; (2) learn the function of consonant sounds and letters in the initial, medial, and final position; and (3) see print in a variety of situations (big books, peer writing, word walls, trade books, basal readers, worksheets, charts, etc.).

Teachers of young children are encouraged to use both oral interaction and direct instruction in demonstrating phonemic awareness patterns that show how sounds in words are manipulated. The following list provides an instructional structure for developing phonemic awareness.

1. *Promote language through different types of oral delivery.* Teachers of young children can use nursery rhymes, riddles, songs, read-aloud books, poems, and other creative ideas that provide sound production. Teachers can demonstrate the same types of activities to parents during the annual Open House/Back to School Night, at parent–teacher conferences, through newsletters, on a Web site, and at various types of parent educational meetings. Children should be asked to respond to questions and statements related to reading selections in both narrative and expository print sources. The teacher or parent can ask questions such as "Which two words rhyme?" "Which two words begin with the same sound?" and "Identify the sounds that you hear at the end of the first two words in the following sentence." Rhyming words are used frequently as an instructional activity for young children, and the teacher should spend time demonstrating that rhyming words sound the same at the end of each word used in the rhyming pattern. In addition, teachers should encourage children to make up their own rhyming word patterns. Older children can be encouraged to create "hink pinks," or riddle rhymes in which they think of a two word rhyming phrase, like fat cat, and then write a riddle question to be answered by it (i.e., What do you call a chubby kitty? A fat cat).

2. *Create games and activities that develop an awareness of sounds in words.* As children begin to develop an understanding of the concept of phonemic awareness, the teacher can purchase or develop games and activities that practice sound patterns in words. As an example, teachers can say a word (or children's names, for example) and ask children to clap the number of syllables heard as the teacher repeats the word. The **Elkonin box** (1963) is frequently used to practice phonemic awareness by placing a picture on an overhead projector or worksheet and drawing the appropriate number of boxes needed to represent the sounds heard in the word. The teacher might have a picture of the word *cat* and three boxes under the picture. Each box represents a sound heard in the word *cat*. Children then place some type of marker (paper clips, plastic counters, pennies, beans, etc.) in each box as the teacher pronounces a word with that sound. As children advance in their understanding of phonemic awareness, the teacher should ask children to write the letter of each sound in the appropriate box. The teacher should have several examples of Elkonin boxes for the children to use.

| c | a | t |

Another activity to help students delete or add phonemes to words is having an ending sound on tagboard (such as "at") with beginning sounds (c, f, m, etc.), which can be flipped in front of the ending sound ("at") to make new words. These flip charts can be teacher constructed on tagboard with the beginning phonemes on a binder ring. Technology programs abound for emerging readers, but a teacher must be sure that he or she uses a variety rather than only programs that are "worksheets" on the computer. One type of technology that helps students with difficulties in spelling in this area is voice recognition programs, where a computer "reports" in writing what a child says. The teacher must also make sure that children are given appropriate grade-level reading activities and assignments.

3. *Design writing activities.* As children begin to develop an understanding of phonemic awareness, the teacher should provide classroom activities that allow children to experiment with language through writing words, phrases, sentences, paragraphs, and longer written segments. The more opportunities children are given to write, the better they will become at understanding and hearing the sounds in words they can use to invent the spelling patterns used to produce a word. As children become capable of segmenting sounds used to spell words, the teacher should encourage children to approximate (or invent) the spelling of words based on the sounds heard in words. Teachers should then provide instruction in classroom settings that will enhance spelling patterns. In addition, teachers can use classroom word walls to display spelling patterns used in vocabulary words, sight words, other frequently used words, and so forth. Teachers should remember to encourage children to use words from the word wall in both oral and written language formats.

Table 2.2   Components of the *Texas Primary Reading Inventory*

Grade	Screening Section	Inventory Section
Kindergarten	Graphophonemic knowledge	Book and print awareness
	Phonemic awareness	Phonemic awareness
		Graphophonemic knowledge
		Listening comprehension
Grade 1	Graphophonemic knowledge	Phonemic awareness
	Word reading	Graphophonemic knowledge
	Phonemic awareness	Reading accuracy and fluency
		Listening comprehension
Grade 2	Word reading	Graphophonemic knowledge
		Reading accuracy and fluency
		Reading comprehension

In classroom settings, teachers can assess a child's ability to use *phonemic* awareness through informal or formal means. Informal assessments that evaluate phonemic awareness include: (1) teacher observations of students' completing phonemic awareness tasks that require them to complete written tasks and produce oral responses, (2) teacher use of rubrics and checklists that identify the level of performance students have acquired using phonemic awareness tasks, and (3) other teacher-generated products that provide evidence of students' growth using phonemic awareness tasks.

One formal assessment instrument, the *Texas Primary Reading Inventory* (TPRI), is currently being used by teachers in Texas to determine children's ability to manipulate sounds in words and to determine how they understand these words. It is used in kindergarten through second grade and has been designed as an early reading assessment to determine young readers' early literacy and comprehension development (Carlson, Fletcher, Foorman, Francis, & Schatschneider, 2001). Table 2.2 shows the components of the TPRI's screening section and inventory section.

The *Yopp-Singer Test of Phonemic Segmentation* is another formal assessment used to measure children's ability to pronounce sounds in spoken words and to spell words. This is a 22-item assessment that requires children to respond to teacher-pronounced words by segmenting each pronounced word into separate sounds. This test allows teachers to identify students who need instruction and practice in phonemic awareness (Yopp, 1995).

Read this activity and respond to the question that follows:

Ms. Nguyen, a kindergarten teacher, asks students to "clap the number of syllables" heard in this list of words:

1. schoolhouse
2. building
3. pony
4. blue
5. Monday
6. hamburger
7. wagon
8. book

What is the purpose of this activity?

A. To determine the development of sight words.
B. To determine the ability to hear syllables.
C. To determine the readiness for teaching reading.
D. To determine the use of capital letters.

This activity allows Ms. Nguyen to determine how effectively her kindergarten children are hearing syllables in orally pronounced words. Therefore, choice *B* is correct.

Standard III: Alphabetic Principle

Competency 003: **Teachers understand the importance of the alphabetic principle for reading English and provide instruction that helps students understand the relationship between spoken language and printed words. (See note after Standard I.)**

The teacher knows the elements of the alphabetic principle, understands individual differences as related to the alphabetic principle, provides instructional activities that assist children in gaining competence in determining sound/letter relationships, and uses a variety of assessment practices that determine skill development. Remember that the TEKS promote instruction that uses a variety of practices for developing print awareness, letter knowledge, word analysis strategies, and fluency development.

Read the following activity and respond to the practice question:

Select the purpose of the activity that follows:

Have first-grade students name the letters of the alphabet. Have one sheet that lists the alphabet in sequence and one sheet that lists the alphabet in random order. Remember to present lowercase letters first in at least a 14-point print size. *The teacher may ask students to repeat the same activity using uppercase letters.*

What is the purpose of this activity?

A. To determine alphabet letter recognition.
B. To determine the use of uppercase and lowercase letter formation.
C. To determine readiness for formal reading instruction.
D. To determine alphabetizing.

The purpose of this instructional activity is to determine letter recognition of both upper- and lowercase letters in sequential and random order. Choice *A* is correct.

This standard focuses on elements of the **alphabetic principle**, which states that there is a one-to-one correspondence between alphabet letters (*graphemes*) and sounds (*phonemes*). The English language does not have a systematic alphabet system that has a one-on-one sound for each of its approximately 44 different sounds (phonemes). As an example, Tompkins (2001) states that "long *e*, for instance, is spelled fourteen different ways in common words. Consider, for example, *me, meat, feet, people, yield, baby*, and *cookie*" (p. 164). In addition to the alphabetic principle, it is important to state that **graphophonemic knowledge** is the understanding that written words are made up of systematic letter patterns that represent sounds in pronounced words. This discussion highlights instruction related to **letter recognition** (the relationship of letters in printed words to spoken language) and instructional activities used to enhance the development of letter recognition. Again, we can clearly see the interrelationship of the components of language arts (oral skills of listening and speaking and reading and writing).

Letter naming, or **alphabetic recognition**, is an important skill to develop, because children use this skill to acquire reading, spelling, and writing ability. It is important to mention that the **alphabet** is a series of abstract marks that are assigned identities and sounds for use in written contexts. As young children develop the skill of naming letters of the alphabet, they must learn to recognize the shapes of the uppercase manuscript letters, lowercase manuscript letters, uppercase cursive letters, and lowercase cursive letters. Young children must also learn to identify letters based on formation, position on a line, length, and size. Children frequently have difficulty recognizing the difference between letters that look similar. As an example, the uppercase letters *E* and *F* and the lowercase letters *b* and *d* often confuse the young reader. Until recently, many children who reversed or confused similarly formed letters (or words that contained similar letters) were considered to have learning deficits. However, today educators believe that constant exposure in a variety of instructional settings assists children in developing the skills needed to overcome many of these somewhat common difficulties.

A good many children enter school naming the letters of the alphabet by rote memory. However, teachers should realize that young children might not understand that these letter names connect to sound and writing. Children need instruction in using the letters of the alphabet in random sequence and to learn, practice, and apply the basic sounds that each letter represents. According to Adams (1990) and Cramer (2004), automatic and instant recognition of letters, presented in sequence and randomly, allow children to focus on learning and applying sound–symbol relationships.

Most educators agree that beginning teachers should come to their classrooms with a variety of instructional methods and activities to teach the young child to recognize and apply letter-name knowledge. As an example, Mr. Robinson may plan a lesson using sandpaper letters and other tactile and manipulative activities, alphabet songs, and books that teach and practice the "letter of the day." Mrs. Jordon may use a multisensory (seeing, hearing, touching, and movement) approach to teach and practice forming the letter of the day by using paints, shaving cream, body-letter formation, different-color markers, clay, sand, and paper and pencil. Both of these teachers understand that children should be encouraged to learn alphabet naming by direct instruction and through many types of exposure, including visual, auditory, tactile, and kinesthetic. Teachers should, in addition, use the consonant-vowel-consonant word pattern (C-V-C; e.g., *bat*) to model blending (see discussion of *blending* under Standard II). The teacher should use pictures to enhance the idea that letter naming connects to the reading of words. For instance, as the teacher introduces the letter *h*, the teacher should show and pronounce the word *hat* and show a picture of a hat. A picture file of many things that relate to this sound is valuable to show children (house, horse, hand, etc.) to increase understanding. Teachers who overload their lessons with the focused "sound of the day" help children remember better. For example, Ms. Vasquez, on her "'*A*' Day," wears an aqua apron with apples appliquéd on it. As she begins her lesson, children gather in the circle area and she takes out of the pockets of her apron a small model airplane, a tiny alarm clock, an apple, an American flag, an animal cracker, and so on. She has the class say each word several times and pass the object around to each child. Later during the day, she tries to speak in sentences with this sound ("I'm ready for lunch. I have such an appetite. I hope they serve apricots."), and when children hear the sound, the first to raise his or her hand receives a prize ticket.

It is also an effective practice for the teacher to adjust instructional pacing to meet the needs of children. As the beginning teacher considers ways to teach concepts that relate to the alphabetic principle, he or she may want to consider the following instructional sequence:

1. Teach letter names in random sequence.
2. Teach the formation and sounds of letters in random sequence.
3. Teach lessons that highlight one letter at a time.
4. Teach the likenesses and differences in letters based on formation and sound.
5. Reteach difficult letters.
6. Provide skill lessons for students experiencing difficulty in learning letters.

Children must also have a rationale to learn. For example, if teachers were on the /t/ sound, she or he might remind children that if they did not know this letter, they might not be able to see that tacos were on the menu at restaurants, or that they had received a note from their classmates, Tommy, Tammie, Tanya, and Tomàs.

As teachers consider ways to assess children's use of the alphabetic principle, it is important to realize that assessment should be frequent so that teachers can address the immediate instructional needs of learners. Teachers should initially assess children to determine their knowledge of the alphabet by asking them to name the written uppercase and lowercase letters of the alphabet presented in random order. This type of assessment allows the teacher to determine each child's knowledge of letter names and plan further instruction. Then the teacher should develop a variety of assessments to use to determine each child's growth and development in identifying letters of the alphabet. These assessments can also include such activities as asking a child to identify specific uppercase or lowercase manuscript letters of the alphabet by naming letters as the teacher points to specific letters, by having the child point to specific letters as the teacher names a letter, or having the child match uppercase and lowercase manuscript letters presented in columns.

Most educators agree that the beginning teacher should ask parents to become involved in the development of the emergent literacy of their young children. Teachers, with the permission of the school's administrative staff, can develop several of the following activities for the purpose of involving parents:

1. Design grade-level workshops to demonstrate ways to assist with decoding words, reading and asking questions, and homework assignments.
2. Develop take-home kits that include books for the child to read, practice worksheets that highlight a specific skill, fun activities, and additional suggestions for things to do in the home. Parents should be encouraged to play many sound games with their children, relating the sound to the letter, and to words the child knows ("Brother is on his bike. What sound do you hear twice? That sound is a B.").
3. Produce a newsletter and a Web site that inform parents about classroom events, new skills that are being introduced, and other academic information. Teacher-made CDs or other recordings can also be an effective way to reach parents, remembering that English may not always be the language spoken at home.

Examine the following as an assessment activity.
Then consider the question that follows:

Mr. Dwyer, a kindergarten teacher, places a teacher-made folder game in the literacy center. The directions ask students to match lowercase letters with the corresponding uppercase letters by pulling a length of yarn from one letter in the uppercase column to its corresponding letter in the lowercase column.

What is the purpose of this activity?

   A. To practice letter association.
   B. To play a game.
   C. To practice writing the alphabet.
   D. To practice writing conventions.

In this instructional situation, Mr. Dwyer could use this activity to allow students to practice upper- and lowercase letter association. Then, following repeated instruction and practice (using games; computer activities; a variety of tactile products employing sandpaper letters, plastic letters, and other raised surfaces; books; or other literacy tools), he uses this type of activity as an assessment to determine students' growth in identifying upper- and lowercase letters. The correct answer is *A.*

Standard IV: Literacy Development

Competency 004: **In understanding that literacy develops over time and progresses from emergent to proficient stages, teachers use a variety of contexts to support the development of children's literacy.**

> *The teacher understands and promotes literacy development of all students and understands the developing reader's growing awareness of environmental print, sounds in spoken words, and uses of print. Knowing that literacy development occurs across multiple contexts in reading, writing, and oral language use, the teacher selects and implements materials, strategies, and activities to enable students to distinguish letter forms from number forms, text from pictures, and to understand functions and concepts about print, including book handling skills, directionality, and the relationship between written and spoken words. The teacher is familiar with a large body of children's literature, and provides multiple opportunities for students to listen to, respond to, and independently read literature of a variety of genres. The teacher also selects and integrates appropriate technology to enable students to select literature for independent reading. Remember that the TEKS promote knowing different types of print sources that teachers can use in instruction.*

Try this practice question:

Which strategies should a teacher implement to foster younger students' enjoyment and appreciation of poetry?

   A. Reading poems, clapping out the rhyme in familiar rhymes, and recording a "Top 10" set of poems for use in a listening center.

    B. Making personal collections of students' favorite poems, requiring memorization of poems, and dramatizing narrative poems.

    C. Illustrating Native American poetry, analyzing sections of poems, and sharing haiku with poetry pals in another classroom.

    D. Choral reading and peer editing.

First, consider which activity would lead to an enjoyment and appreciation of poetry. Because each item contains more than one activity, you must decide if *each* of those activities leads to true appreciation and enjoyment. Let, use the strategy of elimination on this item, so that if one choice does not promote enjoyment or appreciation, mark the entire item incorrect. For each suggested answer, underline or check those activities that would promote enjoyment and appreciation in poetry. In items *B, C,* and *D*, do all activities listed in each choice promote enjoyment? No, not all activities in those choices do. Memorization, poem analysis, and editing would not allow "pure enjoyment and appreciation." *All* of the activities in *A* promote appreciation of poetry for younger children; therefore, choice *A* is the answer.

This standard emphasizes instruction related to literacy development skills, or emergent literacy, and the use of a variety of text structures, such as children's literature and expository text in instructional settings. Teachers should understand the developmental steps that children encounter in learning to become proficient readers in order to identify, diagnose, and prepare for effective instruction. **Emergent literacy** refers to the reading and writing experiences that a child encounters *before* formal literacy instruction begins. These experiences occur in the home, social environments, and preschool settings. During the development of print association, children become aware of different types of print found in their environment. They begin to recognize that print is meaningful, develop the ability to rhyme, engage in reading environmental print (e.g., "read" the names of favorite places when passing these locations in a car), scribble "words," and participate in story discussion during the reading of a favorite book. Children engaging in emergent literacy activities should receive meaningful direct guidance from an adult figure. An adult can provide scaffolding to assist in gaining higher levels of understanding. **Scaffolding** refers to support for a learner as he or she enters a phase of readiness for a new skill. This scaffolding is especially important the moment a child is ready to read. Educators believe that emergent literacy activities include prereading and prewriting activities that develop in a meaningful way. As an example, a young child may imitate an adult by "writing" a letter to an aunt or grandparent, even though that letter may contain scribbles that are meaningful only to the child. Also, the young child may learn to memorize a favorite book because a parent or teacher has read the same book to the child many times. As a reminder, oral language develops in the young child from the early developmental stages of babbling to developmental and mature speech, so even Pre-K children come to a teacher with a variety of experiences with language.

Teachers use a number of strategies for building initial literacy skills, including the use of showing children the parts of a book, and they should often make use of a pointer to demonstrate the left-to-right sequence for reading and helping students understand that sentences are made up of whole words. Teachers can demonstrate these concepts by using "big books" and other types of narrative reading sources in children's literature. As teachers assist children in developing literacy skills, it is important to realize that children are learning the alphabet in non-sequential order, acquiring phonemic awareness skills, developing a sight vocabulary, and learning to decode words that are encountered in isolated lists and in contextual settings. As elementary students develop into more proficient readers, they use a variety of decoding skills (e.g., phonics, context clues, structural analysis), read with varied pitch and intonation, read with increased fluency and rate, develop *orthographic* awareness (correct spelling), recognize a greater number of sight words in both isolated lists and contextual text, and show an interest in a variety of text types. It is important to understand the stages that students experience in becoming capable of reading various text types in order to help students grow. Table 2.3 highlights literacy developmental stages in children from Pre-K to grade 6.

As you study Table 2.3, remember that the teacher should engage children in oral and written language, such as in discussions of books, rereading favorite stories to children, providing books on tape, providing class libraries or centers for choices to encourage more sustained independent reading, providing games and activities that promote language development, modeling and instructing on strategies for determining the pronunciation of an unknown word, modeling comprehension strategies, engaging students in higher-level thinking activities, teaching and modeling the writing process, and producing other effective ways to promote classroom literacy. A **balanced approach to literacy** is recommended.

Table 2.3 Literacy Developmental Stages

Pre-K children begin to do the following:

- Become aware of environmental print
- Recognize signs seen frequently (e.g., a STOP sign)
- Recognize a limited number of letters and numbers
- Interpret forms of their writing that represent their written messages (a child could interpret a series of lines he or she made to mean "I have a new bike.")
- Actively participate in reading and writing activities
- Orally make rhyming word patterns
- Listen to short stories and retell their favorite parts
- Recognize the orientation of print (left-to-right, top-to-bottom, and print use)

Kindergarten children begin to do the following:

- Retell information from narrative and expository text sources
- Write letters of the alphabet (in uppercase form) and numbers
- Recognize the sound that letters make in the initial position
- Make an association with onsets and rimes in one-syllable words
- Write a limited number of sight words
- Engage in invented spelling to communicate in printed form
- Use more descriptive words in oral expression

First-grade children begin to do the following:

- Read stories and discuss stories
- Write stories
- Develop comprehension strategies for getting the main idea, predicting outcomes, understanding sequence, using contextual clues, etc.
- Develop reading fluency
- Use word identification strategies to determine an unknown word
- Use limited punctuation marks
- Use appropriate capitalization in words, such as their first names and the first word in a sentence
- Develop spelling techniques for writing words
- Develop sight words

Second-grade children begin to do the following:

- Increase sight word recognition
- Read a variety of text sources, such as expository, poems, notes from peers, invitations, etc.
- Read for different purposes, such as for general or specific information, fun, relaxation, communication, retention, etc., because we read in different ways for different purposes

(continued)

Table 2.3 Continued

- Read with fluency
- Use effective comprehension strategies
- Use word identification strategies to determine the pronunciation of an unknown word
- Use an increasing number of punctuation marks in written products
- Use the elements of the writing process
- Make the transition from invented spelling to correct spelling
- Use capitalization more extensively
- Engage in self-selected independent reading

Third-grade children begin to do the following:

- Increase sight word recognition
- Read with increased fluency, rate, and expression
- Use word identification strategies to determine the pronunciation and meaning of unknown words
- Use comprehension strategies to gain understanding of text sources
- Use reference sources to gain information
- Recognize the difference between narrative and expository text forms
- Write descriptively in different text forms, such as expository paragraphs, stories, research reports, poems, letters, etc.
- Use the elements of the writing process effectively
- Proofread written products
- Develop and use an increased vocabulary
- Increase their ability to use correct spelling

Fourth-grade children begin to do the following:

- Increase sight word recognition that includes content area subjects
- Read a variety of text sources with increased understanding, fluency, rate, and expression
- Spell correctly in a variety of written forms, such as paragraphs, poems, etc.
- Read longer text sources, such as informational articles and trade books
- Produce effective written summaries
- Expand vocabulary
- Continue to use reference sources
- Use effective comprehension strategies to understand a variety of text sources
- Increase use of punctuation

Fifth-grade children begin to do the following:

- Build on previously learned skills and strategies
- Read widely in both classic and contemporary literature and informational selections
- Recognize persuasion techniques used by a speaker
- Write for a variety of purposes, such as persuasion, entertainment, or information, with increasing ability
- Become more competent in their use of writing mechanics, as well as literary devices, such as dialogue, plot structure, and figures of speech
- Become more proficient in editing their compositions
- Create compositions and projects involving research and the integration of technology

Sixth-grade children begin to do the following:

- Become more proficient at learned skills and strategies
- Read even more widely in more complex classic and contemporary literature and informational selections
- Recognize persuasion techniques used by a speaker
- Write for a variety of purposes, such as persuasion, entertainment, and information, with increasing ability
- Become even more competent in their use of writing mechanics, as well as literary devices, such as dialogue, plot structure, and figures of speech
- Become more proficient in editing their compositions
- Create more advanced compositions and projects involving research and the integration of technology

Teachers should use many different types of children's literature. **Genres** (types) of children's literature include picture books, folk literature, realistic fiction, historical fiction, fantasy, science fiction, informational books, poetry, mysteries, and biographies. *Picture books* are those books in which the text and illustrations combine to form a meaningful whole. A special type of picture book is the *textless*, or *wordless*, picture book that relies solely on the illustrations to tell the story. Included in this genre are alphabet books, counting books, picture books, and *concept books* (books that teach children about concepts or ideas such as shapes, colors, and feelings). Although we often consider picture books appropriate only for our youngest readers, there are many quality picture books that can be creatively and successfully used with upper elementary students. *Folk literature* (folklore) encompasses those tales that were originally told orally. Such styles as fairy tales, tall tales, fables, myths, legends, epics, ballads, and folk songs all are part of folk literature and often engage students in moral lessons about human nature. *Realistic fiction* stories are those that occur in contemporary times and are quite popular with children because they present characters and situations with which they can identify. *Historical fiction* presents stories about characters and events of the past and affords an effective way to introduce children to important periods in Texas, U.S., and world history. *Fantasy* and *science fiction* include stories in which anything can happen and can develop children's imagination, creativity, and sense of humor. *Expository texts* (informational books), or nonfiction literature, can pique children's interest about specific topics and help answer many of their questions on various subjects. *Biographies* and *autobiographies*, books about real people both past and present, introduce children to persons with interesting and often inspiring life stories.

Poetry is another major genre, or type, of children's literature. Teachers often do not include poetry in classroom instruction—either because they have negative poetry memories from their own school days or because they lack knowledge on how to select poetry for their children. Negative memories might include being required to memorize poems and then listen to each classmate recite the same selection in front of the class. This reduces the enjoyment of poetry for many young readers, as does having to overanalyze and determine the "real" meaning of poems (in the upper elementary grades).

Poetry preference studies done since the early 1960s, in particular those by Terry (1974) and Kutiper (1985), show that children have certain likes and dislikes regarding poetry. Children like poems to which they can relate—in other words, poems that deal with familiar experiences. They also like narrative poems, limericks, poems about animals, poems with humor, and poems with lots of sounds in them. When given the choice, children overwhelmingly prefer poems by contemporary writers to those by traditional writers. Sometimes young children do not like to read or hear haiku, although by fourth grade many begin to write, understand, and enjoy age-appropriate haiku.

Poetry is a genre that is meant to be heard. Children benefit from activities that promote listening to or orally expressing poetry. Enjoyment comes from hearing favorite poems read or sung and by sharing them with others. This pleasure can then foster students' desire to create their own poems. Poem patterns, such as *couplets* (composed of stanzas where two lines rhyme), *triplets* (composed of stanzas where three lines rhyme), *biopoems* (an unrhymed poem in which the student describes him- or herself in nine lines or less), *acrostic poems* (in which a name or concept is spelled downward and each letter begins with a word or phrase that relates in some way), *cinquains* (a five-line poem), and *diamantes* (a diamond shaped, seven-line contrast poem), are all simple and fun for students to write. Older children enjoy writing *limericks* (humorous poems of five lines, where the first, second, and fifth lines rhyme and the third and fourth have another rhyme). They can also feel a great sense of accomplishment when their poems are *published*, or shared with others.

Teachers may use many of the genres discussed to explore **seven literary elements**, which include the following:

1. Setting
2. Character
3. Plot
4. Style
5. Point of view
6. Mood or emotional tone
7. Theme, or the "abstract statement about life or humanity reflected in a story or poem" (McGee & Richgels, 2000, p. 116).

Older elementary children should be encouraged to include these elements in their writing.

The **basal reader** is another text source used to develop children's literacy skills. Basal readers are designed to provide a sequence of skills that are introduced, practiced, and applied by having students read narrative and expository text sources. After reading basal reader stories, teachers often have children use corresponding workbooks, skills sheets, and other types of supplementary instructional materials to reinforce skills introduced in each lesson. Most often, basal readers and their accompanying materials (including a teacher's edition) are the "reading books" provided by schools.

Try this practice question:

Mr. Chaparral is about to introduce a unit on the westward movement to his fourth-grade students. Which of the following strategies would be most effective in immersing his students in this subject?

A. Have students read the related chapter in their social studies textbook and answer the questions at the end of the chapter.
B. Organize the class into groups and let each group choose a novel on the topic.
C. Have students read diaries, biographies, and nonfiction books about the westward movement and collaboratively create an illustrated timeline for the bulletin board.
D. Assign everyone to read, with the teacher's assistance, Laura Ingalls Wilder's *Little House on the Prairie* and then have students write a response to the story.

Consider which of the suggested activities would give students the most understanding of the westward movement. Choice *A*, reading the chapter in the textbook, gives the students only one perspective on this historical period (the textbook author's perspective), and answering the questions at the end of the chapter can be tedious, boring, and solitary. Choice *B*, allowing groups of students to select a novel, does not provide a focus for a broader view of this lesson. Choice *D*, assigning everyone to read the same book, does not take into consideration that fourth-grade boys and girls prefer to read about characters that are the same gender they are. Boys would probably prefer to read a book in which there was a male character. Choice *C*, having students get into groups and choose their own book for reading and discussion, gives students responsibility by allowing them to schedule their reading, conduct their discussion, and plan their final presentations to the class. Reading diaries, biographies, and other nonfiction literature pertaining to the historical period gives students a truer perspective of what life was like then. Allowing them to collaborate on a timeline lets children take responsibility for organizing and executing their work. Because this response involves a broad range of related literature, collaborative learning, and student decision making, the correct choice is *C*. The teacher must remember that books should be at the appropriate reading level for elementary children. The answer is *C*.

Standard V: Word Analysis and Identification Skills

Competency 005: Teachers understand the importance of word identification skills (including decoding, blending, structural analysis, sight words vocabulary, and contextual analysis) and provide many opportunities for students to practice and improve their word identification skills.

The teacher, knowing that many children develop word analysis and decoding skills in a predictable sequence but that individual differences occur, understands the importance of word recognition skills, such as decoding, blending, structural analysis, sight word vocabulary, and contextual analysis for reading comprehension, and provides various instructional practices that allow children to develop skill in using these strategies. The teacher teaches phonetic analysis of regular words in a simple-to-complex progression (i.e., phonemes, blending of onsets and rimes, short vowels, consonant blends, other common vowel and consonant patterns, and syllables). Be sure to note this sequence. In addition, the teacher selects and implements strategies, materials, and models to teach students how to decode more complex words, utilizing the alphabetic principle, structural analysis (prefixes, suffixes, and roots), and syllables, along with teaching students how to use dictionaries, glossaries, and other resources to determine the definitions, pronunciations, and derivations of unknown words. Remember that the TEKS promote instruction that emphasizes the introduction and independent usage of word analysis skills.

Educators also frequently discuss the sequence in which word analysis and decoding skills should be introduced to the reader. According to Blevins (1998), the following sequence should be considered when teaching young children to read using **word analysis skills:**

1. Teachers should introduce consonants and short vowels in combination. The purpose of this combination is to develop decodable words that children encounter in print and can transfer to spelling words (e.g., *bat, pet, sip, hot, cup*).
2. Teachers should introduce single consonants before introducing consonant blends or clusters (see the following list for definitions).
3. Teachers should first introduce consonants that have high utility. For example, the letter /t/ has a higher *utility*—or, it is found in more words—than the letter /z/.
4. Teachers should then begin to introduce more complex letter combinations, such as consonant blends (e.g., *fl* in the word *flag*) and diagraphs (e.g., *oa* in the word *float*).

Teachers should know the definition of **word recognition skills** and how to apply these skills in instructional situations. The following list provides significant terms, definitions, and some examples:

1. **Affix.** A structural element added to the beginning or ending of a root or base word in order to alter the meaning, pronunciation, or function. Example: prefixes ("before," as in *un-* [uncontrollable]) and suffixes ("after," as in *-ness* [happiness]).
2. **Alphabetic principle.** The idea that individual letters represent individual speech sounds; therefore, words may be read by saying the sounds

represented by the letters, and words may be spelled by writing the letters that represent the sounds.

3. **Consonant blend or cluster**. Two or three letters in the same syllable that are blended or heard when pronounced. Example: *tr* in *tree*.

4. **Consonant digraph**. A combination of two or more letters that represent a sound that is different from the speech sound that the letters represent individually. Examples: *ch* in *chop, sh* in *shop, th* in *thank, wh* in *whether,* and *ph* in *phone.*

5. **Decode**. Associating printed letters with the speech sounds the letters make to comprehend a word.

6. **Diphthong**. Two adjacent vowels in which each vowel is heard in the pronunciation. Examples: *ou* in *house, oi* in *oil, oy* in *boy,* and *ow* in *brown.*

7. **Explicit phonics instruction**. Providing children with direct phonics instruction that allows them to use decodable text sources that are made up of words and sounds that have been previously taught.

8. **Grapheme**. A written or printed letter symbol used to represent a speech sound (phoneme).

9. **Grapheme–phoneme relationship**. The relationship between printed letters and the sounds they represent.

10. **Logographic awareness**. The first stage children experience when learning about words. Words are learned as whole units that are sometimes embedded in a logo, such as a STOP sign or the arches in the McDonald's sign.

11. **Morpheme**. The smallest meaningful unit of language. Example: *cat* is a morpheme whose pronunciation consists of three phonemes (c/a/t).

12. **Onsets and rimes**. *Onsets* are the consonants that come at the beginning of syllables in words. Example: the *bl* in the word *blend* is an onset. *Rimes* are vowels and consonants at the end of a syllable. Example: *end* in the word *blend* is a rime.

13. **Orthography**. Correct spelling.

14. **Phoneme**. The smallest unit of sound in a language that distinguishes one word from another word. Example: *cat* and *hat* are distinguished as sounding different by considering their beginning consonant phonemes /c/ and /h/.

15. **Phonemic awareness**. The knowledge or understanding that speech consists of a series of sounds and that individual words can be divided into phonemes.

16. **Phonic analysis**. The process of applying knowledge of letter–sound relationships to words. Teachers ask for this when they instruct children to "sound out" a word.

17. **Schwa sound**. In many words that are multisyllabic, one of the syllables receives less or diminished stress. The sound of the vowel in the syllable that receives the diminished stress has a softening of the vowel sound that is identified as a *schwa* sound and often pronounced as the *"uh"* sound. The word *about* contains the *schwa* sound.

18. **Sight vocabulary**. Any words a reader can instantly recognize without having to use any type of word recognition strategy. When a word cannot be taught with any other word recognition strategies, such as onsets and rimes, it is usually taught as a sight word, such as *the, said,* and *what.*

19. **Syllable**. Divisions of speech sounds within words. Each **syllable** has one vowel sound. An open syllable ends in a vowel, and a closed syllable ends in a consonant. Teachers should teach the following rules:

    a. When there are two consonants between two vowels, teach students that the syllable is divided between the two consonants, unless the two consonants are a blend or a digraph. Example: *traf/fic* represents the V-C-C-V pattern where both consonants are the same and *pen/cil* represents the V-C-C-V pattern where the consonants are different. Both have divisions between the two consonants.

    b. When vowel digraphs or diphthongs appear in a word, teach students not to divide between these vowel combinations. Example: *ea/ger* (*ea* represents a digraph) and *pow/der* (*ow* represents a diphthong).

    c. When there is a V-C-V pattern noticed in the middle of a word, divide either before the consonant or after the consonant. When teachers instruct students to divide the word into a syllable before the consonant, students should notice that the first vowel sound is long. Example: *mo/ment* represents the V-C-V pattern that shows a long sound pronunciation of the vowel. When teachers instruct students to divide the word into a syllable after the consonant, students should see that the first vowel sound is short. Example: *sev/en* represents the V-C-V pattern that shows a short sound pronunciation of the vowel.

    d. When there is a compound word, teach students to divide into syllables between the two words. Example: *seahorse* should be divided as *sea/horse*.

    e. When a word has an affix (prefix or suffix), teach students to divide into syllables between the base word and the affix. Example: *remove* should be divided as *re/move*.

20. Vowel digraph. Two adjacent vowels that represent one speech sound. Examples: *ee* in *feet, oo* in *foot, ea* in *meat*, and *ai* in *sail*.

21. Word analysis. An inclusive term that refers to all methods of word recognition. Phonics is one such method. Other methods include *picture clues* (using pictures and graphic aids to assist in word pronunciation and meaning), *context clues* (using surrounding text to aid in word pronunciation and meaning), *sight words*, and *structural analysis* (focusing on root words, base words, affixes, compound words, syllable division, and contractions).

In addition to becoming acquainted with these terms, beginning teachers should teach these skills directly and assist students in applying word recognition skills in a variety of literacy settings. For example, as students read various selections of print orally, they frequently encounter words that they mispronounce in context. Encouraging students to reread the section of print where the mistake (or **miscue**) occurred often produces the correct pronunciation (by using **context clues** that allow meaning to be gained through the other words in the sentences and surrounding sentences). Teachers can also test their children on words that do not make sense (nonsense words), such as *bov, hig, mek*, and so forth, to see if their skills in reading decoding and the alphabetic principles are on target. As students advance, they should be able to use individual fix-up strategies to help with their comprehension. Although teachers should provide students with a wide variety of print sources, they should remember to suggest books that can be read independently and have words that are consistently pronounceable in approximately 95 percent of the text; however, putting students in a position where they obtain overall success with a bit of a challenge is optimal (according to motivational theory). Teachers should always remember to apply the concept of the **zone of proximal development** in reading, which means discovering the place where children can be successful with some assistance from an adult or a capable peer. Allowing time for students to discuss the main ideas presented by the author, other concepts, and the students' own purposes for reading also increases understanding. To further enhance fluency, teachers should encourage students to reread favorite sections of print. Word recognition skills are important; however, teachers should provide significant exposure to new words so that these words become automatically pronounced as sight words.

Try this practice question:

Mitch, a second grade student, reads a word incorrectly in a sentence as he is reading orally to his teacher. After reading two more sentences, he goes back and corrects the error. What strategy did Mitch's teacher observe him using in determining his error?

    A. Application of onsets and rimes
    B. Context clues
    C. Structural analysis
    D. Sight words

Consider the approach Mitch used in determining the need to go back and reread the sentence. What clued him to the need to go back? Because Mitch is in second grade, he should have the ability to apply *onsets* (identification of the consonant at the beginning of a word) and *rimes* (identification of the consonants and vowels at the end of a syllable). However, it cannot be determined if he used this strategy because his self-correction was delayed until after reading two additional sentences. Therefore, choice *A* is not correct. We know that he made a miscue in reading, and we know that his teacher did not stop his reading. He pronounced a word incorrectly but continued to read two more sentences. It appears that the contextual setting gave him a clue as he continued that assisted in determining that a word had been pronounced incorrectly in an earlier sentence. Therefore, it is seen that Mitch used context clues in determining the need to go back to reread the sentence that contained the error, rather than structural analysis and sight words. Therefore, choice *B* is correct.

Now consider the worksheet in Figure 2.1 to answer the following question:

Considering Maria's written responses on the worksheet shown on the next page, what assessment would be incorrect on the part of the teacher about her reading achievement?

    A. She can read words that contain consonant blends.
    B. She can read words that contain vowel digraphs.
    C. She can use structural analysis skills.
    D. She can understand the use of metaphor.

As you think about the correct answer, consider that one function of this standard is to provide information connecting the reader, the text, and the context. Does Maria seem to do this? Yes, because she basically answers the questions correctly. Nicole could have extended her response to question 4 by indicating that she quickly began to feel happy because she thought of a way to come back to the amusement park; however, not including this extension does not make her response incorrect, because the text states that Maria felt sad. The correct response is *D*, because we are looking for the incorrect assessment, and the story contains no figurative language (such as metaphors) and because she reads several words that contain the following decoding elements:

Consonant blends or clusters: *spend, blop, stuffed, train, bring, plays*

Vowel *digraphs* (two vowels together that are read as one sound): *train, feels, Leave (other examples, tea, eat, pea)*

Structural analysis: example of a word from the story: compound word, *doorbell*

Notice that Maria reads other words that are examples of several of the decoding terms included in the list of terms defined under this standard. The answer is *D*.

Read the worksheet below and answer the four questions. (A third-grade student completed this worksheet.)

Name: _____Maria Jones_____   Date: _____April 5, 200?_____

Read the following passage and answer the questions.

Nicole is in a hurry this morning because Whitney's mother is picking her up at 10:00. The girls are going to the amusement park to spend the day. Since Nicole just moved to Simons two weeks ago, she has not been to this park. She hears the doorbell, runs to open the door, and sees Whitney. "Are you ready?" Whitney asks. "I am," replies Nicole.

   As Nicole enters the amusement park, she sees people who look as excited as she feels. She rides on the Big Blop, plays toss the ring and wins a stuffed rabbit, eats a hot dog, rides on the Turning Train, and goes to a puppet show. She tells Whitney's mother that this is the most fun she has had since coming to the new town. Whitney's mom tells the girls that it is time to go to the car for the ride home. As they leave the park, Nicole is sad because she is not ready to leave. Then she thinks, "My mom can bring us the next time."

1. Describe the way Nicole feels when she woke up. Why did she feel this way?

   Happy. She is going to the park.

2. How long has Nicole lived in her new town?

   Two weeks.

3. List the things the girls do at the amusement park.

   rides, plays toss the ring, eats seesastow

4. How does Nicole probably feel as she leaves the amusement park?

   She is sad.

FIGURE 2.1

Standard VI: Reading Fluency

Competency 006: Teachers understand the importance of fluency to reading comprehension and provide many opportunities for children to improve their reading fluency.

The teacher understands that fluency involves accuracy, rate, and intonation and knows the norms for reading fluency that have been established by the TEKS (Texas Essential Knowledge and Skills) for various grade and age levels. Understanding the connection of word identification skills and reading fluency to comprehension and the differences in students' development of word identification skills, the teacher selects and implements instructional practices that develop reading fluency, such as reading independent-level materials, reading orally from familiar texts, repeated reading, partner reading, silent reading for increasingly longer periods, and self-correction. The teacher encourages the development of lifelong learning and reading for pleasure by providing opportunities for students to self select books for independent reading, to engage in silent reading, and for extended reading of a wide variety of materials and literary genres. A teacher who teaches reading also knows how to collaborate with other professionals and families to promote reading fluency. Remember that the TEKS promotes the usage of instructional strategies that enhance reading fluency.

Try this practice question:

Ms. Routt, a first-grade teacher, has noticed that two students have limited knowledge and use of sight words. Which activity would not provide further word recognition development?

A. Provide students with a variety of books at their independent reading levels.
B. Ask the students to select something different rather than to reread their favorite part of a book.
C. Allow the students to look at the print as the teacher reads the book.
D. Have the students read along with taped versions of the books.

Each choice but one promotes literacy development. These children have had limited knowledge and use of sight words that could promote reading fluency; therefore, they must see and use print in a variety of ways and use stories of various types and in many different ways. This can be accomplished if Ms. Routt allows the children to actually see words in print and hear words that make up stories. Therefore, choice *B* correctly answers this question, because the children are asked *not* to reread their favorite part of a book but to select something different. Rereading a motivating selection is an excellent way for students to gain word recognition. In addition, big books, large print, colorful illustrations, and adequate spacing are features that the teacher could use to assist the students in acquiring literacy development. The correct answer is *B*.

Reading fluency relates to a student's being able to (1) orally read a text source by using accuracy in pronouncing words, (2) comprehend effectively because attention is given to textual meaning, (3) provide expression that includes attention to punctuation, and (4) read with a rate that is appropriate for the purpose identified for reading the text source. Table 2.4 provides an explanation of reading fluency components.

Children often experience reading difficulties that affect fluency as it relates to comprehension. A list of the most common reading difficulties that influence reading fluency and instructional practices that address these difficulties follows.

1. *Word-by-word reading* is described as a student's pausing after each word in printed text. This type of reading is often caused by limited sight-word knowledge and overdependence on the usage of phonics. As remediation practices, the teacher could:
   a. assign reading materials at a lower level.
   b. use familiar reading materials that contain known sight words.
   c. have children dictate language experience stories that could be read aloud (review Standard I—LEA).

Table 2.4   The Components of Reading Fluency

Read orally a text source by using accuracy in pronouncing words.

The student can recognize most of the words in the text with automatic and immediate recognition. Students may read text sources at the independent level, which means that approximately 95 percent to 100 percent of the words are recognized and pronounced correctly. However, many students need opportunities to engage in repeated readings of the same text sources before they reach this level of automatic and immediate word recognition.

Comprehend effectively because attention is given to textual meaning and not just to word identification.

The student can comprehend text if he or she does not need to spend a significant amount of time decoding words. The frequent pausing to figure out a word alters the flow of reading, thus causing comprehension to receive less attention on the part of the reader. Basically, **fluency** (continuous flow of word recognition) results in comprehension. It is important to note that some students engage in effective word naming without effectively comprehending the text source. Teachers must remember to evaluate comprehension by asking questions or making statements at various levels, by having students retell sections of print, and by using other strategies as well.

Provide expression that includes attention to punctuation.

The student reads with attention to phrasing, appropriate breathing, voice intonation, tone, and attention to all punctuation marks. **Prosody** is the term frequently used to identify these types of reading considerations (Dowhower, 1991). Think about how you would expect a student to read this sentence: I have a new puppy!

Read with a rate that is appropriate for the purpose identified for reading the text source.

    d. have children read along with taped text sources until fluency is reached.

    e. provide opportunities for children to read at their independent level daily.

    f. suggest reading materials for parents to have in the home that allow children to practice using sight words and new exposure words.

2. *Insufficient knowledge of word recognition skills* refers to limited use of sight word knowledge, context clues, structural analysis, and other skills used to help in pronouncing an unknown word. As remediation practices, the teacher could:

    a. have children use sight words in isolation, phrases, and complete sentences.

    b. have children read a variety of print sources at the students' independent reading levels.

    c. have charts in the classroom that include onsets and rimes that appear in words that could be used in sentences (a word wall could be used).

    d. have available for children common affixes and words that contain the affixes written in complete sentences (a word wall could be used).

    e. have children continue to read text involving an unknown word. Have children consider the word's onset and the print following the unknown word.

3. *Ineffective comprehension* by a student is recognized when he or she is not able to tell about what has been read or is not able to respond to statements and questions posed about text that has been read. As remediation practices, the teacher could:

    a. develop questions and statements that encourage responses at different levels (recall, comprehension, etc.).

    b. encourage note taking and active listening.

    c. enhance word recognition knowledge.

    d. assign reading at appropriate levels.

    e. develop visual aids, such as pictures or felt-board figures, to show the sequence of a story that children are reading.

    f. explain the use of signal words and phrases (such as *first, also, on the other hand, in contrast, in comparison, next, then,* and *finally*).

    g. demonstrate the steps of the Question–Answer Relationships strategy (QARs) that are outlined in the discussion of Standard VII.

Many schools promote reading fluency in programs, such as DEAR (Drop Everything and Read) or SSR (Sustained Silent Reading). These programs ask everyone in the school (including the teacher-as-a-model) to select something from a large variety of reading material and read silently for a period of time—just for the enjoyment of it. Teachers have a part in guiding children to materials that are interesting, exciting, and within their abilities. Another technique for increasing fluency is *guided reading*, where the teacher divides children into flexible groups based on their immediate needs and reading levels. At the beginning, teachers direct students in a mini-lesson on new vocabulary, a *purpose for reading* (looking for specific details, main ideas, or special information; learning "how to"; identifying styles; comparing/contrasting; checking predictions; etc.), or other strategies that they may use to increase fluency. Students then read in the small group as the teacher guides them with prompts/cues and encourages use in some of the strategies that they may have discussed. Finally, the teacher goes back to helping with comprehension of the reading by asking questions and giving feedback.

Consider this practice question:

A second-grade teacher has noticed that Jamie is developing the reading behavior of a word-by-word reader; that is, she reads each word with a pause between it ("The . . . cat . . . ran . . . up . . . the . . . tree!"). Which strategy would be best for the teacher to use with this student?

- **A.** Providing the student with books of interest.
- **B.** Asking literal level questions.
- **C.** Assigning reading material at a lower level of difficulty.
- **D.** Encouraging the student to read orally in a small group.

Allowing a student to read books based on his or her interest (*A*) is an effective practice; however, these books may not promote oral fluency in reading because the books may not be written at the student's independent level. Asking literal questions (*B*) allows the teacher to know if the student understands the stated concepts in a story but does not promote fluency. Assigning reading material at a lower level of difficulty allows the student to encounter known words. This practice and the practice of allowing the student to reread favorite books at the independent level promote fluency. Encouraging students to read orally in a small group (*D*) often promotes anxiety. Therefore, choice *C* is the most effective practice for the teacher to use with Jamie. The answer is *C*.

Standard VII: Reading Comprehension and Application

Competencies 007 (Reading Comprehension and Applications): Teachers understand the importance of reading for understanding, know the components of and processes of reading comprehension, and teach students strategies for improving their comprehension using a variety of texts and context.

The teacher, knowing that comprehension is an active process of constructing meaning, understands factors affecting students' reading comprehension, such as oral language development, word analysis skills, prior knowledge, language background, previous reading experiences, fluency, vocabulary development, ability to monitor understanding, and characteristics of specific texts. The teacher, understanding the levels of reading comprehension, knows how to model and teach skills for literal comprehension (identifying main idea, recalling details), inferential comprehension (inferring cause and effect relationships, making predictions), and evaluative comprehension (analyzing character development and use of language, detecting faulty reasoning). The teacher provides instruction in comprehension skills which support students' transition from "learning to read" to "reading to learn," and uses various strategies to enhance students' reading comprehension, such as making connections between text content and students' lives, connecting related ideas across different texts, engaging students in guided and independent reading, assisting students in generating questions, and applying knowledge of text topics. The teacher teaches strategies that facilitate comprehension of different types of text before, during, and after reading, such as previewing, making predictions, questioning, self-monitoring, rereading, mapping, discussing texts, and using reading journals. Teachers select and use instructional strategies and materials to enhance students' understanding of their own culture and the cultures of others through reading. The teacher teaches the elements of literary analysis, such as story elements and features of various literary genres, and has knowledge of the continuum of reading comprehension skills in the statewide curriculum and grade-level expectations for those skills.

Try this practice question:

Ms. Jones has decided to assign a series of expository paragraphs about "Early Days in San Antonio" to her fourth-grade social studies students to read during class. Which of the following would be most effective to use before having the students read this information?

A. Summarize the paragraphs for students.
B. Determine what students already know about the topic.
C. Read a section to students to foster interest.
D. Give students a series of questions to answer as they read.

Actually, each of these activities could be considered appropriate for Ms. Jones to use with her students. However, we are looking for the most effective method. It is always an effective practice to determine students' background knowledge about a new topic, because it would be difficult for students to gain contextual meaning or, in this case, have an adequate background or understanding of this time in Texas history. By determining students' background knowledge, the teacher can then decide the amount of preparation necessary before the students could begin this learning activity. If the teacher determines that students have either little or no background knowledge, she will realize that they are not yet ready for this activity. Instead, she must provide background knowledge so that they are able to make connections and to comprehend this new information. Therefore, the answer is *B*.

As a discussion of comprehension strategies is presented, it is important to identify and briefly explain literal, inferential, and evaluative comprehension. **Literal comprehension** has readers respond correctly to questions and statements from stated text. For example, a student could read, "The boy ran home from school." The teacher could ask this student to identify the specific details of where the boy had been and where the boy is going. This type of response does not require the student to incorporate any background experience or to consider thinking beyond the print. Other literal comprehension categories that the elementary teacher should implement are: (1) identification of stated *main ideas* in expository text structures (i.e., main ideas in narrative text structures are not usually stated directly for readers; instead, a sequential string of details are provided about characters, their problems, their solutions to the problems, and so on, that require the reader to identify a central theme or the general significance of the total narrative selection), (2) identification of *sequence* of details, (3) identification of *comparisons*, and (4) identification/recall of details.

Inferential comprehension has readers use ideas and information that are stated directly in the text along with their intuition, background, and experiences to reach a conclusion or a hypothesis. It should be expected and accepted that, as students make inferences, their responses may differ from other students' responses. Student responses should be accepted, as long as they are connected to the literal meaning of the text. One category of inferential comprehension that teachers use in instruction is predicting outcomes or ideas. Teachers of young children can ask students, "Predict what you think a story or textbook chapter is about by looking at pictures or reading the title of the chapter," or, as a story develops, "Predict what happens next." One reason for identifying patterns is for prediction purposes. Another category of inferential comprehension involves identifying cause and effect relationships.

Evaluative comprehension requires children to compare information and ideas presented in the text with their own experiences, backgrounds, and values. These responses, given in their own words, might be about *reality versus fantasy, fact versus opinion, use of language, analysis of characters,* and the *accuracy of information* that compares various written sources about the same topic.

Comprehension can sometimes be a little tricky to teach, but teachers must implement appropriate procedures for classroom use that assists students in using text sources effectively. It is also important for the teacher to develop and monitor comprehension before, during, and after the reading of a text source. Mr. Love uses a reading response prior to the book report notebook in which he asks students to record quick notes on their feelings about each book they read. This allows him to see quickly if children really understand the main points of the book and the characters. This is further developed in formal book reports later.

The *Directed Reading–Thinking Activity (DR-TA)* is a technique used to increase understanding of text structures. The DR-TA follows the following steps:

1. Assists students in acquiring the skills needed during the reading of a text source. The teacher and students *survey* the material and make predictions from illustrations and other graphics. The teacher provides instruction by introducing new technical terms in isolation and in contextual settings, and the teacher assists students by providing teacher-directed and student-generated questions and statements to provide purposes for reading the selection.
2. Encourages students to *write responses* to questions and statements as they read silently. Students should write their responses so that they can participate in a discussion in the next step.
3. Continues to develop comprehension by discussing, clarifying responses, and redefining purposes as students *read orally* and *discuss* sections of text that refer to the identified purpose-setting questions and statements.
4. Has students *reread* the sections of the text silently or orally for continued instruction related to critical thinking (making inferences, drawing conclusions, identifying the main idea, making judgments, etc.). The teacher assists students in applying the textual information to real-life situations and in identifying additional instructional needs noticed during the discussion and reading of the text.
5. Expands instruction to include the use of research skills, technology-based activities, related supplementary *recreational reading* from trade books and other sources, and group projects to develop additional cross-curricular cognitive ideas. (Stauffer 1969, pp. 14–15)

K-W-L is a strategy often used to promote comprehension and active learning of expository and narrative text sources. This strategy allows students to use their prior knowledge to identify (1) what they already *know*, (2) to initiate curiosity by generating questions to show what they *want to know* about the topic, and (3) to provide responses about what they *learned* after the lesson is concluded. Ogle (1992), the developer of K-W-L, recommends using the following diagram to record information (although there are a number of variations):

K—What I Know	W—What I Want to Know	L—What I Learned

Repeated story reading is a strategy that young children enjoy because they become so familiar with a text source that they can often read (or engage in pretend reading) on their own. Teachers should repeatedly read the story to children, encourage children to repeatedly read it, provide situations for them to discuss it, provide props (costumes, dolls, puppets, paper characters glued on sticks, etc.) to tell or dramatize it, and provide opportunities for children to engage in other literacy activities, such as drawing and writing about the story.

Story retelling allows children to read or listen to a story that they then retell. This activity allows children to participate in language development, comprehension skill enhancement, and story structure awareness. Children have an opportunity to use their background and experiences in retelling and explaining the main ideas and supporting details of the story; to practice listening skills (because the teacher should give children purposes to promote active listening); to practice the sequencing of what happened first, second, next, and last in the story; and to practice self-expression. Morrow (1989) recommends that when children experience difficulty in retelling a story, the teacher should ask about the story by using such prompts as:

1. What was the story about?
2. Who was the main character?
3. What was the main character's problem?
4. How did the character solve the problem?
5. How did the story end?
6. What was your favorite part?

In addition to questioning for comprehension, is important for teachers to remember that children can retell stories in written form or through drawings and manipulatives. As an example, Gunning (2010) suggests that in retelling a story where a dog ran after the cat, students have representative animals that they can pick up and show what happened, or they may be given a story map graphic organizer with a number of squares in which they draw or note the main events in order.

Summarizing is another skill area that must be considered a significant comprehension strategy. In order to assist students in using summarizing effectively, teachers should (1) demonstrate to students how and why to omit noncontributing information from the text, (2) explain what repeated details are and show why those details could be omitted in summarizing, and (3) continue to assist students in determining the author's main ideas or the overall general significance of a selection that could be used in a written summary. As teachers recognize that children are becoming proficient in developing effective summaries over smaller chunks of materials (paragraphs, subchapters, etc.), they usually begin to expose children to the skill of developing summaries over longer sections of print (summarizing a chapter, story, or novel). This process of combining extended sections to produce connected meanings can enhance understanding of the text.

The teacher always recognizes the importance of modeling and emphasizing all strategies that are used to assist students in identifying concepts and information that they may and may not understand in their reading, writing, listening, and speaking activities. The teacher also recognizes that the cognitive concept of *metacognition*, defined as metacognitive awareness, self-regulation, or thinking about one's own thinking, is related to self-monitoring and provides instruction and activities that allow children to learn to become more independent learners. This encourages children to assess their own cognitive growth, to identify inconsistent "missing areas," and to learn to use those strategies on their own that work best for themselves. As an example, Jody, a third grader, encounters an unknown geographic area that appears in the chapter of a social studies textbook. Jody realizes that ignoring the fact that she does not know anything about this area would alter her comprehension; therefore, she could decide to seek the pronunciation of the geographic area and to determine the location of this area by looking at a map. The correct pronunciation and an understanding of the area's location provide additional background that can enhance comprehension. Other strategies that help children self-monitor what they know include graphic organizers, K-W-L discussions, and other types of activities that help students see what they know and what they do not know, and aid them in centering on the best strategy to help them learn. In addition, the teacher frequently monitors him- or herself. This means he or she reflects on instructional delivery by asking children specific questions to determine if they are comprehending. This allows the teacher to make adjustments, if needed, by using different words to teach the same concept, substituting words in oral delivery, switching strategies, and making directions clearer. In other words, the teacher is trying to make instruction more effective and meaningful for students (not simply repeating or "saying it louder").

In classrooms today, *listening* has become an important part of the daily routine. This is discussed at the beginning of this chapter, but it is also a part of this competency. **Oracy** is the concept that identifies and describes the differences between the skills of "reading and writing" from those of "listening and speaking"; that is, oracy considers those English Language Arts (ELA) skills that are based on the making of sounds (or oral-based skills). Oracy should be considered in classrooms in order to assist students in functioning in an active discussion-based environment (Wilkinson, 1974). Active listening is essential in a classroom because speaking and learning to read are connected to purposeful listening.

Several factors that influence listening instruction should be considered as students become active listeners in school settings (1) the student's background as related to his or her experiences and to a cognitive knowledge base; (2) the level of language development; (3) the instructional level of the material being presented; (4) the speed, pitch, and intonation of the person providing the oral delivery of information; (5) the attention span of the listener; and (6) the instructional preparation of the listener, including having been given a purpose for listening (gain facts, learn directions or "how to . . .," gain points of view, etc.), activities to organize the information, and activities that enhance memory for retaining the information that has been presented (Lundsteen, 1979).

This standard considers the use of listening activities as one way of assisting students in monitoring cognitive structures in classroom settings. It should be clearly noted that effective listening requires instructional attention through various types of activities, such as note taking, questioning, and listening-think-alouds.

Note Taking

Note taking, as mentioned earlier, is one of the most direct listening skills used in classrooms when it is seen as a teacher-produced way of delivering information to children in an oral form. Students must listen to succeed in this task. Note taking is also used when children use multiple sources, such as encyclopedias, textbooks, interviews, charts, and narratives, to collect information and record this information by making lists, answering questions, filling in note-taking forms, and so forth. However, note taking is not stressed often enough in classroom situations. Let's examine a procedure that could be used to connect note taking, reading, and listening for elementary children. The teacher could begin the initial stage of note taking by providing a worksheet that outlines important points that will be expanded on by the teacher later in oral delivery. Let's consider the components of a teacher-delivered talk or mini-lecture in an elementary science class about "How Plants Grow." The teacher has developed a note-taking worksheet to be used by children to serve as purpose-setting points for effective listening. The following chart shows this type of example.

Topic: **How Plants Grow**	
Teacher provides questions for students.	*Each student provides answers to questions.*
1. How do plants start to grow?	Student provides a response.
2. What are the parts of a plant?	Student provides a response.
3. What does a plant need to grow?	Student provides a response.
4. Why are plants important to people?	Student provides a response.

Student summarizes information from the answer section.
Student summary statements are based on information from the student's answers to the questions.

Note taking allows children to learn how to determine significant details and main ideas from information. This type of filtering of significant information helps children determine the major points provided by the teacher. Allowing children to use sample notes developed by the teacher, to compare notes taken in class in cooperative groups, and to make adjustments to individual notes provides children with a self-evaluation method. This type of self-assessment of the notes can often assist children in becoming more critical listeners (and readers).

Other graphic organizers also help children organize information and read for a purpose. Concept mapping shows a major focus (e.g., dogs) in a center circle and "radiates" related information (breeds, use, care, etc.) or details in connecting "bubbles." This helps students see main and subsidiary ideas very clearly. Venn diagrams can be effective in helping students compare and contrast two related topics, such as how a traditional and a modern version of a folk tale are similar and different. Story maps, in which students highlight characters, setting, conflict, resolution, and other story elements not only help comprehension but also enhance students' own story writing ability.

Questioning

Questioning is one of the most used teaching strategies found in today's classrooms. Research, however, indicates that many teachers ask questions only at the literal or knowledge level (remembering). This is lower-level thinking, according to the taxonomy discussed by Bloom and his colleagues (1956) (lower levels include knowledge, comprehension, and application; higher levels include analysis, synthesis, and evaluation—or, as Anderson and Krathwohl discuss in their 2001 text, in the new Bloom's taxonomy, creating/synthesis is the highest level). The first three levels provide basic thinking, but teachers' aims should always be to have children think at higher levels. In language arts, teachers often pose questions and statements as advanced organizers as a way of providing students with purposes for listening to orally delivered information and information found in text sources. These questions and statements should require responses that allow children to identify the main idea of a selection, determine details that discuss the main idea, and identify supporting details that further describe the initial details. The following are specific strategies that can be used by teachers to enhance questions and responses.

QUESTION–ANSWER RELATIONSHIPS (QARS). This is a directed-teaching strategy that develops students' awareness of the process used in answering questions. Steps should include:

1. Identifying "right there" questions that are literal and can be answered from information stated in the book and sometimes found in one sentence.
   a. An example question might be: What is Carmen's job?
   b. Answer that is stated in the text source: "Carmen has worked for the last ten years as a bus driver for elementary school students. She lives in Pasadena, but she works nearby in South Houston."
2. Identifying "think and search" questions, requiring students to draw a conclusion. They are told that the information needed to determine the answer to the question can be found in the text source, but it is in more than one sentence. Students are instructed how to link this information by putting several ideas together to determine a response.
   a. An example question might be: How would you describe Emily?
   b. The answer would come from several sections of text that described Emily. Students would put the description together from the entire text source that describes her.
3. Identifying "author *and* you" questions, requiring students to use text details plus their own background knowledge to make an inference. They must relate what they know to what is in their text source. Answers become more individualized rather than a single correct answer. As an example, children read a paragraph about "Going to the Zoo" on a very hot summer day. In the story, a lady smiles and allows a little boy to go ahead of her on a ride. The children were asked to answer the following question: What type of person is the lady? The reader must determine that the lady is probably a kind person because of her actions.
4. Identifying "on your own" questions connected to evaluative responses, background consideration, and creative thoughts to determine an answer. Children, for example, having read about the life of Abraham Lincoln, could then be asked to identify the characteristics of a leader.

Another way to view questioning is to look at the difference between convergent questions and divergent questions. **Convergent question** responses allow students to use their text source to answer questions because there is only one correct answer to a question. However, **divergent question** responses require students to use the text source, their background knowledge, and their understanding of the information in the text to answer a question. In other words, the teacher could expect to hear a variety of individualized answers that are connected to the text sources—but all of which could be correct.

RECIPROCAL QUESTIONING (REQUEST). Using ReQuest, students learn to pose their own questions and statements about content material being studied. Manzo (1969, pp. 124–125) recommends the following steps:

1. Teacher and students read the same passage silently.
2. Teacher closes the book and is questioned by students.
3. Roles change, and the teacher begins to ask students questions.
4. Teacher assists students in developing logical responses to questions. When the teacher determines that children have an adequate knowledge of question–answer responses, the teacher then allows them to read independently to determine the answers to questions.
5. Teacher conducts a follow-up discussion.

Listening–Thinking Strategy

The purpose of the listening–thinking strategy is to provide a format for teaching students how to develop predictive listening and comprehension. This strategy encourages students to make predictions as the teacher reads the title of a chapter, the beginning, or reads up to an exciting point in a story. The teacher then allows children to change or make new predictions. As the teacher reads to students, he or she uses pitch or intonation variations and storyline discussions to assist students in listening effectively (Walker, 2000).

Many content areas utilize students' reading and writing skills in acquiring knowledge of concepts. It is important for students to understand that informational textbooks, or *expository texts*, contain such features as a preface, a table of contents, appendices, a glossary, and an index. In addition, each chapter within expository textbooks includes an introduction, headings, subheadings, graphics, purpose-setting questions, and a summary. Most expository texts are organized with the most important ideas stated first, and the supporting ideas and descriptive details following in paragraph form. Students who understand this textbook structure can often distinguish the important and significant details from the less important details in reading material (Meyer, 1975). Also, authors of textbooks usually provide connective terms, such as *most important, however, because, after*, etc., to help students connect one idea to another idea as they read information (Halliday & Hasan, 1976). Teaching these format cues can help students locate information more quickly.

Content area teachers should identify specific strategies that can be embedded throughout their lessons in social studies, science, health, and so on. Every teacher should consider him- or herself to be a reading teacher. During prereading activities, the teacher introduces activities that activate a child's schema and establish purposes for reading. As students read silently, teachers provide them with activities that monitor comprehension continuously. After children finish reading, teachers should assist them in determining relevant applications of the new information, in building schema, and in extending comprehension skills by rereading portions of the textbook or other sources that supplement the chapter.

SQ3R: Survey, Question, Read, Recite, and Review

In order to discuss Standard VII, which incorporates the structure of assisting young readers in learning to use expository text structures independently, an overview of SQ3R and its cognitive connections to other study strategies is needed. Also, it is necessary to indicate that this strategy is usually most effective with expository (information-based) text-sources (textbooks, computer sites, journals, etc.). In SQ3R, **S** means *survey*, **Q** means *question*, and **3R** means *read, recite*, and *review*. Let's discuss each separately and make connections with other study strategies such as previewing, note taking, study guides, and test taking.

The *survey* step suggests that the reader, with instructional guidance from the teacher, (1) previews the reading selection and notices the title of the chapter and the titles of the subchapter headings; (2) notices new vocabulary; (3) reads the introduction and summary of the entire chapter; (4) reads the first sentence in each paragraph while considering each subheading and reading both the questions at the end of each subsection and at the end of the chapter; (5) reads sections in bold or other types of selected print; (6) studies graphic and visual information, such as maps, illustrations, graphs, and so on, to become familiar with the purpose of this information; and (7) notices other relevant information. In using this step, readers notice the structure of a chapter, thus allowing them to determine a framework for reading and comprehending the information. In addition, Vacca and Vacca (1986) recommend that, as children preview (by examining the introduction, illustrations, new vocabulary terms, subchapters, the chapter summary, etc.), they can often determine the amount of time it will take to complete a task and determine what they already know about the topic.

The *question* step recommends that the teacher aid readers in determining what questions about the reading material can be answered from the text. These questions provide purposes for reading the selection and are designed to assist readers in paying close attention to the information that is being read. Questions can be formulated in several ways; however, the most common way to formulate questions in this step is to change the stated subchapter headings into questions. As an example, a chapter in a third-grade social studies textbook might be titled "Living in China." In this chapter, students could probably expect to find a subchapter heading titled "The People of China" that could be changed by the student into a question such as, "Who are the people living in China?" This can result in factual information about China but also in a discussion about the differences among many Asian people (Japanese, Korean, Indian, Thai, etc.). Also, the teacher could prepare a study guide (study guides are discussed later in this section) or a list of questions and statements that could be given to the students before beginning to read the text source.

The *read* step requires the student to answer the questions, or in some cases, the statements formulated in the question step. Opening the door to engage children in active reading through the use of questions and statements leads to connections of main idea information, details, and descriptive ideas. Imagine being given a reading assignment and being simply told that "Tomorrow you are going to have a test on this." You and some children already have metacognitive strategies in place that would allow for successful comprehension, but others would get very little from this assignment and would probably not earn a passing grade. One of the reasons that some children might have difficulty passing such a test is that there was not a specific "road map" to follow to determine the understanding of the text material. As teachers, we do not want to always tell students exactly what they should learn as they read, but we do want to scaffold until they have acquired the metacognitive strategies that allow independence in determining comprehension. For some students, this can be accomplished quickly, but for others it takes time to scaffold them on their way to becoming independent learners.

The *recite* step asks students to make either oral or written responses to the questions formulated in the *question* step discussed earlier. As students respond orally to answer these questions, teachers can additionally request readers to identify locations in the text that were used in making these responses, or children can provide written responses to the questions.

The *review* step allows pupils to evaluate the text information by rereading selected segments of the text so that they can verify their responses given during the recite step. Children can either read out loud or read silently the text sections that verify their answers. Remember, readers have had private time with the text source to answer the questions. After they have had an opportunity to read the text silently, it is instructionally appropriate to allow children to volunteer to read sections of the text orally that provide responses to questions generated in the question step. In reminding ourselves of the components of DR-TA, we can remember that this strategy encourages reading out loud to answer questions and to verify responses to answers. However, in SQ3R oral reading comes *after* students have been given an opportunity to read the text source silently.

As we continue to discuss strategies that respond to this standard, the use of adjunct study materials, such as study guides and graphic aids, are discussed in more detail. First, let's see exactly why adjunct study materials are important. According to Vacca and Vacca (1986), adjunct study materials add a way for children to interact and make connections with text material that is unfamiliar or difficult, to analyze and discuss ideas and concepts found in texts, and to scaffold students in comprehending the text being read.

Study guides prepared by the teacher or commercially by textbook authors benefit students during active silent and oral reading. Study guides usually provide a set of questions or statements for children to use as they study text materials. Although there are several types of study guides, three types are discussed here. The **interlocking study guide** is a type of guide that frames (1) a group of literal questions, (2) a group of interpretive questions, and (3) a group of evaluative questions to be answered by readers. The **noninterlocking guide** arranges questions and statements in a nonordered fashion that does not group questions according to literal, interpretive, and evaluative levels but intermingles questions between the three levels. For example, the first question could be an evaluative question, the second question could be literal, the third question could be interpretive, and so on. The last type of study guide discussed here is the **Guide-O-Rama**. Teachers using this type of guide determine the purpose for reading the selection needed to answer specific questions. Teachers do not require students to read the sections of text that do not address the purpose for reading. However, the teacher determines and shows, by signaling, what parts of the text must be used to complete the task. As an example, Mrs. Bell asks her children to read page 127, paragraph 4 to answer a question about a famous woman scientist. This type of signaling is done throughout the chapter to gain specific information that relates to content-specific information.

Yet another study skill is the ability to locate information. The elementary teacher should assist students in learning to use an index by, for example, designing an activity in a fourth-grade social studies class that asks readers to identify headings that contain information about the production of oil. Students identify headings such as oil, production of oil, types of oil products, procedure used in processing oil, and sources of oil. After the list is formulated, children use the textbook's index to determine if the headings are listed. Note that the skill of alphabetical sequencing is necessary for this activity to be completed effectively. Readers identify page references and use them to actually find the information in the textbook. When the concept of locating information using a book index has been mastered, the teacher should encourage readers to use index entries of other reference sources, such as encyclopedias, almanacs, and atlases. In addition, children should be taught to use the table of contents of text sources to locate library sources and to use computer technology to locate various types of information. Older elementary students can be taught to bookmark information and the rudimentary concepts of copyrighting and plagiarism with technology.

Interpreting graphic information is important in increasing comprehension, but children may need special instruction in this area. Readers encounter maps, cartoons, charts, and other types of diagrams in textbooks. Usually there is text association that connects the graphics to the text, but children often do not include graphics in reading of the text information. A map of the regions of Texas, for example, might be included in a fourth-grade social studies book and, to encourage children to interpret the information, the teacher could ask them to do the following on their own maps:

1. Outline the regions of Texas with yellow.
2. Color the water areas blue.
3. Trace the mountain range areas in brown.

This teacher-generated activity promotes graphic interpretation that allows students to make cognitive connections with print.

Test-Taking Strategies

It is also important for the elementary teacher to include test-taking strategies for elementary students. Teachers want to encourage readers to become effective test takers by encouraging them to consider doing the following:

1. Scan the entire test before answering test items to determine the test format, the type of test questions, and the number of points for each item to determine the approximate amount of time to spend on most test items.
2. Answer the questions that you know first.
3. Look for giveaway answers on objective tests and words that indicate extremes in the answer (*best, least, none, never, always,* etc.).
4. Make a graphic organizer, list, or an outline to begin answering essay-type questions. Students should be taught to identify and answer all parts of an essay question by pinpointing information that is required within the question(s).

In addition, Carmen and Adams (1972) designed SCORER as a test-taking strategy that is similar to the strategies above. SCORER stands for and recommends the following: *S* stands for *schedule* and recommends that test takers learn to predetermine the time they believe they will need to complete a test efficiently; *C* stands for *clue* and recommends that the test taker identify words that could assist in answering the question; *O* stands for *omit* and recommends that the test taker omit the hardest questions first and return to these difficult questions after known ones are answered (unless, of course, it is a test with decision sets like some of the TExES formats); *R* stands for *read* and recommends that the test taker read each question carefully to determine if each part is fully understood (if taking an informal teacher-generated test, the test taker could seek clarification from the teacher); *E* stands for *estimate* and recommends that the test taker determine what should be included in a response (e.g., if taking an essay test, the test taker could make an outline of the information needed to complete the response); and *R* stands for *review* and recommends that the test taker read over the test before finally submitting it to the teacher. This strategy allows the teacher to expect a degree of responsibility from students during test-taking situations. One instructional part of teaching in Texas involves preparing children for their state test. Even if you do not teach at a grade level in which the state test is given, you still have the responsibility of assisting teachers who do teach at those grade levels by preparing children with test-taking skills. This is a serious undertaking in Texas because of the amount of recognition and funding attached to test scores. To see more test-taking strategies that are good for children (as well as adults), see Chapter 1.

Consider the following practice questions related to comprehension:

Mr. Guntur, a third-grade teacher, reads a page of print from the science textbook to his students. Which of the following activities would be most effective in helping students gain the information?

A. Have students take notes or fill in a graphic organizer.
B. Give students a set of questions to consider.
C. Have students determine the main idea.
D. Give students study guide questions for homework.

The part that states "Mr. Guntur reads" cues us to consider that this question relates to *listening* skills. We can then decide which activity promotes active listening. Having children take notes or fill in a graphic organizer as they listen to Mr. Guntur read (choice *A*) involves effective listening. Giving a set of questions to consider (*B*) is a good practice *if* questions are provided before reading or during reading. Giving students a study guide for homework (*D*) is also an effective practice, as is determining the main idea (*C*), but it is not most effective for active listening. Therefore, choice *A* is the best answer because it recommends that the children take notes or fill in a graphic organizer as they listen to their teacher read a page of print. Remember, one test-taking strategy that is effective on the TExES is to watch for cue words, such as *most*, as we see in this question. The answer is *A*.

Mrs. Jones's students have completed reading paragraphs on the Battle of the Alamo. Now she wants to help her children extend their understanding of this topic and inferential thinking. Which of the following would be the most effective practice that she could use?

A. Have students reread the paragraphs for determining a different purpose.
B. Have students read information from different sources, such as trade books, computer-generated information, and magazines.
C. Have students develop a dramatic play that identifies fictional or nonfictional characters who lived during the Battle of the Alamo.
D. Have students write a paragraph that identifies the major events of the Battle of the Alamo.

Mrs. Jones has several effective instructional choices here, but which choice best promotes an understanding of the topic that allows children to read, develop purposes, and analyze the information most effectively? Each choice has fragments of knowledge extension; however, choice *C* most promotes inferential comprehension. Having children develop a play would first have them gather knowledge and then create characters based on this factual knowledge. This activity would also promote an integrated usage of the levels of comprehension. The answer is *C*.

Miquel is a good reader who enjoys books on many topics. His teacher, Mrs. Canteo, knows that he demonstrates self-monitoring skills in his social studies class books in order to learn a concept. Which of the following statements does not demonstrate self-monitoring?

A. Miquel asks himself self-structured questions as he reads text silently.
B. Miquel slows down his reading rate.
C. Miquel asks his teacher a question.
D. Miquel does not reread a difficult sentence.

Self-monitoring includes any technique that allows the learner to identify ways to completely understand a concept. Choices *A*, *B*, and *C* could be considered self-monitoring skills because they could be used by the student to determine a way to more effectively learn the concept. The question asks, "What is *not* . . . ?" Therefore, *D* is the correct answer.

Tran, a fifth-grade student, is having difficulty understanding the main idea of sections of a text. Which of the following activities would be most appropriate for the teacher to suggest that Tran use in order to become more effective in determining the main idea?

A. Show an example of a summarized paragraph.
B. Have the student paraphrase major facts and ideas after each paragraph in a section.
C. Teach the student underlining and note-taking strategies.
D. Provide an outline prepared by the teacher.

The best choice is *B*, because the student needs to develop a system for learning to determine the main idea of a selection. Although paraphrasing after each paragraph is time consuming, this strategy allows the reader to use statements or purpose-setting questions to help determine main idea choices. The answer is *B*.

A first-grade teacher, Mrs. Beck, reads a story to her students. Which of the following activities helps the teacher best determine if her students comprehend the story?

    A. Have students tell their favorite part of the story.
    B. Have students write about their favorite character.
    C. Have students illustrate the main parts of the story.
    D. Have students identify the setting of the story.

Consider which activity would give Mrs. Beck the best assessment of how well her students comprehended the story. Because each choice contains an activity, you must decide which is best for understanding the elements of the entire story. In choice *A*, children are being asked to consider only their favorite part of the story. Choices *B* and *D* ask pupils to write only one element of the story; whereas in *C*, they are required to illustrate the main parts of the story. This illustration allows the teacher to assess students' understanding of the whole story rather than just one segment or element of the story. Therefore, choice *C* is correct.

What would be a first-grade social studies teacher's most effective practice in getting students prepared to either read a chapter or to listen to the teacher read (with a purpose) a chapter on "Community Helpers in the United States"?

    A. Have students brainstorm and write (or draw) things they know about "Community Helpers in the United States."
    B. Have students define community helpers by using their textbook's picture and word glossary.
    C. Distribute a mapping activity and have students attempt to fill in information about community helpers.
    D. Have students view a film on community helpers.

This teacher is showing evidence that he or she knows ways to incorporate reading skills in other content areas. Decades ago, a social studies teacher probably would have assigned the reading without any initial preparation. However, today teachers use a variety of strategies to enhance decoding and comprehension. Let's look at the choices. Choice *A* is an effective practice because it investigates students' background knowledge and encourages them to write or draw about what they know. Choice *B* is not an effective practice because students have not discussed this topic; therefore, they may not select the best definition for the term as it relates to their social studies textbook. Choice *C* is not effective because students have not yet been given the type of instruction that would prepare them to fill in a mapping activity. Choice *D* could be effective if the teacher had given students a purpose for viewing a film or if a film had been used as an extension to the lesson. Therefore, *A* is the most effective practice. The answer is *A*.

Mrs. Torres has found that her second-grade students experience difficulty comprehending their science textbook. Much of the difficulty appears related to new vocabulary and terminology presented in chapter discussions. Which of the following language arts strategies could she use to increase understanding of concepts presented in the science textbook?

    A. Students chorally read the text aloud and stop on each page to discuss words that they cannot pronounce.
    B. Students, in pairs, are assigned a vocabulary word from the textbook. They are to paraphrase, or write in their own words, a definition of the vocabulary word, given the context.
    C. The teacher writes a synopsis, or summary, of each chapter in the textbook at a lower reading level to increase student comprehension of the text material.
    D. Students are given a list of words from the text and instructed to look them up in the dictionary and copy the definitions.

Choice *A* does not present a language arts skill that improves comprehension and learning of science concepts; this only promotes phonics knowledge. Choice *C* does not teach a language arts skill because students are not involved except to copy. Students may not know which definition in the dictionary entry is the correct one. Copying all the dictionary definitions for a word is nonproductive busywork. Choice *B* empowers students to use their own language to create meaning of new vocabulary terms and concept knowledge in the science content area. The correct answer is *B*.

Mr. Campo, a sixth-grade teacher, has assigned students to read a science chapter for homework. Identify the most effective procedure Mr. Campo could recommend that students use to begin the assignment.

A. Take 30 minutes to read the chapter.
B. Preview the chapter before beginning to read.
C. Identify a Web site that might have additional information about the chapter that they could access at home.
D. Read the introduction to the chapter.

Remember that students are preparing to read the chapter as a homework assignment, and this means that Mr. Campo is recommending startups to assist in independently reading the assigned text. In this case, he should not suggest a time frame for completing the reading assignment (*A*), because students read at different rates. A Web site (*C*) could provide additional background information for the students. However, the Web site would probably be most effective in the extension section of the lesson, because this question does not indicate that the teacher has established the level of students' background knowledge. Also, remember the possible technology bias from your *Pedagogy and Professional Responsibilities* TExES; that is, many lower socioeconomic status families may not have easy access to technology at home. An effective practice the teacher could recommend is for the students to preview the chapter before beginning to read (*B*). The preview allows students to notice new vocabulary terms, graphic aids, questions, and other features related to the chapter. Choice (*D*) may not be as inclusive. Another consideration is for Mr. Campo to preview the chapter with children before assigning it as homework. Mr. Campo might find that students need assistance with skills such as the pronunciation of several words encountered during the preview. Therefore, *B* is the best answer.

Mr. Baco, a second-grade teacher, has his students gather information about Native Americans from a social studies textbook, a trade book, a Web site, and field trip to a museum. Mr. Baco assigns students to work in cooperative groups to synthesize information found in each source. What is the main purpose of this assignment?

A. To illustrate how people dressed during this time.
B. To notice how different sources describe a topic.
C. To develop a paragraph.
D. To practice reading from a variety of sources.

Mr. Baco obviously intends for the students to gain insight into the topic by using a variety of sources, and it is important to understand that he wants students to synthesize information found in different sources. Therefore, *B* is the correct response, because students can see how different sources discuss and describe Native Americans.

Standard VIII: Reading, Inquiry, and Research

Competency 008 (Reading, Inquiry, and Research): **Teachers understand the importance of research and inquiry skills to students' academic success and provide students with instruction that promotes their acquisition and effective use of those study skills in the content areas.**

The teacher instructs students on how to locate, retrieve, and retain information from a range of content area, narrative, and expository texts and selects and uses instructional strategies to enable students to comprehend abstract content and ideas in written materials (by using examples, diagrams, and manipulatives). The teacher selects and uses instructional strategies to teach students to interpret information presented in various formats, such as maps, tables, and graphs, and also how to locate, retrieve, and retain information from technologies, print resources, and experts. The teacher selects and implements strategies to help students understand, study, and use inquiry skills across the curriculum (using text organizers, taking notes, outlining, drawing conclusions, applying test-taking strategies, previewing, setting purposes for reading). He or she also helps students in gaining skills for locating, organizing, evaluating, communicating, and summarizing information and understands the importance of organizing information from multiple sources for student learning and achievement. The teacher knows grade-level expectations for study and inquiry skills in the TEKS. Remember that the TEKS promote developmental instruction for comprehension that allows children to engage in a variety of strategies.

Try this practice question:

Mrs. Chen wants her sixth-grade students to use graphic sources of information to address research questions. Students are most likely to develop these skills if they have had opportunities to:

A. locate graphic information about a specific topic in an encyclopedia or other reference book.
B. research, collect, and organize information into their own tables and charts and summarize the results of a peer survey on an age-appropriate topic.
C. collaborate with a partner to make an outline of the features of different graphic formats.
D. make accurate copies of tables, charts, maps, and other graphic information provided by the teacher.

Choice *A* requires students to locate information from reference resources but does not require the students to demonstrate research analysis. Choice *B* requires students to do several operations before finally demonstrating that they can summarize the results of a survey. Choice *C* allows students to collaborate with a partner but does not require any type of demonstrated research usage and elaboration. Choice *D* does not require any type of research organization into a form that demonstrates understanding—it is simply copying. Therefore, the answer is *B*.

The development of students' research skills and the encouragement of academic inquiry are integral components to student comprehension and success in all subject areas. The teacher strives to instill within students the ability to (1) conduct research from a variety of sources; (2) form and revise questions for an investigative approach to source material; and (3) organize and synthesize information from multiple sources to ultimately draw their own critical conclusions. Following this process of inquiry, students should be able to (4) summarize their conclusions, (5) present projects and reports in various media, and (6) ultimately put forth new questions and hypotheses that promote a lasting pursuit of learning.

Research-oriented units may require considerable class time and call for access to a variety of resources, but they also encourage collaboration with other content-area teachers if a school is departmentalized. This focus on collaboration provides a good model to the student's ability to self-direct research in the future and cultivates skills that are integral to students' overall academic success. For example, an English/Language Arts teacher might introduce a creative writing lesson involving original historical fiction that centers on the greatest disasters in Texas or U.S. history that allows students to incorporate research and comprehension skills within a historical context. The students are then challenged to brainstorm a list of what they may already know about their chosen or assigned topic, followed by listing what they must know before moving forward with the investigative process. The students' results and conclusions would ultimately inform the creative writing project. Moreover, the utilization of students' research skills, combined with the creative-writing process, satisfies both the need of the English/ Language Arts teacher to teach research skills and the need of the social studies teacher to teach content knowledge.

The TEKS also stress the importance of students' ability to interpret and use graphs, maps, timelines, tables, and so on. Students are expected to use text organizers, such as headings, graphs, and tables, when sifting through various research sources in order to filter this information and ultimately solve an investigative problem. These research skills can be learned through exercises that combine multiple interpretational and organizational elements, encouraging a process that can be applied in all subject areas. For instance, a teacher could develop a project where students set out to research the major political, cultural, and popular events that have occurred since they were born. The teacher could instruct students to begin investigations by starting with their year or date of birth and then have them frame questions to direct their research thereafter ("How many years have passed since I was born? Was there a major event that happened the year I was born? Did anything happen on the day I was born? What happened the next year?" and so forth). This encourages self-directed research and challenges the student to raise new questions for further investigation. Using traditional encyclopedic resources, as well as new technologies, such as the Internet and CD-Rom databases, students must interpret and organize a considerable amount of information and filter out what is not relevant or appropriate for their needs. From there, students could form a timeline of significant events and construct their own narratives from their compiled research.

Note taking, a skill discussed earlier, is another very valuable form of assessing students' research skills. According to the TEKS, students are expected to summarize and organize information from a variety of sources by taking notes. The teacher can evaluate students' progress by having students write notes as they listen to a guest speaker, read from age-appropriate newspapers, or search sources online.

The effective teacher is one who promotes research skills that are integral and beneficial to a students' continued success in all subject areas. Assessing students' comprehension of information from multiple sources and, very importantly, their ability to synthesize information to draw distinct conclusions helps students' ability to process the world critically.

 # Standard IX: Writing Conventions

Competency 009: Teachers understand the conventions of writing in English and provide instruction that helps students develop proficiency in applying writing conventions.

The teacher understands the stages children experience in acquiring writing conventions, understands the relationship between spelling and phonological and alphabetical awareness, and understands the stages of spelling development (prephonemic, semiphonetic, phonemic, transitional, and conventional) and knows how and when to support students' development from one stage to the next. The teacher selects and uses instructional materials, strategies, and hands-on activities for the development of fine motor skills, including a correct pencil grip, necessary for writing skills according to grade level expectations in the TEKS. Knowing writing conventions and appropriate grammar and usage, the teacher selects and uses instructional strategies, materials, and activities to help students correctly use English writing conventions. Remember that the TEKS promote developmental application of the writing conventions.

Children should also be encouraged to write for meaningfulness. When children see a direct link with the real world and writing communication, they are more motivated to learn (rather than filling out a worksheet). Writing letters that are really sent to friends, relatives, or guest speakers requesting or explaining something, communicating with technology, creating, entertaining, and so on, make writing more valuable and meaningful.

It is essential for the teacher of young children to understand that writing is an exciting activity that comes in a variety of forms (scribbles, drawings, and letter or number formations) that often produce reversals, words, and sentences. Parents and teachers who encourage very young children "to write" strengthen the process of understanding that writing is an important activity and the ability to recognize the shape of writing required later. Young children often write from the bottom up (not from the top down), write from right to left (not from left to right), and mix a variety of written forms to spell or invent the spelling of a word. Most young children have some exposure to print and have had the opportunity to observe the conventions of print (parents have read books to them, preschool and kindergarten teachers have used a variety of "big books," and they have had access to books for examination or reading). In order for the teacher to explain the importance of becoming aware of conventions used in writing, he or she should be able to identify the types of conventions that could be used with young children. Spandel and Stiggins (1997) identified several **conventions** that teachers should model and include in instruction. For example, they recommend that teachers demonstrate the following conventions: (1) left-to-right directionality of print usually by pointing as they read orally; (2) the idea that people read and write from the top to the bottom of a page; (3) that space should be left on both sides of a word to show division; (4) that culmination punctuation marks should be used; (5) an awareness of the proper use of lowercase and capital letters; (6) an awareness and growth of correct spelling; (7) use of left and right margins, neatness, developmental grammar use; and (8) the awareness of a storyline. To help start writing conventions, each week, Mrs. Kaye asks one of her very young students to tell the other children a short story, which she writes on a large tablet as he or she speaks. She puts the tablet where all can see, and reads the story back to make sure that the children see that her pointer is going left-to-right and top-to-bottom, that the words fall within the tablet margins, and that each spoken word is a also a written word. Teachers are encouraged to observe growth patterns and to collect samples of writing that document growth in these conventions over time.

Recall from the discussion of *Standard VIII: Development of Written Communication*, that children go through a developmental process in learning to construct meaning by using print. Students who are learning to spell go through a developmental process by using scribbles to indicate spelling approximations. Table 2.5 summarizes the stages of spelling development with the appropriate grade levels in which they occur.

Table 2.5 Stages of Spelling Development

Prephonetic (Pre-K to beginning/middle of kindergarten)

Students use scribbles that show a sense of directionality, symbols, and other forms to present written language. Students often understand the purpose of written forms of language because they see print in books, on signs, and on different items in their environment. However, students do not understand yet the concept of using letters to produce words.

Prephonetic/Semiphonetic (End of kindergarten to middle of grade 1) (some researchers do not include this stage)

Students are aware of some of the sounds of the alphabet. They begin to realize that letters of the alphabet stand for sounds they hear in a word.

Phonetic (middle of Grade 1)

Students understand the regular sounds of the alphabet and begin to use invented spelling. In most cases, words they spell can be interpreted (or read) by others because they spell by using the sounds in a word (e.g., a student could spell *BOOKS* as *BOCZ*).

Transitional (end of Grade 1 to beginning of Grade 2)

Students begin to spell words based on how words sound. They are beginning to spell words based on how words look because they are experiencing more words in printed form. Usually, students place a vowel in each syllable they write, and they are beginning to use limited structural analysis (prefixes, suffixes, and inflectional endings). They continue to use invented spelling, but it is used with some correct spelling. The student might spell *BOOKS* as *BOKS*.

Conventional or Standard (Grade 2 through Grade 4)

Students begin to spell more words correctly and more consistently and seem to understand the meaning of more words. They spell correctly one-syllable words that have a short vowel sound, and they understand and use verb past tense correctly. They have difficulty with dividing words into syllables and spelling words that have double consonants. At this point, the student should be able to spell *BOOKS* correctly.

Conventional or Standard (Grade 5 into High School)

Students begin to spell most words correctly and consistently and begin to use multiple-syllabic words, content-specific words, roots, prefixes and suffixes in written selections that are well organized and logically produced with a critical connection that includes correct forms of most conventions. At this point, the student should be able to spell most words correctly in a fully developed written selection that has been assigned by a teacher.

Source: Adapted from Gentry, 1981.

Try this practice question:

Mrs. Thompson wrote "Excellent" on her first-grade student's story on the next page. Her reasoning included all but:

    A. The student used more than one type of punctuation mark.
    B. The student used left-to-right orientation.
    C. The student illustrated the story.
    D. The student demonstrated correct spelling.

This student correctly used several writing conventions (punctuation marks, left-to-right orientation, spacing, directionality, and capital letters). He did not spell correctly (*D*), but the child would still be in the inventive spelling stage. If these words had not yet been taught during spelling time, the teacher would want to concentrate more on the issues in choices *A*, *B*, and *C*. The child also included an illustration that clearly matches the story. It is important to remember to provide a variety of writing examples to use in classroom settings. For example, teachers can use word walls to display descriptive and other types of words, provide topics for students to use during writing sessions, have a variety of writing products available for students to access, and provide feedback to students for the purpose of developmental growth. Remember that we are looking for the answer that is the *exception* here. The answer is *D*.

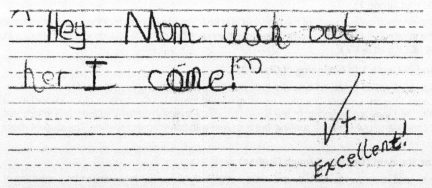

FIGURE 2.2 Why do you think the teacher wrote "Excellent" on this first-grade student's story?

Use the following chart to answer the practice question:

A third-grade teacher has just opened Devin's portfolio (next page). The teacher notices four writing samples (pre-kindergarten, kindergarten, and first and second grades) that are a part of Devin's portfolio. What can the teacher best determine about Devin's writing products?

- **A.** His writing in samples 1 through 3 shows little use of writing conventions.
- **B.** His writing in samples 1 through 4 shows development in spelling.
- **C.** His writing in sample 4 shows development in letter formation and punctuation but also shows errors in spelling.
- **D.** His writing in sample 3 shows that he understands the formation of only uppercase letters.

Think about all you know about children and their developmental stages for writing, spelling, punctuation, and so on. Actually, Devin shows literacy development and progress with each of his portfolio products, so let's think about each of the answer choices. Choice *A* does not give Devin credit for many things he does effectively. For example, in sample 1, Devin uses spacing of scribbles to communicate his thoughts. In sample 2, he is beginning to use uppercase letter formation and number formation, and he continues to demonstrate usage of spacing. In sample 3, he is beginning to show usage of letter–sound association and punctuation. Choice *B* gives Devin credit for showing developmental spelling patterns. Choice *C* gives Devin credit for development in letter formation and punctuation, but sufficient credit regarding spelling is not given. He does misspells two words (he writes *an* instead of *and*, and he writes *kat* instead of *cat*), but credit should be given for letter–sound association. Choice *D* indicates that Devin knows the formation of only uppercase letters. However, he is showing development in spelling and punctuation. Therefore, choice *B* is the best answer.

	Sample 1 Pre-kindergarten (I have a kite.)
	Sample 2 Kindergarten (I am four.)
	Sample 3 Grade 1 (I have a puppy.)
	Sample 4 Grade 2 (I like my dog and cat. My dog is big.)

FIGURE 2.3 Devin's Portfolio Samples

 # Standard X: Written Communication

Teachers understand that writing to communicate is a developmental process and provide instruction that promotes students' competence in written communication.

Teachers teach purposeful, meaningful writing in connection with listening, reading, and speaking, and they know how to promote students' development of an extensive reading and writing vocabulary by providing students with many opportunities to read and write. Teachers monitor students' writing development and provide motivational instruction that addresses individual students' needs, strengths, and interests. Teachers know that writing is a process, and they provide instruction in the various stages of this process: prewriting, drafting, revising, editing, and publication. Teachers provide students with opportunities to write for various audiences, purposes, and settings in various voices and styles. Teachers understand the benefits of technology for teaching writing and provide instruction in the use of technology to facilitate written communication. Teachers know grade-level expectations for writing in the TEKS.

Remember that the TEKS promote using strategies that emphasize developmental writing and elements of the writing process.

Answer the practice question that relates to a classroom situation:

Ms. Keith, a fifth-grade social studies teacher, assigned the following task:

You are to interview a relative or friend who has fought in a war. Use the following as discussion areas during your interview: which country started the conflict, location of the war, time of the war, the causes of the conflict, when and where the major battles were located, the results of the peace agreement (if any), and the role that the relative played. Ms. Keith asks the students to bring their notes to class in one week.

Sidney is excited about this assignment, understands the purpose of the assignment, interviews his aunt who served in the Gulf War, and brings his notes to Ms. Keith early. Ms. Keith notices the following about Sidney's notes: The notes are incomplete in content, words are spelled correctly, and punctuation and other mechanics are basically correct.

How can Ms. Keith best assist Sidney in producing notes that are more complete in content?

A. Have Sidney read examples of interview notes from his language arts textbook.
B. Encourage Sidney to prepare a draft of the notes.
C. Have Sidney reread his notes.
D. Have Sidney explain the purpose of the assignment.

Test taker 1 selected choice *A*, believing that looking at examples from a commercial textbook and allowing Sidney to compare his notes would be adequate. Test taker 2 selected choice *C* because Sidney seemed to skip the initial phases of the writing process, and test taker 3 selected *D* because the teacher engaged Sidney in an oral activity. To answer this question effectively, however, knowledge of the phases of the writing process would be helpful. The logic of the other test takers includes the use of examples from textbooks and teacher connection with a student's product. However, do these ideas address the writing process? The test taker should consider each choice, but the most effective response is *B*. By asking Sidney to prepare a draft of his notes, the teacher is encouraging him to recall the interview with his aunt and get his ideas down first. Later, Sidney can revise and edit his notes. Therefore, *B* is the correct answer.

This standard addresses the developmental process that young children use to learn to communicate in written form. Baghban (1984) suggests that children learn to write in stages that are scaffolded, or supported, by teachers. The **emergent writing stage**, which usually begins before kindergarten, allows the child to produce print in a variety of forms such as scribbling, drawing, and a combination of letter formations and drawings. Teachers of young children should encourage the practice of these beginning efforts in forming letters, as this strengthens the connections of letter recognition in beginning to read, too. Children in the emergent stage should have a number of activities that help them recognize and form letter shapes. As mentioned earlier, these might include having students touch sandpaper letters, make letters out of clay, draw letters in sand trays or on their desks with shaving cream, as well as more traditional methods. Teachers will know if students are able to distinguish shapes through letter matching activities. Children read their drawings in a story format as if they constructed a written source, often reading from left to right and top to bottom because they have observed adults reading to them. In this stage, the child may write his or her first name and may try to produce other popular words often using **invented spelling** forms (e.g., *gone* spelled as *gon* because of the way the child perceives how the word sounds). Children may also write using the name of the letter to communicate (I LV U or U C ME). The beginning writing stage, which usually starts in first grade, allows the child to continue to use invented spelling to label pictures and to write sentences and short stories. The teacher notices that children begin to write sentences that describe personal items, show a developing awareness of correct spelling patterns (word walls are often used to show spelling pattern examples that could be used in both spelling and word pronunciation), and use a story form that shows a description of a beginning and an ending of a story. The **developing writing stage** begins to show a process for writing that is explained in the following section. Teachers need to assess students' writing by using writing products to look for development in **mechanics** (correct formation and use of lower- and upper-case letters, directionality from left to right, use of punctuation, etc.) and for development in spelling (see Standard IX for more information about spelling development). It is useful to remember that children's fine motor skills may not match their knowledge. Teachers who provide a number of materials with which to write (crayons, markers, chalk, dry-erase boards, paints, technology, etc.) may be able to better assess children and then help them. Children who feel frustrated with a traditional pencil and paper may be much more comfortable and skillful with other writing instruments. Teachers, however, must help them develop fine motor skills to help in writing such a fingerplays, cutting, construction with blocks, modeling clay, and many others.

This standard addresses the writing process that is used in the integrated language arts classroom. In times past, teachers approached the process of writing in a much different way, where the focus was on having students produce papers that contained no spelling or grammar errors and that could easily be assigned a letter grade. Currently, teachers are focusing much more on the components of the writing process by using models that scaffold and encourage students to use different genres such as creative stories, poetry, content-specific expository products and other types of narrative products (Ziegler, 1981). They basically want children to enjoy producing ideas on paper first without being punished for mechanics, then revise later in the process. (As an aside, in management, teachers should avoid associating writing with punishment in assigning the writing of "lines" when children misbehave. Teachers should want children to enjoy writing rather than link it to negativity.) Teachers understand that students basically follow a process that is sequential. Most teachers assist children in understanding the phases of the writing process. Therefore, it is important to identify and discuss the following phases of the writing process.

Try this practice question:

Look at the following web Adrian, a fifth grader, created during the prewriting stage.

How can his teacher, Ms. Freeman, best help him write his first draft?

A. Have Adrian redo the web with fewer subtopics.
B. Have Adrian write his story in chronological order.
C. Have Adrian write down something about each of his subtopics.
D. Have Adrian tell his story into a tape recorder and then transcribe it.

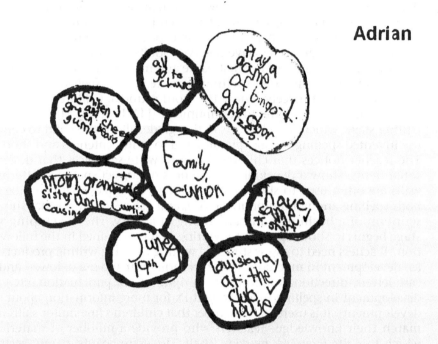

Adrian

Think about what should occur during the drafting stage of the writing process. Adrian has several potentially good subtopics about which to write, and he should be encouraged to pursue each of the topics. Redoing his web (A) at this point would not be productive because his web is fine. Writing the story in chronological order (B) might prevent Adrian from fully recording his thoughts if he is concerned with getting things in correct sequence. Telling his story into a tape recorder and then transcribing it (D) could prove to be time consuming and interfere with the flow of ideas. Adrian should be encouraged to begin writing something about each of his subtopics. Then, during the revision stage, he can include or delete sections to improve his story and look at his sequencing. The answer is C.

Phase 1: Prewriting

This phase allows students to explore topics for consideration, identify ways to gather information about the topic, determine (with their teacher's help) the purpose for the writing assignment (for example, to inform, entertain, persuade, express feelings, explain, evaluate, offer ideas, solve a problem, use a combination of purposes, etc.), determine the intended audience, and select the format of the product (e.g., if the product will be a poem, a creative story, an expository response, other formats). Many teachers find that this is often the most difficult phase because students often cannot begin to get their ideas into written form.

Phase 2: Drafting

The students have gathered information about the topic. Therefore, during this phase they begin to write about the things they have learned. Students are encouraged to write and not be too concerned about mechanics such as spelling, grammar, and punctuation until revisions are made.

Phase 3: Revising

The teacher encourages children to be concerned with revising the content of their writing assignment but not yet consider correcting mechanics such as spelling and punctuation. Students are encouraged to consider their audience by selecting the most effective wording to convey clear meaning, provide supporting details, and present descriptive meaning. During the revision phase, teachers often encourage children to discuss their products with peers and to confer with the teacher. This exchange with peers and the teacher often suggests more effective ways for revising their writing. This phase also fosters repeated exchanges because students continue to redevelop their content by considering comments from peers and from the teacher.

Phase 4: Editing

During the editing phase, the teacher encourages students to proofread their content by looking for mechanical errors, such as misspelled words and incorrect punctuation. Teachers encourage children to collaborate with their peers for the purpose of assisting in proofreading to identify errors. In addition, the teacher often acts as a proofreader.

Phase 5: Publishing

As noted in phase 1, an important consideration for a writer is the audience who reads the content of the product. The writing products can be shared through books, verbal sharing, reports, collections of stories and poems bound by the teacher in book form, or other of types of oral and written forms. Children should also be encouraged to self-assess their progress by looking back at their work over time. This is possible by keeping portfolios.

The previous steps are often part of a **writing workshop** that lasts over several days. The teacher may use a routine format that includes (1) a mini-lesson on a strategy that supports the writing experience [e.g., sequencing, techniques for getting ideas] for about 10 minutes; (2) a statement of purpose (for 3 or 4 minutes) in which students give their goals for the day; (3) a 20- to 30-minute sustained writing block where the teacher can pull out individuals for conferences; and (4) a 5- to 10-minute sharing time (Duthie, 1996).

As teachers help young children develop writing skills, the teacher should allow children to connect reading and writing (by either narrative or expository selections that students read themselves or that the teacher reads to the children). Teachers can accomplish this skill by asking children to reflect on ideas from various types of texts. For example, children may be asked "What if" questions to promote children's thinking about text sources. The "What if" responses can be used as a writing activity. Teachers should encourage written text to include words from word walls and from phonemic awareness instruction (review standards II, III, and IV to connect the usage of word recognition discussions).

Children must have a variety of situations that encourage writing and, the more authentic the task, the better rationale good writing has for children. They should be encouraged to electronically mail (e-mail) pen pals who live in various parts of their state, the United States, and the world, or they can critique a recent television show or movie they have seen. Journal writing provides a way for children to express their literary experiences. They can participate by writing in various types of journals, such as those that center on describing a character from a story or those that have a short "story starter." It is important for the teacher of young children to model effective writing forms by responding to children's writing activities and by assisting them in using the phrases discussed previously in the writing process. Many examples of the types of writing selections that students are encouraged to use should be provided and discussed to develop a critical eye as to their quality. Table 2.6 provides a list, with suggested content, of these writing selections.

Table 2.6   Content for Writing Selections

A summary paragraph should include:

- an accurate restatement, written in one's own words, of the main ideas of the text
- a restatement of supporting details
- omission of unimportant details

A narrative paragraph should include

- descriptive details to develop the characters, setting, and plot
- a clear beginning, middle, and ending
- a logical organization, with clues and transitions, to help the reader understand the order of events (examples of transitions include *first, but, last, also,* and *next*)
- a consistent tone and point of view
- language that is appropriate for the audience
- an explanation of the importance of the events and ideas

A compare-and-contrast paragraph should include

- the subject being compared and contrasted (a Venn diagram is an appropriate graphic aid to use)
- specific and relevant details
- transitional words and phrases that signal similarities and differences
- a conclusion

A conclusion paragraph should include

- a summary of the main points
- a description of personal feelings about the topic or an interpretation of facts or events
- a brief restatement of the thesis

A cause-and-effect paragraph should include

- a statement that includes the cause-and-effect relationship being examined
- a connection between causes and effects
- facts, examples, and other details to illustrate each cause and effect

A problem-solving paragraph should include

- a concise explanation of the problem and its significance
- a workable solution and details that explain and support the solution
- a conclusion that restates the problem

Try this practice question:

Students in Ms. Mitza's fifth-grade science class have been writing descriptive expository paragraphs about "Ocean Life," and the students are using the computer lab to do the assignment. As Ms. Mitza observes her students, she notices that they are composing their paragraphs, frequently doing a word count, and checking their spelling. She wants her students to use a variety of text sources to locate information and organize their paragraphs around main ideas as they revise.

Which of the following instructional strategies would be most effective in achieving this goal?

- A. Providing a lesson on further technology skills.
- B. Modeling paragraph construction.
- C. Asking children if they have described main points.
- D. Encouraging students to graphically organize their paragraphs before beginning to write information.

Choice *C* is correct because the teacher wants her students to construct paragraphs that contain information related to their main topic. It is an effective practice to teach further technology skills as needed and to encourage children to develop their own graphics as they construct their paragraphs. However, it is also important to remember that in the *revision* phase, children are still constructing text without being concerned about editing yet. The answer is *C.*

Standard XI: Viewing and Representing

Competency 011: **Teachers understand skills for interpreting, analyzing, evaluating, and producing visual images and messages in various media and provides students opportunities to develop skills in this area.**

*The teacher understands grade-level expectations for **viewing and representing** visual images and messages (as described in the TEKS), has knowledge of the characteristics and functions of different types of media, and knows how different types of media influence and inform. The teacher evaluates how visual image makers represent meaning and messages, and he or she provides students with opportunities to interpret and evaluate visual images in various media. The teacher also provides students with opportunities to interpret events and ideas based on information from maps, charts, graphics, video segments, and technology presentations. In addition, there should be venues for students to select, organize, and produce visuals to enhance and extend meanings, while encouraging the use of technology for producing various types of communications, such as class newspapers, multimedia reports, and video reports. Students must be helped in analyzing how language, medium, and presentation contribute to the message.*

Try this practice question:

Mrs. Ruiz, a fifth-grade teacher, has students read Hans Christian Andersen's original 1837 story "The Little Mermaid." Following the fairy tale's reading, the teacher has the students watch Disney's 1989 animated film adaptation of the same name. Assuming Mrs. Ruiz would like the students to engage in an analytical exercise of the two media, which activity should she assign her class?

A. Have the children describe the language used in Andersen's original version of "The Little Mermaid," expressing their opinions as to his word choices to depict the protagonist.

B. Have the children make a Venn diagram to show the overlapping similarities of the written and film adaptation of "The Little Mermaid," engaging in an open discussion afterward to explain their diagramming.

C. Have the children mimic Andersen's written style by challenging them to develop a fairy tale of their own, then having them engage in a group exercise afterward to discuss their stories.

D. Have the children discuss the tale's overall meaning, regardless of medium, and write the meaning in one declarative sentence.

The correct answer is *B*, as it asks the children to take their initial observations of both media and expand on those observations through comparison and reflection. The open discussion offers the students an opportunity to share their thoughts and hear those of their peers. The answer is *B.*

The TEKS promote "viewing" and "representing" visual media to cultivate students' ability to be critical consumers of media. The University of Texas Center for Reading and Language Arts (UTCRLA) translates these terms as

- Viewing: Understanding and interpreting visual communications that are conveyed non-verbally.
- Representing: Expressing one's understanding by producing some type of visual media. (*Teaching the Viewing and Representing Texas Essential Knowledge and Skills in the English Language Arts Curriculum*, 2003)

The importance of media literacy and students' ability to understand, analyze, and produce visual representations of written text cannot be overstated. Children today encounter increasingly varied forms of visual media, from traditional art and visual images to print advertisements to electronic and computer technology media. The influx in sources, channels, and forms of news, entertainment, and information of all kinds require students have an ever more sophisticated level of media literacy (Kubey & Baker, 2001; Megee, 1997).

According to findings by Kubey and Baker (1999), there is an increasing need to explore various types of literacies that consider not only print messages but visual messages as well. These researchers note that it is expected that students will spend upward of 2,000 hours a year for the rest of their lives with electronic media, yet some schools may still consider that the only valued forms of expression are novels, short stories, and poems. In addition, Burroughs, Brocato, Hopper, and Sanders (2009) argue that "[b]ecause the media convey, and sometimes constitute, information through artistic expression, students must be taught to become sophisticated in their evaluation, understanding, and consumption of art forms across all media" (p. 155).

The UTCRLA further stresses the importance of media literacy because (1) media dominate our lives; (2) media provide models for our values and behavior; and (3) media literacy increases our understanding, appreciation, and enjoyment of media (Teaching the Viewing and Representing Texas Essential Knowledge and Skills in the English Language Arts Curriculum, 2003). The Viewing and Representing TEKS are broken down into three components: (1) Understanding and Interpreting, (2) Analyzing and Critiquing, and (3) Producing.

Understanding and interpreting visual images, messages, and meanings calls for students to examine, describe, and deconstruct visual representations determine points of view, which ultimately strengthens their media literacy. For example, given the task of describing and interpreting the meaning of the stylistic choices of a premier painter in one of his/her paintings, a student must first consider the elements of design—of balance, color, lines, shape, and so on—before deducing the influence of these choices on the artwork's meaning or message. Developing this observational skill in tandem with the ability to interpret meaning encourages the student's ability to apply this process to other forms of media.

Analyzing and critiquing visual representations allows children the opportunity to build on initial observations of media through reflection, criticism, comparison, and so on. The teacher challenges students to consider media significance and evaluate the ways in which image makers convey meanings (e.g., graphic artists, photographers, illustrators). A compare-and-contrast exercise involving a film adaptation of a written story or novel, given in the previous question for example, utilizes a student's ability to comprehend the same story as manifested in two forms of media. Ideally, this focus on an explicit comparison helps develop a student's critical eye with regards to varied media.

Students' *production* of visual media that communicates to their peers is also an important element of expressing media literacy. Once children have mastered the ability to interpret, understand, and analyze visual media as an expression of written text, the teacher challenges them to utilize their knowledge via their own visual representations. The production of a multimedia report based on a subject covered in class or of a student's own choosing, for instance, allows for a demonstration that may include graphics, video, sound, text, and so on; this culmination of interpretation, analysis, and production of visual representations is critical to students' sufficient media literacy. Kortz and associates refer to this as *TIVA*, or "an acronym that brings together presentations with text, images (pictures and graphics), video, and audio for more complete concept and linguistic development in teaching and learning" (Kortz, Nath, & Parker Braselton, 2011, p. 377).

It should be noted that Viewing and Representing exercises provide ample room for adaptations for students who struggle with reading/writing or those with behavioral/learning disabilities. Collaboration with specialists (vision, auditory, speech/language, technology, etc.) is central to successful modifications or supports to planned lessons and activities. With sufficient preparation, the teacher ought to be able to extend the opportunity to every student to strengthen their media literacy.

Try this practice question:

Ms. McConn, a sixth-grade teacher, is planning a lesson involving print media by analyzing newspapers' use of print advertisement and other graphic visuals to convey meaning. Morgan, a student with visual impairments, can perform most visual tasks, but she has problems with normal print size. Morgan reads very slowly, but she comprehends well. What possible solutions or adaptations should Ms. McConn not worry about employing to ensure she is aiding Morgan's media literacy?

   A. Consult the IEP (Individual Education Plan) and a specialist to understand what preparations can be taken to allow for Morgan's participation in the lesson.
   B. Enlarge the newspaper and use optical aids.
   C. Provide extra time for Morgan to complete the lesson at her own pace.
   D. Allow Morgan to listen to an audio version of the newspaper, completing her response exercises orally.

Choice *A* addresses one of the first steps to be taken by the teacher when considering adaptations for any special education student. The IEP (as a key document) should be consulted when questions regarding the special education student arise, and various specialists (e.g., vision specialist, orientation and mobility specialist, special education teacher, and Education Service Center specialist) should be consulted to facilitate the education of students with disabilities. Choice *B* shows how planning in advance is critical so that resources can be obtained. Choice *C* is an appropriate adaptation, as it has already been noted that Morgan's comprehension is not hindered if she is allowed time to accommodate her slower reading tendencies. The correct answer is *D*, as auditory interpretations of the newspaper neglects the lesson's goal of having students' ascertain differences in print media, specifically. Remember, we are looking for the *exception*. The answer is *D*.

Standard XII: Assessment of Developing Literacy

Competency 012: Teachers understand the basic principles of literacy assessment and use a variety of assessments to guide literacy instruction.

The teacher knows how to select, administer, and use results from informal and formal assessments of literary acquisition, reading comprehension, and writing conventions. The teacher can determine students' independent, instructional, and frustration reading levels, using the information to select appropriate materials for individual students and guiding students' selection of independent reading material. The teacher knows the characteristics of informal and formal reading comprehension assessments and uses ongoing assessment to determine when a student may be in need of classroom intervention or specialized reading instruction and how to develop appropriate instructional plans for this. The teacher analyzes students' errors in reading and in applying writing conventions and uses this information to provide focused instruction to promote literacy acquisition. Understanding the use of self-assessment in writing, the teacher provides opportunities for students to self-assess their writing (for clarity, interest to audience, and comprehensiveness). The teacher understands how to encourage collaboration with families and communicate students' progress in literacy development to parents/caregivers and to other professionals through a variety of means, including student work samples.

Remember that the TEKS promote systematic assessment for the purpose of effective on-grade-level instruction.

Try this practice question:

During an informal assessment, Ms. Enzo recorded the way a first-grade student, Corbin, read the following sentence:

The boy likes to play baseball.

"She ba base."

Based on this sample, where should Mrs. Enzo focus initial reading instruction?

A. Automatic sight word recognition.
B. Picture clues.
C. Compound words.
D. Syllable division.

Ms. Enzo should provide instruction on sight word recognition so that textual meaning can be emphasized. Picture or illustration clues (*B*) could be helpful, but the test item does not provide a picture for Corbin to use. Although baseball is a compound word and can be applied to syllable division, she would help Corbin initially by using instruction that focuses on sight word recognition. Therefore, *A* is correct.

In today's classroom settings, assessment can usually be viewed as either formal or informal. **Formal assessment** often centers on norm-referenced standardized tests. Formal tests are published tests "for which norms based on the performances of large numbers of students have been developed" (McCormick, 1999, p. 80). Norms provide information for educators to compare the test performance of students with large numbers of other students in a similar sample group. For example, in many Texas elementary schools, the Iowa Test of Basic Skills is administered to students. Their scores are then compared to what seems normal for a great number of test takers at that level (e.g., students in a school in Texas are compared to students in the same grade throughout many states). In addition, criterion-referenced tests should be discussed. These can be published tests that provide information about the exact types of skills students have either mastered or not mastered. Criterion-referenced tests can be standardized, but the results are not used for comparison, so this type of test is usually not normed. Scores are not compared to other students but to how well a student knows particular concepts. The TExES test is an example of a criterion-referenced test because scores reflect a percentage of how many questions were answered correctly by a test taker. Criterion-referenced tests are also based on specific objectives that set the level of performance used to determine if a student has or has not mastered a task level. For example, a social studies objective might be stated: The student will demonstrate mastery by correctly identifying and describing five (5) rivers found in Texas. A student must match and describe this information in order to pass this test. Most teacher-made tests are also criterion referenced (e.g., a spelling test on a word list, a test on Chapter 3 in students' social studies book).

The *Reading Miscue Inventory* helps teachers determine if students are reading *miscues* (or words read differently from what is actually written) that prevent them from obtaining correct information from the passage. This assessment assists in determining if children are using background and context clues to assist in reading. The Reading Miscue Inventory stresses that (1) reading is the ability to obtain meaning, (2) reading is not an absolute process because effective readers often substitute words, and (3) teachers should not treat all miscues the same way. Let's look at an example of a miscue that does not basically change the meaning of a sentence: *The boy saw a red automobile* is read aloud by a child as *The boy saw a red car.* The teacher decides if the student has altered a word in a sentence significantly enough to change the meaning of the sentence, and, in this case, he has not. However, if the child had substituted *hat* for *automobile*, then the teacher would have realized that this miscue changed the entire meaning of the sentence and would signal serious difficulties in analyzing words.

Informal assessment (see additional information in Standard II) is a nonstandardized measure that could be an observation, a checklist, a teacher-generated test, an interest inventory, an interview, a research project, a portfolio, an informal reading inventory, a reading miscue inventory, or another type of measure that gives a teacher insight into student performance. Most of these informal assessments and their implementation processes have been a part of your schooling for years and are clearly understood. However, several need additional discussion.

Teachers use a **running record** to identify the number of correct words a student pronounces in lines of print. To conduct a running record, the teacher uses a blank sheet of paper to place check marks, or *ticks*, that represent each correctly pronounced word. The teacher marks, or *records*, miscues and errors by using the same criteria used in marking informal reading inventory responses and miscues (Clay, 1985).

Portfolio assessment has become a much discussed concept in education. A **portfolio** is a collection of student-generated products over a period of time. Calfee and Perfumo (1993) suggest that portfolios could include the following student-generated products in a particular area of literacy: (1) rough, final, and published drafts; (2) content-entry journals; (3) tests and quizzes; (4) illustrations; (5) independent and group-generated projects; and (6) other types of literacy products. Each item should be carefully selected by the teacher or the student or both in consultation. The length of portfolios can vary from long and involved to rather brief. In addition, teachers' written comments should be maintained over time to document children's academic achievement history. Portfolio collections provide a meaningful picture for parents during conferences and for students to self-assess their own progress. Teachers should begin to help students self-assess in many areas, including clarity, interest to their audience, and comprehensiveness.

Another type of assessment is an **Informal Reading Inventory (IRI)**, which contains a series of graded paragraphs followed by a comprehension

Table 2.7   Reading Levels of an Informal Reading Inventory

	Word Recognition Accuracy Percentage	*Comprehension Level Percentage*
Independent	95% to 100% correct	90% to 100% correct
Instructional	90% to 94% correct	70% to 89% correct
Frustration	Less than 90% correct	Less than 70% correct

analysis. Teachers have many types of commercially prepared IRIs from which to select. Most contain the following components: (1) a graded word list to determine the starting paragraph level and basic information about a child's sight word vocabulary; (2) two sets of paragraphs, with one to be read orally and the other to be read silently; and (3) a series of comprehension checks at different levels. The basic purpose of the IRI is to determine a child's (1) independent reading level (students can read at school or at home without assistance), (2) instructional reading level (students are challenged and require instruction from the teacher), (3) frustration level (students are experiencing material that is too difficult to read), and (4) listening capacity level (students can benefit from hearing the teacher read text aloud that is followed by questions). It is important to remember the criteria for determining reading levels as structured by an informal reading inventory (Table 2.7).

Capacity level (also called *hearing level* or *listening level*) is tested by the examiner reading to a child at the next level beyond his or her determined frustration level. The comprehension checks are administered until the child scores less than 70 percent on questions related to the paragraphs that are read aloud to the child. The purpose of the capacity level, which measures listening comprehension, is to determine the level of reading material children could understand if they could read the material themselves (Spring & French, 1990).

Most educators agree that instruction is a cycle that should lead from lesson objectives to effective instructional activities to assessment and back to new objectives that target what the teacher noted during assessment. Let's look at how a first-grade teacher could assess the following written product and use the results to plan instructional activities and additional authentic assessment activities (Figure 2.4)

FIGURE 2.4 A Written Retelling of *The Three Little Bears.*

Let's assume that Mrs. Kumar has read *The Three Little Bears* to her class and has asked Emily to do a written retelling of the story (see Standard VII to review the components of story retelling). The teacher should note that Emily understood the following: (1) the family structure of the bears, (2) the name of the food they were going to eat, (3) what they did, and (4) what had happened to their food when they returned. Mrs. Kumar should assess the written retelling to determine instructional strategies that could be used to help Emily orally retell omitted details about the story. For example, Mrs. Kumar could ask Emily to tell about other characters in the story, other things that happened in the story, where the story took place, the main problem and how it was solved, and so on. In addition, Mrs. Kumar should assess Emily's writing conventions (see Standard IX to review writing conventions) and determine further activities that could be used in instruction. A teacher might plan an additional lesson on using punctuation at the end of a sentence, in which several activities would be given to provide the child practice in using an appropriate punctuation mark at the end of several different types of sentences. This brief discussion highlights that assessment and instructional practices should be used daily to make instructional decisions.

Try these practice questions:

Mr. Orion provides the following information about Patrick's reading performance during a parental conference:

"Patrick reads slightly above grade level. He enjoys reading orally in class and has a positive attitude about learning. There is some concern about the usage of miscues during oral reading. This is causing Patrick to make some comprehension mistakes. This is not necessarily a habit yet, but strategies that will assist Patrick in being more accurate in oral reading should be provided."

Which instructional practices would not be recommended?

A. Establishing strategies that allow Patrick to use his own background knowledge to determine word selection during oral and silent reading.
B. Encouraging him to stop and seek assistance each time he encounters a word he cannot pronounce.
C. Instructing him to use context clues to determine unknown words.
D. Instructing Patrick on how to use metacognitive strategies to ask questions about the readings.

Patrick should have grade-appropriate sight word recognition. However, it would also be an appropriate practice to encourage him to use his own background in determining word choices, to use self-determined questions (using a metacognitive strategy) to assist in meaning, and to use context clues to determine unknown words. Therefore, choice *B* is correct and is *not* recommended so as not to continuously break the flow of his reading, especially during independent reading. The answer is *B*.

Students in Mr. Perez's sixth-grade mathematics class have been writing journal entries to describe the process used in solving math problems. Mr. Perez has just requested that his students give him journal entries submitted over the last five Mondays. Which type of assessment is closest to Mr. Perez's request?

A. Portfolio assessment
B. Informal reading inventory
C. Criterion-referenced testing
D. Norm-referenced testing

Mr. Perez is using modified portfolio assessment considerations in his request to see a rather specific collection of student-generated products that could indicate a pattern of academic or nonacademic growth. For a more complete portfolio assessment, he would want to include many different products and have student input. However, *A* is the closest to his request.

SUMMARY

This chapter discusses the instructional importance of acquiring knowledge about the concepts to be tested on these standards of the English Language Arts and Reading for the EC-6 *Generalist* and should serve as an introduction or as a strong review of information that you have studied in coursework and applied in different types of instructional settings. As you connect this information to your current knowledge base, notice an increase in basic information that assists you in preparing for this examination. In addition to acquiring the knowledge needed to be successful when taking this examination, it is necessary to properly apply it successfully to reach children in classroom settings. These concepts are truly the base for success in all (or many parts) of other content areas, and, as strongly noted in the chapter, every teacher should consider him- or herself a good reading teacher—no matter what subject(s) he or she teaches. The importance of designing effective language arts and reading lessons cannot be overstated. Planning this type of instruction requires the development and use of activities that are theoretically sound, meaningful, and interesting—so that all children can participate in an effective learner-centered classroom environment. Educators who understand the process and reasons for designing and conducting effective instruction for reading and language arts are able to identify and meet these needs for all of their children.

GLOSSARY

You should become familiar with the following terms so that you can establish an effective knowledge base. This knowledge base provides you with more information when considering the most effective response to questions on the *TExES* and in becoming a more professional teacher.

Affix. A structural element added to the beginning or ending of a word in order to alter the meaning, pronunciation, or function (e.g., prefixes and suffixes).

Alliteration. Words in a sentence or phrase that begin mostly with the same letter sound.

Alphabet. The written symbols (graphemes) of a language arranged in a special order. The English alphabet has 26 letters of graphemes.

Alphabetic principle. The idea that individual letters represent individual speech sounds; therefore, words may be read by saying the sounds represented by the letters, and words may be spelled by writing the letters that represent the sounds.

Alphabetic recognition. The ability to name letters of the alphabet.

Balanced approach to literacy. The use of different strategies and approaches to teach reading.

Basal reader. A collection of stories that matches the instructional level of children, usually seen as the reading textbook in schools.

Bilingual education. Instruction that involves presenting reading and other subject area materials in the child's native language while gradually introducing English.

Blending. The skill of combining separate sounds to create a word (/t/ /o/ /p/ = top)

Choral reading. Oral reading, often of poetry, involving more than one reader.

Consonant blend or cluster. Two or three letters in the same syllable that are blended or heard when pronounced (e.g., *tr* in *tree*).

Consonant digraph. A combination of two or more letters that represent a sound that is different from the speech sound that the letters represent individually (e.g., *ch* in *chop*).

Context clues. Words or phrases within a reading passage that give hints to vocabulary meaning.

Contextual. Depending on or pertaining to context (a word's placement in a sentence) that a reader can analyze and use to determine meaning.

Conventions. Certain established patterns in language and writing. For example, in English we read from the top of the page to the bottom, and from the left to the right.

Convergent question. A question with one correct answer (e.g., "What is the capital of Texas?").

Conversation. An activity involving two or more persons taking turns talking about a subject.

Debate. A discussion involving varying viewpoints on a central topic, where sides are supported.

Decode. Deciphering word meaning; associating printed letters with the speech sounds the letters make.

Developing writing stage. One of the patterns (e.g., scribble writing, one-letter labeling, inventive spelling) evidenced by an individual as he or she emerges into writing.

Diagnostic assessment. Prior to instruction, determining students' difficulties or lack of knowledge to decide the path of further instruction that matches students' needs.

Dialect. A linguistic change or variation in speech pronunciation that is different from the standard, or original, pronunciation.

Diphthong. Two adjacent vowels in which each vowel is heard in the pronunciation (e.g., *ou* in *house*).

Discussion. Focused conversations about a specific topic.

Divergent question. A question that could have many correct answers (e.g., "What is the best way to limit pollution?").

Elkonin box. A strategy designed to help a student segment words. The teacher shows a picture of an object to the student and draws a series of boxes to match the number of sounds in the object's name. After hearing the word pronounced and identifying the sounds, the student writes the letters representing the sounds in the boxes.

Emergent literacy. Children's reading and writing development before formal instruction in classroom settings.

Emergent writing stage. Beginning efforts in letter formation (scribbling, drawing, and a combination of these), usually starting before kindergarten age.

English as a Second Language (ESL). An instructional program that teaches English to students whose native language is not English.

Evaluative comprehension. Level of comprehension that requires children to compare information and ideas presented in a text with their own experiences, background, and values.

Facilitative. Skills, such as word analysis, that enable a reader to identify words.

Figurative language. The literal meaning of a sentence is put aside to make writing or speech more interesting and creative; use of figures of speech (simile, metaphor, analogy, hyperbole, alliterations, etc.).

Fluency. Continuous flow of word recognition.

Formal assessment. Published tests, such as norm-referenced and criterion-referenced tests.

Functional. The actual understanding or comprehension of what has been read.

Genre. A description of the type of text being read (e.g., poetry, biography, mystery, fantasy).

Grapheme. A printed letter symbol used to represent a speech sound (phoneme).

Graphophonemic knowledge. Written words are made up of systematic letter patterns that represent sounds in pronounced words.

Graphophonic. Sound–symbol relationship.

Guide-O-Rama. A written guide, with informal notes and thoughts, designed to guide students through a textbook chapter or other reading selection.

Homographs. Words spelled the same but having different pronunciations and meanings; for example: "She is wearing a red *bow*," and "She will *bow* to the queen."

Homophones. Words that sound the same but have different spellings and meanings; for example: "He is wearing a *red* shirt." "He *read* the book."

Idioms. Figurative sayings that have special meanings; for example, "Keep your shirt on!" basically means "Don't get angry."

Inferential comprehension. Level of comprehension that requires children to respond to questions and statements based on ideas and information that are directly stated in the text, along with the use of their intuition, background, and experiences to reach a conclusion or a hypothesis.

Informal assessment. Nonstandardized means of assessment, such as anecdotal records, checklists, rubrics, and portfolios.

Informal reading inventory (IRI). A series of graded paragraphs followed by a comprehension analysis used to determine a child's independent, instructional, and frustration level for reading.

Interlocking study guide. A study guide containing questions in a definite ordered format: literal, interpretive, and evaluative.

Interview. One person asking another questions and recording their responses.

Invented spelling. Temporary spelling patterns young children use to approximate the spelling of words (e.g., a young child might write "It wus a preti da" instead of "It was a pretty day.").

Language experience approach (LEA). An instructional method that incorporates children's experiences and backgrounds as a means of developing instructional reading stories.

Language interference. For ESL children, the use of sounds, syntax, and vocabulary of two languages simultaneously as a child participates in literacy activities.

Letter recognition. The relationship of letters in printed words to spoken language.

Literal comprehension. Level of comprehension that requires children to respond to questions and statements that directly relate to stated text.

Logographic awareness. The first stage children experience when learning about words.

Words that are learned as whole units are sometimes embedded in a logo, such as a stop sign or the arches in the McDonald's sign.

Mechanics. The accepted conventions of correctly written standard English, consisting of spelling, capitalization, punctuation, grammar, and usage.

Metaphor. Comparison of two unlike things without using *as* or *like* (e.g., "The *moon* was an *orange* floating on the *silver platter* of the *sea*.").

Miscues. Words read differently than how they are written.

Morpheme. The smallest meaningful unit of language (e.g., *cat* is a morpheme whose pronunciation consists of three phonemes, c/a/t).

Noninterlocking study guide. A study guide arranging questions in a nonordered format, intermingling questions among literal, interpretive, and evaluative levels.

Nonstandard dialect. Grammatical variations in a language most often associated with a cultural group.

Onsets and rimes. *Onsets* are the consonants that come at the beginning of syllables in words—for example, the *bl* in the word *blend* is the onset. *Rimes* are vowels and consonants at the end of a syllable—for example, the *end* in the word *blend* is the rime.

Oracy. The concept that identifies and describes the differences between the skills of listening and speaking from the skills of reading and writing.

Oral expression. Active speaking, such as conversations, discussions, oral reports, choral reading, and so on.

Oral reports. Individual or group reports delivered orally to an audience.

Orthography. Correct spelling.

Phoneme. The smallest unit of sound in a language that distinguishes one word from another word. Example: *cat* and *hat* are distinguished as sounding different by considering their beginning consonant phonemes /c/ and /h/.

Phoneme isolation. The ability to recognize individual sounds in a word (e.g., *dad* and *dog* have the same beginning sounds, not the same middle sounds, and not the same ending sounds).

Phonemic awareness. The knowledge or understanding that speech consists of a series of sounds and that individual words can be divided into phonemes.

Phonic analysis. The process of applying knowledge of letter-sound relationships to words; teachers ask for this when they instruct children to sound out a word.

Phonics. Using letters and the sounds of letters to determine the pronunciation of a word.

Phonological awareness. The ability to use letter–sound knowledge to identify an unknown word.

Phonology. The study of speech sounds.

Picture books. A book in which text and illustrations unite to form a meaningful whole.

Portfolio. A collection of student-generated products that shows growth, progress, or improvement over a period of time.

Prosody. The rhythm of speech in reading, including phrasing, appropriate breathing, voice intonation, tone, and attention to all punctuation marks.

Puppets. Animal or human characters made from a variety of materials to be held or slipped over the hand and used in dramatic play; often provide shy children with more oral confidence.

Readers' theater. The oral presentation of drama by two or more readers using a printed script; normally used to create motivation and oral fluency.

Reading fluency. The ability to read a text orally at an appropriate rate with correct word pronunciation, expression, and comprehension.

Research. Students conduct investigations, forming and revising questions, while using a variety of sources and drawing conclusions from information gathered.

Rhyming. Producing patterns of rhyming words.

Running record. An informal assessment that provides a record of a child's oral reading development and behavior.

Scaffolding. Support for a learner as he or she enters a phase of readiness for a new skill.

Schwa sound. In many words that have more than one syllable, one of the syllables receives less or diminished stress. The sound of the vowel in the syllable that receives the diminished stress has a softening of the vowel sound that is identified as a schwa sound and often pronounced as the "uh" sound. The word *about* contains the schwa sound.

Segmentation. The ability to identify and separate sounds in words (for purposes of blending); for example, fish = /f/ /i/ /sh/.

Semantic feature analysis. Constructing a grid for a concept (e.g., mammals) where examples of the concept are listed vertically (e.g., cow, bat, squirrel) and their features are listed horizontally (e.g., has fur, swims, flies); students then decide which feature matches each word.

Semantic or concept map (word cluster). A method of expanding understanding by writing a word or concept in the center circle of a cluster, drawing rays, and writing information about the word or concept in the "outer bubbles" to make connections/relationships between the word or the concept.

Semantics. The way one defines a word(s); meaning of words.

Seven literary elements. These seven elements are plot, theme, characterization, point of view, setting, mood or emotional tone, and style.

Show-and-tell. A traditional informal speaking activity in which a child brings something from home that is special to him or her and tells the class about it.

Sight vocabulary. Any words a reader can recognize instantly without having to use a word recognition strategy; many teachers have children personalize a word bank of the sight words they can read.

Similes. Comparison between two things of a different kind or quality using *like* or *as* (e.g., "The rain came down like transparent sheets.").

Syllable. Divisions of speech sounds within words. Example: unbelievable = *un be liev a ble.*

Syntactic. Patterns of phrases, clauses, and sentences. Example: Give the money to Mom and me.

Syntax. Sentence structure.

Text forms. Printed materials.

Textless books *(also known as wordless books).* A picture storybook or concept book with few or no words in which the illustrations convey the story.

Thematic units. Instructionally generated learning activities that center on a topic of interest (such as a variety of content areas teaching various aspects of the topic of "butterflies").

Trade books. Children's literature sources that teachers sometimes use in instructional settings instead of textbooks.

Viewing and Representing. Students understand and interpret visual communications that are conveyed nonverbally, and they can express this understanding by producing visual media. Students can attend to and interpret, for example, the meanings of illustrations and drawings, maps, political cartoons, media messages, performances, and computer graphics.

Vowel digraph. Two adjacent vowels that represent one speech sound (e.g., *ee* in *feet*).

Word analysis skills. An inclusive term that refers to all methods of word recognition; phonics is one such method. Other methods include *picture clues* (using pictures and graphic aids to assist in word pronunciation and meaning), *context clues* (using surrounding text to aid in word pronunciation and meaning), *sight words*, and *structural analysis* (which focuses on root words, base words, affixes, compound words, syllable division, and contractions).

Word recognition skills. Skills readers use to identify printed words, such as *instant recognition* (sight words), context clues, and onset and rimes.

Word sorts. Sorting a collection of words taken from a word wall or other sources into two or more categories; in *closed word sorts*, the teacher gives the categories and the words to categorize (e.g., categories might include nouns and verbs, or words with a long /a/ sound and words with a short /a/ sound); in an *open word sort*, the students are given words but the teacher directs them to divide them into categories with names that make sense to them (e.g., *make, saw, give, say, talk, called* may go into present or past tense verbs).

Word wall. A list of words children are learning (or know) posted on a poster (or an actual wall in a classroom) in a highly visible location so children can access them easily for spelling and/or ideas as they work.

Writing or Writer's Workshop. An extended project that can involve narration of a story to the teacher or, in the case of older children, a writing assignment prompt, instruction on a small area of writing or punctuation, revision/editing, "publishing," and peer sharing. This is normally an interdisciplinary activity and occurs three to five times a week.

Zone of proximal development. Children learn within their instructional level or just beyond their instructional level with scaffolding from an adult or from a capable peer.

REFERENCES

Adams, M. J. (1990). *Beginning to read: Thinking and learning about print.* Cambridge, MA: Massachusetts Institute of Technology.

Anderson, L., & Krathwohl, D. (Eds.). (2001). *A taxonomy of learning, teaching, and assessment: A revision of Bloom's taxonomy of educational objectives.* New York: Longman.

Baghban, M. (1984). *Our daughter learns to read and write: A case study from birth to three.* Newark, DE: International Reading Association.

Barrett, T. C. (1965). The relationship between measures of prereading visual discrimination and first grade reading achievement: A review of the literature. *Reading Research Quarterly, 1,* 51–76.

Blevins, W. (1998). *Phonics from A to Z: A practical guide.* New York: Scholastic Professional Books.

Bloom, B. S., Englehart, M. D., Furst, E. J., Hill, W. H., & Krathwohl, D. R. (Eds.). (1956). *Taxonomy of educational objectives: The classification of education goals, handbook I: Cognitive domain.* New York: David McKay.

Burroughs, S., Brocato, K., Hopper, P. F., & Sanders, A. (2009). Media literacy: A central component of democratic citizenship. *The Educational Forum, 73,* 154–167.

Calfee, R. C., & Perfumo, P. (1993). Student portfolios: Opportunities for a revolution in assessment. *The Reading Teacher, 46,* 532–537.

Carlson, C., Fletcher, J., Foorman, B., Francis, D., & Schatschneider, C. (2001). *Texas primary reading inventory (TPRI) teacher's guide.* Austin: Texas Education Agency.

Carmen, R., & Adams, W. (1972). *Study skills: A student's guide to survival.* New York: Wiley.

Clay, M. M. (1985). *The early detection of reading difficulties: A diagnostic survey with recovery procedures.* Portsmouth, NH: Heinemann.

Cramer, R. L. (2004). *The language arts: A balanced approach to teaching reading, writing, listening, and thinking.* Boston: Pearson Education, Inc.

Cunningham, J. W., Cunningham, P. M., Hoffman, J. V., & Yopp, H. R. (1998). *Phonemic awareness and the teaching of reading: A position statement from the board of directors of the International Reading Association.* Newark, DE: International Reading Association.

Dowhower, S. L. (1991). Speaking of prosody: Fluency's unattended bedfellow. *Theory into Practice, 30,* 165–175.

Duthie, C. (1996). *True stories: Nonfiction literacy in the primary classroom.* York, ME: Stenhouse.

Elkonin, D. B. (1963). The psychology of mastering elements of reading. In B. Simon & J. Simon (Eds.), *Educational psychology in the U.S.S.R.* (pp. 165–179). London: Routledge and Kegan Paul.

Gentry, J. R. (1981). Learning to spell developmentally. *The Reading Teacher, 34,* 378–381.

Gipe, J. (2010). *Multiple paths to literacy: Assessment and differentiated instruction for diverse learners* (7th ed.). Boston: Pearson.

Gunning, T. (2010). *Creating literacy instruction for all students* (7th ed.). Boston: Allyn & Bacon.

Halliday, M., & Hasan, R. (1976). *Cohesion in English.* London: Longman.

Jewell, M., & Zintz, M.F. (1986). *Learning to read and write naturally.* Dubuque, IA: Kendall-Hunt.

Juel, C. (1988). Learning to read and write: A longitudinal study of fifty-four children from first through fourth grade. *Journal of Educational Psychology, 80,* 437–447.

Kortz, J., Nath, J., & Parker Braselton, M. (2011). Technology for Texas teachers. In J. Nath & M. Cohen (Eds.), *Becoming an EC-6 teacher in Texas: A course of study for the Pedagogy and Professional Roles (PPR) TExES* (pp. 347–434). Belmont, CA: Wadsworth/Cengage.

Kubey, R. (Ed.). (2001). *Media Literacy in the Information Age: Current Perspectives* (Vol. 6). New Jersey: Transaction Publishers.

Kubey, R., & Baker, F. (1999). Has media literacy found a curricular foothold? Retrieved May 11, 2010, from http://www.frankwbaker.com/edweek.htm

Kutiper, K. (1985). *A survey of the adolescent poetry preferences of seventh, eighth, and ninth graders.* Unpublished doctoral dissertation, University of Houston, Houston, Texas.

Lundsteen, S. W. (1979). *Listening: Its impact at all levels on reading and the other language arts.* Urbana, IL: ERIC Clearinghouse on Reading and Communication Skills and the National Council of Teachers of English.

Manzo, A. V. (1969). The request procedure. *Journal of Reading, 13,* 123–126.

McCormick, S. (1999). *Instructing students who have literacy problems* (3rd ed.). Upper Saddle River, NJ: Prentice-Hall.

McGee, L., & Richgels, D. (2000). *Literacy's beginnings: Supporting young readers and writers.* Boston: Allyn & Bacon.

Megee, M. (1997). Students need media literacy: The new basic. *Education Digest, 63(1),* 31–35.

Meyer, B. (1975). *The organization of prose and its effect on memory.* Amsterdam: North-Holland.

Morrow, L. M. (1989). Using story retelling to develop comprehension. In K. D. Muth (Ed.), *Children's comprehension of text: Research into practice* (pp. 37–58). Newark, DE: International Reading Association.

National Reading Panel (2000). *Teaching children to read: An evidence-based assessment of the scientific research literature on reading and its implications for reading instruction.* Washington, DC: National Institute of Child Health and Human Development.

Ogle, D. M. (1992). KWL in action: Secondary teachers find applications that work. In E. K. Dishner, T. W. Bean, J. E. Readence, & D. W. Moore (Eds.), *Reading in the content areas: Improving classroom instruction* (3rd ed.), (pp. 270–281). Dubuque, IA: Kendall-Hunt.

Piaget, J. (1973). *The language of the child.* New York: World.

Rey, H. A. (1957). *Curious George gets a medal.* Boston: Houghton Mifflin Company.

Rubin, D. (2000). *Teaching elementary language arts.* Boston: Allyn & Bacon.

Rupley, W. H., & Willson, V. L. (2000). Content, domain, and word knowledge: Relationship to children's reading comprehension. *Journal of Reading and Writing, 8,* 419–432.

Spandel, V., & Stiggins, R. (1997). *Creating writers: Linking writing assessment and instruction.* New York: Addison Wesley Longman.

Spring, C., & French, L. (1990). Identifying children with specific reading disabilities from listening and reading discrepancy scores. *Journal of Learning Disabilities, 23,* 53–58.

Stanovich, K. E. (1994). Romance and reality. *The Reading Teacher, 47,* 280–291.

Stauffer, R. G. (1969). *Teaching reading as a teaching process.* New York: Harper and Row.

Terry, C. A. (1974). *Children's poetry preferences: A national survey of upper elementary grades.* Urbana, IL: National Council of Teachers of English.

Tompkins, G. E. (2001). *Literacy for the 21st century: A balanced approach* (2nd ed.). Upper Saddle River, NJ: Prentice-Hall.

University of Texas Center for Reading and Language Arts. (2003). *Teaching the viewing and representing Texas Essential Knowledge and Skills in the English Language Arts Curriculum: Professional development guide* (revised). Retrieved May 11, 2010, from http://www.texasreading.org/downloads/secondary/guides/2003VR_bw.pdf

Vacca, R., & Vacca, J. A. (1986). *Content area reading.* Boston: Little, Brown and Company.

Walker, B. J. (2000). *Diagnostic teaching of reading.* New Jersey: Merrill.

Wilkinson, A. (1974). Oracy in English teaching. In H. DeStefana & S. Fox (Eds.), *Language and the language arts* (pp. 64–71). Boston: Little, Brown and Company.

Yopp, H. K. (1995). A test for assessing phonemic awareness in young children. *The Reading Teacher, 49,* 20–29.

Ziegler, A. (1981). *The writing workshop, Vol. 1.* New York: Teachers and Writers Collaborate.

A READING LESSON PLAN

Title: The Letter "B"

Grade Level: Kindergarten/First

Main Subject Area: Reading

Integrated Subjects: Art/music

Time Frame/Constraints: 1 to 2 hours

Overall Goal(s): To have children associate /b/ sound with the upper- and lowercase letter *B*.

TEKS OBJECTIVES:

§ 110.2/3. *English* Language Arts and Reading, Kindergarten (B) knowledge and skills (1) Reading/Beginning Reading Skills/Print Awareness. Students understand how English is written and printed; (B) identify upper- and lower-case letters; (2) Reading/Beginning Reading Skills/Phonological Awareness. Students display phonological awareness; (H) isolate the initial sound in one-syllable spoken words; (3) Reading/Beginning Reading Skills/Phonics. Students use the relationships between letters and sounds, spelling patterns, and morphological analysis to decode written English; (A) identify the common sounds that letters represent; (5) Reading/Vocabulary Development. Students understand new vocabulary and use it correctly when reading and writing; (C) identify and sort pictures of objects into conceptual categories (e.g., colors, shapes, textures); (17)

Oral and Written Conventions/Handwriting; (A) form upper- and lower-case letters;

§ 117.2. Art Creative expression/performance. The student expresses ideas through original artworks, using a variety of media with appropriate skill. The student is expected to: (A) create artworks, using a variety of colors, forms, and lines; (B) arrange forms intuitively to create artworks; and (C) develop manipulative skills when drawing, painting, printmaking, and constructing artworks, using a variety of materials;

§ 117.3. Music (1) Perception. The student describes and analyzes musical sound and demonstrates musical artistry. The student is expected to: (C) identify repetition and contrast in music examples.

LESSON OBJECTIVES:

(Note: Objectives should be given to students *after* the Concept Attainment Game).

- Students will draw a picture of something that starts with the letter "Aa."
- Students participate in the Concept Attainment Game on things that start with the letter "Bb."
- Students will listen to a Batman cartoon book or to *Brown Bear, Brown Bear.*
- Students will sing "Bingo," clap the "beat" of the song, and "bark" to the song.
- Students, in groups, will construct a "B-Bag."
- Students will each make an upper- and lower-case "B" with brown beans.
- Students will complete a worksheet in which each correctly circles 8 out of 10 answers of words beginning with the /b/ sound.
- Students will orally identify pictures of animals whose names start with /b/.

Readiness Skills or Prior Knowledge Needed: Know that letters stand for sounds.

Sponge Activity: Students will be asked to draw a picture of something showing yesterday's letter/sound ("A") on a piece of paper.

Environmental Concerns: Remember to go over "glue rules" during bean activity. Students should be in their core groups for the "B-Bag" activity; if not, be sure groups are heterogeneous.

Rationale(s): (To be given *after* the Concept Attainment Game). There are many words that start with the letter "B". If we want to be able to read and write those words, we must be able to recognize and pronounce that letter. How could we write Bobby, Bailey, or Brianna (or "B" names of classmates) if we didn't know about "B"—because all of their names begin with the letter "B"? How could we see if a restaurant had the foods we wanted to eat (burgers, barbeque on a bun, beans, bananas, etc.) if we could not recognize the letter "B"?

Focus or Set Induction: Concept Attainment Game. The teacher has two sets of large cards: (1) with 4–5 pictures of fruits and 4–5 pictures of vegetables [or anything other than fruit] and (2) with at least 10 large pictures of things that begin with the letter "B" (boat, baby, bear, bag, bathtub, books, brown crayon, backpack, bacon, ball, balloon, banana, bell, buttons, etc.) and 10 cards with things that do not begin with "b" (camera, cat, umbrella, truck, dog, elephant, apples, eggplant, etc.). The teacher introduces the game by saying, "Today, boys and girls, we are going to play 'Guess What I'm Thinking.' I am going to show you some pictures that have some examples of what I'm thinking and some pictures that are not of what I am thinking. There are some rules for this game. You must raise your hand and be called on, and you can never say what "it" is (that you believe is in my mind) until the end of the game, but you can guess another example of what I am thinking or you can guess a non-example (or "not it"; that is, something you believe that I'm *not* thinking about). Let's play a sample game, so that you will see how to play." The teacher shows two cards with two different fruits (for example, apples and grapes) and one card with a vegetable and tells students, "I'm going to put the cards that are examples of what I'm thinking of on this side of the board (marked "Yes" or "It"), and the ones that are not of what I'm thinking about on the other side (marked "No" or "Not It"). Now, who can give me another example of what I'm thinking?" When students say a particular fruit, the teacher adds the picture to the "Yes" side (or prints the word on the board if it is not on one of the cards). If it is a non-example, it is placed on the "No" or "Not It" side. If students say "fruit" right away (the concept) you must say, "Well, maybe, but can you give me an example or a non-example to test your guess?" When the cards are finished and it is fairly obvious that most students do know that the concept is fruit, the teacher asks one child to tell out loud what the concept is. If it is not correct, play a little longer. As a practice game, this should not last very long. Move on to the real game. The teacher begins by showing two examples of the /b/ cards and one non-example, placing them under the correct label on the board and asks the class to say the name of each object in the picture out loud. Then

the teacher asks students to give an example ("Yes" or "It") or a non-example ("No" or "Not It"). Place answers in the correct area (either a picture or the printed word). Children should have a few guesses between adding pictures, but if they are off-track, always add a new card to the example side. When the teacher begins to see that children have an idea of the concept, he or she should switch modes to showing children a picture and asking on which side it belongs. Finally, children will be asked to give the concept—"words that begin with the letter 'B.'" If they do not get it, the teacher can have them go through all of the cards again and pronounce all of the words and/or give other hints. Finally, she or he should ask if students know other words that start with the letter "b" that were not mentioned.

MAKING CONNECTIONS:

1. **Connections to Past or Future Learning:** (Do not give until after the Concept Attainment Game). We learned how to make a letter "A" and learned about some of the sounds that "A" makes. Today, we will learn more about the sound that the letter "B" makes and how to make a lower- and uppercase letter "B."

2. **Connections to the Community:** Does anyone know a person whose name starts with the letter "B"? Do you know any businesses that start with the letter "B"? (Burger King; Halfprice Books, bank, bakery, etc.; having pictures is a good idea).

3. **Cultural Connections:** Look at a list of names of people in the class or grade level that begins with the letter "B," research the cultural origin and share with students. Ask them if all languages have a "B." They do not—the Hawaiian language has no words with "B."

4. **Connection to Student Interests and Experiences:** What toys start with the letter "B"? (Barbie, baseball, baseball bat, baton, beach ball, bears, baby doll, balloon).

Materials: 2 sets of cards for Concept Attainment Game (one for the practice game and one for the real game); Batman cartoon book (with lots of words with the beginning /b/ sound) or *Brown Bear, Brown Bear;* brown paper bags; stickers with "B" words and non "B" words; blue balloons and blue ribbons; beans and light brown construction paper; worksheet; PowerPoint slides with "B" words; animal cards.

Activities: Guided Practice: Teacher reads a Batman cartoon (or can make one up) with many "Bat words" or reads *Brown Bear, Brown Bear.* The class sings "Bingo," and the teacher has children "bounce" when they hear the letter "B." Children then clap the "beat" as they sing again, and finally children substitute the word *bark* for all of the words as they sing the last time. Children are grouped to construct a "B-bag." Each group has a brown paper lunch bag. The group is given a number of stickers. They are to pick out the stickers that have words beginning with the letter "B" and glue or stick them on their bags. When they are finished, all members of the group should raise their hands, and the teacher will come and tie a blue balloon onto their bags with a blue ribbon.

Independent Practice: Each child will make an upper- and a lowercase "B" by pasting brown beans on a sheet of light brown construction paper; children will correctly circle 8 out of 10 items on a worksheet that begin with the letter "B."

Assessment: Individuals must complete their "B" sheet with brown beans. Children must circle 8 out of 10 items that begin with the letter "B" on a worksheet.

Transitions: Individual seat to circle. Circle to groups (use song). Group to circle (use "When I call your name, if you can tell me something that starts with "B," you can move back into the circle.).

What will students do who finish early? Children will view a teacher-constructed PowerPoint Presentation with many pictures of items beginning with the letter "B."

Closure: The teacher will tell children that science cannot function without the letter "B," for example, to identify animals. The teacher will hold up animal cards that start with the letter "B" (bat, butterfly, baboon, badger, beetle, bear, bee, bluebird, blackbird, bunny, bugs, etc.) or not (cat, dog, fish, monkey, elephant, giraffe, etc.) and have children identify orally those animals whose names begin with "B."

Modification for Students with Special Needs: Toby will need to sit next to the teacher during the closure to ensure that his attention is directly on the cards. The teacher may need to go back and have Toby identify the cards one-on-one. Travis will need extra help manipulating the beans. The teacher may ask him to put the beans in the sandbox rather than glue them.

Reflection: To be completed after teaching the lesson.

In addition:

Center Connections: This lesson can be tied to centers in the following ways:

1. In the **Art Center**, children create their own *Brown Bear, Brown Bear* page with their choice of an animal whose name begins with "B" to be bound later for a class book.

2. In the **Home Center**, materials (clay, etc.) are available for "preparing" a number of bakery goods with a play oven to "bake" the item (encourage bread, biscuits, bagels, breakfast items, brownies, blueberry muffins, breadsticks, etc.). A "cookbook" should have pictures of "B" bakery products for children to see. Students are required to "bake" something with a "B" and show it to the teacher.

3. In the **Gym Center**, children balance a beanbag on their heads and try to keep their balance along a line of tape on the floor (simulating a balance beam). Children bounce a basketball and toss a beach ball. Children toss the beanbag into a Bozo the Clown's mouth.

4. In the **Science Center**, children use a balance to test many items for balanced weights. Children blow bubbles.

5. In the **Math Center**, children sort buttons by attributes (brown and blue; big and bigger, etc.).

DRAFT YOUR OWN LANGUAGE ARTS OR READING LESSON PLAN

Title of Lesson: _____

Grade Level: _____

Main Subject Area: _____

Subjects Integrated: _____

Time Frame/Constraints: _____

Overall Goal(s): _____

TEKS Objectives: _____

_____

_____

Lesson Objectives: _____

_____

_____

Readiness Skills or Prior Knowledge Needed: _____

_____

_____

Sponge Activity: _____

_____

_____

Environmental Concerns: _____

_____

_____

Rationale(s): _____

_____

_____

Focus or Set Induction: _____

_____

_____

Making Connections:

1. Connections to Past or Future Learning: _____

_____

2. Connections to the Community: _____

_____

3. Cultural Connections: _____

_____

4. Connections to Student Interests & Experiences: _____

_____

Materials: _____

_____

_____

Activities: Guided practice: _____

_____

_____

_____

_____

_____

_____

_____

Independent practice: _____

_____

_____

_____

_____

_____

_____

_____

Assessment: _____

_____

_____

Transitions: _____

_____

_____

What will students do who finish early? _____

_____

_____

Closure: _____

_____

_____

Modification for Students with Special Needs: _____

_____

_____

Reflection: _____

_____

_____

OBSERVING LANGUAGE ARTS AND READING EXPERIENCES/ACTIVITIES

During your visit to an EC-6 classroom, use the following form to provide feedback, as well as to reflectively analyze the room, the materials, and the teaching.

The Classroom Environment	Observed	Not Observed	Response
1. There is ample space for movement by children and adults.			If not, how could the classroom be rearranged?
2. There is evidence that diversity is valued.			If so, describe. If not, what language arts elements could be included to address this issue?
3. The teacher uses activities that promote oral skills.			If so, explain the types of activities observed. If not, what types of activities could be added?
4. The teacher uses approaches that provide instruction in the development of phonological awareness.			If so, describe. If not, which approaches could be implemented?
5. The teacher uses approaches and materials that provide instruction in the alphabetic principle.			If so, describe. If not, what could be added?
6. There is evidence of exposure to print awareness.			If so, describe. If not, what could be added?
7. The teacher uses games, activities, and a variety of other instructional materials to teach and practice word analysis and decoding skills.			If so, list and describe their effectiveness. If not, what could be added?
8. The teacher uses a variety of text sources to promote comprehension skills, higher-level questioning, and critical thinking.			If so, list types. If not, what are some logical additions?
9. The teacher uses instructional practices to promote reading fluency.			If so, describe. If not, what practices could be added?
10. The teacher uses motivating instructional materials to teach the development of the writing process.			If so, describe. If not, what materials could be added?
11. There is evidence of instruction in the conventions of writing.			If so, describe. If not, what opportunities were missed?
12. The teacher uses a variety of informal, formal, and authentic assessment practices.			List and explain the assessment practices and their effectiveness. If not effective, what are some logical additions?

The Classroom Environment	Observed	Not Observed	Response
13. There is evidence that parental involvement in reading and language arts is encouraged.			If so, describe. If not, how could this be encouraged?
14. There is evidence that students have choices to some degree.			If so, describe. If not, how could this be accomplished?
15. There is evidence that state standards are used in lesson planning and implementation.			If so, describe. If not, how could they be incorporated into instructional planning?
16. Student work samples are displayed.			If so, describe. Is this effective? If not, list ideas on how this could become more effective.
17. There is evidence of the integration of technology usage in aspects of language arts/reading instruction.			If so, describe. If not, in what ways could this be accomplished?
18. The teacher engages students in both individual and group work.			If so, describe. If not, how could this be changed?
19. The teacher employs student reading and writing across the curriculum.			If so, describe. If not, describe some methods to accomplish content area integration.
20. There is a language arts/ reading center in the classroom.			If so, describe. If not, describe a center that could be added.
21. The teacher integrates movement into language arts/reading.			If so, describe. If not, how could it be added?
22. The teacher integrates music into language arts/reading.			If so, describe. If not, how could it be added?
23. The lesson begins with a motivating focus.			If so, describe. If not, what could be added?
24. Language Arts/Reading displays are attractively presented in the classroom.			If so, describe. If not, what could be changed?
25. The teacher checks for understanding for *all* children			If so, describe. If not, what children are left out?
26. The lesson is presented in a logical manner.			If so, describe. If not, what should be rearranged and why?
27. The teacher uses an effective closure to end the lesson.			If so, describe. If not, what could be added?

TEST YOURSELF ON LANGUAGE ARTS AND READING

1. Mr. Binca, a second-grade teacher, noticed that Marsha had finished reading her library book. He asked her to select a couple of sentences to read out loud to him, and she read the following:

   The boy and his dad took a trip. They had fun because they went fishing in a pond. Mr. Binca noticed that Marsha hesitated as she began to read the word *fishing* and read the beginning of the word very slowly to sound like *f/i/sh*. Which phonemic awareness skill is Marsha using to read the word *fish*?
   A. Rhyming
   B. Segmenting
   C. Blending
   D. Visual discrimination

2. Mrs. Brown, a first-grade teacher, is providing individual practice for Milake. The teacher slowly pronounces the word *"cup"* phonically as *c/u/p* and immediately asks Milake to pronounce the word, which he is able to do correctly. Which phonemic awareness skill is being used in this situation?
   A. Rhyming
   B. Segmenting
   C. Blending
   D. Auditory discrimination

3. A fourth-grade teacher assigned two writing prompt topics each week for students to use to construct written compositions. The teacher recently noticed that the students were not developing compositions that effectively used the writing conventions. Which of the following ideas might *best* improve the students' use of the writing conventions?
   A. Correct each composition and have the students re-write the compositions using the teacher's edits.
   B. Have students play "conventions detective" and look for their incorrect conventions.
   C. Design a series of PowerPoint presentations that provide instruction and practice games with the uses of capitalization, punctuation, and other mistakes she has seen children making.
   D. Have the students learn to spell a new set of words each week.

4. Miss Binica teaches a Pre-K class and has noticed that two of her students do not participate in whole class oral language discussions. What could the teacher do to encourage the participation of these two students?
   A. Determine several things that these students enjoy doing and incorporate these ideas into her questioning so that she can discretely build the children's answers from short ones into longer ones.
   B. Read a story to the class. After reading and discussing the story, she could ask the two students to draw the sequence of the story and tell their favorite parts to other children in the class.
   C. Ask the students to re-tell their favorite story to another child in the class.
   D. Instruct these two children to individually stand in front of the class to tell about the story that they most liked during the week.

5. A fourth-grade student can instantly recognize, or read, most of the words in the newly adopted science textbook. The student needs to use only word analysis or decoding skills for two or three words. Which reading skill is this student mostly employing?
   A. Context clues
   B. Structural analysis
   C. Sight words
   D. Syllable division

6. A third-grade teacher wants her students to identify summary paragraphs in reading selections and to write summary paragraphs as a part of written compositions. How can this teacher best describe to students the components of a summary paragraph?
   A. There is a consistent tone and point of view.
   B. Descriptive words are used.
   C. The main ideas are restated, and essential supporting details of the text or composition are noted.
   D. The main problem is discussed and a good solution is noted.

7. Mrs. Mendosa, a first-grade teacher, reads *Curious George Gets a Medal* (Rey, 1957) to her students. She wants to develop sequencing skills with her students because she knows this skill can be used in other instructional areas, such as mathematics, science, and social studies. Which of the following instructional activities would allow her to teach this skill?
   A. As she reads the story to her students, she would allow the students to re-tell each part of the story.

B. In small collaborative groups, the students would discuss the characteristics of the main character.

C. As the students write in their composition logs, they would write a summary of the story.

D. As Mrs. Mendosa reads various sections of *Curious George Gets a Medal*, the students would complete a chart that is arranged for them to record the various events that happen in the story.

8. Ms. Jackson frequently reads books to her Pre-K class with rhyming texts. Often she will omit the final word and encourage the children to supply it. On what reading skill is Ms. Jackson focusing?
   A. Auditory discrimination of onsets in words
   B. Auditory discrimination of rimes in words
   C. Use of context clues
   D. Structural analysis

9. Miss Newton works with a small group of kindergarteners using a set of picture cards. She shows a card to the children, pronounces the name of the object, and asks them to say the letter that matches the sound they hear at the beginning of the word. Miss Newton is likely assessing:
   A. understanding of the alphabetic principle.
   B. ability to decode words.
   C. discrimination between onsets and rimes.
   D. sight vocabulary.

10. When Mrs. Rose shares big books with her Pre-K students, she points to the words as she reads the story. Mrs. Rose is primarily teaching her students:
    A. sound–symbol relationships.
    B. the directionality of print.
    C. word boundaries.
    D. orthography.

TEST YOURSELF ANSWERS AND RATIONALES FOR LANGUAGE ARTS/READING

Answer 1: *Phonemic awareness* is the ability to recognize that spoken words are made up of a sequence of individual sounds that contributes to the young reader's ability to recognize and pronounce unknown words (Rubin, 2000). The National Reading Panel (2000) has indicated that phonemic awareness instruction is an essential instructional tool in helping the young reader to learn to independently pronounce words. Choice *B* is correct because the reader was able to pronounce the individual sounds, or phonemes, in segments in the word *fishing*. *Segmentation* is defined as the ability to identify and separate sounds in words (for the purpose of then blending into words). The answer is *B*.

Answer 2: The young child was able to say the word after her teacher slowly pronounced (or blended) the individual sounds, or phonemes, in the word. The correct answer is *C*.

Answer 3: Choice *A* does not necessarily provide a reason for why certain edits were made. Choice *B* could be fun but does not provide instruction, but this could be an excellent *follow-up* activity. Choice *D* does not indicate *how* these words would be used in the instructional sequence of the writing process. Choice *C* is correct because it would provide information and structured application/structured practice for the students to see various ways of using the conventions. The correct answer is *C*.

Answer 4: We should immediately rule out choice *D*. Even though talking about things children enjoy encourages more talking, standing in front of the class would be ineffective and stressful for these children. Choices *B* and *C* would encourage the students to talk to other classmates but not necessarily to speak out in a whole class format. Choice *A* considers using instructional topics that are of interest to the students and builds small successes that can grow into greater ones. Eventually, the students may become comfortable enough to participate in longer discussions. The correct answer is *A*.

Answer 5: The question stem indicates that the student can read "most of the words" in the textbook. This would indicate that the student is using sight words because most of the words are recognized without additional analysis. Choice *C* is correct because the student is recognizing almost all of the words instantly. The answer is *C*.

Answer 6: Choices *A* and *B* are not needed in a summary. The main idea may not necessarily include a problem (*D*). A summary paragraph is an accurate restatement of the main ideas and supporting details. The summary paragraph omits unimportant details. If the summary paragraph is a part of a student's composition, the main idea should be written in the student's *own words*. The correct answer is *C*.

Answer 7: Choices *A*, *B*, and *C* are effective instructional activities. However, the question stem addresses the development of sequencing skills.

The teacher could *best* achieve the development of sequencing skills by using an advanced organizer, such as a sequencing chart or story board, to be sure that they visually see the sequence of each main event. The answer is *D*.

Answer 8: Rhyming words share the same ending sound. By inviting students to provide the missing rhyming word in a phrase or sentence, Ms. Jackson is focusing on the ending part (or rime) of the word. Words with the same rime (or ending sound), rhyme. The correct answer is *B*.

Answer 9: The ability to *decode words* (B) and being able to discriminate between *onsets* and *rimes* (C) are skills that depend on knowledge of the alphabetic principle, but there is an "umbrella answer" here that is better. *Sight vocabulary* (D) consists of words that children must learn to recognize without decoding strategies because they do not follow the rules; that is, they are *irregular*. The students in this scenario are learning that the printed symbol (grapheme) represents a sound (phoneme) (A). This is a very basic understanding in learning to read. The correct answer is *A*.

Answer 10: *Orthography* refers to correct spelling, so *D* would not be the best answer. *Sound-symbol relationships* (A) and *word boundaries* (B) may be taught using big books, but by tracking the print as she reads, Mrs. Rose is demonstrating the *direction* in which a text is read. Shared reading (using big books) enables the teacher to demonstrate one of the *conventions of print*—directionality. The correct answer is *B*.

3 Preparing to Teach Mathematics in Texas

Michael L. Connell
University of Houston–Downtown

Norene Vail Lowery
Houston Baptist University

Rena M. Shull
Rockhurst University

Charles E. Lamb
Texas A&M University

Since the late 1990s, special attention has been placed on the need for effective teachers of mathematics and the development of successful methods in which mathematics is to be taught at all grade levels. If children do not receive a good background in mathematics in their early years, it is unlikely they will progress well in the upper grades. This chapter helps you understand the unique requirements for teaching mathematics behind this focus and the process by which a person becomes a high-quality teacher of mathematics. Included are samples illustrating knowledge and beliefs held by effective teachers of mathematics and how these are reflected in their methods of instruction and in their teacher–student interactions during the process of instruction.

The chapter is organized into three main sections for test takers who are preparing to teach mathematics in EC-6 classrooms. The first section highlights the current emphases placed on the teaching and learning of mathematics. This overview describes the move from traditional and didactic teaching to the hands-on elementary mathematics classrooms of today. The second section presents standards for the TExES, with a brief elaboration on the expectations that the state of Texas has developed for teachers of mathematics. Sample question items that correspond to each area are given, along with information for successful completion of the mathematics portion of the TExES *Generalist* exam. A teaching snapshot follows with practice questions and information addressing both teaching strategies (such as manipulative use, **formulas**, and so on); mathematics content; and other vital information for EC-6 mathematics. This is followed by a third section consisting of a glossary and another set of practice questions that require you to use both content and teaching strategies. An example lesson plan and observation form complete this chapter. Note that words in bold are defined in the glossary in this chapter.

An Overview of Mathematics Education Today

Mathematics is unique in many ways among the content areas. In particular, the nature of mathematics contains both *procedural* (things that you do) and *conceptual* (things that you must understand) elements. A number of teacher candidates typically enter their professional training lacking personal meanings for the conceptual elements of elementary mathematics. In order to teach mathematics, teachers must not only be able to solve the problems themselves but also to explain the mathematical concepts to children. If you lack knowledge and understanding to guide your thinking and find it difficult to design mathematics experiences for children that they are able to easily grasp, it is not surprising that mathematics instructional approaches become predominately traditional, procedural, and *algorithmic* (using step-by-step procedures or formulas for solving a problem) rather than instruction with activities involving using higher levels of thinking in mathematics. Furthermore, as shown later in the chapter, problem solving is much more than the simple recall of rules and application of isolated procedures that traditional approaches most often offer.

Fortunately, recent advances in cognitive psychology and the corresponding emergence of a constructivist approach to teaching and learning promote new methods of addressing mathematics in the classroom (Davis, Maher, & Noddings, 1990) that are in much greater alignment with requirements of Texas standards. In addition, goals for mathematics education with an impact on curricular content, instructional strategies, classroom learning environment, and assessment have been established by the National Council of Teachers of Mathematics (NCTM). Furthermore, National Standards (NCTM, 1989, 1991, 1995, 1998, 2000) for mathematics, the Texas Essential Knowledge and Skills (TEKS), and the Texas Assessment of Knowledge and Skills (TAKS) (scheduled to be replaced by the State of Texas Assessment of Academic Readiness [STAAR]) all promote active learning environments that are learner centered and in which teachers seek to use students' prior knowledge to connect with emerging concepts.

In classrooms based on these principles, there is a marked difference in instructional approaches. For example, questioning strategies are used to develop higher-order thinking skills in children, and the use of cognitive terminology, such as *classify, analyze, predict, create,* and *justify,* is used in learning interactions. Many types of manipulatives are frequently used to assist children in "seeing," "reflecting," and "thinking" to provide a concrete basis for those concepts that are abstract, and learning centers are used to provide relevant, exploratory, and interactive contexts for learning mathematics (both for individual students and in small groups). Opportunities are created that address diversities in learning styles, gender, culture, multiple intelligences, and ability. Learners in these classrooms are not passive but *active* learners in all aspects. The NCTM *Principles and Standards for School Mathematics* (2000) and the organization's Web site (www.nctm.org) provide teachers with developmentally appropriate, grade-level visions of teaching and learning mathematical content and process skills.

Mathematics in today's classrooms should come alive through experiences that inform children of the value and utility of mathematics through historical aspects, present-day professions, and everyday living. Children who do not know when they will ever use the mathematics skills presented rarely engage in or retain their math lessons. The mathematical content and processes of today also emphasize reasoning and authentic problem solving. Lessons should connect mathematical ideas to other subject areas in *interdisciplinary* instruction and join other mathematical concepts in *intradisciplinary* ways. Real-world contexts and applications always help children to value mathematics and see its relevance. Instruction should involve the use of a textbook as one of *many* resources, and children should utilize primary sources of data with manipulatives and physical materials. As technology advances, its many uses in mathematics classes evolve continuously as well. The use of calculators and computers is now well accepted as supporting instruction and the development of higher-order thinking, rather than a means to bypass understanding.

Other suggested strategies for teachers have changed as well. The incorporation of multiple *mathematical representations* (models, tables, graphs, etc.) for the same situation is now widely promoted for children to develop better conceptual understanding of mathematical concepts. Assessment is no longer relegated to the end of the chapter test but is ongoing (formative) and interwoven with teaching by placing a focus on learning processes. Currently, alternative forms of assessment (e.g., observations, checklists, interviews, performance tasks, journals, portfolios) are routinely incorporated in the assessment process.

The picture of a the 21st-century mathematics classroom continues to be refined with the traditional rows of desks and individual seatwork giving way to an active mathematical learning environment with small groups of students engaged in collaborative problem solving. In such a classroom, children are motivated to learn and discuss both the content and processes of mathematics in an interactive, hands-on, minds-on approach. In these classrooms, reasoning and communicating are highly valued components, and the classroom itself is a safe learning environment that supports an active community of thinkers (including the teacher as a co-learner and investigator). This creates a new role for the teacher of mathematics as facilitator to children who are in the process of constructing their own knowledge.

Introduction to the Mathematics Standards

There are currently nine components in the Texas State Board for Educator Certification's Mathematics *Generalist* EC-6 Standards. Within each of these component standards, it is possible to see the vision described previously for improving the teaching and learning of mathematics. Each standard is designed and correlated with the mathematics TEKS (the Texas curriculum) and the state examination that tests students on the TEKS. The first part of this section presents guidelines for Early Childhood, followed by recommended manipulative materials for EC-6 and corresponding introductory information from the EC-6 **set** of Mathematics TEKS. The third part of this section presents the Mathematics *Generalist* EC-6 Standards with sample questions and discussion.

Pre-Kindergarten/Early Childhood Considerations

Mathematics learning builds on children's curiosity and enthusiasm and challenges them to explore ideas about patterns and relationships, order and predictability, and logic and meaning. Consequently, quality instruction occurs in environments that are rich in language, encourage children's thinking, and nurture children's explorations and ideas. These ideas include the concepts of number, pattern, measurement, shape, space, and classification.

1. **Number and Operations:** The concept of *number* is fundamental to mathematics. Fortunately, children come to school with rich and varied informal knowledge of number, as well as the psychological underpinnings on which more sophisticated understandings may be built. A major goal is to build on this informal and developmental base to more abstracted understanding and skills. The following activities help children move from basic **counting** techniques in pre-kindergarten to later understanding number size, relationships, and operations.

   In the classroom, the child performs the following tasks that involve the concept of *number*:
   - arranges sets of concrete objects in one-to-one correspondence
   - counts by ones to 10 or higher
   - counts concrete objects to 5 or higher
   - begins to compare the numbers of concrete objects using language (e.g., *same* or *equal, one more, more than,* or *less than*)
   - begins to name *how many* are in a group of up to 3 (or more) objects without counting (e.g., recognizing two or three crayons in a box)
   - recognizes and describes the concept of 0 (meaning there are none)
   - begins to demonstrate part of and whole with real objects (e.g., an orange, a chocolate bar, a pizza)
   - begins to identify first and last in a series
   - combines, separates, and names *how many* concrete objects

2. **Patterns:** Recognizing patterns and relationships among objects is an important component in children's intellectual development. Children learn to organize their world by recognizing patterns and gradually begin to use patterns as a strategy for (1) problem solving, (2) prediction, (3) forming generalizations, and (4) developing the concepts of number, operation, shape, and space. Furthermore, pattern recognition is the first step in the development of algebraic thinking. The following activities help children move from basic pattern recognition in pre-kindergarten to the ability to use patterns in a predictive fashion in problem solving:
   - imitation of pattern sounds and physical movements (e.g., clap, stomp, clap, stomp)
   - recognition and reproduction of simple patterns of concrete objects (e.g., a string of beads that are yellow, blue, blue, yellow . . .)
   - recognition of patterns in their environment (e.g., day follows night, repeated phrases in storybooks, patterns in carpeting or clothing)
   - learning to predict what comes next when patterns are extended

3. **Geometry and Spatial Sense:** Geometry and spatial sense are essential if children are to represent and describe their world systematically. As children learn to name and recognize the properties of various shapes and figures, to use words that indicate direction, and to use spatial reasoning to analyze and solve problems, they create the context within which much of later mathematics is developed and described. The following activities help children move from basic shape naming and recognition in pre-kindergarten to exploring changes in shape as a tool for puzzle and problem solving:

The young child:
- recognizes, describes, and names shapes (e.g., circles, triangles, rectangles—including squares)
- uses words that indicate where things are in space (e.g., *beside, inside, behind, above, below*)
- recognizes when a shape's position or orientation has changed
- investigates and predicts the results of putting together two or more shapes
- puts together puzzles of increasing complexity

4. **Measurement:** Measurement is one of the most widely used applications of mathematics. Early learning experiences with measurement should focus on direct **comparisons** of objects. Children make decisions about size by looking, touching, and comparing objects directly, while building language to express the size relationships. It is through measurement activities that number concepts become firmly anchored to real world situations, operations are modeled, and mathematical principles may be easily explored.

   The young child performs the following tasks:
   - covers an area with shapes (e.g., tiles)
   - fills a shape with solids or liquids (e.g., ice cubes, water, sand)
   - begins to make size comparisons between objects (e.g., *taller than, smaller than*)
   - begins to use tools to imitate measuring
   - begins to categorize time intervals and uses language associated with time in everyday situations (e.g., *in the morning, after snack*)
   - begins to order two or three objects by size (*seriation*) (e.g., largest to smallest; smallest to largest)

5. **Classification and Data Collection:** Children use sorting to organize their world. As children recognize similarities and **differences**, they begin to recognize patterns that lead them to form generalizations. As they begin to use language to describe similarities and differences, they begin sharing their ideas and their mathematical thinking. Children can be actively involved in collecting, sorting, organizing, and communicating information. These activities help children categorize elements of their world preparatory to the assignment of number and formal numeric operations.

   The young child performs the following tasks:
   - matches objects that are alike
   - describes similarities and differences between objects
   - sorts objects into groups by an attribute and begins to explain how the grouping was done
   - participates in creating and using real and pictorial graphs

Mathematics Manipulatives

Active, "hands-on, minds-on" learning involves the use of manipulatives, or concrete objects. *Manipulatives* provide a concrete basis for understanding abstract concepts and are very effective teaching tools for all students. Most educators support the use of manipulatives to help students' conceptual understanding by aiding visualization and internalization of concepts and ideas. The following guidelines offer some suggestions for management of materials appropriate for all levels of learning and interactions:

- Arrange and prepare the materials beforehand according to the purpose of the lesson.

- Explicit guidelines must be established for what is and is not acceptable behavior for using manipulatives.
- Free time for exploration for several moments before the lesson begins is necessary whenever a new material or new manipulative is introduced. This is also appropriate for when manipulatives are first placed in learning centers.
- Clear expectations must be provided for lesson goals and the use of materials.
- Specific directions concerning the purposes in using the manipulatives are imperative. Teachers and students must understand the purpose of the materials related to the lesson in order to make the connections from models to an internalized idea.
- Teachers should model the use of materials and "think aloud" about what they represent.

RECOMMENDED MINIMUM CLASSROOM MANIPULATIVE MATERIALS.

Kindergarten (Early Childhood)

Interlocking counting cubes (1,000)
Attribute blocks (four sets—60 each): manipulatives that come in various colors (red, blue and yellow), sizes, thicknesses, and shapes (squares, triangles, circles, and hexagons)
Pattern blocks (four sets—250 each with two mirrors): blocks that come in six colors and six shapes
Buttons, shells, keys, and other familiar objects for counting/sorting
Measuring instruments for time (demonstration clock)
Play money

Grade 1

Interlocking counting cubes (1,000)
Attribute blocks (four sets—60 each)
Pattern blocks (four sets—250 each with two mirrors)
Measuring instruments to measure length, **volume**, **mass**, temperature, and time
Play money

Grade 2

Interlocking counting cubes (1,000)
Base 10 blocks (1s, 10s, and 100s for each child)
Attribute blocks (four sets—60 each)
Pattern blocks (four sets—250 each with two mirrors)
Measuring instruments, both metric and customary (to measure length, volume, mass, temperature, and time)
Play money
Two- and three-dimensional geometric models (two sets of common shapes and solids)

Grade 3

Interlocking counting cubes (1,000)
Base 10 blocks (1s, 10s, and 100s for each child, one 1,000 block for each four children)
Pattern blocks (four sets—250 each with two mirrors)
Fraction models—circles, squares, bars, or rods
Measuring instruments, both metric and customary (to measure length, volume, mass, temperature, and time)
Play money
Two- and three-dimensional geometric models (two sets of common shapes and solids)

Grade 4

Base 10 blocks or other place value models (1s, 10s, and 100s for each child, one 1,000 block for each four children)
Decimal models
Fraction models—circles, squares, bars, or rods
Measuring instruments, both metric and customary (to measure length, volume, mass, temperature)
Interlocking centimeter cubes (2,000)
Tangrams—one per child (a seven-piece group of blocks that can be used to copy or design patterns).
Two- and three-dimensional geometric models (two sets of common shapes and solids)
Geoboards—one per child and one for teacher demonstration

Grade 5

Base 10 blocks or other place value models (1s, 10s, and 100s for each child, one 1,000 block for each four children)
Decimal models, including tenths, hundredths and thousandths
Fraction models—circles, squares, bars, or rods
Measuring instruments, both metric and customary (to measure length, volume, mass, temperature)
Interlocking centimeter cubes (2,000)
Gram cubes (1,500)
Pentominoes
Tangrams—one per child
Two- and three-dimensional geometric models (two sets of common shapes and solids)
Polyhedral Dice
Playing cards
Geoboards—both rectangular and circular, one per child and one for teacher demonstration

Grade 6

Base 10 blocks or other place value models (1s, 10s, and 100s for each child, one 1,000 block for each four children)
Decimal models, including tenths, hundredths and thousandths
Fraction models—circles, squares, bars, or rods
Measuring instruments, both metric and customary (to measure length, volume, mass, temperature)
Interlocking centimeter cubes (2,000)
Gram cubes (1,500)
Pentominoes
Soma cubes
Tower of Hanoi Puzzle
Tangrams—one per child
Two- and three-dimensional geometric models (two sets of common shapes and solids)
Polyhedral dice
Playing cards
Algebra tiles
Geoboards—both rectangular and circular, one per child and one for teacher demonstration

Access to a virtual manipulative Web site, such as the National Library of Virtual Manipulatives (http://nlvm.usu.edu/).

TEKS for Pre-Kindergarten through Sixth Grade

An understanding of the expectations for student achievement, as given by the Texas Education Agency (TEA), helps readers to approach the TExES in a competent and confident manner and to become ready to teach children. For all grades Pre-K through 6, the following introductory information to the TEKS describes the learning experiences required for students to meet the expectations in achieving mathematical learning:

> *Within a well-balanced mathematics curriculum, the primary focal points at Kindergarten are developing whole-number concepts and using patterns and sorting to explore number, data, and shape . . .* (§111.12 adopted to be effective September 1, 1998, 22 TexReg 7623; amended to be effective August 1, 2006, 30 TexReg 7471)

> *Throughout mathematics in grades kindergarten through 2 students build a foundation of basic understanding in number, operation, and quantitative reasoning: patterns, relationships, and algebraic thinking; geometry and spatial reasoning; and measurement and probability and statistics. Students use numbers in ordering, labeling, and expressing quantities and relationships to solve problems and translate informal language into mathematical symbols. Students use patterns to describe objects, express relationships, make predictions, and solve problems as they build an understanding of number, operation, shape, and space. Students use informal language and observation of geometric properties to describe shapes, solids, and locations in the physical world and begin to develop measurement concepts as they identify and compare attributes of objects and situations. Students collect, organize, and display data and use information from graphs to answer questions, make summary statements, and make informal predictions based on their experiences.* (§111.12 to §111.14 adopted to be effective September 1, 1998, 22 TexReg 7623; amended to be effective August 1, 2006, 30 TexReg 7471, http://ritter.tea.state.tx.us/rules/tac/chapter111/ch111a.html#111.11)

> *Throughout mathematics in grades 3 through 5 students build a foundation of basic understandings in number, operation, and quantitative reasoning: patterns, relationships, and algebraic thinking; geometry and spatial reasoning; measurement; and probability and statistics. Students use algorithms for addition, subtraction, multiplication, and division as generalizations connected to concrete experiences; and they concretely develop basic concepts of fractions and decimals. Students use appropriate language and organizational structures such as tables and charts to represent and communicate relationships, make predictions, and solve problems. Students select and use formal language to describe their reasoning as they identify, compare, and classify shapes and solids; and they use numbers, standard units, and measurement tools to describe and compare objects, make estimates, and solve application problems. Students organize data, choose an appropriate method to display the data and interpret the data to make decisions and predictions and solve problems* (§111.15 to §111.17 adopted to be effective September 1, 1998, 22 TexReg 7623; amended to be effective August 1, 2006, 30 TexReg 7471, http://ritter.tea.state.tx.us/rules/tac/chapter111/ch111a.html#111.11)

> *The primary focal points at Grade 6 are using ratios to describe direct proportional relationships involving number, geometry, measurement, probability, and adding and subtracting decimals and fractions.*

> *Students should build a foundation of basic understandings in number, operation, and quantitative reasoning; patterns, relationships, and algebraic thinking; geometry and spatial reasoning; measurement; and probability and statistics. Students use concepts, algorithms, and properties of rational numbers to explore*

mathematical relationships and to describe increasingly complex situations. Students use algebraic thinking to describe how a change in one quantity in a relationship results in a change in the other; and they connect verbal, numeric, graphic, and symbolic representations of relationships. Students use geometric properties and relationships, as well as spatial reasoning, to model and analyze situations and solve problems. Students communicate information about geometric figures or situations by quantifying attributes, generalize procedures from measurement experiences, and use the procedures to solve problems. Students use appropriate statistics, representations of data, reasoning, and concepts of probability to draw conclusions, evaluate arguments, and make recommendations. In addition to the problem solving activities described for K-5th, students at sixth grade are expected to use these processes together with graphing technology and other mathematical tools such as manipulative materials to develop conceptual understanding and solve problems as they do mathematics (§111.21 adopted to be effective September 1, 1998, 22 TexReg 7623; amended to be effective August 1, 2006, 30 TexReg 4479, http://ritter.tea.state.tx.us/rules/tac/chapter111/ch111b.html#111.21).

As these excerpts from the Texas requirements illustrate, the curriculum and learning expectations are presented in a spiraling manner. This means that each year provides a foundational basis for further concept development and elaboration for the following year. Students who miss growth during a year because of ineffectual mathematics teaching can be lost each year after that.

Mathematics *Generalist* EC-6 Standards and Sample Questions with Discussions

In this section, the standards are organized around common instructional themes and presented with a brief elaboration that enhances the view of the role of the EC-6 teacher. Following each section are sample questions for readers. Each section gives further discussion in the light of current relevant literature and research. Because some areas of the standards are very broad, the sample items attempt to capture the essence of the standard to its broadest scope and to assess the most important aspects of each standard. To gain more experience, download released TAKS tests at http://www.tea.state.tx.us/index3.aspx?id=3839&menu_id3=793. Currently, tests from grades 3 through 6 are available. It is assumed that when the STAAR replaces the TAKS, this will continue to be the case. These help beginning teachers see on what type of mathematics questions the EC-6 students could be tested (and thus what they should be able to teach).

Standard I (Number Concepts), Standard VII (Mathematical Learning and Instruction), and Standard VIII (Assessment)

Standard I: The mathematics teacher understands and uses numbers, number systems, and their structure, operations and algorithms, quantitative reasoning, and technology appropriate to teach the statewide curriculum (Texas Essential Knowledge and Skills [TEKS]) in order to prepare students to use mathematics.

Standard VII: The mathematics teacher understands how children learn and develop mathematical skills, procedures, and concepts; knows typical errors students make, and uses this knowledge to plan, organize, and implement instruction; to meet curriculum goals; and to teach all students to understand and use mathematics.

Standard VIII: The mathematics teacher understands assessment and uses a variety of formal and informal assessment techniques appropriate to the learner on an ongoing basis to monitor and guide instruction and to evaluate and report student progress.

The beginning EC-6 teacher must be able to plan appropriate activities for all children based on research and principles of learning mathematics. This includes the use of instructional strategies that build on the linguistic, cultural, and socioeconomic diversity of children and that relate to children's lives and communities. Furthermore, developmentally appropriate instruction should be provided along a continuum from **concrete to abstract** *with instruction that address needs of the child provided by the teacher. In order for this to take place the teacher must understand how mathematical learning is supported through appropriate* **use of manipulatives and technological tools.**

The teacher must take care to develop a learning environment within which children are motivated and **actively engaged** *in the learning process using a variety of interesting, challenging, and worthwhile mathematical tasks and by providing instruction in individual,* **small-group,** *and large-group settings. Mathematics instruction within this type of setting uses a* **variety of tools** *to think with (e.g., counters, standard and nonstandard units of measure such as rulers, protractors, scales, stopwatches, measuring containers, money, calculators, software) to strengthen children's mathematical understanding. Appropriate learning goals based on the Texas Essential Knowledge and Skills (TEKS) in mathematics are developed while using these learning goals as a basis for instruction. An important aspect of this environment is to help children make connections between mathematics, the real world, and other disciplines, such as art, music, science, social science, and business.*

As emphasized earlier, the teacher should strive for conceptual understanding and never be satisfied with a correct answer that cannot be explained. In reaching this goal, the teacher should use a variety of formal and informal assessments and scoring procedures to evaluate children's mathematical understanding, common misconceptions, and error patterns. Various questioning strategies should be used to encourage mathematical reflection and help children analyze and evaluate their own emerging mathematical thinking. It is important that the teacher understand the reciprocal nature of assessment and instruction and include both *formative* (ongoing) and *summative* (ending) assessments. An effective teacher does not instruct without assessing—and, likewise, does not assess without instructing. It is important to use assessment results to design, monitor, and modify instruction to improve mathematical learning for individual children, including English Language Learners. The teacher understands how mathematics is used in a variety of careers and professions and plans instruction that demonstrates how mathematics is used in the workplace.

Consider the following question:

Mrs. Jones was teaching her Pre-K class basic volume concepts but could not get students to understand that the amount of liquid in a cup was the same amount as when she poured the liquid into a flat bowl. What was happening? Select the best answer.

A. The children are in the preoperational stage and do not have the ability to conserve yet.

B. The children are in the preoperational stage and do not have the ability to transform yet.

C. The children are in the preoperational stage and do not have the ability to classify yet.

D. The children are in the preoperational stage and do not have the ability to seriate yet.

As could be surmised from these answer choices, children are normally in the preoperational stage at this grade level. *Transformation* (B) refers to the ability to record a process of change. Even though children might watch as a transformation occurs (such as a line of coins, where the teacher moves or lengthens the row but does not add to the number of coins), they are often unable to understand that the actual number of coins remains the same. The preoperational child will say that the lengthened row is now a different row, rather than one that has been changed or transformed.

Although not mentioned in this situation, children at this age also experience a failure of *reversibility* (the ability to mentally undo a change or transformation). *Seriation*, which is mentioned in the problem (D), refers to the ability to order things in a series (e.g., smallest to largest) according to increasing or decreasing length, **weight**, or volume, so, although tempting, this would not be the right answer, as this ability does not appear until the concrete operational level (7–11 years).

Classification (C) is the ability to group on the basis of common characteristics or attributes and, therefore, does not relate to the volume problem described. This allows a child to master ordering more than one object (e.g., $A < B < C$). Classification with more than one attribute appears about ages 7 to 11 years, although children in pre-kindergarten and kindergarten can form simple groups, usually on the basis of one attribute.

The best answer for this situation is choice A (conservation). Children younger than the approximate age of 7 in the preoperational stages do not have the ability to *conserve*, or see that the amount of something stays the same regardless of its shape or container (e.g., a clay ball can have the same amount when flattened into a pancake or a tall glass can contain the same amount as a shorter, wider glass). The lack of this ability makes it difficult for young children to see that the amount of something is the same no matter the number of pieces into which it is divided (e.g., a candy bar divided into halves). As children grow and work with materials such as water, sand, clay, rice, beans, paints, and so on, they are better able to apply the concepts of conservation, reversibility, more/less, bigger/smaller, and the structures and meaning of numbers. The correct answer is A.

The teacher's role is to plan and teach learning experiences that are appropriate for the developing stages of children. By observing and talking with children, teachers are better able to plan appropriate mathematical tasks that encourage progression along this developing continuum for individuals. In order to address situations such as the one presented in Mrs. Jones' pre-kindergarten class, it is important for teachers of young children to understand the intellectual development of the young child. In his theories on cognitive development, Jean Piaget (1896–1980) provides important insights for reference. Piaget believed that cognitive growth occurs as a result of the progressive active construction of logical structures that are constantly modified and combined into ever more powerful logical mental structures. To the teacher, this means that every child in every class is on an individually developing continuum of understandings. Piaget also proposed that as children interact with their environment, they create internal representations to accommodate new experiences based upon their developmentally situated modes of understanding.

A review of Piaget's stages of cognitive development helps you understand mathematics education for young children much more clearly. Before beginning, however, remember that the ages indicated here are approximate, and vary from one individual to another.

In the *sensorimotor stage* (birth to age 2 years), children are egocentric and not aware of things outside their immediate environment. Learning results from pulling, pushing, turning, twisting, rolling, poking, and interacting with many different properties of objects. At this level children require a rich environment with many stimuli. In the *preoperational stage* (ages 2–6), children come to realize that objects continue to exist outside the immediate environment, even when they cannot be seen. Now, learning involves discovering distinct properties and **functions** of objects as they compare, sort, stack, roll, distinguish triangles from squares, and begin to use some beginning abstractions to communicate (*"That is a red square," "The cat is under the table,"* etc.). The ability to conserve often (but not always) begins toward the end of this stage, as students engage in a number of "dump-and-fill" play activities. These include exploration of spaces (going under chairs, into cabinets, etc.) and experiences with volume by emptying and filling spaces (such as cabinets and boxes) with materials such as blocks. Children at this level should interact with a wide variety of objects, items, and materials (buckets, shovels, funnels, sand, water, etc.) to practice describing sorting, reversibility, and finding patterns based on attributes. During the *concrete operational stage* (ages 6–12), children complete the ability to conserve, begin to use symbols, and learn to classify with multiple attributes. They require experiences with touching, smelling, seeing, hearing, and performing. They begin to label and use symbols to describe and communicate as a form of internal representation. They must use hands-on tools to investigate. Children in the concrete operational stage are progressing to abstraction as they are moving to the *formal operational stage* (ages 12 and older). This final stage is not guaranteed by achieving a specific age. The formal operational learner is now able to make use of symbols and logical systems to build new knowledge. At this upper level, children can interpret ideas, think independently, and combine new abstractions to create new ideas. Some students never achieve this level during the school years and/or may never achieve it in certain content areas.

Piaget suggests that there are four broad factors that impact the progression through these stages of cognitive development: (1) maturation, (2) physical experience, (3) social interaction, and (4) *equilibration* (meaning that the mind seeks to resolve questions that occur). Relying on this foundation, learning experiences for children through the age of 12 must involve objects, tools, manipulative experiences, reflection, and social interaction with materials for optimal cognitive growth. A key to successful EC-6 mathematics is planning concrete experiences that facilitate learning. A sound mathematics classroom learning environment and curriculum reflect this cognitive approach to learning.

One way that teachers of mathematics bring concrete experiences to the forefront in their classrooms is by stocking them with a variety of manipulatives. Some of these can be teacher-made or collected, while others must be purchased from teacher supply companies. A listing of some of the more commonly used manipulatives is provided in Table 3.1, along with suggestions of the type of concept they help children develop.

Table 3.1 Common Mathematics Manipulatives

Name	Description	Concept Usage
Attribute blocks	Color, shape, size, and thickness; five shapes, three colors—yellow-red-blue, large and small in size	Classification, grouping, prenumber activities, symmetry, measurement, problem solving
Base$_{10}$ Blocks	Wooden/plastic pre-grouped/trading models	Builds representations of place value, exponents, number representation, operations, geometry, measurement, number theory
Calculators		Problem solving, checking solutions, place value, number magnitude, data to function, graphing, number pattern exploration
Chips, trading	Colored chips with assigned values two-sided, colored	Place value for regrouping in carrying and re-naming, fractions, number sense for decimals and operations, links blocks to algorithms
Counters/Tiles	Many varieties, such as plastic bears, frogs, chips, beans; ceramic tiles	Prenumber activities, number sense, numeration, basic number operations
Cubes • Unifix • Multilink • Wooden	One side connects All sides connect Do not link together	Can be used to develop one-to-one correspon-dence, **subitizing**, counting, sorting, basic operations, geometry, spatial sense, algebra groupable place value
Cuisenaire rods	Color and length determine value	Fractions, basic operations, logic, problem solving, area, perimeter, and more
Geoboards	Square board with pegs—rubber bands used	Area, logical thinking, number concepts, geometric figures, shapes, angles
Miras	Reflective surfaces	Symmetry, rotation, flips, and more
Paper folding	Any area of paper	Fractions, symmetry, recognizing polygons, and more
Pattern blocks	Many shapes and colors—squares, triangles, rectangles, **trapezoids**, **rhombi**, hexagons	Fraction concepts, counting, sorting, matching, logical thinking, problem solving, symmetry

Consider the following question:

Ms. Mehrman wishes to foster critical thinking skills in her first-grade students. Using overhead attribute blocks, Ms. Mehrman places an attribute block on the overhead and has her students identify the four attributes (size, shape, color, thickness) of the block. She then asks the students to select a block that is "one different" from the beginning block (i.e., with only one attribute different from the original block). She places this new block next to the first one and begins to form a "train." The class identifies the four attributes of this new block and justifies that it is one different from the first block. The students are now asked to find a block that is one different from this second block, and the process continues. This activity is most appropriate for developing students' understanding of which the following?

A. There can be more than one answer to a question.
B. It is necessary to recognize the four attributes of each block.
C. The size of the attribute blocks may be large or small.
D. The thickness of the block is very important.

Although students must identify the attributes, this activity develops a deeper development of critical thinking skills. Size is only one of the four possible attributes. Therefore, if Mrs. Mehrman puts up a large red block, students could select a "one away" block that is a blue, yellow, smaller, thicker, and so on block.

Too often, children think that there is only one right answer to a problem. This particular activity helps students realize that there can be many correct answers to a problem, requires children to characterize each attribute block, and has them consider which attribute block has only one attribute different from the block just played. There are many correct answers from which to choose in this activity. The correct answer is *A*.

Asking good questions is an essential skill in the teaching and learning of mathematics. A good question should follow the "Goldilocks criteria" of being neither too difficult nor too easy. A good question typically has links that may connect it to other questions and areas of interest. A good question may even require a full class period for full exploration! Such questions should pose thoughtful responses and reflection and move children from the knowledge and comprehension levels of Bloom's taxonomy upward to application, analysis, synthesis, and evaluation. Through addressing such questions on a regular basis, children can develop thinking that enhances their abilities to analyze, solve, and expand on problem situations. In mathematics, "there should be explorations that have no answers, no precise answers, or that have many answers" (Troutman & Lichtenberg, 1999, p. 386). Asking children to elaborate and justify their responses helps encourage higher-order thinking. Timing is also a factor in better questioning. Asking thought-provoking questions is not effective unless there is appropriate wait time, time for discussion, and time for other processing that allows for children's reflective thought.

Solely answering questions, however, is not enough. It is through *communication* that mathematical ideas are organized, extended, clarified, and realized. Effective communication best occurs in a risk-free learning environment built through careful and reflective planning, questioning, and listening. Teachers should guide children in learning how to talk about mathematics in the classroom, and children should become comfortable and competent in expressing their mathematical ideas. It is through active interaction and communication that children express ideas to peers, teachers, and others and learn to contemplate their own and others' responses. Communicating mathematically also allows teachers to informally and formally assess understanding and progress. As children communicate mathematically, they can also better understand and self-assess their own abilities. They are able to hear explanations from other children on their own level that can enhance a teacher's explanation.

Consider the following question:

Ms. Ismail asks her fourth-grade students to discuss and then package color tiles into individual bags. There are 420 color tiles in the class set and 24 students in her class. The problem involves how many color tiles are in each student's bag and how many are left over. The students decide to divide 420 by 24 and get an answer of 17.5. They are not sure what the answer means. The best response for Ms. Ismail is to:

A. have students recheck their answers.
B. ask students to discuss why they divided and what 17.5 means to this answer.
C. cut some color tiles in half.
D. ask students to round their answers.

Having students recheck their computations (choice *A*) might improve computational accuracy, but it does not foster higher-order thinking. Having students use concrete objects to represent part of the problem (*C*) might cause a deeper understanding of the decimal contained within the answer, but without the teacher guiding the activity, students might not connect this to the larger problem. **Rounding** the answer (*D*) has no application to this question.

Ideally, the teacher should require the students to assess their understanding of **division** and what the **remainder** means. This may be done by encouraging students not just to give a set answer but to continue to question what the answer might mean to a real-life problem when something cannot be divided. The best response for this situation is choice *B*. Situations such as this one are important to address in the classroom because they provide the teacher with opportunities to assess the understanding of mathematical learning informally. Children benefit by talking through their understanding, reflecting on their thinking, and affording them experiences that help them to make sense of the mathematics that they are learning. The correct answer is *B*.

Assessments are a major part of learning in mathematics. Without them, teachers cannot know what children are or are not learning. The role of assessment is changing in today's mathematics classroom. Strict use of pencil-and-paper testing is no longer sufficient for mathematics. When paper-and-pencil tasks are used exclusively for evaluation, it is difficult to determine whether a student understands conceptually or has made inadvertent errors. However, when paper-and-pencil tests are supplemented with student interviews, teachers are able to determine more about their conceptual understanding (Connell, 2009). The students soon come to realize that it is important to search for meanings in assessment when they are evaluated with respect to their understanding, as well as their skill at getting correct answers. Thus, interviewing helps students and teachers by focusing their attention on the things that matter most and allow for better diagnosis of misconceptions that eventually leads to more correct answers.

A variety of approaches to assessment are currently being implemented in the classroom setting, particularly alternative forms that provide a more complete and thorough picture of a child's mathematical understanding. Because children enter school with different levels of understanding and experiences with mathematics, assessment should be used early on to adapt instruction to children's needs. In addition to interviews, checklists and observations are appropriate for assessing even very young children. Writing and drawing in mathematics journals provides children with time for reflecting on the mathematics that they are learning and provides teachers with insight into children's thinking. Performance tasks that challenge children to perform or to apply their learning to new situations or **events** may be used to reveal how children are learning and applying that learning to become successful problem solvers.

It is important to remember that in assessing young children, they may often have difficulty manipulating objects physically. This can affect the validity of how they may be judged. For example, a teacher may believe that a child really does understand a particular mathematics concept, yet an assigned task (e.g., cutting and pasting paper objects) is incorrectly completed, due perhaps to underdeveloped eye–hand coordination rather than lack of knowledge. The EC-6 teacher must be aware that younger children cannot physically do some types of tasks easily, yet they can understand the concept. Using multiple means of assessing children can identify these types of situations. Mrs. Kay, for example, sits with her individual children at times and says, "Okay, I'm going to be the one with the pencil (or manipulatives) this time and you are going to tell me what to do in this problem." At other times, she asks partners to show each other how to work problems as she watches (Ashlock, 1990). Encouraging many forms of representations that reveal children's understanding of mathematics is important for helping children to grow and for making judgments for grading. As mentioned earlier, checklists, open-ended question responses, and the use of rubrics, portfolios, student self-assessment, peer evaluation, interviews, and observations should all be a part of mathematics assessment.

Observation of children's learning mathematics informally provides teachers with unforeseen opportunities (*teachable moments*) to engage in questioning and probing into the child's thinking. Often in the solution of a teacher-posed problem, children generate other related problems. These self-posed problems not only provide insight into the current understanding of the learner but also provide excellent questions to pose for further assessment.

Teachers should not limit assessment to determining children's computation abilities or problem-solving skills. Teachers must also assess the child's attitude and mathematical thinking as applied to everyday problems. In many cases, the most important type of assessment to determine and diagnose error patterns is to challenge the child to do a problem and observe the problem-solving strategies used by the child in working out a solution.

Consider the following question:

Ms. Baumbach is working with the entire first-grade class. She says, "I have put some pennies, nickels, and dimes in my pocket." She places her hand in her pocket. "I have put three of these coins in my hand. How much money do you think I have in my hand?" Many children are confused and begin voicing guesses. In order to facilitate problem solving in this situation, the teacher should not:

A. suggest to the students an approach using trial and error.
B. suggest to the students an approach that uses real coins.
C. allow students to verify their guesses with one another.
D. ask an individual to come to the board and show how she or he got the answer.

Remember that we are searching for an answer that does *not* belong. The teacher wants her students to develop problem-solving skills. Trial and error (*A*) allows students to explore different possible solutions. These explorations foster development and logical reasoning (and application of this reasoning) to real-life situations. Using real coins (*B*) helps students connect the problem to the real world. Students value money and want to become accurate when dealing with money. The use of actual coins makes the problem more pertinent to their everyday lives. Students must verify their guesses (*C*), and this problem helps them develop understanding of the possible answers. This problem should help students realize that there are many possible and correct responses. Students must develop several strategies to become good problem solvers, and choices *A, B,* and *C* are all positive ways to help children.

Teachers should always realize that when one child is working at the board, the remainder of the class is not. Because the question asks that we identify something that is not helpful, the answer is *D*.

Along with the inclusion of realistic and authentic lessons, another area of major importance in mathematics education today is problem solving.

Problem-solving means engaging in a task for which the solution method is not known in advance . . . problem-solving is an integral part of all mathematics learning, not an isolated part of the mathematics program. Students should have frequent opportunities to formulate, grapple with, and solve complex problems that require a significant amount of effort. (NCTM, 1998, p. 76)

In planning for incorporation of problem solving into instruction, teachers should plan learning experiences carefully that are relevant and grade appropriate. Relevant problems help motivate children to solve the problem because they can see a need or interest in their own lives. Grade appropriateness helps the children recognize that they have, or can acquire, the skills to solve it, increasing their motivation to try through self-efficacy. Young children should be introduced to problem solving in play. Ms. Clemens, for example, notices Shak and Brandy playing in the sandbox with cars. "Hm-m-m," she says. "It looks like it might be difficult to drive over to this side because your car might get stuck in the 'river.' What could you do? That's right! You could build a bridge. Which block shape(s) do you think would make the best bridge?"

Teachers can be guided in their selection of grade-appropriate problem-solving challenges through the TEKS expectations. The importance of problem solving is shown by its designation as a process standard by the NCTM (2000). *Process standards*, as defined by the NCTM, are specific skills and strategies used to acquire and use mathematics content knowledge; that is, knowing the **multiplication** facts is not enough—children must know *when* and *how* to use multiplication (or other operations) in real world situations. Problem solving, therefore, is not viewed as a separate entity but as both a skill and an attitude that should permeate the mathematics learning environment. Teachers should encourage their students to solve problems, to apply strategies reflectively, to support student thinking, and to ask carefully worded questions about constructive problems. When this is done, they provide their students with a rich problem-solving experience. This emphasis is reflected in the TEKS of every grade level.

The NCTM Standards (1989) recommended that students develop and apply a variety of strategies to solve multi-step and non-routine problems, including problems in which students "model situations using verbal, written, concrete, pictorial, graphical, and algebraic methods, reflecting on and clarifying their own thinking about mathematical ideas" (NCTM, 1989, p. 78). Additional recommendations include learning experiences that emphasize deductive and inductive reasoning methods, real-world relevancy, and the use of patterns and relationships to recognize, describe, analyze, and extend mathematical situations (NCTM, 1989). Strategies such as drawing a picture, looking for a pattern, systematically guessing and checking (trial and error), acting problems out, and so on, must be taught so that children are able to apply them independently.

It is the teacher who determines the learning environment in a mathematics classroom. This section reminds us that it is the role of the teacher to be the facilitator and a resource person and to provide opportunities to solve relevant problems through meaningful, concrete exploration. Teachers must always encourage children to gain new strategies in order to problem solve.

Standard I: Number Concepts and Standard II: Patterns and Algebra

As might be expected, Standard I also overlaps Standard II: Patterns and Algebra.

Standard II: The mathematics teacher understands and uses patterns, relations, functions, algebraic reasoning, analysis, and technology appropriate to teach the statewide curriculum (Texas Essential Knowledge and Skills [TEKS]) in order to prepare students to use mathematics.

The EC-6 teacher must be able to analyze, explain, and model relationships between number properties, and algorithms for the four basic operations involving **integers**, **rational numbers**, *and real numbers. In helping students toward solutions the teacher should be able to apply knowledge of place value and other number properties to perform mental mathematics and computational estimation. In addition, the teacher must be able to demonstrate understanding of equivalency among different representations of rational numbers and select appropriate representations of real numbers (e.g., fractions, decimals, percents) for particular situations.*

The teacher should be able to demonstrate ideas from number theory (e.g., **prime factorization**, *greatest common divisor) as they apply to* **whole numbers**, *integers, and rational numbers, and use those ideas in problem situations. As a part of this, the teacher should be able to show a variety of models for representing rational numbers (e.g., fraction strips, diagrams, patterns, shaded regions, number lines).*

In discussing numbers the teacher should understand the relative magnitude of whole numbers, integers, rational numbers, and real numbers. In discussing procedures, the teacher should use a variety of concrete and visual representations to demonstrate the connections between operations and algorithms. The teacher should be able to extend knowledge of counting techniques to include combinations to quantify situations and solve problems.

Students should develop organizational skills needed to properly handle larger quantities of data. Choosing an appropriate graphical representation is a fundamental requirement needed to present data in an accurate manner. Not only is it imperative for the teacher to model mathematical terminology, symbols, and communication, it is necessary for the teacher to provide active opportunities for children to do so.

Consider the following question:

Ms. Bell's first-grade class has surveyed the students at Washington Elementary School about their favorite soft drink from a list of Pepsi®, Coke®, Mountain Dew®, and Sprite®. A total of 63 students participated in the survey. Which is the most appropriate graph to use to display this data?

A. A bar graph
B. A line graph
C. A circle graph
D. A pictograph

A **line graph** (*B*) is used to represent continuous data **points**. For example, if one wanted to track how much each drink sold over time with a data point for each year, a line graph would work well. However, this problem deals with discrete and separate objects that have no connection; that is, each drink is a separate item that is not related or connected to any other drink. A **circle graph** (*C*) involves the understanding and application of degrees, ratios, and the use of protractors. These topics are covered in more detail in fifth and sixth grades. A circle graph could be used, but for exactness, each portion of the circle would have to be divided with mathematical tools (such as a protractor), and angles would need to be determined—a task far beyond first graders. **Pictographs** (*D*) are introduced later as another way to represent data because one picture would need to stand for a certain number of each drink (e.g., one picture of a Coke® could equal 5 persons who prefer Coke®). If this were a smaller sample size (instead of 63), a pictograph could be used for this grade level for a one-on-one correspondence. Students are then developmentally ready to code the data.

Bar graphs (*A*) are appropriate for the primary grades. (As an aside, when students are engaging with these types of activities, the teacher must include possible rationales for them other than "Isn't this fun to know?" or "Isn't this a fun activity?") For example, fast-food restaurants clearly would be able to use this type of data to match customer preference, the school carnival committee could use this to provide drinks that people prefer, and so forth). The correct response is *A*.

Consider the following question:

Mr. Batiste distributes color tiles to each student in his kindergarten class and asks the students to sort the tiles by color. Mr. Batiste sorts his set of color tiles on the overhead. When the students have completed the task, Mr. Batiste asks kindergartners to describe the data. Which of the following is the best description of Mr. Batiste's teaching objective?

A. He wants to assess his students' knowledge of color.
B. He wants to assess his students' ability to classify the color tiles.
C. He wants his students to be able to discuss and explain the results of the sorting.
D. He wants his students to work independently.

Color recognition is an important concept for kindergarten students to learn (*A*). However, it is not the best response. Sorting by color (*B*) is also an important process for kindergarten students to learn, as is the ability to work alone is an important learning activity (*D*). However, these answers are also not the best answer. Mr. Batiste is encouraging his students to develop and use accurate mathematics vocabulary to synthesize the results of their sorting activity. The best response is *C*.

Let's try another question:

Ms. Ketkar has been working with her sixth-grade class on ordering decimals. To help students develop an understanding of the "size" of decimal values and to better help them "see" the decimals, Ms. Ketkar should use which of the following representations?

A. An egg carton
B. Cuisenaire rods
C. Dot paper
D. Centimeter grid paper

An egg carton (*A*) has 12 sections and would not be appropriate for fostering the development of the understanding of decimals that are based on **powers** of 10. Cuisenaire rods (*B*) are generally used when comparing and relating lengths. They are often used with fractions, **area**, and **perimeter**. Dot paper (*C*) is often used to help students develop spatial abilities. It is useful when asking students to do pictorial presentations of a concrete shape. The centimeter grid paper (*D*) is based on 100 units, 10 rows and 10 columns. It provides a visual means of developing decimal notations. Regular grid paper can help students understand area relationships to lengths of squares and rectangles. The correct response is *D*.

The initial development of number and numeration concepts should include the ability to recognize numbers of objects, the verbal word associated with a given number, and the symbol corresponding to that word. Later, more sophisticated understandings, including relationships between base, **exponent**, and place value, together with ways of representing numbers and more advanced number relationships, can build on this foundation. This basic knowledge and corresponding skills associated with number and numeration concepts is necessary for all students. Without a strong foundation in these areas, children will not achieve success and thrive in everyday mathematical situations.

Children learn the names of numbers first before ever understanding that a number symbolizes an amount. After learning the names and order of numbers, young children move to understanding one-on-one correspondence by using every opportunity in the classroom to touch and count. Mr. Jenson lines up students to go to lunch by touching them and counting, "One, two, three, ..." He also asks students to get out and put away materials by counting, for example, "One block, two blocks, . . . ," as appropriate. Providing a visual picture of the size of a number enables students to have a concrete method to show representations. Children must also learn to recognize, form, and write the shape of numbers (1, 2, 3, . . . ; one, two, three, . . . , respectively). From this basis, children must have learning experiences that develop meaning for operations and how they relate to each other, along with the use of the four basic arithmetic operations, strategies, and estimation abilities.

Teachers who encourage good number sense teach common sense about numbers. Number sense concepts, when developed as described here, lead to logical and relevant student use of numbers in real-world contexts. Estimation skills, for example, help children think about the correctness of their mathematics. Children should constantly be challenged to think about numbers: "Does this answer make sense? If so, why?" "Is this amount larger or smaller? If so, why?" Good number sense provides a foundation for developing all other areas of mathematics. As the use of technology as a mathematics tool advances, the importance of estimation as a basic skill is even more critical because users must have an idea if their technological computations are "in the ball park." In the real world, a bank teller (or customer) who uses a calculator to quickly add deposits of $525.00 and $280.00 should know to recheck the figures if the calculator answer displays an answer of $1,505.00 because they should be able to quickly round to $500 and $300 and know that their deposit should be "in the neighborhood" of $800. Children should be experienced with the use, development, and application of estimation skills. NCTM (1989) states:

> *(Students) should be able to decide when they need to calculate and whether they require an exact or approximate answer. They should be able to select and use the most appropriate tool. Students should have a balanced approach to calculation, be able to choose appropriate procedures, find answers, and judge the validity of those answers. (p. 8)*

Try this question:

As an introduction to estimation, Ms. Babinoux filled a glass jar with candy balls and told the children that the person who came closest to guessing the correct amount in the jar would win a prize. Children were excited to guess. Some children guessed 1,000 and some children guessed 10. The closest person guessed 100 (there were 90 in the jar). She awarded the prize and then moved to some problems on the board. This focus was:

A. appropriate because it was relevant in showing students the value of estimation.

B. appropriate because it motivated students to use mathematics to get the prize.

C. inappropriate because students used no estimation strategies but just guessed at **random**.
D. inappropriate because it is not age-appropriate to ask children to estimate.

It is certainly appropriate to have children begin to think about the logic of their answers through estimation, so the answer is not choice *D*. The focus did motivate the students, but they did not use correct estimation skills to get the prize (*B*). This focus began the process of showing a rationale for having tools to estimate (*A*). It would have been highly relevant had Ms. Babinoux immediately tied this to why we must have estimation strategies to use in cases like this one and how to make a good estimate (such as counting how many candy balls are on the top row and how many possible rows there are in the jar and multiplying). Unfortunately, she did not use it in that manner. She simply had students guess at random without any follow up or connections. The correct answer is *C.*

By having a solid personal understanding of number and numeration concepts, teachers are better prepared for planning appropriate learning experiences for students. Understanding number and numeration concepts means that teachers should be competent in mathematics by having or developing a solid foundation of number sense and of basic computation of numbers themselves. As noted earlier, test takers and teachers may also review and test their knowledge of mathematical content by taking released TAKS (soon to be STAAR) tests online to help better understand the expected concepts and skills. Children in grades 3–6 all take a state test each year, but Pre-K through second grade teachers help begin the strong foundation for later testing. Readers are encouraged to seek additional resources at:

1. http://www.tea.state.tx.us/student.assessment/taks/index.html
   This Web site highlights the student testing, TAKS (soon to become the STAAR), and describes which mathematics concepts should be taught and assessed at each grade level. Currently, TAKS information booklets with more examples of test questions can be found at this site or at the following sites (put in appropriate grade level at the end). Be sure to go through the grade levels up to sixth grade. We assume that when the new tests become available, there will be a similar Web site for the new STAAR information (http://www.tea.state.tx.us/index3.aspx?id=3693&menu_id3=793; http://ritter.tea.state.tx.us/student.assessment/resources/guides/study/G4MathE-SG.pdf).
2. http://ritter.tea.state.tx.us/rules/tac/chapter111/index.html
   This Web site highlights the student TEKS.

Consider the following question:

To aid her second-grade students in comparing fractions, which manipulative should Ms. Asif use to help her students "see" the size of the fractions?

A. Fraction strips
B. Base 10 blocks
C. Egg cartons
D. Attribute blocks

Base 10 blocks (*B*) are more appropriate in activities involving place value or decimals. Egg cartons (*C*) are appropriate for use with fractions with 12 as a **denominator**. Attribute blocks (*D*) are appropriate manipulatives to use in activities that involve sorting and classifying. The fraction strips can be used with all fractions (*A*). Fraction strips are a set of paper strips that are cut and shaded to represent the relation between and among wholes, halves, thirds, fourths, and other fractional parts of a whole. The answer is *A.*

Try this one:

Ms. Garcia has been working with her kindergarten class on pattern recognition. To assess her students' understanding of patterns, she asks them the following question: "What would be the next number in this pattern? 1, 2, 3, 3, 1, 2, ..."

A. 5
B. 3
C. 4
D. 6

The numbers 5 (*A*) and 6 (*D*) are not in the pattern, and 4 (*C*) is incorrect as well. This means that the correct response is *B*, 3. The pattern is 1, 2, 3, 3, 1, 2, 3, 3. The next activity that she may want to offer these young children is to have them use colors in this pattern (e.g., red, blue, yellow, yellow). The answer is *B*.

Strategies are necessary to effectively analyze data and make accurate predictions. For the elementary teacher, it is imperative that children have opportunities to learn basic concepts of patterns and relationships to build on as they advance in study. Early experiences with patterns, functions, and relationships provide a foundational basis for later development of **algebra** and the study of solutions to equations. The *function concept* is one of the cornerstones of algebra (and later mathematics) and is defined as actions that transform one number into another (e.g., if you add 1 to 3, the 3 is transformed to 4, which allows students to work later on with functions such as $x + 3 = 4$). In later study, students begin to understand functions, reasoning about abstract objects, generalizations, and symbolic notation. These concepts underlie all areas of mathematics and the basis of mathematical communication.

These abilities become crucial when one considers the full scope of algebraic thinking in which teachers must prepare students to participate. Algebraic thinking has expanded in definition to the point where entire courses are devoted to its exploration and development and, although a full description is outside the scope of this book, some general outlines can be provided. Algebraic thinking includes representation of number and **variable**, patterns and functions, inductive and deductive reasoning, and use of mathematical symbols and tools to analyze situations. This is expressed in the following statement:

> *The process of creating generalizations from number and arithmetic begins as early as kindergarten and continues as students learn about all aspects of number and computation, including basic facts and meanings of the operations.* (Van de Walle, 2010, p. 255)

Patterns are a way of helping children organize and order the world. Sorting, classifying, and ordering objects helps students deal with patterns, geometric shapes, and data. Young children are able to identify patterns in their environment to gain understanding of predictions ("What comes next?") and can use this to develop vocabulary such as "first," "second," "last," and so on, to help with time issues. When children generalize patterns to science, social studies, and other real-world problems, they can more easily predict (which, eventually, helps with better decision making). Teachers should always encourage making generalizations about patterns by asking questions such as, "Tell me about that pattern on your sweater." "How do you know that it is a pattern?" "What is the missing part of this pattern?" "How would you make a pattern longer/different?" "Today is Wednesday, so what will tomorrow be?" and "Can you clap this pattern after me?" Children should be encouraged to explore and model relationships using language and, later, notation describing their observations.

As discussed later in the chapter, two key components of algebraic thinking for children are (a) making generalizations and using symbols to represent mathematical ideas and (b) representing and solving problems. Learning experiences in which children make generalizations from observations about patterns, numbers, and operations develop a foundation for this type of algebraic thinking. The use of terminology, such as *associative* and *commutative* (see terms in the Glossary), may not be necessary in the early grades, but teachers should be aware of the algebraic properties used by young children and begin to draw attention to the concept. Studying patterns, functions, and algebra is the beginning of learning about the different uses of variables and how to solve equations.

Standard III: Geometry and Measurement, and Standard IV: Probability and Statistics

The mathematics teacher understands and uses geometry, spatial reasoning, measurement concepts and principles, and appropriate technology to teach the statewide curriculum (Texas Essential Knowledge and Skills [TEKS]) in order to prepare students to use mathematics.

The beginning teacher should be able to apply knowledge of spatial concepts such as direction, size, and shape to identify, use, and develop formulas to find lengths, perimeters, areas, and volumes of basic geometric figures. The teacher should be able to understand concepts and properties of **points**, **lines**, **planes**, **angles**, *lengths, and distances and use properties of* **congruent** *(alike) triangles to explore geometric relationships.*

The teacher should model the uses and properties of **parallel lines** *and* **perpendicular lines** *and be able to demonstrate* **translations**, **rotations**, *and* **reflections** *to illustrate similarities, congruencies, and symmetries of figures. Furthermore, concepts of* **symmetry** *should be expanded to describe* **tessellations** *and to illustrate geometric concepts, properties, and relationship.*

In problem solving, the teacher should use a variety of representations (e.g., numeric, verbal, graphic, symbolic) to analyze and solve problems involving two- and three-dimensional figures such as circles, triangles, polygons, cylinders, prisms, and **spheres**. *Problems should be explored in which the teacher explains, illustrates, selects, and uses appropriate units of measurement to quantify and compare time, temperature, money, mass, weight, area, capacity, volume, percent, and speed using conversions within and between measurement systems as required.*

For sixth grade classes, the teacher should be able to model logical reasoning, justification, and **proof** *in relation to the axiomatic structure of geometry and have students use reasoning to develop, generalize, justify, and prove geometric relationships.*

Standard IV: The mathematics teacher understands and uses probability and statistics, their applications, and technology appropriate to teach the statewide curriculum.

*The beginning teacher should model investigation and exploration of questions by collecting, organizing, and displaying data in a variety of formats. When appropriate, the teacher should be able to demonstrate an understanding of measures of central tendency (e.g., **mean, median, mode**) and **range** and use those measures to describe a set of real world data. **Probability** should be addressed through multiple experiences with data collection, experiments, and simulations, including both simple and **compound events.** The teacher should help the students determine probabilities by constructing sample spaces to model situations and applying probability to make observations and draw conclusions.*

Let's look at this question:

Ms. Fischer plans to introduce the concept of volume to her second-grade class. She wants her children to understand volume through exploration. Which would be the most appropriate for her to use?

- **A.** Color tiles
- **B.** A measuring cup
- **C.** Pattern blocks
- **D.** Attribute blocks

Color tiles (*A*) are used to represent two-dimensional situations. They are often used for perimeter, area, and multiplication **arrays**. Pattern blocks (*C*) are often used for two-dimensional activities such as tessellations and area. They also can be used effectively with fractions. Attribute blocks (*D*) are designed for activities using sorting and classifying. Volume is a three-dimensional quantity, and the measuring cup is the only three-dimensional object presented as a choice. The best answer is *B*.

The application of mathematics is a necessary and important component of the mathematics classroom. The value of connecting what children are learning in the classroom to its application in real-life situations cannot be overstated. "Why is it important, boys and girls, to have a correct lunch count? On a field trip we have 18 children who are on the bus. There are 21 children in our class. Should I tell the bus driver to leave now? Why or why not?" When students are able to address such situations they truly begin to understand what they have learned. As the NCTM puts it, "(S)tudents should not only learn mathematics, they should also learn the utility of mathematics and the interrelatedness of mathematical ideas" (1998, p. 90). This is a relatively easy process, because many areas of learning have components or concepts that can be related to mathematics in some way. Teachers who focus on these relationships can use them to enhance mathematical appreciation and foster student growth.

When mathematics is integrated with other subject areas, its value, understanding, and relevance become greatly extended. Dump-and-fill activities, comparison books, and other activities in which students have an opportunity to see differences (before formal instruction) help young children begin to understand concepts such as more/less, bigger/smaller, greater than/less than, and so forth. Setting up a class store is another easy way to have mathematics relate to the real world. This may also fit with a token economy management system, where children must have so many play dollars or tokens to "purchase" a variety of reward items ("$10" for 10 minutes of free time on the computer, "$50" for being able to eat lunch with friends in the classroom on Friday, etc.).

An **interdisciplinary relationship** exists between mathematics and many subject areas. Science often uses mathematics to explain and extend concepts. This link is through both content and process. For example, much of science relies on patterns of data and measurement. It is also the use of data and **statistics** that helps students clarify issues related to health issues in their personal lives and as consumers. Using survey data, children can link data analysis and statistics to learn more about social studies, and map skills also require working with numbers. In turn, the use of **ratio**, **proportion**, and percentages extend children's understanding of mathematics. Mathematical connections abound in other areas such as in music (patterns [in rhythms] and fractions in note values) and in sports (measurement, geometry, data analysis, and statistics, etc.). Teachers can also find an abundance of literary connections, including wonderful children's books about numbers, predictions, and other mathematical concepts. Using a literature focus can help motivate and stimulate student interest in mathematics. Counting and shape books, rhymes, songs, and fingerplays complement learning mathematics and provide excellent focus activities for mathematics and focus activities with problem solving situations in the upper grades.

Children are motivated and interested when a story gives life to the mathematics they are learning. Dinosaur books such as *How Big Were the Dinosaurs?* or *The Littlest Dinosaur* might be used to introduce a lesson on size or measurement. A teacher may want to take a digital photo of something a child has created in the block center so that the child can describe it, tell a story about it, or write about it (for instance, Carrie wrote: *"This is my tower. I built it with cubes. Lots of people live here. There are some offices here, too."*). Children who create a class survey and then write their own "story" about it are extending mathematics into language arts. For example, after graphing class shoes, Sara wrote, "There were 15 kids who had tennis shoes on. Four had those kinds of shoes with straps. They were girls. I think kids like tennis shoes best. People who make shoes ought to make mostly tennis shoes. I like tennis shoes best, too!" Using mathematics in applied situations leads to deeper understanding. Making tally charts and asking young children to explain them is also a way to have children understand the concept of one-to-one correspondence in naming numbers, and graphs should be used as appropriate organizing tools to make these concepts clearer, to support arguments, make predictions, and draw conclusions together with summary statistics in interpreting data and representing real world problems.

Answer the following question:

Which of the following activities would provide the best opportunity for sixth-grade students to apply measurement skills to a science context?

  A. Investigating the habitat of butterflies
  B. Determining the melting point of an ice cube
  C. Exploring the properties of water
  D. Investigating the properties of rocks and minerals

The investigation of the habitat of butterflies (*A*) would increase students' knowledge of butterflies but is not a measurement activity. Learning about the properties of water (*C*) would not necessarily be a measurement activity but could be associated with volume. However, this is not the best answer. Determining the properties of rocks and minerals (*D*) is not necessarily a measurement activity but could also be associated with volume. However, this is not the best answer either. In order to determine the melting point, students must measure and record the temperatures preceding the melting point. Therefore, *B* is the *best* response.

And this additional question. . .

Margie grouped her fourth-grade students in groups of four and gave each group a piece of yarn. She asked the children to make different closed figures with the yarn and to describe what they thought was happening to the area and perimeter of the shapes. She hoped that the students would discover which property remained the same, regardless of the shape. Which would remain the same?

    A. The area of the figure
    B. The perimeter of the figure
    C. The length of the figure
    D. The width of the figure

Area is the **product** of length times width ($a = l \times w$). As either the length or width is changed, the area (A), or the space inside, changes (for example, the area of a square is different if they change the shape to a circle). Because the yarn is being used to make different shapes, the length (C) and width of the figure change as the figure is changed. The width of the figure (D) varies as the yarn is being moved to create new figures. The perimeter is the distance around the figure. Although the yarn may change shape, the total length of the yarn (representing the figure's perimeter) remains constant. The correct answer is *B*.

Geometry helps students understand the three-dimensional world in which they live. Through the study of geometry, teachers can offer students ways to interpret and reflect on the physical environment with real and abstract methods. Furthermore, many of the more powerful representations used in elementary mathematics are geometric in nature and are weakened when basic geometric knowledge is absent. Learning activities should promote interaction with physical models, drawings, and software. Activities such as these are highly effective in helping children visualize geometric concepts.

> *Geometry and spatial sense are fundamental components of mathematics education. . . . Geometric representations can help students make sense of area and fractions;* **histograms** *and* **scatterplots** *can lead to insights about data; and coordinating graphs can be used to analyze and understand functions. Spatial reasoning is helpful in using maps, planning routes, designing floor plans, and creating art.* (NCTM, 1998, pp. 61–62)

Students must be encouraged to use geometric ideas in representing and solving problems in a variety of contexts. Geometric puzzles, geoboards, and blocks help children understand many-sided figures and circles. Geometry for young children should focus on shape identification, vocabulary development, and physical manipulation of basic shapes. Primary children routinely construct many plane and **solid figures** from blocks, dominos, and even marshmallows or gumdrops connected with toothpicks. When children name and manipulate these objects, they see relationships much easier (two **right triangles** can make a square, etc.). Hands-on and interactive experiences help children learn concepts and techniques that help them interpret their physical world through principles of geometry. By the time a child is in the fourth grade, he or she should be able to identify basic geometric shapes such as the **circle**, **square**, **rectangle**, **triangle**, **quadrilaterals**, **pentagon** (a five-sided **polygon**), **hexagon** (a six-sided polygon), **octagon** (an eight-sided polygon), and solid figures such as the **cube**, **cone**, **pyramid**, **cylinder**, and so forth. When children are introduced to shapes in school, seeing a multitude of the shapes possessing the property being taught is the best instructional policy. The teacher, for example, may put on her hat with a circular brim and her apron with huge circles appliquéd onto it, while children work with paper plates, cut out circles from various materials in centers, draw circles in sand or shaving cream, and construct art projects using only circles. Students come to the circle to sing a "circle song" (which includes making circles with their hands and arms) and are served snacks that are circular (cross cuts of fruit, round crackers, etc.). Basic concepts addressing symmetry, rotation, reflection, and transformation are also learned. Finding the perimeter (distance around) of figures and some area (surface measurement) measurements are taught in the primary grades.

Answer the following question:

Ms. Kim divided her first-grade students into groups of two. She asked each student to fold a piece of construction paper in half. On one-half of the paper, each student was asked to construct a design using pattern blocks. When the students had finished their designs, the students switched places with their partners and were asked to replicate their partners' designs on the other side of the paper. This activity is most appropriate for:

   A. development of skills needed for repetition.
   B. understanding that different students have different designs.
   C. development of spatial ability and awareness.
   D. recognition of properties of polygons.

This activity helps students learn to duplicate shapes (A), and students must recognize the properties of polygons (C), but these are not the best answers. Neither is the understanding that students can use different designs (B). To understand and use geometry, one must develop spatial ability and awareness (D). The correct response is C.

Let's try another question:

Ms. Shanar wanted her first-grade class to develop an understanding of *nonstandard* measurement. She asked her children to measure the distance from the bottom of the classroom door to the doorknob. What would be an appropriate tool to use?

   A. A paper clip
   B. A pencil
   C. A hula hoop
   D. A color tile

A paper clip (A) would be too small and too difficult for first-grade students to try to use for measuring a vertical distance. The hula hoop (C) is round and would not be appropriate for measuring a linear length. The color tile (D) is small. It would be very difficult for students to estimate the vertical distance using the color tile. A pencil would be the most appropriate item to use of the choices presented (B). It is longer than both the paper clip and the color tile and would be easier for young students to use to estimate the distance. Always consider the age of the child when answering questions. The correct answer is B.

Measurement includes length, time, area, mass, and volume or **capacity**. See Table 3.2 to review measurement units, if needed. Measurement is used every day by children as they explore their environment and ask questions such as, "How tall am I?" "How long will it take to get there?" "How much longer until lunch?" "How much do I need?" "How far is it to my house?"

Table 3.2 Geometric Formulas and Measurement Units

P = Perimeter $\qquad$ A = Area $\qquad$ V = Volume $\qquad$ SA = Surface Area for Solid Figures
C = Circumference (b = base, l = length, w = width, h = height)

Rectangle	$P = 2l + 2w$	$A = lw$
Square	$P = 4s$	$A = s^2$
Parallelogram	P = sum of all sides	$A = bh$
Triangle	P = sum of all sides	$A = \frac{1}{2}bh$
Trapezoid	P = sum of all sides	$A = \frac{1}{2}h\,(b1 + b2)$
Polygon	P = sum of all sides	A = depends on shape
Circle	$C = 2\pi r$ or πd	$A = 2\pi r^2$
Prism	$V = Bh$	SA = the sum of the area of each face
Cylinder	$V = \pi r^2 h$	$SA = 2\pi rh + 2\pi^2$

MEASUREMENT UNITS

Customary

Length
12 inches (in) = 1 foot (ft)
3 ft = 1 yard (yd)
36 in = 1 yd
5,280 ft = 1 mile
1,760 yd = 1 mile

Area
144 square in = 1 square foot
9 square ft = 1 square yd
43,560 square ft = 1 acre (A)

Volume
1,728 cubic inches (cu in) = 1 cubic foot (cu ft)
27 cu ft = 1 cubic yard (cu yd)

Capacity
8 fluid ounces (fl oz) = 1 cup (c)
2 c = 1 pint (pt)
2 pt = 1 quart (qt)
4 qt = 1 gallon (gal)

Weight
16 ounces (oz) = 1 pound
2,000 lb = 1 ton (T)

Temperature (Fahrenheit)
32 degrees F = freezing point of water
98.6 degrees F = normal body temperature
212 degrees F = boiling point of water

Time
60 seconds (sec) = 1 minute (min)
60 min = 1 hour (hr)
24 hr = 1 day (da)
7 da = 1 week (wk)
4 wk = 1 month (mth)
12 mths = 1 year (yr)
52 wk = 1 yr
365 da = 1 yr

Metric

Length
1,000 meters (m) = 1 kilometer (km)
100 centimeters (cm) = 1 m
10 decimeters (dm) = 1 m
1,000 millimeters (mm) = 1 m
10 cm = 1 dm
10 mm = 1 cm

Area
100 square mm = 1 square cm
10,000 square cm = 1 square m
10,000 square m = 1 hectare (ha)

Volume
1,000 cubic mm = 1 cubic cm
1,000 cubic cm = 1 cubic dm
1,000,000 cubic cm = 1 cubic m

Capacity
1,000 milliliter (mL) = 1 liter (L)
1,000 L = 1 kiloliter (kL)

Mass
1,000 kilograms (kg) = 1 metric ton
1,000 grams (g) = 1 kg
1,000 milligrams (mg) = 1 g

Temperature (Centigrade)
0 degrees C = freezing point of water
37 degrees C = normal body temperature
100 degrees C = boiling point of water

Students need many experiences using standard and nonstandard measurement to foster their understanding of the physical aspects of the real world. A *nonstandard measurement* is any item that is used to measure other items but is not part of a standardized system of measurement (such as the metric system). For the younger child, this might be a child's finger, a shoe, a book, a paper clip, or a pencil. Using such a nonstandard unit to measure another item, such as the length of a table, allows the younger child to grasp the concept of using a repeated movement or a repetition of that unit to measure. In other words, for the question "How long is the table?" children can use a book, placing the book on the table, making a mark and counting, "One." Then they can **slide** the book further along the table, make a mark and count, then repeat the procedure the length of the table while recording or counting the number of book lengths that are used to measure the table. Although nonstandard measurement helps young children grasp the concept of repeated measurement, it also increases understanding of estimation skills. It is important to remember that what makes a unit *standard* is that it belongs to a *standardized system* of measurement (such as the metric system), not that you get the same results each time you use it. Many children could mistakenly believe, for instance, that the book in the preceding example should be standard because it gives the same result each time it is used, regardless of who does the measuring.

The study of measurement is necessary for everyday life, as well as for connecting other mathematical concepts and other content areas. As measurement often includes number operations, geometric ideas, statistical concepts, and notions of function (NCTM, 1998), measurement can serve an important purpose by linking concepts and applications. For example, the Pythagorean Theorem $(a^2 + b^2 = c^2)$ links geometry, measurement, and algebraic thinking. Learning experiences should provide students with ample opportunities for selecting units, understanding appropriate measurement units, and understanding the techniques, tools, and formulas of measurement. Other components of measurement study should include selecting and using benchmarks to estimate measurement (such as an inch is about as wide as an adult thumb) and **scaling** (making an object smaller/larger or drawing to scale). Older children select and apply appropriate standard units and tools to measure length, area, volume, weight, time, temperatures, and the size of angles. An excellent activity, for example, useful in sixth grade is to create a scale drawing of the school playground. This activity allows for discussion and practice with precision, error, scaling, fractions, and problem solving while reinforcing both measurement and geometry.

Teachers must select learning experiences carefully that foster student understanding of measurement and all associated aspects of applying measurement. This includes understanding that measurements can be approximations and that different units may come to affect the precision of a given measurement. Therefore, sometimes teachers might say, "In Houston, from the school, it is 5 miles to the mall, or about 10 minutes. During the holidays, it takes 30 minutes to get to the mall." Learning to select and use the most reasonable and appropriate unit of measurement is vital for the continuing development of number sense and estimation (e.g., "Just a couple of blocks down the street," without this understanding can turn into a mile walk). The study of measurement is most effectively taught with the use of concrete materials. Children must have opportunities to handle measurement tools and apply concept knowledge to real-world, relevant situations (e.g., the difference in taking a teaspoon rather than a tablespoon of medicine). Children who measure the pet gerbil's cage for paper or the goldfish bowl for water, the bulletin board to put up new borders, space for a new center, and milk and cocoa in a kitchen center for chocolate milk are all learning mathematics for everyday situations. Measurement is a fundamental concept whose processes connect mathematics with itself and to other content areas such as social studies, science, art, health, and physical education.

As mentioned, measurement concepts should first be taught with non-standard units in order for children to grasp the general concept. It is then possible to effectively introduce standard measurement units and scales that are used in everyday life (such as inches, feet, yards, centimeters, meters, quarts, gallons). From this basic understanding, children are better able to understand the need for measuring with standard units and become familiar with customary standard units used in the United States and metric systems. Finally, children need practice in carrying out simple conversions, such as from inches to feet or centimeters to meters, within a single measurement system. Most importantly, children should be able to understand such attributes as length, area, weight, volume, and size of angle and the appropriate type of unit for measuring each attribute (see Table 3.2).

Providing a way for children to experiment with measuring is important for all grades and can be part of a kitchen, shop, garden, science, social studies, or growth center. Older elementary children must develop, understand and use formulas, and develop strategies for determining perimeter, **surface area**, and **volume** of solids in addition to being able to convert between various systems of measurement (e.g., English to metric).

Look at the following question:

Mr. Kurz is interested in having his fifth-grade class understand problem solving in real-world situations. His current problem is determining the amount of decorative wall border needed for putting up a place for students' work. The children are asked to measure the width of their classroom using nonstandard measures. Stephen finds that the classroom is 36 shoes wide. Amy finds the classroom is 9 jump ropes wide. Which mathematical concept should the children apply to convert from one nonstandard measure to the other?

A. Metric measurement
B. Absolute value
C. Area and perimeter
D. Ratio and proportion

Choice *A* implies the use of the metric measurement system with no connection to other types of measurement. **Absolute value** (*B*) applies to the distance from the origin and would be used if direction from the origin were being considered. Absolute value is also often thought of as the distance a number is from zero on the number line. Area and perimeter (*C*) relate to attributes of geometric shapes. Ratio and proportion (*D*) provide a method of converting from one measurement system to another. The correct response is *D*.

Consider also the following question:

Ms. Rubalcava has placed 10 color tiles (8 green and 2 yellow) into a paper bag. She tells her sixth-grade students that there are 10 color tiles in the bag and some are yellow and some are green. She shakes the paper bag and, without looking, picks one color tile from the bag. She asks the students to guess the color of the tile in her hand. She then opens her hand and shows the class the color tile. It is green. Ms. Rubalcava asks a student to record the color on the board with a tally mark. She places the color tile back in the bag and repeats the process

10 times. Her sixth-grade students help her tally her results. After the tenth pick, the tally is 7 green and 3 yellow. She asks the students to guess how many green tiles and how many yellow tiles are in the bag. She repeats the experiment, and this time the tally is 9 green and 1 yellow. She repeats the process several more times, and the students tally the data. Her purpose in this experiment is:

    A. to help her students count.
    B. to show the students that it is impossible to know how many green tiles and yellow color tiles there are without opening the bag.
    C. to help students learn to use probability experiments to solve problems in the real world.
    D. to better understand the concept of **addition**.

Even though the students count the number of green and yellow tiles (*A*), the object of this lesson is to develop an understanding of predicting how many tiles of each color are in the bag. Although the students do not know for certain how many green tiles and yellow tiles are in the bag (*B*) until all the tiles are shown, the students can learn how to give accurate predictions based on several repetitions. The object of the lesson is not to have students count the green tiles and yellow tiles (*D*), but to understand the concept of probability. The students develop an understanding of how to collect data and why it is important to conduct several experiments in order to make a prediction. The correct answer is *C*.

It is possible to help children develop understanding of unknown situations. They can learn to form a rational basis to forecast accurate predictions when absolute certainty is not possible but when other necessary information is presented. As was the case in the Rubalcava question, probability and prediction are often connected to data collection. Children are often interested in questions, such as "What is your favorite color?" "What kind of candy do you like the most?" and so forth. Inquiries such as these may be used to interest children in collecting information (data) and in developing how to best represent the findings of that data (graphing, charting, making a table). Teachers can begin modeling these procedures with very young children as a class effort and gradually build a foundation of understanding which may be used in later grades. Older children enjoy conducting surveys that are part of their everyday lives. For example, they may wish to find out how many children prefer hamburgers or pizza in the lunchroom, and how the cafeteria personnel use such data to plan for these preferences. Students in the upper grades may be interested to present their findings on favorite authors and books to the library or share their preferences for music and vocal or movie stars.

Try this one:

Mr. Webb's fifth-grade class has completed a unit on statistics including measures of central tendency. Frank, one of his students, wants to attain a 92 **average** for the five tests given each quarter. If Frank scored an 86 on his first test, a 96 on his second test, a 94 on his third test, and a 90 on his fourth test, what grade must Frank earn on his fifth test for a 92 test average?

    A. 92
    B. 93
    C. 90
    D. 94

For the goal average, there must be 460 grade points accumulated ($92 \times 5 = 460$). Frank must determine his current grade point by adding the four test sources ($86 + 96 + 94 + 90 = 366$). The difference results in the needed test score of 94 ($460 - 366 = 94$). To check this, the **sum** of the five test scores, divided by 5, result in an average of 92. The correct response is *D*.

In an increasingly technical world, it is imperative that students have experiences with the concepts underlying data, statistics, and probability. Beginning in the primary grades, learning activities should include organizing data into categories, sorting experiences, and other informal activities that encourage refining questions and decision making. Building a foundation in the early grades with these types of activities allows students to further their understanding by interpreting data using methods of exploratory data analysis. Even very young children can question and gather data about themselves and their surroundings; sort and classify objects by attributes; use coins to generate random data; represent data using concrete objects, pictures, and graphs; and discuss events related to their own experiences as "must happen," "could happen," or "can't happen." Children might ask, "How many of us are wearing T-shirts today?" The results may be tallied and put into a chart, or a class picture graph may be created using a T-shirt as the displayed icon, depending on the age and the data numbers, or the teacher may place a small package of M&Ms® on a child's desk and ask them to arrange the colors in a "bar graph."

Predicting the chances of an event can also be done with young children. "Do you think at least five people will score 100 on our spelling test on Friday? Why or why not?" Learning experiences based on data can help students to develop and evaluate inferences, make predictions, create representations, and stimulate communication. Along with these experiences, children must understand and apply basic notions of chance and probability. The goal of a mathematics curriculum such as this is to produce students who are prepared for informed decision making. It is the responsibility of the teacher to provide such a learning environment that encourages and nurtures questions, interpretation, inference, and probability. Only through these efforts will mathematical literacy be achieved.

Standard V: Mathematical Processes, and Standard VI: Mathematical Perspectives

Standard V: The mathematics teacher understands and uses mathematical processes to reason mathematically, to solve mathematical problems, to make mathematical connections within and outside of mathematics, and to communicate mathematically.

The beginning teacher should be able to apply correct mathematical reasoning to derive valid conclusions from a set of premises and use basic principles of inductive reasoning to make **conjectures** *(inferences) and use deductive methods to evaluate the validity of conjectures. This requires the teacher to use both formal and informal reasoning to explore, investigate, and justify mathematical ideas; and recognize examples of fallacious, or incorrect, reasoning.*

Students should be guided to recognize that a mathematical problem can be solved in a variety of ways, including **iteration** *(a process in which a cycle of actions or operations is repeated, generally to get closer to a final answer) and* **recursion** *(a process in which objects [including numbers] are defined in terms of other objects of the same type). A recursive relation is then used to build up large numbers of objects from a relatively small set of initial values and rules needed at the upper grades. They must also learn how to evaluate the appropriateness of various strategies and how to select an appropriate strategy for a given problem. Often it is necessary to develop physical and numerical models to represent a given problem or* mathematical procedure. When this is done, it is important for the students to recognize that assumptions are made when solving problems and that they must identify and evaluate those assumptions. A good way to ensure that this takes place is to investigate and explore problems that have multiple solutions and require the students to apply content knowledge to develop a mathematical model of a real-world situation and analyze and evaluate how well the model represents the situation.

Because mathematical communication and reasoning is an important mathematical process, it is necessary for the teacher to facilitate discourse between the teacher and students and among students to explore, build, and refine mathematical ideas. In accomplishing this, the teacher should use questioning strategies to identify, support, monitor, and challenge students' mathematical thinking and help students interpret the meanings of mathematical statements among developmentally appropriate language, standard English, mathematical language, and symbolic mathematics.

Students should have access to a variety of tools to demonstrate their understanding of mathematics, including calculators and computers (as appropriate). In instruction, the teacher should use visual media, such as graphs, tables, diagrams, and animations, to communicate mathematical information and use the language of mathematics as a precise means of expressing mathematical ideas.

Standard VI: **The mathematics teacher understands the historical development of mathematical ideas, the interrelationship between society and mathematics, the structure of mathematics, and the evolving nature of mathematics and mathematical knowledge.**

The beginning teacher should be able to relate the history and evolution of mathematical concepts, procedures, and ideas for the grades taught. This can be done by referring to key events and knowledge of specific individuals throughout the history of mathematics to illustrate age-appropriate mathematical concepts. This history should include contributions made by different cultures to mathematics and the impact mathematics has on society and culture. It is of utmost importance that mathematics is seen as useful in a variety of careers and professions to avoid the question, "When will I ever use this?"

Within this framework the teacher should then design age appropriate activities that emphasize mathematical contributions from various cultures. This historical development serves an important purpose as it illustrates how mathematics progressed from concrete applications to abstract generalizations. It also allows the teacher to effectively emphasize the role of mathematics in the workplace and to demonstrate how mathematics is used in a variety of careers. The teacher should be able to describe the properties common to the mathematical disciplines within the workplace and implications of current trends and research in mathematics education.

See how you do on the following question:

The students in Ms. O'Shea's fourth-grade class have completed studying addition, **subtraction**, multiplication, and division of whole numbers. To assess their understanding of whole number operations, Ms. O'Shea asks her students to mentally estimate the answer to the following question: 36×98.

It is a number:

1. slightly less than 3,600
2. a lot less than 3,600
3. slightly more than 3,600
4. a lot more than 3,600

This question helps Ms. O'Shea assess her students' understanding of:

A. multiplying a whole number by 100.
B. multiplication as the inverse of division.
C. the fact that when you multiply, the product is always larger than the **factors**.
D. multiplication as a shortcut for repeated addition.

To obtain a product much smaller than the whole number multiplied by 100, the value of the factor must be closer to 1. To obtain a product slightly larger than the whole number multiplied by 100, the factor must be slightly larger than 100. To obtain a product a lot larger than the whole number multiplied by 100, the factor must be considerably larger than 100. When a whole number is multiplied by a number slightly less than 100 (A), the product is smaller than the whole number multiplied by 100. The closer the value approaches 100, the closer the product is to that product. The answer is A.

Students need many opportunities to assess their own understanding of mathematical operations. To do this, various activities should be used that present applications of mathematical operations in many contexts. As one goal of mathematics instruction is computational fluency, children should have opportunities to master **basic facts** and operations and, as always, apply relevant experiences to real-world situations. Rarely does someone approach you in a conversation to ask, for example, for 21 to be divided by 7. Mathematics is normally based in some type of context. Understanding the meaning of arithmetic operations and how they are related to one another and contextual situations is important for students' development.

A large part of a teacher's job is anticipating and diagnosing typical misconceptions that students have about mathematics (Table 3.3). When teachers anticipate particular problems children have, they can design lessons that better help children with understanding these concepts and skills up front. When teachers know and can diagnose common mathematical misconceptions, they can readily help children move pass their errors more quickly so learners do not fossilize their misconceptions.

Table 3.3 Common Mathematical Difficulties for Children

Most difficulties that children have with arithmetic emerge from a lack of understanding of important place-value concepts.

Place-Value Difficulties

- Associating place-value models with numerals
- Using zero when writing numerals
- Using regrouping concepts to represent a numeral
- Naming place-value positions in a numeral
- Giving nonstandard place-value representations for a numeral

Addition and Subtraction Difficulties

- Identifying addition or subtraction situations
- Using counting to find basic addition facts with zeros in computations
- Using counting to find differences that are related to addition facts

- Regrouping when computing sums and differences
- When the two numerals in an exercise have a different number of digits (e.g., 1,244 × 23)
- A sum involving several **addends** or when a sum or difference involves large numbers

Multiplication and Division

- Identifying multiplication and division situations
- Determining the basic facts
- Using the basic multiplication facts to find related **quotients**
- Applying place-value concepts and basic facts to obtain products and quotients of **multiples** of 10
- Using zeros in a product or quotient
- Using the **distributive property of multiplication** over addition when computing products
- Regrouping when computing products and quotients
- Aligning partial products
- Solving word problems "when"

Rational Numbers

Difficulties associated with fractions

- Associating meaning with a fraction
- Using the **equivalent fraction** rule
- Applying appropriate uses of a **common denominator**
- Making appropriate interpretations for mixed numerals (e.g., $\frac{22}{3}$, $\frac{53}{8}$)
- With the meaning of the operations

Difficulties associated with decimals

- Associating meaning with a decimal
- With place value and with the equivalent fraction rule

THOUSANDS			ONES						
Hundred Thousands	Ten Thousands	Thousands	Hundreds	Tens	Ones	.	Tenths	Hundredths	Thousandths
1	2	3,	7	2	3		0	4	9

- With place value and with common denominators in addition and subtraction
- With the meaning of the operations and in distinguishing between various rules for the operations

Reading and writing difficulties

- Mathematical terms and symbols that are based on precise definitions are not generally learned in out-of-school environments
- Sometimes words that have precise mathematical meaning are used ambiguously in everyday conversations
- Mathematical words have other meanings in ordinary use
- Words are used inappropriately in mathematical context
- The names and meaning of many mathematical symbols cannot be determined by looking at the symbols

- Sometimes inappropriate or misleading visual models are given to illustrate the meaning of mathematical terms and ideas
- Mathematical language is more concise than ordinary language
- The organization of mathematical communications differs from the organization of ordinary reading materials

Source: (Adapted from Troutman & Lichtenberg, 1999).

The meanings of *addition* and *subtraction* are the focus of Pre-K through second grade, whereas the meaning of *multiplication* and *division* are the focus of third through fifth grades. Mental math skills are required learning experiences, although drilling students over and over again to memorize facts creates boredom rather than understanding. NCTM (1998) advocates the appropriate use of calculators and computers, but "when the instructional focus is on developing student-generated or conventional computational algorithms, the calculator should be set aside to allow for this focus" (p. 51).

Children should be able to decide which mathematical operations (addition, subtraction, multiplication, division) should be used for a particular problem, how the same operation can be applied to other situations, how operations relate to one another, and what results to expect. (NCTM, 1998, p. 53)

Consider the following question:

Ms. Ashman is teaching her fifth-grade class an alternate method for doing long division. This algorithm was introduced as follows.

```
16 | 89
     −16    |
      73
     −16    ||
      57
     −16    |||
      41
     −16    ||||
      25
     −16    |||||
       9
```

This teaching approach emphasizes an underlying process of division. Which approach is this?

A. The quotient of the **dividend** and the **divisor**
B. Multiplication by the **reciprocal** of the divisor
C. The **inverse operation** of multiplication
D. Multiple subtractions of the divisor from the dividend

Choice *A* uses the standard algorithm for long division. Choice *B* has no relevance to the question, because it applies to division with fractions. Division is the inverse of multiplication and could be used to check the solution. However, *D* is the correct response: Division is a shortcut for repeated subtraction. Groups of 16 are being removed from the original large group. Each tally mark represents the formation of a group of 16. *(89 is the dividend; 16 is the divisor, the answer is the quotient [5], and the leftover is the remainder [9].)* The answer is *D*.

Answer this question:

Ms. Sikka wants to incorporate calculators into her third-grade mathematics curriculum. She distributes calculators to each student. She asks students to enter the number 6,734 into their calculators. She then asks her students, in only one step, to have the number 6,704 show on the calculator display. Ms. Sikka uses this activity to develop her students' understanding that:

A. calculators provide correct solutions.
B. calculators can be used for guess-and-check problem-solving strategies.
C. calculators can be used when an answer is needed quickly.
D. calculators can be used to help understand place value.

Using calculators provides correct answers but not necessarily correct solutions (A) and does not automatically help develop higher-order thinking skills. Having students recognize the pattern in a guess-and-check situation (B) is one solution, but this is not relevant to this activity. Using the calculator to add the numbers quickly (C) is using the calculator as a computation tool. This question assesses students' understanding of place value (D). The calculator allows students the freedom to explore and to verify when they have found the correct solution. The answer is D.

Texas standards show that technology must be incorporated into the mathematics classroom. Calculators provide a means for students to develop higher-order thinking skills in a non-computational setting because they allow children to focus on logic, reasoning, and estimation, rather than becoming bogged down by procedural computation or faulty memorization. This may be doubly so for children with learning disabilities, because calculators may allow them to function very well in problem solving. As such, technology can play a vital role in the development, practice, and extension of problem solving strategies. Table 3.4 gives other strategies for problem solving.

Computers can provide motivating ways to reach children, although teachers should be aware that many programs offer only "worksheets on a screen." For an alternative view of the potential of the computer, you are encouraged to visit the National Library of Virtual Manipulatives found at http://nlvm.usu.edu/.

Table 3.4 Common Mathematical Strategies for Problem Solving

Acting out the problem

Drawing a picture

Systematic guessing and checking (trial and error)

Making a table

Working a simpler problem

Working backward to solve a problem

Use tools (manipulatives, real objects, technology)

Standard IX: Professional Development

Standard IX: The mathematics teacher understands mathematics teaching as a profession, knows the value and rewards of being a reflective practitioner, and realizes the importance of making a lifelong commitment to professional growth and development.

The beginning teacher of mathematics is able to communicate with colleagues to create professional interactions across disciplines at the building and district level. The teacher should exchange content information with mathematics teachers at preceding and subsequent grade levels to ensure continuity in students' mathematics education. Recognizing that professional development is an ongoing process, the teacher should use workshops and professional development activities as an opportunity to keep up with current technology, obtain new instructional materials and ideas, and discover new approaches for delivering mathematical lessons. The teacher should set, as a goal, continuing to learn new mathematics and actively select research-based materials from appropriate publications produced by professional mathematics organizations to develop lesson plans, instructional activities, and assessments. In communication, consider organizing or participation in a variety of methods (e.g., newsletters, Web pages, fundraisers, math nights, volunteer programs, field trips) to promote communication among parents, students, and the community. Local organizations and electronic communities can likewise serve as a forum for exchanging, discussing, and evaluating ideas regarding mathematics and mathematical instruction and can also serve as an opportunity for professional self-assessment.

Consider the following question:

All fifth-grade classrooms are having a pet show next week. Mr. Messick is in charge of the show and needs to know about how many entry forms to print to send home. Mr. Messick gives his fifth-grade class the following problem to help:

> *Seven children have pets at home. The mean number of pets per child is 2. How many pets does each child have? If there are 124 fourth-grade students, how many entry forms must be printed? Write several sentences explaining your answer.*

National curriculum standards recommend open-ended problems like this and the use of multiple solution strategies. Which of these statements best explains why?

A. Problems of this type are best solved by applying algebraic principles (solving for unknowns) to real-world contexts.

B. Open-ended problems like this allow for a variety of solutions and explanations and promote inquiry, reasoning, and communication.

C. In dealing with uncertainty, students have opportunities to collect and analyze data.

D. The teacher can use this problem for an easy assessment of the students' reasoning processes and correct any misconceptions, as there is only one correct answer.

Algebraic applications (*A*) would not be appropriate, as it is beyond the needs of this situation. This situation does provide an opportunity to collect and analyze data (*C*). It also provides for teacher assessment and methods of communication and verification. Choice *B*, however, is the best response. The question provides children with an opportunity to apply classroom knowledge to real-life contexts. This is a major focus for student learning today. It is important that children learn mathematics with relevant, real-world application and contexts. In this situation, some children may have one pet, no pet, three pets, and so on. There is uncertainty of the exact number, just as in real life. Open-ended situations such as this one help to model real-life situations. The answer is *B*.

It is very difficult to teach something as a teacher that you have not yet learned as a learner. Teachers must develop a level of competence and confidence in mathematics to successfully instruct their students. Obtaining a mathematics textbook or workbook for grades 6 and below and then working the problems these books contain will help you assess any areas that may need review, as does working all of the problems in this chapter.

DISCUSSION

Teachers make a difference in student achievement, and this is never truer than in mathematics. One way of ensuring successful young mathematicians is to be sure that children are *active* in the learning process. The following is a list originating from the *Curriculum and Evaluation Standards for School Mathematics* document (NCTM, 1989) and discussed in Van de Walle (2009). These verbs reflect a more appropriate view of mathematics objectives in an *active* manner rather than a traditional view that encourages passive learners:

Explore	Predict	Justify
Formulate	Solve	Investigate
Develop	Verify	Discover
Construct	Explain	Describe
Represent	Conjecture	Use

Classrooms that encourage the use of these processes foster student achievement. Within such a learning environment students are given the opportunity to experience an exploratory setting, pose challenges, and offer the support that encourages mathematical construction. Mathematics educators who subscribe to the constructivist view of teaching (and learning) mathematics acknowledge that learners must be actively engaged in activities that promote this role for the learner.

In 2000, NCTM produced a document that incorporated all three of its previous documents (NCTM, 2000). Two of its principles warrant special notice within this discussion and summary at this time: the Teaching Principle and the Learning Principle. Let's review what we have learned in this chapter through these principles.

THE TEACHING PRINCIPLE

Effective mathematics teaching requires understanding what students know and need to learn and then challenging and supporting them to learn it well. (NCTM, 2000, p. 16)

"More than any other single factor, teachers influence what mathematics students learn and how well they learn it. Students' mathematical knowledge, their abilities to reason and solve problems, and their self-confidence and dispositions toward mathematics all are shaped by teachers' mathematical and pedagogical decisions" (NCTM, 1998, p. 30). This statement has serious implications and designated responsibilities for the classroom teacher. These components include analysis of and reflection on teaching and learning, worthwhile mathematical tasks, the learning environment, and classroom discourse.

Only through thoughtful analysis and reflection can teachers address the myriad of decisions required for successful teaching. In order to be effective, teachers must use their knowledge of mathematics, pedagogy, student learning, questioning, instructional strategies, and more to plan, teach, and assess the learning environment. When teachers apply all their knowledge concerning teaching into practice within the classroom, they create a positive learning environment for learning mathematics (Ball, 1993). Teachers who hold high expectations that all their children can learn mathematics (and who search for and use exciting mathematics lessons) result in children who enjoy mathematics with a high sense of self-efficacy.

Using pedagogical content knowledge allows teachers to draw on theories, previous experiences, and successes to apply to new situations, such as determining worthwhile tasks (Shulman, 1986). Other factors, including curriculum and learning goals, help to shape the mathematical environment with the teacher as a guide and co-learner (vital roles in constructivism). A crucial factor in the learning environment is the teacher's dispositions toward mathematics, learners, and mathematics education. Even young learners can "read" messages that teachers are not approaching a subject wholeheartedly—either because they don't like it or are unsure of mathematical concepts themselves. There must be a "can-do" atmosphere that encourages student interaction and discourse. Teachers must have both knowledge of the content and the resources (curricular frameworks and guides, instructional materials, lesson plans, etc.) to help inform decision making and planning.

Teachers can provide classrooms that promote thinking, but it takes much more than worthwhile mathematical tasks and commitment to discourse. It takes deep insight about mathematics, about teaching, and about learners, coupled with a sound and robust mathematics curriculum and thoughtful reflection and planning (NCTM, 1998).

Teaching in the real world is a highly complex activity that requires knowledge about many things. Children come to the classroom with diversity in prior learning: special needs; special talents; differences in culture, gender, socioeconomic backgrounds; and more. Each student has his or her own perspective of the world, needs that he or she is seeking to be met, and informal experiences with mathematics. Awareness of each individual child's background and needs is crucial to create an effective learning environment. The teacher must ensure that all children have access to materials appropriate for understanding math and the time to explore those materials. It is important not to inadvertently disadvantage any student, including providing advanced methods for gifted and talented children that are needed to reach their full potential in mathematics. Mathematical challenges that celebrate the diversities and multicultural perspectives of the classroom should be created.

Teachers should accommodate learning for all children through planning, questioning, teaching, and assessing. For young children,

mathematics is a natural way to explore their world. This early perspective should be protected and developed. Thus, it is at the early childhood level that diversities can best be addressed before disparities widen. Girls, minorities, and children in poverty are still not reaching their full potential in mathematics, so teachers must provide learning experiences that give all children equal access to mathematical experiences. Assessment in the classroom must focus on the child's understanding, thought processes, and attitudes about learning mathematics. Developing a positive attitude and an excitement about the teaching and learning of mathematics in the classroom helps to promote and foster learning for all children. The following resources appropriately address this vision of teaching and learning in the Texas classroom (but should not be limited to these alone): the TEKS, the state test objectives, and the NCTM Principles and Standards for School Mathematics (NCTM, 2000). Others include selected district textbooks and developed curricula guidelines, the valuable Web site resources as listed at the end of this chapter, veteran colleagues and administrators, quality in-service programs and workshops (many of which are offered in Texas through Regional Service Centers), reputable computer mathematics software and commercial learning programs, and other activity sources that are learner centered.

THE LEARNING PRINCIPLE

Students must learn mathematics with understanding, actively building new knowledge from experiences and prior knowledge. (NCTM, 2000, p. 20)

Learning mathematics is markedly different today than in the past. Today it is believed that networks of knowledge create a whole conceptual organization of learning. Old and new knowledge are connected, and children's prior knowledge and experiences affect new knowledge (Noddings, 1990). Teachers must consider this view in two ways. First, children may come to their class with rich and varied prior knowledge and experiences in mathematics or very little to no mathematical background. Second, teachers have a responsibility to each child to provide all the experiences and knowledge established by the TEKS in their grade level so that children can successfully move through the Texas curriculum.

The sense of a mathematical community is another perspective on learning mathematics that can be used to help guide instruction (Lave, 1991). When teachers successfully create a community of learners where conceptual understanding thrives and procedural proficiency is present, children are able to develop an appreciation and value for the usefulness of mathematics. Students should (a) develop a disposition to see the power of mathematics, (b) become autonomous learners who analyze and reflect, and (c) develop the ability to communicate mathematically. The National Research Council (1989) states, "To understand what they learn, [students] must enact for themselves verbs that permeate the mathematics curriculum: examine, represent, transform, solve, apply, prove, communicate" (pp. 58–59).

A highly effective tool in this effort is the use of learning centers (Table 3.5). These centers are designated areas of a classroom in which the teacher has strategically provided opportunities for children to explore and experience mathematics (as well as other content areas) through different contexts, materials, and events. These are selected based on the teacher's goals for student learning and grade level appropriateness. Learning centers are effective across all grade levels and with inter- and intradisciplinary content areas. Through informal observations of children at work or play in the centers, teachers are able to gain much insight into the levels of the mathematical understanding. Then, other learning centers for exploration and lessons can be planned and put in place by the teacher that are developmentally appropriate based on these

observations. Questions to ask children working with materials might include "How tall is it?" "How can you tell?" "How much bigger is it?" "How do you know?" "Can you show me another way to do this?" "What would happen if . . . ?" and "How are those shapes different?" Mathematics in the early childhood through sixth grades can and should cut across many daily activities. Table 3.5 gives a beginning list of centers in which mathematics can be the main focus or used in an interdisciplinary way.

Children learn better through learning activities that are motivating and challenging within relevant, real-world contexts. This can be achieved through the use of manipulatives, technology and other mathematical tools, active discourse, and group collaboration. In order for teachers to be able to provide such a learning environment, Van de Walle (1998, p. 34) summarizes seven strategies for effective teaching of mathematics.

1. Create a mathematical environment.
2. Pose worthwhile mathematical tasks.
3. Use cooperative learning groups.
4. Use models and calculators as thinking tools.
5. Encourage discourse and writing.
6. Require justification of student responses.
7. Listen actively.

It is now believed that teachers and students together share responsibility for mathematics learning (NCTM, 1998). Through careful and reflective planning, teachers are able to create learning environments that are challenging, motivating, and active communities of mathematical learning.

Table 3.5 Mathematics in Learning Centers

Center or Play Area	Mathematics Concepts	Manipulatives/Representations
Games, puzzles, and regular daily items, sorting trays	Grouping, counting, matching, patterning, ordering	Classification, numeral identification, logic, geometric forms
Housekeeping/Kitchens	Counting, measuring, one-to-one correspondence, estimation	Play money, numerals, labels
Water play/Sand table	Measuring, counting, conservation, estimation, positioning	Can draw numerals in sand, use measuring tools
Music/Puppets	Counting, one-to-one correspondence, patterning, classification, fractions (music)	Create patterns with music, role play mathematical situations
Painting	Grouping, measuring, patterning, classification	Numeral writing, geometric designs
Woodworking	Measuring, counting, patterning, comparing size and shape, classification	Numeral writing, geometric designs, patterns
Block building	Counting, comparing size, one-to-one correspondence, classification, patterning, geometric shapes, positioning, estimation	Blocks as symbols, labels, can be used as many different representations

SUMMARY

Mathematics is much more than arithmetic. Most of us experienced mathematics learning in a much different way than we are expected to teach it today. Mathematics is more than practicing the procedures of arithmetic by working on addition, subtraction, multiplication, and division problems on worksheets. Teaching and learning mathematics requires providing children with many varied opportunities to construct their own concepts of mathematics across all grade levels. Each learner constructs knowledge based on experimentation and observations with real-world materials and situations. The role of the teacher is to provide a learning environment that fosters these experiences. Teachers support the language for the concepts that children are learning by using the correct terminology early and provide the time and materials that best represent a concrete concept. There must be time for hands-on manipulation for learners, and symbols should be introduced only after concepts are well understood by the children.

Learning environments must be created that encourage and motivate all children to want to do mathematics and challenge them to represent and reflect on their mathematical thinking. To emphasize again, an environment must be exploratory, offering children experiences with real-world items (such as items for shopping, money, and sand, beans, rice, water, etc. for measurement), blocks for construction, and other manipulatives that encourage experimentation.

Technology is no longer viewed as cheating within the mathematics classroom, but rather as an important tool for sense making and exploration. The classroom teacher may now select from a multitude of software choices outside drill activities for use in the classroom to support instruction and encourage exploration and practice for developing children's understanding of mathematics.

Successful teachers build on children's everyday activities, incorporate their cultural origins, languages, integrate technology, and focus on strategies. They use a variety of instructional strategies, create meaningful contexts, and provide for active participation to help children learn, develop, and appreciate mathematics in their world. The NCTM Principles and Standards for School Mathematics and the TEKS for Texas schools offer guidelines for what mathematics is to be learned at different levels and the progression of that learning. Effective teachers remember that how mathematics is taught is just as important as what mathematics is taught.

A Snapshot
of Teaching Mathematics in the Elementary Classroom

CLASSROOM SCENARIO

The scenario exemplifies the vision of teaching elementary mathematics in the classroom according to national standards and state guidelines. Highlights of the scenario are represented in italics within parentheses. These comments explain why and how this type of lesson represents the best in teaching mathematics.

This third-grade class has been working on problems that involve separating or dividing. The teacher, Mr. Kaster, is attempting to provide the class with some early involvement with multiplicative situations (using multiplication). Simultaneously, Mr. Kaster wants to include experiences with contexts for deepening students' knowledge of and skill with addition and subtraction. This third-grade class has the knowledge and skill for performing addition and subtraction, but their understanding of multiplication and division is still quite informal. There has been some development of the concept of fractions that connects to their ideas about division. The class has not yet learned the division algorithm (the conventional procedure for dividing).[1]

The twenty-five students in Mr. Kaster's third-grade classroom are planning to share a class treat.
(Mr. Kaster seized this "teachable moment" to engage the students in real-world, relevant problem solving.)

---

[1]Adapted from *NCTM Professional Standards for Teaching Mathematics*, 1991, pp. 58–59.

The problem involves 48 chocolate-iced cupcakes that were provided by a local bakery as a treat associated with the class field trip the previous day. Mr. Kaster has given the class the following problem: If there are 48 cupcakes for our class treat, how many can each child have?

(Mr. Kaster knows that this problem will most likely elicit alternative representations and solution strategies, as well as different answers. This provides a wonderful opportunity for mathematics learning. It should additionally help the students develop their ideas about division, fractions, and the connections between them.)

The students are encouraged to think about the problem individually. After several minutes, Mr. Kaster allows the students to form problem-solving groups.

(To promote collaboration and problem solving, Mr. Kaster has the students work in small groups of three and four to discuss their ideas about the problem. This is a routine practice for this class.)

While the students are working in small groups, Mr. Kaster walks around the room informally eavesdropping on the small group discussions.

(This is a valuable method of informal assessment.)

While walking around the room of small groups working together, Mr. Kaster notices that one group immediately decides to represent the problem with mathematics manipulatives.

(Mr. Kaster always has various manipulatives available at the small group tables, as well as all the full complement of manipulatives that are displayed in the Math Center of the classroom.)

Two groups choose color tiles to be cupcakes and begin to represent the problem. Another follows, but selects pattern blocks. A fourth group begins to draw pictures of cupcakes. Group 5 works with paper and pencil and then sees that other groups have chosen different ways of representing the problem. They, too, select pattern blocks. After much discourse, the sixth group scans the others to see what they are doing. This group also decides to use pattern blocks. As one of the girls is about to choose pattern blocks for her group from the Math Center, another student rushes over and whispers in her ear. She then decides to use fraction circles.

As Mr. Kaster continues to facilitate the small group work, the leader of one group raises his hand.

(This is the system that Mr. Kaster has in place addressing small group discussions. Each member of the group has a role to fulfill. Roles are rotated periodically. Questions that arise must first be addressed in small group discussion. When there is a consensus that no solution is agreeable, then and only then may the group leader raise his or her hand to ask for help. This promotes cooperative collaboration and learning within the groups, as well as facilitating discourse and problem-solving skills.)

Mr. Kaster asks if the "first three and then me" rule has been followed. When answered affirmatively, the student asks if they should include him in the number of people having a cupcake. The other groups overhear this and readily agree that Mr. Kaster should have a treat, too. They agree to change the number of people from 25 to 26 to include Mr. Kaster.

After the groups have worked for about 20 minutes, Mr. Kaster asks if the children are ready to discuss the problem in the whole group. The groups seem to agree. Mr. Kaster asks who would like to begin.

(The teacher allows time for the children to develop their solutions independently, with a few others, and then involves the whole group. By asking who would like to share their solution, he encourages the students to take intellectual risks.)

Two boys, Juan and Mark, come to the front of the class. Using the overhead projector, they write:

$$\begin{array}{r} 48 \\ -26 \\ \hline 24 \end{array}$$

One explains, "There are 25 kids in our class plus Mr. Kaster makes 26, and so if we pass out 1 cupcake to each child, we will have 24 cupcakes left, and that is not enough for each of us to have a second cupcake, so there will be some leftover ones."

(Students are expected to justify their solutions, not just to give answers.)

Mr. Kaster and the students reflect on this solution that was presented. Mr. Kaster scans the class and asks if anyone has a comment or a question about this solution.

(The teacher solicits other students' comments about the boys' solution without labeling it right or wrong. As members of a learning community, Mr. Kaster expects the students to decide if an idea makes sense mathematically.)

One girl, Amanda, says that she thinks that solution makes sense, but that "8 minus 6 is 2, not 4, so the answer should be 22, not 24." She demonstrates by pointing at the number line above the chalkboard. Starting at 8, she counts back 6 from 8 to get 2 using a pointer. The two boys reflect on this information for a moment. The class is quiet.

Mr. Kaster waits.

Then Juan says, "Yeah, let's fix it . . . 8 minus 6 is 2 . . . so 22."

Mr. Kaster listens closely but does not jump into the interactive discourse.

(The mathematical learning environment should be established as a "risk-free" atmosphere. Students should be encouraged to respectfully question one another's ideas. The boys "revise" their solution because they have been convinced by Amanda's explanation. There is no sense here that being wrong is problematic.)

Another student remarks that their group had the same solution as the first one shared.

"Ashley?" asks Mr. Kaster, after pausing for a moment to look over the classroom of students. Mr. Kaster remembers that this group had a different approach.

Ashley states that her group may have found a way to give each student in the class more than one cupcake. Ashley coaxes another group member, Ashok, to go to the overhead with her.

Using small color tiles on the overhead, the students demonstrate that each tile would represent a whole cupcake. The students proceed to divide the entire group of 48 cupcakes into two groups. One group represents the one student—one cupcake idea (26), while the other group (22) represents the leftover cupcakes.

(These actions demonstrate the same subtraction problem of the previous two boys that used the conventional representation of the problem.)

Ashley states, "If we could cut these tiles in half, then each of us would get one whole cupcake and half of another one, we think." Ashok and the rest of that group agree, "Each of us would get one and a half cupcakes."

Another student, Tom, suggests that because the color tiles cannot be cut in half that they try to use the pattern blocks like his group had tried. The class agrees that this is a good idea.

Tom joins Ashley and Ashok at the front of the room. Using pattern blocks, the students demonstrate how 48 cupcakes minus 26 cupcakes leaves 22 remaining cupcakes to divide in half. Using the blocks by exchanging whole blocks (hexagon) for two pieces (trapezoids), they represent the 22 cupcakes as 44 half cupcakes. The group then proceeds to assign each of the 26 people with half a cupcake.

Mr. Kaster asks, "Do you have any leftovers?"

(The students work together to solve the problem. Sometimes they build on the solutions offered by classmates. Mr. Kaster gathers

insights about students through close listening and observation [informal assessment].)

At times, Mr. Kaster takes the responsibility for pushing (facilitating) students' thinking forward.

"There are still 18 half cupcakes or 9 whole cupcakes left over," replies Ramiro.

"What do the rest of you think about this?" asks Mr. Kaster.

(Mr. Kaster expects the students to reason mathematically.)

Several students give explanations in support of Ramiro's solution.

"I think that does make sense," says Mary, "but I had another solution. I think the answer is 1 plus one-half plus one-fourth." Mary is a member of the group that chose to use fraction circles to help in their small group discussion of the original problem.

(Students seem willing to take risks by bringing up different ideas.)

After waiting for the class to have a time of reflection on Mary's comments, the teacher continues.

"I don't understand," Mr. Kaster says. "Could you show what you mean?"

(Mr. Kaster seizes the opportunity to extend the class's thinking about fractions through this real-world problem that has motivated and engaged all of the students into actively thinking mathematically using many approaches and representations of their thinking. This has been done throughout the use of manipulatives, conventional procedures, collaboration, and classroom discourse within a community of learners in a risk-free environment.)

This scenario is just one snapshot of the many ways that teachers of mathematics are able to develop rich mathematical learning environments in their classrooms. This exemplifies a learner-centered classroom. Teaching in this manner helps the teacher facilitate student understanding of mathematics. The use of manipulatives, small and large group collaborative discourse, and active hands-on, minds-on learning experiences help students to value mathematics, as well as to develop conceptual understanding of mathematics. This empowers students to become mathematically literate and leads to successful student achievement and progress.

TEACHING STRATEGIES PRACTICE QUESTIONS

You may want to go ahead and try these questions, or you may want to review the terms in the Glossary before attempting the questions.

Select the best response to each of the following questions.

1. Mr. Morales asked his sixth-grade students to choose their favorite colors from a list of red, blue, green, and yellow. After the students had made their selections, the class tallied their data. Which type of graph would be the most appropriate to use for this information?
   A. A circle graph
   B. A line graph
   C. Box and whiskers plot
   D. A scatter plot

2. Ms. Maxwell wanted to help her second-grade students better understand place value. What would be a good manipulative to use?
   A. Cuisenaire rods
   B. Color tiles
   C. Base ten blocks
   D. Attribute blocks

3. How many lines of symmetry does a rectangle have?
   A. One
   B. Two
   C. Four
   D. Six

4. Ms. Lam is using base 10 blocks with her first-grade class to solve addition and subtraction problems. She asks her students to "show" her, using the blocks, the number 34. A possible solution is:
   A. 3 flats; 4 longs.
   B. 3 flats; 4 units.
   C. 2 longs; 14 units.
   D. 1 long; 14 units.

5. Kanesha spends approximately 45 minutes each school day on homework. If she continues to spend 45 minutes a school day on homework, how much time will Kanesha have spent after 15 days of school?
   A. 6.75 hours
   B. 10 hours, 25 minutes
   C. 11 hours, 15 minutes
   D. 11 hours, 45 minutes

6. Using the metric system, Mr. Coulter asks his class to estimate the length of their desk tops. A "reasonable" estimate could be:
   A. 60 cm.
   B. 60 mm.
   C. 60 m.
   D. 60 km.

7. Use the problem below to answer the question that follows:

$$+\ \frac{\overline{\quad}\ \ \overline{\quad}\ \ \overline{\quad}}{\overline{\quad}\ \ \overline{\quad}\ \ \overline{\quad}}$$

Use each numeral 0, 1, 2, 3, 4, and 5 once. Place a digit on each line so that you will have the largest sum possible.

This problem would be most appropriate for providing students an opportunity to use which problem-solving strategy?
   A. Working backward
   B. Extending the problem
   C. Looking for a pattern
   D. Drawing a diagram

8. Before going on a field trip, Ms. Jurca must decide how many buses to request for all sixth-grade classes with a total enrollment of 315. She orders enough buses to transport all of the students. If each bus carries 60 students, how many empty seats will there be? A calculator is chosen by a one student to help solve this problem. The student divides 315 by 60 for a solution of 5.25. The student is confused and asks Ms. Jurca for help. The teacher's best initial response might be to:
   A. ask the student to explain why he or she divided 315 by 60 and what that answer represents.
   B. suggest that the student use paper and pencil to check the answer.
   C. suggest that the next step should be to multiply and then subtract.
   D. explain that the answer 5.25 means that six buses are needed to transport all of the students.

9. Children in Ms. Baker's fourth-grade class were asked to find the number of cats and dogs owned by the class. There was a total of 12 dogs and 9 cats for the class. Ms. Baker wanted her students to use a pictograph to represent the data. If a square represented three dogs and a triangle represented three cats, how many triangles should the students use to graph the data?
   A. 4
   B. 3
   C. 7
   D. 2

10. Ms. Martin is using rocker scales in her second-grade classroom. She has her students place objects of different weights

on the scales. This activity could best be used to foster her students' understanding of:
A. how to weigh objects accurately.
B. how to predict which object is heavier.
C. how to find the total weight of objects.
D. how to better understand the concepts of less than and greater than.

11. The first step for the teacher to do when developing students' prenumber concepts is to:
A. spend class time working with concrete objects.
B. spend class time working with pictorial objects.
C. spend class time having students write their numbers.
D. spend class time having students recognize the words for the numbers.

A third-grade student is given 12 color tiles and is asked to create as many differently shaped rectangles as possible for each number from 1 to 12. Ms. Longino models these directions with six tiles, making two rectangles, as shown below. Use this information to answer questions 12 through 14.

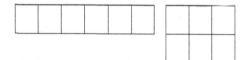

12. Ms. Longino has chosen this activity to help develop Ashauna's understanding of which of the following number concepts?
A. Percentages of whole numbers
B. **Least common multiples**
C. Factors of whole numbers
D. Numeration systems other than base 10

13. If during the activity, a student asks why a 4 × 3 rectangle and a 3 × 4 rectangle have the same shape, Ms. Longino may use this opportunity for a lesson on which of the following geometric concepts?
A. **Right angles** and perpendicular lines
B. Properties of congruent figures
C. Properties of **similar figures**
D. Area and perimeter

14. Ms. Longino wants to encourage the application of higher-order thinking skills. Of the following questions, which is the best question to ask at the end of the activity in question 13?
A. How many more rectangles could you make with 15 color tiles?
B. Which number from 1 to 12 made the most rectangles?

C. For any given number of color tiles, how could you determine how many rectangles can be made?
D. For any given rectangle, how can you determine the perimeter of the rectangles?

****

15. Ms. Jacob divided her second-grade students into groups of four and gave each group a copy of a grocery store advertisement. Students were asked to work as a group and plan a meal for four people that contained one item from each food group. Students were asked to ensure that the meal was nutritious and was the least expensive meal they could plan. Ms. Jacob's objective for this activity is to:
A. help students learn the food groups.
B. connect mathematics to real-world situations.
C. help students develop communication skills.
D. foster collaborative working groups.

16. Ms. DeVillier placed 60 color tiles in a bag: 20 red, 10 blue, 10 yellow, 20 green. She asked her third-grade students to construct a graph to accurately represent the ratios of the color tiles. The ratio of the area for the green tiles to the area of all the tiles should be:
A. 2:4.
B. 1:2.
C. 1:3.
D. 3:1.

ANSWERS TO TEACHING STRATEGIES PRACTICE QUESTIONS

Be sure to look at the information that follows this section if you are unclear about these terms (e.g., attribute blocks are described in Table 3.1, Common Mathematics Manipulations). Other terms are described in the Glossary.

Answer 1: *Circle graph:* This is the best answer to represent this type of data, because the colors create discrete categories. As noted earlier, a circle graph involves the understanding and application of degrees, ratios, and the use of protractors. Although these are not appropriate for younger children, they are expected in the fifth and sixth grades. A line graph indicates continuous data over time. A box and whiskers plot is best suited to display differences between summary statistics for populations. A scatterplot graph shows paired data values. The correct answer is *A*.

Answer 2: *Base 10 blocks:* These are the best manipulatives for place value concepts.

Cuisenaire rods (A) may be used with fractions, ratio and proportion, measuring, and more. Color tiles (B) may be used for counting, probability, fractions, and some place value. Attribute blocks (D) would be used for sorting, classifying, and other activities. The correct answer is C.

Answer 3: *Two: Lines of symmetry divide the shape into mirror images.* A rectangle has two: one from side to side in the middle and the other drawn from end to end in the middle. Lines of symmetry may be formed when a shape is folded. From corner to corner in a rectangle is a **diagonal**, but it is not a **line of symmetry**. The correct answer is B.

Answer 4: *2 longs; 14 units.* This is the best answer. A long has a value of 10 units. Two longs would represent 20 units. Add the 14 units and the total number represented is 34. A flat has the value of 100 units. The correct answer is C.

Answer 5: *11 hours, 15 minutes.* The answer may be found by multiplying 45 minutes by 15 days and converting the total number of minutes to hours and minutes. This is done by dividing the product of 45×15 by 60 (minutes in an hour). The remainder is indicated as minutes left over—after making as many hours as possible. The correct answer is C.

Answer 6: *60 cm (centimeters).* This is the most reasonable answer. Millimeters are too small. A centimeter is about the width of the human little finger. A meter is comparable to a yard, and a kilometer is closest to a mile (although less than a full mile). Meters and kilometers are too large. (An inch is approximately 2.54 cm.) The correct answer is A.

Answer 7: *Looking for a pattern.* The best strategy to apply in a problem such as this is to look for a pattern. The other strategies are more appropriate when there is more information available. For example, if a few digits were placed in the problem, the work backwards strategy would be appropriate. Extending the problem is not a good choice because there is not enough information provided. Drawing a diagram is not appropriate in this case. The correct answer is C.

Answer 8: *Ask the student to explain why he or she divided 315 by 60 and what that answer represents.* This teacher response exemplifies the constructivist approach to teaching mathematics. It allows children to reflect on and justify their responses in order to make sense of the problem at hand. The other response choices here are not appropriate for a learner-centered mathematics classroom. The correct answer is A.

Answer 9: *3. There are 9 cats.* The triangle represents 3 cats, so 9 divided by 3 = 3 triangles needed for the graph. The correct answer is B.

Answer 10: *How to better understand the concept of less than and greater than.* This activity is asking children in general to measure the differences in objects in relation to each other. Understanding the concept of less than and greater than is very well represented in this activity for second grade. Children are able to compare without using a specific measuring scale. The next step would be to ask children to predict which is heavier. The correct answer is D.

Answer 11: *Spend class time working with concrete objects.* Children are better able to understand mathematical concepts by first using concrete objects to manipulate. From there, learning progresses to pictorial or graphic, symbolic, and abstract. The correct answer is A.

Answer 12: *Factors of whole numbers.* As children work with the 12 tiles to make different rectangles, the results create rectangles of different dimensions that are multiplication arrays (1×12, 12×1, 2×6, 6×2, 3×4, 4×3). These represent the factors of 12. The correct answer is C.

Answer 13: *Properties of congruent figures.* By definition, congruent figures have the same size and same shape. Thus, 4×3 and 3×4 are congruent figures. The correct answer is B.

Answer 14: *For any given number of colored tiles, how could you determine how many rectangles can be made?* This question is the best answer because it challenges children to reflect, evaluate, and generalize the concept to another situation that allows many different responses. This has the children thinking beyond the usual recall of information. The correct answer is C.

Answer 15: *Connect mathematics to real-world situations.* It is extremely important that children learn and apply mathematics to real-world contexts to provide relevancy and to motivate students' problem-solving thinking. The correct answer is B.

Answer 16: *1:3.* Students need to develop organizational skills needed to properly handle large quantities of data. Choosing an appropriate graphical representation is a fundamental requirement that students need to present data in an accurate manner. This response gives the ratio of the area of all of the tiles to the area of the green color tiles. This is the correct response: There are 60 color tiles total and

20 of the 60 are green. (In this case, the ratio of the green tiles [20] to the entire group of tiles [60] is written $\frac{20}{60}$. This simplifies to $\frac{1}{3}$ and is written in ratio form of 1:3.) The correct answer is *C*.

CONTENT PRACTICE QUESTIONS

This section includes problems addressing various mathematical concepts to help refresh some basic mathematical thinking and procedures. Answer the following questions and check your responses with the answers. (For further review, visit the Web sites previously listed and/or locate some mathematics textbooks to study.)

1. Which of the following is a **prime number**: 9, 21, 41, or 36?

2. Complete: _____ kg = 3,200 g

3. There are 32 employees at the office. Of the employees, 20 are women. What percentage of the employees are women?

4. Multiply: $-5.2 \times + 2.6 = ?$

5. Write in exponent form: $4 \times 4 \times 4 \times 4 \times 4$

6. Divide: $0.02\overline{)1.576}$

7. What are the coordinates of point A?

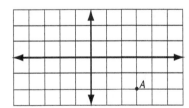

8. What is the LCM of 12 and 15?

9. Rosa spends $\frac{1}{3}$ of her allowance on lunch and $\frac{1}{4}$ of her allowance on entertainment. How much of her allowance is left?

10. What percent of 40 is 35?

11. Find the **circumference**.

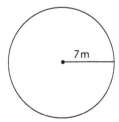

7 m

12. Find the volume.

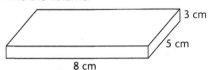

3 cm
5 cm
8 cm

13. A sweater that usually sells for $29.00 is on sale for $26.10. What is the percentage decrease?

14. How tall is the house?

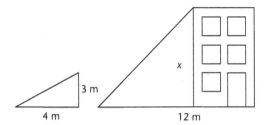

3 m
x
4 m
12 m

15. Subtract:

6 yds 1 ft
−3 yds 2 ft

16. What is the surface area?

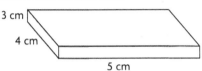

3 cm
4 cm
5 cm

17. Solve for *n*: $5n - 14 = -19$

18. Add: $5\frac{1}{6}$
     $+ 6\frac{5}{8}$

19. Round 68.0719 to the nearest tenth.

20. Jamyce has received grades of 89, 92, and 85 on 3 tests. What grade must she get on the next test in order to have an average of 90?

21. Subtract: $-6 - -5 =$ ___?___

22. Find the perimeter:

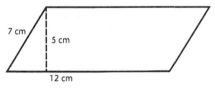

7 cm
5 cm
12 cm

23. Which line is perpendicular to line *AB*?

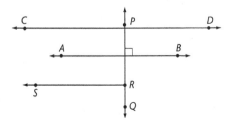

C   *P*   *D*
A   *B*
S   *R*
Q

Use the following **Venn diagram** to answer questions 24–27.

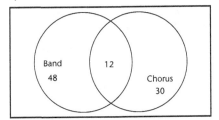

24. How many students are in the band?

25. How many students are in the chorus?

26. How many students are in the band and the chorus?

27. How many students are in the band but not in the chorus?

****

28. How many square meters of carpeting are needed to carpet a room that measures 12 meters by 19 meters?

29. Which ratio is equal to the ratio 3:4?
    A. 4:3
    B. 6:7
    C. 15:20
    D. 20:15

30. Write as a percentage: $\frac{3}{8}$

Use the spinner to answer questions 31–34. Imagine that you spin the spinner. Find each probability.

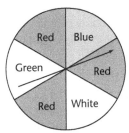

31. *P* (red) (probability of hitting a red section).

32. *P* (not blue) (probability of not hitting a blue section). You toss a coin and then spin the spinner above. Find each probability.

33. *P* (head, red)

34. *P* (tail, red)

****

35. Find the permutation: There are 4 students and 4 chairs in a room. How many different possible seating arrangements are there?

36. Carrie used a leash 3 meters long to tie her dog to a tree. What is the area of the circular region in which Carrie's dog can play?

Use the data below to answer questions 37–40.

85	75	70	70	70
100	90	85	90	65
70	90	80	65	85
75	100	75	95	95
65	90	90	85	90

37. The mode is _____ .

38. The range is _____ .

39. The median is _____ .

40. The mean is _____ .

****

41. Solve: $(6 \times 4) - (18 \div 3)$

42. Solve: $6(4 + 5)$

43. What is the prime **factorization** of 288?

44. How far will a bicycle with a 12-inch wheel **radius** travel in one complete revolution of the wheel?

ANSWERS TO CONTENT PRACTICE QUESTIONS WITH PROCEDURAL RATIONALE

1. *41.* A prime number can be divided only by 1 and itself without a remainder.

2. *3.2.* There are 1,000 g (grams) in one kg (kilogram).

3. *62.5 percent.* 20 is what part of the total, 32? Divide 20 by 32 to obtain the decimal 0.625. The final step requires changing this decimal value into a percentage. Because *percent* literally means "parts per hundred," we multiply this decimal number by 100 to convert it into a percentage.

4. *−13.52.* The product in multiplication of a positive and a negative number is a negative number.

5. *45.* The number of times the number is used as a factor determines the exponent.

6. *78.8.* The decimal point in the divisor and the dividend is moved two places to the left to make the divisor a whole number; then division procedures are followed.

7. *(3, −2).* The first number in a coordinate pair represents the *x*-axis (horizontal) value, the second number is the *y*-axis (vertical) value.

8. *60.* The LCM is the *least common multiple* and is found by listing the multiples of 12 and listing the multiples of 15. Find the **common multiple** from the list that is the least in number.

9. $\frac{5}{12}$. Change $\frac{1}{3}$ and $\frac{1}{4}$ to have a common denominator of 12 ($\frac{4}{12} + \frac{3}{12}$), add to obtain $\frac{7}{12}$. That subtracted from 1 (the allowance) ($\frac{12}{12} - \frac{7}{12}$) is $\frac{5}{12}$.

10. *87.5 percent.* To find a percentage of a number, divide 35 by 40. The decimal answer is then changed to a percentage (0.875 becomes 87.5 percent).

11. *43.96 m.* C = $2\pi r$ ($2 \times \pi \times$ radius); π(**pi**) = approximately 3.14.

12. *120 cubic cm.* The volume is found by multiplying the measurement of each of the edges ($8 \times 5 \times 3$).

13. *10 percent.* Subtract the sale price from the original price ($2.90). Find what percentage that is of the original $29.00 (divide $2.90 by $29.00 to get 0.10, to become 10 percent).

14. *9 m.* This is a proportion problem. The small triangle is similar to the triangle drawn from the building. Similar figures have angles and sides that are in proportion. The given ratios may be determined to be 3:4 and *x* (the unknown) is to 12. 3:4 as *x* is to 12. Cross products may be used to solve. ($4x = 3$ times 12 or 36). Solve for *x*.

15. *2 yd 2 ft.* The 6 yd 1 ft must be renamed as 5 yd 4 ft, because 1 yd is renamed (3 ft) and added to the already 1 ft. Subtract.

16. *94 square cm.* Surface area is the sum of all the areas of each **face** of the figure. In this case, there are 6 faces. Each is a rectangle. $A = lw$ ($4 \times 1, 4 \times 1, 8 \times 4, 8 \times 4, 8 \times 1, 8 \times 1$).

17. *−1.* Add 14 to both sides of the equation. $5n = -5$. Divide both sides by 5; $n = -1$.

18. *$11\frac{19}{24}$.* To add unlike fractions, determine the **least common denominator** (24), then add ($5\frac{4}{24} + 6\frac{15}{24} = 11\frac{19}{24}$).

19. *68.1* Zero is in the tenths place. The 7 in the hundredths place determines that the zero be rounded up to 1.

20. *To obtain an average of 90 from four tests, a student would need a total of 360 grade points.* Add the first three scores to total 266. Subtract this from 360 to get 94.

21. *−1.* To subtract −5 from −6 use the inverse of −5, which is +5. Another method is to change the sign of the second number and add when subtracting like-signed numbers. To begin to teach students this concept, use a number line or use two color counters

and teach making zero pairs (pairing a negative to a positive to make zero).

22. *38 cm.* Add the length of all four sides to determine the perimeter.

23. *Line PQ.* Perpendicular lines form a right angle at the point of intersection.

24. *60 (45 + 12).* This represents only the band members' set.

25. *42.* This set includes those that are members of the chorus and the band and only the chorus. (30 + 12)

26. *12.* This set is only those members that are in the band and the chorus.

27. *48.* This set represents the total of 60 minus those that are in both (12), totaling 48.

28. *228 square m.* To find the area for a rectangle, multiply the length by the width.

29. *15:20.* Two equivalent ratios make a proportion.

30. *37.5 percent.* What percentage of 8 is represented by 3? The 3 is divided by 8. That decimal quotient is changed to a percentage.

31. *$\frac{1}{2}$.* There are three red sections on the spinner out of a total of six sections. $\frac{3}{6}$ becomes $\frac{1}{2}$ in its simplest form.

32. *$\frac{5}{6}$.* There is only one blue section of the spinner and five that are not blue, making it 5 out of 6.

33. *$\frac{1}{4}$.* The probability of spinning a red is 1 out of 2 ($\frac{3}{6}$), for tossing a head is $\frac{1}{2}$. Multiply the two probabilities: $\frac{1}{2} \times \frac{1}{2} = \frac{1}{4}$.

34. *$\frac{1}{4}$.* See answer 33.

35. There are four choices for the first student. Once he sits down, there are only three choices for the second student. The third student has two choices. The last student has only one choice. Mathematically this is represented as $4 \times 3 \times 2 \times 1 = 24$.

36. *28.26 square m.* The leash represents the radius of a circle. To find the area of a circle, multiply π (3.14) by the square of the radius.

37. *90.* The mode is the most often occurring number.

38. *35.* The range is the difference between the largest and the smallest numbers.

39. *85.* The median is the middle number. It is the average of the two middle numbers when the numbers are arranged in order.

40. *82.* The mean is the average. Total all numbers and divide by the number of numbers.

41. *18.* PEMDAS ("Please Excuse My Dear Aunt Sally") is a mnemonic phrase that represents the **order of operations**. Perform operations in parentheses first, then exponents, multiplications, division, addition, subtraction.

42. *54.* See answer 41.

43. $2^5 \times 3^2$. The prime factorization of a positive integer is a list of all the integer's **prime factors**, often expressed using exponents. For this example, we have $288 = 2 \times 2 \times 2 \times 2 \times 2 \times 3 \times 3$, which may be written as $2^5 \times 3^2$.

44. *24π inches.* The distance covered by the bicycle in one complete revolution is equal to the circumference of the wheel. Because circumference is equal to π times the **diameter** ($C = \pi d$) and the diameter is equal to twice the radius ($d = 2r$), the circumference can be found as $C = 2\pi r$. Because $r = 12$ inches, the total distance travelled in one revolution would be 24π inches (approximately 75.4 inches).

PRACTICE QUESTIONS ON CONTENT AND TEACHING STRATEGIES

1. Ms. Burns is discussing the concept of time with her first-grade students. She asks her students to close their eyes, and, when they think 1 minute has passed, raise their hands. Once students have raised their hands, they may open their eyes, but they are to remain quiet until everyone else has raised his or her hand. The purpose of this exercise is to:
   A. have first-grade students practice counting techniques.
   B. have first-grade students realize that there is more than one right answer.
   C. have first-grade students develop estimation skills with regards to time.
   D. have first-grade students realize that some students count faster than others.

2. Ms. Shelledy has placed her second-grade students in groups of four and has given each group a bag of color tiles, a piece of 1-inch-square paper, and markers. She asks each group to separate the color tiles by color and then to make a bar graph to represent their data using the 1-inch-square paper. Ms. Shelledy asks the groups to bring their graphs to the front of the classroom and discuss their graphs. The main objective of this exercise is to:
   A. learn how to work in cooperative groups.
   B. increase students' familiarity with using language to describe data.
   C. give students practice in creating bar graphs.
   D. increase students' ability to sort objects by attributes.

3. What number should replace the blank in the following number sentence?
   $35 \times \_ = 2,450$
   A. 60
   B. 70
   C. 75
   D. 80

4. Ms. Sewell distributes four-function calculators to her third-grade students and asks that they enter the number 7,346. She asks students what number they need to subtract from 7,346 so that they will have the numeral 7,046 on their calculator displays. The main purpose for this activity is to:
   A. increase the use of technology in the mathematics classroom.
   B. have students realize that calculators can be used to add or subtract numbers efficiently.
   C. increase students' understanding of place value.
   D. have students use mental computation.

5. In the following empty box, figure out the relationship and fill in the correct number.

5	10
13	
21	26

   A. 5
   B. 6
   C. 16
   D. 18

6. Ms. McAninch took her first-grade class on a walk near the school. She asked her students to look at the buildings in the neighborhood and to see if they could identify shapes they saw. When the students returned to the classroom, they discussed the

shapes they had seen. The main purpose of this activity was to have children:
   A. learn about the buildings in the neighborhood.
   B. connect mathematical shapes to the real world.
   C. learn that mathematics learning can happen outside of the classroom.
   D. see how many different types of buildings are in the neighborhood.

7. If a clock's hands have an angle of 269 degrees, it would show approximately how much of a turn?
   A. $\frac{1}{4}$
   B. $\frac{1}{2}$
   C. $\frac{3}{4}$
   D. 1

8. The fourth-grade students in Mr. Gomez's class were studying circles and learning how to construct pie charts. What would be the appropriate manipulative for them to use?
   A. Cuisenaire rods
   B. Base 10 blocks
   C. Paper plates
   D. Attribute blocks

9. Look at the following letters and tell which has no line of symmetry.
   A. **C**
   B. **T**
   C. **X**
   D. **L**

10. Ms. Goyal groups her third-grade students into pairs. She distributes a pair of straws to each pair of students and asks them to show her an **acute angle** by arranging the straws on their desks. The best reason for having them work in pairs is to:
   A. give students an opportunity to work with something unusual to make more of an impact.
   B. give students an opportunity to collaborate and share their ideas about angles.
   C. give students an opportunity to demonstrate a visual representation of an acute angle.
   D. give students an opportunity to learn more about geometry.

11. On the following number line, which letter represents two-thirds?

A	B	C	D
0	0.5	$\frac{4}{6}$	1.0

   A. A
   B. B
   C. C
   D. D

12. Ms. Pellegrino groups her kindergarten students into groups of four and gives each group a balance beam and base 10 blocks. She asks the students to place three units on one side of the scale and two units on the other side of the scale. The main purpose of this activity is to:
   A. connect mathematics to science.
   B. strengthen student understanding of the counting numbers.
   C. develop the concept of inequality.
   D. develop the concept of one-to-one correspondence.

13. A veterinarian prescribed medicine for a cat that weighed 12 pounds. How many ounces does the cat weigh?
   A. 144 oz.
   B. 192 oz.
   C. 6 oz.
   D. $1\frac{3}{4}$ oz.

14. Ms. Clemson asks her second graders to draw a picture of a square. Students then share their pictures with their classmates and discuss why they think their pictures represent squares. Ms. Clemson listens carefully to her students' responses, and when the class is through, she discusses what the students have said and corrects misconceptions she has heard. This lesson would be most appropriate for:
   A. students developing a visual representation of geometric shapes.
   B. developing students' van Hiele levels of understanding.
   C. helping students to articulate their responses.
   D. assessment of students' understanding of squares.

15. Mr. Kahn asks his fourth-grade students to discuss multiplication. He distributes calculators to each student and asks them to multiply two counting numbers. The students discuss their answers. Mr. Kahn asks students to generalize the magnitude of their answers. The main objective for this activity is to:
   A. give students practice with multiplication.
   B. give students practice with calculators.
   C. use technology in the mathematics classroom.
   D. develop number sense concepts of magnitude.

16. If Ms. Hong offers her sixth-grade children the same types of candy from a bag, and

there are 6 red pieces, 4 green pieces, and 9 yellow pieces, what is the probability of a child picking a yellow piece?

A. $\frac{9}{19}$

B. $\frac{1}{9}$

C. $\frac{1}{4}$

D. $\frac{10}{19}$

17. Ms. Seo has her fourth-grade students working in pairs with pattern blocks. She asks them to build a square using the green triangles. She then asks the students to build a rectangle that is not a square with the green triangles. The best objective for this activity is to:

A. develop students' spatial skills.

B. help students distinguish between rectangles and squares.

C. familiarize students with pattern blocks.

D. develop students' ability with area.

18. The entire third grade at Oak Hill Elementary has been studying multiplication. Ms. Lewis discusses that 4×5 is the same problem as 5×4. This example demonstrates:

A. the **commutative property for multiplication.**

B. the **associative property for multiplication.**

C. the distributive property.

D. multiplicative identity.

19. Mr. Donaldson has been teaching division concepts to his fourth-grade students. He arranges students in groups of four and distributes base 10 blocks to the groups. He asks the groups to take 10 units blocks and divide them equally into two groups. Then, he asks them to divide the 10 blocks into 5 equal groups. Finally, Mr. Donaldson asks the students to divide the 10 blocks into zero groups. The main purpose of this activity is to show that:

A. division is making groups of equal size.

B. zero can be divided by any number.

C. it is not physically possible to divide a number by zero.

D. when dividing by zero, there will be a remainder.

20. Miss Studer's kindergarten class is working in pairs to sort attribute blocks by large blocks and small blocks. When students have finished sorting their shapes, she asks each student to choose one large block and draw a picture of this shape on a piece of paper. The objective for this activity is to develop each student's:

A. ability to make a choice.

B. drawing ability.

C. ability to transfer a design.

D. ability to understand the meaning of *large.*

21. Mr. Erick's first-grade class is discussing their pets. Mr. Erick suggests that the class develop a graph of this data. He distributes sticky notes for the number of pets each child says that he or she has at home and asks them to write the pets' names and types of animal on their notes. Finally, he asks children to come to the front of the class and place their notes on a chart that has been divided into sections by types of pets that those in the class possess. The main purpose of this activity is to:

A. find out about the types of pets the class possesses.

B. connect the pet data to a graphical representation.

C. connect students' personal data to the classroom.

D. have students move around in mathematics class at a certain point, as is developmentally appropriate at grade level.

ANSWERS FOR PRACTICE QUESTIONS ON CONTENT AND TEACHING STRATEGIES

Answer 1: This problem emphasizes the importance of estimation skills in building number sense for young children. It is increasingly important for teachers to help children "feel" the passing of time periods because successful students, throughout their schooling, are able to gauge the passing of a certain amount of time to a particular task. For example, when a teacher says, "You have 10 minutes left to finish your work," successful students are able to estimate this and vary their work to fit the time allotment. The correct answer is *C.*

Answer 2: Students need practice using mathematical vocabulary to describe data. Explaining to others helps fix a concept in one's own mind. The correct answer is *B.*

Answer 3: One can work this problem by "trying out" or "plugging in" each of the answers but a much better approach is that of using inverse operations (by dividing 2,450 by 35). The correct answer is *B.*

Answer 4: Place value is the most difficult concept for elementary students. Activities are needed to help students understand it better. The correct answer is *C.*

Answer 5: The relationship is 5 numbers more for each set of numbers. Therefore, 18 is 5 more than 13. The correct answer is *D*.

Answer 6: Connecting mathematics in the classroom to the real world allows students to concretely see that mathematics is a part of the everyday world—a strong rationale for learning geometry. The correct answer is *B*.

Answer 7: A clock represents a circle; $\frac{1}{4}$ of a turn is 15 minutes and is a 90 degree angle; $\frac{1}{2}$ of a turn is 30 minutes and is a 180 angle; $\frac{3}{4}$ of a turn is 45 minutes and is a 270 degree angle, and one turn is a full hour (60 minutes) or a 360 degree angle. Because 269 degrees is almost 270, the answer is $\frac{3}{4}$ of a turn. The correct answer is *C*.

Answer 8: Paper plates are appropriate because of their circular shape. The correct answer is *C*.

Answer 9: The only letter that could not be folded over to create a perfect mirror image (or line of symmetry) is L. The correct answer is *D*.

Answer 10: Students solidify their knowledge through peer discussions. The correct answer is *B*.

Answer 11: A = zero, so this cannot be the answer. B = 0.5, or $\frac{1}{2}$, so this is not correct. The correct equivalent of $\frac{2}{3}$ is $\frac{4}{6}$, and one can also see that $\frac{4}{6}$ is placed about two thirds down the number line. The correct answer is *C*.

Answer 12: The scales are an authentic means to demonstrate equality and inequality. The correct answer is *C*.

Answer 13: We must remember that 1 pound equals 16 ounces. Then we can simply multiply 12 × 16 for an answer of 192. The correct answer is *B*.

Answer 14: Through appropriate questioning, students will develop to the next van Hiele level. The van Hiele Model, developed by Pierre van Hiele and Dina van Hiele-Geldof, is a five-level hierarchy of ways to understand geometric thought. The levels are sequential, and appropriate questioning can help students to move to the next level of geometric understanding. The correct answer is *B*.

Answer 15: *Magnitude of numbers* is a number sense attribute that students must develop. One component of having number sense is understanding the relative magnitude of answers. Students need practice in determining the reasonableness of an answer, so students can ask themselves, "Is my answer 'in the ball park,' 'too big,' or 'too small'?" Activities such as these can help build number sense. The correct answer is *D*.

Answer 16: Probability exercises help students decide how "probable" an event is—or how likely it is to occur. Because there are 19 pieces of candy and 9 are yellow, students should realize that the ratio $\frac{9}{19}$ describes the number of yellow pieces of candy in the bag. The child has 9 chances out of 19 of picking a yellow piece. The correct answer is *A*.

Answer 17: *Spatial sense* is an intuition about shapes and the relationship of shapes. Spatial sense can be developed by appropriate activities that help students experience these relationships. The correct answer is *A*.

Answer 18: Understanding that the commutative law applies to both addition and multiplication helps students develop an ease with computation; that is, they can see the relationship between numbers. The correct answer is *A*.

Answer 19: Using manipulatives to develop a conceptual understanding of division enables students to seek logical solutions to problems. The fact that we cannot physically show how to divide 10 objects into 0 piles means that this problem cannot be solved mathematically either. The correct answer is *C*.

Answer 20: Students need many experiences in transferring images. These experiences help students develop their abilities to accurately represent what they see to images they can replicate. The correct answer is *C*.

Answer 21: Mathematics must be connected to the real-world experiences of students. These connections help students to make sense of their world by connecting the vocabulary of math to actual data. The correct answer is *C*.

GLOSSARY

Absolute value. The absolute value of a real number is equal to the numeric value of the number without regard to its sign (e.g., [−3] = 3). Absolute value is often thought of as the distance a number is from zero on the number line.

Acute angle. An angle that measures greater than 0 degrees and less than 90 degrees. ∠

Acute triangle. A triangle that contains acute angles (< 0 and > 90 degrees).

Addition. The mathematical process of combining. It is signified by the plus sign (+).

Addend. A number that is added. In 5 + 8 = 13, the addends are 5 and 8.

Adjacent angles. Two angles with a common vertex, a common ray, and no common interior points. ⊥

Algebra. A branch of mathematics in which arithmetic relations are explored using letter symbols to represent numbers.

Algorithm. A step-by-step procedure or formula for solving a problem.

Angle. Two rays with the same endpoint. The endpoint is called the vertex of the angle.

Arc. Part of the circumference of a circle.

Area. The number of square units needed to cover a surface.

Array. A systematic arrangement of objects, generally in rows and columns.

Associative property of addition. The sum is always the same, even when the addends are grouped differently $(2 + 3) + 4 = 2 + (3 + 4)$.

Associative property of multiplication. The product is always the same when the factors are grouped differently $(2 \times 3) \times 4 = 2 \times (3 \times 4)$.

Average. A number obtained by dividing the sum of two or more addends by the number of addends $(2 + 4 + 6 = 12 \div 3 = 4)$.

Bar graph. A graph using vertical or horizontal bars to display numeric information.

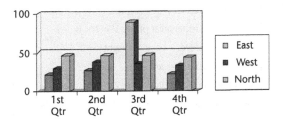

Basic fact. A basic operation performed on two numbers of value 12 or less, such as $7 + 1 = 8$, $15 - 8 = 7, 9 \times 2 = 18, 8 \div 4 = 2, 12 \times 11 = 132$

Bisect. To divide into two congruent parts.

Capacity. The volume of a figure, given in terms of liquid measure.

Circle. A plane figure with all of its points the same distance from a given point called the *center.*

Circle graph. A round graph that uses different-size wedges to show how portions of a set of data compare with the whole set.

Circumference. The distance around a circle (C). $C = \pi d$ or $C = 2\pi r$ where d = diameter and r = radius.

Common denominator. A common multiple of two or more denominators. For $\frac{1}{6}$ and $\frac{5}{8}$, it is 24.

Common factor. A number that is a factor of two or more numbers. A common factor of 9 and 6 is 3.

Common multiple. A number that is a multiple of two or more numbers. A common multiple of 2 and 3 is 6.

Commutative property of addition. Two numbers can be added in either order. The sums are the same $(2 + 3 = 3 + 2)$.

Commutative property of multiplication. Two numbers can be multiplied in either order. The products are the same $(2 \times 4 = 8; 4 \times 2 = 8)$.

Comparison. The process of determining the relative size or quantity of objects of numbers.

Complementary angles. Two angles whose measures add up to 90 degrees.

Composite number. A whole number greater than 1 that is not prime (e.g., 4, 6, 9, 10, 12, . . .).

Compound events. A compound event describes the probability resulting from two or more simple events. When one event has no impact on the other, we say that they are *independent events.* If the outcome of an event has an impact on the outcome of another event, these are *dependent events.*

Cone. A solid with a circular base and one vertex.

Congruent. Having exactly the same size and the same shape, as in a congruent figure.

Congruent angles. Two angles that have the same measure.

Conjecture. A well-thought out guess, prediction, or estimate.

Coordinate system. A graph with a horizontal number line (*x*-axis) and a vertical number line (*y*-axis) that are perpendicular to each other. The point of intersection is called the *origin* and labeled 0 on the graph. An ordered pair (*x, y*) is used to name a point on a coordinate system.

Counting. 1, 2, 3, 4 (naming sequence of numbers).

Cube. A rectangular solid with six congruent square faces.

Cylinder. A solid with two bases that are congruent circles.

Decimal. A number that uses place value and a decimal point to show tenths, hundredths, thousandths, and so on.

Denominator. The bottom number of a fraction, telling in how many parts the whole is divided. In $\frac{1}{3}$, the 3 is the denominator.

Dependent events. Events such that the outcome of the first event affects the outcome of the second event.

Diagonal. In a polygon, a segment that connects one vertex to another vertex but is not a side of the polygon. ◻

Diameter. In a circle, a segment that passes through the center and has its endpoints on the circle. ◯

Difference. The answer for subtraction. In $16 - 9 = 7$, 7 is the difference.

Distributive property of multiplication over addition. The product of a number and the sum of two numbers equals the sum of the two products $[3 \times (4 + 2) = (3 \times 4) + (3 \times 2)]$.

Dividend. A number that is divided by another number. For example, in $36 \div 4 = 9$, 36 is the dividend.

Divisible. When one number is divided by another and the remainder is 0, the first number is said to be divisible by the second number. For example, in the problem $12 \div 3 = 4$, 12 is said to be divisible by 3.

Division. The inverse operation to multiplication. Division ($\div$) is often described as the "goes into" operation, as in, "How many times does 6 go into 18?" ($18 \div 6 = ?$).

Divisor. A number that divides another number. In the example $36 \div 4 = 9$, the 4 is the divisor.

Endpoint. The point at the end of a line segment.

Equally likely outcomes. Outcomes that have the same chance of occurring in a probability experiment; for example, flipping a coin is equally likely to result in heads or tails.

Equilateral triangle. A triangle with three congruent or equal sides and three angles of 60° each.

Equivalent fractions. Fractions that name the same fraction ($\frac{1}{2} = \frac{2}{4} = \frac{4}{8}$).

Even number. A whole number that is a multiple of 2.

Event. The particular outcome one is looking at in a probability experiment.

Expanded form. Expressing a number as factors $[325 = (3 \times 100) + (2 \times 10) + (5 \times 1)]$.

Exponent. A number that tells how many times the base is to be used as a factor or to be multiplied by itself. In 2^3, 2 is the base and 3 is the exponent, meaning $2 \times 2 \times 2$.

Face. A flat surface of a solid figure.

Fact families. The related number sentences for addition and subtraction or multiplication and division that contain all the same numbers (e.g., $2 + 3 = 5$; $3 + 2 = 5$; $5 - 3 = 2$; and $5 - 2 = 3$).

Factor. A number to be multiplied or a number that divides evenly into a given second number is a factor of that number. In $2 \times 3 = 6$, 2 and 3 are factors of 6.

Factor tree. A diagram showing how a composite number breaks down into its prime factors.

Factorization. Writing a whole number as a product of factors. The factorization of 12 is $2 \times 2 \times 3 = 12$.

Frequency. The number of times a score appears in a list of data.

Formulas. The following formulas should be committed to memory:

Perimeter of a square: $P = 4 \times s$
Area of a square: $A = s \times s$
Perimeter of a rectangle: $P = (2 \times l) + (2 \times w)$
Area of a rectangle: $A = l \times w$
Volume of a cube: $V = s \times s \times s$
Volume of a rectangular prism: $V = l \times w \times h$
Area of a triangle: ½ base $\times$ height
Area of a circle: $A = \pi r^2$
Circumference of a circle: $C = 2\pi r$ or $C = \pi D$
Area of a trapezoid: ½ $\times$ height $\times$ (base1 + base 2)

Function. Functions may be thought of as actions that transform one number into another. For example, the process of taking a number and adding 3 to it is a simple function. This particular example could be written as $F(x) = x + 3$. In order to be classified as a function, there must exist only a single result for each operation of the function; if there is more than one result from the action (such as "Take a number and add what you get when you roll dice to it"), the result can be a workable procedure but not a function, as many different outcomes are possible.

Geoboard. A manipulative used to explore basic concepts from geometry, such as area, perimeter, and simple intuitive proofs.

Greatest common factor (GCF). The greatest whole number that divides two whole numbers. (The GCF of 24 and 32 is 4 evenly.)

Height of a triangle. The perpendicular distance from a vertex to the opposite side or base.

Hexagon. A polygon with six sides.

Histogram. A graph showing the results of tabulating the number of items found in defined categories and shown using vertical bars; often referred to as a *bar chart.*

Independent events. If two events *A* and *B* are independent, then the probability that both will happen is *P(A)* × *P(B).*

Integers. The whole numbers and their negatives (e.g., −2, −1, 0, 1, 2).

Inverse operations. Operations that undo each other. Addition and subtraction are inverse operations, as are multiplication and division.

Isosceles triangle. A triangle with two congruent (equal) sides.

Iteration. A computational process in which a cycle of actions or operations is repeated, generally to get closer to a final answer.

Least common denominator (LCD). The least common multiple (LCM) of two denominators (30 is the LCM of $\frac{1}{6}$ and $\frac{1}{15}$).

Least common multiple (LCM). The smallest number that is a common multiple of two given numbers; determined by finding a prime number that can go evenly into each and continuing until no other prime numbers divide into both. (The LCMs of 12 and 16 are 3 and 4.)

Line. A straight path that extends forever in both directions.

Line graph. A graph in which a line shows changes in data, often over time.

Line of symmetry. A fold line of a figure that makes the two parts of the figure match exactly.

Line segment. Part of a line with two endpoints.

Mass. The amount of matter that something contains.

Mean. The average of a set of numbers; the sum of the numbers divided by how many numbers there are; 2 + 5 + 5 = 12, then 12 ÷ 3 = an average/mean of 4.

Median. The middle number of a set of numbers after they have been placed in numerical order. In the set [2, 3, 4], 3 is the median. If there are an even number of numbers, the median is the average of the two middle numbers.

Minuend. The number from which another number is subtracted (e.g., 14 − 8 = 6, 14 is the minuend).

Mode. The number that occurs the most frequently in a set of data. In the set [2, 4, 4, 3, 5], 4 is the mode.

Multiple. A multiple of a number is the product of that number and a whole number. Some multiples of 2 are 4, 6, and 8.

Multiplicand/multiplier. A number that is multiplied by another number. In 7 × 4 = 28, the multiplicand is 7; the multiplier is 4.

Multiplication. For whole numbers, multiplication is often defined in terms of repeated addition, or "jumps" on the number line. For other types of numbers, (such as fractions and decimals) area models are more useful to illustrate multiplication concepts.

Numerator. The top number in a fraction that tells how many parts of the whole are being named. In $\frac{3}{4}$, the 3 is the numerator.

Obtuse angle. An angle that measures greater than 90 degrees and less than 180 degrees.

Obtuse triangle. A triangle that contains an obtuse angle.

Octagon. A polygon with eight sides.

Odd number. A whole number that is not a multiple of 2.

Order of operations. When there is more than one operation and parentheses are used, first do what is inside the parentheses, then the exponents. Next, multiply or divide from left to right. Then add or subtract from left to right (PEMDAS, or Please Excuse My Dear Aunt Sally).

Ordered pair. A number pair, such as (2, 3), in which the 2 (*x*-axis) is the first number and the 3 (*y*-axis) is the second number.

Outcome. Any possible result in a probability experiment.

Parallel lines. Lines in the same plane that do not intersect.

Parallelogram. A quadrilateral (any four-sided polygon) with opposite sides parallel and congruent.

Pentagon. A five-sided polygon.

Perimeter. The sum of the lengths of the sides of a polygon ($P = 2l \times 2w$ where *l* = length and *w* = width).

Perpendicular lines. Lines that intersect at right angles.

Pi. (π) The number obtained by dividing the circumference of any circle by its diameter. Two common approximations for π are $\frac{22}{7}$ or 3.14.

Pictograph. A visual representation used to make comparisons. A key always appears at the bottom of a pictograph or picture graph showing how many each object represents.

Group 1 ☺ ☺

Group 2 ☺ ☺ ☺

☺ = 5 people

Plane. A flat surface that extends indefinitely in both directions.

Plane figures. Two-dimensional figures with flat surfaces, such as squares, rectangles, hexagons, triangles, pentagons, and quadrilaterals.

Point. A location in space.

Polygon. A simple closed figure (square, triangle, hexagon, etc.).

Polyhedron. A geometric figure solid with flat faces and straight edges.

Power (of a number). A number found by multiplying the number by itself one or more times.

Prime factor. A factor that is a prime number. The prime factors of 15 are 3 and 5.

Prime factorization. A composite number expressed as a product of prime numbers ($24 = 2 \times 2 \times 2 \times 3$, or $2^3 \times 3$).

Prime number. A whole number greater than 1 that can be evenly divided only by 1 and itself.

Probability. The chance that an event will occur.

Product. The answer in a multiplication problem (in $36 = 4 \times 9$; 36 is the product).

Proof. A process by which logical steps based on valid mathematical actions and operations are used to establish new truths and understandings from other understandings that have previously been proved or accepted as true.

Proportion. An equality of ratios ($\frac{1}{2} = \frac{4}{8}$).

Pyramid. A solid figure made by connecting the vertices of a polygonal base and a single point not in the same plane as the base. Unless otherwise specified the base is assumed to be a square.

Pythagorean Theorem. In any *right* triangle, the area of the square whose side is the hypotenuse (the longest side and opposite from the right angle) is equal to the sum of the areas of the squares whose sides are the two legs (the sides that meet at the right angle). Where c is the length of the hypotenuse and a and b are the lengths of the two sides, this may be expressed as $a^2 + b^2 = c^2$.

Pythagorean Triple. A set of numbers that satisfy the Pythagorean Theorem, $a^2 + b^2 = c^2$. For example, because $3^2 + 4^2 = 5^2$, the numbers 3, 4, and 5 are a Pythagorean Triple.

Quadrilateral. A four-sided polygon with four sides and four vertices. Common examples include squares, rectangles, and trapezoids.

Quotient. The answer in a division problem. In $10 \div 2 = 5$, 5 is the quotient.

Radius. In a circle, it is a line segment that connects the center of the circle with a point on the circle; it is equal to $\frac{1}{2}$ the length of a diameter. ◯

Random. When a selection is made without looking (i.e., picking an item at random), as in probability problems.

Range. The difference between the highest and lowest values in a data set.

Ratio. A comparison of two or more values ($\frac{1}{2}$, $\frac{4}{6}$; or 1:2, 4:6); or (1 is to 2; 4 is to 6).

Rational counting. The ability to order and enumerate objects in sets.

Rational number. Any number that can be expressed as a fraction $\frac{a}{b}$, where a and b are integers and $b \neq 0$, such as 3, $\frac{3}{1}$, $\frac{1}{4}$, 0.34, and 56 percent.

Ray. Part of a line that has one endpoint and goes on and on in one direction. ⟶

Reciprocals. Two numbers whose product is 1, such as $\frac{2}{3} \times \frac{3}{2} = 1$.

Rectangle. A parallelogram with four right angles.

Recursion. A process in which objects (including numbers) are defined in terms of other objects of the same type. A recursive relation is then used to build up large numbers of objects from a relatively small set of initial values and rules.

Reflection. The mirror images of a figure that has been "flipped" over a line; this process indicates if a figures has symmetry.

Remainder. The amount left over after a division problem. In $\frac{18}{4} = 4$ r2, the remainder is 2.

Rhombus. A parallelogram with four congruent sides.

Right angle. An angle that measures 90 degrees. └

Right triangle. A triangle that contains a right angle (90 degrees). ◺

Rotation. The image of a figure that has been turned, as if on a wheel.

Rote counting. The naming of numbers in order without making any connection between numbers and sets of real-life objects.

Rounding. Expressing a number to the nearest thousandth, hundredth, tenth, one, ten, hundred, thousand, and so on as directed.

Scalene triangle. A triangle with no congruent sides.

Scaling. A transformation that enlarges or diminishes objects.

Scatterplot. A graph showing paired data values.

Segment. Part of a line including two endpoints.

Set. A well-defined collection of objects or numbers.

Similar figures. Figures with the same shape but not necessarily the same size.

Slide. See *translation.*

Solid figures. Three-dimensional figures such as cones, spheres, cylinders, cubes, prisms, and pyramids.

Sphere. A round, solid figure with all points an equal distance from the center (e.g., baseball, Earth).

Square. A rectangle with four congruent sides.

Square/square root. A square number is a product of a number that is multiplied by itself (e.g., $3 \times 3 = 9$ [where 9 is the square] or $5 \times 5 = 25$ [where 25 is the square]. The square root is the multiplicand (3 in the case of 9, and 5 in the case of 25).

Statistics. A branch of mathematics that deals with the organization, description, and analysis of data.

Subitizing. The inborn ability to visually distinguish between groups of 0, 1, 2, and 3 objects.

Subtraction. The inverse of addition (i.e., subtraction undoes the act of addition). This means that if we start with any number and add and then subtract the same number, we get the number we started with. Often called the *take away* operation.

Subtrahend. The number to be subtracted from another number. In $15 - 8 = 7$, the 8 is the subtrahend.

Sum. The answer in an addition problem. In $5 + 3 = 8$, the 8 is the sum.

Surface area. The sum of the areas of all the surfaces of a space figure.

Symmetry. A figure has line symmetry if it can be folded on a line so that the two halves of the figure are congruent (the same). The fold line is called the *line of symmetry.*

Tessellation. Sometimes referred to as a *tiling of the plane.* A tessellation is a collection of plane figures that fills the plane with no overlaps or gaps. Tiles on a kitchen floor can be thought of as a simple form of tessellation. Escher's art is often used to illustrate more advanced tessellations.

Translation. The image of a figure that has been "slid" to a new position without flipping or turning.

Trapezoid. A quadrilateral with one pair of parallel sides. These sides are called the *upper* and *lower bases.*

Triangle. A polygon with three sides.

Unit price. The ratio of the total cost to the number of units.

Variable. A symbol, usually a letter, that stands for an unknown quantity. In $6 \times y = 36$, y is the variable.

Venn diagram. A diagram that uses regions to show relationships between sets of things.

Vertex. The common endpoint of two rays that form an angle, or the point of intersection of two sides of a polygon or polyhedron.

Volume. The number of cubic units needed to fill a solid figure.

Weight. A measure of the force that gravity exerts on a body.

Whole number. Any one of the numbers 0, 1, 2, 3, ... Because of infinity, there is no "largest" whole number. The smallest whole number is zero.

Zero property for addition and subtraction. For any number n, $n + 0 = n$ and $n - 0 = n$. Zero is the additive identity for addition.

Zero property for multiplication. For any number n, $n \times 0 = 0$.

REFERENCES

Ball, D. L. (1993). With an eye on the mathematical horizon: Dilemmas of teaching elementary school mathematics. *Elementary School Journal, 93*(4), 373–397.

Connell, M. L. (2009). Teaching mathematics. In L. A. Saha & A. G. Dworkin (Eds.), *The new international handbook of teachers and teaching* (pp. 947–954). New York: Springer.

Davis, R. B., Maher, C. A., & Noddings, N. (1990). Suggestions for the improvement of mathematics education. In R. B. Davis, C. A. Maher, & N. Noddings (Eds.), *Constructivist views on the teaching and learning of mathematics.* [Monograph Number 4]. *Journal for Research in Mathematics Education,* 187–191. Reston, VA: NCTM.

Lave, J. (1991). Situated learning in communities of practice. In L. B. Resnick, J. M. Levine, & S. D. Teasley (Eds.), *Perspectives on socially shared cognition* (pp. 63–82). Washington, DC: American Psychological Association.

National Council of Teachers of Mathematics. (1989). *Curriculum and evaluation standards for school mathematics.* Reston, VA: Author.

National Council of Teachers of Mathematics. (1991). *Professional standards for teaching school mathematics.* Reston, VA: Author.

National Council of Teachers of Mathematics. (1995). *Assessment standards for school mathematics.* Reston, VA: Author.

National Council of Teachers of Mathematics. (1998). *Principles and standards for school mathematics: Discussion draft. Standards 2000.* Reston, VA: Author.

National Council of Teachers of Mathematics. (2000). *Principles and standards for school mathematics.* Reston, VA: Author.

National Research Council. (1989). *Everybody counts.* Washington, DC: National Academy Press.

Noddings, N. (1990). Constructivism in mathematics education. In B. Davis, C. Maher, & N. Noddings (Eds.), *Constructivist views on the teaching and learning of mathematics.* [Monograph Number 4]. *Journal of Research in Mathematics Education,* 7–18.

Shulman, L. (1986). Paradigms and research programs in the study of teaching. A contemporary perspective. In M. Wittrock (Ed.), *Handbook of research on teaching* (3rd ed.) (pp. 3–36). New York: Macmillan.

Troutman, A. P., & Lichtenberg, B. K. (1999). *Mathematics, a good beginning.* New York: Brooks/Cole Publishing Company.

Van de Walle, J. (1998). *Elementary and middle school mathematics: Teaching developmentally* (3rd ed.). New York: Longman.

Van de Walle, J. (2010). *Elementary and middle school mathematics: Teaching developmentally* (7th ed.). New York: Allyn & Bacon.

Van de Walle, J. (2009). *Texas edition of elementary and middle school mathematics, teaching developmentally* (7th ed.). New York: Allyn & Bacon.

RESOURCES

Artzt, A. F., & Newman, C. M. (1990). *How to use cooperative learning in the mathematics classroom.* Reston, VA: NCTM.

Baroody, A. J. (1993). *Problem solving, reasoning, and communicating (K–8): Helping children think mathematically.* Columbus, OH: Merrill.

Burns, M. (1985, February). The role of questioning. *The Arithmetic Teacher,* 14–16.

Burns, M. (1992). *About teaching mathematics: A K–8 resource.* White Plains, NY: Cuisenaire.

Carpenter, T. P., Carey, D. A., & Kouba, V. L. (1990). A problem-solving approach to the operations. In J. N. Payne (Ed.), *Mathematics for the young child* (pp. 111–113). Reston, VA: NCTM.

Eisenhower National Clearinghouse for Math and Science Education (http://www.enc.org).

This Web site offers mathematics and science Internet links for teachers, stories, and ideas about mathematics and science teachers.

Fennema, E. (1973, May). Manipulatives in the classroom. *The Arithmetic Teacher, 20,* 350–352.

Hope, J. (1989). Promoting number sense in school. *The Arithmetic Teacher, 39*(6), 12–16.

Kamii, C., & Lewis, B.A. (1990, September). Research into practice: Constructivist learning and teaching. *The Arithmetic Teacher, 38*(1), 34–35.

Math Forum (http://www.forum.swarthmore.edu). This Web site includes classroom materials, online mathematics activities, software, articles, and more.

Mathematics Lessons Database (http://www.mste.uiuc.edu/mathed/queryform.html). These lessons in mathematics and programs are related to teaching mathematics.

National Council of Teachers of Mathematics (http://www.nctm.org). This is the national organization responsible for the creation and publication of the mathematics standards.

Stenmark, J. K. (Ed.). (1991). *Mathematics assessment: Myths, models, good questions, and practical suggestions.* Reston, VA: Author.

Texas Education Agency. (1998). *TAAS Mathematics objectives and measurement specifications and the mathematics update 1998–1999: A guide to TAAS and the Texas Essential Knowledge and Skills (TEKS).* Austin, TX: Author.

Thornton, C. A. (1990). Strategies for the basic facts. In J. N. Payne (Ed.), *Mathematics for the young child* (pp. 133–151). Reston, VA: NCTM.

Teachers are also encouraged to seek additional resources for review at the following Web sites:

http://www.tea.state.tx.us/student.assessment/resources/release/index.html. Teachers may review and test on mathematical content by taking released TAAS tests online. Any of the grade-level tests are good reviews.

http://www.tea.state.tx.us/student.assessment/taks/index.html. This Web site highlights state assessment (currently the TAKS).

http://www.tea.state.tx.us/teks/teksfaq/ch111.html This Web site highlights the student TEKS.

A MATHEMATICS LESSON PLAN

Building Fraction Concepts

Grade Level: Fourth

Main Subject Area: Mathematics

Integrated Subjects: Social Studies, Art, and Reading

Time Frame Constraints: 3–4 days

Overall Goal(s): To enable students to identify fractions and what they mean, to name parts of fractions, to determine the magnitude of fractions, and to recognize equivalent forms of the same fraction.

TEKS OBJECTIVES:

§ 111.16. **Mathematics**: (013) (4.2) Number, operation, and quantitative reasoning. The student describes and compares fractional parts of whole objects or sets of objects.

§ The student is expected to:

A. use concrete objects and pictorial models to generate equivalent fractions;

B. model fraction quantities greater than one using concrete objects and pictorial models;

C. compare and order fractions using concrete objects and pictorial models; and

D. relate decimals to fractions that name tenths and hundredths using concrete objects and pictorial models.

§ 113.6. **Social Studies**, Grade 4; (11) Economics. The student understands the reasons for exploration and colonization. The student is expected to: (A) identify the economic motivations for European exploration and settlement in Texas and the Western Hemisphere.

§ 117.14. **Art** (b) **Knowledge and skills;** (4.2) Creative expression/performance. The student expresses ideas through original artworks, using a variety of media with appropriate skill. The student is expected to (B) design original artworks.

§ 110.6. **English Language Arts and Reading**; (b) Knowledge and skills; (15) Writing/purposes. The student writes for a variety of audiences and purposes, and in a variety of forms. The student is expected to: (A) write to express, discover, record, develop, reflect on ideas, and to problem solve.

LESSON OBJECTIVES:

- Students will draw their favorite types of pizzas on a piece of paper and divide it into fair shares.

- Students will observe the concept of "fair shares" and discuss various "fair share" situations.

- Students will, in groups, decide on their best definitions of division.

- Students will orally and on paper use "special names" that tell us how many parts make a whole (e.g., thirds, three parts, etc.).

- Students will recognize that the more parts that are needed to make a whole, the smaller the parts (by constructing and using fraction strips).

- Students will recognize that the **numerator** tells how many parts are being considered, and the denominator tells us how many parts are in a whole by drawing and labeling models.

- Students will recognize that equivalent fractions are another way of naming the same amount by constructing and manipulating fraction strips and manipulating two-colored counters.

- Students will draw a "newly invented" candy bar, design a wrapper for it and show division into ten "fair shares," with each labeled with its fractional name.

Sponge Activity: Students will draw their own pizza with all the ingredients they like.

Focus or Set Induction: The teacher will have a huge chocolate bar that is divided into squares. She will tell children that after the lesson they may have a piece, but that she wants to divide it now. She shows that she is giving one group about $\frac{1}{4}$; and another group $\frac{3}{4}$. If students do not start saying "That's not fair," then she should ask the class if it is fair. Then she will tell students that they will be talking about "fair shares" today. She will then ask them to draw a line on the pizza that they just drew in the sponge activity to show what would be a "fair share" of their pizza if there were two other friends coming for lunch (three altogether). Students should draw thirds.

ENVIRONMENTAL CONCERNS:

Students need to be seated in small groups (three to four) at a table. Materials and supplies should be in the center of the table (paper, markers, fraction strips, two-colored counters).

Materials: Drawing paper, three large chocolate bars (or more, depending on class size), three or more same size bananas and oranges, knife, writing paper, overhead projector, blocks, markers, index cards with hole punched in top left-hand corner.

Rationale: Dividing wholes into fractions is a part of almost everyone's daily lives. If you cook, you must use fractions ($\frac{1}{2}$ cup, $\frac{1}{2}$ t), if you split costs with friends ("Let's buy one bucket of popcorn and split it 3 ways"), if there is a good price on something on sale (a $\frac{1}{3}$ off sale), and so forth. Using rational numbers and fractions also helps in problems with scaling, proportionality, and related rates later.

MAKING CONNECTIONS:

1. **Connections to Prior Knowledge** (using a literacy strategy): Ask students what they already know about division. What is division about? Ask groups to come up with their best definitions of *division*. Share each group's definition with the class and connect division to fractions. Relate that fractions are a division into equal parts.

2. **Cultural Connections:** Do you think that people around the world use fractions? If so, what are some ways (division of food, division of labor, etc.)? Teacher will also talk about how in most of Europe, up until the 1800s, a family's land was always passed on to the oldest son. Was that a fair share for the rest of the children in family? However, what would happen if there were 10 children and each got a fair share (families were big then), then each of those children had 10 children, and they each had 10? What would eventually happen to the land? How much land would a child eventually get? Many families wanted to try to keep their land in one piece. That's why the oldest son received the land, but the fact that people could not have a fair share of land influenced much of the immigration to the New World and to Texas (in the 1800s).

3. **Connections to the Community:** Ask students when they see their community using fair shares. Is the street divided into equal lanes? When you order at a restaurant, do you get equal portions as the other diners for whatever you order? Wouldn't it be terrible if you went to McDonald's, and they gave your friend a whole burger and you only half for the same price (or you got 5 fries and they got 15)?

4. **Connections to Student Interests and Experiences:** See focus. Talk about other things we can divide to make fair shares with our friends or family.

Activities: Guided Practice.

I. **Area Model:** Teacher will draw a rectangle on the overhead and explain that this rectangle represents a "whole." Using this whole, the teacher will draw a vertical line halfway through the rectangle. Class will discuss how many parts there are to the rectangle (two) and that the two parts are each fair shares (the same size). Using the rectangle as a reference, students will say the names of the parts: $\frac{1}{2}$, $\frac{1}{2}$, and the whole is $\frac{2}{2}$. Students will label each part ($\frac{1}{2}$, $\frac{1}{2}$). The teacher will ask children, "What do you think the bottom number is telling us?" and "What is the top number telling us?"

Teacher tells students that there is an easy way to remember how a fraction is written. She shows a banana cut in fourths and asks students to tell how many pieces are there (four). Then she tells children to write that number down (how many pieces make the whole) and put a line over it. Then, she lifts one piece up over the remaining three pieces and asks children to tell how many pieces are on top (1). Now she puts a one over the four. She tells students that to identify fractions, we first count all the pieces that would make a whole or fair shares, and that is called the *denominator*. Then, we put down a line. Next, we count the parts that have been raised up out of the whole (over the line), and that is the *numerator*.

The teacher will draw another rectangle, similar in size to the first rectangle and ask for a volunteer to draw vertical lines so that there are three fair shares. The class will discuss how many parts there are (three) and that each part is the same size. Students will also say names of the parts, using the area model as a reference; $\frac{1}{3}$, $\frac{2}{3}$, and the whole is $\frac{3}{3}$. The students will work in their groups and draw models for fourths, fifths, and sixths. Groups will share their area models with the class and explain why their models demonstrate the fractions and will say the names of their fractions. To discuss fractions larger than one, the teacher will show two models of the same fraction: for example, $\frac{1}{2}$, and students will discuss how many fair shares there are (four) and how to say the parts: $\frac{1}{2}$, $\frac{2}{2}$, $\frac{3}{2}$, $\frac{4}{2}$.

II. **Length Model:** Using the fraction strips, have each student make halves, thirds, fourths, fifths, and sixths—use a different color paper for each fraction. As students finish making halves, ask them to write the fraction $\frac{1}{2}$ on each part of the fraction strip. Then, as a class, say the fraction names $\frac{1}{2}$, $\frac{2}{2}$. Do the same process for thirds, fourths, fifths, and sixths. Each student will have a set of fraction strips.

Literacy Connection: Ask the student to write comments about making the fraction strips. Ask them to write everything they can tell you about these fraction strips.

III. **Ordering Fractions:** Using their fraction strips, students, in groups, will take a piece of each different colored fraction strip (will be one from $\frac{1}{2}$, $\frac{1}{3}$, $\frac{1}{4}$, etc.), and they will be able to place, in order of increasing magnitude, the fractions $\frac{1}{6}$, $\frac{1}{5}$, $\frac{1}{4}$, $\frac{1}{3}$, and $\frac{1}{2}$. Students will then discuss $\frac{2}{3}$ and $\frac{2}{4}$, and so on. In their groups, they will discuss the magnitude of fractions and why when the bottom number gets bigger, the piece gets smaller.

IV. **Set Model:** Using two-colored counters, ask students to show $\frac{1}{2}$, $\frac{2}{4}$, $\frac{3}{6}$, and so on (have students line them up so they can see equivalency). Discuss why if fractions can physically be grouped into smaller sets, the fractions can be simplified ($\frac{2}{4} = \frac{1}{2}$, $\frac{3}{6} = \frac{1}{2}$). If not, the fractions are said to be *relatively prime*.

Literacy Connection: Ask students to write a self-assessment about simplifying fractions. Students will write about what they learned with the chocolate bar. They will discuss what would happen if they divided the chocolate bar into four fair shares. If they gave a friend two fair shares and the student kept $\frac{1}{2}$ of the chocolate bar, would they each have the same amount? Why or why not? Explain.

Independent Practice: Students will draw two pictures on one sheet of art paper. Students will "invent" a rectangular candy bar and design the wrapper for it. They will draw the bar itself and show how their new candy bar will be divided into 10 fair shares (show their rectangle divided into 10 equal areas). They also will mark each piece with the fractional name ($\frac{1}{10}$) and label each portion. Then they will discuss how many portions equal a whole and why.

What will children do if they finish early? Use a paper plate and demonstrate how to divide the area of the circle into three fair shares.

Assessment: Teachers will assess students on their new candy bar. Design elements of the wrapper are to be completed only. Correct use of fractional names and fair share elements must be correct.

Closure: Teacher will show a PowerPoint presentation of various things in real life where fractions are used (bicycle spokes design, road sign that says $\frac{1}{2}$ mile to something, road line dividing road lanes, window panes, house construction, etc.). Teacher will give each student a piece of the chocolate bar and ask what he or she received ("a fair share").

Modifications: (for a student with a learning disability in math) (spatial skills): Ask the student to divide the rectangles into only two fair shares.

Reflection: To be completed after teaching the lesson.

Developed by: Rena M. Shull, Ph.D., Assistant Professor, Rockhurst University; Debra Pellegrino, Ed.D., Associate Professor, Rockhurst University.

DRAFT YOUR OWN MATHEMATICS LESSON PLAN

Title of Lesson: _____

Grade Level: _____

Main Subject Area: _____

Integrated Subjects: _____

Time Frame/Constraints: _____

Overall Goal(s): _____

TEKS Objectives: _____

_____

_____

Lesson Objective(s): _____

_____

_____

Readiness Skills or Prior Knowledge Needed: _____

Sponge Activity: _____

_____

_____

Environmental Concerns: _____

_____

_____

Rationale(s): _____

_____

Focus or Set Induction: _____

_____

_____

Making Connections: _____

1. Connections to Past or Future Learning: _____

_____

2. Connections to the Community: _____

_____

3. Cultural Connections: _____

_____

4. Connections to Student Interests & Experiences: _____

_____

Materials: _____

_____

_____

Activities: Guided practice: _____
_____
_____
_____
_____
_____
_____
_____
_____
_____
_____

Independent practice: _____
_____
_____
_____
_____
_____
_____
_____
_____
_____
_____

Assessment: _____
_____
_____

What will students do who finish early? _____
_____
_____

Closure: _____
_____
_____

Modification for Students with Special Needs: _____
_____
_____

Reflection: _____
_____
_____

OBSERVING MATHEMATICS EXPERIENCES/ACTIVITIES

During your visit to an EC-6 classroom, use the following form to provide feedback, as well as to reflectively analyze the room, the materials, and the teaching.

The Classroom Environment	Observed	Not Observed	Response
1. The teacher elicits prior student knowledge about mathematics.			If so, describe; if not, tell how she or he could have done so.
2. An appropriate and motivating focus is used to begin the lesson.			If so, describe; if not, what could be used?
3. The lesson includes manipulatives.			If so, describe the "tools of inquiry"/manipulatives used. If not, describe what type of manipulatives may have been appropriate for this lesson.
4. Children are given time to manipulate ("play with") concrete items/manipulatives prior to settling into the learning task (if manipulatives are used).			If so, what was the effect? If not, what was the effect?
5. If manipulatives are used, for what percentage of the class do they seem effective?			If they were not effectively used, tell why you believe they were not and give ideas and proper time for effective use.
6. Children are allowed to use manipulatives during independent practice.			If so, about what percentage of the class continued to use them during this time? What was the result?
7. A Math Center is a part of the room.			If so, describe what types of tasks were in the center. Do they appear to be motivating? Why or why not? If not, tell what type of center and tasks might be effective.
8. Mathematics tasks are integrated into other centers in the room.			If so, describe; if not, tell what type of tasks could be included.
9. The learning environment is student centered for mathematics.			If so, describe; if not, how could this be accomplished?
10. The learning environment is motivating for mathematics.			If so, describe; if not, how could this be accomplished?
11. The mathematics lesson is logically presented.			If so, describe; if not, how could this be accomplished?
12. The mathematics lesson is interdisciplinary.			If so, describe; if not, what other content could be included?
13. Real-life problems are used in examples or in work.			If so, describe; if not, what examples could be included?
14. Student-to-student interaction is a part of the lesson.			If so, describe; if not, tell why it should be.

The Classroom Environment	Observed	Not Observed	Response
15. Teacher-led consensus is part of the lesson.			If so, describe; if not, tell why it should be.
16. The teacher addresses children who are in transitional stages according to Piaget.			If so, describe; if not, how could the teacher do this?
17. Many types of visuals are available in the class (charts, checklists, strategies, etc.).			If so, describe; if not, what are some additions that would be beneficial to help children in math?
18. The lesson is presented in a logical manner.			If so, describe; if not, what should be rearranged and why?
19. Math strategies were discussed by the teacher.			If so, describe; if not (and the lesson is appropriate), tell what and how strategies could be included.
20. Children are informally assessed.			If so, is it appropriate? If not, describe how it could be more effective. Were all children "checked for understanding"?
21. Children are formally assessed.			If so, is it appropriate? If not, describe how it could be more effective.
22. Children are authentically assessed.			If so, is this appropriate? If not, describe how it could be more appropriate.
23. The teacher is positive about mathematics.			If so, describe; if not, tell why it would be important.
24. The teacher involves all children in the lesson.			If not, who was left out? Why do you think this student(s) was left out?
25. An appropriate closure was made for this lesson.			If so, describe; if not, how could this have been accomplished?
26. You would have liked to have experienced this mathematics lesson as a child.			Tell why or why not.
27. This lesson is constructivist.			Tell why or why not.
28. You would have learned from this lesson.			Tell why or why not.
29. Modifications are made for some children.			If so, describe them and tell if they are effective. If not, what could be changed?

4 Preparing to Teach Social Studies in Texas

Trenia L. Walker
Texas Tech University

Janice L. Nath
University of Houston–Downtown

The National Council for the Social Studies (NCSS) established a task force on Standards that defines *social studies* as follows:

[T]he integrated study of the social sciences and humanities to promote civic competence. . . . The primary purpose of studies is to help young people develop the ability to make informed and reasoned decisions for the public good as citizens of a culturally diverse, democratic society in an interdependent world. (1994, p. 3)

This NCSS definition was adopted by the Texas Education Agency's (TEA) (1999) Social Studies Center (SSC) when creating its Texas Social Studies Framework. The aim of social studies, as noted above and according to both national and Texas state standards, is civic competence. Mike Moses, a former commissioner of education in Texas stated, "[W]e know that the goal of providing students with the knowledge and skills necessary to assume their roles as leaders in our state and nation in the 21st century rests primarily with the social studies" (TEA, 1999, unnumbered preface). In our classrooms and in the world beyond, we want people to learn to live and work together responsibly. Social studies instruction is critical—both for preparing students to become responsible, thoughtful, participating citizens and to provide students with many of the basic skills that involve geography, economics, and other areas (under the umbrella of social studies) that they need to function in our society today and in the future.

Often reading and mathematics programs are considered the basics in EC-6 education; however, a social studies program is also basic. The Texas Education Code (1995) §28.002 calls for each school district that offers kindergarten through grade 12 to include social studies as part of the required curriculum. This code also specifies that instruction in social studies consists of Texas, United States, and world history, as well as government and geography. Economics, one of the traditional subjects in the social studies, was originally included only as a part of the enrichment curriculum. In 2007, economics was added as a requirement for high school graduation in Texas. The Texas Administrative Code §74.2 goes on to specify that for elementary grades, "The district must ensure that sufficient time is provided for teachers to teach and for students to learn . . . social studies. . . ." (Texas Education Agency, 1996).

Although the state of Texas mandates the instruction of social studies in K–12 classrooms, teachers should truly appreciate the importance of the subject(s). As Parker (2005) points out:

> *Without historical understanding, there can be no wisdom. Without geographical understanding, there can be no social or environmental intelligence. And without civic understanding, there can be no democratic citizens and, therefore, no democracy. This is why social studies matters. (p. 4)*

Regardless of their future career paths, students are citizens of our country and the world. Hopefully, each will grow up to be a thoughtful citizen who will contribute in positive ways to society. Students must also navigate in their city and state and, perhaps, through much of their country and even the world through their understanding of geography. They must understand their personal and national economic situations; their rights and the rights of others; how other nations and beliefs affect this country; references to our history and that of others; how to resolve conflicts; and many other skills that social studies provide. For these reasons, it is vital that EC-6 teachers devote sufficient instructional time to social studies. A good social studies program integrates opportunities to develop students' skills in many other subjects, including reading, writing, mathematics, science, music, and so forth (Chapin, 2006).

Let's now look at the requirements for social studies knowledge and skills that an EC-6 teacher needs—both in order to pass the test and to teach his or her students well. Table 4.1 compares the teacher standards, the Texas Examinations of Educators Standards (TExES) test framework, and the SS Texas Essential Knowledge and Skills (TEKS) for children (currently under revision). Notice the overlap in what teachers should know and be able to do and what children should know and be able to do. If you become familiar with all of these areas, you will do well on the test and be a knowledgeable teacher for your students.

It is beyond the scope of this chapter to provide all the knowledge, skills, and other information necessary for EC-6 social studies. However, every

Table 4.1 A Comparison of Knowledge and Skills for Teachers and Students

Teacher Standards (What teachers should know and be able to apply)	The TExES Framework (What teacher test takers should know and be able to apply)	TEKS Strands (What EC-6 students should know and do)
Knowledge History Geography Economics Government	Social science instruction History Geography and culture Economics Government and citizenship	**Knowledge** History Geography Economics Government Culture
Values Citizenship Culture		**Values** Citizenship Science, technology, and society
Skills Research Intra- and interdisciplinary teaching Recent issues and developments in the field		**Skills** (based on the strands above)

attempt is made to connect the areas shown in Table 4.1 and to provide basic knowledge in social studies. Because there are so many terms, dates, and important names, these are boldfaced rather than repeated in a glossary in this chapter. The social studies test framework for the *Generalist* EC-6 certification (as seen in Table 4.1) is made up of four competencies (numbers 019–023): (019) Social Science Instruction; (020) History; (021) Geography and Culture; (022) Economics; and (023) Government and Citizenship. The State Board for Educator Certification (SBEC) (2008) defines the standards that make up each of these competencies:

Standards I–III: Social Science Instruction. The social studies teacher has a comprehensive knowledge of the social sciences and recognizes the value of the social sciences in society and the world; effectively integrates the various social science disciplines; uses knowledge and skills of social studies to plan and implement effective curriculum, instruction, assessment, and evaluation.
Standard IV: History. The social studies teacher applies knowledge of significant historical events and developments, as well as multiple historical interpretations and ideas, to facilitate student understanding of relationships between the past, the present, and the future.
Standards V and IX: Geography and Culture. The social studies teacher applies knowledge of people, places, and environments to facilitate students' understanding of geographic relationships in Texas, the United States, and the world; understands cultures and how they develop and adapt, and uses this knowledge to enable students to appreciate and respect cultural diversity in Texas, the United States, and the world.
Standard VI: Economics. The social studies teacher knows how people organize economic systems to produce, distribute, and consume goods and services, and uses this knowledge to enable students to understand economic systems and make informed economic decisions.
Standards VII and VIII: Government and Citizenship. The social studies teacher knows how governments and structures of power function, provide order, and allocate resources, and uses this knowledge to facilitate student understanding of how individuals and groups achieve their goals through political systems; understands citizenship in the United States and other societies,

and uses this knowledge to prepare students to participate in our society through an understanding of democratic principles and citizenship practices. **Standard X: Science, Technology, and Society.** The social studies teacher understands developments in science and technology, and uses this knowledge to facilitate student understanding of the social and environmental consequences of scientific discovery and technological innovation.

Elementary Social Studies Scope and Sequence in Texas

Traditionally, EC-6 social studies builds a foundation to support the learning that occurs in later grades. The **scope and sequence** of social studies programs reflects this goal. The *scope* of a program is the depth of the subject (or how far into the subject you go). The *sequence* is the order in which the subject matter is introduced. In Texas, generally, the scope and sequence of social studies is arranged according to an expanding environments model:

Kindergarten:	Self, home, family, and classroom
1st Grade:	Student's relationship to the classroom, school, and community
2nd Grade:	Local community and impact of individuals and events on the history of the community, state, and nation
3rd Grade:	How individuals have changed their communities and world
4th Grade:	History of Texas from the early beginnings to the present within the context of influences of the Western Hemisphere
5th Grade:	History of the United States from its earliest beginnings to the present with a focus on colonial times through the 20th century
6th Grade:	Students study people and places of the contemporary world

Following this type of scope and sequence allows teachers to begin social studies instruction by focusing on areas that are familiar to their students. In the earliest grades, for example, the focus is on students' personal knowledge and experiences that are closest to them (and, thus, more concrete). In later grades, instruction is expanded from close to more distant, either in time (historically) or in place (globally). For instance, one sees that a main focus in kindergarten is on family; therefore, students in subsequent grades may be asked to build on their understanding by learning about families in a previous century or from a distant land. This foundation building for learning subsequent topics is essential. The TEKS for children establish this foundation.

The TEA's Social Studies Center (2000) states that a comprehensive social studies program depends on the integration of eight strands listed in the TEKS. By providing teachers with such a guide, Texas hopes to ensure that students become responsible citizens of the 21st century and that they possess needed factual and conceptual knowledge, intellectual skills, and basic democratic values. The eight strands of the TEKS are (1) History; (2) Geography; (3) Economics; (4) Government; (5) Citizenship; (6) Culture; (7) Science, Technology, and Society; and (8) Social Studies Skills. In the introduction to the TEKS statements, it is recommended that the skills listed in the geography and social studies skills strands be integrated into the teaching of all the other essential knowledge and skills for social studies. More information on the TEKS for social studies can be found at http://ritter.tea.state.tx.us/ssc/teks_and_taas/teks.htm.

Let's now look more closely at the information for the test you will be taking. In the text that follows, each of the standards and competencies that make up Domain III (the social studies component) is introduced with a statement that broadly defines what an entry-level EC-6 educator must know and be able to do. A descriptive statement follows, explaining in more detail the knowledge and skills covered by the standard(s). We also show how content can be taught in appropriate ways for EC-6 students, along with sample questions of the type that might be found on the TExES. It is of value to learn these standards and competency statements well, because they give solid hints about how to answer many of the pedagogy-type questions on the *Generalist* test. For example, the paragraph that summarizes Competency 019 tells us that Texas wants its teachers to know and use the EC-6 Social Studies TEKS to design instruction; thus, if a question on the *Generalist* exam asks what would be a good base for guiding one's social studies curriculum, the knowledge of this competency would clearly point to choosing the TEKS as a good answer. The practice questions should also be used to organize your reading and review the content. Because the standards requiring specific knowledge (history, geography, economics, and government) contain so much information, they have been broken down into smaller, more manageable units. A sample lesson plan is given at the end of the chapter, as well as an additional blank form to write your own. There is also a form that you can use to guide and inform your observations of a social studies classroom and more practice questions.

Standards I, II, and III: Social Science Instruction

The social studies teacher has a comprehensive knowledge of the social sciences and recognizes the value of the social sciences.

The social studies teacher effectively integrates the various social science disciplines.

The social studies teacher uses knowledge and skills of social studies, as defined by the Texas Essential Knowledge and Skills (TEKS), to plan and implement effective curriculum, instruction, assessment, and evaluation.

Competency 019. (Social Science Instruction) The teacher understands and applies social science knowledge and skills to plan, organize, and implement instruction and access learning.

This means that the beginning teacher understands the state's social studies content and performance standards for social studies that comprise the Texas Essential Knowledge and Skills (TEKS) and the vertical alignment of the social sciences in the TEKS from grade level to grade level, including prerequisite knowledge and skills. The teacher should know the implications of stages of student growth and development so that he or she can design and implement effective learning experiences in the social sciences (e.g., knowledge of and respect for self, families, and communities; sharing; following routines; working cooperatively in groups). This should result in being able to select and apply effective and developmentally appropriate instructional practices, activities, technologies, and materials to promote students' knowledge and skills in the social sciences, including currently available technology as a major tool for learning and communicating social studies concepts. This teacher should also understand and use social studies terminology correctly and be able to promote students' use of social science skills, vocabulary, and research tools, including currently available technological tools. Preparation of inter- and intradisciplinary instruction should help teachers relate skills, concepts, and ideas across different social science disciplines and provide and facilitate instruction that helps students make connections between knowledge and methods in the social sciences and in other content areas. The teacher should not only be able to create maps and other graphics to represent geographic, political, historical, economic, and cultural features, distributions, and relationships but also to relate these and other concepts to the practical applications of social science issues and trends and to communicate the value of social studies education to students, parents/caregivers, colleagues, and the community. Finally, the teacher should be able to use a variety of formal and informal assessments and knowledge of the TEKS to determine students' progress and needs and to help plan instruction that addresses the strengths, needs, and interests of all students, including English language learners and students with special needs.

Implication of Child Development in Social Studies

As in other content areas, age and developmental levels play a large part in effective teaching and learning. This is particularly true in social studies, where children need a wealth of concrete and visual items to enhance their development of spatial skills and abstract ideas. The development of social skills and values also depends on children's readiness. Teachers of very young children provide experiences that both tie children together as a group (with their commonalities) and also help children identify traits that make them unique. Early childhood activities that feature name games, focus on physical similarities and differences, and employ family-based themes are all a part of a good developmental social studies program.

Constantly creating situations in which social skills are enhanced is also an important developmental process. It is difficult to have a country in which values are a part of life if children have had very few opportunities to express themselves, feel empathy, belong to a group, and practice other social skills—mostly because they sit all day in individual seats with little interaction. It is difficult to understand democracy in a place where only authoritarianism is seen and where children have few choices and feel powerless. Even small activities, such as voting on tomorrow's snack from a menu of items, sharing in a group, choosing a center or project of their own, or deciding how to show mastery from a list of assessment items, can help increase social studies elements in the classroom. Providing time for young children to **play** in social situations is also a huge step in this direction, as are **directed** or **creative dramatics** (e.g., telephone conversations, pretending to be at the store, doing chores).

Teachers in grades EC-6 must also take into account the developmental changes children experience as they enter early adolescence. Slavin (2009) describes the physical, intellectual, social, and emotional changes that begin to occur around age 11. Children may begin to experience changes in cognitive development moving beyond the concrete operational stage to a formal operations stage. In this stage, individuals begin to think abstractly, reason logically, and draw conclusions from the information available, as well as apply all these processes to hypothetical situations. Teachers of preadolescents should recognize the social and emotional development that may also be affecting their students. Young people desire attention from their peers as they seek their acceptance. As Allen and Stevens (1998) point out, group loyalty may lead to indifference and sometimes cruelty to group outsiders.

Social studies teachers should employ active, cognitively challenging, student-centered instructional strategies. **Role-play**, for example, may provide a powerful learning opportunity for students, particularly with issues that involve emotions, empathy, and decision making. A teacher may ask for an ad-lib scenario, such as this:

Let's pretend that Roberto accidentally tore Janna's paper. How would Roberto feel? What could he say? What could Janna say? Let's have them show us how they would handle it in a positive way.

Drama is also important in social studies, as students play parts in historical plays or skits and gain insight into historical characters by acting out written historical situations. These can be written by professionals, by teachers, or by the students. **Mock trials** for many issues allow children to learn about our justice system as they simulate the courtroom and take on the roles of attorneys, judge, and jury. **Mock meetings** (e.g., town meetings, legislative sessions) help students understand ways for the public to be involved in local, state, and national government. Creating formats for students to work in **cooperative groups** is perhaps one of the most important areas for children and preadolescents to practice social skills. Teachers who structure these groups well are not only teaching content but also helping children gain skills they need to get along in the real world, such as sharing; giving "I" messages ("I feel angry and hurt when you say things like that," rather than "You are so mean!"); learning to listen actively (maintain eye contact, let the other person talk without interrupting, then telling/restating what you think was stated by the other person); learning to give and receive praise; negotiating by taking turns; and using a compromise. It is difficult for children to gain these skills if the teacher constantly resolves conflicts rather than allowing children to work through situations in which they can practice these skills themselves. Therefore, we can see that the EC-6 teacher is constantly teaching social skills parallel to teaching social studies knowledge and skills.

Consider the following practice question:

Ms. Landry noted that Black History Month was fast approaching. In her yearly plan, she had blocked out several lesson periods to focus on this topic in her diverse urban classroom. Which of the following instructional techniques would be her best choice for these lessons?

A. Lecture
B. Inquiry
C. Cooperative groups
D. Independent study

There are two key issues in this question—a diverse classroom and a focus on an event related to multiculturalism. Although you might say that inquiry (*B*) is a worthy part of social studies instruction (and, indeed, it is), a teacher should use cooperative groups (*C*) to teach the principles of multiculturalism. This is particularly appropriate in diverse classroom settings, because "research on cooperative learning and inter-group relationships has shown that students in cooperative learning situations develop great appreciation for cooperative-learning classmates" (Manning & Baruth, 2000, p. 236). Telling, or lecture (*A*), reading about it during independent study (*D*), or even inquiry (*B*) are no substitutes for having students work together to accomplish goals with those who may be different from themselves. The best answer is *C*.

Technology as a Teaching Tool

One of the most important issues in social studies education today is the role of technology in teaching and learning. Technology has played a leading role in connecting the world in unprecedented ways. Instantaneous communication, access to media and popular culture, and globalization have contributed to the interconnectedness of the world. Social studies educators understand the role of technology in the world today and the possibilities for the future. Clearly, technology has a role to play in contemporary social studies education.

There are many technologies that might be incorporated into the social studies classroom: computers, television, videos, audio recordings, CD-ROMs, and other tools. Media such as CDs, VHS tapes, and DVDs (in addition to the Internet) offer many opportunities for students to experience cultures across time and distance to work with many types of maps, play challenging social studies games, visit virtual museums and go on museum tours, and so forth. The TEKS require that children in social studies be using technology to create poems, stories, pictures, maps, graphs, and presentations. Teachers should always be sure to preview media before class presentation to ensure that they are age appropriate in overall content and language, interest, connection to the subject being taught, and presentation.

Computers have been placed in most elementary schools since the late 1970s. During those early days, they were primarily used to provide drill-and-practice opportunities for students. Students were presented problems and entered their responses; the computer would send back a graphic feedback (usually along the lines of a smiley face/sad face). Clearly, this use concerned educators who came to view computers as centers of busy work with the same limitations as a worksheet. Although many of these drill-and-practice computer programs remain, there are many other computer applications that provide powerful classroom learning tools. Some examples include the following:

1. **Word processing, database, and spreadsheet software.** These programs are nearly standard on all classroom and computer lab computers and can be used in the social studies classroom for collection and presentation of data and a variety of writing tasks.

2. **Problem-solving software.** These programs present complex situations in which students face a dilemma, choose from a number of possible alternatives, and arrive at a solution—thus encouraging active exploration and discovery. One of the most popular problem-solving programs for children in grades 3 through 8 is *Where in the World Is Carmen Sandiego?*

3. **Strategy and simulation software.** These programs place students into situations that are as authentic as possible. One of the most popular simulations is still *The Oregon Trail.* It presents a series of decisions that pioneers faced in 1847 as they set out in wagon trains to find new homes in the Oregon Territory. For example, if a student decides to hunt or stop at a fort, they can lose time and may fail to pass through the mountains before the winter snows begin. This could lead to illness or not having enough food. With each decision, children are shown the consequences of their choices. Other classic simulation programs for use in some classrooms are: *SimAnt, SimCity,* and *SimEarth.* In each of these simulations, children are placed into settings in which they describe, create, and control a system. Popular strategy software titles include *Chess* and, for older students, *Civilization* (version V to be released this year). In this game, players attempt to "dominate the world through diplomatic finesse, cultural domination, and military prowess. . . . The game is an addictive blend of building, exploration, discovery, and conquest. Players match wits against some of history's greatest leaders as they strive to build the ultimate civilization to stand the test of time" (*Civilization III* Official Web site, n.d.).

4. **Presentation software.** These programs are communication tools that combine video, graphics, animation, and text. These *authoring* programs enable students to organize and communicate information in more aesthetically innovative ways. Some of the most popular presentation software titles for students are *Flash*, *PowerPoint*, and *KidPix*. Social studies is a perfect place for students to begin whole class, small group, or individual presentations through the use of these tools.

5. **Web-based communication.** Classroom connections to the Internet are common today. With these connections, students can access and create
   - Electronic mail (e-mail)/instant messages (IMs)/text messages
   - Newsgroups and Listservs
   - Web sites, using *Dreamweaver*, *Flash*, and *MS FrontPage*
   - Weblogs (blogs) (simple Web sites that contain personal writing space); students might read blogs that belong to others, including politicians or social activists, or create their own
   - Podcasts (broadcast files)—information is recorded, saved in a compressed file format, such as MP3, and uploaded to the Internet. Listeners can download and play files on an iPod or other portable media player.
   - V-Casts (video casts)—video files can be downloaded from the Internet and played on personal computers or cellular phones.
   - Wikis—formats set up so that all designated users can contribute/edit on the same site.

Children can find and use **experts** as resources, chat with students in their school, city, state, country, and around the world and can also participate in joint social studies projects with other classrooms in their school or elsewhere. When students engage in conversations with similar children, they are able to see from primary sources (with whom they can relate) how much they are the same but also their differences. Social networking sites such as FaceBook, MySpace, and Twitter are popular sites for online conversations. E-mails, e-pals, blogs, podcasts, Wikis, and V-casts can be used to gain and share information, solve problems, increase communication skills, let others know their feelings on issues, and so forth. Students can gain online access to video sites such as YouTube and also live-streaming television and radio programs from stations around the world. They might also use the Internet to access online newspapers from around the world in order to track current events from a variety of perspectives. The Internet should allow children to open the doors of their classroom and interact with people from all over the world—including experts and other students. As these windows of communication open, however, teachers should be reminded that they must always monitor electronic communications carefully.

Intradisciplinary and Interdisciplinary Issues

When social studies is integrative in its treatment of topics, it can cut across disciplinary boundaries in both **intradisciplinary** ways (overlapping within social studies content such as geography and economics or history and government) and **interdisciplinary** ways (overlapping lessons between social studies and other content areas, such as mathematics, science, language arts, music, art, etc.). Traditional-style education, however, emphasizes the separate teaching of individual subjects—language arts, mathematics, science, history, geography, and so on. These subjects are, too often, divided into separate instruction time with very few interconnections. The limited number of hours in the school day often precludes all subjects from receiving equal instruction time, causing social studies educators to be particularly concerned.

Maxim (1999) observes: "If social studies is somehow squeezed into the day's schedule, children are often led through a quick oral reading of a textbook section and a brief question-answer recitation period" (p. 23). To remedy these practices, teachers can seek **themes** and design **thematic units** (in order to **integrate subject areas** with social studies). These themes can cut across numerous disciplines, allowing for learning opportunities that are deeper, not wider. Social studies themes can focus on a particular person or type of person (explorers, community helpers, etc.), continent or country, era, holiday, current event, climate, and so on.

The National Council for the Social Studies (NCSS) (1994) identified five key factors that make for powerful social studies teaching and learning:

1. Meaningfulness
2. Integration
3. Value-based
4. Challenging
5. Student active

Maxim (1999) adds that "social studies appears to be the major area for blending subjects previously taught separately" (p. 24), and Berg (1988) answers the question of where social studies might fit into the integration of subjects. He states:

> *Right in the middle! A major goal of the social studies is to help students understand the myriad interactions of people on this planet—past, present, and future. Making sense of the world requires using skills that allow one to read about the many people and places that are scattered about the globe; to use literature to understand the richness of past events and the people who are a part of them; to apply math concepts to more fully understand how numbers have enabled people to numerically manage the complexity of their world. The story of humankind well told requires drawing from all the areas of the curriculum.* (Berg, unnumbered pull-out section)

Thematic teaching may be an effective way to blend or integrate subjects. Themes can span time and space and integrate knowledge, beliefs, values, and attitudes to action. This type of integrated instruction works to develop knowledge of the evolution of the human condition through time, its current variations across locations and cultures, and an appreciation of social and civic decision making (NCSS, 1994). There are six intradisciplinary areas of social studies commonly found in the lower levels:

1. Geography
2. Anthropology
3. Sociology
4. History
5. Economics
6. Civics

How might planning such lessons work? An example of **intradisciplinary integration** (within the social studies disciplines) might be found in teaching the concept of families. For example, children might be asked to use historical thinking skills to compare what families were like long ago to now. They may use their knowledge and skills in sociology and anthropology to understand how the concept of family works in other parts of the world and use geography to locate those places. Families might be used to springboard discussion and to examine, using a civics skill, how and why decisions are made. Economics could connect well with helping develop students' understanding of needs and wants (and other economic terms) and how those might change in various parts of the country and the world. Teachers who employ intra- and interdisciplinary themes can integrate in exciting ways for children.

Teachers who integrate across all subjects, or use **interdisciplinary integration**, connect concepts across all content areas, not just within social studies. This is true across the curriculum, but social studies connect particularly well with language arts. Meaningful literature selections, especially mass-market books and trade books, can provide exceptional opportunities for students to develop the knowledge and skills that help them examine their opinions and attitudes as they learn outside the textbook and worksheets. Thus, literature is an important tool in a social studies classroom because it can educate and entertain. Huck, Hepler, and Hickman (1993) note, "A history textbook *tells*; [but] a quality piece of imaginative writing has the power to make the reader *feel*" (p. 11). Student motivation may be increased vastly through the use of children's books with social studies content and themes rather than with a social studies textbook alone (Farris, 2007). Other researchers agree that reading social studies-based quality children's literature enhances a child's understanding of social studies:

> *Literary works are packed with conceptual knowledge about the human condition and can supply meaningful content for skill-building experiences. . . . Perhaps more completely and certainly more intensely than with textbooks, a creative teacher can use trade books to engage students in the pursuit of such citizenship competencies as processing information, examining other points of view, separating fact from opinion, and solving problems.* (McGowan & Guzzetti, 1991, p. 18)

Textbooks are primarily concerned with facts; whereas literature is primarily concerned with feelings: compassion, humanness, misfortune, grief, happiness, and awe (Maxim, 1999). Unfortunately, social studies teaching and learning—more than any other subject—is dominated by textbooks (Loewen, 1995). Most of the criticisms aimed at textbooks reference their physical size and weight for young students, the prose style that is bland and voiceless, and excessive coverage of information that makes them boring, but it should really be about targeting the ways teachers use them (Maxim, 1999; 2010). Textbooks are not meant to be the entire social studies curriculum, only a single resource.

There are many books that can be used to develop social studies knowledge and skills. For example, a **mock trial** can follow the reading of the *Real Story of the Three Little Pigs* (or other fairy tales with similar plots). Offering readings with multiple perspective taking is a major goal of the social studies for children. Fairy tales from the past or from other cultures or countries can be analyzed and compared. These tales can reveal a great deal about the people who tell or write them. Themes around books such as *Everybody Cooks Rice* (Dooley, 1992) or *Bread, Bread, Bread* (Morris, 1993) invite reading, tasting, and geographic curiosity. In a unit on the theme of homes, students might begin by reading *Houses and Homes* (Morris, 1992). Young children can orally describe, write about, and draw their own homes and those they find in their neighborhoods. From these tasks, they can investigate the concept of shelter in other parts of the world and discover why people have created different types of houses or shelters to match various conditions and environments. This provides an opportunity to conduct some scientific investigations of building materials. Using spatial skills in a Block Center, children can also investigate how some structures are built, integrating mathematical knowledge and skills. Many other children's books investigate common but meaningful themes.

Other content areas (in addition to language arts) have the potential for connections with social studies. Music and art make social studies come alive for children. Health issues that people have faced in the past and today can be connected. Children can see the rationale behind mathematics skills when coupling them with social studies issues. Environmental studies also combine the subjects of science and social studies. This is true for most of the people-related topics in social studies. However, social studies makes a unique contribution to the curriculum through the following:

- It provides a forum for children to learn about and practice democracy.
- It helps children explain their world in many dimensions, including environmental aspects.
- It assists children with positive self-development.
- It helps children acquire a foundational understanding of history, geography, biography, and the social sciences.
- It promotes a genuine sense of the social fabric.

Interdisciplinary education's greatest strength is its potential for helping children go beyond superficial knowledge. It enables them to develop an in-depth, multidimensional understanding of a topic. Why separate many topics into distinct subjects when they can be multiple dimensions of the same topic? Instead, by integrating subjects through themes, students become involved in activities that are ultimately more meaningful and powerful. Above all, social studies is the only curriculum subject with people constantly at the center of the subject matter (Ellis, 2006). Teachers who employ intra- and interdisciplinary themes can create much more stimulating lessons that help children go beyond the surface across the curriculum.

 ## Engaging All Students

Teachers must have more than knowledge in their content; they must also have an understanding of their students. Four important areas of education have been identified by Grant and Vansledright (2001): (1) learners and learning, (2) content, (3) teachers and teaching, and (4) the classroom environment. Through these lenses, a useful framework for examining social studies classrooms can be considered, and good pedagogy tells teachers that they must know their children. Teachers are increasingly confronted with a wide range of diverse students in their classrooms. Among today's students, there is growing ethnic and cultural diversity, as well as significant differences in socioeconomic backgrounds and intellectual abilities. One of the biggest challenges for teachers is to design quality, thought-provoking, and engaging learning opportunities for all students.

The world inside classrooms reflects today's world. The current inclusion movement seeks to integrate all types of learners into the classroom. Although some may disagree with this idea, advocates (including those who write the TExES standards and competencies) "strongly believe that students with learning disabilities increasingly benefit both academically and socially from placement in the regular classroom" (Farris, 2007, 151). Inclusion might also bring in students identified as gifted. The classroom teacher has the task of reaching and teaching students along this "extensive continuum of skills and abilities" (Farris, 2007, p. 153). Teachers often use differentiated instruction techniques to match learners' individual abilities with instructional methods and materials. Instead of focusing solely on skills development and memorizing facts, teachers should "refocus on interdisciplinary teaching and theme-based units, student portfolios, and cross-grade grouping whenever possible while continually keeping the individual child in mind" (Farris, 2007, p. 155). Learning can often center on inquiry-based activities that develop higher-level thinking skills and interest for all in order to both "raise the floor and raise the ceiling" (Wheelock, 1992).

Assessment and Evaluation

Students, parents, and teachers should all be constantly aware of a student's performance and progress. Assessments should be carefully planned and interwoven with instruction. Teachers gauge, or assess, students' prior knowledge and skills before beginning new lessons or instructional events. Once the lesson begins, teachers apply informal and formative assessments to gain information about student learning on an on-going basis. Teachers generally consider **formative assessments** the most useful type of assessment because they provide both teachers and students with instant information, and teachers can correct mistakes or misconceptions before they are practiced too long; thus, this information provides teachers with the data to decide whether students have understanding of the lesson to that point and are ready to move on or if there is a need to reteach aspects of the lesson that may remain unclear. **Summative assessments** provide information on how a student has done on a particular set of objectives at the end of instruction. **Evaluations**, however, help the understanding of how well the student has done over a long period of time, so the required state test in specified grades contributes to this type of information as a form of assessment.

Although both assessments and evaluations are useful in helping to explain student progress, some assessments can also provide exciting and meaningful learning activities in social studies. Designing these types of assessments can sometimes be a bit different for the social studies teacher because they can require some criteria for performance. Often a rubric is used to identify the performance criteria and also the levels of proficiency (from high to low) that students may demonstrate. Although these assessments do require more of a teachers' time than do some other types of assessments, they may be more rewarding for both teachers and students because they are much more authentic and motivational. At the beginning of any activity, teachers should provide clear expectations through goals and objectives to students and provide them with several varied opportunities to demonstrate mastery. **Authentic** or **performance-based assessments** ask students to create real-world products or to perform, not simply answer a set of questions. These can be particularly exciting in social studies and can make a lasting effect on students. Examples of this type of assessment include debates, Readers' Theatre, creating or participating in plays, dressing-up-in-character day, songs or dances, posters, brochures, persona-taking, advertisements, discussions, projects, cartoons, journal entries, creating models, and so forth.

Reflective Teaching

As a **people-centered** subject, social studies often requires teachers to tackle controversial and often contradictory issues, such as conflict and respect. Savage and Armstrong (1996) write, "Teaching social studies is not for cowards" (p. 8), and note that social studies teachers "tend to be thoughtful people who have a point of view and who are willing to stand up for their commitments" (p. 9). These are important qualities and actions to model for students. Therefore, along with modeling respectful behaviors, social studies teachers must make many decisions daily regarding what roles are taken in instruction. Essentially, they decide what role they take and what roles students play during an activity to increase skills in interactions, as well as in thinking. For example, teachers are **experts** during direct instruction lessons, **consultants** or **facilitators** during cooperative group events, and **coaches** during inquiry, problem-solving, or performance activities. Roles that ask students to be more active than the teacher reap much more meaningful and valuable learning.

Teaching decisions also require **reflective practice**. The most effective teachers are those who regularly examine their own teaching. Grant and Vansledright (2001) believe that teachers should perform "regular examinations of and introspection into what, who, and how you're teaching, and why you choose to do what you do" (p. 265). They must consider how their beliefs and actions influence their students and the subject(s) they teach. This is particularly true in social studies, where teachers may have strong beliefs and values that affect what occurs in the classroom—for example, they must be particularly careful of not including or over- or underemphasizing some perspectives because of their own biases towards some issues, especially those in cultural and political areas.

Part of reflective teaching involves keeping up with changing content and new social studies methods. EC-6 teachers are expected to engage in **professional growth** for social studies. Teaching a discipline such as social studies is not static, but rather in a constant state of transformation, due to both the discovery of new knowledge and the changing political and cultural scenes. Texts are adopted for a number of years, so contemporary information can become outdated quickly. Teachers should be sure to **present current knowledge** and to make use of current events that touch the lives of their children. Teachers cannot become complacent in their thinking about what, who, and how they teach, and they should update their knowledge and teaching methods to match children's needs and the changing times.

Teachers are professional educators and should make connections with others in their field. **Professional organizations** offer opportunities to interact with colleagues and gain insights into current research on teaching and learning strategies and tools for social scientists and for the classroom. Because it is imperative to keep up to date with the latest issues and trends in the field, teachers have numerous social studies resources that help them. For example, in Texas, social studies educators may want to join the Texas social studies listserv (http://ritter.tea.state.tx.us/curriculum/social/sslistserv.html) to get updates from the Texas Education Agency (TEA). The Texas Council for the Social Studies (TCSS) (http://beta.txcss.org) is a professional organization for social studies educators. TCSS publishes a journal, *The Social Studies Texan*, and holds a conference in the fall. At the national level, teachers can consult the monthly and quarterly journals published by NCSS, *Social Education* and *Social Studies and the Young Learner*. NCSS members receive a monthly newsletter and qualify for discounted registration fees for the annual conference held in late fall each year. The NCSS Web site (www.ncss.org) contains a great deal of information regarding social studies teaching and learning, as well as membership information. There are also links to numerous listservs maintained by NCSS members where social studies educators may freely exchange information and ideas. In addition to the national and Texas professional organizations, the Internet and other media are always at one's fingertips. The days of solely relying on older textbooks, out-dated filmstrips or grainy documentary films, or maps and globes depicting countries (such as the USSR) that no longer exist should be gone. Resources, many of them free and available for teachers who make efforts to search them out, include vast amounts of information and supplies, current unit and lesson plans, up-to-date materials for children, and so forth.

Consider the following practice question:

Mr. Hood began to design a lesson on the history of the cattle kingdom era of Texas. He thought about how he could set up his lesson. What would be his best choice?

A. After watching a film clip on the cattle drives, have students use their map colors to draw the main cattle drive trails.

B. Integrate the lesson with mathematics, reading, and music.

C. Have students read the chapter on cattle drives in their well-written social studies chapter on this topic.

D. Invite a guest speaker from a local ranch to come in to speak with children.

Students should be given opportunities to make deeper connections with many topics so lessons will become less isolated and more meaningful. The best answer is *B.* Using mathematics, children should be able to relate the cattle drives to the economy of Texas to understand why the cattle industry flourished during this time period. Also, there were many songs that originated during this era that sat the stage for country and western music. Having students use map skills and seeing a filmstrip (choice *A*) could be a part of the lesson, but failing to integrate other key information makes the lesson less meaningful. Simply reading a chapter (choice *C*) would not make the connections needed for big picture understanding. Having a local rancher (choice *D*) would be an excellent addition, although he or she might not be an expert on the *history* of this topic. The correct answer is *B.*

Standard IV: History and Standard X: Science, Technology, and Society

The social studies teacher applies knowledge of significant historical events and developments, as well as multiple historical interpretations and ideas, to facilitate student understanding of relationships between the past, the present, and the future.

The social studies teacher understands developments in science and technology, and uses this knowledge to facilitate student understanding of the social and environmental consequences of scientific discovery and technological innovation.

Competency 020 (History): The teacher understands and applies knowledge of significant historical events and developments, multiple historical interpretations and ideas, and relationships between the past, the present, and the future as defined by the Texas Essential Knowledge and Skills (TEKS). Because there are so many details, concepts, and vocabulary in this competency, these are listed for the beginning teacher in the following bulleted points:

- Demonstrates an understanding of historical points of reference in the history of Texas, the United States, and the world.
- Analyzes how individuals, events, and issues shaped the history of Texas, the United States, and the world.
- Demonstrates an understanding of similarities and differences among Native-American Indian groups in Texas, the United States, and the Western Hemisphere before European colonization.
- Demonstrates an understanding of the causes and effects of European exploration and colonization of Texas, the United States, and the Western Hemisphere.
- Analyzes the influence of various factors (e.g., geographic contexts, processes of spatial exchange, science and technology) on the development of societies.
- Demonstrates an understanding of basic concepts of culture and the processes of cultural adaptation, diffusion, and exchange.

- Applies knowledge and analyzes the effects of scientific, mathematical, and technological innovations on political, economic, social, and environmental developments as they relate to daily life in Texas, the United States, and the world.
- Demonstrates an understanding of historical information and ideas in relation to other disciplines.
- Demonstrates an understanding of how to formulate historical research questions and use appropriate procedures to reach supportable judgments and conclusions in the social sciences.
- Demonstrates an understanding of historical research and knows how historians locate, gather, organize, analyze, and report information by using standard research methodologies.
- Knows the characteristics and uses of primary and secondary sources used for historical research (e.g., databases, maps, photographs, media services, the Internet, biographies, interviews, questionnaires, artifacts), analyzes historical information from primary and secondary sources, and understands and evaluates information in relation to bias, propaganda, point of view, and frame of reference.
- Applies and evaluates the use of problem-solving processes, gathering of information, listing and considering options, considering advantages and disadvantages, choosing and implementing solutions, and assessing the effectiveness of solutions.
- Applies and evaluates the use of decision-making processes to identify situations that require decisions by gathering information, identifying options, predicting consequences, and taking action to implement the decisions.
- Communicates and interprets historical information in written, oral, and visual forms and translates information from one medium to another (e.g., written to visual, statistical to written or visual).
- Analyzes historical information by categorizing, comparing and contrasting, making generalizations and predictions, and drawing inferences and conclusions (e.g., regarding population statistics, patterns of migration, and voting trends and patterns).
- Applies knowledge of the concept of chronology, or the arrangement of events in correct time order, and its use in understanding history and historical events.
- Applies different methods of interpreting the past to understand, evaluate, and support multiple points of view, frames of reference, and the historical context of events and issues.
- Demonstrates an understanding of the foundations of representative government in the United States, significant issues of the Revolutionary era, and challenges confronting the U.S. government in the early years of the Republic.
- Demonstrates an understanding of westward expansion and analyzes its effects on the political, economic, and social development of the United States.
- Analyzes ways that political, economic, and social factors led to the growth of sectionalism and the Civil War.
- Understands individuals, issues, and events involved in the Civil War and analyzes the effects of Reconstruction on the political, economic, and the social life of the United States.
- Demonstrates an understanding of major U.S. reform movements of the 19th and 20th centuries (e.g., abolitionism, women's suffrage, temperance).
- Demonstrates an understanding of important individuals, issues, and events of the 20th and 21st centuries in Texas, the United States, and the world.
- Analyzes ways that particular contemporary societies reflect historical events (e.g., invasion, conquests, colonization, immigration).

Consider the following practice question:

Mrs. Scott is teaching her third grade students about the Underground Railroad. She wants to make sure the lesson is meaningful, so she plans to bring in a primary source. Which of the following would be considered a primary source?

A. A biography of Harriet Tubman
B. A wanted poster of Harriet Tubman from those times
C. *Follow the Drinking Gourd*, a book by Jeanette Winter
D. The textbook chapter on the Underground Railroad

Choices *A*, *C*, and *D* are all examples of secondary sources because they report or summarize information "second hand." Other secondary sources might include reports from a newspaper or other media sources. Because these reporters or summarizers pick and choose their sources, social scientists caution that their viewpoints can sometimes be biased (e.g., a history of the American Revolution written by an American author and another one written by a British author normally come from vastly biased perspectives). The answer is Choice *B*, because this poster was an actual "witness to the events" of the times. Other primary sources include letters, paintings (made during the times), photographs, diaries, autobiographies, and so forth that originate from people who actually lived during the event. The answer is *B*.

Teaching History

Of the six disciplines of the EC-6 social studies, history has long been dominant in the social studies curriculum. A question often asked is, "Why study history?" Researchers explain that our "history is a fluid continuum. The present in which we live is also the future of the past and the past of the future" (Ellis, 2006, p. 207) and "History should be studied because it is essential to individuals and to society" (Stearns, 1998, p. 5). If we do not know where we have been in our past, it can be difficult to have a clear view of our future. Although almost everyone agrees that history should be taught in the schools, there is a great deal of debate over what should be taught and to whom. Given the huge amount of history that exists for Texas, the United States, and the world, it is impossible to cover everything. Also, rote memorization of mere facts has proved to be insufficient. Students must go beyond simply knowing facts to being able to make sense of those facts and to use them to make good decisions as citizens. Research shows that even the youngest children are constantly considering information and then constructing and reconstructing their understanding of things. Therefore, history teaching and learning is particularly appropriate for elementary school children because they are naturally inquisitive and can use accurate information to make sense of the people and events of the past to connect to their present. Everyone has heard that "History repeats itself." Without doubt, it is important that our children not make the same mistakes as others have before and also reach for the greatness of those who have been successful in raising people up in some manner. Also, as Ellis (2006) explains, "Children living in the present can benefit greatly from understanding the past—the sense of continuity, the inheritance, the traditions, the changes, and the reminders that are all around them" (p. 207).

With all of this said, history at all levels, but especially for young children, must be meaningful (The National Center for History in the Schools [NCHS], 1996). Even as adults, we may not remember when Henry VIII lived, but we remember that he broke with the Catholic church over lust for a new wife (whom he later beheaded). For young children, history should be filled with emotions that they understand, things that can spark their imaginations, causes of good and bad events and their outcomes, ideas and ideals to which they can aspire, and so on. It is this that makes learning history meaningful to children.

Research has shown that children retain misconceptions that make sense to them somehow (Grant & Vansledright, 2001). This can also be true of their understanding of historical events. Events of the past are very complex, and children often oversimplify them. Therefore, it is important that they begin to develop an understanding of how the events of the past influence the present **(cause and effect)** and how our own past connects with that of others. This emphasizes the need to include, as a part of history instruction, a "wide array of knowledge from what are considered cultural areas: arts, literature, music, philosophies, religion, science, technology, and social and political knowledge" (Chapin, 2006, p. 149). This helps students expand their historical understanding and be able to consider events from a broader perspective.

As they broaden their understanding, students learn to think like historians (Wineberg, 2001). The NCHS (1996) explains:

> [R]eal historical understanding requires students to engage in historical thinking: to raise questions and to marshal evidence in support of their answers; to read historical narratives and fiction; to consult historical documents, journals, diaries, artifacts, historic sites, and other records from the past; and to do so imaginatively—taking into account the time and places in which these records were created and comparing the multiple points of view of those on the scene at the time. (p. 14)

Historical thinking skills must be developed sequentially. The first step must be to know the facts about a particular person, place, or event. For example, how could a child argue who is the greater superhero—Superman or Spiderman—and present a valid case for his or her choice, if the child had never heard of either? The same is true for history events and historical persons. A factual foundation of information and ideas must be present for any greater consideration and deeper understanding. According to Anderson and Krathwohl (2001), who adapted and updated Bloom's Taxonomy (1956) for today's classrooms, **productive pedagogies** (those aimed at higher-order thinking by students) center on the **transformation of facts** (meaning breaking them apart to analyze them, evaluating them, or creating something new out of them). In the new Bloom's Taxonomy, more outcome-oriented language is employed. For example, students begin at the lowest level with *remember* rather than *knowledge*. It remains true, however, that essential information must be initially introduced into the process, and then this basic information informs the higher-order thinking transformation process throughout. The highest level of student development in new Bloom's Taxonomy is creating new ideas and information using what has previously been learned, and this should be the goal in social studies.

The standards of history are somewhat similar across grade levels, although teaching methods and objectives may vary. For example, a third-grade class studying the community may use a computer to create a database of historical places in their community. This database might include pictures and descriptions of historic buildings, old homes, and other places of historical interest. Second-grade students may study older forms of transportation used in their communities (walking, horses, trains, etc.) and compare these to newer forms (cars and planes). They, too, could create a database for their information. This allows children to categorize, arrange, sort, select, and display their information. Then they might predict what sorts of transportation would help people in their city in the future. These examples demonstrate how students could meet history standards in different ways.

Many times, teaching social studies, unfortunately, does not encourage students to connect their newly learned concepts with their lived experiences. This often leads students to justifiably ask why they should learn history when it has nothing to do with them. Most classroom experiences are determined by the content of textbooks rather than the pursuit of meaningful knowledge. Levstik and Barton (2001) believe that history for primary grade-level students "rarely amounts to anything more than learning a few isolated facts about famous people connected to major holidays. . . . In fact, when asked why they think history is a subject at school or how it might help them, students sometimes can think of little, except that it might be useful if they were ever on *Jeopardy!*" (p. 14). The authors go on to explain that teachers must provide opportunities for students to make meaningful connections: "To get more understanding from history, teachers must begin with the concerns and interests of students and must help them find answers to questions that grow out of those concerns and interests" (p. 14). Students must begin to see social studies as patterns of human behavior from which much can be learned. History must be made to seem alive! For example, Ms. Hodges, in an inquiry model, asked her fourth-graders if they have ever heard the expression "Your name is mud"? When some replied that they had, she asks if they could guess what the expression means and from where the expression originated. Ms. Hodges told students that she would answer any question they could formulate to find the answer, but she could answer questions only with a "yes" or "no." This caused students to think of their own questions and to also use the questions that their peers ask as resources to get to the answer. Most would say it simply means that one's reputation is "dirty," but the answer goes deeper than that. Dr. Mudd, a physician, fixed the broken leg of John Wilkes Booth, the assassin of Abraham Lincoln, after he shot the president. Most people thought for many years that Dr. Mudd was part of the plot to kill Lincoln, and in fact, he spent some time in prison for being involved. Because his name and reputation were ruined, even though he was finally proved innocent, the phrase became ingrained in American phraseology as depicting a person's actions as especially heinous. NCHS (1996) stresses that teachers should bring history alive by using "stories, myths, legends, and biographies that capture children's imaginations and immerse them in times and cultures of the recent and long-ago past" (p. 3). Documents, witnesses, and physical remains (**artifacts**) offer students clues to historical mysteries. Students may conduct an **oral history** interview with an eyewitness to an historical event to gain a first-hand account. Social studies teachers must provide students with opportunities to apply critical-thinking skills to organize and use information acquired from many of these resources and experts. They should seek out many ways for children to think at higher levels.

Distinguishing fact from opinion is one key thinking skill that students should develop. With this in mind, students must learn to differentiate between primary and secondary sources. **Primary sources** are original records; **secondary sources** use primary sources to deliver information at a later time. Social scientists interpret primary sources, or original records, and convey understanding of the content based solely on the data provided. Secondary sources basically provide secondhand information. For example, suppose a car accident occurred in which a car hit another car from behind. A description of the accident given to the police by an eyewitness is a primary source, because it comes from someone actually there at the time. The story in the newspaper the next day is a secondary source, because the reporter (who interviewed the witnesses and wrote the story) did not actually witness the accident. The reporter is presenting a way of understanding the accident or a summary of events after talking to witnesses or others. Students should be able to locate each of these types of sources, be able to use them, and also understand that both sources can contain biased viewpoints, particularly secondary sources because they were not there. In the previous example, the eyewitness may have been hit by someone else in the past and embellished a bit because he or she is sympathetic to the driver who was hit (as could have been the reporter). The reporter also might not have been able to interview all of the witnesses, so may only be reporting some of the data. Social studies teachers must teach children to analyze all such data for **spin** (or bias)—whether it is intentional or not. In this era, when even photographs and videos can be cleverly altered, it is most important for future citizens to be able to examine multiple primary and secondary sources critically to reach conclusions more truthfully. Children must be able to carry out investigations—just like real historians.

Social scientists gather a great many facts and figures about people's activities (**raw data**). One way that people often self-report information to social scientists is through **surveys**. Data are collected and organized in different ways so that social scientists may observe certain patterns and relationships that lead to useful predictions and conclusions. **Statistics** are numeric, or **quantitative**, data that represent information about a given subject. There are many ways to display statistics or other raw data, and these can be used in all areas of the social sciences. These numbers can become interesting and powerful representations if displayed in ways that allow the reader to make quick and constructive use of them in thematic ways. Graphs are a convenient way of organizing data. An economist could use a **line graph** to show or compare the changes in oil production over time. A political scientist might present statistics in a **bar graph** that shows a comparison of different amounts. A **circle graph**, or **pie chart**, is an easy way to show the parts, or percentages, into which a total amount is divided. The full circle, or pie, represents 100 percent, a half circle is 50 percent, and so on. Circle graphs could be useful for showing the percentage of the population of a large city that each of its ethnic groups represents. For young children, graphs might begin with percentages of each type of pet they have at home, type of lunch desired each day (and thus the importance of ordering food supplies correctly), or type of clothing worn.

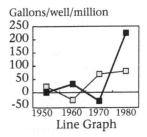
Line Graph

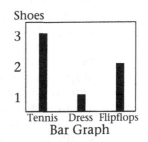
Bar Graph

Pie Chart

Charts and **tables** are also important means for organizing and displaying information. Children should be taught to read and interpret this information and to construct these types of graphs using keys. Most important, they should be taught how people use graphs to make decisions (e.g., a local pet store may look at the data and see that there is a large percentage of cats owned by people in a particular neighborhood, so stocking more cat supplies ensures that the store makes more money and that the local people can always find the products they need).

There are other visual means that are effective in EC-6 social studies teaching and learning. **Timelines**, for example, are graphic representations of a succession of historical events, constructed by dividing a unit of time into proportional segments (Maxim, 2010). A timeline is an effective method of illustrating time spans between events. As children study the past, timelines help them put events into perspective by allowing them to see when important things happened (Maxim, 1999). Because young children relate to time only as it is meaningful to them, their first experiences in grasping prehistory experience is focusing on routines. Calendar time helps bring attention to the day of the week, yesterday, tomorrow, the seasons, and the routine of the day (in terms of teaching after and before and sequencing events). To help young children understand how things change with time, teachers can measure children's height throughout the year, keep a lost tooth chart, have a "baby versus now" photo board, and so forth. Maxim (2010) recommends that for the very youngest students, teachers construct timelines on topics of immediate experience. Routines of their daily schedule can be illustrated on a beginning timeline. Fourth graders are able to understand historical eras and are able to sequence major events over a period of time. For instance, cut-outs of symbols for major holidays in the United States or other events can be pinned or clipped onto a cardboard strip in sequence, or disks with laminated pictures can be strung in order on a length of yarn. The students must decide which symbol comes first, second, and so on as they place the events in proper sequence. Children can also construct and illustrate a timeline of important events of their lives (e.g., birth, birth of a sibling, riding a bike, taking a particular vacation, going to school) by drawing on a long strip of adding machine paper.

Maps are another visual means of representing information and are used to show distances, strategic locations, boundaries, physical features, resources, climate, and so on. In order to effectively use maps, students must learn to read them and even "become" junior *cartographers,* or mapmakers. Learning to read maps is similar to learning to read the printed word. Children must learn to associate arbitrary symbols (a picnic table for a park, a star for a capital city, etc.) with something real in the environment. The "actual symbolic representation on maps is too abstract for kindergarten and early primary-grade children to use," notes Maxim (1999, p. 369); however, this does not mean that young children are incapable of using symbols of any kind as parents soon realize when they are passing the Golden Arches of McDonald's. There are a variety of social studies activities that help students discover relationships between some physical aspect of their environment and its symbol. For example, children can play informally with blocks and other building materials. Playing with blocks helps children conceptualize space as they construct environments that simulate real locations ("In the Block Center today, boys and girls, I want you to try to build our classroom"). Teachers might also take students on a class trip to take pictures around the school or neighborhood. These pictures can then be mounted on blocks of wood and children can be encouraged to play with them as they would their regular blocks to reconstruct their neighborhood. A children's picture book that might be related to this activity is *Block City*, based on a poem by Robert Louis Stevenson (1988). The poem/book begins, "What are you able to build with your blocks? Castles and palaces, temples and docks." **Photographs** can be used to present visual data, and a number of schools are acquiring digital cameras that enhance technology connections. Teachers first take pictures of children in their environment to show them that familiar things can be represented by scale models. Teachers then point out that the pictures are small, whereas the real thing is much bigger. Taking pictures of many of the things in the classroom and asking children to point to the real object leads children to understand that real things can be represented in much smaller ways. This helps children understand small map symbols. **Cartoons** are another way to develop symbolic understanding. Cartoons may be used to depict real people and to express all sorts of ideas and opinions. It is important to remind children that hurtful (or otherwise inappropriate) images or expressions should never be used. The most important thing to remember is to begin with symbols that are familiar to students or are seen often by children (e.g., the heart symbol in "I ♡ Texas," the international symbol for restrooms, or the symbol for "Walk/ Don't Walk").

Teaching standards ask that teachers not only know facts and provide meaningful activities but that they also know and have students involved in the **methods of historians**, such as (1) problem identification (i.e., investigators perceive that a problem is meaningful to them in some way); (2) the ability to gather information from the past; (3) the ability to observe data carefully; (4) the ability to analyze data and make inferences; and (5) the ability to draw conclusions (Seefeldt, 1997). Personal involvement in the problem-solving process helps students acquire a more balanced sense of history; that is, it is not only something one knows but also something that one lives. Children must be given opportunities to explore social studies rather than simply be exposed to it. Students should be allowed to actually "do" history: frame meaningful questions, gather and analyze data from both primary and secondary sources, and disseminate their findings in a variety of ways to a diverse audience (Levstik & Barton, 2001, p. 11).

In summary, to develop our students' interests in history, we must have a firm grasp of not only the content but also how to teach it (Maxim, 1999). Successful history teaching requires that teachers develop their knowledge of people, ideas, and events from the past for a foundation on which to build exciting lessons. Knowledge of history ultimately provides both teachers and students some insight for a better understanding of current problems and conflicts.

Given the extensive nature of the information that this standard covers, it is broken down into the following headings and subheadings:

WORLD HISTORY

United States History and International Relations

Exploration and Settlement
National Unity
Regional Differences
Industrial Growth
Reform Movements
International Affairs
International Relations between the Superpowers
The Present

Texas History

Earliest Inhabitants
Early European Exploration and Development
Revolution, Republic, and Statehood

Consider the following practice question:

What invention helped to fire the sentiments that gave rise to the Reformation?

 A. The pocket watch
 B. The printing press
 C. The cotton gin
 D. The telescope

The Reformation began in 1517, when Martin Luther, a Catholic priest, challenged the authority of the Catholic Church. Word of Luther's challenge (or protest) against many church abuses that were occurring during this time spread quickly due to the printing press (*B*), invented in 1440. This, in turn, led to the birth of the Protestant religion (from the word *protest*), in which Luther's believers (and others later on) moved to a Reformation of church practices and beliefs. The pocket watch (*A*) was not invented until 1675. The cotton gin (*C*) was not invented until 1793, and the telescope (*D*) was invented in 1608, but none of these would have a connection to religious reform. The correct answer is *B*.

KEY QUESTION: *What were the main events in World History?*

- Current paleontologists have located the remains of the first **Homo sapiens** in Africa (near modern-day Ethiopia). Their existence has been dated from about 160,000 years ago. From there, civilizations migrated outward, eventually populating the world. An important concept in development of civilization is the move from hunting/gathering to the domestication of plants and animals. This allowed people to live in settlements rather than have to gather food in a nomadic life. As people remained together longer, languages, governments, economies, specialization of labor, and social networks began to form. These varied from place to place.

- Although evidence shows humans to have been in the Middle East and Asia long before, from 3500 to 2000 B.C.E. ("Before the Common Era" or "Before the Christian Era"), river systems in the Middle East, India, and China saw the rise of **four major river valley civilizations**. One of the earliest was in the Middle East in the region of Mesopotamia (meaning "land between the waters") near present-day Iraq. This land was part of the **Fertile Crescent** and was located between the **Tigris and Euphrates rivers** and extended down along the Nile.

- Also in the Middle East, agricultural settlements along the **Nile River** in Egypt led to the creation of a major civilization in 3100 B.C.E. This began a period of rule by royal kingdoms, which lasted until the 300s B.C.E. Egyptians created a system of communication through written pictorial characters called **hieroglyphics**. We are able to read ancient hieroglyphics because of the discovery in 1799 of the **Rosetta Stone**, carved in 196 B.C.E. This stone contains text written by priests to honor Ptolemy, a pharaoh (a king of Egypt) and continues to explain some governmental decrees. The same text was carved on the stone in two languages (Egyptian and Greek) and used three scripts (hieroglyphic, demotic, and Greek).

- A third major civilization, the **Indus River Civilization**, developed around the same time, 2600 B.C.E., on the coast of the Arabian Sea in present-day Pakistan. Although these people had a written language, it has yet to be deciphered; therefore, little is known about this civilization.

- The fourth major river valley civilization began in China, along the **Yellow River**. By 2000 B.C.E., the Chinese had discovered bronzeworking and were making tools and weapons from iron by 600 B.C.E.

- Around 2000 B.C.E. in what is now labeled as the Middle East, the Hebrews (later known as Israelites and Jews) brought **monotheism** (worship of one deity) to the world. Other civilizations believed in **polytheism** (worship of many gods).

- Between 800 and 500 B.C.E., the Greeks formed dozens of independent city-states rather than a single nation. The Greek word for city-states is *polis*, which is where the word *politics* originates. The largest of the Greek city-states, **Athens**, formed a new type of governmental system in which its citizens (all free men) decided their laws. This was called a *direct democracy*, or rule by the people. The **Greeks** are considered to have laid the foundation of Western Civilization. Greek writers and philosophers such as Socrates (470–399 B.C.E.), Plato (428–347 B.C.E.), and Aristotle (384–322 B.C.E.) are still influential in Western thought. Macedonia, north of Athens, produced **Alexander the Great** (356–323 B.C.E.), who conquered much of the land from Eastern Europe through much of India. His influence spread Greek ideas, including democracy, throughout his empire.

- As the Greek civilization declined, the new powerful civilization of **Rome** arose in the Mediterranean region. As Rome expanded its territory, a series of internal struggles began. Representative government (the **Republic**) started to fail and political power began to be concentrated in a single ruler (a **dictatorship**). **Julius Caesar** was, perhaps, the most famous Roman ruler, followed by the first true dictator of the Roman Empire, **Augustus**. The **Roman Empire** lasted roughly from 31 B.C.E. until 476 C.E. (the "Common Era," or the "Christian Era"; formerly A.D.) and, at times, stretched north to the island of Britain (up to Hadrian's Wall near Scotland), west to Spain, south to Egypt, and also covered much of the Middle East. In 380 C.E. Christianity was made the official religion of the empire by the **Emperor Constantine**. Rome fell in 476 C.E., most often accredited to overextension, the decay of values and morals, corruption in government, over taxation, and sacking by several different Germanic barbarian tribes then and in the prior years.

- Advanced civilization has been tracked in China for more than 4,000 years. The Golden Age of China, lasting almost 1,000 years, began in about 600 B.C.E. and was marked by modern papermaking, development of the compass, paper money, gunpowder, and the teachings of **Confucius** and **Buddha** (from China) and others who established the literary, moral, and religious traditions of Chinese society that would remain for centuries. Beginning about 200 B.C.E., **China** entered the first of its four imperial dynasties. The first emperor to unify the nation was from the Qin (Ch'in) dynasty. The name China is thought to have derived from the name of this dynasty, and it was during this period that the Great Wall was completed. The Han dynasty was one of the most prosperous, the strongest, and longest lasting of the Chinese dynasties, and it was during this time that the **Silk Road** caravan trade route to the West first opened due to the western expansion of the empire. The Sui, Tang, and Song dynasties followed, with the Tang dynasty often considered the high point in China's Golden Age. Peasant rebellions and military disasters destroyed the final dynasty in 906 C.E., and China remained split into several independent states until a single Chinese nation emerged again in the 1200s under Genghis Khan and, later, Kublai Khan.

- In the Middle East a new faith, **Islam**, emerged in the 600s C.E. Founded by a wealthy merchant from Mecca, **Mohammed**, who, following a holy vision, spent his life spreading the message he received in the vision. Like Judaism and Christianity, Islamic faith has only a single deity. The word *Islam* comes from an Arabic phrase meaning "to submit to God." Followers of Islam, called **Muslims** (which comes from the phrase "servant of God"), follow teachings laid out in the Koran (Qur'an).

- After the fall of the Roman Empire, Europe began a period of decline from 500 to 1500 C.E. The beginning of the Medieval period (the term *Medieval* in Latin means middle ages) was known as the "Dark Ages"

(476–1000), a time when it was felt that much ancient knowledge was lost, that little headway was made in civilization, and that it was "dark" because few written accounts survive (or were written) to enlighten us about these years.

- In Medieval Europe, there was no centralized government system. A system of small states with kingships ruled, allowing little mobility for serfs who were tied to the land (fiefs). Wealthy landowners gave peasants their protection; in return, these serfs had to work the land and give most of the products produced by their labors to the owners. This was called **feudalism.**

- In the years between 1095 and 1270, approximately eight Crusades were led by Christian kings and Popes against those (mostly Muslims) who held the Holy Land. Many reasons influenced Crusaders to "take the Cross": religious beliefs to recapture the Holy Land from Muslims or to gain salvation, overpopulation in areas of Europe, stepping stones to riches or nobility, desire to see military action, and so forth. The **Knights Templar**, who were warrior priests, were one group who fought in these wars.

- In England, citizens who had been ruled under an absolute monarchy begin to tire of kings who were wasteful and unjust. The **Magna Carta** (1215), imposed on England's King John by his barons, provided the first checks on the powers of the king. This document is considered to be the forerunner of constitutional law and our own Bill of Rights.

- **Marco Polo** and members of this family were some of the first Europeans believed to have traveled through Asia on the Silk Road. He was said to have lived for many years in China under the rule of Kublai Khan during the 1200s. He returned to dictate about many of the wonders he saw and experienced, and these descriptions and maps of his travels spurred on other voyages and eventual discoveries (such as that of Christopher Columbus).

- Toward the end of the Middle Ages, around 1300, a revival of culture and intellect began in southern Europe, being especially strong on the Italian peninsula. It eventually spread across Europe. This period, referred to as the **Renaissance** (meaning "rebirth" of classical ideas) lasted until approximately 1600. Artists such as Michelangelo and inventors such as Leonardo da Vinci, Copernicus (astronomy), and Newton (laws of motion) led the way to new knowledge and enlightenment.

- The **Protestant Reformation** began in 1517 when a monk named **Martin Luther** protested against the many abuses of the then powerful Catholic Church. He was excommunicated and founded the new Lutheran Church, which was the first of the protestant denominations.

- An examination of any historical issue or event must account for deliberate, frequently violent, or coercive impositions that are products of conscious acts that often—and always, in the end—led to unforeseen consequences. These acts include invasion, conquest, and colonization. An example of this can be seen in the history of Central Asia. This region, located between three major cultural areas, was greatly affected by conquests and trade. The Silk Route, Mongol invasions, state formation, and the diffusion of Buddhism and Islam significantly altered the history of this area.

- An **ethnic conflict** or **ethnic war** is a war between or among ethnic groups and is often the result of ethnic nationalism. **Ethnic groups** are people who identify themselves as a part of particular group through a common cultural past, race, religion, or nation. Not all ethnic conflicts escalate into war. **Belgium**, for example, has a long history of tension between the majority of Flemish speakers (concentrated in the north) and the French-speaking Walloon minority (mostly in the south). Decentralization and power-sharing has allowed the country to survive ethnic tensions for more than 170 years. During that time, Belgium has enjoyed a high level of political and economic development. The same is true in **Canada**, which has longstanding issues with a **secession** movement. Quebec, a French-speaking province, has often thought about withdrawing from Canada. Ethnic conflict, however, has never escalated to the point of war in either of these two countries because ethnic groups are allowed to control the regions of the country where that group is in the majority, while respecting basic minority rights. This prevents a zero-sum power struggle between ethnic groups, which, unfortunately, erupted in **Rwanda** and **Kosovo**. In 1994, the Hutu majority in Rwanda committed **genocide** (deliberately attempting to remove a people by killing or hurting anyone of a particular ethnic, religious, racial, or national group) against the Tutsi minority, killing hundreds of thousands. After World War II, Yugoslavia was a country meshed together from eight other former small countries first under communism, then later strict socialism. Following the death of its president, Marshal Tito, Yugoslavia experienced major ethnic conflicts. Slobodan **Milošević**, a Serb, tried to integrate ethnic groups in the region into a greater Serbia. Many fought the Serbs in order to establish their own independence. Milošević was accused of genocide and was later captured but died prior to the end of his United Nations trial for war crimes. The 1995 Dayton Accords recognized the existence of **Bosnia** as a separate nation, and the ethnic conflict ended there; however, this agreement did not recognize Kosovo as independent. Serbs tried to reassert control of the ethnic Albanians in Kosovo and a war began. In 1999, NATO forces, under the command of American **General Wesley Clark**, began a bombing campaign that drove the Serbs from the region. A NATO force of around 10,000 soldiers is still present in Kosovo. Seven separate nations now exist in that area based mostly along ethnic and religious lines.

- Conquest and immigration influenced the history of Ireland, resulting in centuries of ethno-religious conflicts. Ireland, prior to British conquest in 1175, consisted mostly of groups of smaller kingdoms. The Irish were not keen on British rule, and many uprisings ensued. By the 14th century, the colony of Dublin, which had been the British Capitol, was in trouble. Several British kings tried to subdue the Irish population, depriving the rebellious families of their lands and awarding those lands to British settlers. This was called a **policy of plantation**. When King Henry VIII broke with the Catholic Church, religion entered Irish politics for the first time, with those loyal to Britain being Protestant. In 1534, Irish Catholics began a crusade against the Protestant English king. They were unsuccessful and, as a result, more Irish families lost land and power to the British, whose settlers in Ireland were being rewarded with both. When the **Home Rule movement** (or giving the government back to Ireland) began to gain momentum, those in the northern portion of Ireland with the strongest ties to Protestant Britain resisted. In 1921, Ireland was officially divided into two parts, the six predominantly Protestant counties in Ulster would be known as the North, and the 26 predominantly Catholic counties would be known as the South. The period known as

The Troubles erupted, however, when the IRA (Irish Republican Army) of the North, an underground group of pro-Catholic dissenters, sought to unite Ireland into one country. The British army remained in the north to protect the rights of the northern Protestants, but became the target of much violence. Finally, a cease fire was brokered. The country of Ireland remains divided and, although the violence has mostly disintegrated, much of the north remains segregated along religious and ethnic lines.

United States History and International Relations

Consider the following practice question:

What document is known as the first document of American democracy?

A. The Articles of Confederation
B. The Constitution
C. The Mayflower Compact
D. The Federalist Papers

The Mayflower Compact was signed by the Pilgrim men aboard the Mayflower in 1620 before the colonists moved onto land at Plymouth. It was the official Constitution of the Plymouth Colony for more than 70 years after its signing. In this document, the colonists agreed to govern themselves according to the will of the majority; thus, this compact is the first document of American democracy and the first America State Paper. The answer is C.

I. Exploration and Settlement

KEY QUESTION: *Who were the early European explorers in the Americas?*

- It is now accepted that **Leif Ericsson** and a small group of **Vikings** were the first Europeans to set foot on North America, probably as early as 1000 C.E. in present-day Canada.
- From the 15th through the 17th centuries, European nations explored and settled large parts of the New World. The Spaniards, landing first in the West Indies under the command of Christopher Columbus, established colonies in South America and Mexico. Later, in 1565, Spaniards explored much of Florida and founded a settlement at **St. Augustine** (the oldest settlement to be continuously occupied within the present-day United States). Their explorations were motivated by the search for a route for Far Eastern goods, gold, the desire for expansion of territory, and the wish to convert native populations to Roman Catholicism.
- **Christopher Columbus** argued his case with **King Ferdinand** and **Queen Isabella** of Spain for sailing west to find the riches of the Far East markets. In 1492, his **three ships**, the **Nina**, the **Pinta**, and the **Santa Maria**, made landfall in the New World in the islands of San Salvador. Thinking that he had landed in India, he named the native tribes *Indians*. This was the first of four voyages. Although Columbus was not the first European to touch on the New World, his voyage opened doors to the wave of exploration and conquest by European nations.

- America was named for **Amerigo Vespucci**, who was said to have voyaged with Columbus and to have completed later voyages (which he mapped). Vespucci believed that Columbus had discovered a New World and, afterward, maps called this land *America*.
- **Ponce de Leon**, a Spaniard, was the first European to set foot on land that is currently the continental United States, as he explored Florida in 1513 looking for the famous "Fountain of Youth."
- **Vasco Nunez de Balboa**, a Spaniard, also sailed in 1513 and, after crossing land at the Isthmus of Panama, was the first European to see the Pacific Ocean.
- **Ferdinand Magellan's** ship (under the flag of Spain) was the first to sail around the globe in 1522.
- **Hernan Cortes**, a Spaniard, conquered the **Aztecs** for their riches in Mexico in 1519. Although the Aztecs were strong, they and their king, **Montezuma**, believed that Cortes was a part of an ancient prophecy, thus giving the Spaniards a great military advantage, as they were *first* welcomed as gods.
- **Francisco Pizzaro**, a Spaniard, conquered the **Incas** in Peru and explored much of South America between 1531 and 1533.
- In 1527, **Cabeza de Vaca**, a Spaniard, accompanied by a small expeditionary force (including **Esteban**, an African slave), was the first explorer to land in Texas (having floated on a raft from a disastrous expedition in Florida). In 1536, four survivors finally found their way to Mexico City with mythical tales of Seven Cities of Gold.
- In 1539, **Hernando De Soto** explored much of what are now the southern states of the United States (Florida, Alabama, Georgia, the Carolinas, and Tennessee). De Soto claimed much land for Spain, including much of what is now considered "the South." He explored as far west as the Mississippi River.
- **Francisco Coronado**, a Spaniard, explored in 1540 much of what is now the states of Texas, New Mexico, Arizona, Oklahoma, and Kansas, also looking for the Seven Cities of Gold.
- **Juan de Oñate**, known as the last of the conquistadors, continued the search for cities of gold in the northern part of New Spain. His expeditions led him to become the first governor of Santa Fe de Nuevo Mexico, the province of New Spain that stretched over most of present day New Mexico and some parts of Texas, Utah, Colorado and Arizona.
- **Giovannia da Verrazano**, who sailed for France in 1524, and **Jacques Cartier**, a Frenchman, explored the upper New England coast and Canada for France in 1534. Cartier was searching for a Northwest Passage from France to the Far East. Although he did not locate a passage, he founded trade with Native American Indians. This influenced France's interest in Canada through current times. Quebec remains a province of Canada, and French is still the primary language.
- **Sir Francis Drake** sailed along the Pacific coasts of North and South America, and, on completing his voyage in 1580, was the first Englishman to circumnavigate the globe.
- **Sir Walter Raleigh** established the **first English colony** ("The Lost Colony") in America in 1587 on **Roanoke Island** in Virginia (named for Queen Elizabeth, who was known as the Virgin Queen). Supply ships from England were delayed until 1590 and, when they returned, the colony was deserted. It is not truly known what happened to those early Roanoke settlers, but it is thought that most died and others were absorbed into local Native American tribes.

- By 1580, Spain had basically claimed as **New Spain** all of the land in what is now the southeastern, south central, and southwestern parts of the United States (in addition to most of South America). **Jose de Oñate** explored and claimed New Mexico for Spain in the late 1500s. **José de Éscandón** was known as the Father of the Lower Rio Grande for his colonization of the area. At this time, Spain was the most powerful country in Europe. However, England (under Queen Elizabeth) had many concerns and differences with Spain. In an effort to gain control over the seas, Spain sent a huge **Armada** of ships against England that was defeated by a combination of Queen Elizabeth's navy and horrific weather in 1588. This defeat considerably diluted Spain's power and allowed England and France to become the leading imperialist nations.
- In the 1600s, the French and the English explored the wilderness lands of North America. The French founded colonies in Canada and all along the Mississippi River. They were more interested in staking claims to land and trading in furs and fish than in developing permanent settlements. French explorer **Samuel de Champlain** founded Quebec City in 1603 and built a fort to secure the territory in Canada. The French claim on lands in budding America and the increase in population of settlers expanding across the Appalachian Mountains caused clashes with the Native Americans. Later, from 1756 to 1763, the British colonists in America faced the **French and Indian War**, which resulted in France losing all of its land east of the Mississippi River (except New Orleans) to the British.
- **Henry Hudson**, an English explorer, further investigated the Hudson Bay and Hudson River areas in 1609. Later, he laid claim to New Amsterdam (Manhattan) for the Dutch East India Company, but it was lost to the British several years later.
- **René-Robert Cavelier, Sieur de La Salle**, a Frenchman, explored the entire length of the Mississippi River from its source to the Gulf of Mexico in 1682 and claimed the land and river for France, but there few settlements of any size until the early 1700s, when trading posts such as Detroit and New Orleans were established.

KEY QUESTION: *How did a desire for freedom influence daily life and government in early America?*

- **Jamestown**, named for King James I of England, was established in 1607 by merchants of the Virginia Company of London. The original colonists, 104 men, suffered terrible conditions, and many died. However, the strong leadership of **John Smith** (whose life was saved by **Pocahontas**, daughter of a Native American chief) kept the colony from collapsing. In 1612, **John Rolfe** discovered a new type of tobacco that could be grown in Virginia. This was the first major cash crop of the New World. The need for workers led to the first Africans being brought to Virginia. Initially, they were treated as **indentured servants** rather than slaves. An indentured servant was a person who agreed to work several years for a person or company in return for passage to America. Even though this colony was the **first permanent English settlement** in America, it is not as famous as Plymouth Colony because it did not open the doors to mass immigration from Europe (as did Plymouth).
- The desire for political and **religious freedom** brought many colonists to the New World. Pilgrims, Puritans, Catholics, and Quakers sought the right to worship without government interference.

- In 1620 the **Pilgrims**, a small group of religious separatists led by **William Bradford**, came to America on a ship named the *Mayflower*. They had separated from the Church of England, at whose head was the king or queen, to return to the scriptures alone as a governing authority. Citing continued church corruption, they were persecuted for their beliefs in England. Prior to coming ashore in the New World, they drafted an agreement, the *Mayflower Compact*, committing the settlers of the **Plymouth Colony** in Massachusetts to self-government and majority rule. Thus, this Compact outlined the first form of **democracy in America**. This settlement marked the beginning of permanence and expansion on the North American continent. After the first hard year had passed, the Pilgrims celebrated the first **Thanksgiving** with the Native Americans who had been friendly to them—the Wampanoag tribe. One American Indian who was of particular help to the Pilgrims was **Squanto**.

- In 1629, the **Puritans**, a larger group than the Pilgrims and who sought to purify the Church of England (but not necessarily separate from it), was led by **John Winthrop** to form a joint-stock company they called the Massachusetts Bay Company. A **joint-stock company** raised capital by the public sale of stocks in its company. King Charles I, happy to be rid of the Puritans, granted the group a charter to found a colony in the New World. Winthrop wanted to create a colony that would be a "city on a hill," a model for the world of what a Christian community ought to be. The Puritans carefully organized prior to their journey and settlement, which meant that the **Massachusetts Bay Colony** never went through the "starving years" that earlier colonies had endured in their first years.

- Puritan dissenters began to break away to form their own colonies. **Roger Williams** founded a colony in Providence in 1636, and **Anne Hutchinson** founded Portsmouth in 1638. They received a charter from the English Parliament in 1644 to combine their colonies into what would later become the state of Rhode Island. Connecticut was also founded by a Puritan dissenter, **Thomas Hooker**, in 1636.

- England also offered land grants to other religious groups. **George Calvert, Lord Baltimore**, a Catholic, was granted the first proprietary colony for Maryland in 1632, and **William Penn** was given a land grant in what is now Pennsylvania to establish a colony for Quakers.

- **King Philip's War**—perhaps the most costly war in American history in terms of the percentage of lives lost or destroyed on both sides—broke out in 1675 between the New England colonists and some of the local Native American tribes. Dwindling resources, including land, caused increased clashes between the cultures. Many other American Indians fought with the colonists against Metacom, a Native American who took the English name of King Philip. Although the warring tribes were defeated, it took many years for the colonies to recover from this war.

- One of the greatest Native American governmental organizations was the **Iroquois Confederacy**. Formed sometime during the **pre-contact era** (before Columbus), five separate nations located in the upstate region of New York (the Mohawk, Seneca, Onondaga, Oneida, and the Cayuga) joined together in an association known as a *confederacy* or *league*. Some historians believe that the Iroquois Confederacy is the oldest living participatory democracy in the world, as governance was, in fact, based on the consent of the governed. The **Muscogee Nation** was also a confederacy that began in the pre-contact era. The Muscogee were not one tribe, but a union of several. Tribes established towns in river valleys in the present states of Alabama, Georgia, Florida, and South Carolina. Within this political structure, each tribal town maintained political autonomy and distinct land holdings.

- In 1692, Puritans in Massachusetts were shaken by the accusations of young girls in Salem who believed they were being tormented by several witches who lived in the village. The **Salem Witch Trials** resulted in 20 executions, 19 by hanging and 1 who was crushed by rocks.
- By the 1700s, town meetings were conducted throughout the New England colonies. People voted, created their own laws, and sent representatives to colonial assemblies. **Individualism**, the belief in the dignity and worth of each person, had a firm religious and political base in the British colonies.
- Because many colonial economies experienced rapid growth, settlers worked hard to establish their own farms and businesses. Differing geographic and economic conditions led to three distinctive groups. The **13 original colonies** were divided into New England colonies, middle colonies, and southern colonies.
- The **New England Colonies** of Massachusetts, New Hampshire, Rhode Island, and Connecticut had poor soil and thus developed fishing, trading, whaling, and shipbuilding industries. The majority of those who settled here came from England.
- The **Middle Colonies** of New York, New Jersey, Pennsylvania, and Delaware grew large quantities of wheat and grain on family farms, established flour milling, and participated in some shipping and trading. Most of the settlers in this region came from England, Germany, Scotland, and France (along with some free Africans).
- The **Southern Colonies** of Maryland, Virginia, North Carolina, South Carolina, and Georgia had a climate and soil that favored the development of large plantations on which tobacco, indigo, cotton, and rice were grown. There was also some trading and shipping. These colonies were mostly settled by English, French, Scots, and slaves from Africa (on whom the economy of agriculture came to depend).
- One of the earliest legislative bodies in the United States, the **House of Burgesses**, was established in Virginia. Beginning in 1619 in Jamestown, colonists elected representatives to this assembly.

II. National Unity

KEY QUESTION: *What led the states to adopt a central government in 1790?*

- During the first half of the 18th century, England pursued a policy of **salutary neglect** and did not attempt to exercise much economic or political control over its North American colonies.
- In 1763, however, as a result of enormous debts arising from the **French and Indian War**, England decided to levy taxes on the prospering colonies.
- The **Stamp Act of 1765** was an English tax on newspapers and legal documents. Following colonial protests, this tax was repealed, but this was the seed of unrest that sparked the call of "No taxation without representation" for the colonies. Colonists began to set up correspondence throughout the 13 colonies (committees of correspondence) and meet in like-minded groups such as the **Sons of Liberty**, formed by patriots such as **Samuel Adams**, who at first tried to protest against their lost of rights as Englishmen, but later were alleged to be involved with such acts as the Boston Tea Party.

- In 1766, England imposed the **Townsend Acts**, which required new taxes on tea, glass, paint, and paper. Most colonial legislatures sent protests to the British Parliament. The British Crown initially responded by increasing the number of troops stationed in America. By 1770, tensions between colonists and soldiers ran high. In Boston, the hostility between the two groups led to an incident in which several colonists were killed, including **Crispus Attucks**, an African American. Samuel Adams called the incident the **Boston Massacre**. Parliament repealed all the taxes except the one on tea. This created a significant problem; if the colonies paid the tea tax they would, in effect, be confirming that England had the right to directly tax them. In 1773, a group of angry colonists (dressed up as Mohawk Indians) threw tea from British cargo ships into Boston Harbor. In response to the **Boston Tea Party**, England closed the port of Boston and severely limited self-government in Massachusetts. The fundamental disagreement was over England's taxation of the colonists without having been allowed representation in the British government.
- The British government (with King George III at its head) passed four acts, collectively known as the **Intolerable** (or the **Coercive**) **Acts** in response to the dumping of the tea: (1) the port of Boston was closed until the tea was paid for, (2) the Massachusetts royal governor was given greater authority over the colonial legislature, (3) royal officials accused of a crime could be tried elsewhere, and (4) the Quartering Act required American colonists to house British troops.
- In 1774, Americans formed the **First Continental Congress** in response to the Intolerable Acts. Meeting in Philadelphia, its first act was to draft a petition to the British Parliament to protest the Intolerable Acts. In addition to their protest to England, they began to organize a militia to protect themselves. Up until this time, most colonists considered themselves **Loyalists** (or loyal to King George III). However, some were beginning to join groups such as the **Patriots** rather than remain as Englishmen. Committees of Correspondence were created to communicate throughout the colonies about events that had to do with the current politics.
- Initially, the British government paid little attention to the First Continental Congress. By 1775, the British sent more troops to Massachusetts to arrest the leaders of the rebellion. **General Gage** led 700 British soldiers to Concord on a mission to search for and destroy a reported stockpile of colonial arms and ammunition. The Americans tracked the British troop movements and sent two riders, **Paul Revere** and **William Dawes**, to alert the countryside. This famous ride is immortalized in the poem, **"Paul Revere's Ride"** by Henry Wadsworth Longfellow, in which the signal that the British were coming was given by a lantern in the church tower: "One if by land, and two if by sea."
- When the British arrived at **Lexington**, they found a group of 70 American **Minutemen** (militiamen ready at a moment's notice) waiting for them on the village green. A British officer ordered the men to drop their weapons and disperse. The Minutemen held on to their weapons but did begin to leave the green. At the same time, a shot was fired. This was **"the shot heard 'round the world"** marking the beginning of the Revolutionary War. Later that day, the American **Minutemen** drove the British from **Lexington** and **Concord**.
- A Second Continental Congress came together in 1775, and this Congress formed the **Continental Army** with **George Washington** at

its head. This was a rag-tag army that used guerilla tactics on the British because of the poor odds.

- In June 1775, at the **Battle of Bunker Hill**, the Americans were driven back, but surprisingly, they inflicted huge losses on the British.
- In 1776, **Thomas Paine** published his famous pamphlet **Common Sense**, which gave reasons why it was foolish to believe that Americans could reconcile with England.
- The Congress approved the **Declaration of Independence** on **July 4, 1776**. In this declaration (mostly written by **Thomas Jefferson**), the basic principles of the United States government were set forth, along with the colonists' grievances and the reasons they were to be freed from England.
- George Washington, as commander of the Continental Army, after a year of losing battles and skirmishes to the British, managed to **cross the Delaware River** at night with his army and win the Battle of Trenton in New Jersey.
- In 1777, the Continental Army almost did not make it through the harsh winter at **Valley Forge**. There was little food, clothing, or shelter for soldiers. Morale was low throughout the winter. However, Washington's strong leadership was able to keep the army together to continue the **Revolutionary War**, or the **War for Independence**.
- The French were very helpful to the emerging nation, sending ships, weapons, and officers such as **de Lafayette**.
- In October 1781, the **Battle of Yorktown**, the last major battle of the Revolutionary War, was won by the Continental Army, with help from the French. The British forces, under the leadership of **Cornwallis**, surrendered.
- **Nathan Hale**, during the war, spied on the British for the American army but was captured and executed. His famous last words were, "I only regret that I have but one life to lose for my country." **Benedict Arnold**, a high-ranking American officer, turned traitor to the young country, becoming forever associated with betrayal in American history.
- In 1783, with the signing of the **Treaty of Paris**, the colonies won the Revolutionary War and their freedom from England.
- One of the powerful symbols associated with the American Independence is the **Liberty Bell**. On July 8, 1776, tradition tells that the tolling of the Liberty Bell from Independence Hall in Philadelphia summoned citizens to hear a reading of the Declaration of Independence. In October 1777, when the British occupied Philadelphia, the Liberty Bell was removed from the city and hidden. It was feared that the British would have melted it down and used the iron for ammunition. The bell was returned to Philadelphia in 1778 when the British left the city. Despite cracks in the bell, it was used throughout the period of 1790 to 1800 (when **Philadelphia** served as the nation's capital) to call the state legislature into session, to summon voters to turn in ballots, and to commemorate George Washington's birthday.
- After the Revolutionary War, the colonies became independent states, joined together in a loose association under the first constitution of the United States—the **Articles of Confederation** (ratified in 1781). The Articles established a very weak central republican government (elected representation) with a Congress (but with only one governmental chamber [unicameral]). It could declare war but was not allowed to recruit an army. There was no executive branch, central federal judicial branch, or courts. States taxed each other's goods and used different monetary currencies.

- **Shays' Rebellion**, an uprising of debtor farmers in Massachusetts, showed the states how inadequate the Articles of Confederation were. The central government did not have the authority to put down the rebellion.
- In 1790, the site of the **District of Columbia (Washington, D.C.)** was designated as the nation's new capital city next to the Potomac River. **Benjamin Banneker**, an African American mathematician, surveyed the area, and **Charles L'Enfant** was the architect and engineer who designed the plan for the city.
- Recognizing the many weaknesses of the Articles of Confederation, 55 delegates (now known as the **Founding Fathers**) from the various states met in Philadelphia and eventually drafted the **Constitution of the United States**, adopted in 1790.
- **James Madison**, a politician from Virginia, was one of the principal authors of the Constitution. Madison, Secretary of State under Thomas Jefferson, was a party to one of the most significant court cases in U.S. history, *Marbury v. Madison* (1803), which established the precedent for judicial review; that is, courts review the constitutionality of laws and can strike down laws that go against the Constitution (the supreme law of the United States). As Secretary of State, Madison also officiated over the Louisiana Purchase. Later, in 1808, he was elected the fourth president of the United States. Madison was the first president to have ever served in the U.S. Congress prior to being elected president.
- The Constitution was the result of a series of *compromises* (called the **Great Compromise**). Among the most important of these were representation in the legislature and the method of electing the president. The debate over ratification also divided the nation into Nationalists, or **Federalists**, who supported the Constitution, and **anti-Federalists**, who feared that a strong central government might abuse its power and the liberties of the people and the states. The Constitution consists of the **Preamble** or introduction; the **Articles**, which explain the powers (and limits on power) of the federal government; and the **Amendments**, which change or make explicit elements of the original Constitution.
- The Preamble to the Constitution reads:
  We the People of the United States, in Order to form a more perfect Union, establish Justice, insure domestic Tranquility, provide for the common defense, promote the general Welfare, and secure the Blessings of Liberty to ourselves and our Posterity, do ordain and establish this Constitution for the United States of America.
- There are seven **Articles** in the Constitution. The first covers the powers of the Legislature. Because this is the first Article, many Constitutional scholars believe that the Founding Fathers must have considered the powers of the Legislature extremely important. The articles specify the term of office for **senators** (6 years), **representatives** (2 years), and for **president** (4 years); provide for a **Supreme Court** (with 9 judges with lifetime appointments); and set up the **Electoral College** (a complex system for electing the president that provides for a balance of equality between all the states rather than the actual number of popular votes).
- There are **27 Amendments** to the Constitution. The first 10 of these are referred to as the **Bill of Rights**.
- The promise of a **Bill of Rights**, the first 10 amendments to the Constitution, allowed the anti-Federalists to accept the new government. Anti-Federalists wanted to guarantee that citizens would be protected from the new government, so they wanted many rights specified, including freedom of speech, press, religion, and assembly; the

right to bear arms, to petition the government, to due process in courts, and to a speedy and public trial; to not be forced to quarter soldiers in one's home; and protection from unreasonable search and seizure, self-incrimination, **double jeopardy** (to not be tried twice for the same crime), excessive bail, and cruel and unusual punishment. Finally, the 10th Amendment establishes the concept of **federalism**, which gives states all the powers not designated by the Constitution to the federal government. The 14th Amendment abolishes slavery, the **15th Amendment** grants all U.S. (male) citizens the right to vote (including slaves), and the **19th** grants women the right to vote.

- **Roger Sherman**, an early American lawyer and politician from Connecticut, is the only person to sign all four of the great founding documents: the Continental Association, the Declaration of Independence, the Articles of Confederation, and the Constitution.

- Following the War for Independence, George Washington did not believe that citizens in the United States would want to endure the costs or the political danger of having a standing army in peacetime. However, he made the case that it was often necessary and, in fact, safer for the country to have a **professional army** rather than rely solely on a citizen militia. Washington made the case that a system of **checks and balances** in the Constitution would guarantee the safety of this option. Congress had the power to form an army (Article I, Section 8), but only the president could command the army (Article 2, Section 2). The states retained control of their own citizen militias and could provide an immediate response to invasion (by foreign powers, such as the British or Spanish) or rebellion (by slaves, workers, or farmers). The U.S. army provided security for major harbors and estuaries along the coast, provided experts in exploration and cartography to facilitate westward expansion, and also established and fortified outposts to support that mission. After the American Revolution, it was clear that a better trained army would keep the nation more secure, especially with the War of 1812 on the horizon, so training schools (such as the U.S. Military Academy at West Point) were authorized in 1802. Another military institution was instituted for naval cadets after the Department of the Navy and the U.S. Marine Corps were authorized around 1800. Currently, there are five professional military training academies.

- In some ways, the **War of 1812** with England was a continuation of the Revolutionary War. The British and Americans had not finished with their differences. Great Britain refused to abide by the terms of the Treaty of Paris (which ended the Revolutionary War), supporting the Indian tribes against the United States, and the British navy kidnapped and impressed Americans (forced them to serve aboard British ships). America declared war. In a major setback for the American troops, the British captured and burned down much of Washington, D.C. However, American troops successfully defended an attack on **Fort McHenry** in Baltimore. **Francis Scott Key**, a witness to this battle, wrote a poem to commemorate the event. This was set to music as **"The Star-Spangled Banner"** and became our national anthem. It has had potential rivals for this honor. One challenger is **"America the Beautiful."** In 1893, Katherine Lee Bates was inspired to write a poem about the sites she encountered on a cross country train trip. This poem was originally published on July 4, 1895, and was later set to music composed by Samuel A. Ward, who had been similarly inspired.

- One of the most remembered events of the War of 1812 was the victory at the **Battle of New Orleans** (in 1814–1815) with **Andrew Jackson** commanding the U.S. troops. Although the war had already been declared over, the news had not reached the combatants there.

III. Regional Differences

KEY QUESTION: *How did the territorial and economic growth of the country lead to the War Between the States?*

- During the first half of the 1800s, the United States acquired more land west of the original 13 colonies through wars, treaties, and purchases.
- In 1803, President **Thomas Jefferson** bought territory from the French. Known as the **Louisiana Purchase**, this nearly doubled the size of the United States. Jefferson sent **Meriwether Lewis** and **William Clark** to map out other parts of this purchase. They followed the Mississippi River and then continued west to eventually reach the Pacific Ocean in Oregon. A Native American woman, **Sacagawea**, helped guide them. They returned in 1806, marking the beginnings of the covered wagons full of settlers who moved West to settle on their own land there.
- Protected from Europe by an ocean, American leaders continued to encourage territorial expansion on the North American continent and adopted a policy of neutrality toward foreign powers.
- In 1823, **President James Monroe** emphasized a policy of noninterference to warn European nations against intervening anywhere in the Western Hemisphere in his **Monroe Doctrine**.
- By the 1840s, people began to believe in **Manifest Destiny**, the idea that the United States was "destined" to expand from the Atlantic to the Pacific Ocean, and thousands of settlers began to cross the country in wagon trains. The painting **"American Progress"** (also known as "The Spirit of the Frontier") by John Gast most typifies this by showing settlers moving from east to west, driving buffalo and American Indians in front of them. Over the scene floats the spirit of a young woman in goddess form (representing America) that seems to be guiding them forth.
- As the country grew and prospered, regional differences became more pronounced. The Northeast developed an industrial and trading economy. An **Industrial Revolution** (where mass production was being done with machines) began in the late 17th and early 18th centuries. Inventors, such as **Eli Whitney** (who first patented the cotton gin and helped establish the use of interchangeable parts and division of labor that helped found the American system of manufacturing and begin the U.S. Industrial Revolution), **Thomas Edison** (who experimented with early versions of electric lighting, the phonograph, telegraph, electric railway, and an iron ore separator), and **Robert Fulton** (who invented the steamboat), helped begin the transformation from an agrarian to an industrial society. Finished products found markets easier when the **Erie Canal** (1825) helped open up the Midwest by creating a water route between the Atlantic Ocean and the Great Lakes.
- The South became increasingly more dependent on exporting cash agricultural crops (such as cotton and tobacco) to Europe, and the agricultural basis of their economy increasingly grew to depend on slave labor. In the West, cheap land encouraged smaller family farms.
- The growth of the railroad networks also helped homesteaders move West to work small farms of their own and to send goods back East. The completion of the **transcontinental railroad** from coast to coast in 1869, built mostly with Chinese labor, opened the country to the **Manifest Destiny**, or the dream of a country from the Atlantic to the

Pacific. The joining of the tracks from the east and the west was celebrated by driving the **Golden Spike** into the last rail in Utah.

- Regional differences, however, led to **sectionalism**, with Americans increasingly looking at issues in terms of what would benefit their own region rather than national concerns. Northerners favored **tariffs**, or special taxes, on many imported goods to protect their industries. Southerners, who imported more goods, opposed tariffs. Northerners favored the **National Bank**, which gave them a stable currency and investment funds. Westerners and Southerners favored state banks, which would give them easier credit needed in an agrarian society. Midwesterners wanted federal funds for the construction of roads and canals in order to get their products and produce to market more easily. Southerners favored the extension of slavery to new territories, something Northerners and Westerners both opposed. Growing sectionalism meant that Northerners and Westerners came to view any further extension of slavery as empowering the South at the expense of the slaves. However, many Southerners had heavily invested in slavery for their small or large farms (plantations) and felt that, in giving up their slaves, it would cost them their livelihood and land. Southern states used **slave codes** to designate the kind of work that each slave would do—house work, field work, and so forth. **Abolitionists**, particularly in the North, began to demand a complete end to (or the *abolition* of) slavery. **Harriet Beecher Stowe** wrote *Uncle Tom's Cabin*, which influenced many to become abolitionists. Some abolitionists began to help slaves escape through the **Underground Railroad**, the name for a series of safe houses in which people would help lead escaped slaves to the north and freedom. **Harriet Tubman**, an escaped slave, became a "conductor" on the Underground Railroad and was credited with freeing more than 300 escaped slaves. **Sojourner Truth**, another escaped slave, became a powerful and outspoken abolitionist. **Richard Allen**, also a conductor on the Underground Railroad, established the first independent black denominational church in the United States, formed against discrimination and slavery (on social differences rather than on religious differences).

- With the 1828 election of **Andrew Jackson**, sectional issues dominated national politics. A Westerner, Jackson antagonized Southerners by enforcing tariffs but also alienated Northerners by dismantling the National Bank. Under Jackson, all Native Americans east of the Mississippi River were to be moved to west of the Mississippi. The Cherokee Nation, through a Supreme Court decision, was to be allowed to remain, but instead, Jackson, under the Indian Removal Act, had troops force march them to Oklahoma. This march was termed the **Trail of Tears** because of the sorrow and harshness of the 800-mile journey that left more than 4,000 Cherokees dead along the way.

- Several acts on the issues of slavery were instituted during the 1800s. The **Missouri Compromise** maintained the balance of free states versus slave states by allowing Missouri to come into the United States as a slave state and Maine as a free state, but slavery was prevented in any states above the 36° 30′ parallel (except Missouri). The **Kansas–Nebraska Act** allowed for these states, on entering the United States, to choose for themselves. Sectional disputes further intensified when the Supreme Court, in the **Dred Scott Case**, invalidated compromises over the issues of extending slavery into new territories by providing that a slave continued to remain a slave, even if he or she was transported to a non-slave-holding state. The gap between the industrial North and agricultural South widened as each sought to control the central government.

- In 1848, when gold was first discovered in California at **Sutter's Mill** (near present-day Sacramento), the question of slavery in the Western territories became more critical. The "Forty-Niners" (those who rushed to California for riches when they heard the news) were a rough group, and California became a wild and lawless place during the **Gold Rush** years. As a result, many of the fortune seekers who wanted to move to California were often too afraid to bring their valuable slaves to the area, fearing violence plus suspecting that the lure of gold would cause attempted escapes. These fears contributed to California's application for statehood as a free state in 1849. This posed a significant threat to the balance of free states and slave states in the United States.
- When **Abraham Lincoln** was elected president in 1860, the southern states felt that their interests were no longer represented by the federal government and withdrew, or **seceded**, from the Union.
- Under the leadership of **Jefferson Davis**, 11 states formed the **Confederate States of America** (the **Confederacy**; the **South**), and included South Carolina, Mississippi, Florida, Alabama, Georgia, Louisiana, **Texas**, Virginia, Arkansas, Tennessee, and North Carolina. The four slaveholding border states (Maryland, Delaware, Kentucky, and Missouri) and 19 other free states remained in the **Union** (the **North**).
- The **Civil War** began in 1861, when Confederate soldiers fired on federal troops at **Fort Sumter** in South Carolina. A **civil war** is fought between people who are citizens of the same country or live in the same area.
- The **Union**, or the North, had a decided advantage over the Confederacy, having twice the population of the South and three quarters of the nation's wealth. In addition, it had more factories and railroads.
- In July 1862, the first major battle of the war (the **First Battle of Bull Run**), fought on the outskirts of Washington, D.C., resulted in a victory for the Southern forces. **General "Stonewall" Jackson** led his Confederate troops against the poorly trained Union troops under the command of **General Irvin McDowell**. This led to a shake-up in command in the Northern forces. Lincoln had great difficulty finding someone to command the Union army. From 1862 to 1864, the succession of men Lincoln tried as commander of the Union army included **General George McClellan**, **General Ambrose Burnside**, **General Joseph "Fighting Joe" Hooker**, **General George Meade**, and finally **General Ulysses Grant**. Grant would win the war for the Union (the North); **General Robert E. Lee** commanded the Confederate forces.
- Naval engagements were an important aspect of the Civil War. Early in the conflict, the Confederate navy achieved supremacy with their **ironclad** vessel—the *Merrimack*. Originally, the Northern navy had only wooden ships, which could not compete with the iron-plated ship. In 1862, the South's naval supremacy was ended by the North's new ironclad ship—the *Monitor*.
- In September 1862, the **Battle of Antietam**, technically a Northern victory, resulted in the bloodiest single day of battle in U.S. history. At the end of the day, 22,726 men lay dead, dying, or wounded. **General Sherman** undertook a "scorched earth" policy across the South, including the burning of Atlanta.
- Women participated in the war effort by working in factories or nursing (such as **Clara Barton**, known as the "Angel of the Battlefield" and organizer of the American Red Cross). A few women fought in the war or acted as spies.

- Perhaps the most famous battle of the Civil War took place July 1–3, 1863, at the small town of Gettysburg, Pennsylvania. In the **Battle of Gettysburg**, General Meade led 90,000 Union soldiers against General Lee's smaller Confederate contingent of 75,000 soldiers. Meade was severely criticized for allowing Lee to retreat with his remaining army back into the Confederacy, but the battle so weakened the Southern army that Lee never again attempted a serious invasion of the North. The **Battle of Gettysburg** was one of the costliest battles in history. When the fighting ended on July 3, 1863, there were 50,000 fallen Americans from both sides on the battlefield. The battlefield cemetery was officially dedicated on November 19, 1863. President Abraham **Lincoln** delivered the dedication, beginning with, "Four score and seven years ago our fathers brought forth on this continent a new nation, conceived in liberty, and dedicated to the proposition that all men are created equal." In his relatively short speech, later referred to as the **Gettysburg Address**, he memorialized the Union dead and emphasized the power of their sacrifice. He placed the common soldier at the center of the struggle for equality, as he reminded the audience of the higher purpose for which their blood had been shed, so "that the government of the people, by the people, for the people, shall not perish from this earth."
- On January 1, 1863, Lincoln issued the **Emancipation Proclamation**, freeing the slaves in the Confederacy. Immediately, it freed only a few slaves, but it clearly established for the North that this was a war being fought not only to preserve the Union but also to eliminate slavery.
- By 1865, the Confederacy was defeated. **Confederate General Robert E. Lee** formally surrendered to **Union General Ulysses S. Grant** at **Appomattox Courthouse, Virginia**, and the nation began the hard task of recovery. This recovery period was known as the **Reconstruction**.
- More than 618,000 Americans died in the course of the Civil War—more than all American Wars combined.
- **Abraham Lincoln** was assassinated by **John Wilkes Booth** at the Ford's Theater in Washington, D.C., only 5 days after Lee's surrender. It is theorized that the South would have been treated more positively during Reconstruction had Lincoln not been killed and **Vice President Andrew Johnson** not stepped into the Presidency.
- Southern states, such as Texas, voted mostly for Democrats up until the 1960s in response to the harsh Reconstruction years. **John Tower**, who served in Congress for more than 20 years, was the first Republican senator to be elected since Reconstruction.

IV. Industrial Growth

KEY QUESTION: *What were the effects of industrial growth on farms and cities?*

- **Reconstruction** hit the South very hard economically, as the North sought to punish the region for the war. Many Southerners lost their land because of the inability to pay taxes and produce crops (because of loss of life, limb, and slave workers), so even agriculture was depressed.
- In the South during the Civil War and **Reconstruction**, Blacks were given constitutional guarantees of freedom and protection through the **Emancipation Proclamation** and the **Civil War amendments to the Constitution** (13, 14, and 15). **Carpetbaggers** from the North came down to the South to take over land and businesses that could no longer pay their taxes and also to gain political power. **Scalawags** were White southerners with the same goals.

- As a result of the amendments, Southern states passed **Jim Crow Laws**, which legalized **segregation**, and other laws, labeled as **Black codes**, which succeeded in circumventing the amendments in order to deny Blacks the right to vote, as well as other civil rights.
- Most Blacks in the South became **sharecroppers**, farming other people's land in exchange for a portion of their crops. Others became tenant farmers who leased land.
- Unlike Southern sharecroppers, Western and Midwestern farmers benefited from the rapid industrialization of the period. As agriculture became more mechanized, farmers were freed from backbreaking labor, but they felt they were still denied their fair share of the nation's wealth. Farmers often went into debt to purchase new equipment. Railroads charged them exorbitant rates to transport produce to markets, and middlemen siphoned off much of their profits. Therefore, farmers began to demand government regulation of railroad rates and cheap lending practices to ease their debts. They joined the **Grange**, a movement to press their demands for reform. They also formed the backbone of the **Greenback** and **Populist** political parties.
- In 1880, only one quarter of the population of the United States lived in cities, but by 1910, **urbanization** had almost doubled. Rapid technological advances of the Industrial Revolution fostered the development and expansion of industries. Scientific production techniques, such as the **assembly line**, transformed American industry, the economy, and society. **Henry Ford's** use of the assembly line to produce automobiles saw America go from very few cars on the roads in the late 1800s to nearly 5 million by 1917. In 1916, while Ford was putting more cars on the road, the **Federal Aid Roads Act** established the framework for constructing a national network of highways. Americans became more mobile than ever before.
- Between 1880 and 1910, immigrants as well as farmers flocked to American cities to take jobs in the factories. They received low wages and worked under hazardous conditions. In 1911, a fire at the **Triangle Shirtwaist Factory**, in New York City, focused national attention on unsafe working conditions. Because the exit doors had been locked by management in order to keep out union organizers, 146 people, mainly women, died.
- To help workers, the **Knights of Labor** and other unions were started. **Samuel Gompers** founded the **American Federation of Labor (AFL)** in 1886. Members could vote to **strike** (stop working) or could appoint delegates to bargain for better wages and conditions.
- At the same time, industrial leaders, such as **Andrew Carnegie** and **Cornelius Vanderbilt**, created **trusts** to consolidate their control over America's steel and railroad companies. They virtually eliminated competition (created **monopolies**) so that they could set high prices and control the market for their products. These **robber barons** became active in state and national politics in order to impede attempts to regulate their industries.

V. Reform Movements

KEY QUESTION: *How did reforms change the life of Americans in the first half of the 20th century?*

- From the turn of the 20th century until World War I, members of the **Progressive Movement** sponsored legislation to improve the quality of American life and move away from political corruption.

- Reformers enacted pure food and drugs laws to protect consumers.
- The **Temperance Movement** began to gain support against drinking alcohol, but *bootleg* (illegal) alcohol continued to make its way into American homes and establishments. Temperance supporters hoped that **prohibition** (prohibiting the sale and consumption of alcohol) would solve the nation's poverty, crime, violence, and other social problems.
- Reformers like **Susan B. Anthony** and **Carrie Chapman Catt** supported women's efforts to gain the right to vote (or **suffrage**), which was finally granted in the **19th Amendment** in 1920.
- Women pioneers in male-dominated areas (such as aviation) furthered the position of women in society. In 1932, **Amelia Earhart** became the first woman to cross the Atlantic Ocean, flying from Newfoundland to Northern Ireland in 14 hours 56 minutes. In 1937, she and one other crew member were attempting to circumnavigate the globe from west to east when her plane disappeared somewhere over the Pacific Ocean. What happened to Earhart remains a mystery today.
- The **NAACP** (National Association for the Advancement of Colored People) was founded in 1909 by **W.E.B. Dubois** and suffragette **Mary White Ovington**.
- Although slavery had ended, African Americans in the United States were still denied opportunities simply because of their race. There are many examples of those who overcame this discrimination. One is **Bessie Coleman**, born in Atlanta, Texas, in 1892. She was the first African American woman to become an airline pilot and the first American woman to hold an international pilot license. After being denied admission to American flight schools, Coleman studied French and, in 1920, traveled to Paris to attend flight school. Another African American pioneer, this time in the field of hair care and cosmetics, was **Madam C. J. Walker**. By 1917, hers was the largest business owned by an African American. According to many accounts, Walker was the first female American self-made millionaire.
- Child labor was outlawed, and children were guaranteed schooling under compulsory education laws. **Jane Addams**, who lived in Chicago (and established Hull House for immigrant children with working mothers), was instrumental in protecting children from child labor in the early 1900s. In the early 1920s, she helped found the American Civil Liberties Union and was the first American woman to receive the Noble Peace prize.
- Many huge companies gained **monopolies** (owned all of the goods or services of a particular type), with **Standard Oil** one of the first. In 1904, under the leadership of **John D. Rockefeller**, the oil company controlled more than 90 percent of oil production in the United States.
- The government began to take on a greater role in regulating the economy. **Antitrust laws** were enacted to eliminate monopolies and regulate other unfair trade practices. The **Federal Reserve System** allowed the government to create a central bank that controlled the monetary supply of the United States. This is still done, partly by setting interest rates. At the time of publication, the current Chair of the Federal Reserve Board is **Ben Bernanke**, who was appointed in 2006. He replaced **Alan Greenspan**, who was appointed in 1987 by President Reagan and who served almost 20 years.
- After World War I, Americans grew tired of reforms and wanted a **return to normalcy**, an era in which government would play a less important role in people's lives.

- In the Roaring 1920s the economy boomed, and Americans devoted themselves to the making and spending of money. In this frivolous era of **flappers** and **speakeasies** (clubs where illegal alcohol was served), sports and film stars attracted national attention and jazz music gained popularity. The novel *The Great Gatsby* (1925) by **F. Scott Fitzgerald** came to symbolize the entire era.

- On **Black Tuesday**, October 29, 1929, the **stock market crash** brought national prosperity and good times to a sudden and violent end. Stock prices fell rapidly, thousands of people lost their investments, and businesses and banks closed. The nation and the world were soon in the grip of the **Great Depression**, with millions of people unemployed. Families looked for public relief and charitable assistance. In the cities, soup kitchens and bread lines formed to feed the hungry.

- Rural areas were also hard hit during the Depression. One of the worst droughts in American history began in 1930. The region, stretching north from Texas into the Dakotas, came to be known as **The Dust Bowl**. Overgrazing and overplanting, a steady decline in rainfall, and an accompanying increase in heat turned fertile farm regions into virtual deserts (**desertification**). Many farmers left their land in search of work. One of the classic portrayals of this period is **John Steinbeck's** novel *The Grapes of Wrath* (1939).

- **President Franklin Delano Roosevelt (FDR)** proposed a **New Deal** to combat the effects of the depression. He proposed legislation to offer relief to the unemployed, to prevent economic abuses, and to reconstruct the economy with programs such as the **TVA (Tennessee Valley Authority)**, Social Security, and regulation of Wall Street. Although FDR's legislative proposals eased some suffering, the Great Depression did not end until the country **mobilized** for World War II. American industry returned to full strength to manufacture the military machinery necessary for our entry into the war.

- During the Great Depression, **Eleanor Roosevelt** changed the role of First Lady. When her husband Franklin Delano Roosevelt became president in 1933 during the painful years of the Great Depression, she was keenly aware of the social conditions facing Americans. She supported the New Deal principles proposed by her husband and also worked as a civil-rights advocate, particularly concerned with the status of working women. Appointed as a delegate to the United Nations, she helped to develop the Universal Declaration of Human Rights.

- The **Social Security Act** provided social insurance for the elderly and the unemployed.

- The **Security Exchange Commission (SEC)** was set up to regulate the stock market (on Wall Street).

- The **Works Progress Administration (WPA)** gave jobs to the unemployed.

- The **Tennessee Valley Authority (TVA)** put people to work building a series of dams that provided electricity to one of the most depressed rural areas in the nation.

VI. International Affairs

KEY QUESTION: *What are some key conflicts in which the United States participated after the Civil War?*

- **The Spanish-American War** was fought in part by **Theodore "Teddy" Roosevelt** (who later became president) and his **Rough Riders** in 1898, after Cuba asked the United States for help against

Spain. The U.S. warship *Maine*, sitting in Havana harbor, exploded, which gave the United States the excuse it needed to fight against Spain. The results of the treaty that ended this war freed Cuba and gave the Philippine Islands, Guam, and Puerto Rico to the United States as territories (which it kept until after World War II). The Philippines gained independence after World War II, but Guam remains a U.S. territory and Puerto Rico is a commonwealth of the United States. Roosevelt was instrumental in acquiring and building the strip of land in Panama that opened as the Panama Canal in 1914 and that was kept by the United States until 1999 under Jimmy Carter.

- In **1917**, **World War I** saw the United States fighting with the Allies (France, Great Britain, Belgium, Russia, Serbia, etc.) against the **Central Powers** (Germany, Austria–Hungry, the Ottoman Empire, and Bulgaria).

- In **World War II**, the **Allies** (France, the former USSR, Great Britain, and many others) fought against the Axis (Germany, Italy, Austria, and Japan), beginning in Europe in 1939. Switzerland and others remained neutral. The United States entered the war when Japan bombed **Pearl Harbor** in 1941. The war ended with victory for the Allies in 1945.

- The United States fought the **Korean War** from 1950 to 1953 after North Korea (with the help of some Chinese troops) invaded South Korea.

- **Vietnam** was a long war that began under President John F. Kennedy in the mid-1960s and ended in 1975. Vietnam was divided into two parts: the South, which asked for help from the United States, and the North, under communist control. Initial arguments for the United States entering the war centered on holding the line of communism there rather than having South Vietnam fall and letting communism spread to other countries in the Far East (the **Domino Theory**). Although the United States was by far the more powerful nation militarily, the Cold War with China and the USSR seemed to hold the United States back from completing an all-out victory. The American people began to tire of these types of politics and loss of American lives, and the United States eventually pulled out of the region, leaving Vietnam to the Communists. Many Vietnamese, fleeing from the Communists (some on overcrowded boats), emigrated or attempted to emigrate to the United States during this time.

- The **Cold War**, in which there were high tensions between the West and the Communist Block led by the USSR, basically ended in 1991 with the collapse of the communist government in Russia. Although there were complex reasons, many historians give much credit to President Ronald Reagan's policies against "the Evil Empire."

- The first **Gulf War (Operation Desert Storm)** began in 1990 and was a 42-day war (for the United States), in which the first President George (H.W.) Bush and 28 other nations came to the aid of Kuwait after it was invaded by Iraq under Saddam Hussein. After fulfilling the mission of liberating Kuwait, the United States and other multinational forces withdrew from Iraq.

- The Chairman of the Joint Chiefs of Staff at the time of the first Gulf War was General **Colin Powell**. Currently, General Powell is the only African American to ever serve on the Joint Chiefs of Staff. In 2001, President George W. Bush appointed Colin Powell as Secretary of State, the only African American to have ever served in that position up to this time.

- After the attacks on the World Trade Center and the Pentagon on 9/11/01, the Bush administration identified the Saudi Arabian, Osama bin Laden, as the ultimate mastermind behind the attacks. Administration officials linked the airline highjackers to his Al Qaeda terrorist network. At the time, bin Laden and many members of Al Qaeda were believed to be in Afghanistan under the protection of the Taliban, another radical Islamic group. In 2001, the U.S. military launched Operation Enduring Freedom into Afghanistan to attempt to remove Al Qaeda and the Taliban. This began a new policy of what President Bush referred to as a "global war on terrorism," in which American forces were to confront threats to homeland security before they reached the shores of the United States. In 2003, the United States led an invasion into Iraq to overthrow the dictatorship of Saddam Hussein, who was accused of possessing weapons of mass destruction, human rights violations, and of harboring radical terrorist groups. There was hope of establishing a democratic Iraq that would be a model for political change throughout the Middle East. Although some of these issues against Hussein are still unproven, he was captured, tried, and executed, and the country formed a new constitution and held elections amid continued insurgency. The United States has agreed to withdraw its combat troops from the occupation by 2010. After several years of concentration in Iraq, the focus of the war returned to Afghanistan in 2009.

KEY QUESTION: *What was American foreign policy during the late 1800s to the mid-1900s?*

- From the 1890s to the 1940s, American foreign policy alternated between **isolationism** (retreat from international concerns) and **internationalism** (active involvement in world affairs). The United States also went through periods of **nativism** (a move to restrict immigrants) during the 1880s, due to a large influx of immigrants from many countries. Nativism had appeared earlier in the 1850s after many Chinese immigrants arrived, particularly to work on building the railroads.

- **William Seward**, as Secretary of State in 1897, **purchased Alaska** and the Aleutian Islands from Russia, which turned out to be of great economic profit for the United States when the discovery of **gold** caused a huge rush to that area in the 1890s and when oil was discovered much later.

- In the late 1890s, the United States adopted an activist foreign policy of expansionism toward the Caribbean and the Pacific. It began to pursue a policy of **imperialism**, or expansionism, the political and economic control of other territories for purposes of prestige, protectionism, power, and wealth. Many other nations sought land and colonies during this time, as well. For example, the phrase "The sun never sets on the British Empire" summarized Great Britain's imperialistic exploits.

- In 1898, as mentioned previously, the United States went to war to free Cuba from Spanish rule and to protect American trading interests. As a result of the **Spanish-American War**, the United States gained control of Puerto Rico, Guam, and the Philippines. Cuba was liberated but soon became an American protectorate.

- At the same time (1898), the United States annexed the Hawaiian Islands as a territory.

- In 1914, a Serbian separatist assassinated Austrian **Archduke Franz Ferdinand** and his wife in Sarajevo. Many historians have viewed this as the trigger for World War I. What had been an argument by Serbia wanting to separate (after having being annexed into Austria–Hungary), along with the military buildup of many European countries (and other causes), resulted in an escalation that would become **World War I**. European nations took sides and formed powerful alliances.

- The United States, under **President Woodrow Wilson**, tried to maintain a policy of **neutrality**, but in 1917, Germany's submarines sank unarmed American merchant ships and a British passenger ship, the *Lusitania*, killing 1,200 people, among them 128 Americans. The United States joined the **Allied Powers**—Great Britain, France, and Russia, among others—in fighting the **Central Powers**—Germany, the Austro–Hungarian Empire, and their allies.

- The **American Expeditionary Force (AEF)**, under the command of **General John J. "Black Jack" Pershing**, entered the war in the spring of 1918. He gained the nickname "Black Jack" when he led African American troops during his regular army days. Pershing eventually became the highest-ranking general in U.S. history.

- Several new weapons of war were tested during the **trench warfare** of World War I. Poison gas, rapid-fire machine guns, and the airplane are just a few of these weapons of devastation. The war had become a virtual **stalemate**, with neither side gaining ground, until America entered the war.

- The first major battle in which the Americans participated saw the defeat of the Germans at **Belleau Wood** (June 1918). The entry of America into the war was seen to turn the tide in favor of the Allies.

- When Germany accepted defeat in November 1918, both sides signed an **armistice**.

- In early 1918, Russia signed a separate peace agreement with the Central Powers and left the war because of the **Bolshevik Revolution** in October 1917. The communists, led by **V.I. Lenin**, took control of the country and killed **Czar Nicholas** and his family. This began the communist domination of Russia, which lasted more than 70 years. By the 1930s, it is estimated that Joseph **Stalin**'s regime had killed or persecuted millions of Russians in **gulags** (prisons for political opposition, usually found in areas such as Siberia).

- At the end of World War I, during the treaty making at the French palace at Versailles (**Treaty of Versailles**), President Wilson put forth his idealist **Fourteen Points** to foster world trade and fair territorial settlements. These were ignored by the European powers who sought to severely punish the Central Powers. The United States never ratified the Treaty of Versailles due to Wilson's political miscalculations and subsequent stroke.

- Disillusioned with the peace-making process, Americans returned to an isolationist policy and rejected membership in the **League of Nations**, an international organization intended to settle international disputes peaceably.

- Without the American influence in the peace process, the Allied powers proceeded with their **reparations**, or payment for damages, which became the central focus of the Treaty. Almost immediately, Germans began to experience devastating economic hardships. It was not long until a charismatic leader, **Adolf Hitler**, emerged to rally the German people toward nationalist pride and against the countries who had demanded such staunch reparations.

- With the rise of several militaristic governments (**Adolf Hitler** and his **Nazi Party** in Germany; **Benito Mussolini** and the **Fascists** in Italy; and **Emperor Hirohito** and **Admiral Hideki Tojo** in Japan), the postwar settlements of the Treaty of Versailles did not last long. In the 1930s, these **Axis** powers began to absorb neighboring European countries (such as Czechoslovakia), and Japan invaded China. British Prime Minister **Neville Chamberlain** declared a policy of **appeasement** (giving in to demands and ignoring aggression in order to keep the peace) in response.

- **World War II** finally erupted for Europe in 1939, when German troops marched into Poland, violating their independence. The United States sided politically with the **Allies**, including France, Great Britain, and the Soviet Union against the **Axis** powers (Germany, Italy, and Japan) but continued to remain neutral militarily.

- Following the 7:55 A.M. Japanese bombing of U.S. Pacific Fleet navy ships stationed in **Pearl Harbor**, Hawaii, on Sunday, **December 7, 1941**, President Roosevelt (FDR) declared that the United States would enter the war. In a little over an hour, Japanese planes had surprised and sunk eight battleships and three cruisers, killing more than 2,400 American sailors.

- American forces fought the war in both Europe (mainly on land) and the Pacific (mainly on the seas). The chief military planner for the United States was Chief of Staff **George C. Marshall**. The most decorated soldier of this war was a Texan, **Audie Murphy. Cleto Rodriguez**, another Texan, was a Medal of Honor recipient of Hispanic decent. Others who served in different ways were heroes as well. The **Four Chaplains** (two protestant ministers, a Catholic priest, and a rabbi) who were on the *Dorchester*, a troop transport, helped their men get off the ship when it was torpedoed during World War II. Fox, Poling, Washington, and Goode gave up their life vests when it was seen that there were not enough for everyone, and they went down with the ship. The **Navajo Code Talkers** were a group of young men (some as young as 15), who served in World War II because the enemy were able to so easily break the codes sent in English. Their service saved countless lives because it was difficult for anyone else to learn their native tongue. Other Native American tribes had served as code talkers in World War I (Cherokee, Comanche, Choctaw).

- In 1942–1943, the tide of battle in Europe shifted in favor of the Allies when the German offensive on the **Eastern Front** was stopped at **Stalingrad** by the Russian forces, and the Allied forces, under the leadership of **General George Patton**, recaptured North Africa.

- Hitler's **Final Solution** called for the extermination of Jews (and others he deemed "unsuitable" or not of their "master race"). German Jews were the first to be sent to concentration camps. As Germany occupied other countries, Jewish citizens were identified and sent to concentration camps in southern and central Germany, Poland, and Austria. These camps (such as Dachau, Bergen-Belsen, and Auschwitz) were originally built as "labor camps" but became death/extermination camps. The **Holocaust** claimed the lives of 6 million Jews, almost two-thirds of Europe's Jewish population, as well as many others, such as gypsies, homosexuals, and anyone considered "mentally defective."

- **Oveta Culp Hobby** became the first woman commander in the U.S. Army as colonel of the WAACs (Women's Auxiliary Army Corps). Working tirelessly for the war effort, she later received the Distinguished Service Medal for service to our country. Later, she became the first secretary of the Department of Health, Education, and Welfare under President Eisenhower. The WAACs were trained to free up men to fight and served as Signal Corps operators, suppliers, medical personnel, clerks, drivers, ferry and mapping pilots, and in many other positions. The Women's Airforce Service Pilots (WASPs) were also first trained in Texas to take the place of male pilots in non-combat positions, such as towing targets, transporting cargo, and ferrying planes.

- On June 6, 1944, the commander of U.S. military forces in Europe, **General Dwight D. Eisenhower**, launched the Allied invasion—termed **D-Day**—to liberate France from the Germans. The Germans had expected the invasion to come at the narrowest part of the English Channel and had not prepared extensive defenses on the beaches of Normandy, where almost 300,000 Allied troops came ashore. The D-Day Invasion proved to be one of the turning points of the war, although there were tremendous casualties.
- The land war in Europe ended on May 8, 1945 (**VE Day**), but continued in the Pacific against Japan (**VJ Day**) until August of that year.
- The American strategy in the Pacific could be considered "island hopping." The U.S. Navy and the Marines battled the Japanese on island after island as they moved across the Pacific Ocean toward Japan. Two separate American operations were waged on the Pacific front: **General Douglas MacArthur**, based in Australia, moved from New Guinea to the Philippines, and **Admiral Chester Nimitz**, in Hawaii, directed American attacks on key Japanese-held islands. Primarily, the Pacific Campaign was waged by forces from the United States, Australia, and New Zealand.
- After Pearl Harbor, American anger, fear, and mistrust of the Japanese grew against those who were living in the United States, particularly along the Pacific Coast. FDR authorized **relocation camps** in the U.S. interior to intern citizens of Japanese ancestry who were living on the West Coast, many of whom were U.S. citizens. More than 100,000 people of Japanese ancestry were identified, told to dispose of their possessions, and were moved to these centers. In 1944, their internment was upheld by the Supreme Court. Although most were released in 1945, few were ever compensated for their financial losses.
- As the Pacific front progressed, the Japanese lost four aircraft carriers (compared to one American carrier) in the **Battle of Midway**. This was the first defeat the modern Japanese navy had suffered, and it left the United States in control of the Central Pacific.
- Island fighting intensified as American forces advanced toward Japan. Week after week, the Japanese sent *kamikaze* (suicide) planes against the American ships, sacrificing some 3,500 planes while inflicting great damage.
- In February 1945, the **Battle of Iwo Jima**, only 750 miles from Tokyo, was the costliest battle in the history of the Marine Corps. Nearly 26,000 Americans were killed in this battle. The battle is commemorated by a memorial statue in Washington, D.C., of Marines raising an American flag of victory on Mt. Suribachi.
- The **Battle for Okinawa**, 350 miles south of Japan, was another victory for American forces. The United States and its allies suffered nearly 50,000 casualties on land and sea before Okinawa was taken. More than 100,000 Japanese died in the battle. Many civilians were killed and many others jumped over the island's cliffs after Japanese propaganda convinced them of the terror they would face under American domination.
- On April 15, 1945, President Roosevelt died during his fourth term in office. He was succeeded by his vice president, **Harry S Truman**.
- In May 1945, American forces began a firebombing campaign on Tokyo itself. The **Doolittle Raid** was the first strike to reach the main islands of Japan. Some 80,000 civilians lost their lives from the firestorms started by the napalm dropped on the city by American bombers. Japan still did not surrender.

- In order to end the war and save what he believed to be thousands of American lives, President **Truman** made the decision to use two nuclear weapons against Japan. On August 6, 1945, an American B-29, the *Enola Gay*, dropped an **atomic bomb** on the city of **Hiroshima**. The explosion incinerated four square miles of the city, instantly killing more than 80,000 people. Many more survived to suffer the effects of radioactive fallout and to pass the effects on to their children in the form of birth defects. Japan still did not surrender. A second bomb was dropped on **Nagasaki** on August 9, 1945, inflicting another 40,000 deaths.

- **Emperor Hirohito** persuaded his ministers to surrender unconditionally on August 14, 1945. On September 2, 1945, on board the American battleship *Missouri,* anchored in Tokyo Bay, Japanese officials signed the articles of surrender.

- Germany was divided into Soviet-controlled **East Germany** and free **West Germany**. Its capital, Berlin, was divided into **sectors** for the Soviets, French, British, and Americans. East Germany and the Communist Sector of Berlin were cut off from the West until 1989.

- More than 14 million combatants, not including civilians, lost their lives in World War II. Hitler committed suicide in his Berlin bunker rather than face capture and trial. A war crimes tribunal was, however, set up in **Nuremberg** to bring Nazis who had participated in crimes against humanity to trial.

VII. International Relations between the Superpowers

KEY QUESTION: *How did the United States react to Soviet expansion after World War II?*

- Since World War II until the end of the 20th century, relations between the **Soviet Union (the USSR) and the United States** dominated world affairs. The two nations, along with their allies, kept their wartime pledge to create an international organization, **the United Nations** (located in New York City), to replace the disbanded League of Nations.

- In the late 1940s, the Soviet Union gained control of a number of governments. The boundaries between communist-controlled countries and free nations became known as the **Iron Curtain** and included Poland, Bulgaria, East Germany, Rumania, Yugoslavia, Albania, Hungary, and Czechoslovakia. In many areas, fences and walls were built to keep people from escaping communism. The **Berlin Wall**, the most famous of these, was finally torn down in 1989. German reunification was concluded in 1990.

- The United States responded with a **containment doctrine** to block further Soviet expansion, and the **Truman Doctrine** to provide military and economic aid to countries threatened by **communism**.

- In 1947, the American government offered the **Marshall Plan** to all European nations, delivering assistance if they would work together to rebuild their economies after World War II.

- In 1949, the United States and its Western allies formed the **North Atlantic Treaty Organization** (NATO) to provide for a common military defense against the Soviet Union and its allies. In 1955, the Soviet Union responded by creating an alliance of its own—**The Warsaw Pact**—with the communist governments in Eastern Europe.

- The relationship between the two superpowers, particularly during the late 1940s and early 1950s, has been characterized as a **cold war**, a state of tension and hostility just short of war, in which both sides built up powerful arsenals of weapons (including nuclear weapons) and spied on each other to gain military and political advantages.

- The superpowers have also experienced periods of **detente**, or a relaxation of tensions. During such periods, summit conferences, cultural exchanges, and agreements such as the **Limited Nuclear Test Ban Treaty**, the **Helsinki Accords**, and the **Strategic Arms Limitations Treaties** (SALT) have taken place to bring down the level of fear of another world war.

- Perceiving Soviet threats to the **Third World** (the underdeveloped nations of Asia, Africa, and Latin America), the United States undertook policies of military alliances and economic and technical aid for containment in order to prevent a **Domino Effect** (the fall to communism of one country, leading to the fall of its neighboring countries).

- In Asia, relations between the superpowers were severely strained when communist forces under the leadership of **Mao Tse Tung** won their civil war in China in 1949. The exiled Chinese government of **Chiang Kai Shek** moved its government to Taiwan (Formosa). The United States recognized the Chinese government in Taiwan but refused to recognize the existence of the mainland (Communist) Chinese government until 1979.

- In 1950, the United States fought the **Korean War** to prevent the further expansion of communism. The war ended with an agreement to divide Korea at the 38th parallel. Currently, there are two separate countries on the Korean peninsula: North Korea, which is communist controlled, and South Korea, which is democratic. The United States still maintains a strong military presence at the 38th parallel to enforce the division. North Korea is considered an ongoing threat to South Korea and the United States for its military threat and nuclear weapons program under its current dictator, Kim Jong Il.

- In the 1950s during the Cold War, many Americans feared the threat of communism from within the United States, and Senator Joseph McCarthy led the country in attempting to find, label, and blacklist communists—those whom he saw as being American traitors or spies. Some were guilty and some were not, but many lost their jobs and reputations (**McCarthyism**). The **FBI (Federal Bureau of Investigation)** under **J. Edgar Hoover** helped investigate many of these cases.

- **Vietnam** (Indochina) had been a French territory until World War II. At the end of the war in 1945, communists tried to take over. By 1954, the United States was paying a major portion of the French war costs in Vietnam. When the French suffered their ultimate defeat in 1954, President Eisenhower was not prepared to commit U.S. forces to fight in Vietnam. An international conference held at Geneva divided the country at the 17th parallel. **Ho Chi Minh** gained control of **North Vietnam**, and the French continued to rule in the South. The agreement also stated that an election would be held within 2 years to decide the unification of the country. That election was never held. Instead, the United States took over for the French and installed a new leader in the South, **Ngo Dinh Diem**.

- In 1960, President Kennedy sent the first U.S. military advisors to Vietnam. The United States was there merely to advise the South Vietnamese military in their fight against the Communists in North Vietnam.

- On August 2, 1964, an American destroyer, the *Maddox*, was fired on by North Vietnamese torpedo boats in the **Gulf of Tonkin**. On August 4, the U.S. Navy sent another destroyer, the *C. Turner Joy*, into the Gulf with orders to fire at the North Vietnamese torpedo boats if they were fired on. President Lyndon Johnson also ordered retaliatory air strikes on North Vietnamese naval bases.

- On August 7, 1964, Congress passed H.J. RES 1145, which authorized **President Johnson** to take "all necessary measures to repel any armed attack against the forces of the U.S. and to prevent any further aggression" PBS (1999–2000). This **Gulf of Tonkin Resolution** meant that the United States would become an active participant in the conflict. American combat forces in South Vietnam rose from 16,000 in 1963 to 500,000 in 1968.
- In 1968, the North Vietnamese launched the **Tet Offensive**, a series of attacks beginning unexpectedly during a major Vietnamese holiday (Tet—the Lunar New Year). The U.S. public, watching much of the conflict on the nightly television news, began to doubt whether the United States should remain in the war in Vietnam.
- Richard Nixon, running on an antiwar platform, won the election of 1968. Nixon announced the *Vietnamization* of the war (building up the strength of the South Vietnamese to defend their own country). Withdrawals of American troops began in June 1969. This did briefly quiet public protests against the war. However, in April 1970, Nixon ordered the secret bombing of parts of Cambodia, where enemy forces were situated, attempting to allow time for the United States to withdraw. This was seen by some Americans, however, as widening the war into Indochina. News of the bombing led to widespread protests across the United States. On May 4, 1970, at **Kent State** in Ohio, members of the National Guard killed four students and injured nine others as they were protesting the war.
- The growing antiwar sentiment caused Congress to withdraw the **Gulf of Tonkin Resolution** in December 1970. Nixon, however, ignored the action. Then, in June 1971, the *New York Times* published a front-page story on the history of America's war in Vietnam. The feature was based on the findings of a top-secret Defense Department study—**the Pentagon Papers**. The report confirmed what the public had believed for a long time: the government had been dishonest, both in reporting the military progress of the war and in explaining its own motives for American involvement.
- During this period, the morale and discipline among American troops in Vietnam was rapidly deteriorating. The trial and conviction of **Lieutenant William Calley**, who was charged with overseeing the massacre of more than 100 unarmed South Vietnamese civilians in the village of **My Lai**, attracted widespread attention to the dehumanizing effects the war was having on some of those who fought it, particularly many of those who had been a part of a large military draft.
- In 1973, Henry Kissinger, Nixon's secretary of state, signed an agreement to end the war. Many prisoners of war (**POWs**) were finally released and returned home, but it was not until 1975 that U.S. involvement in Vietnam truly ended (with the famous helicopter evacuation of the remaining Americans and many Vietnamese from the American embassy in Saigon).
- Many Americans remain concerned about the thousands of soldiers who never returned from Vietnam. In 1995, the Pentagon reported that there are still 2,202 American soldiers missing in action (**MIAs**) in Southeast Asia—1,618 in Vietnam. Far more Americans are still listed as missing from the Korean War (8,170) and World War II (78,750), but those missing in Vietnam seem particularly significant. This was partly due to the belief that U.S. soldiers were alive and being held as prisoners.
- In January 1975, forces from the North invaded South Vietnam. **President Gerald Ford** asked Congress for emergency aid for South

Vietnam, but the request was denied. In April, the army of North Vietnam marched into Saigon, and South Vietnam fell to the Communists.

- In Latin America, since 1959, the United States has been unable to oust the Communist regime of **Fidel Castro** in Cuba.

- In the Middle East, American recognition and support of Israel as a Jewish homeland in 1948 antagonized many Arab nations and jeopardized the flow of oil. In 1979, after the fall of the Shah, the Iranians under Ayatollah Khomeini held 63 Americans from the U.S. embassy hostage for over a year.

- President Kennedy, after the disastrous **Bay of Pigs** invasion in Cuba, came very close to war with the Soviet Union when it was confirmed that the Soviets were furnishing Cuba with missiles as a staging area for them to reach the United States. Many nuclear fallout shelters were built in states that were within range, and children in schools practiced nuclear drills. Kennedy placed a naval blockade around Cuba and the missiles were removed.

- In 1987, **President Ronald Reagan** faced off with **Mikhail Gorbachev** (the leader of the Soviet Union) demanding that he "tear down this wall" (referring to the Berlin Wall separating East and West Berlin), meaning that the communist government should allow freedom in their country and in their other puppet states (e.g., East Germany). The 9-year Soviet War in Afghanistan, in which the United States supported the anti-Marxist *mujahidin*, resulted in a Soviet withdrawal in 1989. Factors such as the arms race, the technological revolution in the United States, and a lost war in Afghanistan, among others, caused an economic collapse of the government in the Soviet Union, which dissolved itself in 1991, thus effectively ending the Cold War. Although many of the former Soviet states demanded and obtained independence (Ukraine, Belarus, Armenia, Lithuania, etc.), Russia still remains a powerful nation due to its nuclear arsenal and great oil reserves, and it often opposes the United States in international affairs.

- Currently, Russia supports Iran in international questions about its nuclear capability, although the West has demanded continued inspections of Iran's nuclear facilities. Russia has vast economic ties to Iran.

VIII. The Present

KEY QUESTION: *What sorts of domestic issues has the United States faced in the past 40 years?*

- Since World War II, the U.S. government has been confronted with a variety of problems and challenges. Slowly, the nation moved toward becoming an integrated society. President Truman, for example, desegregated the armed services in World War II by executive order.

- In 1954, the Supreme Court declared **segregation** (the tradition of separate but equal) unconstitutional in *Brown v. the Board of Education of Topeka, Kansas.* The principal attorney in the case was **Thurgood Marshall**. In 1967, President Johnson named Marshall as the first African American Supreme Court Justice.

- In 1955 in Montgomery, Alabama, a seamstress named **Rosa Parks** refused to give up her seat on the bus to a white passenger. The bus driver called the police, and she was arrested. News of her arrest spread rapidly, and the **National Association for the Advancement of Colored People (NAACP)** quickly organized a boycott of the buses in Montgomery. They asked a young pastor named **Dr. Martin Luther King**, **Jr.**, to lead the boycott. For 381 days, African Americans refused to ride the buses. The boycott remained nonviolent. In late 1956, the Supreme Court ruled in response to a lawsuit brought by one of the boycotters that bus segregation was unconstitutional. The Montgomery Bus Boycott proved that ordinary people could unite and organize a successful protest movement through **civil disobedience**. Dr. King wrote his famous "Letter from a Birmingham Jail" against racial segregation after one protest effort.

- When the Soviet Union launched **Sputnik** in 1957, President Eisenhower played an active role in establishing the **National Aeronautics and Space Administration (NASA)** and passing the **National Defense Education Act** to train more scientists and engineers. In 1969, NASA's **Apollo 11** astronauts reached the moon. The first person to step on the moon was Neil Armstrong.

- During the 1960s, Dr. Martin Luther King, Jr., helped make Americans aware of continuing racial injustices. The Civil Rights Act (1964), signed by President Johnson, sought to bring more equality to African Americans, especially in housing rights and in schools.

- Some African Americans did not believe that the Congress had done enough to remedy the centuries of segregation and discrimination. Angry rioters often took to the streets. There was a growing movement that believed that African Americans should take complete control of their communities. One of the movement's leaders was **Malcolm X**. His followers did not take the nonviolent approach that Dr. King's followers had used.

- Although Malcolm X was assassinated in 1965, racial tensions increased. In 1966, **Stokely Carmichael** issued a call for **Black Power**. Also in that year, **Huey Newton** and **Bobby Seale** founded a political party known as the **Black Panthers** to fight police brutality in predominantly African American neighborhoods.

- President Kennedy sent a bill to Congress in 1963 that would guarantee equal access to all public accommodations and gave the U.S. attorney general, Robert Kennedy, the power to file school desegregation lawsuits. To help persuade Congress to pass the bill, more than 250,000 people, including 75,000 Whites, came to Washington. There, Dr. King delivered his most famous oration, the "**I Have a Dream**" **speech**. At that time, the **March on Washington** was the largest demonstration ever held in the United States.

- In 1963, President Kennedy was assassinated in Dallas. **Lyndon Johnson**, the vice president at the time, became the president. President Johnson continued to pursue Kennedy's civil rights agenda.

- In 1968, the United States lost two great civil rights figures. Both Rev. Dr. Martin Luther King, Jr., and **Robert Kennedy** were assassinated.

- Under President Johnson, Congress enacted the **War on Poverty** to provide job training and rebuild inner cities. It also passed **Great Society** legislation such as **Medicare**, which insures healthcare for the elderly. Unfortunately, the cost of the war in Vietnam was responsible for cutting the budget money available for many of Johnson's social programs.

- Congress responded by passing the **Civil Rights Act of 1964**, barring discrimination in housing and establishing the Equal Opportunity Commission.

- Texas Hispanics also fought for civil rights, and **Hector P. Garcia** was the first Hispanic to be awarded the Presidential Medal of Freedom, the nation's highest civilian award in 1984 for his work in desegregation and for his founding of the G. I. Forum, which worked for the rights of Hispanic Veterans, particularly after World War II.

- **President John F. Kennedy** and his brother Robert Kennedy, the attorney general of the United States, were concerned with the needs of the poor. However, important domestic poverty legislation was passed only after President Kennedy was assassinated.

- President Kennedy had vowed to put a man on the moon by the end of the 1960s. In 1969, President Nixon congratulated **Neil Armstrong** when he became the first man to walk on the moon. Although **James Lovell** did not walk on the moon, he flew to the moon twice and was the first to fly into space four times. As the commander of the ill-fated Apollo 13 mission, he, his crew, and NASA are famous for the ingenuity used to bring this crew down successfully. With the explosion of the space shuttle *Challenger* on January 28, 1986, and of the *Columbia* in 2003, American space programs underwent review for a period of time. However, shuttle missions were resumed to complete the building of the International Space Station to be finished in 2011. **Sally Ride** was the first American woman in space, and **Ellen Ochoa** is the first Hispanic woman in space and now serves as Deputy Director of the Johnson Space Center. Texas-born Dr. **Millie Hughes-Fulford** was a part of the first mission for biomedical studies on the Spacelab. **John "Danny" Olivas**, raised in El Paso and of Mexican descent, also flew two missions as an astronaut to the International Space Station.

- Abuse of power became a major problem during Richard Nixon's presidency. Nixon and his advisors withheld and covered up information concerning a burglary at Democratic National Headquarters in the **Watergate** building complex during the 1972 presidential campaign. The president and his aides had also used government agencies, such as the FBI and the IRS, for political purposes. When Congress took steps to impeach him, President Richard Nixon resigned from office.

- Through the efforts of **Rachel Carson** and others, America became aware of the need to clean up and preserve their environment. During the Nixon administration, Congress established the **Environmental Protection Agency (EPA)** and passed legislation to provide clean air and water.

- The economy has been a constant source of worry to American presidents. Under President Johnson, inflation increased at an alarming rate. Presidents Nixon, Ford, and Carter found it difficult to control inflation, especially because Arab oil policies raised the price of energy, thereby affecting the costs of manufacturing and transporting goods. Under President Reagan, inflation was finally halted, but the mounting **budget deficit** became a major problem. **Reagan**, however, had solidly contributed to the end of the Cold War by escalating the arms race with the Soviet Union, which ended in its collapse and opened up many other countries under communist rule (including East Germany).

- **George H. W. Bush** acted to stop the aggression of Iraq when it invaded Kuwait, sending troops (a good many of whom were women) into **the Gulf War** or **Desert Storm**.

- During his first term, President **Bill Clinton** was involved in a number of controversies, ranging from alleged wrongdoing in an Arkansas land deal known as *Whitewater* to charges of sexual misconduct. The strong economy and the lack of a significant Republican challenger resulted in Clinton's reelection in 1996. Clinton became the first Democrat since FDR to be reelected president. In December 1998, Clinton became the second president in the history of the United States to be **impeached**, or legally charged (with perjury). Like President Andrew Johnson, Clinton was tried and acquitted, so he did not leave office.

- Third political parties had not been successful since Roosevelt's time. However, in 1992, Texas billionaire and entrepreneur **Ross Perot** ran what was, at first, a successful third party candidacy against George H. W. Bush and Bill Clinton. After dropping out of the race, then reentering, his bid failed. He ran again unsuccessfully in 1996 against Clinton and Robert Dole.

- In 2000, the Republican Party nominated **George W. Bush**, governor of Texas and son of former President George H. W. Bush. This resulted in one of the closest presidential elections in history. This presidential election was complicated by the media incorrectly proclaiming **Vice President Al Gore** as the winner, the withdrawal of an initial concession by Gore, butterfly ballots, hanging chads, a recount of votes in Florida, and several court challenges. Finally, Bush was declared the winner.

- In 1993, a terrorist bomb exploded in the parking garage of the **World Trade Center**, killing 6 and injuring more than 1,000 people in New York City. Four Islamic militants were tried and convicted in this attack. In 1995, 168 people were killed and around 500 people injured when the **Oklahoma City Federal Building** was bombed. Timothy McVeigh was tried, convicted, and later executed for his role in the attack. His accomplice, Terry Nichols, was convicted of conspiracy and sentenced to life in prison. Other terrorist attacks by Islamist militants have occurred on passenger ships and against U.S. embassies and a naval ship (the *U.S.S. Cole*), and in other places. On **September 11, 2001 (9/11)**, symbols important to the U.S. economy and the U.S. military—the **World Trade Center** in New York City and the **Pentagon** in Washington, D.C.—were attacked by hijackers who flew commercial airplanes into the buildings. The Twin Towers collapsed and thousands died in what has been referred to as the worst act of terrorism in American history. Many **first responders** who came to help those in the buildings also lost their lives and are honored as heroes. Passengers on another plane caused it to crash rather than have it hit another target in Washington, D.C. **Todd Beamer**, travelling on **Flight 93**, planned to overthrow the hijackers. His last words, as he and other passengers made their move, became the motto for many fighting Al Qaeda: "Let's roll!" **Osama bin Laden** was named as the primary masterminded of the attack. President Bush reacted by sending troops into Iraq and Afghanistan, but bin Laden currently remains at large.

- In 2008, Barack Obama was elected as the 44th President of the United States. He defeated **Hillary Clinton**, former First Lady and a senator from New York, to win the Democratic nomination. His election was seen as historic as he became the first African American president. Hilary Clinton became his Secretary of State.

IX. Holidays and Public Symbols

KEY QUESTION: *What holidays and symbols hold importance for people in the United States and in Texas, and why?*

- **National symbols** are representations of people, values, goals, or history intended to unite the people of a nation. There are many national symbols in the United States. One is the **bald eagle**, designated as the national bird of the United States in 1782. The Founding Fathers wanted to choose an animal that was unique to the United States. The bald eagle was selected because it symbolized strength, courage, freedom, and immortality. Its image can be found in many places such as the Great Seal and on the quarter and $1 bill. The **Statue of Liberty** is another symbol of freedom that stands in the harbor of New York City. Presented as a gift to the United States by France on the occasion of the nation's centennial, the base contains a message that symbolizes the place of immigrants in this country: "Give me your tired, your poor, Your huddled masses yearning to breathe free . . ." **Uncle Sam** is one of the most popular personifications of the United States. He is depicted as an old man with white hair and a goatee dressed in red, white, and blue. In 1917, as the United States was preparing to enter World War I, the famous image of **Uncle Sam** appeared on military recruiting posters with the caption: *I Want You for the U.S. Army*. This image may have been based upon a real "Uncle Sam Wilson", who supplied food for the army in barrels with the markings of "U.S." The **rose** became the national flower of the United States in 1986. Roses are found in many colors: red, pink, white, or yellow, and grow naturally throughout North America. The national anthem, "**The Star-Spangled Banner**," is discussed later.

- The national **flag** is a symbol of our country. The flag, established after the Declaration of Independence, included 13 white stars on a blue background and 13 red and white stripes representing the original 13 colonies. Although the red and white stripes were set at 13, each time a new state was added, a new white star appeared on the flag (thus we now have 50 stars).
- The original motto of the United States was "*E pluribus Unum*," meaning "One from many." This references the formation of one government from the many colonies. The current motto is "In God We Trust."
- There are also a number of notable U.S. **landmarks** (places that are identified where famous events took place or that symbolize something special). The Washington and Lincoln Memorials in Washington, D.C. are national landmarks, and the Space Needle is a landmark that symbolizes the city of Seattle. **Mount Rushmore**, on which the faces of George Washington, Thomas Jefferson, Theodore Roosevelt, and Abraham Lincoln are carved, is known as the *Shrine of Democracy* (representing the founding, expansion, preservation, and unification of the United States). The Alamo is a landmark that is a symbol of Texas freedom.
- Songs throughout history have had significance as symbols and also as a means of satire. At the beginning of the Revolutionary War, the song "**Yankee Doodle**," which told an insulting story about an American Yankee "fool," was popular among British troops. Soon the Yankee colonists took the song as their own, and it became a point of national pride.
- In 1906, George M. Cohan's musical, "George Washington, Jr.," premiered in front of a sold-out audience at the Herald Square Theater in New York City. A featured song from the play, "**You're a Grand Ol' Flag**," became the first song from a musical to sell more than 1 million copies of sheet music.
- Visual art and poetry are two forms of cultural expression. The United States collects and celebrates each of these as part of a national culture. The **Poet Laureate** Consultant in Poetry to the Library of Congress serves as the nation's official poet. **Phillis Wheatly** is honored as having created the genre of African American literature and as being the first African American to publish a book. Coming to the colonies as a slave during Revolutionary times, she was educated and freed by her family, and her poetry was lauded by many of the founding fathers. The **National Gallery of Art** was created in 1937 for the people of the

United States. During the 1920s, Andrew W. Mellon began collecting with the intention of forming a gallery of art in Washington for the nation, a goal that came to fruition in 1941.

- The **Presidential Library** system, overseen by the National Archives and Records Administration, is composed of thirteen **Presidential Libraries** beginning with the 31st president of the United States, Herbert Hoover. Presidential Libraries are archives and museums that store the documents and artifacts of a president and his administration. Presidential Libraries and Museums, like their holdings, belong to the American people, and are partially supported by private non-profit organizations.

- The **National Park Service** oversees 391 sites throughout the United States. It was established in 1916, with Yellowstone becoming the first U.S. National Park. In addition to the National Parks themselves, the service oversees national monuments, historical parks and sites, battlefields and military parks, lake- and seashores, recreation areas, scenic rivers and trails, and the White House.

HOLIDAYS

- **Martin Luther King Day**, celebrated the third Monday in January, honors the man who worked tirelessly for equal status for people of color, particularly African Americans. As the main leader of the Civil Rights Movement during the 1960s, he spearheaded nonviolent protests (sit-ins and marches) to help African Americans be treated as first-class citizens in America. Martin Luther King, Jr., committed his life to this cause (he was assassinated for his beliefs) and made it possible for many African Americans to obtain jobs, attend schools, and live in neighborhoods that were previously not open to them. His efforts sparked others in many communities and in other parts of the world to struggle for equality. The entire month of February is **Black History Month**, recognizing many other African Americans who have and continue to make contributions in many areas.

- **Lunar New Year**, observed by Chinese, Vietnamese, Koreans, and other Asians always occurs on the first day of the First Moon of the lunar calendar (usually between the end of January and the middle of February). Although the actual celebrations vary somewhat from country to country, most Asian families see the Lunar New Year as the most important family function of the year. As a time for renewal, every part of one's house must be cleaned, and poems (couplets) on long red paper are put by doors and windows to usher in the spring and good fortune. Debts accumulated during the year are settled by the last day of the year. Particularly important is the tradition of the Kitchen god, who during this time would give a report on the family to heaven. A ritualistic dinner of sweet and sticky rice cakes is an important way to send him off with a favorable report. All foods are prepared prior to the New Year to avoid having knives and other sharp objects "cut" the good luck of a New Year. New Year's Day brings red envelopes with good luck money for children, along with new clothes. Firecrackers, which drive away evil spirits, are heard throughout the first 2 weeks of the New Year. On the 15th day, the New Year's celebration ends with the First Moon and the Lantern Festival. In China, people go into the streets with lanterns for a parade—usually with Dragon Dances.

- **Tet** is the most popular Vietnamese holiday. It is generally celebrated on the same day as the Lunar New Year. Exceptions may arise due to the time difference between Beijing (capital city of China) and Hanoi (capital city of Vietnam). It is held during the full moon before spring planting (usually in January or February). Parades are held, and red and gold colors decorate homes to celebrate the Lunar New Year in Vietnam. Everyone returns to their family homes for nearly a week to issue in luck for the New Year. Ancestors' spirits are believed to return, so graves are decorated with flowers, and those who have passed away are paid respect. Midnight on Tet is marked by gongs and drums and visiting friends. The **Moon Festival** is another popular holiday for the Vietnamese (in the eighth lunar month), particularly because children receive many gifts. Parades, drums, and dances are held, and moon cakes are eaten as the moon moves halfway down the sky.

- **Presidents' Day**, on the third Monday of February, honors, in particular, two of the most famous American presidents—**George Washington** (Revolutionary War commander, hero, and first president) and **Abraham Lincoln** (who preserved the Union of all of the states after the Civil War and who abolished slavery).

- **St. Patrick's Day**, celebrated on March 17, is the anniversary of the death of St. Patrick, the Irish patron saint credited with the conversion of many Irish to Christianity. In modern times on this day, "everyone is Irish," wears green, has a shamrock, and generally celebrates Irish heritage.

- **Passover** is a Jewish holiday commemorating the Exodus of the Jewish people from slavery in Egypt. The Jews left so quickly after their release by the pharaoh that they did not even wait for their bread to rise. In remembrance, Jewish people avoid eating grain products and leavened bread products during this time.

- **Easter** commemorates the day that Christians believe Jesus Christ arose from the dead (the Resurrection) after being crucified and buried.

- **Texas Independence Day** is March 2. It marks the day in 1836 when Texas declared its independence from Mexico during the Texas Revolution.

- **Vaisakhi** is a holiday celebrated in many parts of India, but especially for the Sikhs in the north of the country. The harvest is celebrated with much exuberance, feasting, colorful new clothes, and dances.

- **San Jacinto Day**, April 21, commemorates the final Texas victory over Mexico under Santa Anna in 1836, which led to Texas becoming independent.

- **Cinco de Mayo** (May 5) is the day Mexico won a victory over French troops in the Battle of Puebla in 1862, as France attempted to add Mexico to its empire under Napoleon.

- **Memorial Day**, celebrated in May, honors men and women who gave their lives in the service to our country.

- **Juneteenth**, on June 19, is also called *Freedom Day* or *Emancipation Day* and marks the day in 1865 when African Americans in Texas finally heard that they had been freed from slavery, or emancipated.

- **Fourth of July** commemorates the date on which the Declaration of Independence from Britain was signed during the Revolutionary War in 1776. People throughout the United States celebrate this holiday with parades. Fireworks displays remind everyone about the "rockets' red glare, and bombs bursting in air" from the national anthem written during the War of 1812 ("The Star Spangled Banner") and that these "fireworks" gave proof that the flag was still there (symbolizing the continuation of our country).

- **Labor Day**, celebrated on the first Monday in September, honors America's work force.

- **Celebrate Freedom Week** is the week in which Sept. 17 (U.S. Constitution Day) occurs to educate students on the sacrifices made by the founders of this country and those who sought to preserve its values. During this week, from the third grade on, children are asked to learn and recite the beginning of the Declaration of Independence: "We hold these Truths to be self-evident, that all Men are created equal, that they are endowed by their Creator with certain unalienable Rights, that among these are Life, Liberty and the Pursuit of Happiness—That to secure these Rights, Governments are instituted among Men, deriving their just Powers from the Consent of the Governed."

- **Ramadan** is celebrated by Muslims throughout the world during the ninth month of the Islamic calendar. During this time, Muslims are required to fast from dawn to sunset each day to show their devotion to their religion, to impose self-control, and to experience empathy for those who live in poverty. It is a time to read the Qur'an (Koran), go to the mosque, give to charities, and come closer to goodness. Evening meals during this holiday are usually a time to share with family and friends. The Night of Power, the 27th night of the month, is especially holy and is remembered as the night when Mohammed received the first verses of the Qur'an. Many Muslims spend this entire night in prayer.

- **Rosh Hashana**, usually occurring between Labor Day and Discovery Day, begins the Jewish High Holy Days. A 10-day celebration marks the Jewish New Year as a time to examine the past year and make new resolutions. Also known as the *Feast of the Trumpets* (because it begins with the blowing of a ram's horn), it ends with **Yom Kippur**, the most important of Jewish holidays and a day of atonement and fasting, when one is to right the wrongs that one may have committed during the past year. These are days for services, prayers, and introspection. The Shabbat is a day for prayers and services at a temple. It normally begins every Friday at sunset and finishes on Saturday for Jewish worshippers. It is a day of rest and freedom from labors, and Orthodox Jews have specific restrictions. A Shabbat can also occur on particular holidays.

- **Columbus Day**, a federal holiday on the second Monday in October, marks the day in October 1492 when Columbus arrived in the Americas. Because there has been so much evidence that others came to the Americas earlier, many call this day *Discoverer's Day.*

- **Halloween** falls on October 31, when many Americans dress up in costumes, and children receive candy as they Trick-or-Treat or attend parties. Some controversy in recent years has come about over this holiday because of its association with witchcraft and the occult, although others see it as traditional fun for children.

- **Dia de los Muertos** (Day of the Dead) is a Mexican festival on November 1 (All Saints' Day) in which it is believed that those who have died reunite with their families. It is not like Halloween, a scary holiday, but a day on which the souls eat, drink, and are merry. Because of this, flowers, candles, and favorite foods and drinks are placed on graves, and skeletons of *papier mâché* and candies are found in homes and shops. After prayers for the dead, there are picnics and parties, but in the evening, bells ring all night to summon the spirits. Some relatives keep a night-long vigil.

- **Veterans' Day** is a day set aside on November 11 to honor all of those who have served the United States in the armed forces.

- The origin of the word **Diwali** comes from *Deepavali,* meaning "garland of lights." Many Indian Hindus and Sikhs see it as the beginning of a new year or a celebration of good over evil. The significance of the countless small Christmas-type lights and candles displayed in many homes (along with fireworks in the community) represents light triumphing over ignorance. At temples, *puja* rituals (prayers) are part of the holidays, as is the cleaning of homes, special foods and sweets, and visits to family and friends. Diwali falls on the Lunar New Year, so the theme helps keep the idea of enlightenment aglow on the darkest night of the year.

- **Thanksgiving** commemorates the feast of the Pilgrims after a very hard first year in America. It was not until 1863 that this day became a national holiday. Our current holiday, set aside for the fourth Thursday in November, reminds us of the feast that was shared by Pilgrims and Native Americans after the first harvest in the new land.

- **Hanukkah**, or **Chanukah**, is a minor holiday for Jewish people. It is a festival, normally in late November or December, remembering the Jewish fight against the harsh Greek rule in Israel and the subsequent Temple rededication in Jerusalem in 165 B.C.E. On each of 8 nights, a candle is added to the **menorah** (a special candelabra) to add to the evenings' remembrance of the events. The defiled temple was to be rededicated after the Jewish victory, but priests found only enough ritualistic oil to keep a light burning for 1 day. A miracle occurred, as this oil burned for 8 days—enough time to press and prepare more pure oil. *Latkes* (potato pancakes), jelly doughnuts, and other foods fried in oil are eaten during this time, and small gifts are given to family members. A game using a *dreidel* (a four-sided top) is often played. Jewish holidays fall on the same day according to the Jewish calendar, which is based on the moon cycle, and is about 11 days longer. Therefore, the Jewish holidays do not occur on the same day each year on the standard calendar.

- **Christmas** is the most widely celebrated Christian holiday. December 25 is the day designated as the anniversary of the Nativity, or the birth of Jesus Christ. This national holiday is also associated with gifts brought to children by Santa Claus or St. Nicholas.

- **Kwanzaa** is celebrated from the day after Christmas to New Year's Day. Developed by Dr. Maulana Karenga, Kwanzaa introduces and reinforces seven basic values of African culture that contribute to building and reinforcing the family, the community, and culture among African American people (as well as Africans and those of African descent throughout the world). These values are called the *Nguzo Saba*, a Swahili term that includes unity, self-determination, creativity, collective work and responsibility, purpose, cooperative economics, and faith.

- **New Year's Eve** in the Western world occurs every December 31. Many parties are given to "bring in the New Year," and many people stay up until midnight to celebrate the change from the old year to the new. **New Year's Day** is January 1—a day for food and family.

X. Texas History Earliest Inhabitants

KEY QUESTION: *Who were the first Texans, and in what activities did they engage?*

- In answering this question, it would be wise to realize that data is constantly being found by archeologists to change the way that we think about peoples of the past. However, anthropologists believe that the first Texans, called **Paleoamericans**, or Old Americans, crossed the land bridge that was believed to connect Asia with Alaska roughly 37,000 years ago.

- These Old Native Americans of the Ice Age were hunters who roamed the High Plains of West Texas in search of ancient American elephants, mammoths, mastodons, ground sloths, and giant bison. These bison were twice the size and four times the weight of the modern buffalo. Eventually, the Ice Age ended and the lush land of Texas became hotter and drier. Soon the animals that the Old Americans depended on for food became extinct.
- Before the land bridge disappeared, around 7,000 years ago, a new group of humans made their way across it and eventually to Texas. These people of the Archaic Period were called **Amerinds**.
- These new people, like the Old Americans, were nomadic hunters and gatherers. The Amerinds of North America displayed almost identical racial or physical characteristics to each other, with only minor variations of height or color, but became differentiated culturally. They also split into linguistic stocks but, through time, lost even their mutual languages within each linguistic group. They made their tools and artifacts in different ways. The early Amerinds left 27 different kinds of dart points on the Edwards Plateau alone. Archeologists are currently working at an incredibly rich site, the Gault site near Georgetown, to discover more information on the Clovis people who lived there 13,000 years ago.
- Culturally varied, speaking different languages, nomadic, and constantly impinging on each other, the hundreds of bands of Amerinds could only follow the oldest human logic: many made war. Each new folk wandering from the north invaded already appropriated hunting grounds, and the first wars stemmed from the most logical of reasons, the defense of territory. But a constantly roaming and colliding people soon imbedded the idea and act of warfare deep in their cultural heart. Fighting became a central part of their lives; therefore, the center of society and the most important member was the warrior. Because the male warriors were too busy preparing for war and actually fighting, women performed most of the labor.
- The **Neo-American Age**, around 3,000 years ago, is marked by an *agricultural revolution*. The people of this age began to move from nomadic hunting and gathering to sedentary agriculture, where they remained in one place and domesticated crops, including maize (corn), beans, squash, tomatoes, potatoes, and cotton. These people have been referred to as **Mound Builders** because of the burial and temple mounds they erected in the Piney Woods of East Texas.
- The largest group of these Mound Builders was the **Caddo Nation**, once the largest and most powerful American Indian group in Texas. The Caddo settlements, mostly in East Texas, were relatively permanent. The Caddoan tribes hunted game as a supplement rather than a staple. They grew many varieties of crops and lived in villages made up of large timbered houses, which were domed and thatched. Because they were agricultural, and war was no longer a central part of their culture, they were remarkably amiable to White men in the first years of contact, with disastrous results to their tribe. The Europeans brought with them diseases that had devastating effects on the tribes, which had little or no immunity to them.
- South of the Caddo nation, along the Gulf Coast, lived a number of smaller tribes. One of the most powerful was the **Karankawa**. These Native Americans inhabited an area from Galveston to Corpus Christi in a more nomadic way of life; that is, they were mostly hunters and gatherers.

- West of Karankawa country on a line ranging through San Antonio to Del Rio was the territory of a number of small bands of **Coahuiltecans**. Their territory was one of the harshest in the state. Because of the heat and the dry conditions, there were not enough game animals to support a hunting society. Farming was also futile in this area. These people learned to use almost every native plant that grew in South Texas. They made flour from agave bulbs, concocted "fire-water" from mescal and maguey leaves, and roasted mesquite beans. They also consumed spiders, ants, lizards, and rattlesnakes.

- The Jumano and Pueblo peoples both lived in far West Texas. The Plains Jumano were well-known traders. They lived in a central crossroads territory between two highly developed cultures. Caddo tribes in East Texas and Oklahoma were part of the large Southeastern Indian culture and traded with the Mississippian tribes north and east of them. To the west of the Plains Jumano were the Puebloan tribes living in New Mexico and in northern Mexico. Jumano traders would carry goods in large baskets on their backs and on dogs with packs and travois from one side of the plains to the other. This trade area covered a large part of central Texas and the Panhandle of Texas.

- The **Tonkawa** lived above the country of the Coahuiltecans, over the Balcones Escarpment. They ranged across the Edwards Plateau to the Brazos Valley. They lived by hunting, fishing, and gathering fruits, nuts, and berries. They lived on the edge of bison country in buffalo-hide tepees and used large domesticated dogs as beasts of burden. Horses and cattle, brought by the Spaniards in the 1500s, were still unknown to these early Indian tribes. The Tonkawas did not hunt or raid very far north of the Texas plains. They were relatively confined to the Edwards Plateau by another, fiercer tribe that commanded the largest buffalo territory—the Apache.

- The **Apaches** (or Lipan Apaches) inhabited the High Plains of Central Texas. Here there were millions of bison, elk, deer, and antelope. Each spring and fall, bison congregated on the southern plains and grazed in a northward direction throughout the summer months. Anthropologists believe that the typical buffalo-hunting cultures of the Plains evolved first in Texas and then spread north.

- The **Plains Indians** centered their lives on the buffalo. The great hunts took place in the spring and fall, when small herds were surrounded by men on foot and shot with arrows until all the animals were killed. Immediately, the women set to work with their flint knives. Every part of the buffalo was used. It was believed that they had up to 52 uses of the animal. Most of the meat was roasted and the intestines were cooked to provide a special treat. Some lean flesh was sun dried, or *jerked,* to be eaten over the winter. Some organs were cleaned and dried to be used as bags to store water. Bones were made into picks and other tools. Hides were dried for clothing, shelter, and blankets. Apaches made teepees of buffalo skins and light frames of *sotol* sticks. These were flapped with bearskins for doors, and open at the top for escaping smoke. Fires were built in the centers, and they were furnished with hide blankets. Four to 12 people lived in one teepee. The bison hides were tanned so fine that rain could not penetrate or stiffen them.

- In the hot months, Apaches wore very little. In winter they wore deerskin shirts and heavy buffalo robes. Apaches possessed little besides their clothing, tools, weapons, and teepees. During the hottest months of the summer, the herds moved north to follow the grass and the rains, and avoid the blazing sun. During this period, the Apaches, still hunting on foot, were limited in their pursuit of the herds and were forced to supplement their economy with other foods. They learned to domesticate crops by planting them in small patches along the infrequent rivers and streams. While these crops grew, Apaches settled down for long periods beside the waters. The Spanish called these semi-permanent camps *rancherias*.

- The **Comanche people**, who became exceptional horsemen after the Spanish brought horses into the New World, dominated the Southern Plains of the United States, or what is currently the Panhandle of Texas. Originally, the Comanches migrated south because of the greater access to the mustangs that roamed wild. The warm climate and abundance of buffalo were additional incentives. Like many of the Plains Indians, Comanches were nomadic. The buffalo was extremely important to their way of life, providing them food, clothing, and shelter. They supplemented their meat diet through trade with agricultural tribes such as the Wichita and Caddo. Because of their trading skills, Comanches controlled much of the commerce of the Plains. The Comanches came to the Plains later than other groups, so they became accustomed to conflict. The Apaches and Comanches became mortal enemies.

- The most famous chief and warrior of the Comanche was **Quanah Parker**, whose mother, **Cynthia Ann Parker**, had been captured as a child in a raid on Fort Parker (near present-day Mexia, south of Dallas). After many years, she was recaptured, returned to a white settlement, and held there. She grieved for her lost children and her lost life, often not eating or speaking, as she had become a Comanche.

- In the 1700s, missions and *presidios* (fortified areas) were built with great walls to protect priests, settlers, and native converts from hostile tribes. Throughout the 1800s, **forts** were established throughout much of Texas as protection for White settlers, and the **Texas Rangers**, who are believed to be the oldest state law enforcement agency in the United States (established in 1835 by Stephen F. Austin), were also employed to protect settlers. However, as more settlers came into Texas and the buffalo continued to disappear as a food source through professional hunters and fencing, clashes with Native American tribes escalated with increasing violence. In 1874, the U.S. Army prepared to remove the Plains Indians from the Panhandle area of Texas in the **Red River War**. After more than 20 skirmishes, the Comanche tribe under Quanah Parker surrendered and was removed to a Kiowa-Comanche-Apache Indian Reservation in Fort Sill, Oklahoma, in 1875. This effectively ended the culture of the Plains Indians in North America.

- One agreement with Native Americans—the **Meusebach–Comanche Treaty**—stands apart for two important reasons. Made between the new Texas German community in 1847, it is the only treaty between tribes and private citizens (but was recognized by the U.S. government), and it is the only treaty with American Indians believed never to have been broken.

XI. Early European Exploration and Development

KEY QUESTION: *What was the primary function of the Spanish missions?*

- In mid-1519, sailing from a base in Jamaica, **Alonso Alvarez de Piñeda**, a Spanish adventurer, was the first-known European to explore and map the Texas coastline. This event marked the beginning of **Spain's rule** in Texas and the first of **six flags** that would wave over the state (Spanish, French, Mexican, Texan, Confederate, and United States).

- In 1528, **Cabeza de Vaca** was shipwrecked on what is today believed to be Galveston Island. His small band wandered the area for approximately 6 years, trading with the Indians of the region. He later explored the Texas interior on his way to Mexico City. Once there, he related a legend of the **Seven Cities of Gold. Esteban**, who traveled with him, was the first known African to set foot on the Americas.
- From 1540 to 1542, **Francisco Vasquez de Coronado,** a *conquistador* (or conqueror), led an expedition of more than 300 soldiers, Mexican Indian allies, women, and priests through present-day New Mexico, western and northern Texas, and as far north as Kansas, searching for the cities of gold from the legend. Although he found no gold, he did strengthen Spain's claim on Texas. Coronado claimed for Spain all the territory he explored.
- Priests began to settle and build missions in the conquered territory so that they could "civilize" and convert to Catholicism the Indians of the area (and more firmly claim the land for Spain). The **first Spanish mission** in Texas was **Corpus Christi de la Isleta**, established near **El Paso** in 1682. The missions often had *presidios* (or forts) attached to them or nearby to protect those who lived in the missions.
- The **French** claim to Texas rests on the explorer Rene-Robert Cavelier, **Sieur de LaSalle,** who set foot on Texas soil in 1685. He established **Fort St. Louis** inland from Matagorda Bay, after his ship ran aground with the remainder of 300 colonists with whom he started this disastrous journey. The colonists were beset by further hardships, and those who remained finally left to search for a way back to Louisiana. Two years later, LaSalle was killed by his own men. In 1689, Mexican explorer **Alonso de Leon** reached Fort St. Louis and found it abandoned. It is believed that Indians and disease destroyed the remainder of the French force. In 1995, a team of archaeologists from the Texas Historical Commission discovered *The Belle,* one of La Salle's frigates, in the waters of Matagorda Bay. In 1996, the exact location of Fort St. Louis was pinpointed near Victoria, Texas.
- Alarmed by the French presence in Texas and the French settlements in the nearby Louisiana area, the Spaniards established **Mission San Francisco de los Tejas,** in 1690 as the first East Texas mission.
- Throughout the 1700s, Spain established a number of Catholic missions throughout Texas to (1) spread Christianity, (2) establish permanent settlements for the indigenous people to be socialized, and (3) solidly lay claim to land for Spain. Missions were located near the major population centers of all the major Indian tribes of Texas, except for the Apaches of the higher plains. Most of these missions failed and were abandoned. However, visitors can tour a number of the old remaining mission churches that are still in use along the Mission Trail in San Antonio. **Mission San Jose** still retains all of its defensive walls and outbuildings, so one can see exactly what an entire mission was like.
- European diseases such as measles and smallpox spread rapidly among the Indians and decimated their populations. By the end of the 18th century, the Caddo Indians had almost disappeared. Ironically, the diseases brought by Spaniards and Catholic priests of these missions exterminated the very people they had come to save.
- Around the same time the French founded New Orleans in the 1700s, the tiny Spanish mission of **San Antonio de Valero (the Alamo)** was established. Viceroy San Antonio de Valero, for whom the mission was named, began to build a complex around his mission. For protection

from the French and Indians, he established **Fort San Antonio de Bejar (or Bexar)**, named for his brother.

- More and more people began to move to the San Antonio area. By 1726, there were 200 men, women, and children, not counting Native Americans, living in the town of San Antonio along "El Camino Real."
- Other Spanish towns founded in this same time period are **Goliad** and **Nacogdoches**.
- **Jane Long** became known as the **"Mother of Texas"** because of the birth of her child on Bolivar Peninsula in 1821. She referred to herself as the first English-speaking woman to bear a child in Texas. However, the census between 1807 and 1826 reveals that several children were born to Anglo American women prior to this time.
- By 1800, Mexican colonization of the Rio Grande area affected Texas more than all the missions. This resulted in (1) Mexican cattle kingdoms being established in North America; (2) establishing land titles and other related Spanish laws in the region; and, finally, (3) bringing a new kind of settler to the area—the Mexican frontiersman who came to stay, unlike the priests and soldiers who came before them. Mexicans who moved to the area of Texas were called **Tejanos**.
- In 1821, the year Mexico gained independence from Spain, **Stephen F. Austin**, known as the **"Father of Texas,"** received permission from the Mexican government to settle a colony of 300 families, now known as the **"Old Three Hundred,"** in the Brazos River region in southeast Texas with special land grants. This was the first of the Mexican land grants to Anglos. Stephen F. Austin was continuing the work that his father, **Moses Austin**, a North American from Missouri, had begun the year before. Unfortunately, Moses died before he could complete his plan. The economic motivation for many North American families to settle in Texas was based on the rich and inexpensive land, although Mexico wanted the land to be colonized and settled to deter the French and the Indians. **Martin de Leon** was the only Mexican *empresario* to found a Texas colony. An **empresario** was an agent or contractor who was granted land in Texas by Mexico in return for founding a colony. Most empresarios, like Stephen F. Austin, had brought settlers from the United States. Martin de Leon's colony (near Victoria) was the only colony in which most families were Hispanic instead of Anglo American.
- Austin's settlement was the official beginning of Anglo American colonization in Texas. This trickle became a flood as Americans heard about the fertile land in Texas. **GTT** (Gone to Texas) was a sign left on many doors as settlers moved from other U.S. states and territories to Texas.
- Despite restrictions by Mexico, by 1836, there were between 35,000 and 50,000 Anglo settlers in Texas. Even by 1830, Mexico had become so concerned about the rapidly increasing numbers of Anglo American settlers that the Mexican government banned any further emigration into Texas by settlers from the United States. With the increasing Anglo population, a strain quickly developed in the relationship between the Texans and Mexico due to government, language, tariffs, corruption, and religion.

XII. Revolution, Republic, and Statehood

KEY QUESTION: *How did Texas ultimately break with Mexico and gain independence?*

- In the 1830s, Stephen F. Austin had become increasingly involved in the politics between Texas and Mexico, hoping that Texas would move to a more responsive and more central state government. The state of Coahuila's government (of which Texas was a part) was located in the capital city of Saltillo—more than 500 miles away. Traveling from Mexico City, Austin was arrested and thrown in jail without charges for almost a year. This further angered Texans. Early in 1835, Austin announced that he was convinced that war with Mexico was necessary to secure freedom.

- Growing tension in Texas was the result of cultural, political, and religious differences between the Anglo Americans and the Mexican government. In response to the unrest, Antonio Lopez de **Santa Anna**, the president of Mexico, reinforced Mexican troops in Texas.

- Gonzales, a town in central Texas east of San Antonio, owned a cannon to protect itself from Native American attack. Mexico did not want the town to retain this weapon. A battle was fought at Gonzales on October 2, 1835, in which the Mexican forces were thwarted in their efforts to retrieve it. The famous Texas flag flying over Gonzales bore the words **"Come and Take It."** Although there were earlier minor skirmishes, the **Battle of Gonzales** is generally considered to be the first battle for Texas' independence.

- The Mexican dictator **Santa Anna** then gathered a substantial army to sweep through Texas. **General Sam Houston,** commander of the Texan army, ordered **William B. Travis** to the Alamo. There, Travis made a stand with about 189 men, hoping to give other Texans a chance to organize more men for a stronger defense.

- The **Texas Declaration of Independence**, March 2, 1836, was produced, literally, overnight. One of its principal authors was **George Childress**. The only native Texan to sign the declaration was **Francisco Ruiz**. Its urgency was paramount, because while it was being prepared, the Alamo in San Antonio was under siege by Santa Anna's army of Mexico. The Texas Declaration of Independence is similar to that of the U.S. Declaration of Independence. The declaration contains a statement on the nature of government, a list of grievances, and a final declaration of independence. Separation from Mexico was justified by the Texans who charged that, among other things, the government of Mexico had ceased to protect the lives, liberty, and property of the people.

- The **Battle of the Alamo** lasted 13 days, ending on March 6, 1836, with the deaths of all its defenders (numbering about 189). The mission was defended by Anglo-Texans, Hispanic-Texans, and others from the United States (and even a few from European countries) who had heard about the fight for freedom. The Mexican army of Santa Anna numbered 4,000 to 5,000 during its final charge. Among those who fought bravely and were killed were **David Crockett, Jim Bowie,** and **William B. Travis,** commander of the Alamo. One reason this battle is considered to be one of bravery and sacrifice is that all the defenders knew that they would die because of the overwhelming odds. Travis is credited with "drawing a line in the sand" during the siege and asking that all who would stay with him and die defending the Alamo (rather than surrender) cross the line. All but one did, with even the ill Jim Bowie asking that his cot be carried over. His famous letter to request reinforcements was signed, "Victory or Death." A small number of women, children, and slaves were spared by Santa Anna. Principal among them was the only adult Anglo survivor, **Mrs. Susanna Dickinson**, whose husband, Col. **Almaron Dickinson**, had also been killed in the fighting. **Enrique Esparza**, son of a defender of the Alamo (who would have been about 8 years old at the time), and his mother also survived. These witnesses were told to spread the word of what had happened at the Alamo and to tell Sam Houston that resistance was hopeless. Santa Anna continued to sweep east toward Goliad.

- Texas declared its independence on March 2, 1836, during the fighting at the Alamo. Delegates to the Convention of 1836 at Washington-on-the-Brazos had named **David Burnett** as the interim president until an election could be held. Later, when the first election was held, **Sam Houston** became the first elected president of the Republic of Texas.

- A subsequent execution of **James Fannin** (who surrendered, fearing the same fate for his men as at the Alamo) and nearly 400 Texans who were holding the mission at **Goliad** on March 27, 1836, led to the battle cry of Texas' independence at San Jacinto, "Remember the Alamo! Remember Goliad!"

- As Texans heard about the Mexican advance, many abandoned their property and belongings and headed quickly toward the safety of Louisiana, across the Sabine River border. This evacuation was called the **Runaway Scrape**. The flight was marked by lack of preparation and much panic. The people, mostly women, children, and the elderly, used any kind of transportation they had, and many died on the run. Often they were buried where they fell. This flight continued until the war was over, often just far enough ahead that Santa Anna's campfires could be seen at night.

- **The Battle of San Jacinto** was fought on April 21, 1836, just south of the present city of Houston. Santa Anna's entire force of 1,600 men was killed or captured by **General Sam Houston**'s army of 800 Texans; only 9 Texans died. This decisive battle resulted in Texas' independence from Mexico. **Sidney Sherman**, who brought volunteers from Kentucky to fight for Texas freedom, was credited with the battle cry, "Remember the Alamo!" and with the only flag for the Texans at this battle. Later, he helped establish the office for the Major General of the Militia, an office he held until annexation. The Treaty of Velasco ended the revolution. **Vicente Filisola**, the second in command under Santa Anna, ratified the treaty and was tasked with withdrawing troops from Texas after Santa Anna's capture. Texas was now its own *independent country* (**The Republic of Texas**) and would fly its **"Lone Star" flag** for the next 10 years before becoming part of the United States.

- Envoys from Texas had been meeting with officials from the United States well before the end of the war. The Texans wanted to join the United States once they gained independence from Mexico. However, when the war ended in 1836, many in the U.S. government opposed the annexation of Texas because it would have affected the balance of slave and free states. Representatives from the free states believed that Texas would certainly enter as a slave state, and the Congressional power of those from free states would be diminished.

- Five sites had served as temporary capitals of the country of Texas (Washington-on-the-Brazos, Harrisburg, Galveston, Velasco, and Columbia) before Sam Houston moved the capital to Houston in 1837. In 1839, the Texas Congress first met in the new town of **Austin**, the frontier site selected for the capital of the Republic of Texas.

- In 1845, **President James Polk** followed through on a campaign promise to annex Texas and signed legislation making Texas a state. Texas was admitted as the 28th state on December 29, 1845.

- **Sam Houston** commanded the Texas army during the Texas Revolution and was president of the new country of the Republic of Texas. He also became governor of the state of Texas from 1859 to 1861, and later, a U.S. senator after statehood was achieved.

- Even after the Texas Revolution, Mexico continued to dispute the independence of Texas, and several major incidents occurred where Texans and Mexicans engaged in battles and skirmishes. In 1842, Santa Anna sent a large force under **General Adrian Woll** that captured San Antonio. At the **Battle of Salado Creek, Colonel Mathew Caldwell** was successful in repelling the force. However, nearby another group from the LaGrange area was heavily outnumbered; the event became known as the **Dawson Massacre**, where a number of Texans fell and others were captured, many of whom died in Perote Prison in Mexico. Later that year, another group of Texas militia engaged a large Mexican force at the border of the Rio Grande (Mier City) and was forced to surrender. This became known as the **Mier Expedition** and led to the **Drawing of the Black Beans**. Prisoners who were captured were blindfolded and ordered to draw from 159 white beans and 17 black beans. Those who drew a black bean were executed.
- The **Mexican–American War** in 1846 (after statehood) ignited as a result of these continued disputes over claims to Texas boundaries and continued border incursions. The outcome of the war fixed the Texas southern boundary at the Rio Grande River. 1848 saw the end of this war with the **Treaty of Guadalupe Hidalgo,** which finally recognized the annexation of Texas to the United States and ceded California and nearly all of the present-day American Southwest between California and Texas to the United States.
- Sixteen years after becoming a state, Texas seceded from the Union in 1861, following a vote by the Secession Convention to become part of the **Confederacy**. Governor Sam Houston was one of a small minority who opposed secession. Several Civil War battles took place in Texas (two at Sabine Pass, two in Galveston, and one near the Rio Grande).
- The last land engagement of the Civil War was the **Battle of Palmito Ranch** in far south Texas in 1865.
- In 1866, the abundance of longhorn cattle in south Texas and the return of Confederate soldiers to a poor **Reconstruction** economy marked the beginning of the era of Texas trail drives to northern markets.
- The U.S. Congress readmitted Texas into the Union in 1870.
- The present Texas State Constitution was ratified on February 15, 1876.
- Altogether, six flags have flown over Texas: the Spanish, the French, the Mexican, the Texan, the Confederate, and the United States flags.

XIII. Inventions

KEY QUESTIONS: *What scientists and technological discoveries have affected America's history?*

- There have been many inventions that have changed the lives of Americans. Beginning with **Benjamin Franklin**'s experiment with a kite one stormy night in Philadelphia, **electricity** eventually became one of the most important inventions in history. In the mid-1800s, everyone's life changed with the invention of the electric light bulb.
- **Gail Borden**, who came to Texas in 1829, was an inventor of many interesting items but is best known as the father of the **modern dairy industry**, because he patented the process for condensing milk in a vacuum.
- **Louis Daguerre** of France is, perhaps, the most famous of those who invented the **photographic** process in the mid-1800s.

- **Cyrus McCormick** invented the **reaper** in 1856, transforming the farm industry by allowing fewer people to produce more grain.
- In the early 20th century, **George Washington Carver**, an African American scientist and inventor, was responsible for researching and promoting alternative crops such as peanuts and sweet potatoes to Southern cotton farmers, particularly to establish crop rotation in soils depleted by cotton and to find hundreds of uses for these crops.
- Ancient farmers began the process of adding substances to the soil to increase growing capacity in their fields. This allowed them to move to new uncultivated areas faster. By the 17th century, organized research into **fertilizer** technology began. The industry experienced significant growth after World War I, when facilities that had produced ammonia and nitrates for explosives were converted to the production of nitrogen-based fertilizers.
- During the 1800s in France, **Louis Pasteur** worked in several major areas that aided human beings throughout the world. The most important, perhaps, was the **germ theory** of disease. He also invented **pasteurization** to keep milk from souring, as well as a vaccine for rabies.
- An 18th century American naturalist, **John James Audubon**, was the dominant wildlife artist of this country for at least half a century, painting and cataloging the birds of North America.
- **Maria Mitchell** was the first professor of astronomy at Vassar and was also the first woman to become a member of the American Academy of Arts and Sciences. She was the second woman to have discovered a comet.
- Throughout the history of this country, new modes of transportation allowed people and their products to travel more quickly, beginning with canal systems (such as the Erie Canal that connected one of the Great Lakes to the Hudson River and on to the Atlantic), the railroads (especially the Continental Railroad that stretched across the country), and in the 20th century, interstate roadways and commercial airlines. Early in the 19th century, the **automobile** changed people and society, giving people the freedom to move farther from their workplaces, which, in turn, gave rise to suburbs. Demand for cars resulted in a search for faster and cheaper ways to build them. **Henry Ford's assembly line** and **interchangeable parts** production for Model T cars changed the way the manufacturing industry operated. Support industries developed in response to the mass production of cars, two of which were glass for windshields and rubber for tires. Cars also made the construction of roads necessary. Road, bridge, and tunnel construction, in turn, produced new goods and services industries.
- **Joseph Glidden** was an inventor who changed life in Texas dramatically. In 1874, he patented **barbed wire** that was to bring an end to much of the open-range ranching and the days of the cattle drives. This invention encouraged farming and smaller ranches to flourish.
- **Alexander Graham Bell** first patented his telephone in 1876.
- In 1920, KDKA in Pittsburgh was the first commercial **radio** station to go on the air. By the mid-1930s, almost every American household had a radio. The first successful **television** transmission occurred in New York in 1927, although television sets in homes were not commonplace until the 1950s. These two broadcast technologies soon gave rise to the **advertising** industry.
- Advertising encouraged people to consume things, such as **household appliances**, that dramatically changed the 20th-century lifestyle by

eliminating much of the labor of everyday tasks. Engineering innovation produced a wide variety of devices, including electric ranges, washing machines and dryers, vacuum cleaners, and dishwashers. These and other products gave more free time, enabled more people to work outside the home, and contributed significantly to the economy.

- In 1903, history was made at Kitty Hawk, North Carolina, when **Wilbur and Orville Wright** flew what is credited to be the first controlled airplane. **Charles Lindbergh**, or "Lucky Lindy," was the first to fly nonstop across the Atlantic Ocean in 1927, opening the doors to the era of commercial aviation.

- Willis **Carrier** received a patent in 1906 for his *Apparatus for Treating Air*, the first successful air conditioner. By the 1930s, movie theaters, department stores, office buildings, banks, restaurants, railroad cars, and hotels in the South began to install air conditioning. By the 1950s, cooled air was widespread, particularly in the South. The results were unprecedented in various ways. The mortality rate decreased and economic activity increased. During the 1960s, for the first time since the Civil War, more people migrated to the South than out of that area.

- A major home convenience item, frozen food, was popularized by **Clarence Birdseye** in the late 1920s. The Birdseye name is still prominent in the frozen food industry today in the United States and internationally.

- African American **Garrett Morgan** invented the traffic signal, a hair straightening product, and the safety hood (which eventually was to become the gas mask).

- In the 1950s, **Jonas Salk**, an American, invented a vaccine for the terrible disease of **polio** that had left many Americans and people throughout the world with paralysis.

- The **computer** is a defining symbol of 20th-century technology. It is a tool that has transformed businesses and lives around the world, increased productivity, and opened access to vast amounts of knowledge. Computers are continually becoming faster, more powerful, and more affordable. The **Internet** has changed business practices, educational pursuits, and personal communications. It provides global access to news, commerce, and vast amounts of information. **Wireless** and **mobile technologies** are connecting people in ways that were unimaginable just a few years ago.

- Perhaps the most amazing engineering feat of the 20th century is the human expansion into **space**. Engineers have progressed from the early test rockets to sophisticated satellites. The development of spacecraft has expanded the world's knowledge base and improved man's capabilities. Thousands of useful products and services have resulted from the space program, including medical devices, improved weather forecasting, and wireless communications. **Carl Sagan**, an American astronomer, popularized science with his book *Cosmos*. In 1980, the Public Broadcasting System (PBS) televised a 13-episode series based on the book. This series, one of the most viewed series in PBS history, won both Emmy and Peabody awards. He is most famous for founding the study of *astrobiology* (or *exobiology*), which investigates life on other planets.

- **Nuclear technologies**, although generally controversial, are among the most important achievements of the 20th century. The harnessing of the atom has changed the nature of war forever. Nuclear technologies have also given us a new source of electric power and new capabilities in medical research.

- Medical technologies have also become "miracles" beginning in the mid-1900s. One of the most important modern medical pioneers, perhaps, is **Dr. Michael DeBakey.** Working in Houston, he was the first to perform cardiovascular surgeries in so many new areas (including artificial hearts) that it is impossible to list them all. Much of his research has become standard practice for heart surgeons today.

Consider the following practice question:

Mr. McCarthy assigned his fourth-grade class a research project on the earliest immigrants of Texas. Which of the following groups were first?

   A. Spanish
   B. English
   C. French
   D. Amerinds

Europeans came to Texas beginning in the 1500s, more than 5,000 years later than the Amerinds. The Amerind nomadic hunters and gatherers came to Texas around 7,000 years ago. The correct answer is *D*.

Standard V: Geography, and Standard IX: Culture

The social studies teacher applies knowledge of people, places, and environments to facilitate students' understanding of geographic relationships in Texas, the United States, and the world. The social studies teacher understands cultures and how they develop and adapt, and uses this knowledge to enable students to appreciate and respect cultural diversity in Texas, the United States, and the world.

Competency 021 (Geography and Culture) The teacher understands and applies knowledge of geographic relationships involving people, places, and environments in Texas, the United States, and the world; and also understands and applies knowledge of cultural development, adaptation, diversity, and interactions among science, technology, and society as defined by the Texas Essential Knowledge and Skills (TEKS). The following list includes information that a beginning teacher should know and be able to do.

- Analyzes and applies knowledge of key concepts in geography (e.g., location, distance, region, grid systems) and knows the locations and the human and physical characteristics (e.g., culture, diversity) of places and regions in Texas, the United States, and the world.
- Analyzes ways that location (absolute and relative) affects people, places, and environments.
- Analyzes how geographic factors have influenced the settlement patterns, economic development, political relationships, and historical and contemporary societies, including those of regions in Texas, the United States, and the world.
- Demonstrates an understanding of physical processes, or processes that change the Earth's systems (e.g., [1] those *in the lithosphere*, including erosion, deposition, and weathering; plate tectonics; sediment transfer; or other soil formation; [2] *hydrosphere processes* such as the ocean currents and

water cycle; and [3] exchanges of energy and matter *in the atmosphere* that produce weather, weather patterns, and climate; and [4] *biosphere processes* involving animals, plants, and ecosystems, and their effects on environmental patterns).

- Analyzes how humans adapt to, use, and modify the physical environment (e.g., by clearing land, draining swamps, building dykes or dams and irrigation systems), and how the physical characteristics of places and human modifications to the environment affect human activities and settlement patterns.
- Demonstrates an understanding of the physical environmental characteristics of Texas, the United States, and the world, past and present, and analyzes how humans have adapted to and modified the environment.
- Examines how developments in science and technology affect the physical environment; the growth of economies and societies; and definitions of, access to, and the use of physical and human resources.
- Demonstrates an understanding of basic concepts of culture and the processes of cultural adaptation, diffusion, and exchange.
- Demonstrates an understanding of the contributions made by people of various racial, ethnic, and religious groups and analyzes the effects of race, gender, and socioeconomic class on ways of life in Texas, in the United States, and throughout the world.
- Demonstrates an understanding of relationships among world cultures and relationships between and among people from various groups—including racial, ethnic, and religious groups—in the United States and throughout the world.
- Compares and analyzes similarities and differences in the ways various peoples at different times in history have lived and have met basic human needs, including the various roles of men, women, children, and families in past and present cultures.
- Compares similarities and differences between Native American groups in Texas, the United States, and the Western Hemisphere before European colonization.
- Applies knowledge of the role of families in meeting basic human needs and how families and cultures develop and use customs, traditions, and beliefs to define themselves.
- Understands and applies the concept of diversity within unity.
- Relates geographic and cultural information and ideas to information and ideas in other social sciences and other disciplines.
- Formulates geographic and cultural research questions and uses appropriate procedures to reach supportable judgments and conclusions.
- Demonstrates an understanding of research related to geography and culture and knows how social scientists in those fields locate, gather, organize, analyze, and report information by using standard research methodologies.
- Demonstrates an understanding of the characteristics and uses of various primary and secondary sources (e.g., databases, maps, photographs, media services, the Internet, biographies, interviews, questionnaires, artifacts), utilizes information from a variety of sources to acquire social science information, answers social science questions, and evaluates information in relation to bias, propaganda, point of view, and frame of reference.
- Applies evaluative, problem-solving, and decision-making skills to geographic and cultural information, ideas, and issues by identifying problems, gathering information, listing and considering options, considering advantages and disadvantages, choosing and implementing solutions, and assessing the solutions' effectiveness.
- Communicates and interprets geographic and cultural information in written, oral, and visual forms—including maps and other graphics—and translates the

information from one medium to another (e.g., written to visual, statistical to written or visual).

- Analyzes geographic and cultural data by using basic mathematical and statistical concepts analytic methods.
- Understands and analyzes the characteristics, distribution, and migration of populations and the interactions between people and the physical environment, including the effects of those interactions on the development of Texas, the United States, and the world.
- Demonstrates knowledge of the institutions that exist in all societies and how the characteristics of those institutions may vary among societies.
- Demonstrates an understanding of how people use oral tradition, stories, real and mythical heroes, music, paintings, and sculpture to represent culture in communities in Texas, the United States, and the world.
- Analyzes relationships among religion, philosophy, and culture and their impact on ways of life in Texas, the United States, and the world.
- Understands and analyzes how changes in science and technology relate to political, economic, social, and cultural issues and events.

Consider the following practice question:

Ms. Arcain is teaching her first-grade class about the environment. An important concept in this lesson is understanding resources. She wants to make sure that the students understand the difference between natural (renewable) and nonrenewable resources. For review, she asks students, "Which of the following is not a renewable resource?" Students should answer:

A. Water
B. Trees
C. Copper
D. Wind

Copper is a metal ore that is a nonrenewable resource. In other words, when it is used up, it is gone forever. Resources such as these are also termed *limited resources*. The answer is *C*.

Teaching Geography

Geography does not simply begin and end with maps showing the location of all the countries in the world (Davis, 1992). In fact, maps of this nature are fairly limited in their information. Geography should raise important questions about who people are and how they developed as individual societies and then provide clues to the answers. It is impossible to understand history, international politics, the world economy, religion, philosophy, or patterns of culture without taking geography into account. Unfortunately, many students identify geography as a least favorite subject, just as they do history. Too often, teachers concentrate on recitation and memorization rather than allowing students to make meaningful connections between their lives and geography learning.

Traditionally, a central focus of geography has been on map reading and globe skills. Young children can begin to learn map skills, but globe mapping skills are not age-appropriate for Pre-K or kindergartners. For grades 1–3, globes should be used to pique curiosity and help children understand the physical roundness of the Earth (Seefeldt, 1997). However, young children, ages 5 to 7, are able to begin learning about symbols: something that represents another thing. This is a key concept in understanding maps and globes. Children can begin to learn about symbols by manipulating blocks to represent their classroom, as discussed earlier. Children might next work as a class to draw a representation of their classroom from a bird's view, developing symbols to represent desks, centers, the sink, the clock, and other features. They might compare this to a picture that they draw or a digital photo they take from their own desks to understand how a two-dimensional drawing can represent real life. From this point, students move to map their school, playground, and neighborhood. By third or fourth grade, students are ready to deal with landforms and other geographical features.

The concept of direction should follow the introduction of symbols. Prior to entering kindergarten, many children have only started to learn the basics of direction (left and right, up and down, in front of, beside, behind, over, under, far, near, etc.). Left and right may not come easy to children up until age 9. Many of the games and songs popular with very young children such as "The Hokey Pokey," "Simon Says," and "Mother May I?" can be modified to help them with these specific concepts. Once students understand these simple directions, they will be better able to understand the **cardinal directions** (north, south, east, and west). "Simon Says" and "Mother May I?" can be modified for older students with cardinal directions. Meaningful connections can then be made ("It looks like we have a storm coming from the north. What do you think we should wear tomorrow?"). Once the concept of direction has been learned, students may be given opportunities to construct their own maps of their neighborhoods and other popular sites. Treasure hunts constructed by the teacher and by students offer enjoyable activities in constructing and following directions.

Many trade books can reinforce the concepts of maps and map skills. There are several works of fiction that deal with travel and treasure hunting. Trade books can also be used to help students gain understanding of other people and places in the world. For help in choosing appropriate trade books for geography and other social studies subjects, the National Council for the Social Studies annually reviews new trade books for children. The results are normally published in a special pull-out in the May/June issue of *Social Education*.

 ## Materials for the Social Studies Classroom

There are a number of other materials that should be available for geography skills, for lessons, or to be placed in centers. A globe invites children to explore in primary grades. By the later grades, students should be able to answer questions placed in a globe center (for example, "Twirl the globe and stop it with one finger. In which hemisphere did you stop? If it is a landmass, what continent is it? What country is it? What do you think the weather is like there, and why?"). Classroom maps for older children and age-appropriate map puzzles help children spatially in locating shapes of regions, states, countries, or water boundaries. Spatial skills are a prerequisite for success in geography, so teachers should work with children on these skills often. The TEKS ask children to be able eventually to ask geographic questions, such as "Where is it located?" "Why is it there?" "What significance might this location have?" and "How is that related in some way to other peoples, place, and environments?"

Computer technology is also an important resource for the study of geography, including research and communications through the Internet and hypermedia. Programs such as *Where in the World Is Carmen Sandiego?* ask students to combine geography knowledge and skills to problem solve. There are also many types of maps online, ranging from historical maps to the most current city street maps (that can be accessed through Web sites such as

MapQuest) that students can compare with actual satellite images. There are also interactive historic maps online. These maps offer students the opportunity to not only view maps, but, because they are interactive, also allow students to navigate to other related information such as photographs and newspapers from a particular time or place. Bolick (2006) writes:

> *Social studies educators have long taught with maps in the social studies classroom. The Information Age offers social studies teachers new and exciting methods for using maps to teach history. The Internet provides educators access to historical maps that traditionally have not been used in the classroom, as well as providing teachers and students the opportunity to interact with historic maps in new and innovative ways.* (p. 137)

Students could draw map simulations on the computer with art software such as MS Paint. They could also physically construct landform maps out of materials such as salt, *papier-mâché*, or modeling clay.

Sand and water in a center is especially necessary for increasing physical knowledge of landforms. Adding props (that are safe and developmentally appropriate) such as houses, buildings, cars, trains, and so forth encourage children to build neighborhoods, farms, and cities, along with mountains, valleys, rivers, and so forth. Children should be allowed time to play in this type of center, as well as to be directed to specific tasks at times. Teachers should ensure that sand stays moist for easy construction by adding water when needed. Children can also use the water to discover properties of erosion on the land. Sand centers can be constructed of anything that holds well (rubber or plastic swimming pools, or even a large roasting pan for older children). Blocks have been mentioned. Children should first be allowed to explore all of these materials and then, gradually, begin to construct increasingly complex forms found in their environment. For older elementary children, modeling clay should be used as a manipulative for landforms.

To help young children connect to places and people, props in a center provide for sociodramatic play as workers or community helpers (police hats, an astronaut helmet, doctor's bag, a chef's hat and kitchen items, etc.). These items may also be used to reinforce economics standards that focus on jobs, work, and income. Tools, play furniture, and clothes or uniforms of various jobs or of other eras allow opportunities for students to connect to people and places across time and space. Other props for social studies skills might include play money and a cash drawer for economics, items to "sell" at different kinds of stores, and doll families (of diverse ethnicities/skin colors, of various types of families, and of various ages, including grandparents). The Art Center or art activities can also easily become integrated as a springboard for social studies by providing cultural items or *artifacts* (things people make). During the year, the teacher can insert artifacts into a center or show, for example, a piece of Native American pottery or jewelry, a mask, an ink drawing from Asia, or a picture of a clearly different era for students to interpret and use for inspiration. The Music Center or music activities may work similarly—as the teacher rotates recordings and instruments from various eras or cultures.

Picture files (actual or virtual) are one of the most effective tools for social studies. Teachers and students can gather many examples (and non-examples) of a concept such as transportation (with pictures of cars, planes, cycles, trains, hot air balloons, skis, dog sleds, snowmobiles, etc.). Students can relate means of transportation to historic periods and geographic location. For example, cars have been in existence since the late 19th century but look very different today than they did then. In geography, a mountain picture file widens understanding of this concept by including pictures of volcanoes, forested mountains, snow-capped rocky peaks, island peaks, dry west Texas peaks, and villages in mountains in various countries.

Other resources may consist of community helpers. Speakers involved in jobs related to social studies, field trips, or having various vehicles come to school (and many more related activities) may provide a bridge to the real world and how geography can relate to jobs needed in a particular area.

Geography Content

In general, children are fascinated by our world. It is important that EC-6 teachers encourage this fascination among their students. Geography and culture offer many opportunities for children to explore their world and various peoples who inhabit it. The content in the geography competency (like the history competency) is fairly large. To make the geography content more accessible, it is broken down into the following subheadings:

- The study of geography
- Climates
- Natural resources and the environment
- Texas geography

I. The Study of Geography

KEY QUESTION: *What is geography, and what are two major areas of the study of geography?*

- Geography studies both our planet and the people who live on it.
- There are two main branches of geography—physical geography and cultural geography. **Physical geography** focuses on the Earth and its physical environment. Changes in the Earth's crust have created mountains, plateaus, and other landforms. Factors such as weather, earthquakes, and volcanic eruptions continue to alter these landforms. Also included in physical geography are soils, vegetation, climate, and resources, and anything that pertains to our land, water, or atmosphere.
- **Cultural geography** studies how human groups live and change in relation to the physical environment. Cultural geographers define various useful concepts to aid them in this study. One such concept is **population density**, or the average number of people living within a given amount of space (such as a square mile). Urban areas, or cities, are more densely populated than rural areas. **Migration** is another important concept, because it refers to the movement of groups of people out of (**emigration**) or into (**immigration**) different regions. How people use and transport resources and themselves is also part of cultural geography.
- Physical geography also involves describing position through **absolute location** (precise points on a map or grid) and **relative location** (the ability to express a location in relation to other sites—such as San Marcos is about 25 miles south of Austin) (Brophy & Alleman, 1996). Absolute location is related to **latitude (parallels)**, or the horizontal lines of the Earth's grid that are set up like rungs of a ladder to measure how far north or south from the Equator a location is. The **Equator** is a *parallel line* that cuts right through the center of the Earth horizontally and has a location of 0° (zero degrees). Absolute location also requires the measure of **longitude (meridians)**, or the vertical lines of the Earth's grid that stretch "long-ways" from the North Pole to the South Pole. These measure how far east or west a location lies from the **Prime Meridian** (Greenwich, England), which also has a location of 0°.

Time zones are associated with longitude and change at every 15th meridian (there are 24 time zones altogether). The continental United States has *four time zones* (Eastern, Central, Mountain, and Pacific), each an hour later as one moves from the East Coast to the west. Absolute locations are measured in **degrees** and **minutes** north or south and east or west (e.g., Houston is located at the coordinates 29° 45' North latitude and 95° 23' West longitude).

- The world is divided into **four hemispheres** (or half spheres) based on these absolute locations: the **Northern** Hemisphere (the half of the Earth above the Equator) the **Southern** Hemisphere (the half of the Earth below the Equator); the **Eastern** Hemisphere (the half of the Earth to the east of the Prime Meridian); and the **Western** Hemisphere (the half of the Earth to the west of the Prime Meridian). North America lies both in the Northern and Western Hemispheres. The land masses of North America and South America are connected by a narrow "land bridge" called an **isthmus**.

- There are **seven continents** (or large land masses): North America, South America, Asia, Africa, Antarctica, Australia, and Europe.

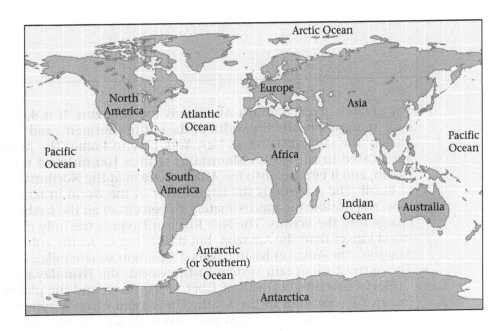

- There are **four oceans**: the Atlantic, the Pacific, the Indian, and the Arctic. Some also consider the Antarctic (also known as the Southern Ocean) to be in this category. Smaller regions of the oceans are seas, gulfs, and bays. A *sea*, generally saltwater, is a secondary body of water usually connected to the larger waters of an ocean. For example, the Bering Sea (near Alaska) is surrounded by the Pacific Ocean, while the North Sea (near the United Kingdom) is bordered by the Atlantic Ocean. A **gulf** or **bay** is also part of an ocean, but is surrounded on three sides by land. The Gulf of Mexico and Galveston Bay are examples.

- By the sixth grade, students should be able to locate the following countries on a map of the world: Canada, Mexico, France, Germany, Great Britain, Italy, Spain, Norway, Sweden, Russia, South Africa, Nigeria, Iraq, Iran, India, Pakistan, the Peoples' Republic of China, The Republic of China (Taiwan), Japan, North Korea, South Korea, Indonesia, and Australia.

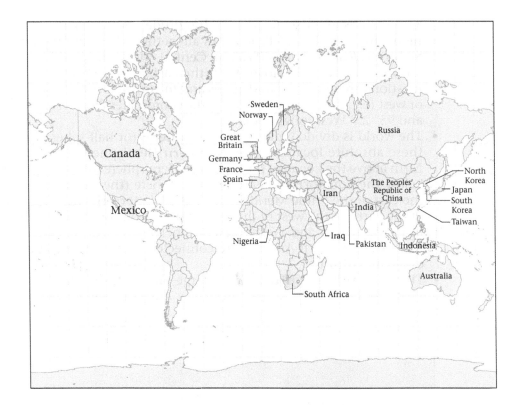

- The greatest river in South America is the **Amazon**. It is 4,000 miles long, spanning nearly the width of the entire continent, and is approximately the same distance as New York City to Rome. The headwaters are located in the Andes Mountains within 100 miles of the Pacific Ocean, and it empties into the Atlantic Ocean at the Northeastern coast of Brazil. The Amazon is the largest river in the world in terms of volume, responsible for approximately 20 percent of all the freshwater discharge into the oceans. The Nile River in Egypt is the only river in the world longer than the Amazon, but it does not equal the volume of the Amazon. The Amazon Basin covers 2.7 million square miles.
- The greatest mountain system in the world, the **Himalayas**, forms a barrier between the Plateau of Tibet to the north and the plains of the Indian subcontinent to the south. The system extends approximately 1,550 miles from east to west and covers about 230,000 square miles. The highest mountains on Earth are located in this range; 110 peaks rise to elevations above 24,000 feet. The highest among them is **Mount Everest**, which has an elevation of 29,035 feet.
- **Relief maps** have *raised* features to show elevation. **Topographic maps** also show detailed elevations and other features or the terrain using contour lines, but are flat. **Physical maps** are also flat but use varied colors (and other details) to show landform features. For example, low elevations are green, whereas the higher elevations are usually indicated by brown (with the highest elevations in white, showing that it could be high mountains covered by snow).
- **Reference maps** (found in atlases, road maps, etc.) show location. **Thematic maps** are those that show various other things about a place, such as its population, vegetation, language spoken, or many other themes. For example, climatic maps may show average precipitation and temperatures, whereas resource or economic maps focus on crops, spending, or other areas of economic interest.

- **Political maps** show boundaries of nations and states with their capital cities.
- The geography of the United States is a result of changes mainly caused by plate tectonics, volcanic activity, and glaciers over millions of years. When viewing a topographical map of the United States from the East Coast to the West Coast, the land that borders the Atlantic Ocean and south around the Gulf of Mexico coastline is mostly coastal plains (primarily lower, flat land). The **Appalachian Mountains** appear next, stretching from the south in Alabama to the Canadian border in the north. This geography caused the New England area and the southeastern states to be settled first, until a way over the mountains (the **Cumberland Gap**) was widened by **Daniel Boone**, an American explorer, in 1775. These mountains open out further west to miles and miles of Great Plains, covering most of the middle of the United States, and stretching from Texas to the Canadian border. In early history, it was in this area where the great buffalo herds roamed (along with many Native American tribes) because this rolling plain was once covered by lush grasslands. The **Mississippi**, North America's greatest river, runs through this plain from north to south, ending in a large delta area near New Orleans. A **delta** is an area of silt formed where a river meets the sea. This deposit usually forms the Greek letter *D*—which is a triangle. These plains are finally broken by the Rocky Mountains, running from their small beginnings in Texas northward into Canada. On the west side of the Rocky Mountains, a great strip of desert stretches from Arizona northward. The high desert area is caused by other ranges of mountains that line the Pacific Coast in the west (the **Sierra Nevadas**, and further north, the **Cascades**). When moisture from the Pacific Ocean hits these mountains, it moves upward, cools, and drops most of its precipitation on the west side of these mountains, thus preventing much rain from reaching the other side.

- The **vegetation regions** of the United States may be divided into four broad categories, with precipitation being the main feature of why each region developed as it did: forests, grasslands, savannahs, and deserts/scrublands. Forests are found across the East, the central and northern Pacific Coast, the higher elevations of the West, and along a

broad band across the interior North. Grasslands are in areas where precipitation is not adequate to support large amounts of tree growth. This occurs in the center part of the country, the Great Plains from Texas and New
Mexico to the Canadian border. Savannahs are areas that often separate
forests from true grasslands and usually border these areas with a combination of trees and grasslands. Deserts, or scrublands, are found in the
Southwest. These regions develop under dry conditions. Vegetation found
in deserts/scrublands usually consists of cacti, chaparral, and mesquite.
- The **Hawaiian Islands**, our 50th state, are the tips of high ocean
  volcanoes.
- Huge **glaciers**, frozen masses of freshwater that move slowly over land,
  cut deep lakes and valleys in the northeastern and northwestern parts
  of the country (such as the **Great Lakes**). In Alaska, Norway, and New
  Zealand, glaciers cut deeply into the land and, as they terminated at the
  sea, the valleys, called *fjords*, filled with water. Some fjords can be
  deeper than the sea they border.
- High mountain ranges were the result of shelves of rock coming together and being forced upward (**plate tectonics**). Some **plateaus**,
  tabletop regions elevated well above the land surrounding them, were
  formed this way as well. **Mesas**, also tabletop landforms, are smaller
  than plateaus. Mesas are hill size, whereas plateaus are mountain size.
- Some educators suggest that the combined physical and cultural study
  of places be coupled with **nine basic human activities**:
  1. Protecting and conserving life and resources
  2. Producing, exchanging, and consuming goods and services
  3. Transporting goods and people
  4. Communicating facts, ideas, and feelings
  5. Providing education
  6. Providing recreation
  7. Organizing and governing
  8. Expressing aesthetic and spiritual impulses
  9. Creating new tools, technology, and institutions
  (Hanna et al., as reported in Brophy & Alleman, 1996, p. 118)
- Other areas of **cultural geography** include the development of political
  systems (e.g., how physical factors such as mountains and rivers help
  set the boundaries of nations), the development of economic systems
  (e.g., how the amount of rainfall in an area helps determine its economy), transportation, languages spoken, and the geography of natural
  resources (e.g., how the presence or absence of resources affects population distribution). **Cultural diffusion** discusses how the exchange of
  ideas, thought processes, inventions, beliefs, agricultures, and so on,
  spread as groups of people come into contact with other groups physically
  or through technology.

Let's try another question:

Ms. La asked her third-grade children to tell which part of the map is the compass rose. What
did children tell her?

A. The compass rose is A.
B. The compass rose is B.
C. The compass rose is C.
D. The compass rose is D.

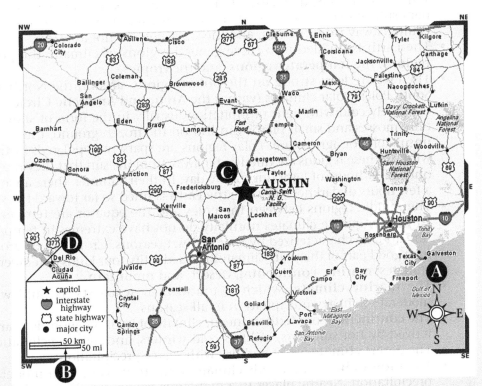

The EC-6 teacher needs to know the elements of a map: the title, the compass rose, the legend, the scale, and the grid system. The *map scale* (as labeled B) on this map gives the reader a clue as to the correspondence of length on a map to real life. For example, 1 inch in the legend may equal 50 miles on the map. A capital city on a map (shown here labeled C) is usually shown with a large star. A map *key* or *legend* (labeled on this map as D) shows all of the symbols used on a map and can also contain the map scale and other information needed to interpret the map. A *grid system* provides the way to locate a particular thing on the map using coordinates. The *compass rose* (as is marked A) gives the reader the four cardinal directions (north, south, east, and west) and often the intermediate directions (northeast, northwest, southeast, and southwest), so the reader can understand the map's orientation. The answer is *A*.

II. Climates: How and Why They Differ

KEY QUESTION: *What are the types of climates?*

- Wherever people live, climate has an important effect on the way of life. It influences the clothing worn, food grown, housing constructed, and transportation used.
- **Climate** refers to average weather conditions *over a long period of time*, taking into account temperatures, wind, and amounts of **precipitation** (rain, sleet, snow). Wind and ocean currents affect climate, as do landforms (such as high mountains) and proximity to the coast.
- **Weather** is the atmospheric conditions *during a short period*; weather may change from day to day.
- To a large extent, climate depends on the amount of the sun's heat that reaches a place. Because the Earth is tilted at an angle as it **revolves** (goes around the sun), the strength of the sun's rays varies in different parts of the Earth and at different times of the year.

- When the Earth is tilted closer to the sun, the rays are stronger and that hemisphere experiences summer. In the winter, that same hemisphere is tilted away from the sun, and the sun's rays are not as warm.
- The Earth is divided into three general regions of climate: the **polar regions**, the **temperate regions**, and the **tropics**.
- The rays are least strong on the **polar regions**, around the North and South Poles. Polar climates (within the **Arctic and Antarctic Circles**) are extremely cold with light precipitation, usually in the form of snow. As only mosses and small plants can live on the frozen ground, the area is unsuitable for agriculture. Polar regions are sparsely populated. In their winters, these regions are tilted so far away from the sun that they receive only a few hours of light during the day. In their summer, there are only a few hours of darkness, because the Earth is titled so far toward the sun.
- The middle regions between the poles and the equator are **temperate zones**. Temperate climates normally do not have extremes in temperature and are characterized by four distinct seasons. Crops can be grown for a good part of the year. Climatologists identify four kinds of temperate climates: **marine**, **continental**, **desert**, and **mountain**.
- The **marine climate**, which is found near seacoasts, is mild with moderate to heavy precipitation in all seasons.
- The **continental**, or Mediterranean, climate of inland regions is characterized by hot summers, mild to cold winters, and light precipitation.
- The **desert climate** is hot and dry with scarce precipitation.
- The **mountain** or highlands climate tends to be cool with moderate precipitation. Nearby places in a highlands region may have rather different climates if they have different elevations or different positions relative to prevailing winds.
- Most of the world's population is found in temperate zones, where the climate is favorable for mental and physical activity, and natural resources for agriculture and industry are accessible.
- The **Equator** is an imaginary circle on the surface of the Earth, equal distance from each pole and dividing the Earth into northern and southern hemispheres. This marks the part of the Earth that is the warmest.
- The **Tropic of Cancer** is an imaginary horizontal circle around the Earth (latitude) north of the Equator (23.5N) that marks the northern boundary of the tropics. This line crosses Mexico, the Caribbean Sea, the Sahara Desert of Africa, central India, Southern China, and the Pacific Ocean just north of Hawaii. Below this line, the climate is normally warm all year round because of its short distance to the Equator. The **Tropic of Capricorn** is an imaginary circle (latitude) south (23.5S) of the Equator that marks the southern boundary of the tropics. This line crosses south central South America, Southern Africa, the island of Madagascar, the Indian Ocean, central Australia, and the Pacific Ocean just south of Tonga. Above this line, the climate is normally warm all year round because of its short distance to the Equator.
- The sun's rays are most strong and direct in the **tropics**, the area near the equator. **Tropical climates** are almost unchanging—very hot, humid, and wet. Jungles and rain forests with their abundant plant life are difficult to clear for agriculture. There are a few arid areas in the tropics as well. The tropics are not as heavily populated as the temperate climates above and below them.
- The circulation of the world's oceans currents are wind driven. Warm ocean currents move from the tropics toward the poles, whereas cold ocean currents move from higher latitudes toward the equator. Seasonal

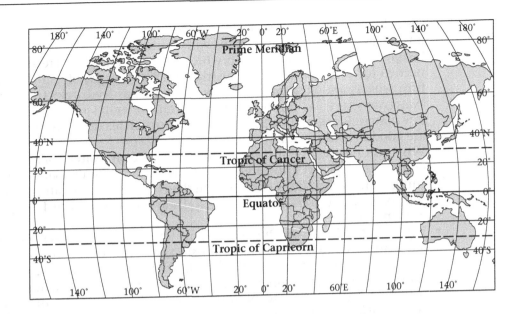

changes in the Pacific Ocean are referred to as **El Niño** if the trade winds in the central and western Pacific are sufficiently weak to allow warm water into the eastern Pacific, and **La Niña** if the normal ocean temperature in this region is cooler.

III. Natural Resources and the Environment

KEY QUESTION: *What are the basic types of natural resources?*

- Any material supplied by the Earth that people can put to use is called a **natural resource**. Resources can be a **pull factor** that attracts people to an area (e.g., a better standard of living, better climate, peace). Lack or loss of resources can be a **push factor**, meaning that people want to leave an area in which they originally settled. There could also be other economic causes (depression, lack of work, etc.), environmental issues (too cold or hot; too wet or dry; etc.), or social reasons (oppressive governments, wars, etc.) that serve as push factors, but resources are an important factor. Other **geographic factors** (landforms, vegetation, water sources, weather and climate, soil, and animal life) also influence settlement. In more recent times, people have been drawn to places with great beauty or where there an available sports (skiing, scuba diving, etc.) or for other reasons. They can populate these areas now because they no longer have to depend on growing local food, they can regulate their inside temperatures, and they can fly or drive great distances quickly.
- **Renewable resources** are those that can be replaced in the foreseeable future. For example, forests can be replanted after trees are cut, and a water supply in a certain area is replenished by rain.
- Examples of **nonrenewable resources** are minerals in the Earth's crust. Metal ores (e.g., iron, gold, silver) and fossil fuels (e.g., oil, natural gas, coal) are among the most important minerals in today's world.
- Researchers are working to find substitutes for some metals that may be used up and to find new energy sources to lessen our dependence on fossil fuels.
- A region's economy develops, in part, according to its available resources. **Arable land** (land suitable for farming) and fertile soil are needed for an

agricultural economy to succeed. In forested areas, the lumber industry is important, as is mining in regions with mineral deposits.

- People usually settle in areas in which water is available. Fresh water is needed for both home and industrial use. The process of using water to turn wheels and generate electricity is known as **hydroelectric power**. Waterways serve as important transportation routes for ships carrying raw materials and manufactured goods. **Port cities** develop where there are good harbors or waterways.

- Wherever people live and work, they affect the air, water, soil, and mineral resources. Dirty (**polluted**) air and water are often unsafe for living things. Industries sometimes pollute rivers, lakes, and oceans by dumping toxic (poisonous) wastes. Oil spills are another hazard for plants and animals.

- Unpredictable **natural hazards** occur when nature creates a disaster such an earthquake, landslide, erosion, an infestation of insects, or weather disasters (floods, tornadoes, hurricanes, droughts, etc.).

- Most air pollution is caused by exhaust from industrial and automobile emissions. In addition to polluting the air, some smoke can combine with moisture in the air to form acids. These acids return in precipitation (**acid rain**) to pollute the land and trees, as well as bodies of water. Acid rain is causing worries over erosion of ancient monuments in places such as Rome and Greece and in forest areas such as the Smoky Mountains. Air pollution is dangerous to health and may cause severe respiratory problems. Local health departments and a federal government agency, the **Environmental Protection Agency** (EPA), monitor air and water and track down polluters. The government also protects the environment by banning the use of cancer-causing chemical pesticides and regulating factory and vehicle exhausts.

- Pollution remains one of the world's most serious problems. Many of our industrialized societies throughout the world are learning to take responsibility for the environment, but developing nations (China, India, etc.) often do not consider this due to the increased costs of reducing pollutants.

IV. Texas Geography (see http://www.tshaonline.org)

KEY QUESTION: *What are the four geographic regions in Texas?*

- Texas is currently the second largest state in both population and in territory. The largest state in terms of population is California, and Alaska is the largest state in terms of territory.

- With an area of 267,339 square miles, Texas is larger than most nations and contains almost every major landform: mountains, plains, plateaus, lakes, rivers, hills, and so forth.

- There are four major land regions in Texas: the **Gulf Coastal Plains**, the **North Central Plains**, the **Great Plains**, and the **mountains and basins (Trans-Pecos Region)**.

- The **Gulf Coastal Plains**, an immense lowland area in the southern and eastern portions of Texas, covers about one third of the state. The Gulf of Mexico provides a long border to the south. Two large port cities in Texas are Houston and Corpus Christi. Houston began its growth as a port city. The Houston Ship Channel, a 52-mile inland waterway, connects Houston to the Gulf of Mexico. The port has been ranked first in the United States in foreign waterborne commerce, second in total tonnage, and sixth in the world.

- At the western edge of the Gulf Coastal Plains stands a line of southward and eastward facing hills. These balcony-like hills, called the *Balcones Escarpment*, mark the boundary between lowland and upland Texas and the beginning of the **North Central Plains**. Part of this area is hillier and rockier than the rest of the Great Plains that extend into northern Texas. This part of the region is often called the *Hill Country*. Most of the land in this area is used for raising cattle.
- The **Piney Woods** makes up the eastern section of the **Gulf Coastal Plains**. The area of vast pine forests and the lands immediately to the west are suitable for diversified farming and livestock.
- The **Valley**, located on the south/southwest border with Mexico and bordering the Gulf of Mexico, makes up the southern section of the **Gulf Coastal Plains**. Cotton, vegetables, and citrus fruits (such as grapefruit and oranges) are among the notable crops grown in the area. Crops can grow all year in this area. The **Rio Grande River** marks the border with Texas and Mexico.

- An **aquifer** is an underground geologic formation that is water bearing or that stores or transmits water. The largest of these, located in the North Central Plains, is the **Edwards Aquifer**, which has been designated as one of the most productive aquifers in the world. It is designated by the EPA as a "sole source" of drinking water for the 1.5 million people of San Antonio and the Austin–San Antonio corridor. The aquifer is also vital to the agricultural and light industrial economy of the region. Springs flowing from the Comal and San Marcos Springs provide water for the tourist and recreation industry.

- The **Great Plains** region extends into the northernmost areas of Texas, including the Panhandle. This region depends on irrigation from underground water supplies and much of this northern area is flat. Some of the areas of the Great Plains offer grasses, weeds, and trees suitable for raising cattle, sheep, and goats. Some areas are developing energy in vast wind farms. Texas has recently taken over the lead in the Western Hemisphere in generating this type of energy.
- The Trans-Pecos region is located in the west/southwest corner of the state where many **mountains and basins** are found. The region is rocky and very dry. With the recent discovery of groundwater reserves there is some limited agriculture production: cattle, cotton, and alfalfa. This region contains most of the state's mountains and best scenery. **Guadalupe Mountains National Park** and **Big Bend National Park** are two such areas.
- Texas has several of the largest urban areas in the United States: Houston, the Dallas/Fort Worth metroplex, and San Antonio are in the top 10, and Austin and El Paso are in the top 20.
- The **capital** of Texas, **Austin**, is located roughly in the middle of the state in an area known as the Hill Country.

Culture

There are many definitions of **culture.** Most, however, synthesize culture into patterns of behavior that take into account a group's beliefs and thoughts, ways of acting/norms, products (artifacts), ways of speaking/language, traditions, and so forth. These are taught to each new generation or gained as one becomes thoroughly assimilated as a part of a particular group; however, culture can also be related to ethnicity and/or race, and religion.

The increasing cultural diversity of the United States challenges educators to understand differing values, customs, and traditions and to provide responsive multicultural experiences for all learners. Currently, one in four Americans is of African, Asian, Hispanic, or Native American ancestry. By the year 2050, that number will be one in three (Duvall, 1994, p. 2). In addition to working with many diverse people throughout their lives in this country, this generation of children will grow up into an ever-shrinking world where trade, travel, and the politics of other countries will become closer than ever before. Without understanding others well, they will always be at risk of reacting negatively to cultural differences.

Teachers must work harder than ever before to educate the diverse children of today's classrooms, because America cannot sustain its way of life and standard of living if many of its citizens go uneducated. According to the Houston Independent School District (H.I.S.D.) Web site, there are more than 90 different languages spoken by students in the city schools in Houston, Texas. Each of these children comes to the classroom bearing his or her cultural norms that may or may not agree with those found in the United States. This situation can act positively or negatively toward a child receiving an equal opportunity for success.

Traditionally, the United States tried to create unity through the public education system by assimilating students from diverse racial and ethnic groups into a single *melting pot* of "American culture." Of course, assimilation requires some self-alienation (denying who you are in order to become someone else). Once everyone was assimilated, all cultures should melt together.

Although the United States is one nation by borders, sociologically we are far from it. Educators can work with children and their families better by gaining an understanding of cultural, ethnic, racial, socioeconomic, and individual differences, especially in light of the wealth of cultural diversity of the nation that increases daily. Although having everyone feel that they are truly American is extremely important, the **salad bowl theory** offers a model for having children retain their heritage and, at the same time, add American heritage. In this theory, various ingredients are mixed together, but the flavor of each ingredient retains its individual flavor.

These issues of multicultural education are different from those of global education. Generally, multicultural education references those who live in America and the many cultures here. **Global education**, however, looks at the connections between *Americans* and the other people in the world. These two entities are not mutually exclusive. They both stand for freedom and universal values, "essential concepts in today's ethnically polarized and troubled world" (Massialas & Allen, 1996, p. 191). Both multicultural education and global education are necessary components of a new multidimensional citizenship that is developing in the world today. Chapin (2006) believes that multidimensional citizenship requires more than just knowledge. Multidimensional citizenship "calls for viewing problems from a global perspective using critical thinking skills" (p. 240). It also involves a commitment to the following convictions:

1. We are all global citizens who share a responsibility for solving the world's problems and for creating the world we desire.
2. We are all members of the family of humankind. We are responsible for understanding and caring for people of cultures different from our own.
3. We are stewards of Earth, which is our home and life-support system. (Chapin, 2006, p. 240)

Instruction can incorporate an interconnective perspective on, for example, ecology, resources, cultures, and human choices. Children should be shown how nations and people depend on each other for survival. A change in a Pacific current such as El Niño, for example, can have ramifications for the entire world. Limiting oil production in the Middle East can automatically cause concern for the rest of the world; the record-setting gas prices in the United States were one consequence. These were nothing in comparison to the gas lines experienced in the United States, Europe, and many other parts of the world when the flow of oil was disrupted in the 1970s. The stock price drop of more than 10 percent in the Hong Kong market in 1997 immediately affected all the stock markets of the world. The eruption of the Icelandic volcano in 2010 disrupted air travel throughout much of Europe and, subsequently, the world. It is difficult, if not impossible, to find any major event in any area of the world without implications for the rest of the world. This makes the rationale for looking at the world with a global view, as well as seeing the value of helping students understand others, incumbent on social studies teachers.

One major connection that the United States has with the world is through popular culture. Popular culture is one of the United States' most lucrative exports. Some reports list popular culture exports second only to the aerospace industry in total revenues from export. U.S. students have access to media that allows them to experience cultures from around the world, and conversely, many of these culture "industries" are U.S. exports. The world's access to American popular culture has exploded, creating what Kellner refers to as a "global popular" (1995, p. 5). The existence of the global popular means that teachers might easily find a common frame of reference or topic when asking U.S. students to consider "others" in the world. One such topic or frame, for example, is popular foods such as pizza. An investigation of pizza may be facilitated by the Internet and the availability of online sites from one of the largest pizza restaurant chains today—*Pizza Hut*. Reading global pizza text as part of the geography and culture curricula offers students the opportunities to apply knowledge and develop skills in a meaningful context, as Kincheloe (2001) recommends. Students learn where people live, their environments, and so on. They also learn that what people eat is determined mainly by location, although occasionally also by religious beliefs (which some historians argue can also be tied in origin to location). For example, they might be interested to see that in the island nation of Japan, one can order a tuna pizza. These things are revealed through an examination of their popular culture, especially noticeable in what they eat on their pizzas (Walker, 2006). Pizza is universal. People around the world use and understand the word, along with cell phones, CDs, jeans, iPods, and so on.

Another way that students might learn about the others who have lived across space and time from them is through non-fiction stories such as **Sadako and the Thousand Paper Cranes**. This story, published in 1977 by Eleanor Coer, told the true story of Sadako Sasaki, a young girl who lived in Hiroshima in 1945 when the United States dropped the atomic bomb. She developed leukemia from the radiation and spent her last years folding paper cranes, believing that if she made 1,000, she would get a wish. Her wish was to live. She made 644 cranes before she died at 12 years old. Other powerful stories are in the form of fables and folktales. Traditional tales exist in every culture. Often these stories began in ancient times and have been passed down from generation to generation through oral retellings. The same basic story often exists in many different cultures; for example, there are many versions of the Cinderella story that are told in countries around the world.

Myths are some of the oldest examples of traditional literature. These are stories that tell of the origins of the world and of nature. The best-known ancient mythologies were created by the Greeks, Romans, and Norse. **Epics** are long stories that are grounded in mythology. These stories always have a human hero who ultimately triumphs over evil. Examples of epics include *Beowulf* and *The Odyssey*. **Legends** are stories that are supposedly based on real individuals or events. There is often a mix of realism and fantasy in these stories. The tales of King Arthur are an example of a legend. **Tall tales** are much more exaggerated and often humorous versions of legends. Some of the most popular tall tales have been about **Johnny Appleseed** (who planted apple trees across the West), **Pecos Bill** (who perfected cowboy skills), and **Paul Bunyan** (who was a larger-than-life lumberjack). **Folktales** are another kind of traditional literature with strong appeal for children. Some reasons for this appeal, according to Lynch-Brown and Tomlinson (2005), may be because the stories are humorous, filled with action from beginning to end, and clearly address issues of justice by rewarding the good and punishing the bad. Some examples of folktales are *Goldilocks and the Three Bears*, *The Three Little Pigs*, *Puss in Boots*, and so forth. Although the terms *folktales* and *fairy tales* are often interchanged, they are not the same thing. Although **fairy tales**, such as *Hansel and Gretel, Sleeping Beauty, Snow White, and Rumpelstiltskin*, share characteristics of folktales, they also contain elements of magic and fantasy (fairy godparents, witches, spells, enchantments, etc.), whereas folktales do not. The most famous collection of fairy tales was published in Germany by two brothers, Jacob and Wilhelm Grimm. The **Brothers Grimm** began collecting fairy tales from across Germany and France in 1803. Between 1812 and 1857, they published seven volumes, for a total of more than 200 fairy tales.

Another type of story with culturally educative value for children is the **fable**. These are stories, typically containing animals as actors, that teach strong moral lessons. Lynch-Brown and Tomlinson (2005) write that throughout history, these stories appealed to both adults and children and, as a result, were the first type of traditional story to appear in print. The best-known collection of fables is **Aesop's Fables. Aesop** (620–560 B.C.E.) was a slave and storyteller who lived in Ancient Greece. He traveled across the region repeating fables such as *The Ant and the Grasshopper, The Hare and the Tortoise, The Town Mouse and the Country Mouse, The Boy Who Cried Wolf,* and so forth. His fables have been translated into many of the world's languages.

Using traditional literature helps children learn lessons about life, moral values, and others. This is a critical component for developing cultural awareness, and teachers should see value in offering their students the opportunity to gain this type of insight.

In addition to understanding how people use oral tradition, stories, and real and mythical heroes as seen through literature, another way of understanding people is through their music, painting, and sculpture. Does the art and music of a people focus on religion, does it turn to realism or attempt to capture beauty and romanticism, or does it have a "hard edge"? Asking these types of questions about a people can open a window onto their hopes, fears, lifestyles, and so forth. This aspect of music is thoroughly discussed at length in Chapter 7, and in art is discussed in Chapter 6. However, it is worth noting that Texas maintains noteworthy cultural representations in many of these areas as well. For example, the Kendall Art Museum in Fort Worth, Texas, the Museum of Fine Arts in Houston, and the Texas Sculpture Garden (the largest private collection of outdoor contemporary art in the world) in Frisco, Texas, house works that many people from around the world come to see. The Sculpture Garden was created for Texas artists. The Museum of Western Art in Kerrville, Texas, attempts to retain the spirit of the cowboy and of Native Americans in the Old West. **Bill Martin, Jr.**, author of *Brown Bear, Brown Bear, What Do You See, Chicka Chicka Boom Boom*, and many other books that are almost required children's reading, lived the last part of his life in Texas. **Alvin Ailey**, a Texas born African American dancer and choreographer, is famous for his work, "Revelations," in which he uses modern dance melded with spirituals and blues. To see a long list of famous Texans in art, music, literature, and in other areas, go to http://en.wikipedia.org/wiki/List_of_people_from_Texas.

Authors and illustrators outside of Texas also make a difference to children's worldview of the past and present. **Laurie Ingalls Wilder** offers great insight into the life of settlers in the 1800s in her *Little House on the Prairie* series of books (also a television series). **Kadir Nelson**, an African American artist and illustrator, collaborated on picture books such as *Moses: When Harriet Tubman Led Her People to Freedom* (Weatherford, 2006) and ***Just the Two of Us*** (Smith, 2005)—both award winning books. He also served as the conceptual artist for Spielberg's *Amistad* and *Spirit: Stallion of the Cimarron*. **Carmen Lomas Garza** is also an exceptional illustrator with her books remembering her Hispanic roots (*In My Family/En Mi Familia, Family Pictures/Cuadros de Familia*, and *Magic Windows/Ventanas Magicas*).

Teachers who make a difference in the lives of children recognize the potential for success for all children. "The primary message from previous research on cultural diversity and learning social studies," Gay (1991) explains, "is that cultural socialization affects how students learn" (p. 154). For the social studies classroom, this means that one of the most important responsibilities of a teacher is to create a classroom environment that respects and supports the unique backgrounds of all children. There are some things to consider that help develop this type of classroom:

1. Cultural perspectives must be integrated into the total social studies curriculum. Teachers should not rely on special days or holidays, weeks, or months (such as Black History Month) to incorporate multicultural perspectives.
2. Understand the existence of the *hidden curriculum* that focuses overwhelmingly on events around Western European experiences. The hidden curriculum is what children learn that has importance but that is not

directly taught (in this case due to emphasis and inclusion—or not). There are many groups who traditionally have been relegated to the margins of U.S. history. These people deserve to be recognized in the main "texts" of history. Even language can create this concept. For example, there would not have been any cave children if there had been only cave*men* in our history. Everyone in the classroom should feel that the contributions they may make to America will be recognized—not just those who belong to certain groups.

The social studies curriculum should include the contributions of the many cultures to American life. Much of the strength of this nation derives from the diversity of its ethnic heritages and cultural origins. The contributions of women to the life, culture, and development of this nation must also not be overlooked nor merely relegated to Women's History Month in March.

Consider the following practice question:

Mr. Chancellor's fourth-grade class was studying the geographic regions of Texas. Students first investigated the different regions and then, in small groups, designed travel brochures for their region. For the group assigned the Valley region, what characteristic of the region should they emphasize?

   A. Orange and grapefruit production
   B. Mountains
   C. Pine forests
   D. Cattle, sheep, and goat ranching

Mountains are found in the Trans-Pecos region (Mountains and Basins) of West Texas; pine forests are found in the Piney Woods region along the border of Louisiana in East Texas and the eastern part of the Coastal Plains; and sheep, cattle, and goat ranching are predominant in the High Plains. Oranges and grapefruit grow in the most southern part of Texas—in the warm Rio Grande Valley near the Gulf of Mexico and the border of Mexico. The answer is *A.*

Standard VI (Economics)

The social studies teacher knows how people organize economic systems to produce, distribute, and consume goods and services, and uses this knowledge to enable students to understand economic systems and make informed economic decisions.

Competency 022 (Economics) The teacher understands and applies knowledge of economic systems and how people organize economic systems to produce, distribute, and consume goods and services. In this competency, Texas expects that the beginning teacher will be able to do the following:

• Compare and contrast similarities and differences in how various peoples at different times in history have lived and met basic human needs, including the various roles of men, women, students, and families in past and present cultures.
• Understand and apply knowledge of basic economic concepts (e.g., economic systems, goods and services, free enterprise, interdependence, needs and wants, scarcity, roles of producers and consumers, factors of production), know that basic human needs are met in many ways, and understand the

value and importance of work and purposes for spending, saving, and budgeting money.
- Demonstrate knowledge of the ways people organize economic systems and of the similarities and differences among various economic systems around the world.
- Understand and apply the knowledge of the characteristics, benefits, and development of the free-enterprise system in Texas and the United States and how businesses operate in the U.S. free-enterprise system.
- Apply knowledge of the effects of supply and demand on consumers and producers in a free-enterprise system.
- Demonstrate knowledge of patterns of work and economic activities in Texas and the United States, past and present, and describe how a society's economic level is measured.
- Demonstrate an understanding of major events, trends, and issues in economic history (e.g., factors leading societies to change from rural to urban or agrarian to industrial, economic reasons for exploration and colonization, economic forces leading to the Industrial Revolution, processes of economic development in world areas, and factors leading to the emergence of different patterns of economic activity in regions of the United States).
- Analyze the interdependence of the Texas economy with those of the United States and the world.

Economics

Consider the following practice question:

Mrs. Laine creates two chocolate "factories" for role play in her fourth-grade classroom. In one, she places four "employee" volunteers: a *mixer* (a person whose job is to take the chocolate out of its container and mix it), a *pourer* (who takes the bowl and pours the chocolate into a mold), a *baker* (who puts the chocolate into the oven and takes it out), and a *wrapper* (who wraps the chocolate in a special foil). The other is a sole proprietorship, where a lone owner does all the jobs, and there is no division of labor. Mrs. Laine provides mixing bowls, forms, and aluminum foil so students can pretend to be doing their jobs. When Ms. Laine calls, "Go," each "factory" goes to work to produce as many chocolates as they can in a specific length of time. The assembly line wins. In the next round, however, she has the mixer "go home sick." The assembly line stalls because no one else knows this job, and the sole proprietorship wins. Mrs. Laine is teaching that:

   A. blue-collar workers are often in assembly-line positions.
   B. specialization of an assembly line also requires cross training.
   C. the demand of a product increases the price.
   D. it would be better to have a corporation.

Mrs. Laine wants to show children that an assembly line works very well, but it can come to a halt if only one worker knows each job because of too much *specialization*. The best idea is to have *cross training* for an assembly line. The answer is *B*.

Teaching Economics

Economics focuses on the production, distribution, and consumption of goods and services. In 2001, as a part of the No Child Left Behind legislation,

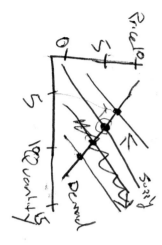

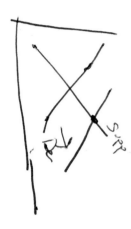

Congress authorized the Excellence in Economic Education (EEE) Act (20 USC 7267) (2001) (U.S. Department of Education, 2009). The EEE "program promotes economic and financial literacy among all students in kindergarten through grade 12." A primary objective of the EEE program is to "increase students' knowledge of, and achievement in, economics to enable the students to become more productive and informed citizens." In Texas, a primary focus of economics in the public schools is on preparing students for the world of work. This school-to-career economics education begins in kindergarten, where students are expected to be able to identify jobs and by first grade to understand the value of work. In 2005, the Texas legislature passed HB 492, requiring that personal financial literacy instruction be integrated into one or more courses required for high school graduation. For young students, however, Schug (1996) suggests concentrating on the following key principles about human behavior: People choose to do the things they think are best for them, and those choices have costs. One way to teach economics concepts to students effectively is through children's literature. Children's literature has, according to Rodgers, Hawthorne, and Wheeler (2007), "been used to describe economic ideas to young people since children's books were first published" (p. 47). In their research, they identified more than 350 picture and easy reader books that have economics concepts as a major theme. Two books that they recommend for teaching "opportunity costs," a key principle of economics (Schug,1996), are: *Mama Is a Miner* (by George Ella Lyon) and *Uncle Jed's Barbershop* (by Margaree Mitchell). In the book *Mama Is a Miner* (1994), the opportunity costs in the story are both personal and environmental. In *Uncle Jed's Barbershop* (1993), the cost to the main character of being able to open his own business was caused by outside forces, unexpected illness of his niece, and a bank failure during the Great Depression that wiped out the remainder of his savings. These books also teach the value of work, identify different types of jobs, and other core elements in a personal finance curriculum.

Economic factors have an important influence on how people in a society live. The economics standard is broken down into more manageable topics as follows:

- Types of economic systems
- Consumer influence
- Structures of business
- Government revenues and expenditures
- Business cycles and government regulation
- International economics
- Economics of Texas

I. Types of Economic Systems

KEY QUESTION: *What is the role of the government in the three different types of economic systems?*

- **Economics** is the study of the ways in which goods and services are created, distributed, and exchanged.
- The **standard of living** of a society is the material well-being of its members. The United States has one of the world's highest standards of living in the world.
- Societies must make decisions about what and how much to create in the way of goods and services.
- A nation's economy can be defined into various types of **industry**. **Primary industry** extracts raw materials (e.g., mining, farming, fishing). **Secondary industry** involves manufacturing finished goods (e.g., chemical and engineering industries, auto makers, construction). **Tertiary industry** provides a service (e.g., banking, healthcare, entertainment) or

markets products from primary or secondary industries. **Quaternary** industry involves research and development industries (e.g., government, information technology).

- Societies also must decide how its goods and services are distributed. The ways in which these decisions are made depend on the type of economic system.
- There are **three major types of economic systems**: communism, socialism, and capitalism. There are also **traditional economies**, as seen (now rarely) in some native groups, who have economies that produce and distribute goods through old customs and beliefs.
- **Communism** is one of the three major types of economic systems. In this system, the government owns all businesses and makes all production decisions. This can also be seen as a **command economy**. All citizens are supposed to share equally in the country's wealth. Communist economies are often planned economies with set national goals for different areas of the economy. For example, many communist countries focus on a high military budget. This type of collectivist government has had little success in increasing overall economic conditions for its people. Cuba, North Korea, and China are currently communist economic systems.
- **Socialism**, a second type of economic system, is based on the idea of a cooperative society in which wealth is more equally distributed and basic social needs are taken care of through the government (mostly through a system of very high taxes). The government controls some basic industries and public utilities, whereas other businesses are owned by individuals. Socialist governments provide many social welfare programs, such as health care and aid to the poor. Sweden is highly socialist; Great Britain is somewhat less, but still, socialist.
- **Capitalism**, as is found in the United States, is a third type of economic system in which *individuals* basically control the means of production, distribution, and exchange. The government usually does not interfere much in business. Capitalism is a **free-enterprise system** or **free-market economy** because, with the exception of some limitations imposed by the government, citizens may engage in whatever business they choose and may produce and charge what they want, to the extent of supply, demand, and price that the market allows. Some individuals, called **entrepreneurs**, may choose to take a risk in return for visionary financial opportunity. These people combine land, labor, or capital to create and market new goods or services. Some famous American entrepreneurs are Benjamin Franklin, Eli Whitney (mass production of cotton), **John Deere** (invented a type of steel plow and founded the largest agricultural equipment company in the world), Milton Hershey (Hershey's Chocolates), Ben Cohen and Jerry Greenfield (Ben & Jerry's Ice Cream), **Wallace Amos** ("Famous Amos" chocolate chip cookies), the Walton family (Wal-Mart), Donald Trump, Oprah Winfrey, and others. **Steve Jobs** and Steve Wozniak created Apple, one of the world's most successful home computers, whereas **Bill Gates** and Paul Allen pioneered Microsoft in the same industry. Some famous Texan entrepreneurs are **Mary Kay Ash** (cosmetics empire), **Stanley Marcus** (Neiman Marcus), T. Boone Pickens (wind energy), and Michael Dell (computers).
- Most modern countries have mixed economies that emphasize one system but use elements of others. For example, the United States has a capitalist system. However, because of the complex nature of our society, the government must exercise some control over business and

industry. There are also government-owned and operated enterprises in the United States, including the Postal Service, the public schools, some railroad lines, and social welfare projects such as public housing developments, Medicare, and Social Security.

II. Consumer Influence

KEY QUESTION: *What is the relationship between the price of and the demand for a product?*

- A **consumer** is an individual who buys or uses goods and services for personal **wants** (he or she would *like* to have an item) or **needs** (he or she *needs* something for survival).
- Consumers buy more of some products and services than others. The ways in which consumers spend their money to buy goods or services (or the **demand**) influence producers' decisions about which goods to produce or which services to provide **(supply)**. When the supply of a particular desired good or service is low, the price normally rises. When the supply of a particular desired good or service is high, the price normally goes down.
- Businesses that make **goods** (concrete products to sell) or provide **services** (work done for someone such as computer, car, or home repair; medical care; teaching; or consulting) must always consider supply and demand in order to make a profit. Thus, if the market is saturated with a good, a company is not able to charge very much for it (unless, for example, everyone wants it and has money to buy it), or if it is a service that many can perform, salaries for the service drop.
- **Supply** is the amount of available goods and services. The development of **assembly lines** has meant faster production of goods and also standardized products. An assembly line is an arrangement of machines, equipment, and workers for a continuous flow of parts in **mass production** operations, where everyone has a specialized job. However, the assembly line can stop if the **division of labor** is too **specialized** (each worker knows only a specified part of a job), and one link of the assembly line is sick or away. All assembly lines should use some amount of **cross training** in order to maintain productivity levels.
- **Demand** is how many people want to buy the product or service. Goods and services can be sold at different prices. Usually, prices affect demand. An increase in price usually results in a decrease in demand. A lower price usually means a greater demand. However, this relationship is not always true.
- The demand for some goods and services is not greatly affected by price. For example, the demand for milk or bread does not change much, even if prices go higher. The demand for these products is said to be **inelastic**.
- In contrast, the demand for many products, such as digital cameras, computers, or new types of phones, greatly increases when the price drops because many more people can afford them. The demand for these products is **elastic**.
- Businesses study the changes in supply and demand for their goods and services to determine an **equilibrium point**—the price at which consumers buy exactly the amount supplied by the producer.
- When there is overproduction, a **surplus** is created, and the saturation of the market causes the demand as well as the price to fall. When there is underproduction, a **shortage** occurs, and prices rise.

- Because of the importance of consumers, businesses try to gain favor for their goods and services through advertising. Consumer protection groups, like **Nader's Raiders** founded by **Ralph Nader**, check the safety and reliability of products and services and the accuracy of the claims in advertisements.

III. Structures of Business

KEY QUESTION: *What elements are needed for the operation of any business?*

- To create goods or services, a business needs four things: (1) natural resources or land, (2) labor, (3) capital or investment [finances], and (4) entrepreneurship. These things are known as **factors of production**.
- **Natural resources** are materials that can be found in nature. Metal ores, water, wood, and land are examples of natural resources.
- **Labor** is the human activity that is required to produce goods or services. Labor can be classified into two types: blue-collar and white-collar. *Blue-collar workers* are manual laborers (e.g., construction workers, electricians, factory employees). *White collar workers* are employed at desk jobs in offices; examples include lawyers, bankers, and journalists.
- **Capital** is wealth used to produce more wealth. Machinery, tools, and equipment are examples of capital. Money also is capital if it is producing more wealth, as in interest-paying savings accounts. Money can be used to buy other capital or to buy natural resources or labor.
- **Business** is any activity in which goods and services are exchanged for profit.
- Businesses are organized in different ways (e.g., sole proprietorships, corporations, conglomerates).
- A **sole proprietorship** is a business owned by one person. Today, sole proprietorships make up almost 75 percent of U.S. businesses. About 8 percent of U.S. businesses are **partnerships**, in which two or more people are owners and operators.
- A **corporation** is a business that is licensed, or chartered, by state or local governments. Corporations are owned by people who buy shares (stock) in the business. Stockholders receive *dividends,* or earnings from the business, based on the number of shares they own. Stockholders elect a board of directors to make decisions for the business. Labor unions are formed by many workers in a particular industry or service to protect the rights of their members against the owners or management. Teachers in some states can belong to a labor union. The largest labor union in the United States is the **AFL-CIO** (American Federation of Labor–Congress of Industrial Organization). **César Chavez** and **Dolores Huerta** organized Mexican American migrant and other agricultural workers in California into the United Farm Workers Union to remedy their harsh working conditions and low wages.
- A **conglomerate** is a corporation that owns or controls companies in many fields.
- Union workers can agree to **strike** (or refuse to work) and protest on picket lines. However, unions must also be careful not to price their companies out of business with demands.
- **Profit** is the excess of income over all costs that a business has in producing its goods or services, including the interest cost of the wealth invested. This is the money made after all expenses.

- **Need** is a specific quantity of a specific good for which an individual will pay almost any price, because these are the basic goods or services a person must have for day-to-day survival.
- **Scarcity** occurs when there is an insufficient supply or amount of something needed. The lack of availability of a particular good affects the price consumers have to pay.
- **Price** is the amount of money, or other goods, that you must give up to buy goods or services.
- **Barter** is an exchange of goods for goods or services without using money.
- **Free enterprise** is a system in which sellers and buyers are free to engage in commercial transactions with little or no government regulation, and in which the **free market** drives *what* and *how much* individuals or companies produce and *for whom* and *in what manner*. Individuals can own private property, can seek a profit, can have voluntary exchange, and, in general, maintain economic freedom. This can occur within a country or between nations.
- *Laissez faire* (with respect to economics) loosely means "hands-off" and is a doctrine of government noninterference in the economy except as necessary to maintain economic freedom.
- **Interdependence** is a term used to describe how one industry depends on the work of another. For example, the building of a house requires several goods and services. Lumber mills, window manufacturers, and so on supply the goods to construct a house. Architects and construction workers provide some of the services required to build a house.

IV. Government Revenues and Expenditures

KEY QUESTION: *What are two main sources of government revenues?*

- The U.S. government raises and spends billions of dollars each year. To pay for its activities, the U.S. government (and state and local governments) accumulates **revenue** (income), mainly through a variety of **taxes**.
- The **personal income tax** brings in the most money. This is money that every citizen who works must pay (usually as a deduction from his or her employment check). The rate of tax is based on one's income. Those who have a low income pay fewer taxes than those who are in the middle and higher income brackets. There are **deductions** that many can make (e.g., how many dependents a worker has).
- The second largest amount of revenue comes from **social insurance taxes** such as that for **Social Security** (a proportional tax taken out of payroll). In turn, those who have paid into Social Security receive retirement and other benefits (such as disability or spousal survivorship if needed). States and communities also collect **sales taxes** on goods that are purchased and **property taxes** assessed on the value of the property one owns.
- Substantial amounts of revenue also come from corporate income taxes, **excise taxes** (taxes on nonessential items [such as tobacco]), customs duties, and **tariffs** (charges levied on imported items), state income taxes, school and property taxes, highway tolls, fines, licensing fees, and sales taxes. Texas does not, at this time, have a state income tax.
- In recent years, government expenditures have been greater than revenues (or the government has spent more than it takes in); this results in a **budget deficit**. The accumulated total of these deficits is called the **federal debt**. The U.S. government can print more money or borrow

money to meet its spending obligations, but as with other loans, the government must pay back the loan with interest. If the federal debt becomes too high, there is concern that the money taken in by the government will simply go toward paying off this interest rather than the actual debt. If this continues over time, other countries around the world may not see the dollar as a strong currency, and the dollar may becomes worth much less against foreign currencies. This can drive up the cost of all things imported into the United States and drive down America's buying power.

- To get some of the money it needs, the government also borrows money through the sale of **bonds**.
- The largest government expenditures are for payments made directly to Americans in the form of Social Security and Medicare benefits (for older citizens), federal retirement pensions (for government employees), unemployment compensation, and social welfare programs.
- **Defense** is the second-largest spending category.
- Interest paid on the federal debt is the third-largest cost and is predicted to be a major expense for taxpayers for many years. Economists and government officials propose different ways to reduce the debt: reducing government spending, raising taxes, or a combination of both of these approaches.
- The government also spends money on public health programs, job training, research, veterans' benefits, grants, and payments to state and local governments to operate publicly funded programs.

V. Business Cycles and Government Regulation

KEY QUESTION: *What methods are used by the government to fight inflation?*

- Most countries experience periodic changes in their economies.
- The movement from one level of economic activity to another and back again is known as the **business cycle**.
- When the economy moves down from prosperity to **recession**, production decreases and unemployment increases.
- A **depression** is a very bad recession, such as the one the United States experienced in the 1930s (known as the *Great Depression*). In a depression, unemployment is rampant, and there are few goods to buy because so many commercial enterprises go out of business.
- Another condition that has an adverse effect on the economy is **inflation**, a general rise in prices. People can buy less with the same amount of money. The real value of the dollar declines.
- During periods of recession or depression, the government tries to stimulate the economy with public works projects, giving "bailouts," and providing low-cost business loans. The government has also examined **trickle-down economics** as a way of getting the economy to recover. The government decreases taxes and increases benefits for companies and businesses so that they can hire more people and make more goods. In that way, the employment rate increases so that workers can find jobs and begin to buy goods again.
- The government can also influence business cycles through monetary policy. The **Federal Reserve System** (or "The Fed"), consisting of 12 regional Federal Reserve Banks, is a regulatory agency with the power to supervise the country's banks and adjust the money supply. The Fed can lower the amount of cash reserves banks must keep, making more money available for loans. Raising the reserve limit decreases the amount of available money.

- The Fed can also adjust interest rates. Higher interest rates mean fewer people and businesses want to take out loans, or if they do, they have less money left over to spend. In this way, the Fed can shrink the money supply to combat inflation.
- The government makes decisions affecting the economy by studying various statistics called **economic indicators**. The **Consumer Price Index** (CPI) is a way of measuring the dollar's value. The CPI is the *average* price of essential goods and services (such as food, housing, and transportation).
- Another important economic statistic is the **Gross Domestic Product** (GDP). The GDP is the value of all goods and services produced *within* a country in a year. The components used to calculate the GDP are personal spending (food, clothing, etc.), government expenditures (defense, roads, schools, etc.), investment spending by individuals and businesses (houses, buildings, inventories, etc.), and net exports. From this, the cost of all imports is subtracted, and this figure is the U.S. GDP. The **Gross National Product** (GNP) is the sum of all goods and services produced by U.S. citizens—no matter where they are produced. For example, if a U.S. factory operates a plant in Mexico, then the profits that the firms earn would contribute to the GNP of the United States. This same factory would contribute to the GDP of Mexico.

VI. International Economics

KEY QUESTION: *Why are protected markets created?*

- Most Americans wear clothes, drive automobiles, consume some foods, or use radios, televisions, or other electronics that were manufactured in other countries.
- As the leading trade nation, the United States **imports** (brings in) and **exports** (sends out) billions of dollars of goods annually. The combination of imports and exports makes up a country's **balance of trade**. A country has a favorable balance of trade when it exports more than it imports. If a country imports more than it exports, then it has an unfavorable balance of trade.
- *Receiving imports* usually means having a greater variety of goods or having consumers purchase some products at lower prices. Currently, **NAFTA** (the North American Free Trade Agreement) between the United States, Canada, and Mexico eliminates many tariffs to promote trade. However, some U.S. industries complain that they cannot compete with foreign manufacturers that are able to produce and sell goods more inexpensively than U.S. companies, particularly because of cheaper labor in foreign countries.
- The United States exports many goods that other countries do not make or cannot produce as cheaply. Many of this country's industries—especially agriculture—depend on exporting for a large share of their profits.
- Although exports increase sales and provide employment for U.S. workers, heavy exports of some goods can sometimes keep prices high at home.
- Countries trade with one another for their mutual economic benefit. However, most countries find it necessary to regulate foreign trade to protect their economies. If the United States imposed no limits on imports of certain products, many American businesses would be forced to close because other countries can produce these products so cheaply. Special taxes, or **tariffs**, are therefore sometimes imposed on certain

foreign goods to make them more expensive so people might choose to buy American-made products instead. When tariffs are used to make foreign goods more expensive than similar items made at home, a **protected market** is created. However, if restrictions that trading partners impose on one another become too severe, both countries can suffer economically.

- Sometimes countries prohibit their usual trade with each other because of a political conflict. A ban that is imposed on trade because of a conflicting foreign policy is called an **embargo**.
- **Transportation corridors**, where people and freight or other goods, such as oil or other energy, food, and so forth are easily moved, are important in trade. When freight, people, and so on move from one type of transportation to another (rail to plane or ship, etc.), it is usually at a **transfer point**. Barriers to transportation corridors can include geographic conditions (mountains, wide rivers, swampy land, etc.) or political barriers, such as country boundaries.

VII. Economics of Texas

KEY QUESTION: *What are the major economies of Texas?*

- Until recently, the Texas economy was land based and colonial in structure. Texas produced, processed, and shipped its agricultural and mineral products to outside markets. Texas was dependent on external demand and the prices paid for its cotton, cattle, or petroleum.
- The first real economy in Texas was created by agriculture. Cotton, a major **cash crop** (agricultural crop destined to be sold rather than used by the farmer), helped shape Texas history. As early as the times of Stephen F. Austin's original colony, the leading export was **King Cotton** (so called because it was the "king" of crops and very valuable). Cotton was barged down Texas rivers to the Gulf of Mexico to be shipped to Europe or the United States. This crop was the heart of the economy during the era of the Republic of Texas and early statehood. After the Civil War, those using the plantation system with slave labor were replaced mostly by smaller farms or sharecroppers. In the early 1900s, the **boll weevil**, a type of beetle, inflicted serious damage on Texas cotton crops. In 1904, an estimated 700,000 bales were lost to the boll weevil at a cost of approximately $42 million. The boll weevil caused a steady drop in Texas cotton yields over a 30-year period. The economy has diversified, but cotton is still an important part of the Texas economy. Texas harvests still account for a third of the total cotton production in the United States.
- The **cattle kingdom**, inherited from the Mexicans, spread across the entire American West in the late 19th century. Initially, the cattle business involved rounding up open-range and stray cattle and driving them north to Kansas railheads. The demand for beef created a link between the Western Frontier and the industrial marketplace. Like King Cotton, the cattle kingdom drew people and money from outside the state and involved agricultural products shipped to distant markets.
- By 1866, cattle had replaced cotton as king in Texas. The abundance of longhorn cattle in south Texas and the return of Confederate soldiers to a poor Reconstruction economy marked the beginning of the era of **Texas trail drives** to northern markets. Cattle that sold for $4 a head in Texas brought $30 to $40 in the North. One of the more famous cattle trails, along with the Chisholm Trail, was the Goodnight-Loving Trail, established by Charles **Goodnight**, who rounded up cattle mostly in

the Panhandle of Texas and drove them north. He was the first to use the chuck wagon. Later at his ranch, he kept a domestic herd of buffalo and crossed them with cattle, creating cattalo, and improved Texas cattle by introducing Hereford cattle to his herds. **Lizzie Johnson**, known as the "Cattle Queen of Texas," was thought to have been one of the first to drive her cattle up the Chisholm Trail.

- **The King Ranch**, which takes up much of the land between Corpus Christi and Brownsville, Texas, was established by Richard and Henrietta **King** as one of the largest ranches in the world. Their new breed of cattle, the Santa Gertrudis, was particularly suited to the Texas range.

- In the 1880s, the **XIT Ranch**, owned by a syndicate, covered 3 million acres and portions of 10 Texas counties and was the largest fenced ranch in the world. The sale of the land financed the construction of the state capitol building in Austin, the largest state capitol in North America. This capitol building is second in size only to the national capitol in Washington, D.C.

- For much of the 20th century, **petroleum** was the basis for the Texas economy. From the first major oil discovery at **Spindletop**, near Beaumont, the production of crude oil and Texas have been synonymous. This huge oil field was discovered by **Pattillo Higgens**, the "prophet" of Spindletop, who initiated the search in the area, and mining engineer Captain **A. E. Lucas**, who brought in the first "gusher" in 1901. Between 1900 and 1901, Texas oil production increased fourfold. In 1902, Spindletop alone produced just over 17 million barrels (93 percent of the state's production). The massive amounts of money involving oil production through the next several decades brought great prosperity and population growth to Texas.

- After World War II, the U.S. market sought cheaper oil in the Middle East. However, the oil embargo by the Organization of Petroleum Exporting Countries (**OPEC**) in 1973, a year after Texas reached its peak in oil production, caused an economic boom during the 1970s as prices were driven upward.

- This boom, of course, was followed by the bust of the 1980s when, in 1986, the price for West Texas crude fell below $10 a barrel. In 1981, the petroleum industry contributed 27 percent of the state's **gross state product** (GSP). Ten years later, in 1991, the industry contributed only 12 percent to the GSP.

- In recent years, the **Texas economy** has diversified from oil and natural gas production, both of which are still very important to the state economy. In 2008, chemical manufactures were the leading economic state export, and petroleum exports were fourth. Agricultural goods are still important (with cotton and cattle still coming first, followed by citrus and other vegetables, grains mainly grown in the valley near Mexico, and grains grown in other areas of Texas). This area of the economy depends on the **crop yield**, or the amount of an agricultural product that can be grown or produced and *actually sold* (due to factors such as weather, pests, and so forth). In 2008, **computers** and **electronic products** were Texas' second largest manufactured goods export. The communications equipment industry, composed primarily of establishments that manufacture telephone, radio and television broadcasting, and wireless communications equipment, is very important to the Texas economy. The import/export industry in Texas also contributes greatly, due to a great number of deep-water ports along the Gulf and its large international airports. The economy and the population of Texas continue to grow due to the warm climate, the favorable taxation, and the lower cost of land and housing in Texas. In 2010, Texas reported the 11th largest economy in the world (Combs, 2010).

Consider the following practice question:

Ms. Henning's fourth-grade class is ending its unit on the different economies of Texas. To ensure their understanding, Ms. Henning asks them the following question: Which of the following is not one of the major economies of Texas?

A. Tourism
B. Oil
C. Cattle
D. Cotton

Remember to read the question carefully. We are looking for the answer that is not a major part of the Texas economy. Oil, cattle, and cotton have been and continue to be important economies for the state of Texas, now adding technology as a major contribution. Although some areas of Texas enjoy a great deal of tourism (San Antonio, South Padre Island, etc.), it is not a major economic factor. The best answer is *A*.

Standard VII: Government, and Standard VIII: Citizenship

The social studies teacher knows how governments and structures of power function, provide order, and allocate resources, and uses this knowledge to facilitate student understanding of how individuals and groups achieve their goals through political systems.

The social studies teacher understands citizenship in the United States and other societies, and uses this knowledge to prepare students to participate in our society through an understanding of democratic principles and citizenship practices.

Competency 023 (Government and Citizenship) The teacher understands and applies knowledge of concepts of government, democracy, and citizenship, including ways that individuals and groups achieve their goals through political systems. This competency asks that the beginning teacher:

- Understands and applies the purpose of rules and laws; the relationship between rules, rights, and responsibilities; the fundamental rights of American citizens guaranteed in the Bill of Rights and other amendments to the U.S. Constitution; and the individual's role in making and enforcing rules and ensuring the welfare of society.
- Comprehends the basic structure and functions of the U.S. government, the Texas government, and local governments (including the roles of public officials), and relationships among national, state, and local governments.
- Demonstrates knowledge of key principles and ideas contained in major political documents of Texas and the United States (e.g., Declaration of Independence, U.S. Constitution, Texas Constitution) and of relationships among political documents.
- Demonstrates an understanding of how people organized governments in colonial America and during the early development of Texas.

- Understands the political processes in the United States and Texas and how the U.S. political system works.
- Demonstrates knowledge of types of government (e.g., democratic, totalitarian, monarchical) and their respective levels of effectiveness in meeting citizens' needs.
- Understands the formal and informal processes of changing the U.S. and Texas Constitutions and the impact of changes on society.
- Understands and promotes students' understanding of the impact of landmark Supreme Court cases.
- Understands the components of the democratic process (e.g., voluntary individual participation, effective leadership, expression of different points of view) and each one's significance in a democratic society.
- Demonstrates knowledge of important customs, symbols, and celebrations that represent American beliefs and principles and contribute to national unity.
- Analyzes the relationships between individual rights, responsibilities, and freedoms in democratic societies.
- Applies knowledge of the rights and responsibilities of citizens in Texas and the United States, past and present.
- Understands how the nature, rights, and responsibilities of citizenship vary among societies.

Consider the following practice question:

Ms. Thompson wants her kindergarten class to understand the importance of rules. How can she best communicate this idea to her students?

- **A.** Require that students memorize her list of five posted classroom rules.
- **B.** Bring a newspaper to class and have students talk about what the president does as chief executive.
- **C.** Ask students to help develop a set of classroom rules.
- **D.** Ask the principal to explain the school's rules to the children.

The best answer is to ask students to help develop a set of classroom rules (*C*). Creating rules and practicing the use of authority help develop a child's understanding and ownership of justice and fairness. Once children have experience in rule making, they may then relate their experiences to understanding how rule making and enforcement occur in the adult world (Chapin, 2006). (*B*). Memorizing (*A*) or telling (*D*) does not create understanding or ownership. Kindergarten children are not yet ready to read newspaper articles and relate them to the fact that the job of the executive branch is to enforce laws (*B*). The correct answer is *C*.

Educational researchers Martorella and Beal (2002) advise that elementary schools are excellent educational environments for developing good citizens. This is because elementary schools are relatively small, and the people in them (administrators, staff, teachers, and students) often form a close community. All of these people become concerned citizens of their classrooms and their schools. Students and teachers are concerned not only with the school's policies and programs but also with the physical appearances of their individual classrooms and the common areas of the building and surroundings.

Teachers should use this sense of caring to foster students' active involvement in their school community. Democratic classrooms are essential to encourage and model activism. In such an environment, teachers begin to teach responsibilities with classroom jobs and rules that allow children to take responsibility for their own behaviors. A simple dictionary definition of *democracy* is "rule by majority or a government of the people." In a classroom setting, democratic ideals such as respect and cooperation are central. Students should play an active role in establishing their goals and rules. On the first day of school, EC-6 teachers should involve students in establishing classroom rules, giving the students a sense of involvement and ownership in their new community.

Playing an active role in establishing classroom rules also gives students the opportunity to understand one of the fundamental principles of democracy— that rights come with responsibilities. Democracies are characterized by hard choices, and choices become difficult when they cause one's values to conflict. For example, if we value freedom, we must also value justice, duty, and responsibility. For example, one has the freedom to speak, but one is not free to yell "Fire!" in a crowd when is no fire. Values can sometimes be hard to reconcile; however, students must learn this most central feature of democracy. Personal choices are most often based on values. In a representative government like that of the United States, people elect representatives that share their values. Therefore, it is essential that children begin to identify and develop their own personal values and understand the role of civic affairs where one is concerned with taking a part in community, state, national, or international issues. Children should ultimately understand the importance of making decisions that provide the greatest benefits to themselves and to the larger society. A key factor in teaching these concepts is that children cannot learn them just from reading a text during social studies time. They must also experience them in classrooms in which these principles are alive and well every day.

In addition, students in all public schools have the opportunity to learn about some aspect of the United States Constitution on September 17 each year. A Federal law passed in 2005 states, "each educational institution that receives federal funds for a fiscal year shall hold an educational program on the United States Constitution." September 17 was chosen to commemorate the signing of the Constitution on that date in 1787. There are many resources to find lesson ideas for teaching the Constitution. One online site is sponsored by the Center for Civic Education at www.civiced.org. Another opportunity for students in Texas to learn about civics and citizenship occurs during the entire week of September 17 during **Celebrate Freedom Week**. In 2007, the Texas legislature passed HB 708 to create a weeklong opportunity to "educate students about the sacrifices made for freedom in the founding of this country and the values on which this country was founded." The Law Related Education Department of the State Bar of Texas has developed curricular materials, as well as online activities and games, which may be used during this week: www.texaslre.org.

The remainder of this section contains content information for government and citizenship that is necessary knowledge for EC-6 teachers who are preparing to teach social studies.

Government Content

The subject of *government* analyzes and compares different types of political systems. Political scientists try to understand decision making in politics and how individuals and groups obtain and use political power. Political systems and concepts are broken down into the following subheadings:

- Foundations of government
- Writing the constitution

- Development of federalism
- Election processes
- Symbols of the United States
- Texas government
- Symbols of Texas

I. Foundations of Government

KEY QUESTION: *What fundamental ideals are expressed in the Declaration of Independence?*

- Any group of people living and working together needs certain laws and services. A **government** acts on behalf of the group, making and enforcing laws and providing for other needs. A democracy does so with the consent of those who are governed. Sovereignty in a democracy, therefore, lies with the people (**popular sovereignty**). The U.S. Constitution provides for majority rule but protects the rights of the minority. **Due process** is forever present to guarantee that the individual is protected through a system of rights in the court system, and he or she cannot be punished arbitrarily.
- **Political science** studies how different types of governments function.
- Governments can be classified by how many people take part in the decision-making process. In a **monarchy**, one person (such as a king, a queen, a shah, or an emperor) usually inherits ruling power. An *absolute monarch* and his or her appointees have complete authority to govern, and this can also be termed an unlimited government. A *constitutional monarch* has limited power and must work with other government officials. Constitutional monarchies still exist today in several European countries, where the king or queen is more of a figurehead than a true ruler; an elected parliament makes most major governmental decisions.
- In a **dictatorship**, or **totalitarian** government, the government is totally controlled by one person or a small group who usually maintains power by force rather than through democratic principles. Extensive control is exercised over people's lives, and all other political parties are disallowed or minimized; thus many freedoms are often curtailed. This is usually termed an **unlimited government** as well, because the leaders have few (if any) limits on their powers. Dictators often rise to power during times of national unrest. Stalin did so in the USSR, Hitler rose to power in Germany and Mussolini in Italy in the years preceding World War II, and Pol Pot gained control in Cambodia in the 1970s. Modern-day dictators include Saddam Hussein in Iraq (prior to his capture and execution), Castro in Cuba, Kim Jong Il in North Korea, and currently, many fear that Venezuelan leader Hugo Chavez is adopting measures that seem to lean in the direction of a creating a dictatorship.
- In an **oligarchy**, a small, very powerful governing class rules. This type of government could have been found in South Africa prior to 1994. Until that time, the Black African majority was ruled by a smaller group of White Western Europeans (apartheid). This may also happen when a country is taken over in a military coup and the new military rulers form a junta.
- **Communist** governments seek, but have rarely succeeded, in establishing a classless society in which everyone has common ownership of the means of production. **Karl Marx**, a 19th-century German political economist, is most associated with explaining the concept of communism. Unfortunately, most nations that have attempted or that currently

have this type of government have developed very authoritarian and repressive governments.

- In a **democracy**, all of the people take part in governing the country and all must follow the laws. This is termed a **limited government**, because the role of the government is limited by its constitution and its people. Ancient Greece was an example of a **direct democracy** because all of its citizens (free males) met to vote on decisions. The United States is a **representative democracy** in which the people elect representatives, such as the members of Congress, to carry out the work of the government. The belief in a republican government (or government headed by elected officials) is why the United States is referred to as a **republic** (as found in the pledge to the flag: "I Pledge Allegiance to the flag of the United States of America and to the *Republic* for which it stands, one Nation under God, indivisible, with liberty and justice for all.").
- When the 13 original colonies decided to free themselves from British rule, the writers of the Declaration of Independence expressed a political philosophy of **individualism** that is still basic to American government today. *Rugged individualism* emerged from those who moved into the New World and carved out the land self-sufficiently as individuals or as families.
- One of the tools that governments (and, of course, businesses) use is **propaganda**, a strategic technique used to persuade another person to believe or act on an idea. By using certain symbols or words in vague generalities, a good propagandist can make people feel angry, sympathetic, apathetic, or any number of emotions. This technique was used often by Hitler's government to cause people to feel patriotic. Other techniques of propaganda also include *name-calling, scapegoating* (falsely labeling individuals or a particular group of people as the reason something bad occurs), *band wagoning* ("get on board" because it is the "in" thing to do), using testimonials or *endorsements* of famous people, and *stacking the deck* (only offering biased reasoning from the opinions that propagandists endorse). Other important concepts to understand are **point of view**, or the perspective from which something is told (i.e., how closely one can be identified as a stakeholder to the issue), and **frame of reference**, which is a structure of concepts, values, customs, or views by which an individual or group perceives or evaluates data, communicates ideas, and regulates behavior. Historians recognize that history is, by and large, written by those who "win." Therefore, it can be a biased prospective, not taking into account the perspectives of those who did not win or even survive. Thus was the case with Native Americans, for example, who for many years were stereotyped as savages in Western movies. The pendulum then swung to view them as a "perfect" culture—at one with nature. Careful study, without bias, finally allows good historians to view these cultures on an individual basis, seeing that some Native American tribes maintained advanced civilizations that were model societies (although their ways were not Westernized), whereas other groups kept slaves, used human sacrifice, and treated women and enemies viciously. However, it is not possible to talk about the settling of America without taking their frame of reference into account. All issues and events should be examined carefully for both point of view and frame of reference to obtain a more objective and factual picture. One way of helping students become more objective is to teach them how to use valid sources. Visual sources include pictures maps, electronic sources, and artifacts, whereas oral sources include conversations, interviews, and even music. Examining these for

truthfulness and bias helps future citizens to interpret them in more useful ways.
- The philosophy of the Bill of Rights emphasizes the equality of all people and the right to "life, liberty, and the pursuit of happiness."
- The U.S. government exists to protect these rights, and the power of the government comes from the consent of the people. If the government ignores the people's will, the people have the right to elect new officials.

II. Writing the Constitution

KEY QUESTION: *At the Constitutional Convention, what compromises were required?*

- Five years after the American Declaration of Independence was written, the first national constitution governing the United States was approved, or **ratified**, by all of the states. This document was known as the **Articles of Confederation.**
- These Articles created a *central government* but with very limited powers. This government could not make laws without unanimous state agreement, nor could it settle conflicts between states or raise revenue through taxes. There was no president or national court system. It soon became clear that these and other weaknesses had to be corrected.
- In 1787, 55 delegates from all the states, referred to as the **Founding Fathers**, met at the Constitutional Convention to develop a new system of government.
- A debate about the nature of representation of individuals and of states was settled by the **Great Compromise**: that is, a two-chamber, or **bicameral**, Congress was created, consisting of a **House of Representatives** (the number of representatives is determined by state population) and a **Senate** (only two representatives from each state are seated). This allowed heavily populated states the advantage in one chamber (the House of Representatives) but all states to have an equal voice in the other (the Senate). To get legislation through, both chambers must approve a bill (and the bill must be signed by the president or overridden by Congress).
- The new **U.S. Constitution** also provided for shared power and responsibilities in three ways: (1) a **separation of powers** that defines three branches of government with distinct powers; (2) a system of **checks and balances** that allows each branch to oversee the other two; and (3) a **federal system** that divides governing power between the national government and state governments.
- The three branches of the federal government are (1) the **legislative branch**, which includes the two houses of Congress (the House of Representatives and the Senate) and makes the laws; (2) the **executive branch** whose main power resides with the president who executes or carries out the laws; and (3) the **judicial branch**, which includes the Supreme Court and lower federal courts who interpret, according to the Constitution, the meaning and validity of the laws.
- **George Washington** was elected the first president of the United States under the new constitution and served for two terms, followed by other Founding Fathers, **John Adams** and **Thomas Jefferson. Abigail Adams** was the wife of John Adams, the first vice-president and the second president, making Mrs. Adams the first Second Lady and the second First Lady—and also was mother of John Quincy Adams, the sixth U.S. president. Her letters to her husband during the Revolutionary War provide an excellent account of the war, but she also served as an early

proponent of women's rights and believed that slavery would threaten the new republic. Indirectly, she was a political force in American politics of the times.

III. The Development of Federalism

KEY QUESTION: *What is federalism, and how does the federalist system provide for the sharing of power between the states and the federal government?*

- **Federalism** refers to a type of democracy in which there is shared power between the national and state governments. After much debate among the Founding Fathers, the **Federalists** (those who favored the ratification [adoption] of the Constitution and the idea of shared powers) and the **anti-Federalists** (those against ratification and who favored states' rights more), the Constitution was finally approved by the required number of states in 1788.

- Because the anti-Federalists were concerned that the Constitution did not provide strong enough guarantees of state power or of individual liberties, the Federalists promised to pass a Bill of Rights during the first Congress. So great was their support for states' and individual rights that **George Mason** and **James Madison** share the title of "Father of the Bill of Rights."

- The first 10 amendments to the Constitution are called the **Bill of Rights**. These include personal, political, and economic rights. Nine of these placed limits on Congress by forbidding it to infringe on certain basic rights: freedom of religion, speech, assembly, and the press; immunity from arbitrary arrest; immunity from the taking of life, liberty, or property for a crime without due process of law; the right to a speedy public trial by jury; no excessive bail or cruel and unusual punishments; and others. The 10th Amendment reserved to the states all powers except those specifically withheld from them or delegated to the federal government.

- Thus far, there have been a total of 27 Amendments to the Constitution. The **13th Amendment** prohibited slavery in the United States. The **15th Amendment** guaranteed the right to vote to all men, no matter their race. The **19th Amendment** guaranteed the right to vote to all citizens, including women. The **24th Amendment** declared poll taxes and similar measures designed to prohibit people from voting were unconstitutional. The **26th Amendment** gave 18-year-olds the right to vote.

- These amendments were proposed following one of the two methods outlined in the Constitution: (1) an amendment must be proposed by two-thirds of both houses of Congress or (2) by two-thirds of the state legislatures. Approval by three-fourths of the state legislatures is needed for the amendment to be *ratified* (passed).

- Powers given specifically to the national government are called **delegated** or **enumerated powers**. There are many, but among them are establishing foreign policy; declaring war and maintaining the armed forces; coining money; establishing post offices and standard weights and measures; creating US courts; and regulating immigration, naturalization, and interstate and foreign commerce.

- Other powers—those not specifically granted to the national government and not denied to the states—are called **reserved powers**, such as the regulation of intrastate trade and the establishment of schools.

- **Concurrent powers** (e.g., tax collection, education) are *shared* by both the national and state governments (raising taxes, borrowing money, maintaining courts).

- Because powers are divided in various ways, no group or part of government can become too powerful **(checks and balances)**. These checks and balances include: (1) the president's ability to **veto** laws passed by the Congress (or legislature); (2) the Congress being able, by vote, to override a presidential veto; (3) and the president making appointments to the Supreme Court when a place is open, but requiring the Congress to approve any nominee. The Supreme Court can also rule on laws passed by both the Congress and the president as unconstitutional. The principles of the Constitution encourage national, state, and local governments to work together to serve the American people.
- The government collects taxes from its citizens and combines those resources to provide for citizens' common good. At the national level, this fund supports our national infrastructure, transportation systems, public health and safety, national defense, and many other important resources. At the state and local levels, this fund maintains public property, such as monuments, parks, beaches, libraries, and schools.

IV. The Election Process

KEY QUESTION: *How does the method for electing the president differ from the way in which members of Congress are elected?*

- Elections and voting are the foundations of U.S. democracy.
- On the federal level, voters elect the president and members of Congress.
- At the state and local levels, voters cast ballots for governors, mayors, state legislators, and city or town council representatives.
- Voters also have opportunities to express their opinions on laws and amendments. Any citizen 18 years of age or older may register to vote and cast a ballot.
- Political parties are not provided for in the U.S. Constitution. However, political differences, beginning early in our history, brought about a two-party system: the Democrats and the Republicans (in more recent times). Despite the strength of the two parties, the history of the United States is filled with third parties (or independent parties) that have achieved limited and temporary successes. The most successful third-party candidate was **Theodore Roosevelt**. His Progressive, or "Bull Moose" Party, won about 25 percent of the popular vote in the 1912 election.
- Today, **Democrats** usually favor a strong federal government involved in economic and social issues. **Republicans** usually want less federal involvement in the lives of individuals and businesses and greater state responsibilities.
- The parties nominate candidates for various public offices.
- In most states, **primary elections** are held to choose **presidential candidates**. In these preliminary elections, voters from each major political party select delegates who, in turn, decide on the parties' candidates for president. These delegates generally pledge to vote for a particular candidate at the parties' national conventions.
- Presidential elections are held every 4 years. According to the Constitution, the president must be a natural-born citizen of the United States, be at least 35 years old, and have been a resident of the United States for 14 years.
- Citizens do not directly elect the president or vice president. Rather, as noted earlier, they choose electors to represent them in the **Electoral College**. This system was set up to avoid having the states with the most popular votes due to their great populations (such as New York

and California) always deciding the presidency. In this system, because each state has a number of electors equal to the total number of its senators and representatives, both population and equality count (much like the makeup of the two-house [bicameral] Congress). A candidate needs a majority of the electoral votes to win. There have been very few instances where the person who won the popular vote did not win the presidency. In 1824, Andrew Jackson received more popular votes and more electoral votes than did John Quincy Adams. However, although he did receive a plurality of the votes, he did not receive a majority. When this occurs, the election must be decided by the House of Representatives, and the vice president is chosen by the senate. The House voted for Adams. In 1876, Samuel Tilden received more popular votes than his opponent; however, Rutherford B. Hayes won the election by 1 electoral vote. In the 2000 election of President George W. Bush, Albert Gore, Jr., received a majority of the popular vote, but he did not have the electoral votes needed to win.

- The **House of Representatives** has 435 members. This total is divided or apportioned among the states according to population. Representatives serve 2-year terms.
- The Speaker of the House is third in line to become President, should anything happen to both the president and the vice president.
- There are 100 **senators**, two from each state. Senators are elected for 6 years, with a third of the Senate being elected every 2 years.
- Both senators and representatives are elected by direct popular vote.
- **Laws are made** by the two legislative chambers of Congress and signed by the president in the following manner: (1) an elected representative (from the House of Representatives or the Senate) proposes a **bill**; (2) legislative committees review the bill; (3) both chambers vote on the bill; (4) if approved by both the House and the Senate, the bill goes to the executive branch (president or governor, if it is a state bill); (5a) if the president (or governor) signs the bill, it becomes law; or (5b) if the president (or governor) vetoes the bill, it is dropped. Congress can override the veto with a two-thirds vote to make it a law.

V. Texas Government

KEY QUESTION: *How is the Texas government similar to the U.S. government?*

- After Texas became independent of Mexico, **Sam Houston** became the first elected president of the Republic of Texas (following **David Burnett**, who was *ad interim* president during the Texas Revolution, when Texas was not yet its own country). The second elected president of the Republic, **Mirabeau B. Lamar** (1838–1841), is called the "Father of Education in Texas."
- **Lorenzo de Zavala**, a prominent politician in Mexico in the government of Santa Anna, immigrated to Texas when it became clear to him that Santa Anna was not going to abide by the Mexican Constitution of 1824. **José Navarro** was prominent in Mexican politics but supported Anglo colonization of Texas and the separation of Texas from Mexico. In 1836, both signed the Texas Declaration of Independence. Navarro served in the Texas government as a strong voice for those of Hispanic descent in Texas who were being isolated after the Texas Revolution and as a voice for annexation for statehood. **De Zavala** was also elected as a vice president of the Republic of Texas.

- The last president of the Republic of Texas was **Anson Jones** (1844–1846).
- When Texas became a state, 10 years after independence, the first governor of the state was **James Pinckney Henderson** (1846–1847).
- In 1874, the election of **Richard Coke** began a Democratic Party dynasty in Texas that continued unbroken for more than 100 years. Many Southerners believed that the Republican party of Lincoln and Johnson had been harsh and punishing during the Reconstruction years following the Civil War.
- In 1888, the dedication of the present **state capitol** in **Austin**, made of pink granite from the Hill Country of Texas and largely financed through the XIT Ranch, ended 7 years of planning and construction.
- **James Hogg** took office as the first native-born governor of Texas in 1891.
- **Miriam A. "Ma" Ferguson**, a Democrat, was elected governor of Texas in 1924. She was the first woman elected governor in Texas and the second woman to serve as a governor in the United States. Because of the date of elections in Texas, she was technically the first woman elected to that office. She served from 1925 to 1927 and again from 1933 to 1935. It wasn't until 1990 that another woman was elected governor of Texas. **Ann Richards**, a Democrat, was the second woman elected Governor of Texas.
- The present Texas State Constitution was ratified on February 15, 1876.
- Currently, the Texas Legislature convenes in Austin for no more than a 140-day regular session every odd-numbered year (unless special sessions are called).
- There are three branches in the Texas government (as in the federal/U.S. government): (1) the executive branch (the governor), (2) the legislative branch (the Texas Senate and House of Representatives), and (3) the judicial branch (Court of Criminal Appeals and the Texas Supreme Court for civil and juvenile cases).
- The **governor** of Texas is elected to a 4-year term in November of even-numbered, non-presidential-election years. There is no limit on the number of terms a governor may serve.
- The governor may call additional 30-day special sessions in which the legislature may consider only the subjects submitted to them by the governor.
- A statewide elected official, the **lieutenant governor** is the presiding officer of the Texas senate and serves a 4-year term. In Texas, the governor and lieutenant governor do not run on a combined ticket as do those who seek the offices of president and vice president in the United States. Therefore, it is fairly common for the governor and lieutenant governor to be from different political parties.
- The **Texas Senate** consists of 31 senators elected to 4-year overlapping terms of office with no term limits. The lieutenant governor serves as president of the Texas Senate.
- The **Texas House of Representatives** consists of 150 representatives elected in even-numbered years to 2-year terms of office (also with no term limits). At the beginning of each regular session, the House elects a speaker from its members to serve as the presiding officer.
- The **Legislative Budget Board** (LBB) primarily develops recommendations for legislative appropriations and performance standards for all agencies of state government. The LBB also prepares fiscal notes and impact statements that provide the Legislature with information and analysis on bills being considered for enactment.
- The **State Auditor's Office** (SAO) functions as the independent auditor for Texas state government. The SAO reviews state agencies, universities,

and programs for management and fiscal controls, effectiveness, efficiency, performance measures, and statutory compliance and compliance with administrative rules and regulations.

- Among other Texas firsts, in 1972 **Barbara Jordan** became the first African American woman from a southern state to serve in the U.S. House of Representatives. She represented Houston's 18th Congressional District. When she died in 1996, she was buried in the Texas State Cemetery, becoming the first African American woman to be interred there.
- In 1981, **Henry Cisneros** became the first person of Hispanic background to be elected mayor of a large U.S. city. At the time he was elected as mayor of San Antonio, it was the ninth largest city in the United States.
- Other famous Texas politicians include **Henry B. Gonzalez**, who served first in the Texas Senate, where he filibustered for more than 20 hours against segregation, then served as a U.S. Representative for more than 30 years from the San Antonio district. **Sam Rayburn**, a Democrat, was elected to the House of Representatives, where he served for 48 years (and with eight presidents), many of those as the Speaker of the House or as the Minority Leader under Republican control of the House. **Irma Rangel** of Kingsville was the first Mexican American woman legislator to serve in the Texas House of Representatives. **James A. Baker, III**, a Texan, has been a key leader in government under three presidents (Ford, Reagan, and George H. W. Bush), serving as campaign manager, chief of staff, Treasury Secretary, and Secretary of State. **Kay Bailey Hutchison** is the first female senator from Texas and is currently the most senior Republican female senator. U.S. presidents born in Texas have included Dwight D. Eisenhower and Lyndon Johnson, and those considered Texans include George H. W. Bush and George W. Bush.

VI. Texas State Symbols

KEY QUESTION: *What are the symbols of Texas and the main features of Texas?*

- State Capital: **Austin**, named after Stephen F. Austin, who gained land grants for the first group of American colonists in Texas ("The Old Three Hundred").
- Motto: **Friendship**, coming from the original word for Texas (*Tejas*), which is what the Caddo Nation called its tribes—friends.
- State song:

*Texas, Our Texas**

Texas, our Texas! All hail the mighty State!
Texas, our Texas! So wonderful so great!
Boldest and grandest, Withstanding ev'ry test;
O Empire wide and glorious, You stand supremely blest.
Refrain:
God bless you, Texas! And keep you brave and strong,
That you may grow in power and worth,
Thro'out the ages long.

*Words by Gladys Yoakum Wright and William J. Marsh. © 1925 by William J. Marsh. Copyright renewed 1953 by William J. Marsh. Used with permission of Southern Music Co., San Antonio, Texas

- State bird: the **mockingbird**.
- State flower: the **bluebonnet**, the brilliant blue wildflower that covers a great part of the state in the spring, giving some fields almost the

allusion of being a lake of blue. **Tomie dePaola** wrote ***The Legend of the Bluebonnet***, a poignant tale of a young Comanche girl's sacrifice for her tribe. DePaola also wrote *Strega Nona*.

- State tree: the **pecan tree**, which can grow in all counties in Texas and is native to 150 counties.
- State pledge: **Honor the Texas flag; I pledge allegiance to thee, Texas, one state under God, one and indivisible.**
- Symbol of Texas freedom: **the Alamo. Clara Driscoll**, philanthropist, was known as the "Savior of the Alamo" when she found that it was in ruins and parts were to be sold and converted into a hotel property. **Adina de Zavala** also helped to save the Alamo's convent area, where much of the fighting occurred, even barricading herself into the barracks area to prevent destruction. De Zavala also organized the Texas Historical and Landmarks Association, which started with marking 38 historical sites in Texas, and is credited with saving the Spanish Governors' Palace in San Antonio.
- State flag: the **Lone Star** flag was adopted in 1839 as the flag of the Republic of Texas. When Texas became a state, the Lone Star flag remained the state flag. Its colors are "Old Glory" red and blue (the same colors as the U.S. flag) and white, representing bravery, loyalty, and purity.
- Nickname: the **Lone Star State** (after the flag).
- State mammals: **longhorn** (large); **armadillo** (small).
- Highest mountain: **Guadalupe Peak** in the Guadalupe Mountains of West Texas.
- Largest ranch: the **King Ranch** is the largest ranch in the world (825,000 acres) but is divided into four divisions and not a contiguous plot of land; the **Waggoner Ranch** at 520,000 acres is the largest ranch in Texas inside one fence.
- Borders: **New Mexico** (northwest), **Oklahoma** (north) (Red River), **Arkansas** (northeast), **Louisiana** (east) (Sabine River), **Mexico** (west) (Rio Grande River), **Gulf of Mexico** (south).
- Longest river: **Rio Grande River.**
- **U.S. presidents from Texas**: Lyndon B. Johnson (LBJ), Dwight Eisenhower, George W. Bush (although he was governor of Texas, he was not born in Texas).
- **Mission San Jose**: known as Queen of the Missions, it was founded during the mission period of Texas. It is located in San Antonio and was built so well that it was practically impregnable. Even today, one can view much of the practical, yet beautiful, work that went into its construction. All of the outer walls, dwellings, workshops, and mill are still intact (as well as the church, which is still in use).
- **San Jacinto Monument**: the world's tallest obelisk was built as a memorial column on the land where the Battle of San Jacinto (which brought Texas independence) was fought.
- Texas local government: **254 counties.**

Consider the following practice question:

Mr. Sprayberry's sixth-grade class was discussing how difficult it seemed for the Congress to come together to get anything done. He reminded them that our Founding Fathers had to make the Great Compromise to adopt the Constitution, even in the beginning. What two issues were most prominent in this compromise?

A. Breaking away from Great Britain
B. Shared powers and states' rights
C. Establishing a king or having a president
D. Representation based on population or representation of an equal number

The Great Compromise (or the Connecticut Compromise) helped the Founding Fathers come together to adopt the Constitution by ending the argument of how each state would be represented. The proposal was accepted for a two-house (bicameral) legislature of the House of Representatives (by population) and a senate (with equal numbers from each state). Both houses must approve for a bill to be passed on to the president. The answer is *D.*

 # Citizenship

Many of the important decisions affecting our lives are political decisions. Citizenship is a very important concept, especially when there is a government ruled by the people, as we have in the democratic republic of the United States. Thomas Jefferson believed that people must be educated to assume this "office of citizen." What are the rights and responsibilities of citizenship? The state of Texas reinforces the importance of educating for citizenship. According to the Texas Education Code (Texas Statues, 1995), Chapter 4.001 Public Education Mission and Objectives:

> *Objective 5: Education will prepare students to be thoughtful, active citizens who have an appreciation for the basic values of our state and national heritage and who can understand and productively function in a free-enterprise society.*

Unfortunately, interest in citizenship seems to be waning, as evidenced, in part, by the voting rate. According to the census bureau, in the November 2004 presidential election, only 60 percent of the voting-eligible population cast a ballot. The voting percentage rate was a bit higher in the 2008 election at 62 percent; however, nearly 40 percent of the voting eligible population did not vote. In so-called *off-year elections* (those without a presidential election), the rates are even lower. For example, the Congressional election in November 2006, only 40 percent of citizens who were eligible to vote actually did. Maxim (1999) explains that "to most students and adults, the study of the institutions and processes involved in these matters is confusing and uninteresting" (p. 302), but Brody (1989) is convinced that apathy toward civic life (the public life of a citizen) is the result of a failure of civic education; "Americans fail to see connections between politics and their lives because they have not been taught that the connections exist and are personally relevant" (p. 60). Maxim also notes that democratic education has traditionally studied the structure and functions of government without regard to how they affect one's life. Essentially, democratic education was equated with democratic knowledge. However, "if democracy is to sustain itself," Barber (1989) argues, "a richer conception of citizenship is required" (p. 355). Barber calls this richer concept *strong democracy,* and describes it as follows:

> *If the point were just to get students to mature into voters who watch television news diligently and pull a voting machine lever once every few years, traditional civics . . . would suffice. But if students are to become actively engaged in public forms of thinking and participate thoughtfully in the whole spectrum of civic activities, then civic education and social studies programs require a strong element of practical civic experience—real participation and empowerment. (p. 355)*

Thus the role of citizens in a strong democracy "includes real, active participation in civic processes (such as helping with a local effort to provide shelter for the homeless) and institutions (such as volunteering to lead a group of Girl Scouts)" (Maxim, 1999, p. 302), in addition to the other important areas mentioned. Active participation of informed and responsible citizens is the ultimate goal of democratic education. Students should also learn of figures in history who have exhibited these elements of good citizenship, such as **Florence Nightingale**. She was born into a wealthy British family living in Italy in 1820. During these times, nursing was not a distinguished occupation; therefore, Nightingale's decision to become a nurse met with the intense disapproval of her family. She also became an advocate to correct the appalling level of care for poor and indigent people. In 1854, she and a staff of volunteer nurses went to Turkey to care for British troops wounded in the Crimean War, becoming known as the "Lady with the Lamp." As a result of this experience, Nightingale wrote a 1,000-page report to Queen Victoria and the Royal Commission on the Health of the Army, which ultimately resulted in the creation of an Army Medical School and a major overhaul of army medical care. An example of good citizenship from an American is **Helen Keller**. Born in 1880, many people know her only as a deaf–blind scholar; however, she was also an important activist for people with disabilities, for women's suffrage, the working class, and other causes. Qualities associated with good citizenship are also evidenced by many young people. **Ruby Bridges**, for example, as a young girl, bravely helped begin the integration of segregated schools in the South in 1960. **Juliette Gordon Low**, despite limited hearing, dedicated much of her life to founding the Girl Scouts. The Web site for the My Hero Project (www.myhero.com/myhero/home.asp) tells the inspiring stories of many young people who exhibited extraordinary courage and exemplary citizenship.

In order to effectively participate in a strong democracy, citizens must be able to think critically in order to make reasoned decisions and to work out societal problems as part of their civic responsibilities. By providing students opportunities to learn and practice the decision making process, teachers set the stage for this. First, students must be made aware of the process used in decision making. Next, teachers afford students the opportunity to see that every decision has both alternatives and consequences (positive and negative) that must be examined. These higher-level thinking skills help students to become thoughtful citizens. Decision making also requires values education (Parker, 2009). Citizens, particularly in a diverse society such as ours, need many opportunities to practice effectively resolving values conflicts. These conflicts, Parker (2009) writes, are an "inevitable and necessary part of democratic life" (p. 80).

Several teaching techniques, *discovery learning, inquiry, problem solving, inductive thinking, critical thinking*, and *questioning skills*, are aimed at developing students' decision-making processes. Social studies teachers incorporate these techniques into their teaching in order to encourage students to actively seek out their own answers to complex and open-ended questions. Our knowledge about subjects can change, fade, or become obsolete, but our ability to think remains constant, even improving with practice. Practice in the decision-making process allows us to both acquire necessary knowledge and apply it thoughtfully. One of the goals of social studies education is to foster effective higher-order thinking skills needed outside the classroom by all members of society, particularly when it relates to citizenship. This can be expanded by careful instructional decisions on the part of the teacher by including student active strategies such as debate, mock trials, role play, and other hands-on/minds-on thinking models.

*At the time of writing this chapter, the social studies TEKS were being revised and were in draft form only. The authors have made every effort to match revisions during this time. It is recommended to check the revised TEKS for possible later additions.

SUMMARY

As you have gathered by now, many of the competencies covered in the social studies section of the TExES overlap in their coverage. This makes organizing these principles an important consideration as you prepare to take the TExES *Generalist*. Knowledge of both the TExES social studies competencies and the social studies TEKS for children is incredibly important on this test—along with knowing how to teach them. Understanding the interrelatedness of the TExES standards, the competencies, and the TEKS should facilitate your study of the types of social studies questions that may appear on the TExES *Generalist*. We hope that what you gain here helps you move easily from a preservice teacher into your role as a knowledgeable classroom teacher (or from an "out-of-state" teacher to a Texas teacher).

Teachers today have the tremendous responsibility of shaping the future through their work with children. This is an awesome responsibility, because our children today will become tomorrow's voters and leaders. Thinking of education merely in terms of the present is no longer sufficient. It is important for all teachers to have a vision of the future for the children they teach—and for the country and world in which we all want to live. This vision should reflect a teacher's passion to work with children and give purpose and direction to their decisions about good social studies instruction. We hope that you carry this vision throughout your days as a teacher of social studies.

REFERENCES

Allen, M., & Stevens, R. (1998). *Middle grades social studies: Teaching and learning for active and responsible citizenship.* Needham Heights, MA: Allyn & Bacon.

Anderson, L., & Krathwohl, D. (Eds). (2001). *A taxonomy of learning, teaching, and assessment: A revision of Bloom's taxonomy of educational objectives.* New York: Longman.

Barber, B. (1989). Public talk and civic action: Education for participation in a strong democracy. *Social Education, 53,* 355.

Berg, M. (1988). Integrating ideas for social studies. *Social Studies and the Young Learner, 1,* unnumbered pullout section.

Bloom B. (1956). *Taxonomy of educational objectives, handbook I: The cognitive domain.* New York: David McKay Co., Inc.

Bolick, C. (2006). Teaching and learning with online historical maps. *Social Education, 70(3),* 133–137.

Brody, R. (1989). Why study politics? *Charting a course: Social studies for the 21st century* (pp. 59–63). Washington, DC: National Commission on Social Studies in the Schools.

Brophy, J., & Alleman, J. (1996). *Powerful social studies for elementary students.* New York: Harcourt Brace College Publishers.

Chapin, J. (2006). *Elementary social studies: A practical guide* (6th ed.). Boston: Allyn & Bacon.

Civilization III Official Web site. (n.d.). Retrieved May 19, 2010, from www.civ3.com

Combs, S. (2009). Comptroller's economic outlook. Retrieved May 19, 2010, from http://www.texasahead.org/economy/outlook.html

Davis, K. (1992). *Don't know much about geography: Everything you need to know about the world but never learned.* New York: William Morrow.

Dooley, N. (1992). *Everybody cooks rice.* New York: Scholastic Books.

Duvall, L. (1994). *Respecting our differences: A guide to getting along in a changing world.* Minneapolis: Free Spirit Publishing.

Ellis, A. (2006). *Teaching and learning: Elementary social studies.* Boston: Allyn & Bacon.

Farris, P. (2007). *Elementary and middle school social studies: An interdisciplinary, multicultural approach.* Long Grove, IL: Waveland Press.

Gay, G. (1991). Culturally diverse students and social studies. In J. Shaver (Ed.), *Handbook of research on social studies teaching and learning* (pp. 144–156). New York: Macmillan.

Grant, S., & Vansledright, B. (2001). *Constructing a powerful approach to teaching and learning in elementary social studies.* Boston: Houghton Mifflin Co.

Huck, C., Hepler, S., & Hickman, J. (1993). *Children's literature in the elementary school.* Boston: McGraw Hill.

Kellner, D. (1995). *Media culture: Cultural studies, identity and politics between the modern and the postmodern.* London: Routledge.

Kincheloe, J. (2001). *Getting beyond the facts: Teaching social studies/social sciences in the twenty-first century.* New York: Peter Lang.

Levstik, L., & Barton, K. (2001). *Doing history: Investigating with children in elementary and middle schools.* Mahwah, NJ: Lawrence Erlbaum.

Loewen, J. (1995). *Lies my teacher told me: Everything your American history textbook got wrong.* New York: New Press.

Lynch-Brown, C., & Tomlinson, C. (2005). *Essentials of children's literature.* Boston: Pearson Education.

Lyon, G. (1994). *Mama Is a Miner.* New York: Orchard Books.

Manning, M., & Baruth, L. (2000). *Multicultural education of children and adolescents.* Boston: Allyn & Bacon.

Martorella, P., & Beal, C. (2002). *Social studies for elementary school classrooms: Preparing children to be global citizens.* Upper Saddle River, NJ: Merrill Prentice Hall.

Massialas, B., & Allen, R. (1996). *Crucial issues in teaching social studies K–12.* Belmont, CA: Wadsworth Publishing Company.

Maxim, G. (1999). *Social studies and the elementary school child.* Upper Saddle River, NJ: Prentice-Hall.

Maxim, G. (2010). *Dynamic social studies for constructivist classrooms: Inspiring tomorrow's social scientists* (9th ed.). Boston: Allyn & Bacon.

McGowan, T., & Guzzetti, B. (1991). Promoting social studies understanding through literature-based instruction. *The Social Studies, 82,* 16–21.

Mitchell, M. (1993). *Uncle Jed's barbershop.* New York: Simon and Schuster.

Morris, A. (1992). *Houses and homes.* New York: Harper Collins.

Morris, A. (1993). *Bread, bread, bread.* New York: Harper Trophy.

The National Center for History in the Schools. (1996). *National standards for history.* Los Angeles: Author.

National Council for the Social Studies. (1994). *Expectations for excellence.* Washington, D.C.: Author.

Parker, W. (2005). *Social studies in elementary education* (12th ed.). Upper Saddle River, NJ: Prentice-Hall.

Public Broadcasting Service. (1999–2000). Return with honor. Primary sources. Retrieved May 17, 2010, from http://www.pbs.org/wgbh/amex/honor/filmmore/ps_tonkin.html

Rodgers, Y., Hawthorne, S., & Wheeler, R. (2007). Teaching economics through children's literature in the primary grades. *The Reading Teacher, 61,* 46–55.

Savage, T., & Armstrong, D. (1996). *Effective teaching in elementary social studies.* Englewood Cliffs, NJ: Prentice-Hall.

Schug, M. (1996). Introducing children to economic reasoning: Some beginning lessons. *The Social Studies 87,* 114–119.

Seefeldt, C. (1997). *Social studies for the preschool-primary child* (5th ed.). Upper Saddle River, NJ: Merrill.

Slavin, R. (2009). *Educational psychology: Theory and practice* (9th ed.). Upper Saddle River, NJ: Pearson.

Smith, W. (2005). *Just the two of us.* Scholastic Inc.

Social Studies Center. (2000). *Texas social studies framework.* Retrieved on January 14, 2007, from http://socialstudies.tea.state.tx.us

Stearns, P. (1998). *Why Study History.* Retrieved December 6, 2006, from American Historical Association [AHA] Web site: http://www.historians.org/pubs/Free/WhyStudyHistory.htm

Stevenson, R. (1988). *Block city.* New York: Penguin Books, USA, Inc.

Texas Education Agency [TEA]. (1999). *Texas social studies framework: Kindergarten–Grade 12: Research and resources for designing a social studies curriculum.* Austin: Author.

Texas Education Agency. (1996). Retrieved April 26, 2010, from http://ritter.tea.state.tx.us/rules/tac/chapter074/ch074a.html#74.2

Texas Statutes/Education Code [TEC] (1995) *Chapter 4.001 Public Education Mission and Objectives.* Retrieved May 14, 2007, from Texas Statutes Education Code Web site: http://tlo2.tlc.state.tx.us/statutes/edtoc.html

United States Department of Education [DOE]. (2009). Subpart 13—Excellence in Economic Education SEC 5532(a)—Aims and Goals. Retrieved Oct 19, 2009, from http://www.ed.gov/policy/elsec/leg/esea02/pg78.html

Walker, T. (2006). Global toppings: What pizza tells us about the world. *Engaging the American past: A monthly chronicle of news and events for history partners.* Vancouver, WA: Educational Service District 112 Teaching History Grant Partnership Newsletter.

Weatherford, C. (2006). *Moses: When Harriet Tubman led her people to freedom.* Hong Kong: Hyperion.

Wheelock, A. (1992). The case for untracking. *Educational Leadership 50,* 6–10.

Wineberg, S. (2001). *Historical thinking and other unnatural acts: Charting the future of teaching the past.* Philadelphia: Temple University Press.

A SOCIAL STUDIES LESSON PLAN

Constructing and Using a Timeline

Grade level: Third

Main Subject Area: Social Studies

Integrated Subjects: Language Arts/Reading, Art

Time Frame/Constraints: Two social studies class periods

Overall Goal(s): To help children understand, use, and create a timeline.

TEKS OBJECTIVES:

§ 113.5 **Social Studies** (b) Knowledge and Skills (1) History (3)(b) create and interpret timelines;

§ 117.11 **Art** (b)(1)(A) identify sensory knowledge and life experiences as sources for ideas about visual symbols, self, and life events;

§ 110.5 **English Language Arts and Reading** (3) Listening/speaking/audiences/oral grammar. The student speaks appropriately to different audiences for different purposes and occasions. The student is expected to: (A) choose and adapt spoken language appropriate to the audience, purpose, and occasion, including use of appropriate volume and rate (K-3).

Lesson Objectives: Students will view out-of-order events and write corrections on a sheet of paper.

Students will view PowerPoint presentations and, as a whole class, put various scenes from a person's life back in order and label them.

After viewing a timeline from the activity above, children construct their own timelines about important events in their lives on adding machine tape.

Students will, as a whole class, help the teacher explain the uses of a timeline.

Pairs of students will construct timelines of the main events of a famous person's life.

Each student will explain one or two of these events to the class.

Readiness Skills or Prior Knowledge Needed: Must understand that events happen in an order; must understand that some events are more important than others.

Sponge Activity: Teacher has children look at a timeline on the overhead where the dates and simple school events during the year are placed out of order and asks children to see if they can see anything wrong and, if so, how would they fix it (write on a sheet of paper).

Environmental Concerns: Partners will need to have space to work together on their timelines.

Focus: Discuss and show the correct timeline of school events from the sponge. Ask children if they think it is easier to think about and remember events when they are in order or out of order. The teacher shows a PowerPoint presentation of pictures (a baby, a toddler, an elementary student, a middle school student, a high school graduation, a college graduation, an adult holding a baby, an old person, etc.) which are out of sequence, all with the years the pictures were taken shown below the picture (the teacher may have pictures and a timeline of her own life to share, if desired). The teacher asks children if this is a good way to show the person's life and why or why not. The children are asked to help the teacher put them in order, label the pictures, and reconstruct a good timeline to go with the pictures. Show the "redesigned" PowerPoint presentation in order and discuss the difference from the first showing. Show an example of a constructed timeline of these events (and include pictures on the timeline, if possible, by shrinking them and placing with the year and the event).

Rationale: Events take place in a certain order of time. A timeline is a good tool to record, help understand logically, and remember the order of events (sequencing). Cause-and-effect can often be established by looking at a timeline. Show children a short timeline of four events in which this is the case (could be a classroom issue, a school issue, or a real or "made-up issue" to illustrate the point). For example, it could be as simple as: *Carrie called Brandi a name on Monday, and Brandi called Carrie a name on Tuesday. There was hitting between the two girls on Wednesday, and the teacher called the girls' parents, who came to school on Friday. There was no television or video games for the girls for the next month at home.* (Teacher should quickly construct a timeline

with the main events and ask students to show how a timeline can show cause and effect, or even prediction.)

MAKING CONNECTIONS:

1. **Connections to Past or Future Learning:** How many of you have seen a timeline in your social studies book before? What was the topic? What did it show? Why do you think the book authors put in it your social studies book? What did it help you understand?

2. **Connections to the Community:** Do different groups in your community have a calendar of events? This is like a virtual timeline in "real time." Are they different for different groups of people? Are different groups of people in your community more interested in certain events (for example, who might have Cinco de Mayo on their timeline of events)?

3. **Cultural Connections:** When we study other parts of the world and history, it can sometimes seem like a puzzle because, at the same time something important is happening in one part of the world, something important is also happening in another part of the world; it is difficult to see that without timelines.

4. **Connections to Student Interests & Experiences:** Have you ever heard anyone tell a story or seen a movie that did not tell everything in order? How difficult was it to understand when your mind had to go back and forth to try to make sense of things? (Teacher could actually tell a story with several events out of order to make this point.)

Materials: Adding machine tape, colored pencils, PowerPoint presentations, simple biographies, bookmarked Internet sites of currently popular people, card paper for accordion timelines.

Activities: Guided Practice: As an example, the teacher shows another simple biography/timeline of an important person (depending on the time of year, choose Martin Luther King, George Washington, etc.) on a PowerPoint presentation. The class will brainstorm important events that may have happened in their own lives (year they were born, the year [or age] when a sibling was born, they learned to ride a bike, traveled to a special place, started school, began to first grade, played on a team, went to second grade, etc.). Students are given two strips of adding machine tape (one for a draft). They are asked to draw pictures of the important events and label them in order of the year and/or age they were when the event happened.

Independent Practice: Partners will pick from a menu of interesting people and design an accordion timeline (strip of paper folded into four sections) of the major events of the life of the person whom they select, based on a short (or prepared) biography or bookmarked Internet site. Each partner will explain one or two important events on the timeline orally to the class.

Assessment: *Informal:* Teacher will check for understanding by questioning students on their personal timelines and after the oral presentations of events from biographical timelines. *Formal:* Students must include at least four major events on their "famous person" timelines (40 percent); events must be in correct sequence (40 percent); drawn picture must be representative of the event (10 percent); and dates must be included (10 percent).

What Will Students Do Who Finish Early?

Have students go to the computer and look up timelines of Harry Potter or other characters at http://www.hp-lexicon.org/timelines/timeline.php (or another current movie with a similar Web site).

Closure: Students will share their personal timelines with a partner, pointing out one or two of the most important events. The teacher will ask students what makes a timeline correct and useful.

Modification for Students with Special Needs: Sara's partner (who is currently working with the speech therapist) will present orally for her partnership.

Reflection: To be completed after teaching the lesson.

DRAFT YOUR OWN SOCIAL STUDIES LESSON PLAN

Title of Lesson: _____

Grade Level: _____

Main Subject Area: _____

Integrated Subjects: _____

Time Frame/Constraints: _____

Overall Goal(s): _____

TEKS Objectives: _____

_____

_____

Lesson Objective(s): _____

_____

Readiness Skills or Prior Knowledge Needed: _____

_____

Sponge Activity: _____

_____

_____

Environmental Concerns: _____

_____

_____

Rationale(s): _____

_____

_____

Focus or Set Induction: _____

_____

_____

Making Connections: _____

1. Connections to Past or Future Learning: _____

_____

2. Connections to the Community: _____

_____

3. Cultural Connections: _____

_____

4. Connections to Student Interests & Experiences: _____

_____

Materials: _____

_____

Activities: Guided practice: _____

_____

_____

_____

_____

_____

_____

_____

_____

_____

Independent practice: _____

_____

_____

_____

_____

_____

_____

_____

_____

_____

Assessment: _____

_____

_____

What Will Students Do Who Finish Early? _____

_____

_____

Closure: _____

_____

_____

Modification for Students with Special Needs: _____

_____

_____

Reflection: _____

_____

_____

OBSERVING SOCIAL STUDIES EXPERIENCES/ACTIVITIES

During your visit to an EC-6 classroom, use the following form to provide feedback as well as to reflectively analyze the room, the materials, and the teaching.

Name: _____ Grade Level Observed: _____ Date(s) _____

Title or Short Description of Lesson or Activity:_____

The Classroom Environment	Observed	Not Observed	Response
1. The seating arrangement is flexible (versus students remaining in straight rows).			Describe the arrangement. What are some advantages and disadvantages?
2. A center is designated for role-play and simulation activities. This could include costumes, props, a variety of types of currency from the U.S. and other countries, and other materials related to social studies.			If so, describe. If not, describe what an age-appropriate Social Studies Center might include.
3. There are images placed around the room that depict people who have exhibited courage and/or good citizenship.			If so, describe. If not, describe images that might be included and why.
4. There is a Geography Center.			If so, describe. If not, describe what an age-appropriate center might look like.
5. There are materials such as modeling clay, *papier-mâché,* and salt, available for hands-on use by students to construct geographic landforms, historical models, or human-made structures.			If so, describe. If not, what materials could be added?
6. Graph paper, markers, colored pencils, and other map-making tools are available for student use.			If so, describe. If not, what materials could be added?
7. There are geography manipulatives, such as maps, puzzles, and globes, available for student use.			If so, describe. If not, what could be added?
8. If there is no Geography Center, are these types of activities integrated within other centers or areas of the classroom?			If so, describe. If not, what could be changed?
9. There are numerous picture files available for students depicting people, places, and events from other times and places.			If so, describe. If not, what files could be added?
10. There are trade books that support the teaching of social studies in the class library.			If so, describe. If not, what titles might be included?
11. The class library contains biographies, factual stories of places and events, and cultural narratives.			If so, describe. If not, what titles might be added?

The Classroom Environment	Observed	Not Observed	Response
12. The class library contains traditional literature, such as myths, epics, legends, tall tales, folktales, fairy tales, and fables.			If so, describe. If not, what titles or types of books might be added?
13. There are artifacts, images, or other resources from other cultures or societies displayed in the classroom.			If so, describe. If not, what could be added and why?
14. Displayed artifacts, images, and other materials are positive depictions that are attractively displayed.			If so, describe. If not, give ideas for what could be added or omitted and why.
15. Social studies topics are connected to other social studies areas in an intradisciplinary way (for example, geography and economics).			If so, describe. If not, give ideas for what areas could be logically connected.
16. Social skills are a part of a lesson.			If so, describe. If not, what skills could be appropriately included?
17. There is a current events reader (such as *Weekly Reader*) in the classroom.			If so, describe how it is used. If not, describe how this type of resource might be used.
18. Technology is available in the classroom.			If so, describe any links to usage with social studies. If not, in what ways could technology be logically added?
19. There are advanced technological tools available for teacher use (overhead computer projector, document camera, digital camera, etc.).			If so, describe how they are used. If not, how might they be incorporated?
20. Students have the opportunity to use various technologies in classroom presentations.			If so, describe. If not, how could they be incorporated?
21. Students use presentation tools in an effective manner.			If so, describe. If not, how could this element be included?
22. There are electronic media, such as a television, DVD player, a cassette player, or a CD player, in the classroom.			If available, describe their use in the classroom. If not, what could be added?
23. The social studies text and other instructional materials used are up to date.			Describe if so, or if not, tell in what ways they are dated.
24. The social studies textbook or other instructional materials shows different genders and cultures.			If so, describe. If not, what is not included?
25. The teacher's media library contains films, music, and other recordings for social studies.			If so, describe. Are these available for student use? If not, what titles might be included and tell how they might be used to further students' knowledge and skills in social studies?

The Classroom Environment	Observed	Not Observed	Response
26. There are student-created recordings in the media library.			If so, describe. What is the value of having these in the media library?
27. Students use the computers primarily for word processing and for Internet research.			If so, describe. What other social studies activities could they use?
28. Various social studies software titles are available for student use.			If so, describe. If not, what titles might be appropriate, and why?
29. Students make decisions in their classroom on major or minor issues (assignments, rules, etc.).			If so, describe. If not, what are some choices that the teacher could give to them?
30. The social studies lesson begins with a motivating focus.			If so, describe. If not, what could be used?
31. The social studies lesson is presented in a logical manner.			If so, describe. If not, what could be rearranged and why?
32. The social studies activities are motivating.			If so, describe. If not, explain why not.
33. The social studies activities involve higher levels of thinking.			If so, describe. If not, what could be added?
34. The teacher uses an appropriate closure to end the social studies lesson.			If so, describe. If not, what could be added?

TEST YOURSELF FOR SOCIAL STUDIES

1. Mrs. Wickcam had her fourth graders design questions for an interview to find out information on the Vietnam War from their grandparents or others of that generation. Mrs. Wickcam is having her students do:
   A. qualitative research.
   B. quantitative research.
   C. inquiry.
   D. survey.

2. Mr. Jackson asked students to find how much rainfall parts of West Texas received for the last year. Students are most likely to find this information in:
   A. an atlas.
   B. periodicals.
   C. an almanac.
   D. a gazetteer.

3. The children in Mrs. Momin's third-grade room have been asked to describe some of the cities, the rail system, and the temples of Japan. They are being asked to describe:
   A. a region.
   B. physical characteristics.
   C. human characteristics.
   D. location.

4. Mr. Poteet's children are asked to show the largest natural region in Texas on a large classroom map. To what region should they point?
   A. Mountains and Basins
   B. Great Plains
   C. (North) Central Plains
   D. Coastal Plains

5. Ms. Baba called on Jamie to tell the class about topography. Which of the following is not a part of topography?
   A. Glaciers
   B. Rivers
   C. Plateaus
   D. Dams

6. Fifth graders were asked to guess at the climate of a city if it was located as follows: ocean, a short strip of coastal plain, mountains, city. They should answer that it would probably be:
   A. very wet.
   B. very cold.
   C. very dry.
   D. very hot.

7. Mrs. Day wanted Julia to point to the country of Panama and tell the class what type of landform was located there. Julia pointed Panama out on the large map and told them that it was a(n):
   A. mesa.
   B. fjord.
   C. isthmus.
   D. delta.

8. Ms. Klein's class was involved in an activity in which she divided the class into two groups. One group was labeled the *Settlers* and the other was labeled the *Texas Native Americans.* The question they were to answer was, "Who should have the land?" Each group researched the conflict between the two groups during the 1800s and came up with reasons why their group should have the land. One group presented their reasons while the other listened, followed by the other group presenting their reasons. After the initial presentation, each group gathered again to decide any rebuttals, and in a second round, presented them to each other. After this presentation, each group went back to see if they could develop a compromise(s) for the situation on which they felt both sides could agree. Each group presented their compromises, then went back to their groups to discuss whether or not they could accept what was offered. Finally, each group told what they could or could not accept to the other. This social studies activity is a(n):
   A. oral history.
   B. case study.
   C. learning center.
   D. conflict resolution debate.

9. Ms. Alvados wants her second-grade children to look up Web sites related to their local community. One of the first things she should do is:
   A. go online and look at the sites and bookmark them, if necessary.
   B. have children do a search on their own to see how many sites come up.
   C. ask the technology specialist to go online to see what is available.
   D. examine the URL address.

10. Mr. Kahn showed his students the following map and asked, "Who can tell me what city is located at 29° 45' North latitude and 95° 23' West longitude?" What is the answer?
    A. Shanghai, China
    B. Mexico City, Mexico
    C. Karachi, Pakistan
    D. Houston, Texas

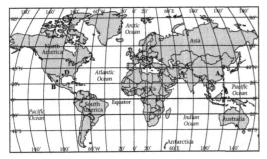

11. On a map, Ms. Lymes asked children to identify the mouth of a river. Which letter should they pick?
    A. A is the mouth.
    B. B is the mouth.
    C. C is the mouth.
    D. D is the mouth.

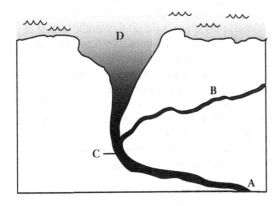

12. Mrs. Delgado's class was studying the ranching days of Texas. Mrs. Delgado asked students to identify the largest Texas ranch that had covered all or parts of 10 Texas counties during that time and that had much of its land sold for the building of the Texas capitol building. They should answer:
    A. the King Ranch.
    B. the XIT.
    C. the Waggoner Ranch.
    D. the JA Ranch.

13. Mr. Elliot's sixth-grade class on world cultures has been examining the rise of the major river valley civilizations that were the start of civilizations. Which of the following civilizations would not have been included?
    A. The Fertile Crescent (present-day Iraq)
    B. Mediterranean Region (present-day Rome)
    C. Indus River (present-day Pakistan)
    D. Yellow River (present-day China)

14. Prior to beginning a lesson on the Constitution of the United States, Ms. Myers conducted a pre-assessment of her fifth-grade students to gauge their previous knowledge on this document. She asked

her students to identify the type of government we currently have in the United States. The best answer is a(n):
    A. monarchy.
    B. direct democracy.
    C. a republic.
    D. oligarchy.

TEST YOURSELF ANSWERS AND RATIONALES FOR SOCIAL STUDIES

Answer 1: *Quantitative research* (B) involves quantities of numeric data. Students might examine statistical information, for example, on how many men were drafted for this war and how many volunteered. *Inquiry* (C) refers to the way that many social scientists go about completing a study. This involves developing a question and a hypothesis, collecting and analyzing data, drawing conclusions, and developing a generalization. For example, Mrs. Wickcam might ask students to investigate the question of whether or not this had been a popular war. Students might hypothesize it was not. They might gather data on war protests and other historical data and conclude that, although many Americans may have thought that the Domino Theory (when one country is taken over by communism, others nearby will fall) was worth fighting for, by the end of this war, most Americans did not feel that it had been worth the many American lives lost. Students might generalize that wars cannot be continued or won if they are not seen as important by most Americans. Although a survey (D) can be conducted orally, a *survey* usually gives written category choices rather than has the participant talk at length about a question. The answer is *qualitative research*, a type of research that uses methods such as interviews, observations, questionnaires, and so on, to collect data that is *in words* rather than numbers. The answer is *A*.

Answer 2: *Periodicals* (B) are sources such as magazines and newspapers. A *gazetteer* (D) deals with population and related statistics. An *atlas* (A) contains maps. Sometimes one finds rainfall maps in an atlas that gives a generalization for the area, but normally one would look in an almanac (C) for specific information for a particular year. An *almanac* is a yearly account of information, such as rainfall and other weather trends, ocean tidal tables, sunrise/sunset tables, information on moon phases, planting guides, and a host of other information (both scientific and folk). The answer is *C*.

Answer 3: These terms all have different definitions. A **region** (A) is an area that is different from another, differentiated by either physical differences (such as a mountain region versus a coastal region) or by differences in culture and language (for example, the Southwest United States is a region known for its cowboy/Old West culture). If students had been asked to describe the many islands of Japan, the rivers, or Mount Fuji, they would have been describing the **physical characteristics** (*B*), which can also include other landforms, bodies of water, types of vegetation, climate, and so forth. **Location** (*D*) refers to the place where something is situated on the Earth, normally using the **grid system** of latitude (parallels) and longitude (meridians). Here students are being asked to describe *human characteristics,* which include all of the things that change a place through *people's* actions. The answer is *C.*

Answer 4: Texas is divided into four natural regions, as listed in the question. The *Mountains and Basins* area (located in far West Texas and containing El Paso) is the smallest region (*A*). The (North) *Central Plains,* is located along the border of Oklahoma, and is the second smallest (*B*). The *High Plains* runs from the Panhandle of Texas (in the north) down through much of the Hill Country in the middle of Texas. This is the next largest region (*C*). The largest region, however, is the *Coastal Plains* (*D*), which encompasses all of East Texas and stretches along the coast of the Gulf of Mexico through the Valley. The answer is *D.*

Answer 5: *Topography* is defined as all of the landforms in a region and may include hills, mountains, valleys, peninsulas, plains, lakes, and so forth. Choice *D* (dams) is a human-made structure, so it is not a part of the topography. Humans modify the physical environment by clearing land for urban development or agriculture, draining swamps, building roads or other areas for transportation infrastructure, drilling for oil, draining wetlands, building dams and irrigation systems, and so on. The answer is *D.*

Answer 6: We would not be able to tell if the climate would be cold (*B*) or hot (*D*) without first knowing the latitude. However, we could guess that the climate would be very dry (*C*) because, most often, moisture-laden winds from the ocean blow across the coast and up the mountains. At this point, the air cools and moisture condenses and turns to rain. Thus, most of the moisture usually falls on the "ocean side" of the mountains, and there is little moisture left by the time the winds arrive on the other side of the mountain, where the wind also warms up. There would be little moisture left for a city on the opposite side of these mountains.

That is why we see the coastal side of California as more lush and fruitful and, on the other side of the mountains, Arizona as mostly desert. The answer is *C.*

Answer 7: A *mesa* (*A*) is a landform that means "table" in Spanish. Mesas look like steep hills but are completely flat on top and are mostly found in the Southwestern United States. A *fjord* (*B*) is a landform that is a very deep bay leading out to the ocean with mountains around three sides. Fjords are formed by glaciers cutting the land through to the sea and are found in colder areas of the world such as Norway, Alaska, and New Zealand. A *delta* (*D*) is a landform that is formed by a river throwing out its silt for many years where it meets the sea. The letter *D* (or delta) in Greek looks like a triangle, and large rivers (such as the Nile or the Mississippi) often build up this landform just at the end of the river where they flow out into the sea. An *isthmus* (*C*) is a landform that is only a sliver of land connecting two greater masses of land. This is the case where North America and South America are connected in Panama. There is a theory that, at one time, there was an isthmus between Alaska and Asia across the Bering Sea where ancient peoples and animals were able to walk across. The answer is *C.*

Answer 8: All of these activities are excellent for teaching social studies. However, *oral histories* (*A*) have students read or listen to *first-hand accounts* or gain first-hand accounts through interviews of people about an era of history or an event. A *case study* (*B*) centers on a person, place, or problem to show a particular example of something under study. For example, students might do a case study on the Mount St. Helen's eruption to show what happens to people during such a disaster by collecting video clips, statistics, oral accounts, and so forth. *Learning centers* (*C*) are small established areas where students go to reinforce information, gain enrichment, and so forth. For example, Mrs. Klein has a Texas Revolution Center where children have pre-arranged tasks such as arranging representative pictures of each event of the Texas Revolution on a timeline, listening to songs from that era, as well as more modern songs like "The Alamo," identifying where the major events took place on a map, matching heroes of the revolution with their deeds, and so forth. However, the activity described in the question is a *conflict resolution* debate, because students are working on a compromise. The answer is *D.*

Answer 9: To be sure that the sites are safe for viewing for young children, the teacher should first go online to look at the sites and bookmark them, if he or she wishes to use them (*A*). It might be interesting for children to see how many sites come up in a search and have them select the best sites, but a teacher must be very careful that none of these are adult sites. It is also necessary for a teacher to identify the purpose of a Web site and determine if the Web site matches his or her goals and objectives. This can be done by looking at the URL address (*D*) to see the expertise of the author, the date the information was entered on the site, and so on, to help establish any bias in information. As children grow, they can be taught these skills as well. The teacher might do this in collaboration with the technology specialist in his or her school, but it is still the responsibility of the teacher to make sure that the sites match the curriculum and that they are safe for children. The answer is *A*.

Answer 10: Remember a memory model for latitude (it is like the rungs of a "*latter*" or ladder [they go horizontally across the world]). They also tell us how far north or south from the Equator a place is located. Longitude measures distance east or west from the Prime Meridian in Greenwich, England, so *long*itude lines run *long*wise. Therefore, the city that matches Mr. Kahn's question is Houston, Texas (*D*). Shanghai, China (*A*) is located at latitude: 31° 14′ North and longitude: 121° 27′ East. Mexico City, Mexico (*B*) is located at latitude: 19° 28′ North and longitude: 99° 09′ West; and Karachi, Pakistan (*C*) is located at latitude: 24° 51′ North and longitude: 67° 02′ East. The answer is *D*.

Answer 11: Letter *A* shows the *mouth* of the river, or its *beginning*. Letter *B* shows a *tributary* (or another smaller river or stream that connects with the main river. Letter *C* shows the *channel* of the river, and *D* shows the *delta* (or the end of a river, which dumps silt out into the ocean or gulf in the form of a Greek letter *D*, or a triangle shape). The answer is *A*.

Answer 12: The *King Ranch* (*A*) was originally smaller (covering about 800,000 acres) than the *XIT* (*B*), but the King Ranch (located west of Corpus Christi in South Texas) has remained intact, so is the largest today. The XIT was located in the Panhandle and owned by a syndicate of investors. During the 1800s, it covered about 3,000,000 acres and was the largest ranch in Texas during its time—prior to much of its land being sold to finance the state capitol building in Austin. The *Waggoner Ranch* (*C*) and the *JA Ranch* (*D*) were also both large ranches but not nearly to the extent of the XIT or the King Ranch. The answer is *B*.

Answer 13: Remember that we are looking for the *exception*. The *Fertile Crescent* (*A*) was one of the earliest major river valley civilizations. It was located between the Tigris and Euphrates rivers and included the region of Mesopotamia (meaning land between the waters). The *Indus River Civilization* (*C*) developed on the coast of the Arabian Sea. It began around the same time as another major civilization developed in the valley of the Nile River in modern day Egypt. The *Yellow River Civilization* (*D*), known as the cradle of Chinese civilization, was the last of the major river valley civilizations. People who lived in this area, located in present day China, discovered bronze-working by 2000 B.C.E. and were making tools and weapons from iron by 600 B.C.E. A powerful civilization began to grow in the *Mediterranean Region* (*B*) in about 700 B.C.E., which became known as Rome. Although this civilization was extremely important in the history of the world, it was not one of the very early major river valley civilizations. The answer is *B*.

Answer 14: A *monarchy* (*A*) is ruled by one person who usually inherits ruling power. Queen Elizabeth II, for example, has been the monarch of the United Kingdom since 1952. The Queen, however, does not have absolute authority over the government because the United Kingdom is a *constitutional monarchy*. This means that the monarch is mainly a *figurehead* and that an elected legislative body, the Parliament in the case of the United Kingdom, makes most major decisions. In a *direct democracy* (*B*), all of the people who are eligible to participate in government decisions gather together to make decisions. This type of democracy existed in Ancient Greece. The only people eligible at that time to participate were free men. This type of government can be difficult to maintain in a large geographic region. A republic, or *representative democracy* (*C*) allows citizens to elect others to represent their interests in the government. As a representative, that official must reside near those he or she represents in order to have greater familiarity with the local issues. This is known as *direct representation*. An *oligarchy* (*D*) is a rare form of government that establishes rule of a small minority over a larger majority of the population. Prior to 1994, this type of government was found in South Africa, where an apartheid government, a minority government made up of Western Europeans, ruled over a majority of Black African citizens. The answer is a republic that is balanced by individual rights and checks and balances of the government. The answer is *C*.

5 Preparing to Teach Science in Texas

Mary E. Wingfield
University of Houston–Downtown

Lynn S. Freeman
University of Houston–Victoria

This chapter contains information about teaching science in the elementary classroom. Many new teachers approach teaching science with trepidation because they may not remember their own science classes as inspiring, but new materials, technology, and approaches can now make this area one of the most exciting for you to teach and your children to learn.

A brief introduction to science education provides the theoretical basis for the state's standards. Each of the science standards is then discussed, along with an opportunity to test yourself on some relevant practice questions. Discussion of the standards should also include Competencies 24–41, which are the science competencies for the *Generalist*. A model science lesson and a lesson evaluation using the standards, a resource list, and references are presented, followed by another lesson plan, a form to draft your own lesson plan, an observation sheet, and more practice questions.

According to the National Science Education Standards (National Research Council, 1996), "Lifelong scientific literacy begins with understandings, attitudes, and values established in the earliest years" (p. 114). Therefore, teachers of EC-6-grade children must remember how important it is to foster a sense of wonder, design investigations, ask questions, and promote curiosity about science in their classrooms. Today's science teachers benefit from newly designed curriculum materials, kits that include developmentally appropriate manipulatives, and enhanced technology applications. Appropriate instructional strategies should be employed that encourage inquiry, problem solving/higher-order thinking, cooperative learning, and concept attainment.

Science education reform efforts have relied on research studies from a number of professional organizations, including the National Science Teachers Association, the American Association for the Advancement of Science, and the National Science Foundation. The effort to improve science education in schools has resulted in the establishment of state guidelines and National Standards. Texas teachers see these reform efforts detailed in the Texas Essential Knowledge and Skills (TEKS) for science for each grade level (access at http://www.tea.state.tx.us/teks). The format of the TEKS reflects national reform efforts throughout each grade level.

Texas children have been formally evaluated on their knowledge of the elementary TEKS on the TAKS test (Texas Assessment of Knowledge and Skills), which is soon scheduled to change to the STAAR (State of Texas Assessment of Academic Readiness) test. Even though every grade level is not currently tested in science, teachers who must give children the state test count on all teachers at every grade level to have readied students. To see how this exam is set up for children (and to test your own knowledge), it is possible to download a released science TAKS test at the TEA (Texas Education Agency) Web site (http://ritter.tea.state.tx.us/student.assessment/resources/release/tests2009/taks_g05_science.pdf). After the change in tests, we assume that a similar STAAR site will be made available.

The state test focuses on an understanding of scientific processes, the nature of science, and the content strands of life, Earth, and physical science. Correlations with the National Standards, the TEKS, and district guidelines ensure that students are benefiting from a concerted effort to provide meaningful, inquiry-based, student-centered, hands-on science instruction. The next section of this chapter highlights each of the 11 Texas science standards for the *Generalist* EC-6 TExES and Competencies 24–41.

Standard I

The science teacher manages classroom, field, and laboratory activities to ensure the safety of all students and the ethical care and treatment of organisms and specimens.

Competency 24: Safe and Proper Laboratory Processes

The beginning teacher considers safety considerations as essential in the hands-on science classroom of today. Curiosity and immaturity combine to present hazards with even the most common materials. This standard requires that the teacher know and understand safety regulations and guidelines, procedures for responding to an accident in the laboratory, including first aid, legal issues associated with accidents, potential safety hazards, and modification of equipment for students with special needs. In the classroom, the teacher employs safe practices by arranging the space for storage, traffic flow, and access to each student. The teacher is responsible for reading the **Materials Safety Data Sheet (MSDS)** *and other chemical labels and for ensuring that safety equipment, including an eye washer (for washing any chemicals in the eyes immediately and for about 15 minutes), a fire blanket, and a fire extinguisher, is available. The teacher must check all materials prior to use, and must create an environment where rules and safety procedures are important. Potential hazards in the field, such as insect bites, poisonous plants, and allergies require planning and preparation. Those hazards should not, however, be used as an excuse for avoiding field investigations listed in the TEKS at each grade level. Finally, classroom pets are a wonderful way to promote responsibility and encourage scientific observations. Considerations must be given to the possibilities of allergies, appropriate instruction in care and treatment, and extra supervision to ensure the careful handling of animals.*

Consider the following practice question:

Ms. Davis, a third-grade teacher, intends to continually reinforce the importance of safety in the science classroom and makes sure that:

A. safety rules are posted in the room.
B. the class previews each activity together to identify potential hazards.
C. signed safety contracts are required at the beginning of the year.
D. safety is part of each student's grade.

The teacher realizes that even if grades are used (*D*), safety rules are posted (*A*), and safety contracts are signed at the beginning of the year (*C*), students need constant reminders for all activities because they may include specific hazards. The correct answer is *B*.

Laboratory safety begins in the planning stages, where activities must be evaluated and risks minimized. Plastic containers are substituted for glass, mercury-containing objects should no longer be used, food allergies are considered, and appropriate management, preparation, and positive measures are employed. The teacher is always on the watch for situations that could become dangerous, such as electric cords that could cause a student to trip. Unsteady tables or desks that could easily tip over should never be used for equipment or liquids.

Numerous sources are available for additional safety information. Each campus should have a copy of the "**Texas Safety Standards**" (can be found at http://www.utdanacenter.org/sciencetoolkit/safety). Once at this site, click on *Texas Safety Standards for Kindergarten–Grade 12*. The major safety points to remember include the following:

• Obtain and review all state and district guidelines and policies.
• Provide appropriate safety instruction, including a safety quiz and safety contract for students and parents to sign.
• Instruct students on proper use of safety equipment—goggles, fire extinguishers, fire blankets, eyewash station, sink area, a safety shower, and so on.

- Provide practice sessions for safety rules and procedures.
- Identify potential hazards and provide appropriate safety precautions before each activity.
- Instruct students to immediately report any personal injury, damaged equipment, and hazard potentials.
- Do not permit students to handle science supplies or equipment until they have been given specific instruction in their use.
- Prevent loose clothing or hair from coming into contact with science supplies, chemicals, or equipment.
- Instruct students in the proper care and handling of classroom pets and organisms.
- Expect the unexpected and never take safety for granted.

Try the following practice question:

After using cabbage juice, vinegar, lemon juice, egg white, and baking soda to identify acids and bases with litmus paper, the teacher should:

- **A.** dismiss students to their next classes immediately.
- **B.** instruct students to return unused chemicals to their original containers.
- **C.** instruct students to clean work surfaces and wash their hands.
- **D.** move students away from tables so that the teacher can clean the area properly.

Returning unused chemicals to original containers (*B*) might lead to contamination. Other labeled containers should be used to store unused chemicals. Answers *A* and *D* fail to promote safety consciousness and appropriate practices, leaving little responsibility to students. The correct answer is *C.*

Standard II

The science teacher understands the correct use of tools, materials, equipment, and technologies.

Competency 024: Safe and Proper Laboratory Procedures

The beginning teacher knows and understands concepts of precision and accuracy in the process of data collection. The teacher can use grade-appropriate equipment and technology for gathering, analyzing, and reporting data. This includes the use of the International System of Measurement (i.e., the metric system) and the ability to perform conversions within measurement systems. Scientific communications include the teachers' ability to organize, display, and communicate data in a variety of ways (e.g., charts, tables, graphs, diagrams, written reports, oral presentations).

Consider the following practice question:

After providing laboratory equipment for her fourth-grade students, Ms. Estrada notices that the triple beam pan balance is not even. She should:

- **A.** instruct students to add a few gram masses until the balance is even.
- **B.** use that balance for weighing only large objects, because it is not accurate.

C. level the balance by using the adjustment dial.
D. use a different balance.

The triple beam balance has an adjustment dial that balances the pan with the beam masses. Adjustment is necessary after the balance has been relocated. Choices A and B might work as solutions, but they do not model the importance of accuracy in science. The correct answer is C.

Scientists use many tools in the collection of data through observations. Below are listed many of the tools that can be found in classrooms where science is taught.

Magnifying hand lenses	Journals/ notebooks	Calculators	Prisms	Beakers
Microscopes	Hot plates	Computers	Mirrors	Funnels
Telescopes	Petri dishes	Cameras	Magnets	Pans
Collecting nets	Terrariums	Aquariums	Cups/bowls	

Measuring Devices

Meter sticks/metric rulers	Thermometers (Celsius & Fahrenheit)	Stopwatches
Graduated cylinders		Calipers
Spring scales	Test tubes	pH paper
Double-pan or triple-beam balances	Clocks	

Equipment for the EC-6 classroom needs to be developmentally appropriate. For example, **double-pan balances** in early grades are used to indicate less-than and more-than relationships, and cups and bowls are used for sorting. Teachers must also be familiar with the correct terminology and use of the equipment so they can instruct their students. For instance, a liquid tends to adhere and curve upward on the sides of **graduated cylinders**. Teachers should know that measurements must be taken by reading the bottom, called a **meniscus**, of this curved liquid (rather than the outer edges) in order to obtain an accurate measurement. This must be done at eye level, and measurements taken only as accurately as the instrument allows. Some measuring devices (e.g., spring scales) require **calibration** (e.g., adjusting with a known standard) before use.

Try the following practice question:

Mr. Landry starts a lesson on the proper use of a microscope and first has children:

A. identify the parts of the microscope: the stage, eyepiece, and arm.
B. make slides to view under high magnification.
C. explain the difference between high- and low-power magnification.
D. predict the total magnification power of the instrument.

The students must correctly identify and name the parts of the microscope first. This procedure facilitates subsequent important instructions for microscope use. Although Choices B, C, and D might be appropriate at some point in the lesson, the students need the microscope terminology to use and follow directions. The correct answer is A.

Data collection and interpretation are included in this standard, and the teacher is expected to promote scientific communication. It may be necessary for the teacher to describe the data using basic descriptive statistics including range, frequency, mean, medium, and mode. The *range* refers to the numeric span between the high and low data collected. The *frequency* refers to how many times something occurs. The *mean* refers to the average of all data collected. The *medium* refers to the data point located midway between the highest and lowest points. The *mode* refers to the most frequently occurring data.

The TEKS include the following student expectations related to scientific inquiry: "construct graphs, tables, maps, charts to organize, examine, evaluate information," "analyze and interpret information to construct explanations from direct and indirect evidence," and "communicate valid conclusions." Students are able to interpret graphs easily if they have had experience in constructing them. Teachers should provide numerous opportunities for students to collect and organize data. **Bar graphs** are used for data of groups, sets, or categories. For example, the early grades often collect categorical data and organize bar graphs for types of weather, car and bus riders, types of shoes, preference of drinks, birthday months, and so forth. **Line graphs** are useful for comparing two sets of continuous numbers and finding the relationship between those data; for instance, school attendance could be charted along a line to see in which months attendance was the lowest. Technology can also be used to collect data on simple spreadsheets and to design graphs, and students can communicate results using presentation software.

Let's look at the pie chart (Figure 5.1) used by Mr. Gray's students to show the percentage of weight recycled by each grade. Note that these data would best be represented as a **pie chart** because it represents proportions of a whole.

Suppose students wondered how the paper recycling amounts changed each week. A data table would best suit this purpose. A data table lists information or observations and should be titled and labeled for clear understanding (Table 5.1 on the next page).

This information could also be visually represented on a line graph (Figure 5.2 on the next page) because the data for both variables (time and weight) are continuous and numeric.

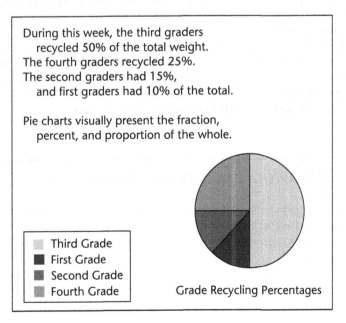

During this week, the third graders
   recycled 50% of the total weight.
The fourth graders recycled 25%.
The second graders had 15%,
   and first graders had 10% of the total.

Pie charts visually present the fraction,
   percent, and proportion of the whole.

Third Grade
First Grade
Second Grade
Fourth Grade

Grade Recycling Percentages

FIGURE 5.1 Pie Chart

Table 5.1	Class Data Table: Paper Recycling Each Week
Week	Weight Each Week (lbs)
1	480
2	820
3	1200
4	780

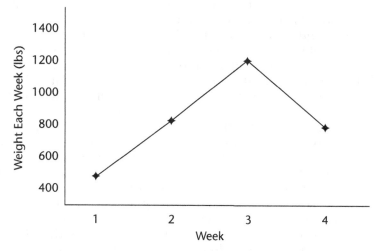

FIGURE 5.2 Line Graph

The **manipulative variable (MV)** is always plotted on the *x*-axis (horizontal), and the **responding variable (RV)** is plotted on the *y*-axis (vertical). Line graphs allow us to determine increasing and decreasing trends (e.g., the weight of recycled paper increased from Week 1 to Week 3) and to determine data values that fall between collected data points on the graph line. For example, what was the weight halfway between Week 1 and Week 2? (The answer is 650 lbs.) Teachers should ask many questions, including which week had the highest weight, the lowest weight, and so forth. They can also ask the students to (1) *identify patterns* and *trends*—which week looks different than the rest; (2) *make inferences*—explain what happened to the weight between Week 3 and Week 4; and (3) *make predictions*—what do you think will happen to the weight in Week 5? Thus, the line graph is the best format to depict the recycled paper weight data for Mr. Gray's class.

Try the following practice question:

During a kindergarten science lesson on animals, Ms. Lowe gave each student a box of animal cookies and asked them to sort the animals by shape. These data on animal cookies could be visually represented best as a:

    A. data table.
    B. line graph.
    C. pie chart.
    D. bar graph.

The categorical data (type of animal) would be the manipulative variable (MV) on the *x*-axis (horizontal), and the number in that category would be the responding variable on the *y*-axis (vertical). A data table (*A*) *could* list this same information in numeric form, but it is not a good visual. A line graph (*B*) is used for continuous, numerical data. A pie chart (*C*) helps show data collected as *parts of a whole*. The bar graph would clearly show which type of animal was most represented and which was least represented. The correct answer is *D*.

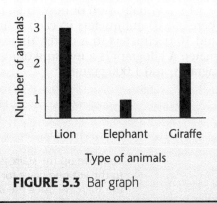

FIGURE 5.3 Bar graph

Consider the following practice question:

A first-grade teacher wants to introduce the concept of measurement to her students. She gives each group of students five objects to observe and asks them to compare the objects to a:

A. metric ruler.
B. standard ruler.
C. student's shoe.
D. yard stick.

First-grade students should use measurement aids without numbers to compare and develop greater than and less than concepts. Upper-grade students should use standard measurement tools—such as in choices *A, B,* or *D*—where divisions and markings are clearly understood and are appropriate for the task. Because the question involves young children, the correct answer is *C*.

Finally, this standard on tools, equipment, and technologies includes emphasis on measurement in the metric system. Scientists use measurement to quantify their observations. For example, an observation of a "large" butterfly has no frame of reference, but a butterfly with a 4-centimeter wingspan is more specific. Scientists are careful that the measuring instrument is appropriate for the task. For example, a graduated cylinder with 1 milliliter markings is more accurate than a beaker with 50 milliliter lines. **Graduated cylinders** are designed and manufactured specifically for liquid measurement. Measurements should be repeated often and averaged to increase their validity (i.e., *accuracy*) and reliability (i.e., *consistency*).

The *International System of Units*, or the **metric system**, was adopted internationally for use in 1960. All but two countries, including the United States, quickly made the conversion to the metric system, and this system is used internationally for commerce and scientific work. The metric system was designed to relate mass, distance, and volume for pure water. For example, a cubic box that is 1 centimeter on each side has a volume of $1 \times 1 \times 1 = 1$

cubic centimeter (volume = length × width × height). The amount of water that it takes to fill this box is defined in the metric system as 1 milliliter, and this same box has a mass of 1 gram (at standard temperature and pressure).

The metric system makes use of base units—**gram** for mass, **meter** for length, and **liter** for volume. Prefixes (e.g., kilo-, deci-, milli-) modify the base units. Converting within the metric system is as easy as adding a zero or moving the decimal point, because each prefix represents a factor of ten. The staircase depicted in Figure 5.4 is a visualization of how these prefixes are related. For example, because there are 10 millimeters in each centimeter, 10 centimeters in each decimeter, and 10 decimeters in a meter, there are 1,000 (10 × 10 × 10) millimeters in a meter. A kilogram is a measure of mass that represents 10 hectograms, 100 dekagrams, and 1,000 grams.

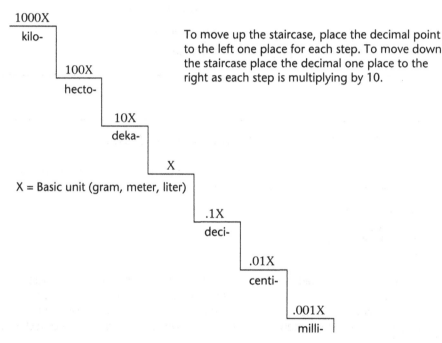

FIGURE 5.4 Metric Ladder and Directions

Try the following metric conversions:

_____ centiliters (cl) = 4 liters (L)   27 meters (m) = _____ millimeters (mm)
_____ dekagrams (dkg) = 50 grams (g)   5 liters (L) = _____ centiliters (cl)
_____ kilometers (km) = 140 hectometers (hm) 0.05 kilometers (km) = _____ meters (m)
_____ centigrams (cg) = 75 dekagrams (dkg)   65 kilograms (kg) = ____ dekagrams (dkg)

Answers: 400 centiliters = 4 liters; 5 dekagrams = 50 grams; 14 kilometers = 140 hectometers; 75,000 centigrams = 75 dekagrams; 27 meters = 27,000 millimeters; 5 liters = 500 centiliters; 0.05 kilometers = 50 meters; 65 kilograms = 6,500 dekagrams. Also note the abbreviations used.

Several common but important measurements and their metric values are as follows:

- Boiling point of pure water at sea level: 100 degrees Celsius (212 degrees Fahrenheit)
- Freezing point of pure water at sea level: 0 degrees Celsius (32 degrees Fahrenheit)
- Normal human body temperature: 37 degrees Celsius (98.6 degrees Fahrenheit)

Try the following practice question:

Mrs. Henry is teaching her third-grade students to measure mass in the metric system. Which of the following measurements represents the smallest mass?

A. 0.045 grams
B. 78 milligrams
C. 0.009 kilograms
D. 0.333 hectograms,

The least amount of mass cannot be determined until all choices are converted to the same unit. For example, 1 yard (36 inches) is more than 27 inches, even though the number 27 is greater than the number 1. Apples must be compared to apples to make a comparison. Converting all the choices into grams yields (*A*) 0.045 grams, (*B*) 0.078 grams, (*C*) 9 grams, and (*D*) 33.3 grams. Clearly, 0.045 grams is the least value. The correct answer is *A*.

Standard III

The science teacher understands the process of scientific inquiry and its role in science instruction.

Competency 025: Scientific Inquiry, History and Nature of Science

The beginning teacher understands that the type of scientific investigation used depends on the questions to be answered. Teachers can help students to know that some questions are outside the realm of science because they deal with phenomena that are not scientifically testable. The teacher understands the use of technology in scientific research and the principles and procedures used in conducting descriptive studies, controlled experiments, and comparative data analysis. The teacher links prior knowledge and experience to the investigations and focuses inquiry-based activities from questions and issues that are relevant to the students. The teacher models the processes of scientific inquiry by using combinations of the following:

- *Asking a scientific question, then formulating a testable hypothesis.*
- *Selecting appropriate equipment and technology for gathering information.*
- *Making observations and collecting data.*
- *Organizing, analyzing, and evaluating data to find trends and patterns and making inferences.*
- *Communicating and defending a valid conclusion about the hypothesis under investigation.*

Consider the following practice question:

Mr. Lopez has completed a fourth-grade unit on the environment and intends to assess students' ability to use higher-order thinking skills to draw conclusions based on experimental data. Given a graph of alternative fuels and the resulting air pollution, the students would be able to:

    A. evaluate which alternative fuel would be best for the environment.
    B. describe the process of measuring resulting air pollution.
    C. predict what new alternative fuel will be invented in the future.
    D. list three alternative fuels.

As this is an evaluation-level question, the student is required to use knowledge and synthesis to think at a higher level. Reading the graph correctly *could* include answer *D*, but the listing task requires only the *lowest* level of knowledge. Basing the conclusions from the graphed information, in this case, would not enable the student to describe the process (*B*) or to predict (*C*) future events. The correct answer is *A*.

      Science teachers are able to promote scientific attitudes related to inquiry and skepticism through careful investigations and analysis of results. Challenging students to (1) make predictions; (2) develop research questions; (3) form hypotheses; (4) conduct descriptive, experimental, and correlation investigations; and (5) correctly analyze the results enables them to become problem solvers and critical thinkers. Questions from all levels of Bloom's taxonomy (http://www.kurwongbss.eq.edu.au/thinking/Bloom/blooms.htm) allow students to use the knowledge of facts and vocabulary to build comprehension through explanations in their own words and applications of the knowledge in other contexts. Higher levels of thinking include *analysis*—taking apart, comparing/contrasting; *synthesis*—putting together, designing/creating; and *evaluation*—recommending/judging based on selected criteria. Assisting students in developing higher-order thinking prepares them for the level of scientific literacy they need (e.g., to read a newspaper story about a new medical discovery and question the report's authors, their sources of information, the investigation's methods, and the interpretation of the data). In an effort to promote the science educational reforms that produce a scientifically literate society, students need authentic experiences with critical thinking and analysis in real-world contexts. Teachers should promote conversations between young scientists to encourage them to see each other as resources and demonstrate that more is learned when scientific information is shared.

Try the following practice question:

During a second-grade science lesson about states of matter and heat, Ms. Curtis allows children to observe the physical changes of an ice cube placed in a sunny spot on the playground. Which one of the following questions regarding the melting of the ice cube are most effective in encouraging students' use of higher-order thinking skills about the effect of heat on matter?

    A. What is the amount of time it takes for the ice cube to melt?
    B. What would happen if the ice cube was placed in the shade?
    C. Why does the melted liquid look bigger than the original ice cube?
    D. What is the temperature of the sunny spot?

Making predictions would require students to use their observations to hypothesize about the amount of heat and the effect of the heat on the ice cube in the shade. Although the time (*A*) and temperature (*D*) could be recorded, these answers do not require higher-order thinking. Choice *C* allows students to make predictions, but it does not directly involve the effect of heat on states of matter. Making use of students' questions is a good way for teachers to advance higher-level thinking and problem solving. Teachers should be flexible, as they continue the investigations and promote student inquiry. The correct answer is *B*.

Consider the following practice question:

Mrs. Glenn, a first-grade teacher, wants her students to understand the scientific process of classification. She provides a container of different rocks to each group of students. What question should she use first to direct her students?

- **A.** How many rocks does your group have?
- **B.** Can you explain how the rocks can be sorted into two groups?
- **C.** Can you tell where each of these rocks came from?
- **D.** How can you find out more about each rock?

Although choices *C* and *D* might be interesting and appropriate for instruction, the objective is to practice classification. Choice *A* requires a response based on low-level knowledge, one that does not require classifying. The correct answer is *B*.

Teachers realize that scientific inquiry is promoted through the practice and use of science process skills. Each of the TEKS grade levels begins with an emphasis on science process skills that can be used in the classroom on a daily basis.

The *basic science process skills* include:

- **Observing:** Using the five senses to describe objects and events. Observations can be *qualitative* (e.g., color, shape) or *quantitative* (e.g., length, mass, volume).
- **Classifying:** Sorting objects or events into groups based on common characteristics or attributes.
- **Measuring:** Determining the length, volume, mass, temperature, or area to describe and quantify objects.
- **Communicating:** Sharing observations and explanations of objects or events with others.

The *integrated process skills* include:

- **Inferring and predicting:** Explaining or drawing conclusions about an object or future event based upon observations.
- **Using variables:** Studying effects of manipulating and controlling variables.
- **Representing data:** Organizing observations and measurements to make data useful.
- **Experimenting:** Using the process skills necessary to ask a question, plan an investigation, collect data, and form a conclusion.

All children can use their curiosity to observe the natural world around them. Children must be encouraged to use their senses to make observations and gather data. When children are able to use their own senses to gain information, they remember it much longer than they would if it had simply been told or read to them. Science with the senses literally comes alive. Even Pre-K students and kindergartners can routinely communicate selected weather conditions at calendar time, classify their results, and represent the data through pictures or graphs. Teachers can often integrate these skills throughout other content areas by infusing prediction into a reading assignment, measuring into a mathematics lesson, or observation into the fine arts.

Consider the following practice question:

The second-grade TEKS expect children to observe, measure, record, analyze, predict, and illustrate changes in size, mass, temperature, color, position, quantity, sound, and movement. The teacher supplies thick and thin rubber bands stretched over cardboard box lids. The students design a controlled experiment with a testable hypothesis to find out if sound produced by plucking the thick and thin rubber bands is different. The experimental design must include all of the following except:

A. manipulative variables—thick and thin rubber bands.
B. responding variables—same or different sounds heard.
C. controlled variables—same-size box lids, and same person plucking each rubber band with the same force.
D. a diagram like a pie chart or line graph.

Although a diagram could be a part of the lab results, the actual experiment must include choices A, B, and C. Controlled experiments should also be repeated and the data averaged when necessary. Remember that the question is asking for the exception. Because it is not required, the correct answer is D.

Scientists use specific processes and criteria to investigate and interpret the natural world. This procedure is called the **scientific method**, and it involves seeking observable evidence in a systematic process. This process begins with **observations** that can be gained from the senses or enhanced through technology. For example, a thermometer provides a quantitative measurement rather than a vague sense of feeling hot or cold.

For scientists, observations lead to questions about "Why?" or "What if?" These questions lead to the examination of existing knowledge on the subject in order to learn more about the phenomena they are questioning. This research step is important because the problem may have already been studied or an answer discovered, or new findings could possibly lead the scientists toward a different **hypothesis**, or educated guess, about the solution. The **experiment** is a means of comparing an unknown set of circumstances to one that is known or controlled. A **variable** is a factor that affects the outcome of the experiment. **Manipulative variables** are able to be changed—such as changing the thick rubber band to the thin one to see what new outcome in sound occurs in the preceding question. An ideal experiment tests only one variable at a time and compares the result to a **control** setting (where a particular variable is not present or consistent). This method helps clarify or examine the outcome, identify possible cause-and-effect relationships, and make predictions for further study. After a hypothesis has withstood repeated testing and experimentation, the hypothesis can be called a **scientific theory**—a general explanation of a group of related phenomena. Scientific theories (as opposed to scientific laws) are still subject to change as new evidence is revealed. Most science theories change over time; this reflects the tentative nature of science knowledge. Science is based on *empiricism*, the view that reality is observable. Thus, new evidence might support or confirm an existing theory, or it might necessitate that the theory be modified to take the new evidence into account. Further, the new evidence might necessitate that the theory be rejected (e.g., Lamarck's theory that acquired characteristics are inherited). The history of science reflects theory building, testing, and modifying, thus attempting to build valid theories that take into account all the evidence available at the time.

Science often uses **models**, both conceptual and physical, as a tool to understand natural events (e.g., ocean waves). For instance, a water wave tank can be used to study the generation, movement, patterns, and forces associated with waves. This model makes wave investigation convenient. Nevertheless, a human-made model cannot duplicate all the variables and their interactions at work in nature. Thus, models are useful, but the results are limited because they cannot fully predict or explain natural events. The wave tank simulation is a physical model. There are also conceptual models (e.g., the structure of an atom, structure of chromosomes) and mathematical models (e.g., paths of hurricanes). These models provide predictive utility, but they must be viewed as incomplete and limited because they are human-made representations.

Teachers should continuously use events and activities that stimulate students' questions and curiosity. Students should have opportunities to explore these events. Sometimes this exploration can be unstructured and more like play. This format is conducive for the investigation procedures described previously. This instructional approach is often called **inquiry-based** or **discovery**. Its goal is to foster engagement, scientific thinking processes, and student-generated generalizations.

Consider the following practice question:

Third-grade students notice that recently planted bushes near the edge of the playground have all turned brown. The teacher uses their observations to promote inquiry about plant growth and environmental conditions. What step should they take next to follow the scientific method?

   A. Research the plant type to determine its ideal growing conditions.
   B. Write a report for the school newspaper about their observations.
   C. Formulate a testable hypothesis or an educated guess.
   D. Plant some new bushes and add water daily.

The students' observations lead to questions, and now they must undertake research to narrow their possible explanations. Then they can form a testable hypothesis (C) and set up an experiment in which water, soil conditions, sunlight, or temperature can be investigated. The cause of the plants' condition may not be a matter of water (D), and their scientific reporting (B) should be undertaken *after* they have tested their hypothesis. They should find out about the situation first, so the correct answer is A.

Standard IV

The science teacher has theoretical and practical knowledge about teaching science and about how students learn science.

Competency 028: Instruction: Theory and Practice

The beginning teacher knows the developmental characteristics of students and how that influences science learning. Piaget and other researchers have identified exploratory, concrete experiences as the foundation of cognition and learning. Vygotsky's research highlighted the role of language and discourse in concept formation. Thus, the combination of concrete experiences and verbal descriptions and explanations at the appropriate developmental level are critical for learning science. The teacher understands the importance of play for the Pre-K child at a water table and the need for manipulatives and concrete experiences for the young child. Teachers use developmentally appropriate methods to plan and implement inquiry-based science programs. They understand the advantages and limitations of using models. They establish a collaborative scientific community that supports actively engaged learning and make accommodations for the needs of all students. Teachers must use strategies that assist students in the development of content-area vocabulary; word meaning in content-related texts; and comprehension before, during, and after reading content-related texts. Teachers must understand common student misconceptions in science and learn theories about how students develop scientific understanding. Misconceptions often confound science learning (e.g., many children think that a whale is a fish). In the classroom, teachers sequence learning activities in a way that allows students to build on their prior knowledge and challenges them to expand their understanding of science. This can be done through lab and field investigations that promote curiosity, openness to new ideas, and skepticism.

Teachers use a variety of instructional strategies to ensure that all students have access to science and that all students develop reading comprehension of content-related texts. They assist students in locating and retaining content-related information from a range of texts and technologies. Teachers also help students to locate the meanings and pronunciations of unfamiliar content-related words through dictionaries. Teachers respect student diversity and use questioning strategies to move students from concrete to more abstract understanding. As a facilitator, teachers expect students to be active participants through individual, small group, and whole-class strategies. Working with others provides a model of the scientific community where researchers often communicate and share findings.

In order to teach effectively, the teacher needs an understanding of the science concepts and definitions presented to the student at each grade level. A review of the TEKS for science at http://www.tea.state.tx.us/teks, teachers' manuals, and curriculum guides is a good place to start. Other resources include textbooks, dictionaries, CD-ROM encyclopedias, and Internet searches for key terms. Although the TEKS at all grade levels begin with a stated emphasis on (1) classroom and field investigations, (2) scientific inquiry, (3) critical thinking and decision making, and (4) tools and process skills of science, they also include examples of developmentally appropriate concepts and content. Stated concepts at lower grades may be studied again in upper grades in greater depth in a spiraling curriculum. For example, a kindergarten student is expected to record observations about parts of plants, including leaves, roots, stems, and flowers. The fifth-grade student also studies plants but is expected to identify that radiant energy from the Sun is transferred into chemical energy through the process of photosynthesis.

The following are examples of *science concepts* included in the TEKS for grades K–6:

- **Kindergarten:** Studies **changes** (weather, seasons, life cycles); explores the **natural world** (rocks, soil, water); and observes and describes **living organisms** (plants, animals).

- **Grade 1:** Studies **natural sources of water** (streams, lakes, oceans); compares *characteristics of living organisms;* identifies and tests ways that *heat* may cause change; manipulates objects to show relationship between **parts to the whole** showing that all parts of a system must be present for the whole to work (for example, a flashlight needs batteries to make it "whole"; a plant needs roots to make it "whole"). Mechanical parts, when put together as a whole, can do much more than they can separately.
- **Grade 2:** Collects information using **tools**, including meter sticks; describes and illustrates the *water cycle;* demonstrates change in *motion* by applying force (push or pull); observes and identifies how magnets are used in everyday life; observes and records patterns, including the appearance of the moon; and studies functions of *plant and animal parts*.
- **Grade 3:** Studies the Sun and planets in our *solar system;* investigates *magnetism* and *gravity;* observes **states of matter** (solids, liquids, and gases); explores different forms of energy; investigates rapid changes in Earth's surface; and compares *adaptations* and *needs* of organisms, including habitats.
- **Grade 4:** Constructs *complex systems* (an electric circuit); draws conclusions using *fossils;* identifies the Sun as a major source of energy; studies **properties of matter** (such as *density*); studies renewable and nonrenewable resources and responsibility of recycling; investigates relationship of producers/consumers in food webs; compares differences of inherited and learned traits.
- **Grade 5:** Designs investigations that promote inquiry and critical thinking; identifies the boiling point and freezing points of water on the Celsius scale; explores the uses of energy and alternative energy resources and properties of light (reflection, refraction); studies the formation of sedimentary rocks and fossil fuels, the significance of carbon dioxide–oxygen cycle to the survival of plants and animals, and the structures/functions that help organisms to survive.
- **Grade 6:** Classifies physical and chemical changes; interprets the Periodic Table and chemical formulas; studies energy transformations, including photosynthesis, food webs, and the efficiency of simple machines; compares/contrasts cell structures/functions; distinguishes between dominant and recessive traits and predicts the probable outcomes of genetic combinations; studies Earth systems, including the rock cycle and atmospheric components; and gains knowledge of the solar system.

Consider the following practice question:

Ms. Peters has been teaching her second-grade science unit on dinosaurs by reading about dinosaurs and having students color pictures. Which activity should she add to be the most consistent with developments in science education about how students learn science?

- **A.** Have a geologist visit the classroom with her fossil collection.
- **B.** Include hands-on measurement activities to compare dinosaur size to animals of today—lifting strings with helium balloons to show and compare the heights of some dinosaurs.
- **C.** Include use of computer technology to visit an archeological site to watch a dinosaur excavation.
- **D.** Show a movie about dinosaurs and have students color more pictures of dinosaurs.

Choice *A* emphasizes careers but is not student-centered. Choices *C* and *D* stress technology, and a computer archeology site would provide a visual of authentic science. Choice *B*, however, is developmentally appropriate and in keeping with research about how second graders—who are concrete learners—best learn. The correct answer is *B*.

Understanding how students learn and making modifications, as needed, in instructional strategies are hallmarks of an effective teacher. The learning theories of Piaget and Vygotsky stress the importance of the *construction of knowledge* by the learner. Unlike a blank slate to be filled by the teacher, the child comes with experiences and prior schema (sometimes misconceptions or naïve ideas) that must be challenged. For example, many children believe that humans coexisted with dinosaurs or that changing the shape of matter changes its mass. Another important aspect in teaching science is modeling—not only modeling scientific tasks but modeling a positive attitude toward the science as well. Social learning theory tells us that children learn vicariously, so the teacher who displays scientific attributes such as curiosity, excitement about discovery, willingness to examine new ideas, skepticism, and so forth will have more success with children who will, hopefully, take on these attributes toward science, too.

The instructional strategy of the *learning cycle* fits the view of constructivists' learning theory. Often described as the *5Es*, the steps are

> Engage
> Explore
> Explain
> Elaborate
> Evaluate

First, the teacher gains attention and uses a focus to introduce the lesson. Asking questions generates curiosity about the concept, **engages** the learner, and can be a means to assess prior knowledge. By using a *KWL chart* (what I know—what I want to know—what I learned), for example, the teacher can identify concepts and misconceptions. Next, students **explore** the materials—a natural response that encourages curiosity and stimulates more questions. As a facilitator, the teacher challenges students' observations and prompts discussions. In the third step, **explaining**, it is the teacher's role to define vocabulary, clarify results, and help draw conclusions. The **elaboration** step allows the student to use and transfer the concept knowledge in a new way. These are usually extension activities or try-at-home examples that students design on their own. Finally, **evaluation** includes the ideas and examples in Standard V, which follows.

In the classroom, there are numerous programs and opportunities to include technology and enhance learning. Virtual field trips, information searches on the Internet, CD-ROM and simulation activities, data collection, and participation in programs like the international GLOBE (http://www.globe.gov) all help compress or expand time and space while ensuring safety and availability of experiences.

Consider the following practice question:

Ms. Helms recognizes that her students are struggling with a social studies chapter and the concept of community when one student declares, "Look, it's like the ants in our ant farm. Some work, some take care of the young—but together, everything can get done." Ms. Helms's best response is:

A. "Good point. But ants are animals, and people are people."
B. "Well, yes, how else can you compare these two systems?"
C. "Well, yes, but ants are just acting out of instinct."
D. "Good point. But we're studying social studies now—not science."

Using an ant farm in the first place was an excellent science lesson for Ms. Helms' students. Integrating the concrete example as a model for the abstract concept of community is developmentally appropriate and cognitively beneficial for students. Higher-order thinking through analogies establishes more cognitive connections for students. Answer *D* does not promote interdisciplinary learning, a concept supported throughout this entire test. Answers *A* and *C* do not enable students to make connections in learning. The correct answer is *B*.

Standard V

The science teacher knows the varied and appropriate assessments and assessment practices to monitor science learning.

Competency 029: Assessments and Monitoring Practices

The beginning teacher knows the relationships among curriculum, assessment, and instruction and understands the importance of monitoring and assessing students' science knowledge and skills on a regular, ongoing basis. In the area of assessment, the teacher knows the importance of validity, reliability, and absence of bias. Also, the teacher knows the purposes and uses of various types of assessments, including diagnostic (before), formative (during), and summative (after). Teachers know strategies for assessing students' prior knowledge and can use assessment to adjust instructional practice. They share evaluation criteria with students and engage students in meaningful self-assessment. In the classroom, the teacher can use formal and informal assessments of science performance, including rubrics, portfolios, journals, and checklists.

Consider the following practice question:

Mr. Garcia's fifth graders are expected to describe and illustrate the details of the water cycle. The teacher provides numerous hands-on activities for students to observe evaporation, condensation, and precipitation related to the water cycle. He asks questions during the activities and reteaches when necessary. How should the teacher grade the students on their understanding of the objective?

A. Have students complete a final written test with matching items.
B. Have students write definitions of the vocabulary.
C. Have groups present posters that describe the water cycle.
D. Have students do a self-assessment.

The teacher should grade students' understanding of the objective through multidimensional means (rather than by a single attribute [*A*]). Although definitions (*B*) might be part of the instruction, they do not allow the student to *describe or illustrate* or show understanding of the water cycle. Self-assessment (*D*), could be a factor—but not the entire grade. The presentation can be used to grade students on their activities, questions and answers, cooperative group participation, and understanding. The correct answer is *C*.

Reform efforts in science education include mandates for instruction and for assessment. We cannot continue to evaluate students with one unidimensional measurement. Knowledge and understanding should be accessed through *formal* (e.g., paper-and-pencil, standardized tests) and *informal* (e.g., journal responses, observation of labs, checklists, question/answer sessions) means. *Authentic assessment* includes observations by the teacher with a shift from a behavioral to a cognitive view of learning. Teachers should use tasks that represent meaningful instructional activities that tap productive thinking and problem-solving skills. Children should be encouraged to collect their work over time and develop portfolios or presentations of their knowledge. With multiple learning styles comes assessment through audio, visual, tactile, and kinesthetic means. For example, a student performance of the water cycle could include a skit of a water drop, the Sun, a cloud of water vapor, a thundercloud full of water, and rain, with all the processes of evaporation, condensation, and precipitation clearly represented through materials, songs, and hand motions. Assessment should also include rubrics, student profiles, pre-testing, reviewing student journals, monitoring, discussion, asking good questions, and so forth.

In addition to using a wide variety of assessments, teachers must also make sure that each measures what it says that it should measure (is valid), has consistency in measurement over time (reliable), is free from any types of bias, and has clarity of language. This enables a science teacher to gain solid evidence on exactly what children know and enables students to feel that their knowledge is measured fairly.

 **Standard VI**

> The science teacher understands the history and nature of science.
>
> **Competency 025: Scientific Inquiry, History and Nature of Science**
>
> *The beginning teacher knows the limitations of the scope of science and the use and limitations of physical, mathematical, and conceptual models to describe and analyze scientific ideas about the natural world. He or she knows that science ideas and explanations must be consistent with observational and experimental evidence but realizes that science is a human endeavor influenced by societal, cultural, and personal views of the world. Teachers understand that scientific theories are constantly being modified to conform more closely to new observational and experimental evidence about the natural world. They understand how logical reasoning is used in the process of developing, evaluating, and validating scientific hypotheses and theories. They appreciate the principles of scientific ethics and the role of publishing and peer review in the development and validation of scientific knowledge. Teachers understand the historical developments of science and respect the contributions that diverse cultures and individuals of both genders have made to the body of scientific knowledge. In the classroom, teachers can analyze, review, and critique the strengths and weaknesses of scientific explanations, hypotheses, and theories using scientific evidence and explanation. Viewing science as a way of knowing, they can provide students with opportunities to examine types of questions that science can and cannot answer. Teachers use examples from the history of science to demonstrate the changing nature of scientific theories and knowledge. They can analyze ways in which personal or societal bias can affect the direction, support, and use of scientific research and should design instruction that accounts for the contributions of individuals from a variety of cultures.*

Science is often viewed as a body of knowledge that has resulted from years of experiments. Formal science training often included the memorization of endless concepts, terms, and formulas. Today, *science education* is viewed as a verb—as a way of thinking and acting and as an expanding body of knowledge that cannot possibly be memorized. In fact, estimates of the knowledge explosion predict that scientific information doubles every 2 to 5 years. Teaching students how scientists developed their experiments and analyzed their results is much more useful than simply memorizing a definition that they may not understand. Learning about the people involved in the production of scientific knowledge gives students a sense of career awareness. They need role models, guest speakers, and diverse cultural examples to make science come alive. Learning about the struggles of science teaches lessons of persistence, patience, and the excitement of creativity and discovery.

Teachers must recognize that science is a societal enterprise that affects and is affected by society. Furthermore, scientists are human beings and capable of errors. For example, Lamarck's incorrect theory states that characteristics that beings *acquired* during their lifetimes were inherited. Errors, incomplete theories, discrepancies, hunches, guesses, new technology, and new discoveries and theories all generate new scientific activity. Governmental funding (needs of society) has greatly influenced the foci of science since World War II (e.g., nuclear energy and weaponry, the Internet). Public and private research grants have supported and directed scientific inquiry, as well as advancement in the areas of space exploration, global climate change, the human genome project, and alternative fuel production.

Numerous resources are available for the teacher to integrate the history and nature of science into the classroom. The National Public Radio presentations of Dr. John Lienhard's "Engines of Our Ingenuity" are broadcast twice daily and are available from the Web site at http://www.uh.edu/engines. A simple Web search of "scientists" gives links to women in science at http://www.astr.ua.edu/4000WS/4000ws.html, to African Americans in the sciences at http://webfiles.uci.edu/mcbrown/display/faces.html, and to numerous pages on familiar scientists such as **Albert Einstein** (theory of relativity), **Thomas Edison** (electricity), **Sir Isaac Newton** (laws of motion), **Madame Curie** (radioactivity), **Antonio Novello** (first Hispanic surgeon general), **Mae Jemison** (first African American woman in space), **Dr. Daniel Hale Williams** (African American doctor who performed the first successful heart surgery), **Louis Pasteur** (pasteurization), **Barbara McClintock** (only woman to win an unshared Nobel Prize in Physiology or Medicine for genetic research), and many others.

Students should know that **Lewis Latimer**, the son of slaves who escaped to freedom in Boston, drew the patent for **Alexander Graham Bell's** original telephone, and Latimer himself invented the carbon filament for the incandescent electric light. They should realize that **Charles Drew**, another African American, was a pioneer researcher in the area of blood plasma preservation, saving thousands of soldiers' lives in World War II through the establishment of blood banks. We can have a greater appreciation for the contributions to science made by people who overcame discrimination. Women like **Rachel Carson**, who wrote *Silent Spring* in 1962, testified before Congress and withstood the attacks of the chemical industry, who denounced her as a hysterical woman for her attention to environmental issues. Women like **Sally Ride**, who became the first U.S. woman to go into space, serve as examples for females in the classrooms today.

Consider the following practice question:

French microbiologist **Louis Pasteur** (1822–1895) is known for his development of the germ theory of disease. He used the results of his early work with the swan-neck flask and his research to show that the growth of microorganisms was responsible for spoiling beverages.

He promoted sanitation procedures for surgical equipment, and at some personal risk, he tested a rabies vaccine on a young boy. A class discussion of Louis Pasteur's swan-neck flask experiment should conclude that

A. fermentation is caused only by the growth of airborne microorganisms.
B. emergent growth of bacteria is not due to spontaneous generation but rather to biogenesis; that is, life comes from life.
C. microorganisms were present only in the boiled broth solutions.
D. legal and ethical risks of vaccines were not a concern in his day.

Using a controlled experimental design in the swan-neck experiment, Pasteur demonstrated that the popular idea of spontaneous generation was incorrect. The correct answer is *B*.

Standard VII

The science teacher understands how science affects the daily lives of students and how science interacts with and influences personal and societal decisions.

Competency 026: Impact on Societal and Personal Decisions

The beginning teacher knows the role that science can play in helping to resolve personal, societal, and global challenges. The teacher understands how human decisions about the use of science and technology are based on factors such as ethical standards, economics, and societal and personal needs. Teachers understand the properties of natural ecosystems and how natural and human processes can influence changes in the environment. They know about concepts related to changes in populations and to characteristics of human population growth that impact consumption on the renewal and depletion of resources. Finally, they understand that scientific concepts and principles relate to personal and societal health, including the physiological and psychological effects and risks associated with the use of substances and substance abuse. In the classroom, the teacher can use situations from students' everyday lives to develop materials that investigate how science can be used to make informed decisions. They can apply scientific principles to analyze factors that influence personal choices concerning fitness and health and factors that affect the probability and severity of disease. They can demonstrate how factors such as population growth, use of resources, overconsumption, technological capacity, poverty, and societal views can influence changes in the environment. Finally, they can demonstrate how science can be used to make informed decisions about societal and global issues through the analysis of advantages and disadvantages of a course of action. Science attempts to generate new knowledge. The goal is always knowledge. However, society using political or economic activity determines if, how, and when that knowledge will be used.

Understanding the relationship among *science-technology-society* (STS) helps students appreciate the need for science in their daily lives. If they can observe the pollution problems from automobiles and factories (technology) and realize that government decisions about air quality and emissions testing are possible societal responses, they can use their science information to make informed decisions. Cutting down the rainforest, using land indiscriminately for energy exploration, transporting oil in tankers that spill and pollute the oceans, overpopulation, and overconsumption are current events issues that strongly impact the future. Students can access data collected from other students throughout the world or establish their own research sites. The international GLOBE program (http://www.globe.gov) trains teachers to work with their students in authentic inquiry. Activities from tracking El Niño temperatures, tree budding times, acid rain values, and possible global climate conditions can be accomplished by classroom scientists. Teachers can also choose numerous texts that emphasize STS issues, including *Investigating and Evaluating STS Issues and Solutions* (Hungerford et al., 1997), that enhance critical thinking and problem-solving strategies by providing sample vignettes to analyze and rubrics that identify skills. Hopefully, these same students will become knowledgeable citizens of the future who can make informed and factual choices about environmental policies, land use, and government regulations that balance the needs of nature with the needs of humans.

Consider the following practice questions:

Ms. Nguyen's class is researching the effects of oil spills on the environment. She decides to focus on two incidents: the *Exxon Valdez* incident in 1989, in which an oil tanker spilled almost 40 million liters of oil into the Prince William Sound in Alaska and the British Petroleum (BP) explosion in the Gulf Coast in 2010.

The first study topic is the effects of the oil on the Alaskan environment and wildlife and on the Gulf Coast seafood industries. Which of the following activities best illustrates the effects of oil on these environments?

A. Students compare and contrast different grades of oil using a beaker and several grades of motor oil.
B. Students compare the density of oil and water using a cylinder, oil, and water.
C. Students compare results of a feather, an egg, and a sea shell that are dipped first in water and then in oil.
D. Students access video clips on the *Exxon Valdez* incident and from the BP oil rig that exploded and hear interviews about how these incidents may have occurred from scientists and engineers.

Even though the first two answers involve comparing and contrasting, which are higher-order thinking skills, they do not answer the question of which concerns the environment. The last answer is neither student centered nor addresses the question. The correct answer is *C*, which involves experimentation with actual materials and allows the student to see clearly how these incidents may have affected various animal life in the immediate environment.

Ms. Nguyen continues her study on the *Exxon Valdez* oil spill and how society can influence environmental policies as a result of such occurrences. She suggested reviewing positive outcomes that resulted from the *Exxon Valdez*. Of the many changes that resulted from the incident, which action demonstrates the effectiveness of societal actions to prevent future oil spills from occurring?

A. More volunteer sanctuaries established by the state to clean the affected animals.
B. More effective methods developed by chemical companies for cleaning oil spills.
C. Exxon establishes alternate transportation routes for oil tankers.
D. Double-hull oil tanks mandated by the federal government as a result of grassroots letter writing campaigns.

The first three answers involve changes initiated by a state or private entity. A policy being legislated as a result of citizens involved in a letter writing campaign is an example of the effectiveness of societal efforts. The correct answer is *D*.

Standard VIII

> The science teacher knows and understands the science content appropriate to teach the statewide curriculum (Texas Essential Knowledge and Skills) in physical science.
>
> **Competency 030: Physical Science (Forces, Motion, & Relationships)**
>
> **Competency 031: Physical Science (Changes in Matter—Physical & Chemical)**
>
> **Competency 032: Physical Science (Energy; Interactions of Energy & Matter)**
>
> **Competency 033: Physical Science (Energy Transformations; Conservation of Matter & Energy)**
>
> *The beginning teacher has a basic understanding of physical science concepts and processes. These include properties of objects and materials; concepts of force and motion; concepts of heat, light, electricity, and magnetism, as well as conservation of energy and energy transformations. In the classroom, the teacher conducts demonstrations and facilitates experiments and experiences that promote understanding of these ideas.*

The following lists provide key science ideas selected from concepts included in the elementary TEKS. Further explanations of these concepts can be found in biology, chemistry or physics text books, encyclopedias, and online searches and sites such as http://www.visionlearning.com/library.

Physical Science: Chemistry and Physics Key Ideas

- **Matter** is anything that occupies space and has mass. Mass and weight are not the same. **Mass** is the amount of matter in an object. **Weight** refers to the gravitational force between objects and the Earth (or another planet). For example, a person who weighs 130 pounds on Earth would weigh 275 pounds on Saturn, but only about 18 pounds on the moon; yet his or her mass would remain constant. **Density** is the ratio of mass/volume and helps explain how objects sink or float. Things that are denser contain more mass in a given volume. A bar of gold is denser than a bar of soap.
- Matter is made of basic particles called *atoms*. **Atoms** contain protons (positive charge) and neutrons in the nucleus and electrons (negative charge) in orbits outside the **nucleus** (the core of the atom). **Elements** are composed of only the same kind of atoms and cannot be broken down further by chemical processes. Molecules and compounds have combinations of two or more kinds of atoms that are sharing electrons in ionic or covalent bonds. *Ionic* refers to bonds formed when electrons are donated from one atom to another. *Covalent* refers to electrons that are shared between atoms. The bonding process creates an imbalanced electrical charge (positive and negative) between the atoms. The opposite charges attract, holding the molecule together. The **periodic table of elements** is arranged by metals, nonmetals, and metalloids, and by families with similar properties. **Metalloids** such as boron and silicon have properties of both metals and nonmetals (e.g., they are not magnetic like nonmetals, but they conduct electricity like metals). (Review the periodic chart at http://periodic.lanl.gov and http://www.chemicalelements.com/index.html.)
- **Matter** is found in four states—solid, liquid, gas, and plasma. *Plasma* is an electrically neutral, ionized gas mixture (e.g., neon signs, lightning bolts, stars) that is affected by magnetic fields and emits light. Matter converts

from one state to another by heating or cooling. When matter is heated, the **molecules** (combinations of atoms) move faster and spread farther apart so that the material expands. When cooled, most materials contract. Changing the states of matter (freezing, melting, etc.) or changing other physical characteristics is called **physical changes**, but these changes do not affect the composition of the matter at the atomic level. The atoms in water remain the same, whether boiling, frozen, or liquid, and the states can be reversed. Thus, the *properties* are not changed. **Chemical changes** do change the substance at the atomic level and can require or give off energy (such as burning, rusting, etc.), and this change cannot be reversed.

- **The Law of Conservation of Matter** states that in ordinary **chemical reactions**, matter is neither created nor destroyed but is only changed from one form to another. All the existing molecules recombine into new combinations. Chemical reactions often produce heat, gas, a color change, or a precipitate. In a **neutralization reaction**, an acid and base produce a salt and water. This law of conservation of matter, however, does not apply to radioactive substances in which atoms can break down into subatomic particles.
- **Mixtures** (e.g., saltwater) can be separated physically and are not chemical combinations. In a **solution**, the substance that dissolves (salt) is the **solute**, and the substance that does the dissolving (water) is the **solvent**.
- **Energy** is defined as the ability to do work. Energy can be changed from one form to another. Stored energy is **potential energy**. When stored energy is released, it is changed to **kinetic energy**, or motion energy. Kinetic energy depends on the mass and the speed of the object.
- **Forms of energy** include *light, heat (thermal), sound, chemical, nuclear* or *atomic, mechanical,* and *electric*. Physical interactions typically convert one form of energy to others. For example, a flashlight converts electrical energy to light and heat energy. An automobile engine converts the chemical energy in fossil fuels to mechanical energy (chemical→mechanical), and running water (potential energy) may be channeled into turning mechanical turbines that can produce electric energy.
- Energy resources can be classified as **renewable** (i.e., trees for burning), **nonrenewable** (e.g., fossil fuels, coal, oil), or **inexhaustible** (e.g., solar, wind, tides, geothermal). Our future energy use emphasizes converting from nonrenewable to inexhaustible energy sources.
- **Electricity** is a form of energy from electrons that provides light and heat. Two types of electricity are **static electricity** (when two materials rub together, and electrons are transferred) and **current electricity** (when electrical energy flows through a conductor in a circuit). **Conductors** are materials that allow the energy of electrons to move easily. **Insulators** are materials that resist the electrical flow of energy. Some types of electrical wire have conductors on the inside (the metal) and insulating materials (a plastic coating) on the outside.
- **Heat** is a form of energy that transfers from one object to another by **conduction** (contact among moving molecules in solids), by **convection** (contact among moving currents of liquids and among gases), or by **radiation** (waves from the Sun or other sources).
- **Magnets** exert a force (a push or a pull) within a region called a *magnetic field*. The **Law of Magnetic Attraction** states that two unlike poles attract each other, and two like poles repel each other. An **electromagnet** is a coil of conducting wire wrapped around a metal core. As electric current flows through the wire, the core becomes a temporary magnet. The flow of electricity in the circuit creates a magnetic field around the circuit. This field then causes the metal to become magnetic.
- **Newton's Three Laws of Motion**, established in the 1700s, explain forces (i.e., pushes or pulls). The **First Law of Motion** states that an object at rest

remains at rest unless a force acts on it to move it—that is, all objects have **inertia**, the tendency of an object to resist a change in the state of motion. This rule explains the importance of seat belts in auto accidents. **Acceleration** is any increase or decrease in the speed or direction of an object. It is related to mass and force in the following equation: $F = ma$ (force = mass × acceleration). When two forces are acting on an object, the greater force dominates. The **Third Law of Motion** states that for every action there is an equal and opposite reaction. This rule explains the forces operating in a rocket launch; that is, as the force of the combusted fuel pushes down, the rocket is pushed up. Newton's laws opened the door for scientists to determine other laws that control our world and the motion of planets in our solar system.

- **Velocity** relates the speed and direction of a moving object. **Speed** is the distance an object moves in a given period of time.
- **Gravity** is the force that pulls (attracts) all physical objects toward each other. It is the force that governs the motion and organization of our solar system.
- **Work** is force multiplied by the distance an object moves. In the metric system, force is measured in **Newtons**. Thus, work is measured in **newton-meters**, more commonly called **joules**.
- **Simple machines** change how work is done by increasing/decreasing the amount of force or speed of force applied, changing the direction of the force, or transferring the force from one place to another. Examples of simple machines include (1) *levers*—three classes of which differ by position of the fulcrum; (2) *pulleys*—fixed and movable; (3) *wheel and axle;* (4) *inclined plane;* (5) *wedge;* and (6) *screw.* **Compound machines** contain one or more simple machines.
- **Waves** are described by their wavelength (frequency), speed, and amplitude. The *electromagnetic spectrum* is an arrangement of light and other electromagnetic waves of different frequencies. The **visible spectrum** includes the seven colors of light—red, orange, yellow, green, blue, indigo, and violet. **Opaque** objects are the color of light reflected; a **transparent** object is the color of light transmitted. Light (as wave and particle) travels in a straight line until it strikes a smooth surface and is **reflected** or travels from one medium to another and is **refracted** (bent). *Laser light* is an intense, narrow beam of light of one wavelength.
- **Sound** is created by the vibrations of a material and is transmitted via a material medium that can be a solid, liquid, or gas. Solids transmit sound waves more effectively because the molecules are more densely packed. Sounds are described by their pitch (high or low) and intensity (loud or soft).

Consider the following practice questions:

Using a relevant application for science knowledge, Mr. Allen explains that the construction of homes built in the southern United States differs from those built in the northern United States in many ways. The placement of the heating/air-conditioning vents in Texas homes and buildings is usually in the ceiling because:

A. cold air is less dense than warm air, and conduction can occur.
B. warm air needs to be forced to circulate to the ceiling.
C. warm air is less dense than cold air, so it doesn't move.
D. cold air is denser than warm air, and convection can occur.

Cold air is denser than warm air and sinks to the floor as the warmer air rises, producing a convection current that moves air within the room. If the cold air is released from floor vents, the air will not circulate because the warmer, lighter air remains near the ceiling. Using knowledge of density and convection in a real-world context shows students that science is relevant to their lives. The correct answer is *D*.

In order for a force to move an object, there must be an unbalanced force applied so that the force is stronger in one direction than in the other. What happens if two people are pulling at opposite ends of a rope (as in a game of tug-o'-war), and the stronger person is pulling with a force of 5Newtons, whereas the smaller person is pulling with a force of 3Newtons?

A. Both people will fall down.
B. The smaller person will be pulled toward the stronger person.
C. The stronger person will be pulled toward the smaller person.
D. A net force of 2Newtons will be applied in the direction of the smaller person.

The unbalanced force results in a net force of 2Newtons in the direction of the greater force (the stronger person). Therefore, *B* is the correct answer.

Standard IX Life Science

The science teacher knows and understands the science content appropriate to teach the statewide curriculum (Texas Essential Knowledge and Skills) in life science.

Competency 034 Life Science (Structure & Function of Living Things)

Competency 035 Life Science (Reproduction & Mechanisms of Heredity)

Competency 036 Life Science (Theory of Evolution; Adaptation of Organisms)

Competency 037 Life Science (Relationships between Organisms & their Environment)

The beginning teacher knows and understands the fundamental concepts and processes of living systems, including the ideas that different structures perform different functions, that organisms have basic needs, and that organisms respond to external and internal stimuli. Important life science concepts include an understanding of the life cycles of organisms, the relationship between organisms and the environment, and how species and populations evolve and adapt over time. The teacher provides activities and examples and describes stages in the life cycle of common plants and animals. Through observations, students identify adaptive characteristics and explain how adaptations influence the survival of populations or species. Students compare inherited traits and learned characteristics and explain how hereditary information is passed from one generation to the next. Students can use Punnett squares to predict the probability of phenotypes based on genotypes. Students also analyze the characteristics of habitats within an ecosystem, identify organisms, populations, or species with similar needs, and analyze how they compete with one another for resources. The following provides more explanation of these ideas.

Life Science: Key Ideas

- **Living things** are able to reproduce, grow, respond to change, eliminate waste, and die. Living things **adapt** (change) to the unique conditions of their environment. They interact with and affect their environment, and the environment affects living things. Living things inherit and transmit the characteristics of their ancestors. Further, populations of living things in a particular abiotic setting (e.g., desert, salt water, soil, forest) are adapted to the physical and chemical aspects of that environment, and they also interact with other populations to transfer energy (e.g., predator–prey relationships) and cycle nutrients (e.g., carbon, nitrogen). This pattern of organization is called an **ecosystem**. Cycles that connect ecosystems with the environment permit nutrients to be reused continuously. Energy transferred through populations in an ecosystem is gradually reduced.

- Living things are currently classified in one of **six major kingdoms**: (1) **animals**, (2) **plants**, (3) **protista** (including protozoans, algae), (4) **eubacteria** (true bacteria), (5) **archaebacteria**, and (6) **fungi** (including various types of fungus, molds, mushrooms). The kingdoms are further classified into increasingly smaller groups, including **phylum**, **class**, **order**, **family**, **genus**, and **species** (then varieties and hybrids). For example, a dog's classification is:

    Kingdom—Animalia
    Phylum—Chordata (animal with backbone)
    Class—Mammalia (animal with body hair)
    Order—Carnivore (animal that eats meat)
    Family—Canidae (animal with dog-like features)
    Genus—Canis
    Species—familia

- All plants and animals are made of **cells** that come from other cells. Each cell is surrounded by a **cell membrane (or plasma membrane)** that controls what enters and exits the cell. Plant cells have a **cell wall** (an outer, rigid covering). Cells can be classified by the presence of a nucleus (*eukaryotic*) or absence of a defined nucleus (*prokaryotic*). The **nucleus** contains chromosomes made of the genetic codes called **DNA** (deoxyribonucleic acid) and controls the cell's activities. Cells obtain energy through a reaction involving **ATP** (*adenosine triphosphate*). Plant and animal cells also contain ribosomes that are crucial to producing proteins. Cells undergo the processes of **mitosis**, or the producing of two new identical cells. **Meiosis** in sex cells produces two new cells with half the original chromosomes. Groups of cells that work and function together are **tissues**. A group of tissues working together is called an **organ**, and a group of organs working together is called a **system** (e.g., the digestive system, the respiratory system). Plants, as part of their cells, also have chloroplasts that carry out the process of turning light energy into chemical energy (*photosynthesis*) and cause the plant to appear green because they contain green pigmentation.

- Living things reproduce in two ways: *sexually* and *asexually*. **Asexual reproduction** occurs in simpler species (yeasts, bacteria, etc.) when one organism (parent) produces new offspring without the involvement of another. **Sexual reproduction** occurs with male and female organisms and enhances variation in the genetic diversity, which enhances the long-term survival of the species. Gregor Mendel's work with pea plants in the 1860s identified factors such as height and color that are **inherited** (passed on to the offspring). Because the offspring inherits one factor from each parent, he began the explanation of dominant and recessive traits (genes) and the understanding of probabilities of **phenotypes** (physical appearance) based on **genotypes** (genetic combination/makeup). The Punnett square can be used to show the **probability** of inherited characteristics that are based on the maternal and paternal alleles. Depending on the characteristic, a complete dominance or an incomplete dominance (*blended inheritance*) may be exhibited. The following example shows a complete dominance situation, where the dominant alleles for round pea seeds are represented with the upper case letter (R) and the recessive allele for wrinkled pea seeds represented with the lower case letter (r). In this crossing, each parent is **heterozygous** (having both R and r alleles) and the possible combinations for offspring with one allele from each parent would be:

25% homozygous (RR) genotype is a round pea phenotype, where both parents contribute the same types of alleles

50% heterozygous (Rr) genotype is also a round pea phenotype, because R is dominant

25% homozygous recessive (rr) genotype, which is the only way this allele is expressed as a wrinkled pea phenotype

	R	r
R	RR	Rr
r	Rr	rr

- Plants undergo several life processes. **Photosynthesis** is very important because it is the sole chemical process that captures, converts, and stores solar energy. Further, it is the source of oxygen in the atmosphere. Photosynthesis involves the ability of green plants with chlorophyll to trap the Sun's energy, take in carbon dioxide and water, and produce food (carbohydrates) and oxygen. Plants, just like animals, undergo respiration using oxygen and releasing energy and carbon dioxide as byproducts. Plants also use the processes of **digestion** to break down and use nutrients, the process of **transpiration** (the evaporation of excess water through stomata, or pores, in leaves), and **capillary action** (the transportation of materials within the plant parts).
- Plants have behavior and structural **adaptations** for survival in their environment and for various other functions. Major structures for growth include **roots** (for anchoring the plant and for taking in nutrients from the ground), **stems** (for support and transportation of nutrients), and **leaves** (for making food and oxygen). Major structures for flowering plants' reproduction include (1) the **stamen** (carries the pollen on threadlike filaments within the flower), (2) the **pistil** (center tube of the flower), (3) the **petals**, and (4) the **sepals** (green structure at the very base of the flower). Fertilized egg cells from the ovary divide and multiply, eventually forming **seeds**. Each seed consists of stored food, a seed coat, and the tiny plant called an **embryo**. Seeds need favorable conditions to germinate and grow. Temperature, water, and air are all external variables that affect seed germination. These factors and sunlight affect plant growth.
- Animals are commonly divided into two groups—animals with backbones, called **vertebrates**, and animals without backbones, called **invertebrates.**
- The vast majority of animals are invertebrates and include the phyla of *arthropods* (insects, crayfish), *mollusks* (clam, oyster, snail), *echnioderms* (starfish, sea urchins), *annelids* (earthworms, leeches), *aschelminths* (hookworms, pinworms), *platyhelminths* (tapeworm—a parasite living and feeding in its host), *coelenterates* (jellyfish, coral), and *poriferans* (sponges).
- **Insects** have three body parts—the *head* (with a pair of antennae), the *thorax* (with three pairs of legs and two sets of wings), and an *abdomen*. Some insects undergo complete **metamorphosis** with four stages of change—egg, larva, pupa, and adult, where the adult looks very different from the other stages. Other insects undergo *partial* (or *incomplete*) *metamorphosis* with three stages—egg, nymph, and adult. Often, the adult may not change very much in appearance from the nymph except for

developing wings. Some insects are social and live in colonies with genetically defined, specialized roles (bee societies that include the queen, drones, and workers). **Spiders** (class arachnida) are not insects; they are arthropods with eight legs.

- The chordate phyla have backbones and include classes of fish, mammals, reptiles, birds, and amphibians.

- **Fish** breathe through gills located on each side of the head that exchange the dissolved oxygen in the water and release carbon dioxide, a byproduct of cell respiration. Fish are cold-blooded animals with fins; their body temperature is the same as that of surrounding water.

- **Amphibians** (including frogs, toads, and salamanders) are also cold-blooded and live in water in young stages but live on land near water as adults.

- **Reptiles** (including turtles, snakes, and alligators) are cold-blooded, breathe through lungs, and have rough, thick, dry skin.

- **Birds** have porous or hollow bones that make them lighter and able to fly. They are **warm-blooded**, which means that their body temperature remains the same regardless of the temperature around them. Many birds migrate, or move at different times during the year, because of unfavorable weather conditions. **Egg incubation** is the process of adults' sitting and warming the eggs until they hatch.

- **Mammals** have hair (even a whale has a few bristles), have lungs for breathing, are warm-blooded, and usually have live young that are fed milk through mammary glands. Mammals have many adaptations for living in different environments. Some of those adaptations are very similar from animal to animal, and some are very different. Bats use a guided flying process, detecting objects through sound echolocation. Whales, dolphins, and porpoises have lungs but live only in oceans. Some mammals (e.g., woodchucks) hibernate all winter. Others (e.g., bears, skunks) have a long winter sleep during which inactivity and slowed breathing allow survival using stored food during harsh weather. *Survival of the fittest* means that those animals that have adapted to the conditions in which they live often are able to continue the species.

- **Humans** are mammals and use other animals to do work and to provide food and clothing for them. Many humans have also tried to protect animals that are **endangered** (few in number) and have worked hard to prevent **extinction** (no longer exist on this planet). Human activity has resulted in many endangered and extinct plants and animals. Climatic changes have also resulted in extinction of many plants and animals throughout the history of the Earth (e.g., the dinosaurs). Dinosaurs and other plants and animals lived long before humans, but **fossils** can show us evidence of many of these and are able to tell us much about the environment during the time in which they lived.

- The human body is made of millions of tiny cells that undertake specialized work. Five main types of tissues include *muscle, nerve, epithelial, connective tissue,* and *blood.* The main *body systems* include: *skin, skeletal* (femur, radius, etc.), *muscular* (triceps, pectoral muscles, etc.), *digestive* (stomach, liver, etc.), *circulatory* (heart, blood, etc.), *respiratory* (lungs, trachea, etc.), *excretory* (kidneys, bladder, etc.), *nervous* (brain, spinal cord, etc.), *reproductive* (gonads, ovaries, etc.), and *endocrine* (pituitary, thyroid, etc.).

- Three main areas of the body are the head, or *cranial cavity,* which holds the brain; the chest, or *thoracic cavity,* which includes the heart and lungs; and the *abdominal cavity,* which contains the stomach, intestines, liver, pancreas, kidneys, bladder, and reproductive organs.

- The human **heart** is strong muscle tissue that acts like a pump by contracting and relaxing. It has two sides separated by a wall called the *septum.* It has four chambers—two *atria* and two *ventricles.* The right atrium receives blood from the veins and pumps it into the right ventricle, where it is then pumped into the lungs to exchange carbon dioxide (a by-product of cell respiration) for oxygen (necessary for respiration). The blood returns to the left atrium and is pumped to the left ventricle and into parts of the body through a large artery. The heart, arteries, and veins along with small, branching capillaries make a closed **circulatory system**.

- The **respiratory system** includes the nose, nasal passages, throat (*pharynx*), windpipe (*trachea*), voice box (*larynx*), *bronchial tubes* (bronchi), *alveoli* (clusters of little air sacs), and the lungs.
- Knowledge of genetics, antibodies, vaccines, and immunity continues to give us new procedures to protect us from bacteria and viruses. The history of medicine provides examples of how scientists obtain, modify, and advance their knowledge.

Try the following practice questions:

Ms. Garcia's third graders are studying animal habitats and food chains. She wants her children to know that the herbivores in an ecosystem depend on which of the following organisms for their survival?

A. Carnivores
B. Omnivores
C. Producers
D. Decomposers

In a food chain, *producers* (plants) use the Sun's energy to make their own food. *Consumers* eat either the producers (plants) or other consumers to obtain energy. Consumers can be classified as *herbivores* (plant-eaters), *carnivores* (meat-eaters), or *omnivores* (eating both animals and plants). For example, the hamburger patty that you may eat (as a consumer—omnivore) came from a cow (a consumer—herbivore) that ate grass (a producer). The grass trapped the energy of the Sun in order to grow, and this energy is passed throughout the food chain. The correct answer is *C*. (Review food chains and energy transfer at http://www.marietta.edu/~biol/102/ecosystem.html and at http://www.usoe.k12.ut.us/curr/science/sciber00/8th/energy/sciber/intro.htm)

Organisms survive in their environments because of inherited traits and learned behaviors. Which of the following characteristics of a dog is most likely inherited from its parents?

A. Obesity
B. Limping
C. Fur color
D. Ability to bark on command

Although a dog may exhibit all of the characteristics listed, only fur color is *inherited*—passed on through the genetic material of the parents. The other traits are *acquired* during the dog's lifetime and are not able to be inherited. The correct answer is *C*.

Standard X Earth and Space Science

The science teacher knows and understands the science content appropriate to teach the statewide curriculum (Texas Essential Knowledge and Skills) in Earth and Space science.

Competency 038 Earth & Space Science (Structure & Function of Earth Systems)

Competency 039 Earth & Space Science (Cycles in Earth Systems)

Competency 040 Earth & Space Science (Role of Energy in Weather & Climate)

Competency 041 Earth & Space Science (Characteristics of Solar System & Universe)

*The beginning teacher knows and understands the properties of Earth materials, as well as changes in the Earth system. Students should participate in investigations of properties and uses of rocks, soils, and water. For example, they can test properties of soil, including texture, capacity to retain water, and the ability to support life. Students should describe characteristics of weather and collect data with simple weather instruments. The teacher assists students with models that demonstrate changes in the Earth's surface due to earthquakes, weathering, glaciers, and so on. Finally, the teacher can describe the basic characteristics of the Sun, moon, and stars—especially the position of the planets in relation to the Sun and the consequences of the moon's orbit around the Earth (**phases of the moon** each month), the **Earth's orientation** (23 degree tilt) and movement around the Sun (a year), and the **Earth's rotation** (spin) on its axis (day, night). The **Earth's tilt** increases the amount of direct sunlight striking the sections of the Earth that tilt toward the Sun (in summer) and decreases the amount of sunlight in those sections tilted away from the Sun (in winter). As the Earth moves (**revolves**) around the Sun every 365 days, the sections receiving more-direct and less-direct sunlight change and reverse. The combination of tilt, revolution, and energy transfer act together to cause weather changes and seasons. The Earth's rotation on its axis moves a given position on the Earth's surface into the path of sunlight and then away from that path. Sunrise, daytime, sunset, and night are the result.*

Earth Science: Key Ideas

- The solid section of the Earth contains four major layers. The **inner core**; the **outer core**; the **mantle**, consisting mainly of rock; and the **crust**, which is the thin (3 to 30 miles) outer layer on which life exists.
- There are three basic types of rocks found on Earth—**igneous** (rocks formed from cooled magma such as granite), **sedimentary** (rocks formed by pressing soft sediment together, such as sandstone), and **metamorphic** (rocks formed from other types of rocks that have been heated and pressed together, such as marble). All are formed of one or more minerals. The rock cycle is a description of the mixing and changing of rock material found in the Earth (e.g., some sedimentary rocks under pressure become metamorphic rocks). These changes result from heat, melting, cooling, chemical reactions, and pressure. Rocks are classified by physical characteristics and rated by *luster* (shine), *specific gravity* (mass/volume), and *hardness* (on the **Mohs scale**). The mass (weight) of rocks can also be measured using a balance scale.
- **Continental drift** refers to the theory that all land masses were once joined together as a single unit called *Pangaea* and have since moved apart to form separate continents. The evidence includes the apparent "puzzle-fit" of the current continents, the similarity in fossil record among continents, and similar climate and mountain range locations.
- Studies of the age and appearance of the ocean floor helped scientists form the theory of **plate tectonics**, explaining that the upper layer of the Earth's surface is made of approximately 20 huge plates that move in different directions causing spreading, colliding, and fracture/fault

boundaries. The major tectonic plates include Eurasian, African, Indo-Australian, Pacific, North American, and South American.

- **Earthquakes** and **volcanoes** occur most often at plate boundaries as the plates push against each other. Volcanoes can arise from these pushing forces, forming *shield*, *cone*, and *composite cones* and releasing hot, molten rock materials, as well as sulfurous gases as soot and dust particles. *Shield volcanoes* are large, gentle rounded shapes lined with vents where very fluid lava flows for long distances (e.g., Mauna Lea in Hawaii). *Cone volcanoes* eject cinder particles (rock fragments) from a single vent. The particles fall directly around the vent, building into a typical cone shape (Paricutan, Mexico). *Composite cones* are steep-sided and made of layers of lava and cinders that build over time (Mt. St. Helens). Earthquakes also can result from plate pressure. Their intensity is measured by a seismograph and compared on the Richter scale.

- Other Earth processes that cause change include the formation and **movement of glaciers** and **weathering** by **wind erosion**, **water erosion**, and *freezing* and *thawing*. Ancient glaciers are responsible for cutting deep gashes in the Earth's surface, sometimes hundreds of miles long, that can fill with water (fjords, the Great Lakes). Other forces can also create landforms. Silting creates *deltas* where large rivers flow into the sea. *Canyons* are carved mainly by water erosions, and *sand dunes* are created by wind erosion.

- Earth's **atmosphere** is divided into several layers. The **troposphere** (closest to the Earth and the layer in which we live) consists of 78 percent nitrogen, 21 percent oxygen, and 1 percent other gases, including helium and carbon dioxide. The next layer is the **stratosphere**, with its ozone layer that absorbs the Sun's ultraviolet radiation, a health risk to many living things. The next layer is the **mesosphere**, followed by the **ionosphere**, and finally the **thermosphere**.

- The **water cycle** consists of the movement of water between the Earth's surface and the atmosphere. The water cycle includes (1) **precipitation**—the collecting and falling of water from clouds to the Earth (rain, snow, sleet, hail, etc.); (2) **accumulation**—the movement of surface and ground water in streams, lakes, underground tables, rivers, and oceans; (3) **evaporation** from the water's surface (almost 80% to 90% from the oceans) due to heat or wind; and (4) **condensation** of water vapor in the air to water droplets due to cooling, forming clouds. The Earth's surface, land forms, air temperature, and wind (caused by uneven heating of land and water surfaces) all contribute to our climate and weather conditions. **Acid rain** is the result of environmental pollutants in the atmosphere that combine with water in the water cycle. The acid conditions can be damaging to metals, sedimentary rock, aquatic habitats, and plants and animal life.

- Our planet (Earth) is just one of eight in our **solar system** that also includes *moons* (natural satellites that orbit a planet), *asteroids* (space debris that drift around the Sun, particularly between Mars and Jupiter), dwarf planets, *comets* (space debris believed to consist of rock, ice, dust, and gases that presents with a vapor tail), and *meteors* (space matter that enters the Earth's atmosphere, creating a shooting, or falling, "star" as it burns). In orbit around the Sun are the inner planets—Mercury, Venus, Earth, Mars—and then the gas giants—Jupiter, Saturn, Uranus, and Neptune. Our Sun is a **star** (a giant ball of glowing gas) radiating energy (heat and light).

- Our solar system is located in one of the spiral arms of the Milky Way galaxy—one of many **galaxies** (large grouping of stars, gas, and dust held together by gravity) in the universe.

- Our **moon** is a satellite of our planet that revolves around the Earth and reflects the Sun's light. The moon has nine phases each month (new, waxing crescent, first quarter, waxing gibbous, full, waning gibbous, last quarter, waning crescent, and new again), depending on its position. The gravity of the moon pulls the water on Earth, causing high and low tides.

Consider the following question:

In which of these ways can volcanoes build up new land?

    A. Add heat to expand the Earth's surface
    B. Add lava to the Earth's surface
    C. Create gases and water vapor
    D. Change the type of rock on the Earth

Volcanoes can form new land through the process of eruption of lava (molten rock) that cools. Remember the question asks how volcanoes can add new land. Although volcanoes do all of the choices shown, the only way that actual land is added is when *magma* (molten rock below the surface of the Earth) is expelled. When it is above the surface, it is termed *lava*. The correct answer is *B*.

Try this practice question:

Which of the following factors causes seasons on Earth?

    A. The Earth's rotation on its axis and size of the Sun
    B. The Earth's magnetic field and distance from the Sun
    C. The size of the solar system in relation to the Sun
    D. The tilt of the Earth's axis and its orbit around the Sun

The **seasons** of the Earth are a result of its tilt on its axis and its orbit around the Sun. When the Sun's rays are more direct on the Northern Hemisphere, it experiences summer and the Southern Hemisphere is in winter. The reverse happens when the Sun's rays are more direct on the Southern Hemisphere (summer) and less direct on the Northern Hemisphere (winter). The correct answer is *D*.

Standard XI Unifying Themes

The science teacher knows unifying concepts and processes that are common to all sciences.

Competency 027 Unifying Concepts and Processes

The beginning teacher knows that scientific literacy relates not only to facts and information but also to understanding the connections that make this information useful and relevant. The teacher knows how the concepts and processes that follow provide a unifying framework across science disciplines:

- *Systems, order, and organization*
- *Evidence, models, and explanations*
- *Change, constancy, and measurements*
- *Evolution and equilibrium*
- *Form and function*

Teachers realize that systems and subsystems can be used as a conceptual framework to organize and unify the common themes of science and technology. They know that patterns in observations and data help to explain natural phenomena and allow predictions to be made.

In the classroom, the teacher can apply the systems model to identify and analyze common themes that occur in physical, life, Earth, and space sciences. They can analyze a system (the ocean, a cell, a flashlight) and general features of a system (input, process, output, feedback). They can analyze the interactions that occur between the components of a given system or subsystem and can use the system to model and analyze the concepts of constancy and change.

Consider, for example, a human being as a whole. The whole can be broken down into an organization of systems (e.g., circulatory, nervous, excretory). These systems have interacting subsystems (e.g., circulatory system has a gas transfer subsystem [lungs], a liquid transfer subsystem [blood with plasma and various cell types], a transportation subsystem [arteries, veins, and capillaries], and a distribution center [the heart] that sends and receives blood). This system works in dynamic equilibrium, perhaps at about 75 heartbeats per minute in normal physical activity. This equilibrium rate changes as activity changes (decreases during sleep and increases during physical exertion). The human heart has changed over evolutionary history into a four-chambered structure that works effectively and efficiently with the system components (i.e., the form is functional). Two heart chambers receive blood; two heart chambers send blood; and valves control flow between the chambers. Heart muscle tissue contracts, pushing the blood from a chamber. In general, the concepts listed at the beginning of this section can be applied across disciplines in a variety of natural events.

In the classroom, **interdisciplinary emphasis** (between content areas— e.g., science and math are discussed in the AIMS program at http://www.aimsedu.org) enables the teacher to reinforce learning and fit curricular pieces together. This can help children see how no content area "stands alone" in real life. Every science teacher is also a reading teacher who is able to help children with skills, such as how to find content-related vocabulary terms in resources such as the dictionary, a thesaurus, a glossary, and through technology. Science should also have an **intradisciplinary** focus that is relevant and meaningful (lessons that combine many of the sciences; not just separate life, Earth, and physical lessons).

Consider the following practice question:

A new fourth-grade teacher is challenged by the demands of district curriculum guides, low state test scores, and preparation for all the content areas of a self-contained classroom. The teacher proposes the following solution at a team meeting:

A. Have the principal hire a science specialist.
B. Have all the fourth-grade teachers share ideas and develop integrated units.
C. Have all the fourth-grade teachers concentrate only on content areas assessed on the state test.
D. Have guest speakers come in more often.

The fourth-grade TEKS require students to identify patterns of change, such as in weather, metamorphosis, and objects in the sky. An **integrated unit** about weather could include science process skills of observation and data collection, organizing, and reporting. It could also engage students in writing, reading, and research (language art requirements). Fiction and non-fiction trade books could also be added for the students' enrichment. The data collection and graphing provide authentic opportunities in mathematics and social studies for investigations of science careers, severe weather's impact on society, and climates and conditions around the world. Science is a part of our daily lives, and its integration with other content areas can only help students to learn more. It is not an option to not teach science (*C*). Although speakers (*D*) and specialists (*A*) could be used for additional instruction, the self-contained classroom teacher best knows how to maximize effective content connections. The correct answer is *B*.

A TExEs Science Assignment

In the classroom, a teacher facilitates the following long-term investigation of mealworms Your task now is to analyze and evaluate this student-centered science activity for its compliance with the standards. The results yield examples of the unifying concepts of systems, change, properties, patterns, models, and survival, all embedded within the format of this investigation.

MEALWORM INQUIRY PROJECT FOCUS. Children are given a "critter" population (5 to 10 mealworms). Their task is to diligently observe and record what they see and learn. This population will change over the next few weeks.

DIRECTIONS TO THE STUDENTS. You need a wide-mouth, transparent container with a small amount of dry oatmeal. The critter (mealworms) population should be maintained at room temperature and sustained with a small slice of apple or potato. The slice should be changed regularly. Because the population cannot escape, a lid is not needed. The population might, however, be transferred temporarily to a flat surface (like a shoebox lid or wax paper) for easier study. The critters are not harmful; they do not transmit disease. They are, however, fragile and must be handled with care. The log/diary will be submitted for grading after at least 6 weeks of observation.

THE LOG SHOULD:

A. contain a minimum of two to three observation entries per week, noting changes and behaviors of the critters. The observations should be dated and organized into a systematic format of your choice.
B. reflect an inquiring mind. Communicate questions, feelings, speculations, predictions, and intuitive leaps that you experience as you are, indeed, thinking about what you see.
C. communicate evidence of informal "sciencing." Devise and try simple experiments. Report what you tried, what happened, and what you learned. You should also communicate ideas you would like to try but could not, given consideration of the animal, safety, time, or equipment.
D. contain a number of simple labeled drawings that visually communicate observations.
E. contain a one- to two-page summary of what was observed and what was learned about these critters. A small group will meet and report/share findings in order to coordinate a master report to be presented to the class.

Lesson Evaluation Using the Standards

The critter assignment is inquiry based and student centered, encouraging higher-order thinking, as well as promoting curiosity and independent student sciencing. Obviously, the basic science concept of metamorphosis is investigated, as well as basic needs requirements and care for living things. Use of laboratory and instructional materials is encouraged, and metric rulers, scales, and magnifying lenses are all available. The assignment addresses safety with regard to the harmless nature of the critters and the materials used for observation. The science process skills are emphasized as observations are used to make and test hypotheses. Students must take measurements to collect and organize data and, finally, to present findings through scientific communication.

The assignment is authentic and parallels how scientists would approach the process of learning about the natural world. The observations lead to experimental designs with testable hypotheses that can be repeated. Students can find out if the critters prefer light or dark, respond to sound, and eat more oatmeal or cornflakes. Students can also answer other original questions. The assignment stresses interdisciplinary learning as it integrates language arts through journal writing and reporting, mathematics through measurement and graphing, and fine arts through drawings with details.

Recent developments and research in science education have reinforced the use of discovery, inquiry, cooperative group reports, science process skills, and the use of technology for research. Mealworm information can be found online at http://www.reachoutmichigan.org/funexperiments/quick/eric/mealworm.html.

REFERENCES

Heller, R. (1995). *How to hide a meadow frog*. New York: Grosset & Dunlap.
Hungerford, H. R., Volk, T. L., & Ramsey, J. M. (1997). *Science-technology-society. Investigating and evaluating STS issues and solutions.* Champaign, IL: Stipes Publishing.
National Research Council. (1996). *National science education standards*. Washington, D.C.: National Academy Press.
Texas Essential Knowledge and Skills (TEKS) access at http://www.tea.state.tx.us/teks

RESOURCES

Information for science teachers working with students with disabilities includes
- National Science Teachers position statements at http://www.nsta.org
- Ed Keller's Internet page: Inclusion in Science Education for Students with Disabilities at http://www.as.wvu.edu/~scidis

A SCIENCE LESSON PLAN

Title of Lesson: Camouflage (How Organisms Utilize Camouflage for Survival)

Grade Level: Third or Fourth

Main Subject Area: Science

Integrated Subjects: Science, Mathematics, Language Arts/Reading, Technology

Time Frame/Constraints: One science period

Overall Goal(s): To help students understand how important camouflage is for animals' survival and how environmental changes can cause animals to change and/or become endangered.

TEKS OBJECTIVES:

§ 112.5.3.9. (3.9) **Science**: Science concepts. The student knows that species have different adaptations that help them survive and reproduce in their environment. The student is expected to: (A) observe and identify characteristics among species that allow each to survive and reproduce; (B) analyze how adaptive characteristics help individuals within a species to survive and reproduce; (3.10) Science concepts. The student knows that many likenesses between offspring and parents are inherited from the parents. The student is expected to: (B) identify some inherited traits of animals;

§ 110.5. **English Language Arts and Reading** (b) Knowledge and skills; (29) Listening and Speaking/Listening. Students use comprehension skills to listen attentively to others in formal and informal settings. (30) Listening and Speaking/Speaking. Students speak clearly and to the point, using the conventions of language. Students are expected to speak coherently about the topic under discussion, employing eye contact, speaking rate, volume, enunciation, and the conventions of language to communicate ideas effectively. (31) Listening and Speaking/Teamwork. Students work productively with others in teams (20) Writing/Expository and Procedural Texts. Students write expository and procedural or work-related texts to communicate ideas and information to specific audiences for specific purposes. Students are expected to: (i) establish a central idea in a topic sentence; (ii) include supporting sentences with simple facts, details, and explanations; and (iii) contain a concluding statement.

§ 111.15. (3.13) **Mathematics**: Probability and statistics. The student solves problems by collecting, organizing, displaying, and interpreting sets of data. The student is expected to: (A) collect, organize, record, and display data in pictographs and bar graphs where each picture or cell might represent more than one piece of data; (B) interpret information from pictographs and bar graphs;

§ 126.2. **Technology**: Technology Applications (5) Information acquisition. The student acquires electronic information in a variety of formats, with appropriate supervision. The student is expected to: (A) acquire information, including text, audio, video, and graphics.

LESSON OBJECTIVES:

(Note: As a discovery lesson, the teacher should not give the objectives to the students until after students are able to go through discovering the concept.)

- Students will watch a puppet demonstration on "hungry birds" and participate in a relay to collect "worms" (yarn pieces) of different colors.
- Students will listen to *How to Hide a Meadow Frog* (Heller, 1995).
- Students will classify data and compare graphic results with other groups.
- Students, in groups, will search in magazines and on the Web for camouflaged animals to construct a poster of at least eight animals (four examples and four non-examples).
- Students will write at least four sentences in a paragraph describing his or her camouflaged animals using correct terminology of predator/prey. Students will predict the survival of a camouflage/non-camouflage organism.
- Students will orally present their posters.
- Students will watch a PowerPoint presentation, find camouflaged animals, and vote on the best camouflaged animal.

Readiness Skills or Prior Knowledge Needed: None

Sponge Activity: Children quickly draw their favorite bird.

Environmental Concerns: Lesson plan is written in the 5E's (constructivist's framework). It needs to be a nice day with dry ground. (Safety issues: check outside area for glass or other dangerous items on the ground; explain relay rules—no pushing; one "worm" only per turn).

Rationale(s): There are many, many animals that live in our neighborhoods—even if we live in a city. Many other animals live in the rural areas of Texas. One way that they stay alive is by blending in with their environments so no one sees them easily. Because animals are sometimes difficult to see because of camouflage, we must be careful about animals and their environments so that they can continue to live in their home areas (*habitats*).

Focus or Induction Set: The teacher should go outside prior to the lesson and scatter the "worms" (yarn pieces) on the grass. Using a bird puppet, the teacher should question students about why the puppet "is crying" (it is hungry and needs to look for food). On a KWL chart, the teacher should quickly write down what students know about the diet of birds and how baby birds are fed (making sure *worms* is on the list). The teacher asks children to pretend that they are birds and go outside and find some food. The teacher then sets up relay teams of three or four members to go outside to hunt for food. Because the little bird is a puppet, the teacher should tell students that he likes "yarn worms." Students run the relay quickly for the previously scattered "worms." (The discovery should be that children realize that predators cannot easily see prey that is the same color as the environment (blends in)—but this should come out later.)

MAKING CONNECTIONS:

(Give after the concept has been discovered.)

1. **Connections to Past or Future Learning:** Do you see or hear the word *camouflage* related to man in anyway? Show pictures of soldiers and equipment from Iraq or Afghanistan with camouflage uniforms, and ask why they think the army selected these types of uniforms.
2. **Connections to the Community:** What animals live in your neighborhood? Are they easy to see or not? If so, how are they camouflaged?

3. **Cultural Connections:** Can you think of any cultures that use camouflage and why? (Tribes in rainforest areas are hunters, and they do not want their prey to see them; they do not have grocery stores to do shopping, so they must hunt for everything they eat; many tattoo their bodies in patterns so that they blend in with the forest).

4. **Connections to Student Interests & Experiences:** What type of camouflage would you wear if you wanted to hide in your room? On the playground? Why?

Materials: Multi-colored yarn "worms"—2-inch pieces (50 each; try to have one set of worms that matches the color of the ground); party hats for beaks, markers, graph paper, nature magazines/pictures with animals.

Activities: Guided Practice:

Explore: Have each team organize their data showing the number of each different color worm and make a graph. Have groups share and compare graphs, noting how they are the same and different. Make a class graph with all the data and do more comparison of each group's graph.

Explain: (concept introduction, terminology) Using the class graph, explain that there were 50 of each color worm that were scattered in the habitat and discuss the conditions of the habitat—green grass, partially brown dirt areas, and so forth. Read the book *How to Hide a Meadow Frog* (Heller, 1995) and explain the terminology *predator/prey, endangered/extinct*. Explain how the green and brown worms were able to hide in the habitat and, therefore, are better able to survive and reproduce. The yellow, red, and blue worms were more obvious and were hunted to the point of being endangered or extinct.

Elaborate: (concept application—camouflage works in nature, as well as in the colored yarn activity). In groups, have students cut out pictures from nature magazines or print pictures that show examples of animals using camouflage and non-examples of animals not camouflaged and paste them on a poster.

Independent Practice: Each student writes a short paragraph about his or her animal, including where it lives, what preys on it, how it protects itself through camouflage, and why it is more likely to survive than the non-example. Each paragraph should contain at least four sentences and include the words *predator* and *prey*. Each student shows and orally describes his or her poster.

Assessment: Each student must have at least two pictures in his or her "square" (an example and a non-example). Each student should write a short paragraph about their camouflaged animal (including where it lives, what preys on it, and how it protects itself through camouflage). Each student gives correct information orally about his or her camouflaged animal and why it is more likely to survive.

What Will Students Do Who Finish Early? Students will go to the following Web site and pick out a camouflaged animal, print out the information for the chosen animal, and follow the directions for coloring: http://www.enchantedlearning.comcoloring/camouflage.shtml.

Closure: Prepare a PowerPoint presentation that shows a number of camouflaged animal pictures and have students try to "Find the Critter" (similar to http://www.longhorncattle.com/camo2.html). Students will vote on the best camouflaged animal.

Modification for Students with Special Needs: Brianna will only write two sentences for credit.

Reflection: To be addressed after teaching the lesson.

DRAFT YOUR OWN SCIENCE LESSON PLAN

Remember that discovery lessons should be taught often in science. When using discovery, be sure to think of the 5 E's and deliver instruction so that Explanation follows Exploration. If using discovery, be sure to share objectives or other parts of the lesson that might give the concept away only *after* the discovery activity.

Title of Lesson: _____

Grade Level: _____

Main Subject Area: _____

Integrated Subjects: _____

Time Frame/Constraints: _____

Overall Goal(s): _____

TEKS Objectives: _____

_____

_____

Lesson Objective(s): _____

_____

_____

Readiness Skills or Prior Knowledge Needed: _____

_____

_____

Sponge Activity: _____

_____

_____

Environmental Concerns: _____

_____

_____

Rationale(s): _____

_____

_____

Focus or Set Induction: _____

_____

_____

Making Connections:

1. Connections to Past or Future Learning: _____

_____

2. Connections to the Community: _____

_____

3. Cultural Connections: _____

_____

4. Connections to Student Interests & Experiences: _____

_____

Materials: _____
_____
_____

Activities: Guided practice: _____
_____
_____
_____
_____
_____
_____
_____
_____
_____
_____

Independent practice: _____
_____
_____
_____
_____
_____
_____
_____
_____
_____
_____

Assessment: _____
_____
_____

What Will Students Do Who Finish Early? _____
_____
_____

Closure: _____
_____
_____

Modification for Students with Special Needs: _____
_____
_____

Reflection: _____
_____
_____
_____

OBSERVING SCIENCE EXPERIENCES/ACTIVITIES

During your visit to an EC-6 classroom, use the following form to provide feedback, as well as to reflectively analyze the room, the materials, and the teacher.

The Classroom Environment	Observed	Not Observed	Response
1. Science lessons are taught with other content area (or integrated) on a daily basis.			If so, about how much time is spent on science? If not, how could some other content areas be integrated into the lesson?
2. The science lesson is clearly inquiry based.			If so, was it effective? If not, what could be changed to make it effective?
3. A demonstration was included in the lesson.			If so, describe. Was it effective? If not, what type of activity might be included?
4. A hands-on lab was included.			If so, describe. Was it effective? If not included, how did children participate?
5. Safety issues were discussed prior to the lesson (if inclusive of a lab or other needed activity).			If so, describe. If not, what should have been included?
6. Lab materials were ready for students.			If not, what was the result?
7. The teacher demonstrated the process for a lab.			If so, was it effective? If not, what could be changed to make it effective?
8. The teacher had written guidelines for the lab for students.			If so, were they effective? If not, what could be changed to make them effective?
9. The lab had an assessment component.			If so, was it effective? If not, what could be changed to make it effective?
10. The teacher monitored students during the lab.			If so, what was the result? If not, what was the result and what should change?
11. Formative assessment was conducted.			If so, was it effective? If not, what could be changed to make it effective?
12. The seating arrangement allowed for all children to be able to see any demonstrations.			If not, what should be changed to make it more effective?
13. There are Science Centers in the room that include hands-on materials for free experimentation in science.			If so, describe. Do they seem interesting and appropriate? If not included, or not interesting, what materials and activities could be included?
14. Long-term Science Centers are set up in the classroom (aquariums, terrariums, insect metamorphosis, etc.).			If so, describe and tell if they are well cared for and well presented. Do children have a part in their care? If not a part of the classroom, what could be added?
15. A classroom pet or other animal is set up in the classroom.			If so, describe. Do children have a responsibility in the care? If so, is it appropriate? Why or why not? If not, what type of classroom pet would be easy to add?

The Classroom Environment	Observed	Not Observed	Response
16. If a classroom pet or other animal is available, there are rules for its care posted or known by all children.			If so, describe. If not, what should be added?
17. Science safety equipment is readily available for teacher and student use.			If so, describe. If not, what should be added?
18. The environment of the classroom during science is one of encouraging multiple answers.			If so, describe. If not, what could be changed?
19. Higher-level questioning was a part of the science lesson.			If so, describe. If not, what should be added?
20. An exciting focus opened the lesson.			If so, describe. If not, describe one that could have been employed.
21. Trade books and other reading materials on science (both factual and "sci-fi") exist in a classroom library.			If so, describe. If not, what materials could be included?
22. All science equipment in the room is set up safely for use (no unsecured electrical cords, materials are easy to reach, etc.).			If so, describe. If not, describe how the room could be made safe.
23. Technology is integrated with the science lesson.			If so, describe. If not, how could this change?
24. Technology is available for students' use in science lessons or in science centers.			If so, describe. If not, how could this change?
25. The science lesson took into account children's developmental levels according to Piaget (e.g., with issues of conservation, reversibility, transformation, concreteness).			If so, describe. If not, what aspects should be addressed?
26. The teacher involved all children in the lesson.			Describe the balance of involvement. If not all were involved, what kinds of children were not?
27. The teacher was positive about science.			If so, describe. If not, tell why it is important to be positive.
28. There was student-to-student interaction during the lesson.			If so, describe. If not, tell why it is important to have this type of interaction.
29. An appropriate closure is used to end the lesson.			If so, describe. If not, what could be used?
30. The teacher used the 5 E's in the science lesson.			If so, describe. If not, how could these be added?

TEST YOURSELF ON SCIENCE

1. Mrs. Cronin's fourth-grade class is studying hermit crabs. Her class has two hermit crabs in an aquarium habitat. During spring break, the school will be closed for a week. Which of the following solutions is the best one to care for the hermit crabs during the vacation?
   A. Put a weeks' worth of food and water out for the hermit crabs; place near a window and provide shade.
   B. Ask a responsible student, with parental permission, to take care of the hermit crabs into his or her home.
   C. Ask the custodian, with the principal's permission, to check and feed/water the hermit crabs.
   D. Release the hermit crabs on the school grounds.

2. One day a hermit crab escaped from the aquarium and traveled across the classroom. What unit of measurement would the students use to determine how far the hermit crab traveled?
   A. Meter
   B. Ruler
   C. Gram
   D. Liter

3. Use the table to answer the following question:

Milligram (mg)	1,000 mg = 1 g
Gram (g)	base unit
Kilogram (kg)	1,000 g = 1 kg

   Mrs. Cronin's students wanted to fill the hermit crabs' aquarium with sand. She gave them a sack of sand that weighed 3 kilograms. How many grams did the sack of sand weigh?
   A. 30 grams
   B. 300 grams
   C. 3,000 grams
   D. 30,000 grams

4. Mr. Lewis is teaching his first-grade students about living organisms and non-living objects. Which of the following activities promote critical thinking in his students?
   A. A scientist visits the class and discusses the differences between plants and rocks.
   B. Students copy and color pictures of a leaf, a rock, a flower, and an insect from their textbooks.
   C. Students are given a pumpkin, a rock, a snail, and a coffee mug to compare and contrast.

   D. Students review Web sites that discuss the characteristics of living organisms and non-living objects.

5. Coral is found in warm ocean waters and provides protection and a habitat for many ocean organisms. Coral is classified as a(n)
   A. animal.
   B. shell.
   C. plant.
   D. rock.

6. Mr. Huckebel was teaching a lesson on weather patterns to his sixth-grade class. He told them that the Earth's atmosphere is a mixture of gases structured in layers. He asked them to name the layer of the atmosphere where most of the Earth's weather occurs. Antonio correctly answered the
   A. stratosphere.
   B. troposphere.
   C. mesosphere.
   D. thermosphere.

7. Which of the following statements about the Sun is false?
   A. The Sun, the closest star, is 93 million miles from the Earth.
   B. The Sun is made of flowing magma.
   C. The Sun's energy reaches Earth through radiation.
   D. The Sun is a fusion reactor in which hydrogen fuses to form helium.

8. The history of space exploration has yielded knowledge and prompted questions about our place in the universe. Which U.S. space program in the 1960s and 1970s focused on investigating the moon?
   A. Viking
   B. Pioneer
   C. Apollo
   D. Sputnik

9. Sound travels fastest in which medium?
   A. Iron
   B. Air
   C. Water
   D. Vacuum

10. Mr. DeLeon's class is studying ecosystems. He discusses the forest and the interdependency of the owl, fox, bird, grasshopper, mouse, and flowers. Which activity would be the best assessment of the concept of *interdependency*?
    A. Create a mural of a forest scene with each organism represented.
    B. Write a journal from the perspective of the mouse.

C. Discuss how the ecosystem of the forest is different from that of a desert.
D. Create a food web using pictures of each organism and yarn that shows the flow of energy.

11. Students are getting ready for a performance at a PTO program that requires moving some sets from the floor up to the stage. Mrs. Bowman's class is studying simple machines. Which of the following simple machines could help accomplish this task?
A. Wheel and axle
B. Screw
C. Inclined plane
D. Gears

12. Carbonic acid, also known as carbonated water (H_2CO_3), is a major component is most soft drinks. It is the result of a chemical reaction between which two compounds?
A. $HO + C_2O_3$
B. $HO_2 + CO_3$
C. $H_2O + C_2O$
D. $H_2O + CO_2$

13. Mrs. Johnson is conducting a lesson on energy conversion using batteries. Which of the following anticipatory sets (Engage, see p. 306) exemplifies discovery learning?
A. Each group is given a flashlight and assorted batteries and is asked to combine the flashlight and batteries so that the flashlight will shine.
B. Each student reads Chapter 4 silently.
C. Each student draws and labels the parts of the flashlight and battery.
D. Students discuss different types of batteries used in the home.

14. The lynx has heavy fur, long legs, and wide thick foot pads with claws for walking on snow and catching prey. Its body is an example of
A. a learned behavior.
B. camouflage.
C. adaptation.
D. instinct.

15. The snowshoe hare is the main prey of the lynx. The hare's coat turns white during the winter when it snows and remains brown the rest of the year. It is anticipated that because of possible climate changes, there might be less snow to camouflage the hares during the winter. What would be a probable outcome for the survival of the snowshoe hares?
A. Over generations the snowshoe hares will starve themselves into extinction.

B. Over generations a few snowshoe hares will acquire mutated genes that allow them to stay brown longer.
C. Over generations a few lynxes will acquire a mutated gene that will allow them to turn white like the snow.
D. Over generations the lynx will have more competition for prey.

16. Mia made a wooden picture frame and got a splinter in her finger when she rubbed the sides of the frame hard with sandpaper to make it smooth. The resistance she felt as she rubbed the sandpaper against the wood was due to which of the following physical force?
A. Gravity
B. Magnetism
C. Electricity
D. Friction

17. Teaching a second-grade lesson on states of matter, Ms. Tyson instructs the class to demonstrate the differences between a solid, a liquid, and a gas. The class divides into groups, and each group mimics the actions of atoms of one of the states of matter. One of the groups does not move and stays close together. Which state of matter is this group portraying?
A. solid
B. liquid
C. gas
D. plasma

18. Ms. Rosa's class was discussing the basic needs for plant survival. Which of the following is not a basic need for plant survival?
A. nutrients
B. heat
C. moisture
D. air

19. Sandstone is an example of which rock classification?
A. Sedimentary
B. Igneous
C. Volcanic
D. Metamorphic

20. Mrs. Nasser is demonstrating a solar eclipse using models for the Sun, moon, and Earth. In what order should she put the three models to demonstrate a solar eclipse?
A. Sun, Earth, moon
B. Moon, Sun, Earth
C. Moon, Earth, Sun
D. Sun, moon, Earth

TEST YOURSELF ANSWERS AND RATIONALES FOR SCIENCE

Answer 1: The teacher is ethically responsible for providing an environment that most closely resembles the organism's natural habitat. With the possibility of the lights, water, or air conditioning/heating not being available at the school or on its premises during vacation, a student should take the hermit crabs to his or her home. (As an aside, this will be popular with students, so teachers should be ready with a selection process for volunteers.) The correct answer is *B*.

Answer 2: Choice *B* is a measurement tool, not a unit of measurement. Choices *C* and *D* do not measure length. The distance the hermit crab traveled would be measured in meters. The correct answer is *A*.

Answer 3: A kilo is the metric designation for 1,000. A 3-kilogram sack of sand contains 3,000 grams of sand. The correct answer is *C*.

Answer 4: Activities that promote critical thinking skills require the student to be actively involved in such experiences as observing, comparing, contrasting, and drawing conclusions. The only choice that allows students to engage in active inquiry is *C*. The correct answer is *C*.

Answer 5: Coral is a simple, delicate animal that secretes and lives inside a hard limestone coating made from calcium in seawater. The correct answer is *A*.

Answer 6: The layers of the Earth's atmosphere from the surface outward are troposphere, stratosphere, mesosphere, and thermosphere. The troposphere is the layer closest to the Earth. The correct answer is *B*.

Answer 7: Magma is hot, melted rock. The Sun, our nearest star, is not made of molten rock but is a hot mass of glowing gases. The Sun is about 93 million miles away. We get warmth from the Sun through radiation, and the Sun is a fusion reactor. Remember that we are looking for the false statement in this question, so the answer is *B*.

Answer 8: The Apollo program put Neil Armstrong and Edwin Aldrin on the moon in 1969. The unmanned Viking program landed on Mars in 1976, and the Pioneer program circled Venus. Sputnik was the Russian program that launched the first man into space in 1961. The correct answer is *C*.

Answer 9: Sound, as a vibration, travels faster through solids because the molecules are more closely packed (rather than in non-solids like air and water). Sound does not travel in a vacuum because there are too few molecules to transmit the vibrations. Iron is a solid, so sound can travel rapidly through it. You may have seen movies where someone puts their ear on the railroad track to determine if a train is coming. One can hear sound through the iron rails much sooner than through the air. The correct answer is *A*.

Answer 10: In order to assess student understanding of *interdependency*, the activity must include not only the organisms but their relationship to one another as well. The only option that addresses both is *D*. The correct answer is *D*.

Answer 11: An inclined plane (a simple, sturdy board placed to create a ramp) allows them to slide the sets up from the floor to the stage. The simple machine in this case allows them to use less force (but over a longer distance). The correct answer is *C*.

Answer 12: Carbonic acid is the result of a chemical reaction between carbon dioxide (CO_2) and water (H_2O). The correct answer is *D*.

Answer 13: The only option that involves exploration and experimentation, which is an important component of discovery learning, is *A*. The correct answer is *A*.

Answer 14: The physical characteristics of an organism are inherited, not learned (*A*). The characteristics of the lynx listed here are not ones that indicate camouflage (*B*). Instinct is a natural impulse or behavior, not a physical characteristic (*D*). The examples listed indicate how the lynx has adapted to its environment. The correct answer is *C*.

Answer 15: The lack of camouflage would not affect the hares' ability to find food (A), and whether the lynxes have the ability to turn white or have greater competition for prey does not affect the snowshoe hares' survival as a species (*C*) and (*D*). In order to survive in an environment with less snow, the hares' genes must mutate to stay brown longer, thus providing greater camouflage from predators. The correct answer is *B*.

Answer 16: *Friction* is a force that results when two objects are in contact with each other. In this example, it is the result of the contact between the sandpaper and wood. Gravity (*A*), magnetism (*B*), and electricity (*C*) are forces that can result even when two objects are not in physical contact with each other. The correct answer is *D*.

Answer 17: The atoms of a gas (*C*) are very active and have the most kinetic energetic. The atoms of a liquid (*B*) do not have as much kinetic energy and do not move as far or as quickly as those of a gas. The atoms of a solid have the least kinetic energy and are held in position. The correct answer is *A*.

Answer 18: The four basic needs for plant survival are nutrients, water, air, and light. Many plants grow in very cold conditions (basic needs for survival of animals include nutrients/energy, water, food, oxygen, space, and the ability to maintain *homeostasis* [or keep the body's conditions stable]). Because heat is not a basic need for many plants, the correct answer is *B*.

Answer 19: Igneous rocks are a result of volcanic activity (*B*) and are also known as volcanic rocks (*C*). Metamorphic rock is formed by both heat and pressure, deep within the Earth (*D*). Sandstone is a sedimentary rock formed by the erosive processes that may occur as both sediment and silt settle at the bottom of river beds. The correct answer is *A*.

Answer 20: A solar eclipse occurs when the moon passes between the Sun and the Earth. In order for the moon to block light from the Sun, it must be in between the Sun and the Earth. The correct answer is *D*.

6 Preparing to Teach Art in Texas

Sara Wilson McKay
Virginia Commonwealth University

Carrie Markello
University of Houston

Janice L. Nath
University of Houston–Downtown

As long as art is the beauty parlor of civilization, neither art nor civilization is secure.

John Dewey, 1934, p. 344

This chapter addresses the art standards of the EC-6 comprehensive exam. These standards range broadly to include art objects and their relationships to their makers and their cultures. As Dewey points out, the role of art should not be limited to what is simply beautiful. Rather, art plays a considerable role in how civilizations perpetuate themselves. Accordingly, this exam explores more than just what young students construct in the classroom. Even at the early childhood and elementary levels (EC-6), students are expected to engage in ideas about how art is created; explore art histories of diverse cultures; and learn to analyze, interpret, and evaluate works of art. In order to achieve these expectations, *generalists* are required to be knowledgeable about cognitive and artistic development of EC-6 students. This knowledge forms the building blocks for well prepared teachers to implement meaningful art instruction and assessment.

Art in the EC-6 classroom plays an important role in the learning and development of young children. Gardner (1983) maintains that art allows perception, awareness, judgment, and expression of ideas to occur in ways that are not purely linguistic or mathematical (such as in reading, writing, science, and technology). Such alternate ways of knowing help children attend to their environment, imaginations, and emotions. Art experiences enable children to develop their minds to perceive subtleties in their experiences, differentiate concepts, and understand complexities in their world (Eisner, 2002). These alternative ways of knowing may be most visible in young children who are not always able to clearly express themselves verbally (Wright, 1997). Early childhood specialist Malaguzzi (1993) identifies a stumbling block in early education, citing that spoken language is increasingly imposed on children through imitative mechanisms that are typically devoid of meaning. In contrast, Malaguzzi advocates that children learn best through strong imaginative processes linked to their experiences and to the problems of these experiences. Art, especially when it is integrated into a learning program rich with problem-solving projects, involves precisely the kind of imaginative processes advocated in the elementary classroom. Wright (1997) continues by suggesting that art provides "a powerful means with which to promote future-oriented learning, particularly for young children, because [it] involves nonverbal, symbolic ways of knowing, thinking and communicating" (p. 365). Through art, young children play active roles in the processes of discovery, self-awareness, personal communication, social interaction, perception, skill use, analysis, and critique. These goals for children in art are consistent with the standards for the visual arts addressed in the EC-6 comprehensive TExES exam. The understanding of artistic development as a domain of human growth, like development in the cognitive or social domain, points to the important role of high-quality art education at the elementary level (Kindler, 1996). This crucial role is underscored by the clear standards EC-6 teachers are expected to meet.

Consistent with the design of the previous chapters, this chapter is structured with an overview of the various art standards that are, in turn, correlated to the Texas Essential Knowledge and Skills (TEKS) for Fine Arts. Each is followed by a discussion of the competencies. In addition, for each standard, there are sample items with responses. A sample lesson plan, a sheet for drafting your own plan, and an observation sheet are also included.

TEKS-Related Correlations

There are five art standards for the EC-6 comprehensive exam. The art section may be an obstacle for many test takers. Perhaps the difficulty stems from the incredible breadth of what is included in the term *art* and a general lack of emphasis on art content throughout the present educational system. This may be the case because of the fear expressed by John Dewey in his quote at the beginning of this chapter. All too often, art is viewed as an extraneous and frivolous endeavor. So much more than decoration, art, as a fundamental part of human activity, has many functions. Such purposes include visually communicating personal, spiritual, social, and political ideas, as well as designing objects for daily life, and reflecting on human activity throughout time and across a variety of cultures (Preble & Preble, 2004). Thus, in addressing these standards, you find that they go beyond a single limited view of art; therefore, a broad perspective about art helps in thinking about these proficiencies. In addition, these standards are in line with the TEKS for Fine Arts for students and are, therefore, critical information for early childhood through sixth-grade teachers.

The TEKS for Fine Arts are designated in four basic strands:

- *Perception:* The student develops and organizes ideas from the environment.
- *Creative Expression/Performance:* The student expresses ideas through original artworks, using a variety of media with appropriate skill.
- *Historical/Cultural Heritage:* The student demonstrates an understanding of art history and cultures as records of human achievement.
- *Response/Evaluation:* The student makes informed judgments about personal artworks and the artworks of others.

The TEKS chapter 117 for Fine Arts goes on to say:

Four basic strands—perception, creative expression/performance, historical and cultural heritage, and critical response/evaluation—provide broad, unifying structures for organizing the knowledge and skills students are expected to acquire. Students rely on their perceptions of the environment, developed through increasing visual awareness and sensitivity to surroundings, memory, imagination, and life experiences, as a source for creating artworks. Students express their thoughts and ideas creatively, while challenging their imagination, fostering reflective thinking, and developing disciplined effort and problem-solving skills. By analyzing artistic styles and historical periods, students develop respect for the traditions and contributions of diverse cultures. They respond to and analyze artworks, thus contributing to the development of lifelong skills of making informed judgments and evaluations.

In the discussion of the various standards outlined that follow, watch for correlations among these TEKS strands and what the test covers. There are significant overlaps that require a broad understanding of what art is.

Art *Generalist* EC-6 Standards

The Texas Education Agency (TEA) requires the EC-6 teacher to understand the concepts, processes, and skills involved in the creation, appreciation, and evaluation of art and be able to apply that knowledge to plan and implement effective and engaging visual arts instruction (Competency 042). This competency applies to the following five standards.

Standard I: Perception in Art

The EC-6 teacher understands how ideas for creating art are developed and organized from the perception of self, others, and natural and human-made environments.

The EC-6 teacher assists students in their ability to perceive and reflect on the environment. The teacher uses correct terminology for the art elements (i.e., color, texture, shape, form, line, space, value) and the art principles (i.e., emphasis, contrast, pattern, rhythm, balance, proportion, unity) in order to help students analyze art and their environment. The teacher constructs art lessons that foster creative thinking and problem-solving skills. The EC-6 teacher also plans lessons that encourage observation and reflection on life experiences, and he or she identifies visual symbols that can be analyzed and compared in both natural and human-made subjects.

> *The teacher demonstrates how the elements and principles are used to convey perceptions in the art of different cultures. Additionally, the EC-6 generalist develops ideas from direct observation, imagination, and personal experience.*

This standard relates directly to the first of the TEKS, requiring teachers to emphasize student *perception* of their environment for both art-making and evaluation of art. It requires that teachers understand the value of multisensory experiences for EC-6 students and necessitates that teachers know that life experiences and imagination are sources for artistic creation. Along with Gardner's theory of multiple intelligences, perception often governs young children's views of reality and can be the basis for their developing logic (Wright, 1997). The EC-6 teacher who is knowledgeable of this standard understands the important role of perception in education and knows that the basic elements of art and principles of design aid students in gathering and assessing what is perceived. *Perception* is our view (or mental interpretation) of something based on the combination of sensory stimuli and influenced by our past experiences, knowledge, mental state, motivation, and so forth (Slavin, 2009). Knowledge of the elements and principles of art helps *generalists* understand how artworks are organized. Through the perception of elements (such as shape and color) and principles (such as unity and pattern), artworks are analyzed. *Generalists* should know how to recognize the relationships among these elements and principles in works of art. In addition, understanding how critical thinking and creative problem solving are applied in perceiving artworks is important for implementing this standard.

Consider the following example:

The following reproduction of Marcel Duchamp's *Nude Descending a Staircase* (1912) best shows:

A. texture. C. balance.
B. movement. D. line.

Test taker 1 picked choice *C*, claiming the reproduction has equal amounts of visual weight on each side. Test taker 2 selected choice *B* because her eye went from the top left corner to the bottom right and that showed her movement. Test taker 3 answered with choice *D* because she saw a lot of lines. Test taker 4 selected choice *B* because of the title of the work, *Nude Descending a Staircase*. Test taker 5 also chose choice *A* because he knows paintings sometimes have texture.

To answer this question correctly, a limited knowledge of the elements of art and the principles of design is helpful. In choice *A*, although the definition of texture indicates any surface can be described in terms of its texture, and certainly there is visual texture in this work, this artwork does not emphasize texture. Because the artist does not use a variety of visual or actual textures emphasizing this element in the artwork, there are better choices.

Choice *B*, *movement*, is supported with visual evidence, and the test taker stated it well by identifying how her eye reacts when looking at the reproduction. Noting that her eye moved from one side to the other gives the test taker visual evidence for her answer (not to mention the title of the artwork). Choice *C* is a valid choice, but is it the best choice? This is an asymmetrically balanced artwork. When looking at this work of art, do you feel an overwhelming sense of balance? No. That is not the perception. When a question asks you for what it shows *best*, it is looking for what is overwhelmingly exemplified. Keep this in mind when selecting answers for art questions. Choice *D* actually falls in the same category as choice *C.* A reproduction that best shows the *use of line* (D) most likely consists primarily of clear, overt lines, not ambiguous lines that are hard to follow. If they are hard to follow or hard to identify, they might be suggesting something else is important (such as in this case with the emphasis on movement). The correct answer is *B.*

1950: 134–59. Duchamp, Marcel, "Nude Descending a Staircase, No. 2" Philadelphia Museum of Art. The Louise and Walter Arensberg Collection. Used with permission.

In order to be able to address this standard about perception, we must pay special attention to what art encompasses. In one respect, art uses a common language called the *elements of art* and the *principles of design.* Following are definitions of the major building blocks of art and descriptions of how they can be arranged in a composition. There is also a chart that may be helpful in trying to understand how an artist uses various elements of art in order to achieve certain principles of design. For example, using contrasting shades of color might suggest conflict in a design, whereas using similar shades of color might suggest unity in a design. This is just an example of the kinds of things to look for when one analyzes a work of art using elements and principles of design.

The Elements of Art

Line: The path of a moving point, a mark made by a tool or instrument as it is drawn across a surface.

Shape: A two-dimensional area that is defined in some way, perhaps with an outline or solid area of color. Shapes may also be implied.

Form: Objects that have three dimensions (length, width, and depth), and therefore have mass and volume.

Space: Shapes and forms exist in space. On a flat surface, artists can employ various means to imply the illusion of three-dimensional space, such as modeling to show volume, objects diminishing in size as they move to the background, overlapping, and showing more detail and brighter colors in the foreground with duller colors and less detail in the distance.

Texture: The way a surface feels or appears to feel if you could touch it; texture can best be learned by touch whenever possible.

Color: The aspect of objects caused by the varying quality of reflected light. Color is possibly the most expressive element of art but the most difficult to describe. Colors appeal directly to our emotions and can stand for ideas and feelings. The *primary colors* are red, yellow, and blue. The *secondary colors* (formed by mixing two primary colors) are green, orange, and purple. In the color chart on the next page (Figure 6.1), one can see which primary colors are mixed to form the secondary colors (i.e., red and yellow make orange, blue and yellow make green, and blue and red make violet/purple). The *tertiary colors* (mixed from a primary and a secondary color) are yellow-green, blue-green, blue-purple, red-purple, red-orange, and yellow-orange.

Value: The relative lightness or darkness of a work or part of a work, whether in color or in black and white.

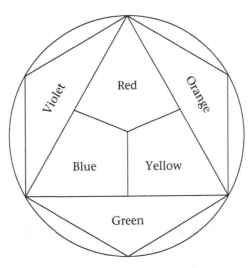

Figure 6.1 This color chart depicts the three primary and the three secondary colors that result from mixing primary colors.

The Principles of Design

Pattern: The repetition of visual elements such as shapes, lines, or spaces to create a natural, accidental, or planned organization of elements.

Rhythm and Movement: The repetition of visual elements such as shapes, lines, or spaces. Visual rhythm and the sensation of movement as the viewer's eyes follow the "beats" through a work of art.

Balance: The arrangement of elements in works of art. This may be symmetrical (formal), asymmetrical (informal), or radial (coming from a center point).

Proportion: The relative size of one part to another.

Contrast: The degree of difference between colors, shapes, tones, or other elements in a work of art.

Unity: Allows the viewer to see a complex combination as a complete whole. If all the parts are joined together in such a way that they appear to belong to a whole, the work of art is unified.

Emphasis: Center of interest in a picture; the focal point. Artists generally designate the most dominant part of the work by using some of the elements discussed here to emphasize the most important point.

And now, let's try this:

In a kindergarten class, how can a teacher best relate art to daily life?

A. Have an Art Center in which students draw whatever they feel in their journals.
B. Ask students where they see art in the world.
C. Give students 15 minutes of free art time at the end of the school day.
D. Ask students to describe specific aspects of their environment in terms of colors, shapes, and light.

Choice *A* is not appropriate, because there is no specific assignment that asks students to look at their surrounding culture in the form of daily life. Similarly, choice *C* gives children no direction in using that free time. Consequently, there is very little learning about the relationship of art to daily life. Choice *B* is a good question to ask; however, for kindergartners it is too broad and vague. This question allows students to use their homes, the outside world, school, and so on to identify art. The problem, however, lies in the fact that these choices might overwhelm a kindergartner, who might not know where to focus first. With the prompting of various settings and good questions, teachers might be able to salvage this choice and get to larger connections of art and daily life, but this is not the best answer. The most specific way to address the connection between art and life with kindergartners is to use the informal way of describing art suggested in choice *D*. This choice is the most concrete answer needed to let children's imagination expand; plus, the variety of answers inherent in the question means that discussion of possible student responses will yield a rich understanding of the multiple ways art is reflected in daily life. The best answer is *D*.

 # Standard II: Creative Expression in Art

The EC-6 teacher understands the skills and techniques needed for personal and creative expression through the creation of original works of art in a wide variety of media and helps students develop those skills and techniques.

The EC-6 teacher demonstrates a basic understanding of techniques used to create various forms of art, including drawing, painting, printmaking, construction, ceramics, fiber art, and electronic media. The teacher is also able to help students use the art elements and principles in making art in various media and understands age-appropriate activities. The EC-6 teacher helps students see their artworks as personal expression and based on relevant ideas in students' lives (i.e., ideas, experiences, knowledge, and feeling). Also, the EC-6 teacher helps students differentiate between copy art and original works of art, focusing on the use of critical and creative thinking while making art. The teacher also demonstrates safe and appropriate use of materials and equipment. The EC-6 generalist describes, models, and provides examples of the range of expression (personal, social, political) available through various art media, as well as examples of objects designed for everyday life.

This standard basically corresponds to the second point of the fine arts TEKS that pertains to *creative expression*. This requires that teachers know how to differentiate between two- and three-dimensional forms of art and that they are familiar with the qualities and uses of various media used to produce artworks (e.g., paint, crayon, chalk, clay). The EC-6 teacher knows how the art elements and principles are used to create art in a variety of media. The teacher also understands the ways personal, social, and political ideas are expressed through works of art and encourages the use of experience, memory, and imagination as sources for making original art.

Consider the following example:

Third-grade students are exploring pattern and repetition found in Native American art. How might a teacher best extend this knowledge from two- to three-dimensional media?

   A. Let students make prints from Styrofoam plates.
   B. Have students experiment with weaving by making bracelets.
   C. Ask students to create shoebox houses and decorate the outsides with patterns they draw.
   D. Have students make a whistle out of clay.

Choice *A* is incorrect because printmaking is a two-dimensional medium. Choice *C* is a poor choice because students merely apply flat (2-D) designs on top of a 3-D model; therefore, they do not use pattern and repetition in the construction of the three-dimensional part of the artwork. Choice *D*, although definitely a three-dimensional product, makes no mention of how pattern or repetition might be used in constructing the artwork. Had there been mention of using Pre-Columbian patterns on the whistles, it may have been a stronger answer, but as it stands, weaving is the most direct translation of repetition and pattern from two dimensions to three dimensions. The best answer is *B*, because the motions of weaving reinforce the idea of repetition in making various patterns in the bracelets, which are three-dimensional. Make sure to include *all* of the elements requested in the art questions. The correct answer is *B*.

In addition to needing to know the basic vocabulary of art, the teacher should be familiar with ways of art-making for the classroom and the fact that visual creations are forms of communication and personal expression. In general, one should be mindful of what is required of the student and whether the emphasis is on process or product. An art project that results in 24 identical valentines, although popular in February (but not for educational reasons in art), is not an appropriate art-making lesson because there is no individual input from the student. "Recipe-oriented" art activities that require children simply to do what the teacher does (or wants) do not allow children to develop artistically (Szyba, 1999). In addition, some students may not be able to relate to the relevance of particular products due to their own life experiences. In trying to conceptualize appropriate art-making lessons, think through the techniques listed next that, when paired with solid content and student input, are strong activities where the students' process is augmented and the students' communication is enhanced. In working with young children, teachers should welcome, even encourage, conversation among the children as they are working and praise original ideas to help children understand that expressing their own feelings and ideas are valued. This will hopefully motivate each child to find his or her own way of working with the art material or the problem posed (Szyba, 1999). The following are ways of **art-making**.

Drawings: Making marks on a flat surface of material, usually paper. Contour drawings trace the outside edge of an object, and gesture drawings are quick drawings to get the idea of an object. Use charcoal (black chalk-like substance), colored chalk for paper (not for chalkboards), conte crayons (available in black, brown, and sienna), pen and ink, pencils or wax crayons, and pastels (similar to chalk but finer and available in a wider range of colors).

Painting: Typically allows for more color exploration than drawings. Paint media include (1) oils—slow drying, requires good ventilation, not appropriate for early childhood or elementary classrooms; (2) acrylics—quick-drying, water-soluble; (3) tempera, used frequently in schools, dries quickly, is opaque, inexpensive, water-soluble; and (4) watercolor—transparent, used with soft brushes, and results are better when used with heavier weight or watercolor paper.

Printmaking: An original artwork made in multiples. Images are raised or scratched into a surface (like scratch-foam, linoleum, wood blocks, potatoes, or erasers) to make a plate or a stamp, and ink is rolled or otherwise placed onto the surface. Either the raised part or the nonscratched part is then pressed or stamped onto paper or fabric. The image plate can be re-inked to make identical prints. Making fingerprints or fingerprint art is also a basic form of this art technique.

Collage: Paper, fabric, and various other materials are combined to adhere to a surface. Making a collage is not just cutting things out of a magazine and randomly pasting them on a surface. Collage involves applying elements and principles of design in conjunction with a central idea.

Sculpture: Wood, metal, stone, clay, paper, and various other materials are used to construct a free-standing, three-dimensional form that is viewable from all sides. Sculptures can be made by: (1) carving (stone or wood either cut or chipped to create a form), (2) modeling (clay shaped into a form—ceramics), (3) casting (a form is created, a mold is made and then filled with melted metal, plaster, or paper pulp, and (4) assembling (found objects or a variety of materials are collected and joined to create a form).

Constructions: Also known as *assemblages*; made from materials, such as paper, wood, or found objects to create a collage on a canvas or board, or a three-dimensional object (Clements & Wachowiak, 2009).

Ceramics: Moist clay formed into three-dimensional or relief sculptures or two-dimensional tiles. Once dried, the clay is baked or fired at extremely high temperatures. Color is added by painting with ceramic glazes and then refired.

Fiber arts: Use of textiles, fabrics, yarns, threads, and so on to produce weavings, quilting, needlework, basketry, and fiber sculpture. Fiber arts also can include spinning of yarn and thread from raw materials.

Electronic media: Technology-assisted image making. This may include draw-and-paint software programs, as well as more sophisticated software such as Adobe Photoshop. Issues regarding copyright and originality must be explicit when working with this kind of media and should be taught to children.

General age-appropriate art-making activities include:
(Note: Safe art materials should be identified by consulting the material safety labels.)

For kindergarteners:
• Make spontaneous drawings and paintings
• Scribble images and name them
• Combine ordinary things to design imaginative places (Szekely, 1999)
• Use and identify primary colors
• Choose color based on emotional appeal, not realism
• Identify and use patterns and textures

For first and second graders:
• Use different kinds of lines, spacing, shapes
• Build forms with clay or wood to develop concepts
• Use more realistic color
• Mix colors in painting
• Repeat shapes in a rhythmic flow
• Create patterns
• Make rubbings of various textures

For third and fourth graders:
• Make lines with a variety of tools
• Create contour (outline) and gesture (very quick drawing to capture the form of a subject) drawings
• Understand concept of shading to create form
• Realize various points of view
• Recognize emerging themes like permanent versus temporary or natural versus human-made (Miller, 1999)
• Mix colors, shades (adding black to a color), and tints (adding white to a color)
• Use a compass for radial balance
• Organize compositions using the principles of design (Linderman, 1997)

For fifth and sixth graders:
• Use lines to create movement and perspective
• Experiment with detail, cartooning, and calligraphy
• Use basic geometric and organic shapes
• Practice creating two-dimensional versus three-dimensional space
• Understand how to select contrasting colors for various effects
• Know how to apply elements and principles of design (Linderman, 1997)

These guidelines do not suggest that there are no exceptions to these activities; they are provided for general age appropriateness. However, teachers designing art-making lessons for students should emphasize engaging content and opportunities for individual expression, and encourage thoughtful process and open-ended criteria, allowing for many "right" answers. These components provide children avenues for successful visual communication.

Now, try your hand at this assessment item:

Which of the following techniques is best for showing pattern and creating texture in a first grader's artistic composition?

A. Crayon rubbing of the bottom of student's shoe
B. A tempera painting using primary colors
C. Perspective drawing showing depth
D. Sculpting a figure out of wire

Shoe rubbings (*A*) typically show patterns (the repetition of visual elements) and textures (the way a surface feels or appears to feel if you could touch it). If enough paint was used in tempera painting, one might get some texture, but a painting could have primary colors without having patterns. Perspective drawings (*C*) are too advanced for first graders and do not necessarily include pattern and texture. Wire sculptures (*D*) are also not likely to show texture or pattern. Therefore, the best answer is choice *A*. Based on what we learned about pattern and texture from the elements of art and the principles of design, crayon rubbings are the most age-appropriate technique for showing pattern and texture. The correct answer is *A*.

Standard III: Appreciation of Art Histories and Diverse Cultures

The EC-6 teacher understands and promotes students' appreciation of art histories and diverse cultures.

The EC-6 teacher describes, compares, and contrasts art of different periods and cultures and explores reasons why different cultures create and use art. The teacher can describe the role of art in everyday life and is able to describe the main idea in works of art from various periods and cultures. The EC-6 teacher is aware of the role of art in storytelling such as that which is found in prehistoric cave paintings or stained glass windows in Gothic cathedrals and documenting history. The capable teacher is able to demonstrate how ideas are expressed using different media in various cultures and at different times. The EC-6 generalist analyzes the cultural contexts of artworks and ways in which history, traditions, and societal issues are reflected in artworks from the United States and other societies. The teacher can describe the role of art in different careers and the use of art skills in various jobs. Additionally, the EC-6 teacher identifies vocational (career) and avocational (artistic activity that provides a personal sense of accomplishment and enjoyment) opportunities in art.

The capable teacher meeting this standard understands the characteristics of a variety of art forms of multiple cultures from both Western and non-Western traditions. This standard requires that teachers know characteristics of art from various historical periods, including various reasons cultures created and used art and continue to do so. Teachers are knowledgeable about careers in the arts, and they understand the various **roles of art** (e.g., storytelling, documentation, personal expression, decoration, utilitarianism, inspiration, and social change) in different cultures.

This standard directly relates to the historical/cultural heritage strand of the fine arts TEKS. The teacher's understanding of the roles of history and culture and their relationships with art is intrinsic to being able to help students experience and explore diverse cultures through the arts. Meeting this standard entails inquiring into art and its origins and seeking connections across cultures. Educators advocate that developing art appreciation in young children deepens their understanding of the world and enriches their daily lives (Epstein, 2001). Simple discussions with children about the choices involved in designing a storybook or the design of tiles on the floor develop young children's ability to discuss art in the context of their cultures (Johnson, 1997). These kinds of discussions reinforce the value of talking with even the youngest of learners about art in their daily lives, as well as art they see from various cultures.

Consider the following example:

Use the reproduction of *Green Coca-Cola Bottles* (1962) by Andy Warhol to answer the next question.

A third-grade teacher wants to show that art can reflect a society's beliefs. In the context of this painting, the teacher could best do this by asking the students to suggest why:

A. the Coke® bottles are full.

B. there are 7 columns and 16 bottles in each row.

C. the artist chose Coke® bottles as his subject, and the bottle is repetitive.

D. the artist did not use Pepsi® cans.

First, let's look at the suggestions that might be given. Choice *A* focuses on a detail of the artwork that is more of a descriptive fact than something to be interpreted about society. If, however, one of the bottles was deliberately empty or half-full, then this might be interesting question, but, as it stands, it gains the student no insight about social beliefs. Choice *B* is the same situation as choice *A*. Choice *C* has students consider what repetition might represent. This allows students to interpret multiple possible meanings from this overwhelming element in the artwork. The entire artwork consists of repetition of manufactured products. Warhol uses repetition to bring attention to the impact manufactured products and advertising had on daily life during the 1960s. Choice *C* similarly asks students to interpret the other main feature of this work of art, the subject matter. This entire work of art uses Coca-Cola® as its subject matter. It is appropriate, then, to ask questions about the significance of this choice. One test taker understood the importance of the subject matter choice for artists such as Andy Warhol, who focused on consumerism to gain the correct answer from this knowledge. Choice *D* asks students to essentially exchange apples for oranges, Coca-Cola® for Pepsi®. Although this may be interesting, the shift to consider Pepsi® in place of Coke® does not significantly shift the social beliefs regarding consumerism communicated in this work. Therefore, choice *C* is the best answer.

Andy Warhol 1928–1987, Green Coca-Cola Bottles, 1962 Oil on canvas. 82½ × 17 in (209.55 × 144.8 cm) Whitney Museum of American Art, New York. Purchased with funds from the Friends of the Whitney Museum of American Art 68.25.

Teachers should recognize art, regardless of whether it is labeled "fine" or not, as a product of its culture. Independent of exclusive criteria, art reflects its producing culture in the questions it asks, in what it holds up as art, and in what content it chooses to represent. An understanding of the relationship between art and culture is probably one of the most important things the EC-6 teacher can pass on to young students, as it is an understanding that results in the creation of a window into others' worlds. In order to have some sense of the historical events that are contemporaneous with the developments and movements in art, Table 6.1 presents a very brief overview of a primarily Western history of art (but with many non-Western references), which is organized to show how art reflects principal social and cultural ideas of its time. This overview is in no way meant to represent all that is "important" about art and history. Rather, it is intended to provide a way of recognizing the manifestation of social and historical issues in the art of a particular culture. One can use the Internet or additional print resources, including museum materials, to explore artistic time frames and topics further.

The most important element in thinking about art and culture is to be aware of the ever-reflective relationship of art and the society that produces it. In relating art and its culture to students, one should be sure that children can relate aspects of their own culture (the world around them) to the cultural aspects of the artwork in question. Also, students should be asked to look at their own surrounding culture to identify possible sources of art, but teachers must be sure that this is specific and appropriate for each grade level. Young students have varying understandings of what culture is as they progress through their grade levels, depending on their social development. For example, in general, second graders are going to be less aware of fashion trends than sixth graders, simply because of how these two groups think about their surrounding social environment. Kindergartners are more likely focus on their immediate family as culture, whereas fifth graders begin to generalize to state and national levels. This varying understanding of culture is important to remember in making age-appropriate cultural connections to artworks.

Table 6.1   Art Historical Periods and Influences—An Overview

Period/Style	Social Issues and Historical Events
Paleolithic (30,000–2,000 B.C.E.): First examples of pigment placed on a surface (cave drawings). Abstract sculptural figures in stone. (For example, see http://arthistory.about.com/cs/arthistory10one/a/paleolithic.htm)	"Magical" explanations for natural phenomena, including procreation. Shelter limited to cave dwellings or other pre-existing natural forms of protection.
Pre-Columbian Art: Olmec (1200 B.C.E.–400 C.E.): Built pyramids and sculpted large stone statues. (For example, see http://www.artlex.com/ArtLex/p/precolumbian.html)	Hereditary rulers, religious leaders, and artisans supported by farmers' food production. This art is termed *Pre-Columbian* because it predates its discovery by explorers in the age of Columbus.
Early Asian Developments (5000–300 B.C.E.): Animal style prevalent in early bronzes. *Bi* discs carved from jade reveal Chinese desire for unity. In India, dome-shaped shrines house relics of Buddha. (For example, see http://www.metmuseum.org/toah/hd/shzh/hd_shzh.htm.)	Development of Confucian principles for living. Advent of *Taoism*, Chinese philosophy. Birth of Buddha in 537 B.C.E. Rise of Buddhism, with its belief in reincarnation and Nirvana.
Egyptian (3500–30 B.C.E.): Proportion in figurative art—rigidity reflects the strength of Pharaohs. (For example, see http://www.visual-arts-cork.com/ancient-art/egyptian.htm.)	Development of pyramids. Pharaohs are divine and immortal, and the focus is on life after death.

(continued)

Table 6.1   Continued

Period/Style	Social Issues and Historical Events
Greek Art (500–325 B.C.E.): Art and architecture reflect concerns with order and rationality. Unparalleled naturalistic style in sculpture. (For example, see http://www.historyforkids.org/learn/greeks/art/greekart.htm.)	Beginning of Western culture as we know it. Human body elevated to highest ideal. Gods given human form and human weaknesses. Advent of philosophy, democracy, medicine, geometry, algebra, and astronomy.
Roman Art (500 B.C.E.–330 C.E.): Contribute realism in figurative sculpture and painting. Massive temples, baths, and other government buildings decorated with reliefs and other sculpture. The triumphal arch celebrates victories of war. (For example, see http://www.historyforkids.org/learn/romans/art)	Takes over Greek and Etruscan culture and adopts it. The idea of republic developed further.
Early African Art (500–1400 C.E.): Terracotta heads of humans and animals (Nok, Central Sudan); life-size terracotta heads for ritual use (southern Africa); bronze casting, ceramics, and copper and iron artifacts for functional and ritual use, such as bowls, swords, altar stands, and pendants (lower Niger); monolithic soapstone ancestral shrines using bird symbols as communicators between earth and sky (Great Zimbabwe, Southern Africa). (For example, see http://vos.ucsb.edu/browse.asp?id=3623.)	The large continent of Africa includes diverse topography, ecology, and groups of people with distinct language, cultural, and ethnic backgrounds. Pageantry and mystery often cultivated through art by political, social, and religious leaders.
Pre-Columbian—Mayan Art (300–900 C.E.): Influenced by Olmec traditions, narrative relief sculpture dominates. (For example, see http://www.worsleyschool.net/socialarts/mayan/art.html.)	Adopts the Olmec hierarchical system of hereditary rulers, religious leaders, and artisans.
Byzantine Art (527 C.E.–1453 C.E.): Domed churches; mosaics become a highly developed art form. Naturalism and realism are lost completely. (For example, see http://www.artlex.com/ArtLex/b/byzantine.html.)	Beginning of Byzantine culture and Eastern Orthodox religion. Gradual decline of Western (Roman) empire. Muslim empire gains strength.
Islamic Art (600–1600 C.E.): Shift from figurative representations to use of complex abstract patterns. Principal form of Islamic architecture is the mosque, featuring a tower (*minaret*) used in calling to prayer. Extensive use of mosaics and pattern covering an entire surface, such as building wall. (For example, see http://www.lacma.org/islamic_art/intro.htm.)	Muslim forces overtake the Byzantine Empire. Islamic empire expands. Crusades begin.
Art in China (600–1279 C.E.): Silk Road opens for Western access to China. Ceramics, jade and ivory carving, and lacquer techniques commonly used by artists. Landscape painting held as pursuit of the founding principle of the universe and is, therefore, the highest art form. Under Mongol rule, exiled artists make political art showing bamboo that bends but does not break, and orchids that flourish without soil around their roots. (For example, see http://academic.brooklyn.cuny.edu/core9/phalsall/texts/chinarts.html.)	Marco Polo visits China in 1275. Mongol ruler Kublai Khan rules as a tyrant and forces artists into exile. In 1368, Mongols are overthrown.
Native American Art—North America (200–1900s C.E.): Prior to 1300 C.E., Anasazi cliff dwellings, Mississippian effigy mounds built to resemble animals. After 1300 C.E., Anasazi dwellings include spiritual center *kivas,* or male council houses decorated with mural paintings of gods. Navaho sand paintings and weavings complement prayers. Hopi *katsina* figures represent good spirits, Pueblo coil pottery uses abstract designs of natural forces such as clouds, wind, and rain. Northwest Coast artists create totem poles, masks, and rattles.	Prior to 1300, diverse cultures developed in North America. After the arrival of Columbus (1492), the development of these cultures is subjected to the conquests of the explorers that follow. U.S. government does not grant citizenship to Native Americans until 1924.

Gothic Art (1140–1530 C.E.): Pointed arch introduced, along with buttress system, lending extraordinary height to the interior. Images mostly religious; reflecting religious stories and stories of major events. Architecture "carries the eye up" to God. (For example, see http://history-world.org/gothic_art_and_architecture.htm.)

Abbot Suger of St. Denis equates light in architecture with ethereal presence.

Aztecs (1300–1500 C.E.): Celebrated calendars with connections to nature and body systems. Create life-size terracotta sculptures, turquoise mosaics, and gold artworks. (For example, see http://www.aztec-history.com/ancient-aztec-art.html.)

Aztecs conquer and control the Valley of Mexico until its discovery by Cortés in 1519. Spanish conquerors destroy Aztec artifacts or evangelize them (incorporate them into their own religious objects).

Renaissance (1350–1650 C.E.): Ever-increasing naturalism (*David, The Mona Lisa*) religious themes (Sistine Chapel, various Madonnas), linear perspective invented; exactness and order are reborn from the classical Greek and Roman times. The importance of the individual is emphasized. These new ideas move to Germany and the Netherlands. (For example, see http://www.artlex.com/ArtLex/r/renaissance.html.)

Humanism: A philosophy that emphasizes the value of each person; no limits to arriving at the level of genius. The popes commission artworks reflecting balance, serenity, perfection, and beauty. Trade and the printing press encourage intellectual freedom and exploration. Important artists are Michelangelo, Leonardo da Vinci, Raphael, Titian, Botticelli, and Donatello.

Baroque (1600–1700 C.E.): Most notable for its theatricality and drama in art achieved by use of light, monumentalizing, and elaborate ornamentation. Rembrandt, Van Dyck, Frans Hals, Vermeer, and Rubens are noted as painters, as is Bernini in sculpture. (For example, see http://www.ibiblio.org/wm/paint/glo/baroque.)

To combat rising Protestantism, the Vatican intends to turn Rome into the most magnificent city in the world and demands that religious art "speak to and impress" the masses with its grandness. Art becomes a commodity to the large group of middle-class bourgeoisie, especially in Northern Europe.

Rococo (Early 1700s C.E.): Curvilinear style of the Baroque is modified and refined to be more delicate. Painting and sculpture begin to reflect sensuality, and extreme ornamentation is the norm in most art forms. (For example, see http://www.artcyclopedia.com/history/rococo.html.)

Decadence of France under Louis XVI and Marie Antoinette, who lead needlessly extravagant lives. Aristocratic values are at their crest.

Romanticism (1750–1850 C.E.): Color and expression of subject matter reign supreme. The worship of nature is foremost. Painting shows passion of subject. In landscape paintings, humans' insignificance in the face of the infinite is called the *sublime*. (For example, see http://www.huntfor.com/arthistory/c17th-mid19th/romanticism.htm.)

Individuality and the power of the individual mind become prevalent social themes. Writings by Thoreau and Emerson contribute to renewed interest in nature.

Realism (1850–1900 C.E.): Romantic idealism fades in favor of depiction of reality—the "here and now"—where real ordinary things and people became worthy subjects. (For example, see http://wwar.com/masters/movements/realism.html.)

The advent of democracy, developing science, and photography bring about a new vision of society. Social inequities are examined in art and literature. Marx writes the *Communist Manifesto*.

Impressionism (Late 1800s C.E.): Marks beginning of modern art. Focuses on the pleasures of life, backing off from Realism and Social Realism. Leisure is the main subject. Optical mixing used and the "fleetingness" of a moment becomes key to represent. Often associated with "dots" of light colors, Manet, Monet, and Renoir are of this period. (For example, see http://www.huntfor.com/arthistory/c19th/impressionism.htm.)

Progress of industrialization creates a "leisure class." Artists' sole occupation is to observe the habits of a city and comment on their observations with flair.

Post-Impressionism (Late 1880s C.E.): No dominant visual style, but there is an increase in the expressive possibilities of color. Artists critique modern life and the elitist qualities of the Impressionists. There is a new emphasis on space and form. Van Gogh, Gauguin, and Cezanne represent this style. (For example, see http://www.metmuseum.org/toah/hd/poim/hd_poim.htm.)

Travel to the outskirts of cities and even to islands is possible. The World's Fair in Paris creates impetus for social critique of the elite.

(continued)

Table 6.1 Continued

Period/Style	Social Issues and Historical Events
Cubism (Early 1900s c.e.): Attempts to see the three-dimensional world in two-dimensional terms. Emphasis is on trying to see the world in terms of the cylinder, the cone, the sphere, and the cube. Picasso painted and drew many works of this type, but he is also considered a modernist. (For example, see http://www.metmuseum.org/toah/hd/cube/hd_cube.htm.)	Much industrial progress occurs, such as the first airplane flight, first radio transmission, and the opening of the Henry Ford plant. Also, Einstein's theory of relativity in 1905 brings up a new notion of time and space.
Futurism (1909–1929 c.e.): Champions speed, motion, energy, and the machine. Painting and sculpture show movement. (For example, see http://www.artlex.com/ArtLex/f/futurism.html.)	World War I begins, and there is a celebration of the new science of the 20th century.
Dada (1915–1923 c.e.): Art reflects a nihilistic point of view and a horror of war. Nonsensical juxtapositions of ideas attack traditional Victorian values and challenge the status of art's sacred or precious images. (For example, see http://www.huntfor.com/arthistory/C20th/dadaism.htm.)	World War I ends with nearly everyone feeling the effects of great loss. Women's suffrage gains strength in the United States.
Surrealism (1924–1945 c.e.): More positive than Dada; exploration of dream images and incorporation of chance events into compositions. The most famous of these artists are Salvador Dali and Miró. (For example, see http://www.huntfor.com/arthistory/C20th/surrealism.htm.)	Surrealists explore theories of Freud and his "dreams" and the significance of the subconscious. The Great Depression takes place, and Hitler begins his rise to power.
Abstract Expressionism (Mid 1940s–1950s c.e.): Energetic use of line and color along with the ability to document the actions of the artist. Jackson Pollack represents this period.(For example, see http://www.artlex.com/ArtLex/a/abstractexpr.html.)	In response to World War II with the Holocaust and the atomic bomb, artists turn inward to abstract representations of feelings. The center of the art world moves from Paris to New York.
Pop Art (Late 1950s–1960s c.e.): Art reflects more humorous, less serious approach. Common images from popular culture, advertising, television, magazines abound. The transformation of the commonplace into the monumental is a dominant theme. (For example, see http://www.arthistoryarchive.com/arthistory/popart.)	Postwar United States is highly commercialized and consumer oriented. Fast food is inaugurated with McDonald's and the TV dinner. Artists such as Andy Warhol use a photo-like technique to emphasize consumerism.
Minimalism (1960s–mid-1970s c.e.): Artists seek to simplify in the face of the excess of 1950s culture. The notion of space and the material presence of shape and form are key in what some term *hard edge*. (For example, see http://wwar.com/masters/movements/minimalism.html.)	With the beginning of the "Space Race" at the Soviet launch of Sputnik, schools and art take a backseat to the basics approach to life.
Postmodernism (1960–present c.e.): Pluralistic art incorporates diverse ideas and cultural values. Art reflects new and old technologies intermixed; reevaluation of traditional canons of art history, particularly roles of women artists. The question of identity is key, along with other social and political issues. (For example, see http://www.visual-arts-cork.com/postmodernism.htm.)	The Civil Rights movement, the military involvement in Vietnam, the assassination of Martin Luther King, the feminist movement, the AIDS epidemic, and the collapse of the Berlin Wall all signify the pluralistic state of current society.

Source: Adapted from Sayre (1997), Kleiner & Mamiya (2005), and Atkins (1993, 1997).

Try the following item:

A sixth-grade class is studying masks from a West African tribe. The teacher explains that the symbols and colors of the masks have different meanings depending on the ceremony for which they were created. Masks celebrating a good hunt have different symbols and colors than masks celebrating a birth in the tribe. Which of the following activities is the most appropriate and effective art activity for supporting students' understanding of this subject?

   A. Students randomly choose West African mask symbols to use on their own masks.
   B. Students think of an important ceremony in their life and make a mask for that ceremony using symbols they believe relate to the ceremony.
   C. Students make a detailed copy of an African mask and then paint it.
   D. Students make Mardi Gras masks, using symbols from African masks.

Choice *A* is incorrect because it does not make the connection of important cultural symbols to a ceremony. Rather, it devalues the African symbols by encouraging students to fabricate their own masks with random African symbols. Likewise, choice *D* devalues the symbols by transferring them to a nonrelated event, Mardi Gras. Choice *C* does not challenge students to make any connection through the replication of these masks. It is simple copying, which rarely serves any educational purpose. Choice *B* is the best choice, because it incorporates students' own experiences, as well as some African history; it encourages students to personalize this knowledge; but most of all, it creates understanding about why African masks are important to tribes. In addition, this choice stresses the importance of ceremony and ensures that students understand West African culture before making their own masks. The best answer is *B*.

Standard IV: Analysis, Interpretation, and Evaluation of Art

The EC-6 teacher understands and conveys the skills necessary for analyzing, interpreting, and evaluating works of art and is able to help students make informed judgments about personal artworks and those of others.

The EC-6 teacher assists students in developing age-appropriate skills necessary for appreciation of art through analyzing, interpreting, and evaluating works of art, as well as the visual world around them (visual literacy). The teacher also helps students to substantiate their understanding and interpretations by determining and describing their own personal criteria for interpreting and evaluating the main idea in artworks. The EC-6 generalist assists students in developing the skills necessary to evaluate and make informed judgments about their own and others' artworks. Additionally, the teacher provides models for students to develop a portfolio of their work.

This standard directly relates to the fourth strand of the art TEKS—focusing on critical evaluation. Today's highly visual world requires even young students to be able to process and make meaning from the barrage of images that make up our image-laden culture. Because of this, **visual literacy**—or the ability to make meaning from what is seen—calls for young children to be given the tools needed to create meaning from the bombardment of imagery, such as television or the Internet, in order to become critical citizens. The tools required to accomplish this task relate directly to the development of higher-order thinking skills in the visual realm. The conscientious EC-6 teacher applies all of this knowledge to encourage critical thought.

In the EC-6 classroom, critical evaluation requires teachers to develop meaningful art experiences for young children. They should avoid potentially harmful activities requiring children to work with pre-formed objects, such as templates or coloring book pages that subliminally tell children there is only one best way to create or interpret (De la Roche, 1996). Teachers must respond with genuine interest to student examinations of artworks. Respectful responses to children's observations about artworks by adults and their peers teach children to value the aesthetic concerns of others. These aesthetic observations stem from easy conversations about common objects, such as cups or chairs (for example, "Why is one more comfortable to hold or to sit on? Which one is nicer to look at?"). There are no "right" or "wrong" answers to either of these questions, but it is these types of questions that give students the tools to justify their own critical responses in positive ways. In addition, discussions about which of a child's artworks should be kept or discarded help young children articulate their own value systems and their own criteria for evaluating art—again, a transferable skill to our own consumer culture, which often preys on children's inability to discern what they like and why (Johnson, 1997).

Consider the following example:

A third-grade teacher wants to encourage students to apply skills of interpretation and aesthetic awareness in a visual context. Which of the following activities is not effective and appropriate for achieving this goal?

A. Asking each student to write a short poem and then to create a small drawing that expresses the feeling of the poem.
B. Showing an artwork to the class and then having each student write a story that he or she thinks the artwork is telling.
C. Having students look at two portraits in two widely differing styles and then discuss what mood is expressed in each portrait and how the mood was created.
D. Having each student complete a coloring sheet. Then have children critique each other on how well the directions were followed.

Choice A requires students to interpret their poems by translating the ideas in their poems into a visual form. It follows that students then must evaluate their artwork aesthetically to see if they adequately expressed the intended emotion. This activity achieves the teacher's goal. Choice B clearly allows students to construct their own meaning or interpretation of the artwork by evaluating the work aesthetically. Choice C asks students to evaluate moods and compare and contrast. It takes these skills into the visual realm by asking students to tell how, in each painting, that mood was created. This also clearly achieves the teacher's objectives. All three options allow room for students to interpret, or draw their own meaning from, the visual art in some way. However, Choice D offers an activity that has no creative value and, therefore, does not address the goal of interpretation and increasing aesthetic awareness. A teacher may use such an activity to help students learn to follow directions, but this is not an activity that enhances interpretation and creativity. The answer (and the exception) is D.

Any standard that addresses higher-order thinking skills requires a quick review of Bloom and Krathwohl's (1956) taxonomy in terms of art outlines the relationship between art thinking and levels of critical-thinking skills:

Lower Levels of Thinking
- *Knowledge,* in which students recall art terminology, titles, dates, and such; recognize, name, identify, label, define, examine, show, and collect information.
- *Comprehension,* in which students explain, describe, translate, interpret, and summarize collected information.

- *Application,* in which students go beyond the concept or principle they have learned and use that principle or technique. Here they can think creatively, make preferences, and project ideas. They can experiment, predict, imagine, and hypothesize as they attempt to solve problems.

Upper Levels of Thinking
- *Analysis,* in which students make connections and establish relationships, categorize, compare and infer, classify and arrange, and organize and group information.
- *Synthesis,* in which students critically design, plan, combine, construct, and produce something original.
- *Evaluation,* in which students critically examine their own work and the work of others as they learn to criticize, judge, appraise, and make decisions.

Art in the early EC-6 classroom is an excellent way to build skills in each of these cognitive categories. As the TEKS advocate, critical evaluation for students requires teachers to be confident interpreters of works of art, taking into account important contextual information about the art in question. Teachers who critically challenge their students must also approach art critically. They must take on the responsibility to elevate art instruction beyond activities such as holiday art or take-home projects that all resemble the teacher's model. These close-ended activities fail to engage the students in critical decision-making processes in their art-making, viewing, and talking about art experiences. In fact, there is an art criticism model in use in many elementary classrooms that help teachers build skills. The *Feldman Model of Art Criticism* suggests four steps to engage with works of art meaningfully: (1) *Describe*—observers take visual inventory of a work of art; (2) *Analyze*—observers think of how the parts relate to the whole; (3) *Interpret*—observers create possible stories and meanings from visual evidence; and (4) *Evaluate*—observers think through the "whys" of the artwork, ultimately developing their own criteria for judgment about the work of art (Feldman, 1992). There are obvious correlations among Bloom and Krathwohl's higher-level thinking and Feldman's steps for art criticism. Look for such correlations in Table 6.2.

Table 6.2 Sample Questions to Stimulate Higher-Order Thinking

Recalling (Knowledge and Comprehension)—generally straightforward questions
(not usually higher-order thinking skills)

	Example Questions
Naming	What is the title of this painting?
Listing	What do you see at the top, bottom, and sides of the painting?
Describing	What are the figures in the boat doing?
Matching	Which picture goes with the word *sad*?
Defining	What is meant by *cool* colors?
Observing	What is the woman wearing on her head?
Identifying	Which building is the lightest value of blue?
Counting	How many apples are in the still life?
Completing	This type of artwork is called (sculpture, landscape painting, portrait painting, etc.).

Processing (Application and Analysis)—open-ended questions
(some are geared more to higher-order thinking than others)

	Example Questions
Comparing	How is this mask like (or unlike) that mask?
Explaining	Why did the artist place the horizon so high (or so low)?
Inferring	From looking at these paintings, what can we infer about space and diminishing sizes?

(continued)

Table 6.2 Continued

Sequencing	Arrange the paintings in order, from those with the brightest and most intense colors to those with the dullest colors.
Classifying	Which sculptures of figures are most realistic? abstract? expressive?
Explaining cause and effect	How did the artist use repetition and pattern to emphasize the face?
Contrasting	How does the texture on the helmet differ from the fur collar?
Making analogies	Can you think of another artist (or culture) who produced art similar to this piece?

Application (Synthesis and Evaluation)—hypothetical questions and personal interpretations (higher-order thinking skills)

	Example Questions
Forecasting	If this artist had lived 50 years longer, how do you think his or her style might have changed?
Predicting	Which artist, in this group of six, do you think will be best remembered for his or her technique in 100 years? Why do you think so?
Judging	Which painting do you think shows the most artistic merit?
Imagining	How do you imagine this artist would have painted a horse? Would he or she have used the same style and technique as in painting this landscape?
Applying	How would you paint a cubist picture of a penguin?
Hypothesizing	How do you think this sculpture would have looked if the artist had painted it with bright colors?

Source: Adapted from Herberholz & Herberholz (1998).

In thinking through some of these questions, the key to determining whether higher-order thinking skills are employed is to look for the kind of student action required. Those that require children to go beyond mere copying, describing, and naming to a level of application, synthesis, and evaluation are going to be more effective in addressing higher-order thinking skills.

Now let's try an assessment item to see whether the relationship of art to higher-order thinking skills is clear:

A fourth-grade teacher shows students a painting of a serene landscape and then a wild abstract gestural painting (one in which quick sketches of the human body or parts of the human body indicate movement). Which of the following questions about these two pieces best promotes students' use of higher-order thinking skills?

A. Have you ever seen these paintings before, and where did you see them?
B. Are the colors used in the second painting also used in the first painting?
C. How does each artwork make you feel, and why do you think they make you feel that way?
D. What would you name each of the paintings?

Choice *A* is merely a recalling exercise. Choice *B* is a comparison question. Choice *D* might require some degree of creativity in coming up with the titles, but there is no place for the student to explain the name that was created. Choice *C* asks students to account for their feelings, thereby requiring the most student action. Thus, choice *C* is the best answer because of the kind of effort required by the student.

Standard V: Cognitive and Artistic Development

The EC-6 teacher understands how children develop cognitively and artistically and knows how to implement effective, age-appropriate art instruction and assessment.

The EC-6 teacher is able to evaluate and assess curricula and instruction in art, as well as the skills and abilities of individual students and those children with special needs. The teacher is able to address the strengths and needs of each child and monitor and encourage growth of students' thinking in art. Teachers recognize and utilize the valuable interdisciplinary structure of the early childhood through sixth-grade classroom, keeping in mind stages of mental, social, and physical development. Teachers also engage in professional development in art, including most recent research and contemporary practices about art teaching at the early childhood level. Teachers communicate effectively about the value of quality art programs in the EC-6 curricula.

This standard is basically the rationale for why the state TEKS in fine arts were deemed necessary to develop and worthwhile to teach. Teachers who meet this standard know about children's stages of development (cognitive/intellectual, social, emotional, and physical) and how these apply to the art curriculum and an interdisciplinary curriculum with art. We have just discussed the place of art in thinking skills, but this section continues to examine other issues related to development in art and for other related issues, such as how materials in the curriculum affect how children develop. For example, Wood and Attfield (1996) tell us that children will use whatever is available in art, but "if all that is available is pre-mixed drippy paints with thick stubby brushes and poor quality paper," we could hardly expect that

> *their work would become anything but repetitive and unchallenging. In our experience children benefit from learning to use a variety of brushes and paints as well as a wide range of media in their efforts to become real world artists. They are capable of mixing paints and using thin brushes and benefit from being able to decide consciously which media are appropriate for a task. In learning to use these tools creatively and efficiently, children then go on to play with the media and develop new uses and combinations. . . . A curriculum which denies and constrains . . . [rather than provides] a range of contexts limits their creativity, their ability to experiment, take risks, test out possibilities, reflect on action, and make connections between areas of learning and experience. (p. 92)*

This statement deals specifically with painting materials, but it should apply across the board to various types and quality of art materials with which children should have experiences—weaving, beads, colored pencils, clay, and so forth.

Just as in writing, children go through a number of stages in art development. Those who teach art should know how children develop their artistic abilities over time. Teachers can use this information as a general guide for planning art lessons and evaluating children's artistic production. Stages of artistic development (Lowenfeld, 1982) suggest that very young children begin with *scribbles* between the ages of 2 to 4 years. By ages 4 through 7, scribbles come to represent figures and objects in the environment. For example, people might be represented with large, circle-like heads and simple stick legs and arms without fingers or toes and are usually floating in space. This is known as the *pre-schematic stage*. As children move from the pre-schematic stage into the *schematic stage* at approximately 7 years of age, they develop some basic shapes they feel comfortable using again and again with some modifications. For example, "mom" may always be about the same as "teacher," "dad," and "sister," (but with different clothes and hair) because there is a drawing schema or a concept for representing "people." Later in the schematic stage, figures become more developed and recognizable, with head, body, legs, arms, hands, and feet, and stand on grass or another baseline (rather than float in space). Each child has his or her own set of symbols to represent various forms. As children develop further into this stage, they begin to add background and weather conditions (usually the sun, which may not always be yellow). At around age 9, children begin to see that the symbols, or schemas, they developed for certain things are too limiting for the real world. As a result, they want to make their drawings much more natural, but their skills often do not allow this. This stage, known as *dawning realism*, occurs between the ages of 9 and 12 years and is one of the most important for art instruction (such as for teaching perspective, contrast, space, and other elements) to help children move past their frustration of not being able to make their art look real. As the children become more concerned about their peers' perceptions of their work, they often become more inhibited and critical of their own artwork. If teachers are not able to help students develop artistically and value their own mark making, many children may stay frustrated with their attempts to draw, move into creating private drawings only, or give up drawing entirely. Teachers should know the stage in which a child is working and judge it accordingly. Teachers must be watchful of students who are in various stages of art development to monitor for considerable delays that may indicate problems in other areas (e.g., delayed fine motor skills, perception difficulties) and be ready to seek help from other school professionals to help further evaluate children in such cases. Even though it is important for teachers to be knowledgeable about the stages of artistic development, it is also important to recognize that these developmental stages were determined some time ago with children raised in Western cultures and, therefore, non-Western children may not demonstrate the same artistic stages of development.

Assessment of children's artwork also involves teaching children to evaluate and critique their own artwork and the work of others. How can teachers begin to encourage effective critical evaluation among their students and peers? They can ask good questions to get the child to talk about his or her work: What would have happened if you turned your pencil on its side here (or used a big brush)? If you put this color in this area instead of that color, what effect would it have? Tell me about what you see when you look in this corner of the picture. I can see many details here, but can you tell me about each? How did you manage to get the effect of dog's hair here? What do you like about this work? What is happening here? What would you change next time? Art assessment for children also focuses on knowledge of art fundamentals (art elements, materials, techniques, etc.), interpretation (analyzing and discussing plausible reasons for the artistic decisions made by the artist to represent specific ideas), and evaluation (assessing artwork in terms of its technical quality and its purpose, whether to tell a story, convey a message, or please the eye). Emphasis should be placed on the process as well as the product and growth over time. Portfolios help document this type of growth. Digital cameras and portfolios can be employed to record and store artworks that children wish to take home to share with family.

Many may believe that art is all talent and that children are naturals—or not. Instead we should embrace learning through artmaking as

> *a form of inquiry that depends on qualitative forms of intelligence. . . . Thinking in the arts is a form of qualitative inquiry in which sensibility is engaged, imagination is promoted, technique is applied, appraisal is undertaken. It is a complex and delicate process that depends upon the ability to experience the nuanced qualities with which one works.* (Eisner, 2002, p. 232)

All children are deserving of quality, comprehensive art instruction that reaches them developmentally and encourages them to reach their full potential as young inquirers and learners.

One resource that helps teachers understand what is expected in arts is the TEKS, as mentioned earlier. A teacher's ability to teach the TEKS to students in the best manner possible also requires that he or she knows the most current developments in the field. Knowledge of professional development sources for art education is one way to stay current. The Texas Art Education Association (TAEA) (http://www.taea.org/taea/default.asp) and the Center for Educator Development in the Fine Arts (CEDFA at http://www.cedfa.org) are extremely useful resources for the EC-6 teacher. Teachers may also find many museums and their Web sites to have excellent art education sections which serve as resources for visits, virtual visits, and for lessons. Technology also provides plentiful Web sites that include information on various techniques (some with movie clips) used in art-making, art history and examples of artists' work.

Consider the following example:

Which statement reflects current thinking about art education in the elementary school?

A. Developing students' technical skills by having them select and then work with a single art medium for an extended period of time.

B. Developing students' drawing skills by having them view and attempt to copy reproductions of drawings by famous artists.

C. Developing students' knowledge of art history by having them focus on important periods of artistic achievement before moving on to other areas (e.g., perceptual awareness).

D. Developing students' critical skills by encouraging them to reflect on their own artwork in the act of creating what they have done so far to guide what they do next.

Choice *A* exemplifies past modes of art education, where the emphasis was on technical product. However, current thinking of art education in the elementary school values the *process* of the art-making over the end product. The emphasis in choice *B* on drawing by copying does not allow students to develop cognitive skills at the same time. Current thinking in art education emphasizes purposeful art-making. Choice *C* is a partial component in current thinking in art education because there is an emphasis on art history, in addition to art criticism, aesthetics, and art-making. This choice strays from current thinking in the field by separating history from perceptual awareness, as well as other areas. This choice does not support integrated art education that is emphasized in the field. Choice *D* encourages critical thinking by having students engage in reflective art-making, where they are able to compare what they did with what they are doing now. This kind of art education is congruent with teaching students art in ways that make them critical and reflective about their own activities (which current thinking supports). The answer is *D*.

Discipline-Based Art Education (DBAE)

Successful EC-6 teachers are aware of **Discipline-Based Art Education (DBAE)** and its goal of applying learning from the arts across curricula.

Discipline-Based Art Education (DBAE) incorporates four strands or disciplines of art: *art history, art-making, art criticism,* and *aesthetics* (or the philosophy of art) that encourage learning across curricula. The four strands of this approach relate to the TEKS four basic strands for Fine Arts: Perception,

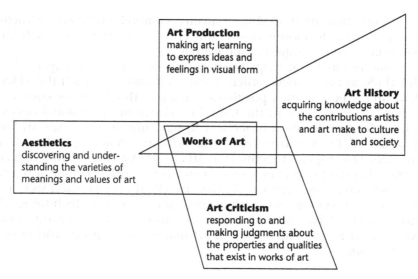

FIGURE 6.2 The relationship of the four art disciplines to works of art.

Creative Expression/Performance, Historical/Cultural Heritage and Response/ Evaluation. Consider the diagram in Figure 6.2 (adapted from Wilson, 1997).

DBAE is:

- different from past approaches to art education that generally focused on students' free expression and art-making
- not a set curriculum, but rather a set of principles based on the domains or disciplines that contribute to creating and understanding art: art criticism, art history, art-making, and aesthetics (the philosophy of art)
- a holistic, comprehensive, multifaceted approach to art education, focusing on artworks at the center of thematic inquiry and instruction

Through DBAE, students:

- make art
- view and study art (original and reproductions)
- respond to and discuss art
- speculate about meaning and value in art
- read and write about objects that have cultural significance
- develop multiple skills and capacities for making art and responding to art, as well as interpreting and evaluating their own art and the art of others
- view and study works of art from many cultures and times, including fine arts, folk arts, and applied arts
- learn how art relates to the rest of the school curriculum, how art influences culture, and how culture influences art

From the preceding list, it is easy to see how easily DBAE mirrors and incorporates the TEKS for art. Curricula should enable children to develop their creative abilities for making art (also called **studio art**), to understand art's cultural and historical context and the contributions that artists make to society **(art history)**, to respond to and evaluate the qualities of visual imagery **(art criticism)**, and discover and understand the varieties of meanings and values of art **(aesthetics)**. DBAE uses adult role models from each of the art disciplines as sources for ideas and methods. This enables the teacher in a DBAE classroom to provide students opportunities for a much wider encounter with art than has traditionally been the case in programs that only emphasize art production activities. Through cumulative learning, students in grades K–12 are able to experience art at many different levels with increasing competence and sophistication.

Artworks play an important role in DBAE; they are at the center of this art education approach and are the link between the four art disciplines. Works of art are selected for study because they have relevance to both the actual communities and the communities in which students live. Images from a child's lived experience may include examples of visual culture, such as a toy from a Happy Meal® or a recent animated movie. These examples of visual culture can serve as appropriate subjects for integrated art study (Freedman, 2003). Students can be encouraged to create works of art in which the themes, topics, and subjects and ideas found in the works of artists are adapted to children's interests and the interests of contemporary society. The use of artworks, including examples of visual culture, activates a big idea approach to art learning, encourages inquiry, knowledge, competence, caring, freedom, well-being, and social justice, which some educational reformists cite as the "moral purpose" necessary for reform (Fullan, 1993; Walker, 2001; Freedman, 2003).

Appropriate student lessons in a DBAE format include the following questions, some of which obviously should be reworded for use in a particular grade level.

Art-Making

- What might have been the sources of the artist's visual idea, and how are these eventually manifested in a given art object?
- What are the steps involved in working in a given art medium to make it ready for the artist to use?
- What are the impacts of work habits on the production of art objects?
- Is the artistic impetus or idea a new one, is it a variation on an old or established idea, or does it build through elaboration or revision of other works or traditions?
- What processes does the artist appear to utilize in order to work out a visual solution?
- How might the creative work of artists depend on the character of their lived experiences?

Art Criticism

- What is the subject or theme of the work, and what does the work say about the intentions, interests, or social or political concerns of the artist?
- What are the significance and meaning of the objects, nonobjects, or visual effects in the work?
- How do the visual elements and principles contribute to an effective and meaningful statement?
- What do critics say the work means, and how is the work regarded overall in the development of the artist and of other artists?
- How do different audiences relate to or interpret this work, and how does its context influence its meanings?
- Does this work sustain attention and involve active discovery of new things?

Art History

- Where, when, why, and by whom was the work made?
- What are the traditional meanings of the objects and symbols in the work?
- What are the distinguishing characteristics or qualities that identify the work and relate it to other works of art?
- Who and what in the artist's life affected him or her most?

Aesthetics

- How can we assign value to what various perceivers say about works of art?
- Should artworks deemed sacred, privileged, or private by groups within one culture be publicly displayed by another culture for all to see?
- To what extent should a viewer substitute his or her own personal perceptions, ideas, and judgments for expert and academic testimony?
- Is the alteration of a work of art the destruction of an existing work of art, or the creation of a new one?
- Should we honor the deathbed request of an artist who wants his or her unsold works destroyed?
- Do citizens have the right to remove public artwork, paid for through taxes, if some members of the public find it offensive? Who decides? What arguments would make the case one way or the other? (Dobbs, 1998)

These questions should help in understanding the goals of DBAE. In general, we can characterize current thinking in art education as a shift from product to *process*, an emphasis on connected, integrated learning in and through art and a multifaceted approach to art education.

Interdisciplinary connections are key ways to making art education classrooms meaningful. As Howard Gardner suggests in his *Frames of Mind* (1983), students who engage with the arts have the opportunity to be smart in different ways because of the different perspectives that art encourages. Consider the following:

> *The arts contribute to an overall culture of excellence in a school. They are an effective means of connecting children to each other and helping them gain an understanding of the creators who preceded them. They provide schools with a ready way to formulate relationships across and among traditional disciplines and to connect ideas and notice patterns. Works of art provide effective means for linking information in history and social studies, mathematics, science and geography . . . opening lines of inquiry, revealing that art, like life, is lived in a complex world not easily defined in discrete subjects.* (Wolfensohn & Williams, 1993, p. 7)

Because our lives do not naturally fall into 50-minute segments during which we focus on one subject at a time, it is important that teachers integrate multiple disciplines in their instruction, with an eye on making learning more meaningful for students (Cornett, 1999).

It is imperative, moreover, that teachers focus on the word *meaningful* used in Cornett's sentence. Teachers should be cautioned that artworks should not be used merely to illustrate topics and concepts (Wilson, 1997). Critical-thinking skills in the arts are transferred to other subjects (Boyer, 1995) and should be recognized and used as such. Projects or assignments that are purported to be interdisciplinary but only address the educational objectives of one subject matter are not using the arts meaningfully. In successful interdisciplinary connections, students are challenged both in a content area and in art. Look for this dual feature in the following interdisciplinary examples. In evaluating the artistic component, bear in mind the other standards already addressed as guidelines. The greatest issue with regard to interdisciplinary art is that there should be openness to allow for more than one way to produce an assignment, even though set criteria are used for assessment.

Relating Language and Art

- Write poems and stories and create artworks to complement them, or vice versa.
- Make paintings, drawings, and murals that reflect books that you have read.

- Play a game that practices different types of language use, such as using gestures, action words, or facial expressions instead of words to suggest a mood or feeling. Practice drawing these gestures, actions, and expressions.
- Create puppets that offer opportunities for interpretations and expressions of ideas, thoughts, and feelings.
- Draw, rather than write, a book report.
- Dramatize a book in dance using costumes, music, and art.
- Make art using news articles as the impetus.

Relating Science and Art

- Study and draw the anatomy, structure, and workings of natural forms, such as the human figure (or part of the body such as a hand, foot, ear, etc.), and label features/parts functions.
- Make sculptures using the principles of balance, gravity, and kinesthetics.
- Design *touch pictures* and *feeling boxes* (pictures and boxes made from various textures and materials).
- Design and build bridges and buildings.
- Study how scientists use various chemicals to clean and restore paintings and sculptures (such as the Sistine Chapel).
- Draw natural objects from observation.

Relating Mathematics and Art

- Draw pictures that show mathematical problems and solutions that involve weight, balance, measurement, and geometry.
- Introduce games that offer visual and spatial planning, such as chess and checkers. Relate spatial planning to drawings.
- Create optical art by dividing spaces on paper.
- Use mathematical tools, such as rulers and compasses, to create drawings and designs.
- Engage in art activities that require measurement and planning, such as weaving and architectural models.
- Use technology to create graphic arts.

Relating Social Studies and Art

- History becomes alive through art by visually interpreting (i.e., draw, sculpt, or paint) historical events or developments.
- Study the history of a country (or a state) through artists' paintings and sculptures and functional objects such as furniture or clothing.
- Draw and compare similar artifacts of various cultures.
- Create maps of a city as seen through the eyes of an architect and a city planner. (Linderman, 1997)

Many teachers, in examining the TEKS, wonder how to include art when they must teach so many other subjects with requirements for state testing. As the demands on educators' time and other expanding responsibilities encroach, teachers must see interdisciplinary learning and art inclusion as a solution instead of cutting out one area in preference for another (Dobbs, 1998). The result is stronger learning in both the arts and the subject area because learning must be transferred cognitively from one domain to another within the same lesson, thus requiring the student to be more fully engaged in the learning process. In addition, incorporating art ensures a visually rich, hands-on learning environment that is motivating for students.

Again, Gardner's (1983) theory of multiple intelligences confirms the EC-6 teacher's knowledge of sound art instruction for their students. There are multiple forms of cognition, visual and spatial being two of them. Art instruction that is mindful of this strengthens cognitive growth across the board (Wright, 1997). Logically, what follows is an interdisciplinary approach to learning through the arts. This means applying these very same standards in the realm of art, with an eye for establishing connections between art and other subject areas. Connections to the arts should figure prominently in any cross-curricular endeavor, because thematic links transport the arts into everyday experiences (Pitri, 2001). In terms of the TEKS, cross-curricular connections encourage children to put their knowledge of the arts to work in reinforcing their learning. For example, perception skills (where students perceive and respond to their environment) align to students' language arts verbal and written skills. Creative expression tied to history and cultural heritage encourages art-making with a purpose. Furthermore, historical and cultural heritage take on a broader significance by virtue of their connections with other social studies. Architecture and graphic design require mathematics skills. Drawing significance from links among other content requires critical evaluation.

One last assessment item:

A teacher wants to link his or her second-grade science curriculum with art. The best example of a lesson that accomplishes this goal is one in which:

   A. children make a papier mâché mobile of the solar system.
   B. children draw, color, and label the stages of metamorphosis of a caterpillar into a butterfly.
   C. children enlarge and paint encyclopedia drawings of flowers and diagram their parts.
   D. children imagine an animal to which they assign certain characteristics and create a three-dimensional habitat for it.

Although students may enjoy doing both choices A and B, these are not the best answer. Choice C clearly promotes little learning in either science or art. Little is gained in the process of copying. Both choices A and B result in students' most likely creating relatively similar products. This aspect is completely avoided in choice D, wherein students creatively design animals with characteristics that require them to practice their knowledge of adaptation and animal habitats in a creative process. Certainly, it is excellent to give students hands-on activities to reinforce learning such as in choices A and B, but be careful to differentiate between a hands-on activity and an interdisciplinary lesson. Because choice D involves critical application of both scientific and artistic knowledge, this choice is the best interdisciplinary lesson. The answer is D.

SUMMARY

This chapter explores the foundations of art education within the context of the EC-6 TExES exam. The hope is that the components discussed here help you understand the five standards for the Visual Arts section so you put them to good use when you enter the EC-6 classroom. This chapter should serve as a review for the comprehensive exam but, more importantly, should be useful in the classroom setting. The standards addressed here are not meant to stand outside of classroom practice. Rather, these strategies are solid ways to ensure that art plays an important role in your curriculum.

Early childhood through sixth-grade educators have identified 10 distinct barriers to establishing a strong base for later learning in the arts for young children. They are: (1) succumbing to stereotypes, (2) assessing children's work in terms of personal ability, (3) reducing art to following instructions, (4) concentrating on precociousness, (5) searching for exotic materials, (6) forgetting who creative teaching is for, (7) avoiding the fine arts, (8) believing that creativity and chaos are synonymous, (9) failing to teach techniques, and (10) neglecting professional development in the arts (Jalongo, 1999). Given the discussion of this chapter, a *generalist* teacher should always strive to overcome barriers to his or her students' future learning in the arts. Using one's knowledge to break down these road blocks and to clear the way for constructive art play should be a meaningful part in the EC-6 classroom.

Art should play a crucial role in curriculum development for many reasons, including those rationales given within the discussion of the various standards. However, let's return to Dewey's words from the beginning of this chapter about art ensuring civilization. In particular, contemplate the following association of art and democracy: If democracy is a fundamental value of this country, art must play a central role in education. It is art that encourages critical thought and respect for diverse points of view. It is art that practices novel solutions to age-old problems and encourages freedom of expression (Dewey, 1934). It is art that allows us a window of understanding into those around us. The practice and study of art enacts democracy where diversity is valued and respect is instilled even in the earliest learning years. Seriously consider the role art can and should play in your EC-6 classroom. Democratic civilization is not secure without it.

REFERENCES

Atkins, R. (1993). *Art spoke*. NY: Abbeville Press.

Atkins, R. (1997). *Art speak*. NY: Abbeville Press.

Bloom, B. S., & Krathwohl, D. R. (1956). *Taxonomy of educational objectives: The classification of educational goals, by a committee of college and university examiners. Handbook I: Cognitive domain*. New York: Longmans, Green.

Boyer, E. L. (1995). *The basic school: A community for learning*. Princeton, NJ: The Carnegie Foundation for the Advancement of Teaching.

Clements, R. D., & Wachowiak, F. (2009). Emphasis art: A qualitative art program for elementary and middle schools. (9th ed.). Boston: Allyn & Bacon.

Cornett, C. E. (1999). *The arts as meaning makers: Integrating literature and the arts throughout the curriculum*. Upper Saddle River, NJ: Prentice-Hall.

De la Roche, E. (1996). Snowflakes: Developing meaningful art experiences for young children. *Young Children, 51,* 82–83.

Dewey, J. (1934). *Art as experience*. New York: Perigee Books.

Dobbs, S. M. (1998). *Learning in and through art: A guide to discipline-based art education*. Los Angeles: The Getty Education Institute for the Arts.

Eisner, E. W. (2002). *Arts and the creation of mind*. New Haven, CT: Yale University Press.

Epstein, A. S. (2001). Thinking about art: Encouraging art appreciation in early childhood settings. *Young Children, 56,* 38–43.

Feldman, E. B. (1992). *Varieties of visual experience*. New York: H. N. Abrams.

Freedman, K. (2003). *Teaching visual culture: Curriculum, aesthetics, and the social life of art*. New York: Teachers College Press.

Fullan, M. (1993). *Changing forces: Probing the depths of educational reform*. London: Falmer.

Gardner, H. (1983). *Frames of mind: The theory of multiple intelligences*. New York: Basic Books.

Herberholz, D., & Herberholz, B. (1998). *Artworks for elementary teachers: Developing artistic and perceptual awareness*. Boston: McGraw Hill.

Jalongo, M. R. (1999). How we respond to the artistry of children: Ten barriers to overcome. *Early Childhood Education Journal, 26,* 205–208.

Johnson, M. (1997). Teaching children to value art and artists. *Phi Delta Kappan, 78,* 454–456.

Kindler, A. M. (1996). Myths, habits, research, and policy: The four pillars of early childhood art education. *Arts Education Policy Review, 97,* 24–30.

Kleiner, F. S., & Mamiya, C. J. (Eds.). (2005) *Gardner's art through the ages*. (Vols. 1-2). Belmont, CA: Wadsworth/Thompson Learning.

Koster, J. (2001). *Bringing art into the elementary classroom*. Belmont, CA: Wadsworth Thomson Learning.

Linderman, M. G. (1997). *Art in the elementary school*. Madison, WI: Brown & Benchmark.

Lowenfeld, V., & Brittan, L. (1982). *Creative and mental growth* (7th ed.). New York: Macmillan.

Malaguzzi, L. (1993). History, ideas, and basic philosophy. In C. Edwards, L. Gandini, & G. Forman (Eds.), *The hundred languages of children* (pp. 41–90). Norwood, NJ: Ablex.

Miller, S. A. (1999). Shape it! Sculpt it! *Scholastic Early Childhood Today, 13,* 46.

Pitri, E. (2001). The role of artistic play in problem solving. *Art Education, 54,* 46–51.

Preble, D., & Preble, S. (2004). The nature of art. In *Artforms: An introduction to the visual arts* (pp. 2–14). Upper Saddle River, NJ: Pearson Education, Prentice Hall.

Sayre, H. M. (1997). *World of art*. Upper Saddle River, NJ: Prentice-Hall.

Slavin, R. (2009). *Education psychology. Theory and practice* (9th ed.). Upper Saddle River, NJ: Pearson.

Szekely, G. (1999). Designing BRAVE new worlds. *Arts & Activities, 126,* 46–47.

Szyba, C. M. (1999). Why do some teachers resist offering appropriate, open-ended art activities for young children? *Young Children, 54,* 16–20.

Walker, S.R. (2001). *Teaching meaning in artmaking*. Worcester, MA: Davis Publications, Inc.

Wilson, B. (1997). *The quiet evolution*. Los Angeles: The Getty Education Institute for the Arts.

Wolfensohn, J., & Williams, H. (1993). *The power of the arts to transform education: An agenda for action*. Los Angeles: J. Paul Getty Trust.

Wood, E., & Attfield, J. (1996). *Play, learning, and the early childhood curriculum*. London: Paul Chapman Publishing Ltd.

Wright, S. (1997). Learning how to learn: The arts as core in an emergent curriculum. *Childhood Education, 73,* 361–365.

AN ART LESSON PLAN

FAMILY TRADITIONS

Grade Level: Fourth Grade

Main Subject Area: Art

Integrated Subjects: Social Studies, Language Arts

Time Constraints: One hour, 30 minutes (2 sessions)

Overall Goal(s): To explore the variety of family gatherings/traditions through the artwork of Carmen Lomas Garza.

TEKS OBJECTIVES:

§ 117.14. **Art**, Grade 4. (b) Knowledge and Skills (4.1) Perception. The student develops and organizes ideas from the environment. The student is expected to: (A) communicate ideas about self, family, school, and community, using sensory knowledge and life experiences; and (B) choose appropriate vocabulary to discuss the use of art elements such as color, texture, form, line, space, and value and art principles such as emphasis, pattern, rhythm, balance, proportion, and unity. (4.2) Creative expression/performance. The student expresses ideas through original artworks, using a variety of media with appropriate skill. The student is expected to: (A) integrate a variety of ideas about self, life events, family, and community in original artworks; (B) design original artworks; and (C) develop a variety of effective compositions, using design skills; (4.3) Historical/cultural heritage. The student demonstrates an understanding of art history and culture as records of human achievement. The student is expected to: (A) identify simple main ideas expressed in art; (B) compare and contrast selected artworks from a variety of cultural settings; and (C) identify the roles of art in American society. (4.4) Response/evaluation. The student makes informed judgments about personal artworks and the artworks of others. The student is expected to: (A) describe intent and form conclusions about personal artworks; and (B) interpret ideas and moods in original artworks, portfolios, and exhibitions by peers and others.

§ 110.6. **English Language Arts and Reading,** Grade 4. (4.27) Listening and Speaking/Listening. Students use comprehension skills to listen attentively to others in . . . informal settings. Students continue to apply earlier standards with greater complexity. Students

are expected to: (A) listen attentively to speakers, ask relevant questions, and make pertinent comments. (4.28) Students speak clearly and to the point, using the conventions of language . . . . Students are expected to express an opinion supported by accurate information, employing eye contact, speaking rate, volume, and enunciation, and the conventions of language to communicate ideas effectively. (4.17) Writing. Students write about their own experiences. Students are expected to write about important personal experiences. (4.18) Writing/Expository and Procedural Texts. Students write expository and procedural or work-related texts to communicate ideas and information to specific audiences for specific purposes. Students are expected to: (i) establish a central idea in a topic sentence.

§ 113.6. **Social Studies,** (Social Studies TEKS are currently under revision.) Grade 4. (b) Knowledge and skills. (4.20) Culture. The student understands the contributions of people of various racial, ethnic, and religious groups to Texas. The student is expected to: (A) identify the similarities and differences within and among selected racial, ethnic, and religious groups in Texas; (B) identify customs, celebrations, and traditions of various culture groups in Texas; and (C) summarize the contributions of people of various racial, ethnic, and religious groups in the development of Texas. (4.23) Social studies skills. The student communicates in written, oral, and visual forms. The student is expected to: (A) use social studies terminology correctly; (B) incorporate main and supporting ideas in verbal and written communication; (C) express ideas orally based on research and experiences; (D) create written and visual material, such as journal entries, reports, graphic organizers, outlines, and bibliographies.

LESSON OBJECTIVES:

Students will : (1) discuss images depicting family gatherings painted by Carmen Lomas Garza in a whole class discussion; (2) compare Garza's family gatherings to their own; (3) identify the elements and principles of design used in Garza's paintings and explain how her design choices relate to her main idea; (4) formulate questions and interview a classmate about their family gatherings; (5) use the information gathered in the interview to write a five-sentence summary about their classmate's family; (6) create a watercolor composition based on their own family's tradition about which they were interviewed; (7) create a classroom exhibition with artworks paired with corresponding stories; and (8) in a whole class discussion, students discuss the content of their artworks, the elements and principles and materials used to create them, and read the summaries aloud.

Readiness Skills or Prior Knowledge Needed: Students participating in the Family Traditions lesson should have prior knowledge of the elements of art and principles of design and how these components can be used for analyzing and creating compositions. They should also have experience formulating plausible interpretations for artworks, as well as some experience comparing artworks from a variety of cultural settings. Readiness for this lesson includes the capability to create thumbnail sketches, knowledge of mixing water colors, and laying down a watercolor wash. Prior knowledge of how to formulate effective interview questions and how to write descriptive sentences that summarize an oral interview is necessary. Students should also have some prior knowledge of various cultural groups in Texas.

Sponge Activity: Students create a list of times and reasons for family gatherings on the whiteboard or chalkboard. Each student is encouraged to add to the list.

Rationale(s): Students benefit from learning about cultural traditions through artworks such as Carmen Lomas Garza's Mexican-American family traditions. This lesson helps students explore their own, their classmates' and Carmen Lomas Garza's cultural traditions. Art can be an excellent way to see inside other cultures, and it is important for students to understand and value diverse expressions of family traditions as participants in a democratic society.

Focus Activity or Motivation: Look at *Cumpleanos de Lala y Tudi* and *Tamalda* from Carmen Lomas Garza's book entitled *Family Pictures/Cuadros de Familia: Fifth Anniversary Edition* (ISBN: 089239-209-1) and/or website www.carmenlomasgarza.com. Students discuss: (1) What is happening in these paintings? (2) What family gatherings did Garza choose to paint? (3) Why do you think so? (4) What elements and principles can be found in her work, and how do they relate to the ideas of the artist? (5) What do you do in your own family traditions? What colors do you see at that time? What sounds do you hear? Are there special foods? (6) What time of that special tradition is the most important to you? Why do you think so? (For example, is it blowing out the birthday candles, is it opening the first or last gift? Is it everyone sitting at the table for a meal, or is it helping to cook a special dish?)

MAKING CONNECTIONS:

1. **Connections with Past or Future Learning:** Ask students to describe family traditions that may take place at family gatherings. Ask students if they have seen Garza's artworks. If so, the students discuss what they know about her work. While looking at *Cumpleanos de Lala y Tudi* and *Tamalda,* students determine what makes Garza's two images similar and different. Students identify elements and principles in Garza's artwork.
2. **Connections to the Community:** Discuss how family gatherings relate to a community. Why might some traditions vary in different regions?
3. **Cultural Connections:** The students discuss birthday traditions in Mexico (www.birthdaycelebrations.net/mexicanbirthdays) and other traditions such as La Tamalada (www.austinchronicle.com/gyrobase/Issue/story?oid=oid%3A525862).
4. **Connections with Student Interests & Experiences:** How does your birthday celebration or family gathering compare to Carmen Lomas Garza's paintings?

Materials: Carmen Lomas Garza's book *Family Pictures/Cuadros de Familia: Fifth Anniversary Edition* (ISBN: 089239-209-1)

Images: *Cumpleanos de Lala y Tudi by Carmen Lomas Garza and Tamalada* by Carmen Lomas Garza.

Art Materials: scratch paper for interviews and sketches of ideas for images, 12″ × 18″ heavy white paper or watercolor paper, pencils, extra fine–point markers, watercolors, water, paper towels.

Other: Computer and LCD projector to project Garza Web site images.

Activities/Instructional Input: Discuss examples of tradition and possible scenes to depict in their artwork. Demonstrate light pencil sketch as basis for painting. Teacher demonstrates laying down a wash for background and foreground, mixing watercolors for more detail, and using extra fine point markers for addtional detail.

Activities: Guided Practice: Students generate a list of questions to interview a classmate about a family gathering or tradition. Students make a list of family gatherings/traditions that they could talk about when interviewed by a classmate. Students discuss with peer group and teacher the family gathering/tradition most suitable for the interview and painting. Students decide what aspects of their family gathering/tradition are most important to depict. Students create thumbnail sketches of the tradition of which they depict.

Independent Practice: Students conduct interviews with classmates and summarize the interview content in five sentences. Students choose the most important and inspiring scene from thumbnails and do their light pencil sketch. Then students lay down their watercolor wash for background and foreground. Next they mix colors for detail and use fine-point markers for final detail.

Assessment: Students complete interviews, paintings, and write at least five sentences to summarize their interview of a classmate's family gathering/tradition. Students title their artwork and discuss similarities and differences of family gatherings/traditions based on interviews, as well as on Garza's, their peers, and their own artworks. Assessment is also based on participation in a discussion on similarities and differences in their use of elements and principles, painting materials, and techniques.

What will students do who finish early? Develop their interview into a story or write a story about one of Garza's images.

Closure: Student work is displayed with written summaries. Students participate in a discussion of their artwork and read aloud the interview summaries created by their classmates. The elements and principles of design used to convey their ideas are identified.

Modification for Students with Special Needs: Brushes will be wrapped in foam rubber for a student who has difficulty holding brushes.

Reflection: To be completed by teacher after teaching the lesson: What modifications are needed to improve the lesson?

DRAFT YOUR OWN ART LESSON PLAN

Title of Lesson: _____

Grade Level: _____

Main Subject Area: _____

**Subjects
Integrated:** _____

Time Frame/Constraints: _____

Overall Goal(s): _____

TEKS Objectives: _____

_____

_____

Lesson Objective(s): _____

_____

_____

Readiness or Prior Knowledge Needed: _____

_____

_____

Sponge Activity: _____

_____

_____

Environmental Concerns: _____

_____

_____

Rationale(s): _____

_____

_____

Focus or Set Induction: _____

_____

_____

Making Connections:

1. Connections to Past or Future Learning: _____

_____

2. Connections to the Community: _____

_____

3. Cultural Connections: _____

_____

4. Connections to Student Interests & Experiences: _____

_____

Materials: _____

_____

_____

Activities: Guided practice: _____

_____

_____

_____

_____

_____

_____

_____

_____

_____

_____

Independent practice: _____

_____

_____

_____

_____

_____

_____

_____

_____

_____

_____

Assessment: _____

_____

_____

What Will Students Do Who Finish Early? _____

_____

_____

Closure: _____

_____

_____

Modification for Students with Special Needs: _____

_____

_____

Reflection: _____

_____

_____

OBSERVING ART EXPERIENCES/ACTIVITIES

During your visit to an EC-6 classroom, use the following form to provide feedback, as well as to reflectively analyze the classroom, the materials, and the lesson(s).

The Classroom Environment	Observed	Not Observed	Response
1. Looking at, making, or talking about art is part of a thematic lesson or unit.			If so, describe. If not, what connections to other content could be added?
2. A variety of art materials are used in open-ended art lessons.			If so, describe. If not, what could be added? How could more artistic choices be encouraged?
3. The selection of materials coincides with artistic exemplars, lesson objectives, and age of students.			If so, describe. If not, how could the materials be better suited to the lesson and students?
4. Children are encouraged to use a variety of materials.			If so, describe. If not, what could the teacher provide?
5. Children are asked open-ended questions to promote dialogue about their own and the artworks of others.			If so, describe. If not, what could the teacher do to encourage discussion?
6. Artwork exhibiting a variety of techniques is displayed in the classroom (painting, sculpture, prints, collages, crafts, jewelry, etc.).			If so, describe where and how. If not, what changes could be made?
7. Art exemplars shown to children are of high quality (e.g., a clear prints or a large slide presentation where the details of art can be clearly seen).			If so, describe. If not, what changes should be made?
8. Art and technology connections are made in some manner (digital stories, digital photography, etc.).			If so, describe. If not, how could it be integrated?
9. Children have sufficient time to think about an art project.			If not, describe how long they were given. What was the result? How long do you think they might need?
10. Children have sufficient time to complete an art project.			If not, describe what was the result. How much longer do you think they might need, and why?
11. Teacher directs children in art lessons with specialized art vocabulary (elements and principles of design, identifies methods and materials, etc.).			If so, describe. If not, what opportunities were missed to do so? What vocabulary could be added?
12. Students are encouraged to reflect on their art-making experience in discussion or in writing.			If so, how was this led by the teacher? If not, what could be encouraged, and how?

The Classroom Environment	Observed	Not Observed	Response
13. Teacher provides structure for children to view and discuss their art and that of peers.			If so, describe. If not, describe a possible scenario.
14. Teacher uses art examples from various cultures, genders, time periods, and age groups.			If so, describe. If not, give ideas for what could be added in a developmentally appropriate way.
15. Higher-level questions are asked about art.			If so, describe. If not, what questions could be added to encourage higher-level thinking?
16. The teacher models new techniques in art to be used as problem-solving strategies for art projects (versus asking children to copy examples).			If so, describe and tell if it is effective. If not, what was the effect on student products?
17. The teacher and students create an environment that demands honoring their own work and the work of others.			If so, describe. If not, give ideas for what could be changed in developmentally appropriate ways.
18. The teacher provides opportunities for students to experiment with art materials/techniques in Art Centers.			If so, describe. If not, give ideas for what could be included in a developmentally appropriate way.
19. There is evidence that the teacher changes materials/ techniques/exemplars in the Art Center.			If so, describe. If not, tell why not and what seems to be an effect of this.
20. The Art Center allows for age-appropriate, artistic, and independent choices.			If so, describe. If not, what is the effect? What could be changed?
21. Other centers/lessons integrate tasks or materials connected with art.			If so, describe. If not, what centers/lessons could be integrated with art, and how?
22. The teacher monitors art projects, discussing progress and giving suggestions.			If so, describe. If not, what is the result?
23. The teacher uses appropriate assessment methods for art activities.			If so, describe. If not, comment on what assessment could have been used and why.

TEST YOURSELF ON ART

1. Mrs. Nomeni wants to include an art lesson in her third-grade science class. What is the best idea from those in the following list?
   A. Draw a picture of the class experiment from an illustration in their books.
   B. Draw a series of pictures of what happened in the experiment that was conducted in class.
   C. Color and label a worksheet on the experiment.
   D. Draw a picture of something that impressed them about the experiment in class; then tell or write about the drawing.

2. Mrs. Henderson teaches her third graders a thematic lesson on animal habitats. As part of the integration, based on the habitats each child was studying, the children choose a corresponding animal to create in clay. First, however, she shows children a number of pictures of animal sculptures in various styles and has children compare and contrast these. She demonstrates basic clay hand-building techniques. Next, she gives students the clay and asks them to create their animals, noting that they have 15 minutes to work on their projects. At the end of the lesson, she is disappointed in their work; she believes she provided a good lesson. What element had she not considered?
   A. Motivation to learn about animal habitats and clay sculpture
   B. Knowledge of artist styles and clay building skills
   C. Production of three-dimensional clay animal sculptures
   D. Planning time to consider application of skills to student-generated ideas

3. Mr. Kendricks has his fourth-grade class think about landforms that involved water (lakes, rivers, oceans, creeks, etc.) in his social studies time. He has students, in groups, draw and color a picture of each of these concepts. What is the best pre-activity for student success on this project?
   A. Creating a concept web with the whole class, brainstorming and organizing ideas and descriptions about these concepts
   B. Reading a story to the class about a child's adventures on a boat
   C. Asking children to close their eyes and imagine they are aboard some type of craft on each of these water forms and to describe how they think it would feel as they float along
   D. Asking children who have seen each of these forms to describe the concepts and their experiences

4. Ms. Tomás wants to integrate art into her kindergarten class. What is the best activity for her to put in a center?
   A. Have children sort cards with primary colors.
   B. Have children sort the work of several different artists addressing the same theme or topic.
   C. Have children sort art of different historical periods.
   D. Have children sort concepts illustrated by different artists in different times.

5. The Pre-K teachers meet at the beginning of the year to talk about the supplies they must order to complete the units they plan to teach. They discuss the art activities that they want children to complete, how age appropriate they are, and how they fit into their goals and objectives. What area is the most crucial to discuss before ordering?
   A. How much children would be motivated by the activities
   B. How much money they have in their budget
   C. Safety and disposal
   D. Establishing good rules for working with art this year

6. Mr. Kim wants to set up a good art evaluation plan for students in his self-contained elementary classroom. What is best for him to use?
   A. Test scores
   B. Rubrics
   C. Checklists
   D. Portfolios

7. At Thanksgiving, Ms. Ortiz decides that her first-grade students should integrate art, math, and science in a project by painting a picture of a pumpkin using orange for the pumpkin, brown for the stem and green for the leaves. Later, the students will cut open a real pumpkin, count the seeds, bake the seeds, and sample them. This could best be described as:
   A. an excellent integration because it has students focus on the details of the pumpkin for later.
   B. not an open-ended use of art.
   C. a motivating focus activity.
   D. a project that is not time efficient.

8. Mr. Howell wants to introduce his third graders to rhythm and movement, balance, proportion, contrast, variety, unity, and emphasis. These concepts make up:
   A. the principles of design.
   B. the elements of art.
   C. the ways of art-making.
   D. Discipline-Based Art Education.

9. Which of the following is not true?
   A. Red + yellow = orange
   B. Blue + red = violet
   C. Blue + yellow = green
   D. Yellow + black = brown

10. Mrs. Barrera plans to teach her sixth-grade students about careers and avocational opportunities in art. Which of the following best describes an art avocation?
    A. Portrait photography
    B. Fashion design
    C. Scrapbooking
    D. Architecture

TEST YOURSELF ANSWERS AND RATIONALES FOR ART

Answer 1: Choices A and C are mindless; they involve copying, a lower level activity. Choice B is better, but basically involves only recalling the steps. Choice D, however, requires the learner to select a meaningful part of the experiment and describe its meaning after the illustration is completed. This activity benefits both art and science, because higher levels of thinking are required to reflect and evaluate on a part of the experiment through drawing, verbalizing, and writing. The best answer is D.

Answer 2: Koster (2001) tells us that there are seven points to consider in the creative process: (1) motivation, (2) problem-finding (3) knowledge, (4) skills, (5) immersion, (6) incubation, and (7) production. Mrs. Henderson provides images and information about artists to motivate the students (A) and knowledge (B) through the integrated lesson. Students clearly produced three-dimensional sculptures (C), although student products did not meet the teacher's expectations. However, there was no time for students to really plan for applying their new knowledge in a meaningful way for a successful production. Creative production in any area (music, language arts, science, etc.) must always include time to think deeply about ideas and plan for their implementation (Koster, 2001). The correct answer is D.

Answer 3: All these activities could add some interest to the lesson. However, we are looking for the best one for a successful project. The activity that most helps students with their drawings is choice A, creating a concept web, which includes details and descriptions of each landform. For example, the bubble for oceans on the concept web might have spokes with words such as *most of the Earth, waves, tropical, blue, green, Arctic, fishing, big ships, whales,* and *hurricanes.* For lakes, the spokes might be *huge (like Great Lakes), shipping, small, enclosed (landlocked), waterskiing,* and *fishing.* These details help children both in social studies and in art. Reading a story such as the one described in choice B does not include all of the concepts needed for the assignment. Choice C, imagining, is a good activity, but it probably does not provide many of the details needed for a successful drawing. Choice D provides an element of "connecting children's background experiences to new learning," which is stated as a good practice numerous times in the competencies; however, many children probably have not seen all of the concepts that are needed in this lesson. The best answer is A.

Answer 4: Age appropriateness is important in every content area, including art. Choices C and D are a bit too difficult for kindergarten children without quite a bit of prior instruction. Choice A is an activity that helps students learn their colors. To really integrate art, however, Choice B is the best. For example, the teacher could select pictures of a animals to sort, done in various mediums (paintings, ink drawings, watercolors, sculptures, cave paintings, etc.) or different types of transportation or landforms; whatever the concepts that were being learned. Sorting concepts with artworks increases students' vision of the concepts and shows a wide range of how artists depict them. The best answer is B.

Answer 5: It is good to look at all these areas prior to making decisions. Teachers should always consider children's motivation (A) and classroom management (D) with special areas such as art, in which children may ruin clothes or cause possible concern with materials and tools. Of course, the budget is a determining factor in ordering supplies (B), although, many times, caregivers can contribute art supplies that are not within a budget. Within the budget, teachers should think of the value of certain art supplies over others (e.g., good brushes should be placed ahead of some supplies because they are an investment that can be used for many years, whereas certain types of paints and papers are expensive, when simple products will do for elementary-age projects). However, a *crucial* discussion before ordering supplies should be safety and disposal issues. Teachers can consult the *MSDS (Material Safety Data Sheet)* required by schools and most often used for science, but it should also tell about the safety of art materials as well. There are many safety issues for teachers to think about with art supplies (Koster, 2001): The need for storing particular supplies in a safe place for young children, the air quality of a classroom (to avoid fumes), reading warning labels to determine safe use guidelines, identifying possible toxic poisons, changing quality as art materials age, risk of misuse for younger children, and so forth. Younger children are particularly at risk, because they often experiment orally (putting things in their mouths), and their physical and mental development can cause them to misuse products and tools because of lack of control. Another concern is the health status of children in the class who may have particular allergies (although teachers may not know this at the time of their discussion), but teachers must concern themselves with chalk dust, for example, when using pastels; with skin allergies with paints and clays; and other toxins that may cause difficulties. A final safety concern that teachers must consider is to check the school's fire code or other safety codes prior to displaying any art in classrooms and in the halls. The answer is *C*.

Answer 6: The best way to evaluate children in art is through portfolios (*D*), which could contain all of the other assessment instruments listed and others (test scores, rubrics, checklists, task assignments, self-evaluations, anecdotal records, products, etc.). The portfolio lends itself not only to teacher evaluation but also to student self-evaluation and reflection. The best answer is *D*.

Answer 7: This lesson could contain a very good integration of art (*A*), as well as a motivating focus activity (*C*), and a time-efficient project (*D*) (although we have no information to support this choice, either positively or negatively). However, the problem here is not with the activity, but with the art project. This is not an open-ended art activity. Creative thinking is not encouraged when certain colors are expected to be used in a certain way. Teachers should

introduce various problems to solve and then allow children to select how they represent the subject. For example, the students could be taught to mix colors, paint while observing the real pumpkin, and then paint what they thought they might find after cutting the pumpkin open. The answer is *B*.

Answer 8: Mr. Howell is introducing the *principles of design* (*A*). The *elements* of art (*B*) consist of color, form, shape, space, line, texture, and value. *Ways of art-making* (*C*) include drawing, painting, printmaking, collage, sculpture, fiber arts, and electronic media. *Discipline-Based Art Education* (DBAE) (*D*) is an approach to teaching the four stands of art together: art history, art-making, art criticism, and aesthetics. The correct answer is *A*.

Answer 9: Choices *A, B,* and *C* are all true. *D* is not. Therefore, the answer is *D*.

Answer 10: Choice *A* is a career that requires artistic and technical knowledge of lighting and photographic equipment. Choice *B* is an occupation that requires understanding of design and fabrics for making garments. Choice *D* requires study of art related to design and materials used for the construction of buildings. Choice *C* is a popular form of art-making that relies on knowledge of art and provides personal satisfaction but is not likely to become a career. There are many other vocations that one can pursue in art. For example, one can work for a museum or gallery as a curator or director managing art exhibitions and collections. Jobs such as fashion designer, industrial designer, graphics designer, jewelry designer, interior designer, and landscape architect require specialized knowledge of art design. Fine arts and crafts careers are made up of such vocations as painter, sculptor, printmaker, photographer, jeweler, weaver, and ceramicist. Other examples of art careers include animation, film making, art historian, and art education. Any art endeavor enjoyed as a *non-professional* is considered *avocational*. These personal art experiences might include, but are not limited to, photography, painting, creating visual journals, or jewelry making. The best answer is *C*.

7 Preparing to Teach Music in Texas

Janice L. Nath
University of Houston–Downtown

Teachers who take the EC-6 *Generalist* test should be familiar with many aspects of music, as the state of Texas has established music standards for these ages of children. Under each music standard, Texas has provided information that includes *Teacher Knowledge* (what teachers should know about music) and *Application* (what teachers should be able to do when teaching music at their particular grade level). These standards are presented in this chapter, but they can also be downloaded in chart form from http://www.sbec.state.tx.us/SBECOnline/standtest/standards/EC_6_standardmusic.pdf.

Many of you may have been placed in a classroom for field experiences, are teaching in, or have grown up in a school where there is a special teacher for music classes. If so, you are probably wondering why the state of Texas requires "regular" elementary teachers to know about teaching music. You may not realize that there are no specialized music teachers in many Texas schools, particularly in the lower grades. Therefore, if any music is to be taught in those schools, it is you—the regular classroom teacher—who is responsible. I hope you agree that it would be a terrible thing for children to grow up without learning about music—in the sense of joy that it brings, of appreciating the wide range of music the world has produced, and in learning the songs and music that bind our culture. You may be the one person who opens the door for a child's love for music, special musical talents, or even a career in music.

Because music is such a significant part of the human experience, Texas wants to offer students the opportunity to have a teacher who can bring music into each classroom, even if a district is not able to provide a music specialist for each school. This chapter is written not only to help those teachers who have had little, if any, music training but also to provide a good review for those who may have had some experience with music. In addition, it should help teachers begin to create music lessons, gain resources, and understand what is needed to help children learn about music.

Because the standards often ask that the teacher recognize music concepts aurally (through listening), a number of Websites are given that allow you to hear an example that is described. Most often, examples of songs or music have been listed that should be familiar to teachers who have grown up in American classrooms; however, if you did not grow up here or if you are unfamiliar with the examples, please pull up the site and listen carefully. Websites change, so if a site is not available, search for another using the name of the song or instrumental title. One Website, http://www.songza.org, offers the opportunity to search and listen to a multitude of music (just type in the title). However, do be aware that the Websites listed in this chapter have been carefully selected as exact examples. Artists can arrange music in many different ways, so interpretations other than those listed may not be a direct match with the concept as described in the chapter. *Interpretation* refers to the same song or piece of music being played in various styles using different musical expression (including sound levels, phrasing, speeds, choice of instruments or voice, and regional expression or style). Also, these Websites are normally meant to be an opportunity for you to listen to an example, but if you were going to teach with the examples given or others from these listening sites, you must make sure that copyright laws are followed.

The standards are introduced in this chapter in an order seen as more logical for learning about music and about teaching music, rather than the numeric order in which they are given by the state. Let's take a closer look at the standards tested here.

Standard I: Visual and Aural Knowledge

(Note: All music standards are covered under Competency 045.)

The music teacher has a comprehensive visual and aural knowledge of musical perception and performance.

The EC-6 teacher should know and understand the standard terminology used to describe and analyze musical sound. Thus, he or she should be able to identify and interpret music symbols and terms, use standard music terminology, and identify different rhythms and meters. In addition, she or he should be able to identify vocal and instrumental sounds and distinguish among timbres; recognize and describe the melody, harmony, tempo, pitch, meter, and texture of a musical work; and identify musical forms. Teachers' knowledge and ability should also include how to demonstrate musical artistry both through vocal or instrumental performance and by conducting vocal or instrumental performances. The teacher should be able to perceive performance problems and detect errors accurately and, in addition, use appropriate techniques of musical performance for instruments and voice.

There are many concepts in music that you should know as a beginning teacher of children in these grade levels because you may be required to teach music as one of your subject areas. The main concepts of this standard center on reading music and include duration, rhythm, pitch and melody, form, dynamics, tempo, timbre and tone color, and musical instrument families. The next several sections cover the basics.

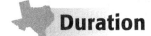 Duration

One of the first concepts about which young children learn in music is **duration** of sound—that is, there are *long sounds* in the world all around us (sirens, mooing cows, etc.), and there are also *short sounds* (a jackhammer, the clicking sounds of a computer keyboard, etc.). These variations of length of sound (or duration) are also found in music and can be represented by symbols or *musical notes*. Each symbol, or written musical note, represents a certain length (or count) that the sound should last, as well as a particular pitch (as we discuss later). The longer the count or length held, the less "darkened, encumbered, or decorated" a note is when written. For example, the symbol for the longest tone in music is called a **whole note** and looks like a hollow circle—almost the same as the letter *O*. If we sing one tone, or note ("la-a-a-a," for example), while we slowly count to 4 in our heads, that is about the length of a typical whole note's duration. To begin to teach very young children this concept, you may want to begin with long animal sounds and have them "sing" whole notes.

O   **O**   **O**   **O**

Moo-oo!   Moo-oo!   Moo-oo!   Moo-oo!

There is an easy connection in determining duration of musical notes to mathematics (fractions, to be exact). If the whole note gets 4 equal counts in a certain piece of music, then we read the next shorter tone as getting 2 counts. The symbol for this tone is called a **half note**. If you divided the whole note that you sang before into two half notes, they would sound like "la-a" "la-a" (if we count 1–2 in our heads for the first "la-a" and 3–4 for the second "la-a"). Half notes are described as hollow circles with a stem. The half note tones can then be divided into shorter **quarter notes**, which are sung or played as "la," "la," "la," "la," as each receives 1 short count (1, 2, 3, 4). The quarter note looks like a half note with a stem, but the circle is filled. To continue to teach young children about the length of sound here, it may be beneficial to have them continue with less sustained animal sounds.

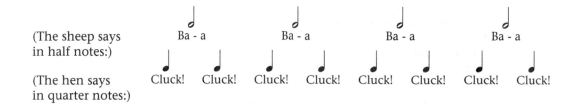

(The sheep says in half notes:)

(The hen says in quarter notes:)

We can continue to divide these length/duration symbols into eighth notes, sixteenth notes, and so on, each note getting half as much time as the note before. Remember that the shorter the note, the more that it is darkened in and the more "flags" it has attached. Let us see how this might look in music. As you sing "la" to yourself, hold each note as long as the count below it shows.

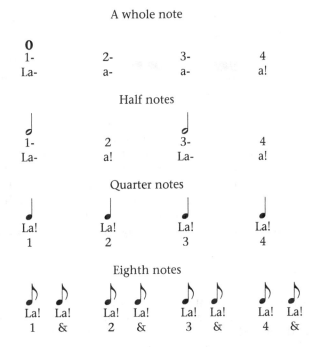

A whole note

0
| 1- | 2- | 3- | 4 |
| La- | a- | a- | a! |

Half notes

| 1- | 2 | 3- | 4 |
| La- | a! | La- | a! |

Quarter notes

| La! | La! | La! | La! |
| 1 | 2 | 3 | 4 |

Eighth notes

| La! | La! | La! | La! | La! | La! | La! | La! |
| 1 | & | 2 | & | 3 | & | 4 | & |

To continue to explain this concept to children, you could, for example, compare a whole note to a telephone ring or siren. The half notes are similar to the length of a grandfather clock's "bonging" on the hour. The quarter notes are like a clock ticking or a car blinker, and the eighth notes are like someone typing rapidly on the computer. You can see how these symbols work in the song "Old MacDonald" (http://www.youtube.com/watch?v= PR3UCF4QGEw or http://www.boowakwala.com/kids/boowakwala-world-farms-farmsong.html). Try singing the song by counting the numbers below the notes rather than the words and you will have an idea of how the shape and design of the note tells you how long to hold it.

| Old | Mac- | Don- | ald | had | a | farm | E | I | E | I | Oh—! | **0** |
| 1 | 2 | 3 | 4 | 1 | 2 | 3-4 | 1 | 2 | 3 | 4 | 1-2-3-4 | |

| On | his | farm | he | had | some | chicks, | E | I | E | I | Oh—! | **0** |
| 1 | 2 | 3 | 4 | 1 | 2 | 3-4 | 1 | 2 | 3 | 4 | 1-2-3-4 | |

There is also a symbol for when no music should be played or sung—the **rest**. When you see a rest symbol, it means to "rest" your voice or instrument by not singing or not playing for a certain time period. Rest symbols (or notations of silence) correspond to the values of musical notes, so we see (1) whole rests, (2) half rests, (3) quarter rests, (4) eighth rests, (5) sixteenth rests, and so forth. Again, these symbols indicate a period of time when there is no sound for an established duration. Each rest appears very different from the others (unlike the notes we saw earlier to which flags and darkening are added as the note gets shorter in length or duration). Rests with their counts are shown next. Remember that there is a length of silence for each rest, according to its value.

whole rest	half rests	quarter rests	eighth rests
1-2-3-4	1-2 3-4	1 2 3 4	1&2&3&4&

One important thing to remember in teaching the duration of notes and rests is that the sound (or, in the case of rests, no sound) occupies the entire space in time until the next note or rest value is written. If one is singing or playing a whole note with the value of four counts, for example, each count must be equal—including the last count. One cannot count, "One—two—three—fo—One—two—three—fo—One—. . . ." Each must receive its full value. It must be, "One—two—three—four—One—two—three—four—. . . ." In the former example, it is like singing, "Old MacDonald had a fa—."

Rhythm

The concept of **rhythm**, or sound organized in time, is an important one in music and strongly relates to the previous discussion. If you have ever marched, played a "pat–slap" game, chanted while jumping rope, or participated in a rap, you have experienced the beat, or *pulse*, of music. This pulse of the music can be easily felt through toe-tapping or dancing and is, perhaps, the most fundamental (although not the whole concept of rhythm). For example, sing the words to "Baa Baa, Black Sheep" and tap your foot at the same time (http://www.youtube.com/watch?v=gBEHFFnV3RY or http://www.kididdles.com/lyrics/b001.html). You experience a very *steady beat* in sets of 2's (count "1, 2" over and over as you hum the tune). Notice that each set is divided by a bar. The distance between bars, in music, is called a **measure** and separates sets of beats into groups—in this case, sets of 2 beats per measure.

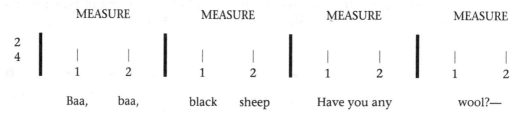

In "Twinkle, Twinkle Little Star," there is a steady beat, or foot tap, in sets of four (http://www.musictechteacher.com/flash_piano_lesson_twinkle.htm).

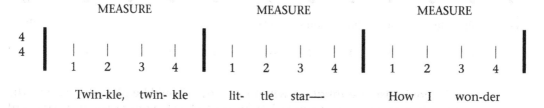

In most Native American music, there is a very steady pulse of four beats. In stereotypical Native American music, such as we hear in Wild West cartoons, a very *strong beat* comes on the first of the four beats (ONE-two-three-four, ONE-two-three-four) (http://songza.org; then search Native American Chants and select The Moon-Red Sky). Think of the drum beat associated with stereotypical Native American music and see if you can tap it out in the following example. In authentic Native American music, this loud-soft-soft-soft rhythm is not so distinct.

The beat changes, however, in "On Top of Old Smoky" (http://toneway.com/songs/on-top-of-old-smoky) and "Happy Birthday" (http://www.youtube.com/watch?v=E2Pr1vC3CSo). When you toe-tap to either song, you should feel beats in sets of three with a very strong beat on the first beat (ONE-two-three, ONE-two-three). This is a rhythm also seen in many waltzes.

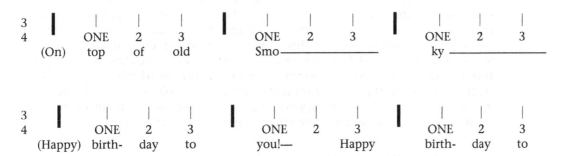

Try tapping or patting each of these songs to see if you feel the beat.

Another type of music that has a strong beat is a march. This type of music is easy for many people to follow (as in a marching band or military group) because it helps people walk in time together: "left, right, left, right; 1,2,1,2." "Yankee Doodle" is a march that demonstrates this beat. Try to move your feet to feel this rhythm as you count to the melody.

One way to see if you are keeping the beat regularly is to set a **metronome**, an instrument that sounds like a loud clock and ticks to the beat that a composer has written or that a musician has selected for each piece of music. It takes the place of a director when playing or singing alone, so that one does not inadvertently speed up or slow down the music. Thus, a singer or instrumentalist can be sure to practice the correct beat in a very steady manner throughout a piece of music.

Now that you have a feel for what beats are all about, how do composers tell players or singers to follow what they intended? At the beginning of each piece of music, as shown next, is the **meter** sign that indicates how many beats per measure the composer desires to be played. This is indicated by two numbers that are one on top of the other called the **time signature**. The number on top of the time signature indicates how many beats there are per measure, or, for our purpose, divided "foot-tap or pat–clap sets." The bottom number tells what kind of note gets one beat. For example, a "2" on the bottom means that a half note gets one beat, but a "4" on the bottom would mean that a quarter note gets one beat. There can be many combinations, but here we deal with only the most common time signatures. Go back to the last six lines of music that we examined previously and note the meter sign on the far left. Let's look at the following signatures.

$\underline{4}$ There are four equal quarter notes to a set in a measure (Count: 1-2-3-4; 1-2-3-4).
4 The 4 on the bottom indicates that a quarter note gets one beat (or think math again: a $\frac{1}{4}$ of a whole note gets a beat = a quarter note).

$\underline{2}$ There are two even quarter notes to a set (Count: 1-2; 1-2), as in a march.
4 A quarter note gets one beat.

$\underline{3}$ There are three even quarter notes to a set (Count: 1-2-3; 1-2-3), as in a waltz.
4 A quarter note gets one beat.

If we now combine these two concepts, we can see that the notes have a *value length* (duration) and that the composer can arrange a *set of notes* together in a rhythm pattern. When we tapped the beat of "Baa, Baa, Black Sheep," we were in $\frac{2}{4}$ time, "Twinkle, Twinkle Little Star" was in $\frac{4}{4}$ time, and "On Top of Old Smoky" and "Happy Birthday" were both in $\frac{3}{4}$ time. A question in the exam may ask you to determine time or meter for a familiar piece of music.

Sometimes music changes time signatures in the middle of a song. If you see measures that look like those shown next, you can see that the beat pattern changes. Using *time signature* changes is the way in which composers tell us that the beat of the song should change, for example, from a waltz beat to a march beat. This does not happen very often in popular vocal music, but we frequently see, hear, and feel the change in instrumental music.

Time signature change

There are also *asymmetric* time signatures. These irregular times signatures are rare but can be seen as $\frac{5}{4}$, $\frac{9}{8}$, and so forth. *Ride of the Valkyries* is a famous piece of music with an asymmetric time signature (http://www.youtube.com/watch?v=V92OBNsQgxU). Just as in the previous description, in $\frac{9}{8}$ time, an eighth note receives one beat, and there are nine beats per measure.

In addition to the beat or pulse and the duration of notes and silence, another element that contributes to rhythm is the patterns of accented and unaccented sound that occur in music. We can also find these in poetry. For example, in "Jack and Jill went up the hill," there is a heavy accent on the words Jack/Jill/up/hill with other less accented words between, although there is still a steady 1-2/1-2 beat that we can tap. The same occurs in music. This concept might be compared to our heart providing a steady, consistent beat while we go about running, jumping, stopping, stepping, and so forth. In music, all of this organization of sound is **rhythm**.

Children seem to develop musical abilities as they mature–just as they do in other areas of learning. Between the ages of about 7 to 9, rhythmic coordination improves dramatically, and by the fourth grade, most children should be able to discriminate among elements of duration and meter. The ability to perceive, recall, and reproduce musical elements precedes the child's ability to read music, or decode, and make sense of rhythmic phrases and other musical features. Just as a child can speak before he or she can read, a child can sing without the ability to read music yet.

To help children learn about rhythm, first promote the natural tendencies of children in rhythmic play when they are moving to the music, then use direct music instruction to teach the elements of rhythm. Thus children should first internalize "how the music feels" before they are introduced to the process of decoding music symbols. Clapping, patting, stamping, and so on to music or having students listen to a beat played by the teacher helps them feel the rhythms. Relating words to rhythm is also helpful, as discussed previously. All words have a rhythm, so select words to match rhythms you wish to teach. For example, say the following words in a rhythmic pattern—"Hou-ston, Dal-las, Wich-i-ta Falls!" This activity also helps young readers determine syllable division. Can you perceive the rhythm of each word and of the phrase as a whole? Model such patterns often, and then ask students to echo or clap what they hear. This is an excellent way to introduce the idea of rhythm, and young children love pat–clap or echo games and follow along easily. As with other content areas and domains, it is best to break instruction and performance into small tasks and relate them closely to that which is already known by the learner. At first, children should discriminate rhythm examples within songs they know rather than using abstract or unknown music. As children grow in their abilities with rhythms, they can be asked to differentiate between rhythm patterns, explain their thinking, or sort out several patterns.

National and state standards tell us that children should, as they grow older, be able to create, notate, and perform simple rhythmic patterns. Another good way to help children understand and perform the concept of rhythm is to have rhythm instruments available. These instruments can be real or can be created from anything that students can beat, rattle, or shake to the beat. Some typical instruments for beginning rhythm activities might be rhythm sticks, hand drums, bongos, maracas, guiros (ridged gourd instruments), jingle bells, tambourines, claves (hardwood sticks), sand blocks, wood blocks (hardwood blocks with a hardwood striker), slit drums, cowbells, hanging cymbals, finger cymbals, triangles, resonator bells, and glockenspiels or xylophones. As an aside, some of these instruments can be rather expensive, but this is an excellent time to begin to teach children the value of taking care of instruments and treating them with respect. Computers and other technologically based devices, including keyboards, sequencers, synthesizers, and drum machines, can also be used. Having a variety of instruments gives students choices in improving or creating their own sound composition.

Pitch and Melody

The next concept or idea about music is, "How do you know what tone to sing or play?" This question is related to another beginning musical concept for younger children: some sounds are high, and some are low. Again, this is a concept that you would first want to compare with sounds that are familiar to children. For example, a mouse usually has a high squeak whereas a cow has a low moo. High and low sounds go together to form a **melody**. When you hum specific high and low tunes together, you hummed the melody, or the tones or pitches that are put together to create a unique piece of music that is recognizable as a particular song. Thus, if asked to sing or hum "Mary Had a Little Lamb," you are humming or singing the melody of that song. The melody may have other parts of music that are added, but if these other parts are played or sung alone, we cannot recognize it as that particular song. Think of the melody as the "main plot" of a song. As in a story, there can be many details that you could add in the telling; but if you tell only the details, no one can follow the storyline. Also, as in literature, there may be a **musical theme**. A melody may, thus, have a pattern that occurs several times throughout a piece of music. This is usually recognized at once and serves to bring the piece of music together as a whole. If you know the popular instrumental song "The Entertainer," you will quickly catch the idea of theme and of how the same melody patterns are repeated to create a theme (http://www.youtube.com/watch?v=jcznaE2BDz0 or go to http://www.youtube.com/watch?v=DDGibUnfGK8 and note the repetition of phrases).

A good way to begin to teach children about melody is to have children move their hands up and down as they sing a melody, or they may draw a graphic representation. For example, a part of the melody of "Jingle Bells!"

("Jingle bells! Jingle bells! Jingle all the way!") might be drawn (or have hand motions follow) like this: (http://www.links2love.com/christmas_songs_20 .htm or http://songza.org; then search for "Jingle Bells" with Lyrics).

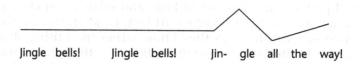

Jingle bells!   Jingle bells!   Jin- gle all the way!

Each musical **note**, or symbol of sound, not only shows us length (as discussed in the section on *duration*), but is also given a name from the musical alphabet based on its tone—or how high or low the sound should be. The musical alphabet uses only seven letters—*A* though *G*—then repeats itself in tones higher or lower. An *octave* is a set of eight tones from a named tone (such as a C note) to the same tone (C), only higher or lower. For example, sing the first two notes of "Somewhere Over the Rainbow," and you have an octave (listen on http://www.youtube.com/watch?v=MXJ2Q0F8H80&feature=related). Then, go back to the lower C note and hum all the notes in between, step by step ("do, re, mi, fa, so, la, ti, do"), to the higher C, and you discover that, altogether, you have hummed eight notes. An octave can be from any starting note, but it must end on the same note eight tones higher or lower (e.g., C, D, E, F, G, A, B—to a higher C; C to C is an octave). A piano and a harp are two instruments with a great number of octaves, although many instruments do not have such a great range.

However, now the question becomes, "How do you know what key or string to play?" The answer is where a note is located on a musical staff. The name/pitch of a note is related to the place where it is found on a **musical staff** (the five lines and five spaces on which all music is written). There is a treble staff and a bass staff in music. The staff for high notes/sounds is called the **treble** and is marked by a **treble clef** symbol, whereas the staff for low notes/sounds is marked by the **bass clef**. Note the symbols for each clef:

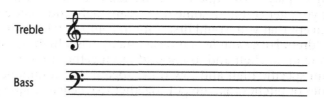

Treble

Bass

Usually (but not always), the melody in music for elementary schools is written on the treble clef. If you are singing a part written for a **soprano** (high voice) or **alto** (mid-high voice), usually for a female or young boy's voice, or if you were playing an instrument with a high sound (such as a flute, a violin, or a clarinet), the music is read from the treble clef. If you have a male mid-range (**tenor**), mid-low (**baritone**), or very low (**bass**) voice or are playing an instrument with a lower sound (e.g., tuba, trombone, string bass), music is read from the bass clef. Instruments like the piano, with many pitches available (both high and low), use both the treble clef and the bass clef. In simple music, we may only see the staff with the melody on it (usually the treble clef). When other notes are added in a more complicated piece for harmony, there is a staff of music for treble and one for bass, each marked with its clef sign. Naturally, because these staffs (or *staves*) are written one on top of the other, the treble clef (for high sound) is on top, and the bass clef (for lower sounds) is on the bottom.

Part of understanding how music is produced involves understanding the relationship among three elements of making sound: (1) size, (2) length, and (3) tension. The higher the sound, for example, the smaller and shorter the vocal chords, the instrument, or the strings, and vice versa. Children's voices are high because their vocal chords are still very small. As noted, if you are playing an instrument that has both high and low notes, such as the piano, two clefs are presented—the treble on top and the bass clef on the bottom. When you open up the top of a piano, you can see that the high notes are played by a hammer striking shorter, thinner strings, but the low notes are much thicker and longer (thus the shape of a grand piano accommodates the different size strings). If you also look at the strings of a guitar, you see that the higher notes (treble) are played by the fingers strumming the thin strings, whereas the lower notes (bass) are played on thicker strings. The same is true with a harp. The lower the note, the longer and thicker the string. *Tension* is also considered in pitch. When a trumpet or trombone player wishes to play a higher pitch, he or she blows air through tautly stretched lips, but a player produces lower tones by blowing through relaxed lips. A singer also uses tension. For example, note the tension of your vocal chords increasing as you singer higher and higher. **Pitch** is caused by vibrations of the materials of the instruments or by the vocal chords. The higher the pitch, the faster the vibrations; the lower the tone, the more slowly the vibrations move.

Music is designed so that pitch is easily read. Each musical note written on a staff has a particular *pitch*, or tone of sound, that is high or low and that is associated with its name. For our purposes, we learn only the names of the notes where the melody is most often found—the treble clef. Beginning music students have always remembered the names of the notes written on the treble clef by two easy methods. The notes arranged in the spaces (between the lines) of the treble clef spell "FACE" (from the bottom up). The notes arranged on the lines of the treble clef are EGBDF ("Every Good Boy Does Fine" or "Every Good Boy Deserves Fudge") from the bottom up. By remembering these placements on a staff, you can easily read the name of each note and may need to do so on a test question. Vocalists can read, then remember, and sing the correct pitch, whereas instrumentalists play the note by reading it from the staff. Remember that these five lines and four spaces are known as a *musical staff*. There are also notes above and below the staff, continuing in the order of the musical alphabet. Look at each staff that follows.

Note names in spaces (FACE)	Note names on lines	Together
E C A F	F(udge) D(eserves) B(oy) G(ood) E(very)	F D B G E

You may have heard the song "Do-Re-Mi" from *The Sound of Music* (http://www.youtube.com/watch?v=WkBepgH00GM or do a search for the song title) or heard someone sing a *scale* (the eight notes of a musical octave) "do, re, mi, fa, sol, la, ti, do," where each note gets progressively higher. Many music texts teach students to sing using the concept of these tone names first rather than the alphabetical name of the notes.

Steps, leaps, and repeated tones are important concepts in music. When you hear a **scale** (do, re, mi, fa, sol, la, ti, do) and back down or even a part of a scale (do, re, mi), you are hearing an example of notes or tones arranged in **steps**—that is, the sound moves from one note to another without skipping a tone. However, if a tone does not change its pitch, it is called a **repeated tone**, such as you hear in the first few notes of "Jingle Bells" ("Jingle Bells, Jingle Bells, . . ."). Sing this first line of the song. Note that your voice does not change its tone at all—that is, your voice does not go up or down. This is a repeated tone.

There is another way that tones are arranged—in **leaps**. When tones leap, the pitch moves up or down, but it skips the tones in between as it moves. As you continue to sing "Jingle Bells," the next few words are "Jingle all. . . ." This line of music has a high leap, then a low leap ("Jingle all"), then ends in steps with the words ("the way"). Think about how this whole first line of music puts together *repeated tones, leaps,* and *steps* to form a *melody.* The following may help you to see that visually.

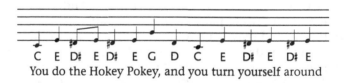

Music also can be arranged in half steps or tones. When you see a piece of music that has a symbol known as a **flat** (♭) or a **sharp** (♯), the composer means that your voice or instrument should only move up a half step or tone for sharps or move down a half step or tone for flats. When a composer wants to indicate a flat or sharp in the middle of a piece of music, it is called an *accidental.* Note how the following accidentals (in this case, sharps) are written in this example: (http://kids.niehs.nih.gov/lyrics/hokey.htm).

C E D♯ E D♯ E G D C E D♯ E D♯ E
You do the Hokey Pokey, and you turn yourself around

A composer can also indicate a sharp or flat every time a particular note is played or sung in his or her piece of music by placing a flat or sharp symbol at the very beginning of a piece of music on the line or space of the note desired where the note(s) is normally written. In the example below, we see that the composer wants us to play or sing a B flat *every* time we come to a note on the B line. In the second of these examples, we can see that the composer asks us always to play a sharp when we come to F notes, as a sharp symbol has been placed on the line where the high F is normally found (EGBDF). If we skip down to the second line of music on the next page, we can see that the composer chose to put three flats into this composition. By looking at the lines and spaces, we can see that we have a flat on the line where B is located (Every Good <u>B</u>oy . . .) and the spaces where A and E are (F<u>A</u>C<u>E</u>) located. Therefore, when we are reading this music and we come to B, A, and E, we would automatically play or sing half steps or tones instead of whole steps.

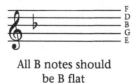

All B notes should
be B flat

All F notes should
be F sharp

The composer could begin with three flats. He or she can change this in the middle of a piece of music as well. In other words, the composer may say, "I want this music to start out with all B flats, but in the middle, I want to change to all B flats plus all E flats. This is called a **key change**, and it makes a difference in the sound of the music. The music can change from no flats to one to seven flats or no sharps to one to seven sharps (one half tone up or down for each note in the musical scale—A, B, C, D, E, F, G). A key change usually creates an emotional surge in music. The staff below shows a *key change* from three flats to one flat. (In "Memories" from the musical CATS there are two dramatic key changes (http://www.youtube.com/watch?v= 4-L6rEmOrny or go to http://www.songza.org and type in "Cats-Memories). Notice the key change after "And a new day will begin" and later after "another day is dawning."

Key and *key changes* are important concepts for other reasons. Have you ever started to sing a song and found that the tone on which you started made it impossible to hit the high notes (or maybe the low notes) as you continued singing along? This is a fairly common occurrence in singing "The Star-Spangled Banner" (http://www.brownielocks.com/starspangledbannerWAVE.html). What did you do when you discovered that you couldn't make those higher or lower notes as you continue into the song? Usually, if you were singing alone, you probably began again—either on a higher note or lower note, which would have helped you hit those notes that you could not sing the first time. This whole concept is related to the key in which a song is played or sung. You may have seen a movie where a singer is trying out for a musical part, and she or he asks the piano player to accompany him or her in a certain key ("Can you play it in C?"). Almost all simple children's songs are written in the keys of C, F, or G. These keys are the most popular because they offer easy accompaniment on many instruments, and the voice range is fairly good for singing.

All of the arrangement of the tones discussed so far creates a melody. Again, *melody* is a unique sound pattern that often allows us to sing or hum along easily with a piece of music or to recognize a particular composition when we hear it played.

 **Form**

Music is written with an overall plan, structure, or **form**. The elements that help shape music into forms are (1) repetition, (2) contrast, and (3) variation. For example, a **melody pattern** is one that can be heard to be repeated several times throughout the music. We use the letters of the alphabet or even shapes to help us identify form, where contrasting parts of music are heard. For example, a song might have an ABA pattern or an ABAB pattern:

One can see this very easily in simple popular songs that have verses but come back to one chorus or *refrain* (part of the song that repeats). Looking again at "Jingle Bells," we know that the song begins with one melody pattern (*A*) and ends with a different melody pattern in the refrain or chorus (*B*), thus the form is *AB*:

A   Dashing through the snow, in a one horse open sleigh
O'er the field we go, Laughing all the way
Bells on bobtails ring, Making spirits bright;
Oh, what fun to ride and sing a sleighing song tonight!

B   Oh, Jingle Bells! Jingle Bells! Jingle all the way!
Oh, what fun it is to ride in a one horse open sleigh!
Oh, Jingle Bells! Jingle Bells! Jingle all the way!
Oh, what fun it is to ride in a one horse open sleigh

(http://songza.org and select Diana Krall — Jingle Bells).

"Oh, Susannah!" is another good example of a song with a different form. It is written in *AAB* form, where there the pattern is three sections; the first and second verses repeat the same melody, while the ending verse (refrain or chorus) is different (go to http://songza.org, type in the title "Oh Susannah" and select the first one).

A   Oh, I come from Alabama with my banjo on my knee
I'm going to Louisiana, my true love for to see.

A   Oh, it rained all day the night I left, the weather it was dry
The sun so hot, I froze to death, Susannah don't you cry.

B   Oh, Susannah! Don't you cry for me,
For I come from Alabama with my banjo on my knee.

"The Bear Went over the Mountain" is a simple example of *ABA*:

A   The bear went over the mountain,
The bear went over the mountain,
The bear went over the mountain,
To see what he could see.

B   To see what he could see,
To see what he could see.

A   The other side of the mountain,
The other side of the mountain,
The other side of the mountain,
Was all that he could see.

(www.gfes.tpc.edu.tw/board/abc-song/bearwent.swf or http://www.youtube.com/watch?v=RmUp2jyHd9Y)

Music can be written in any of these combinations (even adding other forms such as *C*, *D*, etc.). A **rondo** refers to a musical form that has different sections and where the *A* pattern is repeated after each different section (e.g., *ABACA*) (for more information and to listen to a rondo form, go to www.classicsforkids.com/teachers/lessonplans/kodaly/Kodaly230.asp). This occurs in songs and in instrumental music where the *A* form "holds" the entire piece together.

When singing or playing songs with repeated forms, we often see repeat signs. A **repeat sign** (:||) is a handy symbol that tells the musician when to go back and play or sing a passage again. The musician either goes back to the beginning of the music and repeats all of it or finds this sign (||:) and begins from that point again.

Why is form important to know as a musician? First, it is very useful for singers. If a singer masters the melody of one section, such as the melody of form *A* in "Oh, Susannah!" and knows that the next verse is exactly the same form, then he or she can easily repeat the melody. It is also easier to *sight read*, or sing by reading the music without the help of a musical instrument, when that form appears. For instrumentalists, it is the same. However, knowing form really helps musicians memorize their music. In instrumental music, form can be of great importance in arranging more sophisticated orchestra pieces.

Teaching children about melody is much like teaching rhythm. By about age 8, children should be able to have a fairly stable tonal recall ability. To help children learn about melody, first promote the natural tendencies of children in already known and invented melodies, then use direct music instruction. Model melody patterns often, then ask students to copy what they hear, as in echo melody games. As with rhythm, break instruction and performance down into small tasks. Ask students to differentiate between melody patterns and to explain their thinking as to why they are different, and then help them sort out several patterns. Again, when giving direct instruction on melody, isolate examples of melody within songs children know rather than offering examples with which they are unfamiliar. Have them recognize the same melody pattern played on different instruments or sung by different voices. Encouraging students to invent short melodies and write them down so that someone else could read/sing/play them helps children understand the decoding process. Learning to match the exact pitch of a song is usually the last element of acquiring a song (as you may well know from trying to sing along with your favorite vocalists on the radio). Begin with a concentration on the words, then melody contours, and finally work on matching exact pitches.

Dynamics

We are not yet through with the way we decode written music. There are some other very important ways that a composer shows us to how read music. For instance, another question (when we want to play or sing) is, "How loud or soft should the whole piece or a particular part of the music be?" Composers indicate volume by writing terms or abbreviations of those terms into a piece of music. They are usually seen in italics and in Italian, so if you speak that language, you are already ahead in knowing about **dynamics** (how loud or soft the music should be). The most common words relating to dynamics, or volume, are *forte, mezzo forte, mezzo piano,* and *piano*. The symbols for those are *f* (forte), *mf* (mezzo forte), and in contrast, *mp* (mezzo piano), and *p* (piano), and they are simply written right under or, in some cases, above the notes of the music. *Forte* means forceful, loud, or with strength (as in "That is really my *forte*," or my strength). *Mezzo* is medium or between two sounds (as in a *mezzanine*, or the floor in a building between two floors), so *mezzo forte* is medium loud or moderately forceful. *Piano*, however, indicates softness, so *mezzo piano* means to play or sing in a moderately soft manner. What do you think *ff* or *pp* is? As you might guess, it means doubly loud or very soft. If you think of most expressive music that you know, you realize that a song does not stay at one level of sound but changes *dynamics* within the song just as a "dynamic speaker" varies his or her voice by "building the voice" or having it gradually "fall" rather than having it remain monotone. There is a way to indicate this in music as well. The composer simply uses **crescendo** (gradually become louder) or **decrescendo** or *diminuendo* (gradually become softer) or the symbols for these words. A teacher may say to children that they should think of the small end of these symbols, as shown next, as the smaller sound and the large end as the larger sound. These symbols have the same meanings in mathematics. Look at the notation mark in the following example:

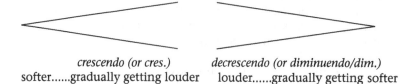

crescendo (or cres.)   *decrescendo (or diminuendo/dim.)*
softer......gradually getting louder   louder......gradually getting softer

| The sound on this end should be *less than* the other end. | The sound on this end should be *greater than* the other end. | The sound on this end should be *less than* on the other end. |

Another way to indicate a change in volume is with an **accent mark**. When an accent mark is used below a note, that note should be stronger, louder, and more forceful (or more emphasized) than the sounds around it. Think again of the stereotypical Native American drums, where the accent is on the first beat or note.

ONE two three four   ONE two three four

The competencies in this area note that teachers should teach their students to sing or play with expression. Concepts found under dynamics are of particular importance in singing or playing expressively.

Tempo

Another Italian lesson comes with determining the **tempo**, or speed, of the beat—that is, how fast or slow the music should be played. Some of these terms are *largo* (very slow, as most *large* things move slowly), *adagio* (slowly), *andante* (walking speed, not fast, or as "an ant walks not *too* fast" as a memory model) or *moderato* (moderate). In contrast, *allegro* (quick or merry), *allegretto* (very lively), and *presto* (very fast, as when you are pressed to hurry), show when the beat should be played quite rapidly. Sometimes music speeds up during the song. Thus, it might be marked *accelerando* (get faster gradually, as in *accelerating*) or vice versa with *ritardando* (or slow down gradually, or *retard* your speed).

Yet another type of contrast in music is indicated by more Italian terms. For example, you may want to sing or play *legato* (smoothly) with a blended connection between notes, or a musical piece may require distinct precision in a way that each note is **staccato** (detached or separated). For example, in "Row, Row, Row Your Boat," the first part of the song is often sung or played smoothly with connection between notes (*legato*) (http://www.manythings.org/pp/row_your_boat.html). Contrast that sound with the "Alphabet Song" (A, B, C, D, E, F, G, . . .) where the voice or instrument clearly separates notes (*staccato*), much like a prancing horse (see exercises 1 and 2 at http://www.studybass.com/lessons/bass-technique/legato-and-staccato/exercises).

Let's look at how many elements are combined now to allow us to read music. At the top of the next page, we have a song written in *treble clef* with one *flat* with *three beats* per measure. It is to be played at a *moderate speed* and *loudly* in the second measure. The melody notes read GFA, CAG, and the first notes of each of the two measures are accented.

Instrument Families

Elementary students usually begin to identify musical *instruments* of bands, orchestras, and even of other lands both visually and *aurally*, or by hearing their unique sound. One way of identification involves classifying or grouping musical instruments into families. There are four main families: percussion, woodwind, brass, and strings. The **percussion** family of instruments, for example, are those that are played by beating, shaking, scraping, or striking. Drums, tambourines, rattles, rasps, triangles, and xylophones are some examples. The piano, too, is often classified as a percussion instrument, because the player's fingers strike the keys and, in turn, small hammers inside the piano strike the strings to make sound. Many of the percussion instruments are used to keep a strong beat in music, such as the strong beat you hear when drums are played in rock and roll bands, the strong beat of Native American music, or the big bass drum being struck as a marching band goes by. These are instruments are very old in the history of civilization, probably because many are easily constructed. They are often the first instruments that children learn to play, for most have just one tone (called *unpitched instruments*), although instruments such as timpani drums and xylophones do have many tones and are known as pitched instruments. By using unpitched percussion instruments, children are able to easily learn to read the rhythm and length of notes first, before they must worry about reading the names of notes for a melody.

Another group of instruments is known as the **woodwind** family. At one time, all these instruments were made of wood, although now you find these made of plastic and metal. Woodwind instruments are played by blowing air into a tube, such as in the clarinet, oboe, saxophone, bassoon, pan pipes, English horn, flute, and piccolo. Many (but not all) of these instruments have a mouthpiece where a sliced piece of reed is fastened. This reed vibrates as the wind passes down through the tube to create a unique sound.

The **brass** family, obviously, has instruments that are made of tubes of brass. These long metal tubes are curled around and around, usually ending in a bell shape that "flowers" to the outside. Brass players make sounds by putting their lips tightly together and buzzing them inside the small, bell-shaped mouthpiece and moving a slide or pushing on valves to create different pitches. The trumpet, trombone, French horn, and tuba are all examples of brass instruments.

The last family is called the **strings**, and includes the violin, viola, cello, and string bass. Of course, all of these have strings, and many are played with a bow that is drawn across them to vibrate the strings, thus creating the sound.

Another important concept to review when thinking about instruments is how the pitch is created for each instrument. The guideline is that the smaller the instrument, the higher the sound. Therefore, the small flute makes a much higher sound than the much larger tuba. To hear many instruments, go to http://www.dsokids.com/listen/instrumentlist.asp.

Timbre and Tone Color

Each instrument has its very own characteristic sound, "voice," or **timbre**. A bell, for example, has a ringing sound that it does not share with other instruments, whereas the cymbals do not share their clash with other instruments as well. There is no mistaking the sound of either of these instruments. Another name for this individual sound is **tone color**. Individual singers also have their own tone color, as most have a unique voice that is recognizable as theirs alone (although we have all tried to imitate the tone color of our favorite popular singers, usually in the privacy of our showers). Combinations of instruments often create a unique sound as well. The choice of how a composer puts sounds together is as important as an artist's selection of colors. In Native American music, for instance, one often hears a combination of drums, rasps, rattles, and flutes that, when heard together, almost always creates a mental picture of this culture. The same is true of country and western music with guitars and fiddles, or of Spanish music with castanets and guitars. Also, there are many special instruments with unique sounds that are often associated with one particular area of the world. The samisen from Japan is one such instrument; the bagpipes from Scotland are another; and the didgeridoo from the Aboriginal people of Australia is yet another example. There are many such unique instruments from Africa and other areas of the world. You can hear many of these instruments at http://www.worldmusicalinstruments.com.

All of the elements that we have spoken about up to this point—*tempo* (speed), *dynamics* (loudness), *meter* (beat), *key*, and *choice of instruments* or *unique voice*—affect the overall **mood** of the music or the feeling that a piece of music creates for the listener. A lullaby, for example, makes us feel quiet and gentle, while a march or rap song makes us feel excited and ready to move our feet. Each person may have a different reaction to the same composition, just as we may react differently to books, movies, and other art forms. However, it is not difficult to explain certain feelings when hearing certain types of music. The brooding mood of bagpipes accompanying "Amazing Grace" (http://songza.org/?gclid=CK2gi4O8npsCFRMhnAodX0tPpQ or go to http://songza.org and type in "Amazing Grace bagpipes and Top Sound & HD") contrasts with the toe-tapping happiness of the fiddle, banjo, and guitar in "Turkey in the Straw" (http://songza.org and type in "Banshee Ceilidh Band Cotton Eye Joe Turkey in the Straw"). Great compositions or even popular songs often have contrasting moods within the same piece as the elements discussed previously work together. Emotion is the true power of music.

Another way that mood is created in music is through use of what we term *key*. There are two major types of key in Western music (versus music from the Far East)—major and minor keys. Most Western music is written in major keys and sounds happy or normal. The main difference when you hear a song written in a **minor key** is that you can recognize that it often sounds "bluesy" or sad. Three famous examples that you may know that are written in minor keys are "When Johnny Comes Marching Home Again" (go to www.songza.org and type in "When Johnny Comes Marching Home," then select the Finger Style Guitar version), "Summertime" (http://songza.org and type in "Summertime" and then select the Fantasia Barrino version), and the popular theme from the movie "Titanic," "My Heart Will Go On" (http://www.youtube.com/watch?v=3ESshQv4gjo, or at www.songza.org, type in the title, and select the Celine Dion version). Many of these are also available on www.youtube.com by searching for song titles and artists as well.). Other information on minor keys can be found at http://cnx.org/content/m10856/latest/. **Ballads**, or songs that tell stories, are often (although not always) set in a minor key, especially when they tell sad stories. Another term that is related to major and minor keys (and other terms that are beyond the scope of this chapter) is *tonality*. Some modern abstract music is *atonal* (i.e., there is no key that can "center" the piece of music).

Also related to mood (and to texture as well, discussed later) is the number of voices or instruments included in a composition. When one instrument plays or one voice sings a main melody, it is called a **solo** performance, even though an instrument or instruments may accompany it in the background.

Elvis Presley was, perhaps, the most famous solo male vocalist of the 1950s, although he was always accompanied by a guitar or group of musicians. The only time a solo singer or **chorus** (a large group of singers) has no instrumental accompaniment is when an arranger indicates that the voices should be **a cappella**, or for voices alone with no instrumental accompaniment. This term comes from voices "in the chapel," where nuns or monks sang or chanted without instruments. When there are two or more musical instruments playing different pitches together, when one instrument is playing different pitches at the same time (such as the piano, autoharp, or guitar), or voices are singing different parts, harmony is created. **Harmony** means that two or more different tones are being played or sung together. For an example, see http://www.songsforteaching.com/store/row-row-row-your-boat-song-download-pr-7125.html where a man and woman sing harmony together. When instruments of a band or orchestra are playing together or a choir of many people are singing different parts together, the harmony is usually very rich because there are many tones being played at once. A barbershop quartet usually has a four-part harmony. When three or more pitches are played together, we call this a *chord*. When a singer is accompanied by a guitar, autoharp, or piano, you are most likely hearing chords of a harmony being played (http://www.ehow.com/video_2375051_finding-minor-basic-piano-chords.html).

There are other ways to create harmony. An *ostinato* is created by singing or playing a rhythm pattern over and over again throughout a song, usually as a part of the background. For example, in "Frère Jacques" ("Are You Sleeping?") (http://www.kiddiddles.com/lyrics/f010.html), one voice or part can sing the lyrics of the whole song, while a second, *ostinato* voice sings only the following words and melody over and over again, "Are you sleeping? Are you sleeping?" throughout the song, even though the main voice continues with the rest of the song. *Partner songs* also add harmony. This occurs when two different songs are sung or played together. A famous example of this is "Scarborough Fair" by Simon and Garfunkel (http://www.youtube.com/watch?v=bwldn3ET53E&feature=related or at http://songza.org, type in "Scarborough Fair Simon and Garfunkel"). Two different songs are actually being sung at the same time, yet they blend together well. Singing or playing *rounds* is a very easy way to create harmony as well. This occurs when one group of musicians begins a song, and others wait to start until the group before it has finished the first musical phrase. There can be three to four groups waiting to sing at different starting points in a round. Most of us have sung "Row, Row, Row Your Boat" in a round. In a *counter melody*, a song is sung or played, but a different melody is also being played or sung at the same time. If you know the famous "The Stars and Stripes Forever" march, you may recall the end of the piece where the very high piccolo trills a counter melody against the main melody as it continues (www.youtube.com/watch?v=nyPc_sZTZUs or http://songza.org currently, it is the "Stars and Stripes Forever with piccolo animation"). You will have to wait until almost the end of the piece to clearly hear the piccolo's counter melody. You can also follow this melody on the accompanying video (see blue on top).

These terms also affect the **texture** of music—that is, how one voice (or instrument) alone sounds versus how different voices (or instruments) sound together. The quality produced by the number and kinds of instruments put together (or instruments and voices) also refers to texture. You can think of musical texture just as you might think of the weave of a cloth. Some weaves are thick and sturdy, while others are thin and delicate—and everywhere in between. The same is true of the texture of music.

Another term that you should know relates to music belonging to particular cultures—**musical conversation**. In African American spirituals, for instance, one may often hear a solo voice ask a question or make a statement while the refrain/chorus comes behind to answer or reinforce it. In "Deep

River," for example, the musical question asked is, "Oh, don't you want to go to the Gospel feast, that Promised Land, where all is peace?" The answering phrase comes next, "Deep River, my home is over Jordan . . . I want to cross over . . ." (http://songza.org and type in "H. T. Burleigh Deep River"). A well-known musical conversation asks, "I looked over the Jordan, and what did I see?" "Comin' for to carry me home. . . ." The answer is, "A band of angels comin' after me." (http://songza.org and type in "Swing Low Sweet Chariot Marion Williams).

All the terms discussed in this section help us begin reading music. There are many more terms in music, but those discussed here are the basics to help you begin. It is easy to access a number of other musical terms by typing in "music+theory" in a search engine on the Internet. For example, go to http://www.essentialsofmusic.com and select the glossary to find definitions and play-back examples.

In the next section, we look at some elements that help teach children music and help us be better teachers of music.

First, test your knowledge on some sample questions from this section:

Mrs. Cottle had her first-grade students first clap their hands to a song, then stand up and march in time to the music. She was trying to teach them about:

A. timbre.
B. dynamics.
C. rhythm.
D. instrument families.

Choice *A* cannot be correct, because *timbre* distinguishes the way one instrument or voice sounds differently from another. A tuba has a different timbre (a very different sound to our ears) than a violin. Choice *B, dynamics*, refers to how loud or soft music is played or sung, so this cannot be the answer. Choice *D* cannot be correct, because there was no mention of the different instruments being played here that would allow us to classify them into families such as the strings, brass, percussion, or woodwind families. Choice *C*, however, is correct. Having children clap or walk to music is a very good way to have them feel the rhythm of a piece of music. They would, hopefully, begin to feel the beat, an element of *rhythm*. The correct answer is *C*.

Ms. Botetourt wanted to teach her children about music with a strong beat. She selected a march to demonstrate two strong beats per measure, a Native American piece to demonstrate four strong beats per measure, and a waltz. How many steady beats per measure does a waltz have?

A. 5
B. 1
C. 8
D. 3

A march demonstrates two strong beats per measure, as it helps people (particularly in the military) march together. Because we have only two feet, a march has a beat for each: left, right, left, right; 1, 2, 1, 2. Native American music is often presented with a very strong ONE-two-three-four beat (http://songza.org and type in "The Moon Red Sky Native American Chant"), whereas a waltz has three strong beats per measure (or set), often with a very strong first beat (ONE-two-three, ONE-two-three). The correct answer is *D* (3 beats).

Students in Mr. Spellman's class were given a writing assignment to describe a churning seacoast. He waited for a stormy day for this assignment to set the mood. In addition, he put on a piece of music to heighten the effect. Before having students write, he asked, "Listen to how the composer used the string family and the percussion family to create a swirling, crashing mood. What instruments do you think you hear from the percussion family in this composition?"

For what type of instruments were students supposed to listen?

    A. Instruments such as the tuba, the trumpet, and the French horn.
    B. Instruments with strings like the violin and the cello that are often (although not always) played by drawing a bow across the strings.
    C. Voices accompanied by woodwind instruments.
    D. Instruments that are struck, beaten, shaken, or scraped, such as the timpani drum, cymbals, bass drum, and triangle.

Choice *A* is not correct, because the tuba, French horn, and trumpet are members of the musical instrument family that are all made of brass and are a separate family from the percussion family. Choice *B* is not correct because, although he was probably going to ask them next about the string family instruments, he asked first about the percussion family instruments. Choice *C* is wrong, because although it mentions a family of instruments, it does not discuss the type of instruments in that particular family, and Mr. Spellman does not talk about voices. Choice *D* is correct, because instruments in the percussion family are those that are played by striking, beating, crashing, shaking, or scraping. Many orchestras use percussion instruments such as the timpani drums and cymbals to indicate dark, brooding power—such as in a storm. Cymbals often imitate the sound of crashing lightning, timpani drums sound like rolling thunder, and the triangle can be struck lightly to sound like raindrops. The correct answer is *D*.

Standard II: Singing and Playing

The music teacher sings and plays a musical instrument.

The teacher must know methods and techniques for singing or for playing a musical instrument and must be able to sing or play an instrument alone or in a group while demonstrating accurate intonation and rhythm. Generalist teachers are expected to be able to perform a varied repertoire of music representing styles from diverse cultures and styles, including music of the United States (covered in Standard V later in this chapter).

This standard also overlaps with Standards I and III, as the teacher must first understand all of the information contained within those two standards so that the information and knowledge contained there can be applied to either playing an instrument or singing. Note however, the important message of this standard: The teacher is expected to sing or play with his or her children often and in a way that maintains an accurate pitch and correct beat of the music. You may not have had the opportunity to take music lessons or be a part of a band or choir, but that does not mean that it is too late for you to learn to read music in order to sing or play an instrument and to teach children to do so. In days long past, there was often a piano in every elementary classroom, and the teacher played while children gathered around to sing. Excellent recordings (often *karaoke*-style), along with easy instruments, have replaced this concept in many classrooms. Again, Texas expects you to be able to sing or play in order to teach children about music! One suggestion is that if you do not already play an instrument that is conducive to accompaniment, it is worthwhile to invest in an autoharp or guitar. An *autoharp* is a stringed instrument that is very easy to play—you simply push down buttons that, in turn, create automatic chords for harmony, then simply strum for accompaniment. A guitar is a bit harder, as you must learn which strings to press to create chords for accompaniment, but both are excellent instruments for the classroom. It does take practice to feel comfortable, but the rewards of singing with your children and adding the harmony of an instrument are well worth it. Both instruments offer the opportunity for children to gather in front of you or in a circle where you can easily see them. With knowledge of only a few chords, you can sing and play a large variety of easily learned children's songs, and there are many songs that enrich the curriculum in various ways. You should pay close attention to the information in the other standards for information on singing or playing an instrument.

Standard III: Music Notation

The music teacher has a comprehensive knowledge of music notation.

The EC-6 teacher must know how to read, recognize aurally, interpret, and write standard music notation. This includes use of clefs, keys, and meters. This would also include being able to interpret rhythmic and melodic phrases and music symbols and terms both aurally (from listening) and from notation (from reading music). Finally, this standard requires the EC-6 teacher to sight read simple melodies in various modes and tonalities and read and write music that incorporates simple, complex, and asymmetric meter.

You have been introduced to these concepts in Standard I in reading, interpreting, and writing music notation. Please review each, as this overlap indicates that these concepts are of particular importance. The other emphasis in this standard, however, is recognizing musical concepts when you hear them—that is, aurally. Of course, that is difficult to determine in a paper-and-pencil test, but as a teacher of musical concepts, you should be able to point out the concepts given in Standard I, such as texture, mood, beat, and so forth, as you listen to music with children or as they sing or perform for you. For example, as they sing, you should be able to say, "Children, if you *crescendo* (get louder gradually) right at this point in the music, it gives more power to the song," or, as you listen to the song "Memories" (from the musical "CATS!") together, you should be able to say, "Boys and girls, doesn't that key change in the middle of this song just work to give you goose bumps! What a wonderful technique by the composer!" Begin to listen to music with a musician's ear and notice each of the concepts discussed in Standard I so that you can bring them to the attention of children. Music book series often group several examples of these concepts on tapes or CDs. This makes it easy for you to hear and teach examples to your children.

Consider the following questions:

Ms. Glymph examined the sheet music that she wanted to teach her class for the PTO program next month.

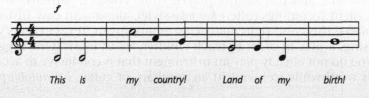

1. How does the dynamics symbol on the first line of this music tell her it should be sung?
   A. Slowly
   B. Rapidly
   C. Loudly
   D. Softly

2. How many beats per measure does this song have, and what note receives one beat?
   A. Two per measure, and a whole note receives one beat.
   B. Four per measure, and a quarter note receives one beat.
   C. Four per measure, and an eighth note receives one beat.
   D. Two per measure, and a whole note receives one beat.

3. For how many beats would the word *birth* be held in this line?
   A. One
   B. Two
   C. Three
   D. Four

In the first question, she should look for the dynamics symbol written in line with the notes that are affected. This is an *f*, or *forte*, so the song begins loudly (*C*). In question 2, she should look at the time signature. In this music, it is $\frac{4}{4}$. The top number tells her that there are four beats per measure, and the bottom of the time signature tells her that a quarter note gets one beat (*B*). In question 3, the measure with *birth* is represented by a whole note. In this song, a quarter note gets one beat, so a half note receives two beats, and a whole note receives four beats (*D*). Children should hold *birth* for four full beats. The answer is *D*.

Generalists are not responsible for Standard IV.

Standard V: Texas and American Music History

The music teacher has a comprehensive knowledge of music history and the relationship of music to history, society, and culture.

The EC-6 teacher should know how music can reflect elements of a specific society or culture and be able to analyze various purposes and roles of music in society and culture. This should include a knowledge and understanding of music of various genres, styles, and cultures. Being able to recognize and describe the music that reflects the heritage of the United States and Texas is an important element in this area. Teachers should also know and be able to explain various music and music-related careers. Finally, it is required that teachers be able to identify concepts from other fine arts and their relationship to music concepts.

Why should every child know about music? It is a universal human experience, although individuals and cultures certainly react to music in their own unique ways. Consider that humans may be somehow "wired" for music, because music has been a part of human life since the beginnings of history, and music has been associated with almost every element of human life. Music was often a means to preserve history and stories orally, as well as to entertain. It was (and still is) used to honor people, places, events, and ideas. Music motivates people to do things, such as support a cause, fall in love, worship, or even march into war. Music is used as comfort or to express a range of emotions such as joy, laughter, nonsense, longing, anger, sorrow, protest, and celebration. In fact, music can be associated with and can express every human emotion. Just think about how bland your favorite movies would seem without the sound track enhancing the emotions that are being acted out. Imagine the emptiness of a wedding, graduation, or other ceremony where there was no traditional music as an accompaniment. We find that the rhythm of many kinds of labor has also been expressed through music, as well as the joys of play and diversion after work was done. People have used music to express traveling to new places and experiencing new things but also to remind them of their homelands and their lives before. Many different cultures of people share and express their music in distinctive ways and celebrate their traditions and holidays in song and dance. Music helps unify people as a culture. To understand the musical part of a people is to understand them better as a whole.

The same can be said in reference to historical times. By analyzing instruments and the expressions of music from different periods of history, students can understand more easily the people who lived in those times. For example, is the music heavy and angry, or is it delicate and light? Does the music tell us that its people danced and sang, or that they marched to war? Are the words set to music carefree, romantic, sad, fearful, or purposeful in some other way? Is the majority of the music of a population or period of time patriotic in nature? Were there certain types of music and dance for different classes of people? Were musicians revered, or seen as servants? Elements such as these can tell us much about a society or culture and its times. However, music can also transcend cultures, times, and ages. Good music may be enjoyed for centuries and by many different cultures throughout the world, thus becoming an instrumental or vocal classic. Music should be considered a universal human endeavor, because so many people of the world have created and enjoyed some type of music and musical traditions.

Texas Music

One requirement noted by this state standard asks you to teach children about our state and national music. As you drive through Texas today, scan radio stations and listen to the many kinds of music that the people of Texas love. Texas music is truly a reflection of the many cultures that exist here today and the rich history of Texas.

The word *genre* has been applied to types of music and should become a part of your vocabulary as a teacher. There are almost too many music genres and styles to list separately, but you will become aware of many in the next two sections (such as country and western, rock, rhythm and blues [R&B], spirituals, Dixieland, jazz, rap, gospel, lullabies, and marches). The terms **genre** and *styles* are sometimes treated as the same, but other music theorists categorize *genre* as an umbrella term (such as African music, folk music, classical music), placing *styles* underneath. For example, under *folk music*, some theorists might further categorize the styles by region and time considerations, so folk music of America and of Europe would be different styles; folk music of early America would be a different style than that of the 1960s; and so forth. There are many genres and styles of music even within Texas music.

The first people of America and Texas were Native American tribes. We know little about some of these tribes, but others still exist and have recordings and videos of song and dance that can easily be accessed through various Websites by searching for "Native American music." Although each Native American nation has developed its own unique music, musical instruments of Native Americans most often include various drums, handmade flutes, and rattles. Voices often accompany songs and dances in sing-song chanting in their tribal languages. Generally, there is a strong beat. Native American songs exist for almost every aspect of men's and women's tribal life—work, planting, hunting, social dances, celebrations, and other rituals of a people. Honor songs are sung to pay special homage to those who are deserving. Still today, *powwows* (gatherings) are nearly always opened with an exciting array of music and dance. Gender roles are normally a part of Native American music and dance, so, in general, one sees separate dances and songs for males and females. Much Native American music deals with the forces of nature, myths, legends, and the spiritual aspect of life and was often used to pass down the oral history and culture of the tribe. In current times, the *Encyclopedia of North American Indians* online tells us that Native Americans have melded together certain types of music that many tribes can share (*pan-tribal music*) such as those for powwows, peyote songs, and the Ghost dance (http://books.google .com and type in book title). Although there has been some melding of Native American music by young modern Native American groups, by and large this music has been affected very little by other cultures.

Following along through the history of Texas, we note the exploration and settling of Texas by those from Spain and, later, Mexico. During these early days when the flag of Spain, then Mexico, flew over Texas, religious festivals were held throughout the year honoring the saints and events found in the Roman Catholic religion—the religion of those of European descent living in Texas at that time. Many of these continue throughout Texas today, particularly in communities with Hispanic traditions and ties. *Las Posadas*, for example, commemorating Mary and Joseph's search for shelter in Bethlehem, is a popular combination of religious and mariachi-style music that remains as a part of San Antonio's December celebrations. Barges carrying performers of the pageant and of many other choral groups cruise the river singing Christmas songs. Mariachi music, typically joyful and exuberant, is very typical of Mexico and is heard often in Texas communities throughout the state. Musicians in traditional black and silver Mexican cowboy (*charro*) costumes stroll and sing in Spanish to the accompaniment of guitars, violins, *guitarrons* (bass guitars), and trumpets. They often sing *corridos* (Mexican folk ballads), *rancheras* (ranch songs), and *boleros* (romantic songs), often with much harmony (for examples, go to http://songza.org and type in "Jose Alfredo Jimenez Rancheras"). Many schools and several universities in southern Texas offer study in mariachi music. *Conjunto* (or *ñorteño*) music is also a Hispanic-based sound heard often in Texas. Created by the working class along the border in the early 1900s, it is a bright and happy sound of Mexican-style music that has borrowed both its main instrument (the accordion) and some of its style (polka) from the Texans of German descent (http://www.lib.utexas.edu/ benson/border/arhoolie2/raices.html). Two famous Latina vocalists, *Lydia Mendoza* and *Chelo Silva,* known as the "Grandes de Texas" (Texas Greats), were best selling recording stars on both sides of the border up until the 1980s in *ñorteño* music. With *conjunto* as its roots, the more modern *tejano* music today is currently defined as *popular* Hispanic-style music (rather than a very specific type of sound). Made famous by the tragic death of its star, Selena, it has gained a considerable following in the past few years (type in "Selena Quintanilla" in http://songza.org). One can hear all of these types of Hispanic-based music daily throughout most of Texas, but the focus of the Hispanic community in Texas often centers on El Cinco de Mayo, a holiday celebrating a battle won in Mexico's fight for independence. During this holiday, there is a great deal of music and folk dancing, and grand balls are held in some parts of Texas.

Music was an important part of the lives of the early settlers and colonists who came from the United States as well. It is said that Texans went into the Battle of San Jacinto (the battle that won Texas independence from Mexico) singing, "Will You Come to the Bower?" Early settlers who came from the United States to Texas brought ballroom dancing that was mixed with folk dances from the many European countries of their ancestries. During the early 1800s, upper-class circles of early Texas colonists and officials in the Mexican government attended sophisticated balls, while *fandangos* were street entertainment with music, dancing, and other activities. At *shindigs*, settlers with little or no formal music or dance instruction attempted polkas and schottisches, dancing in an even more informal and frolicking way. In the formal dances of higher circles, groups danced to figures or quadrilles in the European style, and reminders about what to do next were often called out to the dancers. Over time, the person responsible for this became the *caller*, and dancing depended less and less on the formal steps, thus merging into the style that we know as the *square dance*. One folk dance that was popular during this part of Texas history was the *play-party game*. Dancing to musical instruments was not considered proper among some religious leaders and groups, so the accompaniment to dances was sung or called, and the dance itself was called a *game*. This game also had to serve when little or no music was available. Quite often in the early years of Texas there may have been only a single fiddler at a function. The World Champion Fiddlers' Contest in Crockett, Texas, shows how important this type of musician was to the roots of Texas music.

Although Texas now boasts several of the nation's largest urban areas, much of Texas still has deep roots in its cowboy heritage and music. This was music first sung and played by cowboys on the many cattle drives that originated on the ranges of Texas and moved north to Kansas railroads and markets in the mid-1800s. After the Civil War, many settlers moved west from southern states, bringing the traditional music of the South with them (ballads, hymns, and minstrel songs). Some of these became blended with the Old West–flavored songs of the range, and many of these blends succeeded in becoming American classics. Adaptations of these old songs of life on the range formed the basis of western swing in the 1930s, creating the roots of our modern country and western music. Related to this music, folk dancing in Texas developed its own style. The Cotton-Eyed Joe, for example, is a popular dance step that many Texans still learn (type in "Evil City Stringband Cotton-Eyed Joe" in http://songza.org). As radios became available, the traditional types of dances in Texas began to fade, replaced by the more popular American dances and music of the times during World War II (the Jitterbug, the Lindy, the Swing, etc.). Later, rock and roll moved to the popular front. However, country and western music and dance has always been a part of many Texas communities and has made a resurgence since the 1970s with popular country singing stars topping the charts. Several popular movies featuring country-style line dances and songs that have a more updated rock and roll rhythm helped keep this music in the hearts and minds of many Texans and Americans.

In the later part of the 1800s, many Germans began to leave Europe, fearing the rising militarism of Prussia and desiring to own land of their own. With them they brought their own unique music. Today, the *ohm-pa-pa* of German music is heard throughout many parts of central Texas, especially in the Hill Country area (the region most settled by these groups). During the mid-1800s festivals centered around the homes and communities of German immigrants. In New Braunfels today, *Wurstfest* is always held in October and features German music, dancing, and food. Polka-style music, played most often by small brass bands in German communities, is also still heard in many Texas Czech communities.

Texans also hear and enjoy music that has its roots in African American cultures. You may have heard the expression *King Cotton* in reference to Texas prior to the Civil War. Many parts of eastern and central Texas were optimum for growing cotton and, because Texas was a Southern slave state, many African Americans were brought here to work. With them, they brought their music. After *Juneteenth*, when Union forces brought the news to Texas that the slaves had been freed, many of these emancipated slaves began to look for work. Theirs was a hard life, and most went into either sharecropping or became migratory workers. All hoped to find a place where discrimination and racism were not part of their day-to-day existence. The *blues*, the sound that emerged from these times, was a way for these people to express extreme feelings of sorrow, dejection, suffering, and, yet, even hope and humor (http://www.pbs.org/theblues/classroom/cd.html#null and click on to "Lost Your Head Blues"). During the early 1900s, African American composers contributed greatly to other genres of music. Scott Joplin from Texarkana, known as the King of Ragtime for his "Maple Leaf Rag," pioneered the energizing, lively sounds of ragtime (http://music.minnesota.publicradio.org/features/9905_ragtime/index.shtml#timeline). Jazz followed and formed a backdrop for rhythm and blues and rock and roll. This led the way for R&B performers such as Texas-born Janis Joplin in the 1960s.

Attending festivals throughout the state gives Texans an opportunity to hear music and see dancing from many Texas immigrants' historical backgrounds. The Lebanese–Syrian festivals in Austin, the National Polka Festival in Ennis, and the Greek Festival in Houston are only a few events at which the sounds of the cultures that make up Texas can be heard. In addition, certain cities and towns highlight other music. The Texas Folklife Festival is, perhaps, the most inclusive of all the festivals and is held annually at the Institute of Texas Cultures in San Antonio. Round Top is home to a renowned classical music festival each year, Palo Duro Canyon hosts the outdoor musical "TEXAS" each summer, and the musical extravaganza "Fandangle" is performed at Fort Griffin in Albany, Texas. Several cities, including San Antonio, Corpus Christi, and Houston, host excellent jazz festivals. Houston also has a renowned opera season, and famous musicals can be seen in most large cities or on many university campuses throughout Texas.

Following are some of the many other famous singers and composers from Texas who have contributed to Texas and American music.

Tex Ritter	Roger Miller	Trini Lopez	ZZ Top
Gene Autry	Kris Kristofferson	Roy Orbison	Johnny Mathis
Dale Evans	Freddie Fender	Lyle Lovett	Buck Owens
Willie Nelson	Waylon Jennings	Selena Quintania Pérez	Kenny Rogers
Beyoncé &	George Strait	Tanya Tucker	Clint Black
Destiny's Child	Janis Joplin	Buddy Holly	

Our state song, "**Texas, Our Texas**," can often be heard and/or sung during morning announcement times, at assemblies, at some football games, and at other opening ceremonies at many Texas schools and community events (http://www.senate.state.tx.us/kids/Trivia.htm and click on Trivia). Texas teachers should learn it in order to teach it to children and to help them understand the respect that Texans hold for their state's symbols.

American Music

Both national and state music standards ask that students relate music to history, society, and culture. Because we can say that music is often a reflection of the times in which it is produced, it is helpful for you to know not only about the genres of American music but also about the period in history from which they come and what was happening in America during those times. Little is learned when a teacher just says, "Here is a song from . . . (colonial America or from another culture or another country, etc.)." The investigation of what makes that particular piece *so unique* is what brings children to better understand a historical period or culture, both ours and that of others.

American music has a long history that parallels much of European musical history, as well as the course of events that shaped our country. The first Pilgrim colonists were a very pious people who thought of music mainly for the part it could play in their religion. They used only a few traditional English hymn tunes to sing a number of psalms. However, as the colonies quickly became settled, America took three turns in its music—one direction for the more wealthy and cultured; another direction for those pioneers who lived more isolated, rural lives; and yet another for the slaves who were brought here early in our nation's history.

Where cities prospered, Americans integrated popular European music and dances into their colonial life. Many of the wealthier class listened to and danced European-style minuets and gavottes, mainly to the tunes played on harpsichords. The English and American aristocracy wished to replicate life they remembered from European courts on their rural land holdings and by hosting and attending balls in flourishing urban areas. This type of music was from the Baroque era and lasted almost until the Revolutionary War. In Europe during this time, Bach wrote many of his fugues (mainly for organ), and Handel wrote his famous oratorio *The Messiah*, still a part of many Christmas programs (particularly its "Alleluia Chorus"). An *oratorio* is an opera without costumes, scenery, or action, and is normally religious in nature. Vivaldi also wrote the set of four works known as *The Four Seasons*, along with many other compositions. You may have seen Baroque architecture that exuberantly "fills every space" with movement. Baroque music is very much the same in nature—highly ornate (http://www.youtube.com/watch?v=xozvnMZ7Jq4). This music was usually characterized by a single mood. If the work began with a mood such as sorrow or joy, that single feeling was maintained throughout most of the work.

Settlers soon began to move out from the East Coast into small and isolated rural homesteads (where not even a tavern supported music). In their own homes they sang folk ballads from their original homelands, mostly without accompaniment. If there was a musical instrument, it was probably a fiddle, a mouth harp, or a homemade lute.

Slaves were brought to America very early in its history and from many different African areas and countries. Slaves were forced to adapt to an unfamiliar world that led to a difficult new way of life, a new language, and a new religion. Music became a way of life as slaves united the many cultures and sounds they brought from various parts of Africa and used music to pace their work, communicate, express feelings, and sing songs of worship and of hope. Often, one singer started a song and others answered (*field hollers* or *cries*) or joined in on the refrain after a verse was sung. This music was mainly unaccompanied—sung with voice only (*a cappella*). *Spirituals*, religious songs that were really folk music in nature, first developed as work songs and later combined with impressions of hymns. A number of slave songs (such as "Follow the Drinking Gourd" at http://www.followthedrinkinggourd.org/Appendix_Recordings.htm) are believed to have carried secret codes for instructions for the slave populations to escape on the Underground Railroad. Spirituals often retold Bible stories in a dialect more common to slaves and ex-slaves. Spirituals were eventually accepted into the general population and sung by Americans of many cultures, becoming widespread with the popularity of religious camp meetings in the later 1800s.

Let's return to earlier times again to look at a different type of music. In the early days of America, England sent troops to its colonies. For the military, music was mostly from fife and drum, but the coming War for Independence against England brought out popular American songs such as "The Liberty Tree" (America's first patriotic song at http://www.youtube.com/watch?v=fOUzQ9Di6jQ) and "Yankee Doodle." The latter was composed as a mockery used by the British to make fun of the "backwoods colonists" before and during the war, but it became so much a symbol of defiance and pride that it was practically the national anthem for years following the Declaration of Independence. As the United States became more settled and people began to travel along established trails, rivers, canals, and seaports, many public houses, inns, and taverns began to appear. These provided a place besides church to go where people could hear and share music together. People also gathered to celebrate festive occasions, and dance was often a part of those occasions. The folk dances of America that developed during this time were the *play-party game* and *square dance* (discussed earlier in Texas music). *Long-ways* and *circular formation* dances (such as the Virginia Reel) developed, along with other round dances in which the general movement of all partners goes around the room (such as in the polka or schottische). **Square dancing** is very much seen as a true U.S. folk dance.

For those who remained in touch with the culture of Europe during these times, the Baroque era in Western music was followed by the Classic Period (1750–1820), whose main composers were Mozart, Haydn, and Beethoven. As during the Baroque period, most of these works were commissioned by the wealthy in Europe. The main composers were influenced by popular tunes of the times. A characteristic of this music is *a range of emotions* and themes displayed in each piece rather than maintenance of one mood throughout. The **symphony**, emerging from this period, was an orchestral work of four movements, typically lasting from 25 to 45 minutes with a fast section, a slow section, a dancelike section (like a minuet), and an emotional, fast ending. *Chamber music*, using only a small number of instruments, also emerged from the aristocrats' or merchant classes' musical evening's entertainment. The signers of our Declaration of Independence probably attended soirees where the popular dance sounds of Mozart were played.

As time marched on in Europe, the age of Romanticism in music (1820–1900) was full of uplifting aspirations and beautiful ideals. Music was no longer written just for commission but to fulfill an inner need for self-expression, particularly of yearning love. Also, composers began to look at national feelings—both their own and that of other countries—and draw on folk songs, dances, legends, and history for inspiration. Indeed, there was a great individuality of style based on the concept of nationalism in many works of famous composers of the times, such as in those of Tchaikovsky and Chopin. *Program music*, based on a story, legend, or scene, was a popular style, as we see, for example, in Tchaikovsky's *Romeo and Juliet*. Interest in formal music boomed in the United States, and concert halls (such as Carnegie Hall) were built in many larger cities in the later part of the 19th century.

A more informal type of musical entertainment began during the early 1800s in the United States, termed the *minstrel show*, and these venues became an important type of entertainment for a number of years. During these shows, a variety of entertainment, such as comedy, dances, and songs, were performed first by white entertainers with blackface makeup, but later by African Americans. Dances were normally jigs and clog dances that later developed into **tap dancing**—another truly American form of dance. Accompaniment was often played by the fiddle, tambourine, and banjo, whose rapid, upbeat sounds subsequently influenced ragtime. As these programs became more elaborate with many performers, this type of entertainment eventually became known as *vaudeville*.

During the mid-1800s, a famous composer was working on a style of music that belonged to the United States alone. *Stephen Foster* wrote folk songs that articulated the American character and spirit of work and the home. Much of his work vocalized plantation life and the life of African Americans during these times. The United States became embroiled in the staggering Civil War just following this time period. From the Civil War, we remember songs from both sides such as "The Battle Hymn of the Republic" (the anthem of the North) (http://www.youtube.com/watch?v=pmTWVJ_pXBk) and

"Dixie" (from the South) (on http://songza.org type in "Dixie Anthem of the Confederate States of America" or http://www.musicanet.org/robokopp/usa/oiwishiw.htm). Beginning in the very late 1800s (well after the war), reasonably priced, wholesome, popular music and stage dance was presented in vaudeville shows such as the Ziegfeld Follies. Songs that were carefree and innocent, such as "A Bicycle Built for Two," were written and performed during this period when the United States was mostly at peace. *Victor Herbert*, sometimes called the father of popular music, wrote light operettas such as "Babes in Toyland" up through 1920. The marches of *John Philip Sousa* from this period, including "The Stars and Stripes Forever," also became world famous (http://www.youtube.com/watch?v=nyPc_sZTZUs, or http://songza.org and type in "Stars and Stripes Forever by John Phillip Souza.").

The years of the 1900s to the present have seen many styles of music. This was the age when the United States, like other nations, was changing from a rural, agricultural country to urban, industrial centers. The symbolism and expressionism created in modern art during this period was often mirrored by concert composers, as they experimented with unconventional, dissonant sounds and rhythms. In addition, George Gershwin and Aaron Copland, who composed during this time, are two of the most famous U.S. composers. Gershwin, with his "Rhapsody in Blue," bridged popular music (jazz) with music for the concert hall (http://www.youtube.com/watch?v=8QxWxsK8_3s). Copland, with his nationalistic agenda, wrote expansive music representing specific scenes of the United States and parts of American life that is still popular with adults and children today. Some of his most famous and familiar compositions are "Billy the Kid," "Appalachian Spring," and "The Red Pony" (on http://songza.org, type in "Pittsburg Symphony Orchestra Billy the Kid" or "Billy the Kid Aaron Copeland" and select Hoedown or others). Spirituals were also changing to become *gospel songs*. These newly composed religious songs were more upbeat, with lively voices full of movement, accompanied now with instruments and (often) hand-claps.

Jazz, an American sound created from predominately African American roots, probably began early in the 1900s. To hear examples of many types of jazz, visit http://www.carnegiehall.org/honor/history/index.aspx. The contributing elements were slavery and the hard life after Reconstruction. The heart of jazz lies in *improvisation* (creating music on the spot), *syncopation* (an unexpected accent), and *call and response* (where a voice or instrument is answered by other voices or instruments). The styles of music in their era included *ragtime* (a player piano sound), the *blues, Dixieland*, and *boogie-woogie* (with its "walking bass" sound). In the 1920s, many young people danced the Charleston to some of these sounds. In the 1930s, radio brought music into American homes throughout the country and allowed many people to hear more popular music. *Swing* (big band sound) of the World War II years, *bebop* or *bop*, and *cool jazz* of the early 1950s continued the jazz heritage. The years during World War II were filled with popular songs that remembered those who waited and worked on the home front but who also portrayed a clear determination to win the war. The popularity of glitzy musical movies with song and dance also swelled during this era as a way to escape from the hardships of the war and the Great Depression that had preceded it. U.S. musical theater boomed with the new genre of *musical plays*, particularly those of Rodgers and Hammerstein (*Oklahoma, South Pacific, The King and I, Carousel, The Sound of Music*, and others). In the 1950s, Leonard Bernstein became king of this genre by writing *West Side Story*.

The late 1940s also saw *rhythm-and-blues* emerge from the African American communities, with artists such as Little Richard and T-Bone Walker. Later, *country and western* music from rural communities appeared, along with *rock and roll*. In the mid-1950s songs like "Rock Around the Clock" (http://www.youtube.com/watch?v=F5fsqYctXgM) and others by stars such as Buddy Holly (from Lubbock, Texas) and Elvis Presley rocketed rock and roll to the top of popular music. *Rhythm and Blues (R&B)*, however, remained the main source of movements in pop music throughout the century. These genres influenced the evolution of *rock*. The event that ensured that rock would remain as an influential popular style was the first U.S. tour of the Beatles in the mid-1960s. Television programs like *The Ed Sullivan Show* and *American Bandstand* also brought not only music but also the faces of popular singers to the U.S. public, eventually leading to the development of music videos like those shown now on MTV. Along with the more electric sounds of *rock (classical rock, psychedelic rock, acid rock)* came the folk influence of many of the protest songs of the "atomic age" and the Vietnam War. Softer folk songs of these times were reflected by such artists as John Denver, who often sang about our states in such songs as "Country Roads" (http://www.youtube.com/watch?v= oN86d0CdgHQ) and "Rocky Mountain High" (http://www.youtube.com/ watch?v= OwARpaKHx_w). The reverberations of R&B and gospel united somewhat to produce the popular music called *soul* from the African American community. The 1970s saw a returned interest in partner dancing with the *disco beat*, and *country rock* became a popular form in many areas of the United States. *New wave, reggae,* and *heavy metal* sounds continued into the 1990s, and *rap* began to emerge as a hard, angry, chanting sound from urban African Americans and spread through the pop culture of all ethnicities through the first decade of the new century. The television hit "Dancing With the Stars" more recently spurred the resurgence of ballroom music and dance. As music moved from jazz to rock and rock to rap, melody became ever less important than the beat. However, most popular styles of this period have not lasted very long before being taken over by a new beat, so it will be interesting to see what kind of "new" modern style will evolve.

Other more regional styles of music are a part of our national music history as well. Until recent times, the isolation of the Appalachians and other eastern mountain regions kept their folk music pure and uncorrupted by other types of music. The stringed dulcimer accompanies most of these songs, which have an Old English or Scottish sound, whereas the *bluegrass* sound of this region has a faster, upbeat mood with banjos, guitars, and other instruments. Cowboy and Native American music were previously discussed in the section on Texas music. *Cajun music* from Louisiana is another unique type of music from the United States. Cajun's sad ballads are grounded in the forced migration of the Acadian French from Canada by the British, although the more exuberant sounds of their dance songs came from the mix of those who settled there long ago (from France, Africa, and the Native Americans of the area). The accordion, fiddle, and lyrical mix of French and the local dialect produce a sound that is unique (http://www.metacafe.com/watch/yt-B35NgCMTb28/dewey_balfa_nathan_abshire_jolie_blon or search metacafe for jolie blon). *Hawaiian music* is another type of indigenous music that belongs to the native islanders of our 50th state. In old Hawaiian music, chants with heavy rhythms were accompanied only by percussion instruments such as a hollow gourd (*ipu*) or bamboo sticks (*pu'ili*) (http://www.youtube.com/ watch?v=o8RtRGkzuy and http://www.youtube.com/watch?v= puelcyhsXQ0), although the more modern sound comes from a coupling of the Portuguese guitar (now the ukulele), steel guitar, and missionary hymns (http://www.hunawai.com/music.html). Current trends combine traditional folk songs of the islands, modern instruments, and themes of life surrounded by water and the beauty of nature all around. The native dance, the *hula*, can be slow and graceful, fast and furious, or light and comical. Native Hawaiians love their children to be included in music, and there are many charming hulas for children that can be brought to our classrooms.

Each of the genres (and composers) discussed earlier—and too many more to mention here—is described at length in music books and on the Internet.

In fact, much of the information for this standard comes from an excellent source, *The Handbook of Texas Online* (http://www.tshaonline.org/handbook/ online/search1.html?cx=partner-pub-7401801628149776%3Ama1ejqd5eiy& cof=FORID%3A9&ie=ISO-8859-1&q=music#963) or on the tshaonline home page for music. It is important, however, for you to *hear* these different sounds. As a teacher of music and as an American, you should try to learn and understand our country's musical styles and history for all the richness music offers. Music in the United States will continue to change, but we should try to understand this part of our history and culture well.

As a note, when tragedy struck as a result of terrorists' actions in New York, Pennsylvania, and Washington on September, 11, 2001, it was our patriotic songs such as "God Bless America," "America the Beautiful," "The Star-Spangled Banner," and others that helped to unite us as a nation (http://www. brownielocks.com/godblessamericaWAVE.html, http://www.brownielocks. com/AmericaELVIS.html and http://www.brownielocks.com/starspangled bannerWAVE.html). Every child in Texas deserves to feel that bond of belonging through knowing and being able to sing these American songs.

As a teacher, one should also note that some religious affiliations maintain their Constitutional right for their children not to stand for the *Pledge of Allegiance*, considering it nationalism (in which they do not believe). This extends to teachers not requiring these children to stand for our national anthem, "The Star-Spangled Banner," or to sing other patriotic songs. Parents who belong to these affiliations will let you know. Other children should be reminded of the respect that stopping activity, standing, and placing one's hand over the heart, shows for our national anthem in particular.

Musical Careers

Yet another element of this standard (and another rationale for teaching music) is teaching students about the many areas of employment that involve music directly and indirectly. Certainly, children should understand that people can grow up to become music educators/teachers of general music, to play a particular instrument, or to be a member of a band or choir, but they may not realize that there are many other occupations in which music is the focus. Some of the following could be leisure or volunteer activities (avocational), but many are also employment opportunities (vocational) for the future:

- Member or director of a symphony, stage band (or crew), chamber orchestra, band pit orchestra, or popular music band.
- Member or director of vocal work or dance in a(n) chorus, choir, musical, opera, ballet, folk dancing group, or other performance show, or as a choreographer. (Musicians might work or enjoy performing in city or national organizations, religious institutions, theme parks, cruise ships, restaurants and private parties, weddings, radio, television, or movies.)
- Employment in the recording industry, such as composing, publishing, as a member of a road crew, in law, in studio technology, as an arranger, as a coach, as an equipment engineer, or as a composer for background music in television, radio, or movies.
- Employment in technology, such as in software designer, electronic instrument designer, sound manager, or as a producer.
- Other areas include composer, music historian, professional music critic, disc jockey, instrument maker or repairer, music therapist, music store owner, college professor, advertising (jingles), or tuner.

There are many areas that could involve music both recreationally and as a way to make a living.

Standard VI: Evaluating Musical Performances

The music teacher applies a comprehensive knowledge of music to evaluate musical compositions, performances, and experiences.

In this competency, it is important for teachers to know and understand the criteria used to evaluate and critique musical performances and experiences. Therefore, they must be able to recognize accurate pitch, intonation, rhythm, and characteristic tone quality. Teachers should also be able to diagnose performance problems and detect errors accurately. Finally, they should be able to apply knowledge of musical forms.

Teaching Children to Sing

As a music teacher of younger children, a fair number of your activities involve children in singing. Here are some tips that you may want to use in teaching children to sing—and, it is hoped, to sing well.

The first goal in music is to have children participate. Shyness or other reluctance is often overcome by providing inviting activities in a pleasing environment with musical games and lightness, rather than forcing children to perform. Songs should be selected in which children can find an interest and that they easily handle within their limited voice ranges (i.e., songs where the pitches are not so far apart and notes are not very high or very low). If a song can be integrated with other topics, that often creates interest as well, but one of the most compelling ways to involve young children is to use songs in which their names are inserted in some way. Children (and the teacher) are usually more confident in a circle, where closeness gives the confidence to sing out. Good music instructors should treat the introduction of a song as they would a motivating introduction to a new book by setting the stage or a mood of inquiry ("Let's listen to this song, boys and girls, and afterward, I want you to tell me what kind of person [in what occupation] you think may have sung it originally, and why you think so."). Memorizing a song is important so that you can maintain eye contact while teaching it. Then, introduce the whole song as it is supposed to go, so children catch the exact spirit of the music. Do not forget that songs often introduce new vocabulary or words that, when sung, may not sound like exactly like spoken words. Explain new vocabulary, and talk to children about the importance of pronouncing consonants clearly (e.g., the third line of "Silent Night" is not "All is sprite" but "All is bright").

When seriously teaching a song, use your voice without accompaniment first. If you find it difficult to sing melodies, use a tape or a CD as you sing along. It is important that students, at some point, have good models to imitate (sometimes adult and sometimes children's voices), but your singing with children is required by these competencies, so plan to "go for it" with enjoyment and fun in mind. Imitation is the main way children learn to sing. Give the correct beginning pitch (using a key on an instrument, if needed, a pitch pipe, or your voice) and begin the song. Then repeat the song several times during the introduction phase so that children are not only introduced to the song, but so they also get well acquainted with it. Even though you may feel it is monotonous, do not hesitate to keep songs going for young children through many repetitions—sometimes singing, sometimes humming and doing motions, if applicable. Repetition, however, does not always work without other motivation techniques to keep children involved. The teacher who creates a reason for listening to the music (by asking questions about the music to heighten perception, playing a game, using dramatization or motions, etc.) will find that students remain interested. The younger the child, the better to teach by *rote* (imitation) only and use short repetitive songs, chants, echo songs, or poems in which only one or two things change in each verse and in which children's names are inserted often. Again, much repetition helps children learn to sing a song and enjoy many types of music. Young children do not value the unfamiliar in music—either in singing or instrumentals. However, if they do not hear certain types of music or sing certain songs often, they will not be familiar with (or value) those forms.

Songs that combine movement and motions are developmentally good for children (see the section later entitled "Teaching Children to Move"). Songs can be used to enhance concepts, teach directions, and so forth. Do not be concerned with singing or listening to a great variety of songs during a particular music time. Most children are more satisfied with one or two songs or musical activities that they find gratifying rather than glossing over many half-done experiences or practicing for very long periods of time. Let the mood of children be your guide, when possible, as they gain more from the experience if they are enjoying it. If children are getting too active, use a quiet song to bring down the level of activity, or invigorate a waning time with an exciting, active song. Also, do not be worried that very young children do not sing along all the time. A Music Listening Center may encourage young children to listen or sing quietly on their own. We may not be sure how very young children are truly reacting to music. They may want to get up and leave a singing circle or move in different ways. Do not be too concerned, as they may just be discovering and reacting in a different way than adults might expect. They may also be singing alone or at home.

There are some other factors that can encourage children to sing better as they grow. One common quality error in singing well occurs because the vocalist cannot sing whole phrases without breaking for a breath. During the learning process, have students read or speak sentences, noting where they should finish and take a breath, then do the same by singing. Finally, move to having children sing whole phrases. Because it is also very important that a singing voice project out to the audience, have older children repeat this process to someone across the room to encourage projecting one's voice as his or her voice remains controlled. However, forced projection can result in an unpleasant tone quality with younger children, so it is better to emphasize breath support and use of breath. This will eventually lead to more natural projection. During any musical performances requiring projection, use a larger group of children or have a microphone available rather than force voice projection. It is also very important for students who are performing to stand or sit straight with both feet on the floor in order to get a full breath of air. If standing, children should also be straight, perhaps with one foot slightly in front of the other and resting on the ball of the foot with the chin tilted at a lower angle. This helps them learn to control their breath from the diaphragm rather than the chest, so they can hold notes out for extended periods or sing whole musical phrases or sentences rather than gulp for air in the middle. Some voice trainers suggest that singers draw in air for singing as if sipping through a straw, filling their rib cages well with air, then exhaling as if they were blowing to cool some hot food. Children should not tense up when singing but keep their shoulders relaxed. Doing some stretching exercises helps the whole body become ready to contribute. Singing with a tight jaw is also not desirable, so exercises that have students begin a yawn or slow repetition of vowels and try to sing in a relaxed way are beneficial.

Very young children should not always be expected to sing a tune on correct pitch, but by about the age of 7, they should begin to grow into this ability.

If they are not able to do so, there are several things that might help. Young children tend to sing loudly, sing as they speak (using a speaking voice), or even shout rather than use the light voice that a child should have while singing. Singing on key can be improved by practicing with the Kodaly system of Curwen hand signals that indicate on which tone the singer should be. In this system, each note has a hand signal that represents its tone and name. A teacher can have students match their voices to the tone indicated by the hand signal (you may have seen this in the old movie *Close Encounters of the Third Kind*—as scientists matched hand signals to the famous five tones played as communication by the spacecraft) (http://www.wguc.org/content/display.asp?id=34 and http://www.youtube.com/watch?v=tUcOaGawIW0). Having children listen to recordings of children's voices singing (rather than adults all the time) and having children sing more softly should also assist. Echoing pitch games with speaking and singing also helps, as does playing tapes of familiar voices in the school speaking and singing (e.g., other teachers they know, the principal, friends). Playing a pitch on an instrument, having the student first "think the correct pitch," and then having the child sing can be beneficial, too. Having those who use their speaking voice (rather than a singing voice) imitate other sounds such as animals, sirens, or trains, along with a range of human sounds (whispers, hisses, hums, or shouts) develops a more flexible singing voice and an increased range.

As mentioned, *diction* is also an important part of singing. If you hear children singing in a shrill or throaty manner, it may be because of faulty diction. Students can work on uniform production of vowel and consonant sounds. Clear articulation by the teacher helps the listener understand. Sometimes teachers present a song at such a fast-paced tempo that it is difficult for students to understand the words or carry the melody well. After letting children hear the song in "real time," singing in slow motion can be a remedy. Also, have children practice singing words or phrases with pure vowels so that they can feel how their tongue operates if they are to sing clearly. Just as practicing an instrument is important in mastery, so is practicing singing correctly. Again, by selecting songs that have a limited range of tones, rather than very high to very low, children can often grasp those middle sounds. Sometimes we laugh about family or peers who are tone deaf, but some of our young singers are as well. They may just need attention to tone and practice. Discuss with them the importance of being a good listener so that they can be a good "repeater" of things they hear. Train students to watch the teacher for hand directions (conducting), especially if you should be working on a program presentation. Having children distinguish sound by taping and playing a large variety of sounds for children to listen to and identify is, again, very beneficial for children who are having difficulty with pitch. Echo games, mentioned several times, are a must for practicing various pitches and diction. If a child has continued problems with tone, it is also worth checking medical records to see if there is any reason this should be occurring. Telling a child he or she cannot sing or should not try to sing (unless, of course, there is a temporary or permanent medical condition) can create a stigma carried through life, diminishing the joy that singing can bring.

Teaching Children to Move

Development in the *physical domain* is another rationale for having a music program. Children, through musical response, learn how to control their bodies and refine large and small movements with the body and the voice. By using movement, many areas are heightened, such as dramatic response, imagination, and spatial perception. When songs are selected with simultaneous movements in a group, for example, students become more aware of the space around them, of their balance, and so forth. A teacher should realize, however, that developing physical skills takes time and considerable repetition for young children, especially to fine tune various movements. Finger plays, as well as playing correct rhythms with percussion instruments, require a great deal of repetition to coordinate eye–hand or eye–finger control. These are an important part of development, without doubt, for young children, and music can make it an enjoyable process. Remember that young children are individual in their stages of development in the physical domain and that very young children may have some difficulty with movements such as skipping to music. Although most mid-elementary children can skip and hop, they may still have difficulty with control in dance steps until the later elementary years. To encourage movement, offer opportunities for both structured music and for free creative movement. Be certain that plenty of safe space is provided for freedom of movement. Also, without setting limits on appropriate movements, set limits on behavior *before* movement activities that make movement lessons disintegrate. Demonstrate a variety of movements to children to give them guidance and choices—swaying, creeping, galloping, rocking, whirling, and so forth—both with and without various types of music. When teaching a lesson in movement, children need to hear the music before they are asked to respond. This allows them to imagine and make judgments on what their movements could be before they actually try it. Brainstorming ideas about "what the music is asking us to do" also aids in creativity. Again, and most important would be multiple opportunities for many types of movement: finger plays, singing games, and creative and free responses. At times, children should be encouraged to do what they feel like to the music. Those who feel the music will do so, and other children may look to see what the teacher is modeling. Therefore, the teacher should be a participant, too. At other times, you, as the teacher, may make suggestions such as, "Can you feel the heavy sounds? Can you move slowly like an elephant?" Provide opportunities to move in games or with groups, as well as individual opportunities.

Consider the following question:

Mrs. Conde wants to help her young children get ready for a spring choral program. Currently, her children do not sing very well. Which of the following steps will not help her children sing better and put on a better performance?

A. Selecting songs for the program that have a limited range.
B. Demonstrating a variety of movements before the music is played so that children can imagine and make judgments before they are asked to perform themselves.
C. Having students stand up straight and tall.
D. Speaking or reading sentences, noting where they would normally finish and take a breath.

Mrs. Conde wants to have her children sing better, so movement would not be of importance in this question (*B*), although this method helps with teaching children how to move to music. Choice *A*, selecting songs where children could have better success with their limited voice range (not too high, not too low), is important in a successful performance and in preventing children from straining their young voices or from having them project too loudly as they try to reach pitches. Having students stand up straight and tall also help them with their singing (*C*), as does working on their phrasing so they do not gulp for air in the middle of a phrase (*D*). There are a number of other ways to help children be more successful listed in this section as well. Remember that the question asks for the exception. The answer is *B*.

Standard VII: Planning and Implementing Effective Music Lessons

The music teacher understands how to plan and implement effective music instruction and provides students with learning experiences that enhance their musical knowledge, skills, and appreciation.

Teachers should know and understand the content and performance standards for music that comprise the Texas Essential Knowledge and Skills (TEKS) and the significance of the TEKS in developing a music curriculum. They should be able to use the TEKS to develop appropriate instructional goals and objectives for student learning and performance and provide students with multiple opportunities to develop music skills specified in the TEKS. By knowing the appropriate sequencing of music instruction and how to deliver developmentally appropriate music instruction, teachers should be able to provide students with an experience that is delivered in developmentally appropriate ways that encourage active engagement in learning and make instructional content meaningful. Teachers should know a variety of methods for developing an appropriate and effective curriculum and lesson plans for the music class and be able to adapt their instructional methods to provide appropriate learning experiences for students with varied needs, learning modalities, and levels of development and musical experience. Also, teachers should know learning theory as it applies to music education and be able to provide instruction that promotes students' understanding and application of the fundamental principles of music. They should understand the importance of helping students develop music skills that are relevant to their own lives and provide each student with opportunities to contribute to the music class by drawing from their personal experiences. Teachers should provide each student with varied opportunities to make music using instruments and voice, to respond to a wide range of musical styles and genres, and to evaluate music of various types. Teachers should provide each student with a level of musical self-sufficiency to encourage lifelong enjoyment of music and be able to use varied materials, resources, and technology to promote students' creativity, learning, and performance. Teachers know strategies and benefits of promoting students' critical-thinking and problem-solving skills in relation to music and can provide students with frequent opportunities to use these skills in analyzing, creating, and responding to music. While knowing procedures and criteria for selecting an appropriate repertoire for the music class, she or he also teaches students to apply skills for forming and communicating critical judgments about music and musical performance using the appropriate terminology. Using technology and various other materials and resources available for use in music education is an important part of a teacher's knowledge base. Teachers should help students develop an understanding and appreciation of various cultures through instruction related to music history and discussion of current events related to music that ties music to the past and present. They should also incorporate a diverse musical repertoire into instruction, including music from both Western and non-Western traditions. Both knowing appropriate literature to enhance technical skills and the value of and techniques for integrating music instruction with other subject areas is needed. Promoting music can be an integral element in students' lives, whether as a vocation or as an avocation, and encouraging students to independently pursue musical knowledge should be a part of a teacher's mission in music. Finally, teachers should be aware of and teach students proper health techniques for use during rehearsals and performances.

National standards for music suggest that there are four basic strands in which children should be involved in music: perceptions, creative expression, historical and cultural heritage, and critical evaluation. However, involvement is the key for children in each case at this age, because they learn by doing.

Music in the Domains

Although good music instruction works to support all major domains (the physical, the emotional, the social, and the cognitive), the domain most touched, perhaps, in music is the *affective*—that of feeling, emotions, and appreciation. The five stages of the *affective domain* are (1) *receiving* (actively attending), (2) *responding*, (3) *valuing* (demonstrated by individual choices made), (4) *organization* (ranking in importance), and (5) *characterization by value* (acting consistently with one's values). You may see how this might work easily in the music classroom. Initially, in order for children to learn to love, appreciate, and critique music, they must first be given numerous opportunities to listen or actively attend, then respond to it. Because children develop feelings about the many types and facets of music (through either good or bad examples), the teacher should be sure that encounters with music are positive in all ways possible. Teachers should also provide students with effective tools for judging the value of music. If children cannot actively talk about and use the elements, structure, and effect of a variety of musical examples (presented in Standard I), it is difficult for them to evaluate and value choices.

Other domains are also part of music. The *cognitive domain* in music involves the acquisition of musical theory and history and the higher levels of analyzing, synthesizing (creating), and evaluation. The *physical domain* centers on both body movement and motor skill development (both gross/large and fine). Music enhances athletic skills of growing children through movement. Musical finger plays and movement games should be a part of the physical and spatial development of every early childhood classroom, as children progress from common movements, such as patting or clapping, to the imitation of other animals or inanimate things to role-play and, finally, to organized musical games and dances. Music provides a backdrop for kinesthetic learners by coupling learning to their developmental processes. Older elementary children should not be denied the kinesthetic modality either. The following example is a "silly song" that represents both the use of music as a memory model for remembering landforms concepts in social studies and a song that has students access kinesthetic movement to help in the learning process. It is written to "If You're Happy and You Know It" (http://pbskids.org/barney/children/music/happyand.html).

I'm a mountain and I know it, climb my rocks! (*Children first make a "peak" with their hands, then do a "climbing motion" with their hands.*)
I'm a mountain and I know it, climb my rocks! (*Repeat motions.*)
I'm a mountain and I know it, and I've got steep sides to show it. (*Children form a peak with their hands, then with their right hands point to the left "steep side."*)
I'm a mountain and I know it, climb my rocks! (*Repeat first motions.*)

Other verses and motions include:

Verse 2: I'm a plateau and I know it, flat on top! (*Children form a "table top" plateau with their hands and arms.*) (*. . . and I'm flat on top to show it . . .*)
V 3: I'm a peninsula and I know it, I stick out! (*Children form a "peninsula" by sticking an elbow out to the side.*) (*. . . water's on three sides to show it . . .*)

V 4: I'm a hill and I know it, round on top! (*Children form "hill" above head with hands.*) (. . . *and I round on top to show it . . .*)

V 5: I'm a valley and I know it, a deep "V"! (*Children form a "V" by crossing their forearms almost at the elbow in front of them.*) (. . . *and I'm "V"-shaped to show it . . .*)

There are many memory songs through out the curriculum to integrate into various content areas and for many grade levels (see http://www. songsforteaching.com or http://www.writingfix.com/ipod_prompts.htm).

Social skills develop when children are engaged in any musical activities involving groups or partners. The teacher should be a sharer of and co-experiencer of each activity, but the learner him- or herself must listen, react, create, and perform in order to gain. All children have the potential to develop their skills and their appreciation for music, given opportunities by a Texas teacher.

Remember Your Pedagogy

When teaching music, foremost, do not forget other pedagogy from your *Pedagogy and Professional Responsibilities (PPR) TExES*. Provide a classroom that is warm and open and that invites discovery, creativity, and improvisation. Establish rules and routines that help students become accepting of each other during performances, and give directions that show respect for instruments, equipment and each other in movement. Positively encourage children at all times, especially in performance and creative areas. Provide for continuity and relevance for young children by sharing music from their home/community/culture. Create and follow lesson plans (both long-range and daily), as you would with other subject areas, that help students understand the objectives and the rationales for a musical experience. Download and use the music TEKS as a guideline for preparing goals and objectives for which you are responsible at the grade level in which you teach. Texas expects that you do this for every subject, including music. Allow for both whole-class and individual experiences and for integrating other arts and subject areas whenever possible. Make judgments in terms of your objectives on how well children are progressing, and use those assessments to reflect on what impact it has on what you plan for the next time in class. Good pedagogy also demands having children think at all levels, particularly at higher levels. Such activities at the synthesis level might include creating musical introductions and accompaniments to stories or poems, improvising or writing short songs or simple operettas, composing new musical accompaniments to songs children already know, designing a new movement to a certain song, creating their own instruments, and so forth. Teachers should also use questioning, just as they would with other subject areas. For example, Ms. Hall wants to play a selection from a CD to her fifth-grade class. First, she shows them the cover of the CD and asks about its title and the possible connection to the song titles on the CD. She asks students to also tell her about the cover design and how it projects the mood of the CD. She then gives students the title of the song she wants them to hear. From the title of the song, she asks students to project what they expect to hear in the lyrics. Finally, she asks students to see if the song fits with the "whole package," and why or why not. Using a similar appropriate technique with a music video, Mr. Payne asks his sixth-grade students to watch and then tell about the setting, dress, and other people seen in the video. He asks students to determine the mood and evaluate if the song matched the visuals in establishing the mood. Students were asked to determine if there was an overall message, and, if so, did the video succeed in projecting it. For other critical thinking exercises, see http://bellevuecollege. edu/lmc/ilac/curric/jamieson/jam2.html.

For successful experiences, all music should be *age appropriate* in terms of ability, subject matter, and in terms of development (intellectual, social, and physical). As a reminder, an important part of learning theory tells us that stages of each domain are not always tied to an exact age, so students may move through these stages at different rates. In addition, the *zone of proximal development* (where children can function with help from an adult or capable peer) should be a part of music planning as well; teachers want to challenge young children with music rather than overwhelm them with concepts and skills that they cannot yet handle. Many concrete and manipulative experiences combined with visuals should be an important part of music instruction. Remember also that some movements that older children can accomplish to music are not yet appropriate for the coordination of the young child.

On a serious note about subject matter, teachers must consider that much of our popular music today no longer contains lyrics or messages appropriate for children. Listen carefully to *all* songs that you plan to play in class. You do not want children to hear some songs or repeat lyrics that would lead an angry parent or administrator to your doorstep. Children should be allowed to bring their own music to share, but do establish parental knowledge and rules for appropriateness.

Good pedagogy asks teachers to provide variety. Select a variety of music throughout the day, even though children will or may already have begun to develop preferences. Although certain types of music are not appealing to young children, your opinion matters, so if you also indicate distaste in certain music, young students may imitate your modeling.

There are other important reasons for teachers to understand the basics of music for the elementary classroom. The greatest potential for helping children develop musical interests and skills lies in the years of early childhood and elementary school. Also, multiple intelligence research identifies musical intelligence as one of several intelligences. As such, those children who have talent and intelligence in music should be provided a way to shine as they develop their talents more fully in the classroom. For other students, we know that to offer experiences in an intelligence area (such as music) is to develop new physiological pathways (according to recent brain research). Children who learn best in kinesthetic or tactile ways also often shine during music classes, although, again, *all* children's skills in these areas can be enhanced. Music is one subject that can be developed both for playing, movement, and singing skill, as well as for appreciation. In the early childhood years, a tremendous amount of musical growth can occur—if that growth is nurtured by a caring teacher.

Music is emotional in nature, and teachers can take advantage of that aspect. As with the background music to movies, classroom music can also heighten students' experiences with certain subject areas, such as writing and reading literature, or it can encourage a student to become a part of another land or era. For example, playing Native American music in the background as students enter their social studies classroom can set a mood for the day's lesson on tribes and can continue to involve students as they work on an independent project later in the hour with Native American music as a backdrop. Playing a focus song to lead into an activity can create considerable interest or can close a lesson in a way that helps the lesson linger in the minds of students. For instance, a teacher who was planning a science-heavy unit on the *Titanic* might open or close with the popular theme song from that movie to connect science to the reality of human tragedy. And what student could not write a more vivid descriptive piece or poem on spring, for example, with Vivaldi's "Spring" from *The Four Seasons* playing softly in the background (http://www.youtube.com/watch?v=iSw7CcAXPWk)? Many songs can be found to introduce specific topics or concepts. Because music touches the emotions so easily, it can be used by a creative teacher to enhance the mood of the classroom and to increase creativity and learning across the curriculum.

Often, music text series seek to combine works of art and poetry with works of music. This helps to further develop the affective domain, as students can relate to how a painter suggests feelings and emotions with color, lines, and shapes, to how a poet does the same with words, to how a musician does so with many variations of sounds. For example, a atonal piece could accompany an abstract art painting. Technology can enhance this integration because teachers can create slide shows of a number of different art pieces of an era accompanied by famous musical compositions of those times. Several of these types of examples have already been put together on the Internet (e.g., see http://vodpod.com/watch/647683-leslies-artgallery-women-in-art-by-eggman913).

Making Connections with Music

Music has also been tied to learning in different subject areas in other ways. For example, you may have grown up with songs that helped you remember the alphabet, seasons, holidays, and sequencing of letters and numbers. This is investigated in detail later in the chapter. You have already seen reasons why mathematics has a direct tie with music, particularly when looking at fractions. The study of the production of sound can easily be tied to science lessons, and in social studies there are many small and well-written operettas published for children about various historical periods and famous people from the past. These provide students with motivating preludes to find out more about these times and persons.

When boys and girls begin to learn about people around the world, multicultural studies and music go hand-in-hand. Simple songs written in other languages, may, for example, be a child's first experience with foreign language; they also help a child understand that many peoples throughout the world are the same in that they express similar feelings (and often do so through music). As discussed earlier, music tells us much about the peoples of the world, as well as the different regions of the United States. Music provides exciting differences for a child to see from place to place and from era to era, depending on who writes it, who performs it, for what occasions music is made and performed, and the different instruments and ways of singing that exist. The state music standards in almost every grade level require children to investigate diverse cultures by playing or singing songs or participating in musical games of other cultures. For young children, this aspect of introducing other cultures is extremely inviting. A unit on Japan, for instance, can include a tea party with traditional music of the country playing in the background as students sip their tea, learn about the new country, and create a haiku. Other multicultural experiences and events should often include related music.

There are other content areas that music enhances. Very compelling is the fact that as children follow along with choral lyrics, a very safe way of reading is provided for those who may struggle. In this low-risk read-along situation, music can add to student confidence, and literacy is promoted through voice/print pairing. This can also be particularly helpful for English as a Second Language (ESL) students. Music, when played as a backdrop for reading or drama as a mood setter, can enhance student creativity in dramatic roles. A play can be enhanced when students, using simple instruments, create a musical motif or theme for each character. The matching musical motif is played each time the character enters or begins to speak. As the story becomes more involved and exciting, so does the instrumentation.

Art and music often fit together naturally, as the teacher selects background music that relates in some way to an art project while students work, or the teacher may ask students to "let the music tell them" what to paint or draw. As mentioned, art is often combined as a part of music texts as a way for students to understand comparisons between art and musical elements such as texture, shape, and line.

Music can help us to learn facts and acts as an aid to memory, as also mentioned earlier. Governmental processes, grammar, and math concepts have been set to music as an entertaining way for countless students to remember specified material (e.g., how a bill goes through Congress). Many of you may still be able to name all the states by singing a song such as "Fifty . . . nifty . . . " (http://www.youtube.com/watch?v=k_HeLofy7IE). Such productions as *Schoolhouse Rock*, for example, provide many songs about facts on social studies, grammar, money, multiplication, and science (http://www.youtube.com/watch?v=mEJL2Uuv-oQ for "I'm Just a Bill", or see other lyrics at http://www.schoolhouserock.tv). For example, one song, "Conjunction Junction," tells students, "Conjunction Junction, what's your function? Hooking up words and phrases and clauses" (http://www.youtube.com/watch?v=mkO87mkgcNo). Music can also be used as a memory model for students, as the teacher finds or composes words to popular melodies (or helps students create their own) that relate to a subject at hand. Many of you already know how a certain song or piece of music triggers a memory of a place, a date, a time period, or a particular person. As a memory model for students, the teacher can find or make up words to songs (as noted earlier in the song, "I'm a Mountain and I Know It") with particularly popular melodies that relate to a subject at hand. These lyrics can be quite serious or very silly. For example, a sixth-grade classroom was being observed while taking a test. Earlier, the student teacher had taught her children a song that she had made up to help them remember simple machines and their functions. Students did very well on the test, but interestingly enough, there was quite a bit of humming of the "Machine Song" going on in the classroom that day, as students "accessed" their lyrics and, thus, their definitions of the machines. Older elementary students also love to create these types of lyrics related to the various curriculum areas and put them to popular melodies, rap rhythms, and so forth, whereas younger children love to sing these types of songs because the melody is often already familiar. Do remember, however, that students coming from outside the United States may not readily know these tunes. It may be necessary to teach the originals first.

Having students create their own music as an activity, of course, involves having them work at the synthesis level, a higher-level of thinking. For example, in composing, students can create various rhythms or construct sound stories around a theme (holidays, a person, a trip, feelings, or another concept) in which sounds that represent the theme to the child are collected on tape. A sound tape of human vocalizations (hums, whispers, hisses, sighs, shouts, etc.) that students write and record makes an interesting composition. They may create a poem, lyrics or melodies, short operettas, chants, raps, finger plays, dance or body movements, or a story backdrop (e.g., for a rain forest book, a sound tape for each animal) of their own.

A methodology, *Suggestopedia*, created by Bulgarian Georgi Lozanov, has been used since the 1970s in teaching foreign language in an accelerated manner. In this technique, Baroque music is used to relax the mind, as his research shows that a tense mind closes in learning languages. However, with music, learning in a new language can be easily accepted, because mental barriers do not go up so often when music and relaxation are part of the lesson. Using the *Suggestopedia* techniques, the teacher often uses music in tandem with guided visualization or imaging. A scene is read containing a considerable amount of contextual clues along with known vocabulary. From this, students are able to gain understanding into the new vocabulary in a relaxed manner. Carrying this idea a step further into our elementary classrooms, new vocabulary in many different subjects may be "Greek" to our students, so the same method can be applied in various areas of study. For example, in a modified version of *Suggestopedia*, a teacher may play one of the many nature CD selections that are available of rain forest sounds combined with relaxing music. She or he asks students to relax, close their eyes, and "take a journey with her" into the rain forest. As the music plays, the teacher delivers a script that is full of contextual clues and repetition with new vocabulary words embedded within. New vocabulary and concepts are shown in boldface:

Close your eyes and relax and come with me now to the rain forest of Central America. The first thing that overwhelms our eyes here is the green **vegetation**—*the incredible number of growing plants! Everywhere you look the* **vegetation** *is so green, and many of these plants have beautiful flowers. This green* **vegetation** *grows all year long—because the location is so warm and* **humid**—*that is, sticky and damp. About nine feet of rain falls here every year! How* **humid** *it is here! I am already sweating, and my clothes are sticking to me. Most places in Texas receive only about one to two feet of rain each year. There is so much rain in the rain forest that it cannot evaporate, so the* **humidity**, *or moisture in the air), remains high all the time. Think about how it feels in Texas in the summer on a day when the* **humidity** *is high—you feel sticky, sweaty, and damp. In the rain forest, there is even more* **humidity**! *That's one reason for so much green* **vegetation**. *The* **vegetation** *gets so much moisture. Also, the* **vegetation** *never freezes like it does in many parts of Texas. It is very warm here, so the* **vegetation** *grows and grows and grows! That is why, when we look down upon the rain forest from above, we view a "sea of green." So much* **vegetation**!

Speech and music also go hand-in-hand, as the spoken word has rhythms of which the child is not often aware. Singing, chanting, and rhyming words in the context of music help the child develop better speaking skills and understanding of pronunciation. Encouragement of experimentation of all types of verbal sounds helps the child to become more sensitive to his or her own speaking voice and develop that voice in a more dynamic manner.

Music can also be a mood adjuster for behavior. Teachers who have students enter a classroom where calming music is playing can often feel a difference in the way the class begins to focus. Conversely, music can invigorate a class after a long period of academic work or can help relieve some of the stress accompanying long test periods. Cute musical transitions have always been used by kindergarten teachers to move students from one activity to another, but clever teachers in all grades find that age-appropriate music creates the perfect routine for changing activities or moving to new work areas in a more conducive manner. Listening can also be used as a reward. Young children need the consistency that certain songs can give, so teachers establish songs that build familiar routines for them during the day (a "Come to Circle Song," "Clean-Up Time Song," etc.). Use familiar music before going on to the unfamiliar so that children feel safe in branching out to explore the new.

In summary, there are many ways to connect music to many parts of the classroom each day. Thinking about music can give children enjoyment and can help develop and reinforce thinking. In addition to the ways mentioned previously, music can be a higher-level thinking activity in and of itself, as students compose or create their own compositions or think about sound in creating their own instruments. Boys and girls can analyze and evaluate music to determine their reasons for liking or disliking a song or composition and can interpret what a composer is trying to say through music. After comparing and contrasting, they can choose meaningful alternatives. Older elementary students can investigate music in association with other activities and happenings. Thus, music becomes an integral part of students' lives in many areas—rather than, "It's time for music class now!"

Try this practice question:

For one musical activity, Miss Larson wanted a permanent Music Center in her early childhood class. She and a friend built a huge three-sided box with a short door in one side that was comfortable enough for one or two students. The open side could be pushed up against the wall, so that when Miss Larson wanted to change the center, she could just pull it out from the wall. Light inside was provided by several holes in the top. Inside she placed only one or two instruments at a time (some with multiple tone capability, some that were monotone). For example, one week she placed two drums inside, each with a different tone, whereas the next week she set up *resonator bells* (bells with three pitches and of three different sizes) with a mallet. Sometimes instruments were homemade (a durable box with seeds that could be shaken), and sometimes there were ordinary items (pot lids). She gave directions that mostly focused on the care of the instruments.

This center was:

- **A.** inappropriate because children do not know what to expect or do with the instrument(s) because no proper instruction has been given on how to use them.
- **B.** inappropriate because young children cannot be expected to take care of the instruments when they are not in sight of the teacher, and they already have a chance to play with ordinary things at home.
- **C.** appropriate because it provides time and space for young children to explore and create music spontaneously.
- **D.** appropriate because young children need private time, and the center is constructed so as to combine music with time away from others.

Choice *A* is not correct for young children because, at times, they should be able to experiment independently in music. We would not select choice *B* either, because we expect that children will take care of the instruments, and, as music teachers, we continuously instruct and enforce this concept. We also cannot be sure that students have the opportunity at home to experiment (*B*). Choice *D* is incorrect, because the center is constructed to ensure that at least two students are insulated when they are noisy (which we expect here) rather than creating private time. Let's return to *C*. Choice *C* is correct, because this type of center provides an inquiry-based time and space for young children to perceive information about the instrument (i.e., to experiment for data), analyze, and to come to some conclusions on their own. An important part of experimenting with sound is discovery (*C*). As new instruments are switched, children apply learned information to the new experience. Too many instruments at once is overwhelming to the young child and does not give the child an opportunity to focus. One follow-up activity is to have children make their own instruments, some of which may find their way to this center. Another is to ask questions that make children think (How is this instrument similar to last week's? In what kind of movie scene could this instrument be used? How is it different when played softly and loudly?).The answer is C.

Let's try another question:

Mrs. Bradford's social studies class has been working on a unit on Africa for almost 2 weeks. Students have read about the continent of Africa, researched it on the Internet, seen videos, worked on art projects, and focused on African music as well. Tomorrow, Mrs. Bradford will give a test on this unit.

However, on this day she first had children put away their things and relax. She put on a CD softly in the background entitled "African Safari" and proceeded to involve the class in a Concept Development model. She first asked students to brainstorm all the words that they could think of when they heard the word *Africa* and felt the music playing. As students thought of words, she wrote them on the board. Among the many examples that students contributed were:

Drums	Plains	Tigers	Singing	Flutes
Lions	Safari	Chants	Many tribes	Cheetahs
Hunting	Elephants	Waterfalls	Flamingos	Nile
Ivory	Gold	Lost Cities	Desert	Jungle
Homemade instruments	Big cities	Colonies	Many countries	Hippos
"The Lion King"	Dancing in the villages	Big mountains	Zebras	Diamonds

As the music was replayed, she asked her cooperative tables of students to classify the terms on the board into groups that belong together for whatever reason they think. Then, they were to label these groups with a name. They could also add any terms that they had left out that might belong in their categories. One cooperative group came up with the one of the following classifications and labels:

African Music	**They added to this category:**
Handmade Instruments	Hunting Dances
Drums	Story Dances
Flutes	Masks
Dancing In The Village	Chants
Singing	

Other categories emerged into land forms, African animals, and so forth. As each group read their categories, the class was asked to add anything else that came to mind about Africa. Mrs. Bradford then asked each cooperative table to select one category and create two to four sentences using all of the words they listed. The cooperative group that selected African Music wrote, "In lots of villages in Africa, instruments like drums and flutes are handmade. The village uses these when they sing and dance. Lots of African music is just voices chanting without any instruments. The people there sometimes wear masks to act out stories—like a hunt."

The music added all but which of the following important elements to this lesson?

- **A.** Memories triggered of what students had seen about Africa in movies, videos, photos, and so on, so it acted as a part of scaffolding and tapped into past experiences.
- **B.** Added another modality to the lesson.
- **C.** Added interest to the lesson, so it helped with motivation.
- **D.** Helped increase students' ability to read music.

The Concept Development model, as shown in this example, is an excellent way for teachers to determine what students know about a concept as a class. It is also helpful to begin teaching a lesson on a new concept. It helps a teacher determine prior knowledge so that students are not bored by the reteaching of information they know. As in this case, it is also extremely useful as a review for a unit test so students can self-monitor what they have gained prior to testing, and the teacher can see what she or he might need to reteach. The music gives this lesson an added dimension in all of the areas mentioned in choices *A, B,* and *C.* In addition, if the teacher puts the same music on during the test, *Suggestopedia* experts believe that students will be able to access much more information. Although this model helped to increase vocabulary that has to do with some musical terms (drums, chants, etc.), there is nothing in the lesson that deals with decoding, or reading, music. The correct answer is *D.*

Technology and Music

Technology has opened the doors wide to engage students in music. Not only does advanced technology in listening allow us to hear music more clearly than ever before but also, as mentioned earlier, it allows students to hear their own music immediately, make judgments, and make alternative decisions to refine their performances. Electric instruments and sound equipment also allow for amplification and purer sound. Music that is totally created through the use of *synthesizers* (electronic devices that create sounds) or music or sounds that are altered in some way by electronic devices is termed *electronic music*, as opposed to music played on electronic instruments, such as the electric guitar or other amplified instruments. Music synthesizers that allowed sounds to be produced in almost any way a composer desired first became available in the 1950s. Through the next decades, computers made the process of composing increasingly easier. Currently, software programs work with computers to create sounds similar to almost any musical instrument, to save a composer's music, to recall it for editing later on, and so forth. There are many excellent technology packages for budding musicians. Still other software packages teach students how to read music easily or play using the computer (Switch Ensemble, BoardMaker, etc.). Although working with MIDI (Music Instrument Digital Interface) is sometimes complicated, this is a program that can open a whole new world of possibilities with synthesizing. The MIDI allows electronic instruments to communicate together and with a computer. To hear what the computer can do, go to the following Web site and select from the types of music that you would like to hear: http://www.philharmonia.co.uk/thesoundexchange/make_music/samples/library/. Companies such as eJamming offer the online or in-class ability to play music with others in real time with MIDI instruments. Super Duper Music Looper at www.sonycreativesoftware.com/products/sdml/sdml/asp also allows children to be creative. A recent invention, Siftables®, are sophisticated, interactive minicomputer blocks with displays that children can manipulate to create a variety of compositions simply by moving the blocks to various positions. Do not forget the Internet as a source for many types of music, biographies of composers, music history, and other pertinent information. Technology allows children to communicate about music, to use listservs, access bulletin boards, participate in online groups, contact fan clubs, find out more about artists, keep compositions digitally, download to iPods, and so forth.

 ## Resources for Music Teachers

One question that you must be asking if you do not have a considerable background in music is, "How do I know what to teach, and where can I get ideas?" Many schools have music book series such as Silver Burdett, McGraw-Hill, and so on, eventhough you may have to share one set per grade level. These series may come with student texts at all levels of elementary music instruction. Some investigation as to where these music series might be found in your building (or district) may be in order, but it is worthwhile for your children. Teachers' editions offer clear examples of appropriate scope and sequence, along with many valuable activities. Most important, if these series are provided by your school, they often come with excellent, high-quality recordings (with both children's and adults' voices), written music for accompaniments or classroom instruments, charts and other visuals, and cross-indexes for convenience.

The TEKS (Texas Essential Knowledge and Skills) for music students is also a guide for teaching scope and sequence of skills and is a requirement for teachers to follow in Texas. There are TEKS expectations and elements for teachers in music (under Fine Arts) by grade level, and these can be accessed online. The TEKS for music are available for downloading at http://www.tea.state.tx.us/rules/tac/chapter117/index.html. National Music Standards for young children are also available at http://www.menc.org/resources/view/national-standards-for-music-education.

Libraries can also be important places for you to find music resources. You can find song and musical activity books, books about young musicians, biographies of famous composers, and recordings to check out for many age levels. Many university libraries have sets of teachers' editions or examples of student texts of music series from major textbook publishers to investigate.

People (human resources) can also add much to your music program. The school district in which you work may have a musical specialist who oversees many schools. Other teachers in your school may also be sources of ideas and materials. Be sure to ask your principal about teachers in your building who could become musical resources to you. It is most important for you to maintain a school-wide network for the music program as well. Other teachers may want to share in various aspects of a program or performance, so be sure to communicate what is happening musically in your school. Other district schools (especially "feeder" schools) can be resources for sparking interest in music for students, as musical groups from intermediate, middle, and high schools are asked to perform in your elementary school or class. Musical interest can be ignited in your children as they see teachers in upper grades conducting exciting performances with older children. The popularity of the series of "High School Musical" movies and plays attests to this observation. Be sure to inform your children and their parents about musical performances in your district or community that provide a source of interest and entertainment. Most school bands and choirs perform concerts and musicals during various times of the year, so making sure that you are a part of the information network (and can pass this information on) should be part of your commitment to music and your community. A quick guide to musical events around the state, along with other information, can be found at http://www.texasmusicguide .com. Also, parents can be excellent resources for musical experiences, as well as people from the community who take an interest in children and music. Ask parents through notes, emails, or calls, and be resourceful in your community in searching for professional or amateur musicians who might add to the musical experiences of your children by volunteering in some way.

For teachers, the Internet offers a wide variety of resources, from finding suitable materials for any type of music desired, to finding organizations for music teachers, to locating quick examples of instrumental sounds. The Texas Music Educators' Website at http://www.tmea.org and the Texas Music Teachers Association's Website at http://www.tmta.org are two such sites that provide information and links to many other sites. The Internet has a vast variety of clickable songs and musical pieces from all eras and regions. Musical histories and biographical information on great composers can be found at a moment's notice, and online music stores offer all types of musical recordings, as well as books and sheet music for purchase. There are also a number of tapes and CDs suitable for these grade levels available from retail stores, school supply catalogs, or teachers' stores. There are several journals that may act as resources of interest to teachers of music, such as *American Suzuki Journal, British Journal of Music Education, General Music Today, Kodaly Envoy, Music Educators Journal*, and the *Orff Echo*. As with all subject areas, music has organizations—both national and state—to which teachers belong, many of which publish good resource journals or offer beneficial conferences. The Texas Music Teachers Association (http://www.tmta.org) and the Texas Music Educators Association (http://www.tmea.org), along with the National Association for Music Education (http://www.menc.org) and the Music Teachers National Association (http://www.mtna.org), all have Websites for membership and information and act as good resources. The site for the National Association for Teachers of Singing is http://www.nats.org. There are many other excellent sites for organizations or resources that may be useful. Be creative and persistent in your Internet searches, and you can find what you need.

The Home, Community, and Music

One accepted element of pedagogy asks that the teacher links the culture of parents and the community with instruction. This is also true with the music curriculum as a scaffolding issue—that is, children first relate to the type of music with which they are familiar. In planning, therefore, look carefully at the culture of the community and its unique engagement with music. In Texas, for example, we mentioned that there are rural communities that are of German and Czech descent whose children grow up learning to polka, whereas in other communities, children can two-step with country and western music almost before they begin school. Young African American children in many communities may have considerable experience with gospel music, whereas many young Hispanic students know the sounds of *tejano* very well. Of course, there are communities and individuals everywhere in between who relate to many types of music. One mission of schools is often seen as "supporter of cultures." Therefore, the mission of music in schools is not only to expose boys and girls to a wide variety of music but also to help students develop musical skills and songs that they can enjoy in their own world—that of their community's culture and that of their family and friends. Again, it is important for teachers to know what musical events are offered in the community around the school and capitalize on these connections. Parents are more likely to support programs with which they are comfortable musically, although most want their children to have a well-rounded education in music as well. Most young children love to perform, so school programs offer an excellent bridge to draw parents to the school. You may even have parents who are knowledgeable and willing to help with your programs—a great resource!

Health and Safety in Music

There are some issues to which teachers must attend in music regarding the health and well-being of their students. Most important, if a teacher is lucky enough to have a classroom or school set of *recorders* (beginning instruments that look much like a clarinet), much care must be taken to ensure that these instruments are thoroughly cleaned in order to avoid having bacteria build up inside from warm breaths and to stop the passing on of germs and illnesses if children must share. Make sure to use a sanitizer that does not react with plastic after each session. We know that germs can be easily spread through hand contact, so when children are holding hands during musical activities or trading rhythm instruments, cleaning hands prior to and after the activity may save children from passing colds and other germs during epidemic times of the year.

The loud volume of music can also be of concern. The hearing of children should be considered, especially those who are forced to continuously sit next to speakers or loud instruments. Another safety issue concerns instruments that are played with mallets or strikers. Establish strict rules about the appropriate use of these.

During musical movement exercises, song games, or dances, the teacher is responsible for making sure that space is cleared so that students do not trip over desks, chairs, cords, students' belongings, or other items as they become involved. Special concern for children with exceptionalities, particularly those with physical challenges, should be made here.

If students are going to be on stage or use risers for special programs, establishing rules and practicing moving on and off are musts for safety. During performances, legible emergency procedures must be posted. The stage must be safe (no dangerous cords, rickety risers, trap doors that are not secured, etc.). If lights are to be off at any time, fluorescent-type lights or tape or painted signs must be used to mark exits and other areas of concern. Adequate adult supervision, first aid, fire extinguishers, and so forth must be available, and sufficient rehearsals must have taken place so that children are able to move safely on-, off-, and backstage.

 ## Special Needs Children at Music Time

Classrooms may have children who are differently abled who are a part of the classroom all day or may be mainstreamed for some subjects by reason of Public Law 94–192. If a child has been placed in a regular classroom for music as a part of the least restrictive environment, teachers should make sure that they include those children and modify their objectives, if applicable, on their Individual Education Plans (IEPs). This is required by law, so that these students can participate to the fullest of their abilities. Learn as much as you can about the child and his or her abilities and needs ahead of time, and do not be afraid to call on the help of specialized teachers and parents as resources. If a child is coming to a self-contained classroom only for music, be sure to have music times set out clearly to work in coordination with the schedule of the special needs teacher. Your manner of acceptance and welcome is the model for your students to follow.

Many children with mental differences or learning disabilities may need special attention in the music class with regard to the introduction of instruments, as the sounds may startle, cause sensory overload, or confuse them. Because music is emotional, these students may sometimes overreact during listening times to certain pieces or instrument sounds. Note short attention spans and be ready to change approaches if a child becomes too excitable or too bored. Clear structure and repetition (if children are unable to read long passages) is also a necessary part of instruction for some children with special needs, even in music class. Work on small portions of music at a time with immediate feedback to help eliminate failure. Establish clear signals to end musical selections, as some students may become so involved that they do not stop. Also, try to begin and end the class in a routine way (perhaps with one particular welcome or greeting song and a particular farewell song). Children should be expected and encouraged to participate to the fullest of their abilities and praised well and often for their efforts.

For students with hearing difficulties, the teacher of music must go to further lengths to help in relating the lesson visually, through vibration in a tactile manner (by having students touch) and kinesthetically (through motions). Seating is especially important for these children so that they may see visuals, feel vibrations, and catch the rhythms of movements. Many may not be totally impaired, so seating close to the music source or having a non-pitched instrument close to an ear may be vital, although it may depend on whether their hearing loss involves clarity or loudness (frequency) difficulties. Individual modification may be necessary for distortion in hearing devices for music and group singing. Be certain that these students can see your face and speech movements during all instruction and singing, and use clear, distinct articulation. If a child has near or total impairment and signs, signing the lyrics is also encouraged. Often these types of children face speech difficulties, too, so help in language development (diction, rhythm, etc.) is important in music class.

Students who are visually impaired may be able to participate fully in most lessons, although lessons that focus on listening and rote learning of songs, along with tactile aids for some activities, increase learning. Children with visual difficulties may need physical guidance in any movements to music. If not fully impaired, large visuals in black and white or large-print song books may be provided. If students are learning Braille, see if there is a way to obtain Braille songbooks so they can follow along with the words or assign buddies that can help in creative composition activities. When entering the classroom for music, always warn these students of new placements of sound equipment or instruments or of the fact that you have moved chairs in anticipation of an activity.

Children who are orthopedically challenged may need help with alternative movements, if applicable to the lesson, but they can often participate in most other ways. Sometimes the class can be very helpful in creating a design that helps these students move about and participate more easily. Watch phrasing of words used in movement activities so that all children can participate, depending on the particular circumstances; therefore, provide alternatives for movements such as, "Stand up and skip around in a circle," for example, with children in wheelchairs. When playing rhythm instruments, special accommodations may be needed to help children hold a mallet or stick in some way.

Musically gifted students also require special attention. Some larger school districts have magnet schools for musically talented children, although most are left to the school or classroom teacher. Be sure that you are providing opportunities for these children to work at their accelerated levels through enrichment experiences.

There are other special needs and combinations of special needs not covered here. Students who have learning disabilities that affect other subject areas have the same difficulties in music classes (reading, sequencing, etc.). One important issue that teachers need to remember is that, according to law (PL 94–192), documentation must be provided for evaluation purposes on objectives set by the Admission, Review, and Dismissal (ARD) team. Continue to seek out resources to help with each type of need, and remember that each child is truly an individual and has specific abilities that affect the extent to which he or she can participate. Music may offer children with special needs an avenue of communication not open to them in many subject areas. It is often a nurturing force in their lives, as well as an expressive one.

Consider the following practice question:

Ms. Mitchell tells students that tomorrow would be a special writing day. They are going to experience a concert in class, then become music critics by writing about what they judge to be good or poor quality for two of the four pieces they would hear. They will choose two compositions and evaluate what they hear, what they like, what they do not like, and tell why.

"To go to a concert," she tells them, "tickets must be purchased. During certain times of the day today, you can to go back to the 'ticket booth' desk in the back of the room and select your seating for tomorrow's concert from the seating chart map. You will each get an envelope with 'money' for a seat." All envelopes contain different amounts of money, so students must make a decision on where they will buy their seat based on the money in their envelopes. As students purchase tickets, Ms. Mitchell puts their names on those tickets in order to hand out tickets quickly the next day.

Ms. Mitchell then goes over the expectations for concert behavior: Wait for the usher to seat you, no changing seats because each person has paid for a particular seat, no talking once the concert has started so all can hear, no getting out of one's seat during the music (and if you are not seated by the time the concert begins, you may not go in until there is a break) because it will be dark. Concert goers can show one's appreciation by clapping (and calling out "Bravo," if the performance is very good). She also tells them about the sequence of events for the orchestra: warm-up of the musical instruments at the beginning, applause at the entry of the concertmaster (first seat violinist), tuning of the instruments, entry of the conductor (applause), possible entrance of soloists, applause at the end of each piece, and applause at the end of the concert with standing ovations reserved for outstanding performances. She also reminds them of some longer pieces that they had already listened to in class that had different movements with silence in between. She laughs in telling them that sometimes audience members who do not know the music well may start clapping between the movements—but the music is not really over yet! A good guideline, she notes, is to wait to see if lots of others begin applause, and if still unsure, wait until the conductor actually steps down. She also tells them that they should look particularly nice tomorrow. Although everyone who attends concerts does not dress up, it does show respect for the performers to look nice. Refreshments will be served during intermission (with conversation), so all those who follow the rules will have a snack and be able to chat at that point. Finally, she quickly goes over a bit of information on the composers whose music they will hear.

The following day, Ms. Mitchell has students line up at the door and gives out their tickets with programs. She has two students role-play ushers who seat students in their correct seats for the concert. She then introduces the music and has several students role-play the entrance of some of the orchestra members, and, finally, she has students listen to two exciting pieces of music. Punch and cookies are served at intermission, followed by flashing the lights, reseating, and the playing of two other pieces of music. At the end of the concert, Ms. Mitchell asks students to quietly return to their own seats to review the elements needed for critiquing and begin the writing process as she replays the selections.

This music class contributes most to:

A. introducing students to some of the great composers.
B. having students understand concert etiquette.
C. having students use thinking skills of comparing and contrasting.
D. the integration of mathematics and writing with music.

Standard 7.10s asks Texas teachers to teach concert etiquette. Role-play is the perfect introduction to a real concert (B). It is hoped that one field trip during the year for every school in Texas might be to a musical performance of some type. Ms. Mitchell also integrated this activity into her writing class, as she is asking students to compare and contrast the different pieces of music, so choice C is a good second choice. Although this lesson does integrate some mathematics and writing (D), the main focus is music. The music that she selects for listening could be from the great composers (A), but it could also be chosen more for the enjoyment of this grade level. The emphasis here, however, is on the concert etiquette. Role-play might include any one of the many types of concerts that children might attend: symphony orchestra, chamber orchestra, recitals, choral performances, operas, or ballet. The correct answer is B.

Generalists **are not responsible for Standard VIII.**

 # Standard IX: Assessment

The music teacher understands student assessment and uses assessment results to design instruction and promote student progress.

The teacher knows the skills needed to form critical judgments about music. He or she knows techniques and criteria for assessing students' musical knowledge and skills and can use multiple forms of assessment and knowledge of the music TEKS to help determine students' progress in developing those music skills and understanding. Continuing, the teacher uses an understanding of ongoing results of assessment to continuously develop instructional plans. The EC-6 teacher can use standard terminology in communicating about students' musical skills and performance and can give constructive criticism when evaluating skills or performances. Meaningful prescriptions to correct problems or errors in musical performances can be easily offered.

The state provides several ways of helping teachers to know what is expected of children in Texas EC-6 classrooms. Teachers can use these guidelines to judge if their children are receiving the information and experiences needed to meet these expectations and how well children are achieving in music. For example, the online *Texas Music Curriculum Guidelines* for 3- and 4-year-old children show that children should express themselves through singing and movement and by playing simple instruments, and they should learn to experiment with music concepts, volume, tempo, and sound. Children should also begin to appreciate different types of music.

The child:

- participates in classroom music activities.
- begins to sing a variety of simple songs.
- begins to play classroom instruments.
- begins to respond to music of various tempos through movement.
- begins to distinguish among the sounds of several common instruments.

As another example, the TEKS for music/fine arts can be downloaded at http://www.tea.state.tx.us/rules/tac/chapter117/index.html. The following example shows some of the expectations for kindergarten (other grade levels can be found there as well).

Knowledge and skills:

1. **Perception.** *The student describes and analyzes musical sound and demonstrates musical artistry. The student is expected to:*
   A. *identify the difference between the singing and speaking voice, and*
   B. *identify the timbre of adult voices and instruments.*
2. **Creative expression/performance.** *The student performs a varied repertoire of music. The student is expected to:*
   A. *sing or play classroom instruments independently or in a group, and*
   B. *sing songs from diverse cultures and styles or play such songs on musical instruments.*

Teachers should be sure that they are using these Texas expectations for their grade levels to design short- and long-range music plans to include all of the TEKS at their grade level because teachers are accountable in this area. Using these as a base, teachers can begin to assess whether or not their children are receiving opportunities in all areas and if the quality and quantity of the experiences can be measured and reported. Criteria for judging individual achievement should be built into plans (as with other subjects that are taught). As children participate in experiences, plans should either reflect progression or reteaching of information or skills in music.

Assessment and Evaluation

What areas should be included in music assessment and evaluation? Texas says that information on all the domains on which EC-6 music touches should be included: (1) development of *physical skills* based on the ability to sing, play, and move at expected levels, along with observed growth in perception through sensory responses or the ability to respond to musical differences; (2) growth in conceptual/*cognitive development* or thinking skills related to the elements of music, history of music, and so forth; (3) growth in the *affective domain* in terms of musical participation (both planned and free), musical preferences, creativity, and expressiveness; and (4) growth in the *social domain*, interpersonal skills, and communication gained through musical participation.

Some responses to music are *overt* (or observable) but, more often than not, they are *covert*—that is, they take place within the individual through the affective domain. For that reason, assessment and evaluation can present some difficulty for teachers in music. However, teachers must be able to communicate to children and their parents about a student's growth in music—as is the case with other subject areas. With Pre-K and kindergarten children, this can be challenging because of widespread developmental differences. Young children do not respond well to paper-and-pencil testing, and children often know and can do much more than they can verbalize. However, parents appreciate and expect teachers to inform them about strengths in musical areas (e.g., Can a child coordinate a marching beat? Does the child have good short-term memory in repeating rhythms? Does the child have an excellent sense of imagination in creating new sounds? Does he or she have a clear, pleasant singing voice?). These and other factors that the teacher can glean from music class are also hints that may help a teacher understand how the student is developing in other subject areas, as well. Supporting budding talent may also be a joint venture with the home, if parents know their child is interested or talented.

As with other subject areas, teachers may evaluate the child in music *diagnostically* (to examine specific problems), *formatively* (during a period of time), and *summatively* (at the end of a specified period of time). Anecdotal records or observation sheets are favored by many teachers in music (especially for special needs children), whereas other teachers use checklists or rating scales that help more with issues of quality. Singing and using both directed and improvisational movement-to-music activities provides a way for the teacher to see what children are hearing and then translating into observable movements. A portfolio of audio- or videotapings may also be used to show development. Oral questioning provides a great deal of information, and paper-and-pencil sheets on the elements of music might be used for older students as they are asked to begin learning to read and write music.

Excellent performance in music involves a degree of talent, and some children may have the talent to become world-class performers, whereas others simply do not. However, because instruction and training can make a difference in how children appreciate music all their lives, teachers must be careful to use assessment in music in ways that are helpful and not hurtful. For that reason, we must use music terminology mentioned in the standards with constructive criticism, such as, "Listen carefully to the pitch that you hear now and try to match your voice carefully to it. Now try to make your voice go up just this much more (show hand signal)," or "Your audience will really appreciate hearing rising dynamics during this part, because it makes the piece more powerful," rather than general comments such as, "You are hurting my ears today!" or "Can't you sing louder there?" Teachers alone may be responsible for a child loving or hating music. Teachers can affect children's desire for participation in music for the rest of their lives through the use of good critique and assessment.

Assessing learning in music can be both written and performance based, but having children become good judges of music, including their own, is the best way for them to gain a lifelong appreciation of music. In addition to a teacher's assessments, children should critique their own performances by listening to their own tapes and by listening to many sources. Let them tell you, the teacher, how to make their performance(s) better. Following are some questions that may help young musicians begin to think critically (depending on the instance):

Was your musical performance played/sung on key?
Was/were your instrument(s) in tune?
Did your choice of instruments fit the music well?
Did your piece or performance fit together with its forms?

Did your piece/performance project a mood? (How did you feel when you performed it?) If a mood was intended, did it succeed? If it did, how well? If it did not, why not?

Did the tempo of the music contribute to the correct mood?

How resourceful were you in creating a unique piece?

Was the tempo/speed of the music correct to easily sing or play along?

Was the tempo consistent or regular if so written?

Was your choice of dynamics correct to express what the composer wanted?

Was your sound too loud or too soft to be effective?

Were the lyrics expressive?

Was there enough variety in the music to make it interesting?

What are some ways that you could have sung/played this song differently?

What else could you or the composer/performer of a piece have chosen or done to make the music better?

The same questions (and many more) could be asked of other selected examples of music that a teacher introduces, including questions such as why a particular piece of music was interesting, with the criteria centering on the musical elements and what these elements do for music (e.g., intensifying and declining dynamics; feelings of tension and release; introduction, climax, and closure; elegance and appeal of the notes of the melody). Focusing on these elements helps students become excellent critics. It is difficult for children to understand how to describe their feelings without excellent modeling, however. The teacher should remember to model carefully what she or he hears in music often in order for children to be comfortable in their own assessments.

Standard X: Professional Responsibilities

The music teacher understands professional responsibilities and interactions relevant to music instruction and the school music program.

Teachers must know the legal and ethical issues related to the use or performance of music in an educational setting and be able to comply with copyright laws to make appropriate and ethical decisions. They must be able to comply with federal, state, and local regulations concerning the use or performance of music. In another area of professional responsibility, teachers must know and use strategies for maintaining effective communication with other music educators, the value of continuing professional development in music education, and the types of professional development opportunities that are available to music educators. Knowing strategies for and maintaining communication with students, parents/caregivers, and others in the schools and community about the music program and its benefits are also a part of being an EC-6 teacher (as previously discussed in Standard VII).

Copyright Laws and Music

This section discusses laws that regulate copying sheet music and recordings, playing music for performances, adding music to Websites, and so forth. All teachers are tempted, at times, to take care of their needs for copies of sheet music or recordings easily and quickly. However, copyright laws help composers, musical artists, recording studios, and music publishers make their living. Without royalties, no money is received from their work. Some older music is not copyrighted, but, if a work is, the teacher must follow guidelines stated in laws. Most modern works are copyrighted, even if not specifically marked.

The following guidelines may help you better understand copying music. Teachers are allowed to copy a single copy of a book chapter, article, short story, essay or poem, chart, graph, diagram, cartoon, or picture, but making multiple copies is a bit more complicated. Teachers can make multiple copies on a one-time basis, but not more than one copy per student is allowed, and the copyright must be included. The process must also meet a brevity test. Copying music, too, falls into this category. A music teacher can copy a part of a musical work (one per student) but not the whole work (no more than 10 percent). The teacher must also not take more than one short poem, article, or story per author (or two excerpts), or take more than three items from a collected work. Copying should not be for more than one course per term, or there should be no more than nine instances of multiple copying per class term. When in doubt, buy multiple copies, or request permission, because the composer, publisher, or recording company can seek monetary damages. If you have just made the decision to use an item based on its value to the lesson and could not expect to get permission quickly, then you may follow the guidelines as discussed here. You may also make emergency copies to replace purchased copies that are not available for an impending performance. A music teacher may make some alterations to music and copy them, but not so much that the fundamental nature of the music or lyrics is changed. When using copyrighted music, teachers may record student musical performances and retain them for evaluation and rehearsal purposes only. One sound copy only of a copyrighted piece of music may be made and retained for rehearsal, exercise, or examination purposes, if already owned by the teacher or the school. A music teacher may not make copies that, in essence, create his or her own music series or book or replace collective works. The copyright must always appear on the copy. Students or teachers may not include copyrighted songs or music on a Website without permission. When adding any music to technology-based projects, permission must be obtained if the music is copyrighted. These serve as only very brief guidelines, and as we know from the legal battles in which Napster (a company that allowed music to be downloaded from the Internet) was engaged not long ago, legal issues change. Most of those who are involved in music are very glad for teachers to use materials, but they must be given the chance to agree. Several Websites, such as http://mpa.org/copyright_resource_center, http://www.pdinfo.com/copyrt.php, http://www.law.cornell.edu (then search for music copyright), or http://www.music.indiana.edu/music_resources/copy.html give more complete details of copyright laws and information on how to obtain permission to copy. There is some royalty-free music (see, e.g., http://www.royaltyfreemusic.com/free-music-program/elementary-schools.html); however, when in doubt, be sure to check the details.

In addition to these laws, there may be other local policies and regulations that might affect performances in music. If you plan on children performing in another area outside of your school, you must check carefully to make sure you have followed local guidelines. Communicating with parents and your school district about what music will be performed and in what context is also an important part of musical performance, as parents and the district have the right to exclude their children from certain types of musical performance. If you are planning a large performance, it is better to know sooner rather than later that a number of children may not show up at the performance or that your selections must be changed at the last moment.

SUMMARY

With the information offered here, you should have a good grasp of what you might need to pass most TExES questions about teaching music. Learning the concepts in this chapter should also help you get started teaching music, should you not have a specialized music teacher in your building. Even if you have never played an instrument (or have had others request of you, "Please don't sing!"), you should be encouraged to bring music to the classroom. Children honestly do not care about the quality of your voice (although they also need to hear good models during your time with them), but they will learn to be embarrassed by their voices if you show embarrassment over yours. However, children react positively to an enthusiastic singer, even if one's voice is less than professional, and they will join in at a moment's notice.

In the push for good test scores, many schools without music teachers may encourage teachers to drop everything but the basics. As a creative teacher, however, you should be encouraged to use music in every way to support and enhance basic subjects rather than treat them as separate areas—for the many reasons stated in this chapter. Music is a lifelong joy for most humans, and it can be more appreciated and enjoyed if there is some sort of background for understanding.

There is much more to be learned about music and many more musical terms. This introduction, however, can help you through the basics. It is difficult to only talk or read about these terms and genres. Listen when your radio is on at home or in the car for the musical terms and types of music that you have read about here, and try to seek out as many examples as you can. If you are the only music teacher your children have, we hope this chapter encourages you to teach music in the best ways possible! Enjoy musical times with your children—it makes your day much richer, too!

A MUSIC LESSON PLAN

Cattle Trails in Texas

Grade Level: Fourth

Main Subject Area: Music

Integrated Subjects: Social Studies, Reading, Math, Art

Time Constraints: 3 hours (Music, Social Studies, and Reading)

Overall Goal(s): To familiarize students with an era of Texas history and representative music of this era to appreciate the past and present work in an important area of the Texas economy.

TEKS OBJECTIVES:

§ 117.15. Music (b)(4.5) Historical/cultural heritage (A) identify aurally presented excerpts of music representing diverse genres, styles, periods, and cultures; (C) perform music representative of American and Texas heritage; (D) identify connections between music and other fine arts; (4.2) Creative expression/performance. The student performs a varied repertoire of music. The student is expected to: (A) sing or play a classroom instrument independently or in groups (B) sing songs from diverse cultures and styles or play such songs on a musical instrument; (4.4) Creative expression/performance. The student creates and arranges music within specified guidelines. The student is expected to: (A) create simple accompaniments; (4.1) Perception. The student describes and analyzes musical sound and demonstrates musical artistry. The student is expected to: (A) categorize a variety of musical sounds, including children's and adults' voices; woodwind, brass, string, percussion, keyboard, and electronic instruments; and instruments of various cultures;

§ 111.16. Math (a) (2) make estimates . . . ;

§ 117.14. Fine Arts (4.2)(B) design original artworks; (4.4)(B) interpret ideas and mood in original artworks;

§ 110.6. English Language Arts and Reading (9) Reading/Comprehension of . . . Culture/History. Students analyze, make inferences and draw conclusions (in) . . . historical . . . contexts. . . .(14) Writing . . . Students are expected to: (B) write short poems;

§ 113.6. Social Studies (currently in revision) (b)(4)(B) explain the growth and development of the cattle . . . industries.

Lesson Objectives: After observing a map of the major cattle trails in the 1800s, students will pick one trail and estimate the length of time it took for the drive from Texas; students will write their estimates on a card that the teacher will pick up later.

Students will complete a "quick draw" as they listen to "On the Trail" (*Grand Canyon Suite*) and participate in a discussion on its mood. Students will have only 5 minutes after the music has finished to complete their drawing.

Students will share their quick draw with a partner and evaluate the mood captured with the music.

After viewing Western art, students will orally identify connections of music to art.

Students will listen to, read, and sing three songs from the trail drive days.

Students will view (and listen to) a PowerPoint presentation of instruments (guitar, banjo, fiddle, and harmonica) that come from this era and will discuss orally the tone color of each and texture of these instruments together.

Students will read a short selection from the perspective of a young person during this era.

Students will select and use rhythm instruments as they sing the songs again and orally make judgments of created sound.

Students will complete a four-line verse to the melody of a traditional song (one of the three listened to earlier) with a minimum of two pairs of rhymes.

Students will listen to a current country music selection and compare and contrast traditional trail music with the modern selection (using a Venn diagram).

Readiness Skills or Prior Knowledge Needed: Students should understand mapping skills, estimations skills, cattle industry history, mood, texture, tone color (in music), and rhyming.

Sponge Activity: Students view trail maps of major Texas cattle trails, pick one, and estimate how long it would have taken from start to finish. Students will write their estimates on "pick up cards."

Environmental Concerns: Teach during Rodeo Week (if relevant to a school). Integrate three periods back to back. Could also add more mathematics with measurements for cooking trail menus.

Rationale(s): The cattle industry in Texas set up an important economy for the state and had a considerable effect on music in Texas and the West that continues today. Learning these songs gives us an insight into this era. Many of the songs that came from this era are considered American classics that Texans (and other Americans) know and sing. Western music continues as a considerable industry today, but it has its roots in this era.

Focus or Set Induction: Give students the actual mileage of the trail drives and the average miles per hour and have them refigure their estimates. Teacher will pick up cards and acknowledge the children who came closest. Teacher will talk about life on the trail and the use of music to pass the time and soothe restless cattle to avoid stampedes (especially at night).

Students listen to "On the Trail" from the *Grand Canyon Suite* (go to http://songza.org and type in "On the Trail Grand Canyon Suite") and ask students to "quick draw" what they hear/see in their minds. Go back and discuss the instruments used, the mood of the music, and how it was achieved. Students will show their drawings to a partner and discuss how well the artist captured the mood of the music. While the teacher repeats the music, show students some cowboy art (posters such as "Lifetime in the Saddle," "Horse Roundup," "Place in the Sun" and others by Jack Sorenson); these can sometimes be found at: http://www.art.com/gallery/id—a6960/jack-sorenson-posters_p3.htm?ui=372A6FB9AC864780B81EB32396320401 or http://www.allposters.com (search site for "Place in the Sun"); and pictures of sculptures by Remington http://www.westernsaddle.com/wesscul.html (search site for Remington) or http://www.largeart.com; Remington sculptures, or other oils and photographs; and briefly discuss the style and mood of these works of art. Tell students about the Cowboy Artists of America Museum in Kerrville, Texas.

MAKING CONNECTIONS

1. **Connections with Past or Future Learning:** What famous movies or television shows have you seen that have included cattle drives? Have you been to a rodeo? What kinds of music do you hear associated with rodeos or trail drives? Do people still do this kind of work with cattle? Is the cattle industry still a major economy of Texas? Why do you think singing was a part of trail drives? What kinds of songs were useful on these trails and why?

2. **Connections to the Community:** Does your community have a rodeo? Have you ever seen (or seen on the news) one of the trail rides from many parts of Texas that end in Houston to kick off the rodeo? (There are normally some Websites that include pictures and information; search for Salt Grass Trail, Houston Trail Riders, or others). Have you or your family listened to any modern country music? Are there any country radio stations in this area? Do you think that there are many current songs about driving cattle? Why or why not?

3. **Cultural Connections:** The first Texas cowboys were *vaqueros* (or "cow men") who came from Mexico to Texas to work on ranches owned by Spaniards and Mexicans before the Texas Revolution. Much of the dress and equipment we associate with cowboys originates from these *vaqueros*.

4. **Connection to Student Interest and Experiences:** Many dude ranches still exist (some in Texas) where you can go on trail rides or cattle drives. Many Texas communities have rodeos. Many schools have a Rodeo Day or Rodeo Week. Many Texans enjoy modern-day country music. Have you participated in any of these? Have you seen the award ceremonies on television for country music artists? What did you like about any of these experiences?

Materials: Trail drive map, cards for estimation; *Grand Canyon Suite;* Western art posters, photos, sculpture, or other art; art paper; real instruments or pictures of them (guitar, banjo, harmonica) and sounds of each instrument; sheet music of three traditional songs (and CD, if needed); list of new vocabulary words; PowerPoint presentation of instruments; rhythm instruments; current popular country song; reading sheets on a young person's experience of a trail drive.

Activities: Guided Practice: Students will listen to and sing three songs from sheet music from the cattle drive era of Texas history ("The Old Chisholm Trail," "Bury Me Not on the Lone Prairie," and "Get Along Little Doggies"). The teacher will introduce vocabulary that is not familiar, and all will discuss the message of each song. Students will return to the map from the sponge activity and trace the "Old Chisholm Trail." The teacher will discuss the guitar, fiddle, harmonica, and banjo with students and explore why these may have become popular instruments in Western music. The teacher will show a PowerPoint presentation of these instruments (with each instrument playing alone). Discuss the tone color of each and their texture together. Discuss what animals and animal sounds relate to the instruments and the rhythm, if applicable. In paired reading, students will read a short description of a young person on a cattle drive. Students will discuss, select, and use rhythm instruments that they feel will enhance the songs and use those in singing the songs once again.

Students will orally judge if the instruments helped to enhance the song or not and explain why or why not. Ask students to think and tell which instruments, in general, seem to best represent Western music and make it unique, how certain instrument sounds cause us to think of the West, and which of the three songs they liked best and why.

Independent Practice: Students will compose a four-line verse (that could have been from the era and that can be sung to the melody of one of the songs learned). The teacher should first review rhymes and have students pick out some rhymes in the songs. Be sure to have students write on their papers which song/melody the verse matches. Invite students to share their verses.

Assessment: Individuals will participate in singing and playing rhythm instruments (checklist), participate in discussions (checklist), play an instrument (checklist), and complete a four-line verse that matches the rhythm of one of the three traditional songs sung and discussed previously with at least two sets of rhymes.

What Will Students Do Who Finish Early? Students will expand their quick draw artwork into an art composition, search on the Internet for trail drive vacations, or create their own new trails for a cattle drive from their town or city to a market.

Closure: Students will listen to a current country song and they, as a whole class, will use a Venn diagram to quickly make comparisons. Ask children if they like current country songs and which country songs they might know. Ask if the themes are the same or different from the old-style cowboy music. The teacher may want to bind children's verses for the classroom library and to sing with the melodies later on.

Modifications for Students with Special Needs: Tomás has hearing difficulties and will be placed closer to the music sources.

Reflection: To be completed after teaching the lesson.

DRAFT YOUR OWN MUSIC LESSON PLAN

Title of Lesson: _____

Grade Level: _____

Main Subject Area: _____

Integrated Subjects: _____

Time Frame/Constraints: _____

Overall Goal(s): _____

TEKS Objectives: _____

_____

_____

Lesson Objective(s): _____

_____

_____

Readiness Skills or Prior Knowledge Needed: _____

_____

Sponge Activity: _____

_____

_____

Environmental Concerns: _____

_____

_____

Rationale(s): _____

_____

_____

Focus or Set Induction: _____

_____

_____

Making Connections: _____

1. Connections to Past or Future Learning: _____

_____

2. Connections to the Community: _____

_____

_____

3. Cultural Connections: _____

_____

_____

4. Connections to Student Interests & Experiences: _____

_____

Materials: _____

_____

_____

Activities: Guided practice: _____

_____

_____

_____

_____

_____

_____

_____

_____

_____

Independent practice: _____

_____

_____

_____

_____

_____

_____

_____

_____

_____

Assessment: _____

_____

_____

What Will Students Do Who Finish Early? _____

_____

_____

Closure: _____

_____

Modification for Students with Special Needs: _____

_____

Reflection: _____

_____

OBSERVING MUSIC EXPERIENCES/ACTIVITIES

During your visit to an EC-6 classroom, use the following form to provide feedback, as well as to analyze the room, the materials, and the teaching reflectively. If students go to a specialized music teacher, you should follow your class. However, it will also be valuable to see if many of these elements are employed in the regular EC-6 classroom.

Name: _____ Grade Level Observed: _____ Date(s): _____

Title or Short Description of Lesson or Activity: _____

The Classroom Environment	Observed	Not Observed	Response
1. All children are encouraged to participate in musical experiences.			If so, describe. If not, what children were left out, and how could they be encouraged?
2. Ample space allows children and adults to move around freely and safely during a musical experience (if applicable).			If not, what could be changed?
3. A center is designated for listening to music.			If so, describe. If not, describe one that could appropriately and easily be included.
4. A center is designated for other musical experiences (creating instruments, exploring sounds, etc.).			If so, describe. If not, describe in detail at least one center that could be easily included.
5. If there is no designated Music Center, music activities are integrated within other centers.			If so, describe. If not, describe exactly how music could be included in other centers.
6. If there is music-related equipment freely available to children, the equipment is developmentally user friendly.			If so, describe. If not, what could be added?
7. The regular classroom contains technology related to music (e.g., electronic keyboard, software for music on computer).			If so, describe. If not, what could be easily included?
8. The regular classroom contains rhythm instruments (rhythm sticks, hand drums, tambourines, triangles, etc.).			If so, describe. If not, what could be added?
9. Children use rhythm instruments or wind instruments.			If so, describe. If not, how could the teacher easily add this element?
10. If children use rhythm instruments or wind instruments, the teacher discusses elements of proper use (care of the instruments, safety, sanitation, etc.). Are expectations for use posted?			If so, describe. If not, what could be added?
11. The teacher encourages creativity with music in some way.			If so, describe. If not, how could the teacher encourage creativity?

The Classroom Environment	Observed	Not Observed	Response
12. If music is available for free listening, there are a variety of music/sounds available for free choices.			If so, describe. If not, what could be added?
13. Music is integrated during whole group time in a developmentally appropriate way.			If so, describe. If not, how could this be accomplished?
14. Music is integrated during circle time in a developmentally appropriate way.			If so, describe. If not, give ideas for how it could be done.
15. Music is integrated during independent or teacher-led small group time in a developmentally appropriate way.			If so, describe. If not, give ideas for how this could be accomplished.
16. Music is used as a memory model for children.			If so, describe. If not, give some ideas on how this could be incorporated.
17. Children are comfortable singing and singing with motions without prompting.			If so, describe. If not, how could the teacher better encourage this?
18. Children are comfortable dancing or participating in gross-motor movement with music.			If so, describe. If not, how could the teacher better encourage this?
19. Movements for dance or other musical participation are modeled by the teacher.			If so, describe. If not, what changes could be added?
20. Movements for dance or other musical participation movements are physically developmentally appropriate.			Explain why or why not, if applicable.
21. Listening to music is used for a reward, at times, in a management plan.			If so, is it appropriately done? If not, how might it be added?
22. The teacher offers a variety of musical experiences during the day.			If so, describe. If not, what could be added?
23. There is a set of publisher-prepared music books for each classroom or for each grade level in this school.			If available, describe. If not, describe any written music materials the teacher uses.
24. There is a set of publisher-prepared tapes/CDs or other listening materials for each classroom or for each grade level.			If available, describe. If not, describe any listening materials that could be added.
25. The teacher uses standard musical terminology to describe and analyze musical sounds (makes references to musical symbols, terms, rhythms, meter, mood, texture, etc.).			If so, describe. If not, describe when and what language/terms could be used.

The Classroom Environment	Observed	Not Observed	Response
26. The teacher engages children in learning to read music in some manner that is developmentally appropriate.			If so, describe. If not, could he/she do so? Why or why not?
27. The teacher teaches children a new song.			If so, is it taught effectively? If not, how could she/he be more effective?
28. If music is integrated with other subject areas, the connection is a logical one.			If so, describe. If not, how could this be more logically connected?
29. Children are assessed on their skills or knowledge of the musical element of the lesson or experience in an appropriate way.			If so, describe. If not, what type of assessment could be appropriate?
30. The music/songs are age appropriate.			Why or why not? Describe.
31. The teacher includes hand actions with appropriate songs.			If so, what is the result? If not, what could be included?
32. The teacher discusses new vocabulary or articulation of words in a new song.			If so, describe. If not, what descriptions or vocabulary could be included?
33. The teacher discusses with children the issues concerning the quality of their singing (appropriate volume for young voices, proper projection, breathing through a phrase, proper position, etc.).			If so, describe. If not, what are some appropriate additions?

TEST YOURSELF ON MUSIC

1. The symbols underneath the musical staff shown here tell the musician to:
   A. play or sing this piece of music loudly.
   B. play or sing this piece of music softly.
   C. gradually increase the volume of the instrument(s) or voice(s), then decrease the volume.
   D. gradually decrease the volume of the instrument(s) or voice(s), then increase the volume.

2. Ms. Thomas is using the school's set of fifth-grade music books with CDs to teach her class a song. Halfway through the song, the music is marked *a cappella*. This means that:
   A. the song should become a duet.
   B. all sound should become *andante*.
   C. voices should stop singing and only the instruments should be heard.
   D. the instruments should stop playing and only the voices should be heard.

3. Ms. Miller's third-grade class is reading a story about two children in the 1800s who were taken on a cattle drive from Texas to the market in Kansas City, MO. Miller realizes that this is a perfect time to teach children some of the more well-known songs from this era, so she begins to search for them and is able to find three ("The Old Chisholm Trail," "Oh, Bury Me Not on the Lone Prairie," and "Get Along Little Doggies"), but only in one book in the local library. She finds the lyrics on some Websites, but she wants the written music so students can see the melody lines. The songs in the book that she found also have chords marked where she can play along with her guitar or autoharp. Which of the following statements is correct?
   A. She can legally make a copy for each child in her class this year.
   B. She cannot legally copy these pages for her students.
   C. She can legally copy one song for her class.
   D. She can legally make a copy for all of the third-graders for this year because all the third-grade teachers share lessons.

4. If a musician wants to indicate that no music should be played or sung for a moment, which symbol is used:

5. Ms. Phan often plays particular instrumental music as focus or closure activities in her social studies class when she talks about various cultures. For example, when her lesson is about Japan, she plays a CD with the sound of the *samisen*, and when she talks about Australia, she pulls up some *didgeridoo* music from the Internet. She always asks children to discuss how the sound of that country's instrument has its own characteristics. This element of music is called:
   A. harmony.
   B. timbre.
   C. mood.
   D. texture.

6. The state song of Texas is:
   A. "Texas, Our Texas."
   B. "The Eyes of Texas Are Upon You."
   C. "Deep in the Heart of Texas."
   D. "The Yellow Rose of Texas."

7. A type of true American dance that developed from formal European quadrilles is:
   A. tap dance.
   B. square dance.
   C. fandango.
   D. hula.

8. What type of music is best known for its improvisation, syncopation, and call and responses?
   A. Swing
   B. Classic rock
   C. Gospel
   D. Jazz

9. Stereotypical Native American music is often played with a drum and is written as follows:

The symbol underneath the first beat of every measure is called a(n):
   A. repeat sign.
   B. crescendo.
   C. accent mark.
   D. staccato mark.

10. Mrs. Ganesh asks her children to identify the form of "Rudolph the Red-Nosed Reindeer." It is:
   A. *ABCA*
   B. *AABA*
   C. *ABCD*
   D. *ABBA*

TEST YOURSELF ANSWERS AND RATIONALES FOR MUSIC

Answer 1: The musical symbols underneath this staff have to do with *dynamics* (how loud or soft music is to be played). These symbols reflect a *crescendo* (<) followed by a *decrescendo* (>). These notations indicate that the musician should first begin to increase the volume, and then decrease the volume; therefore, choice *C* best describes the notation. If the composer wants to play or sing the whole line *loudly* (A), he/she writes an *f* for *forte* at the beginning. If he or she wants the line to be played or sung softly (B), the composer writes a *p* for *piano* (soft). If he or she wants to decrease the volume then increase the volume (D), the notation is > <. The answer is *C*.

Answer 2: A *duet* (A) is a song for two voices or two instruments only, just as a *trio* is for three, a *quartet* is for four, and so forth. *Andante* (B) is a musical notation, indicating *tempo* (or speed) and meaning that the music should be played not so fast or about walking speed (versus *largo*, which is very slow; *adagio*, which is slow; *allegro*, which is quick; or *presto*, which is very fast). *A cappella* refers to "voices only." The answer is *D*.

Answer 3: Copyright law is important in sheet music and in copying recordings. There are several issues at stake when copying written music. The law allows a teacher to copy up to no more than three items from a single work, so she is safe in this respect; therefore, choices *B* and *C* are not true and can be eliminated. She can copy, but she is only allowed to copy for one class, so we must eliminate *D*. Her situation meets the guidelines that say if a teacher decides that an item is very valuable to a lesson and it is impossible to get permission before the lesson is to be taught, a teacher can copy for one time only. She can copy for this instance (A), but if she wants to use these songs next year, she must seek permission if there is a copyright. The answer is *A*.

Answer 4: Choice *A* is a symbol for the *treble clef*, which means that higher instruments and higher voices read the music from this staff (versus the bass clef, which is for lower voices or instruments). Choice *C* shows *eighth notes*, which means a voice or an instrument plays or sings very short sounds at that particular pitch. Choice *D* is a *time signature* that shows four beats per measure (from the 4 on the top) with a quarter note receiving one beat (from the 4 on the bottom). Choice *B* is a *quarter rest*. A rest means that no voice or instruments should play or sing. Because this is a quarter rest, there should be no sound during the last beat of this measure. The answer is *B*.

Answer 5: *Harmony* (A) refers to two or more different tones being played together. Although there may be harmony in the music she plays, she is asking for special distinguishing characteristics of each instrument. *Mood* (C) is made up of many elements of music (*tempo* [speed], *dynamics* [loudness], *meter* [beat], *key*, and choice of instruments) that affect the overall feeling generated by the composer to the listener. Although the selections that she plays may also have "a mood" (e.g., bagpipes can have a very sad mood or a rousing military mood), she wants to narrow down the characteristic sound of each instrument. *Texture* (D) refers to how the sounds of different voices or instruments are "woven" together to create a piece of music. Again, in the question, she is asking for children to talk about the very specific characteristic sound (or voice) of an instrument that is not shared with any other instrument. This is known as the *timbre* of an instrument. The answer is *B*.

Answer 6: "Texas, Our Texas" is the state song (A). The words can be found in the social studies chapter of this book (p. 273). Choices *B*, *C*, and *D* are all popular Texas songs, but they are not the official state song. Listen at http://www.senate.state.tx.us/kids/Trivia.htm. The answer is *A*.

Answer 7: Although tap dance (A) is considered a true style of American dance, it developed as a part of minstrel shows that originated in the United States. Fandangos (C) and shindigs were dancing events in the early settlers' days of Texas, rather than a type of dance. The hula is the original dance of the native Hawaiian people, but it is based on Polynesian (not European) roots. Choice *B*, square dancing, is considered a true American style of dance that originated from European formal figure dances such as the quadrille and the minuet. Early on, reminders about which figure came next were often *called out* in America, leading to the role of a *caller* in square dancing. Gradually, the music changed, and the dance depended more on following the caller versus memorizing the exact order of the figures, leading to what we know now as the American square dance. The answer is *B*.

Answer 8: Swing (*A*) is associated with the Big Band sound during and right after World War II, and it is normally played as written. Early rock (or rock and roll) follows an exact written form rather than improvisation, although in later psychedelic rock and acid rock, improvisation is used. Gospel (*C*) was a forerunner of jazz and sometimes uses call and response, but the best answer is jazz (*D*). The heart of jazz is improvisation (or creating music on the spot), call and response (where one instrument or voice answers or echoes another), and syncopation (an unexpected accent). The answer is *D*.

Answer 9: A repeat sign (*A*) tells the musician to go back and repeat a section of the music again and is written as :||. A crescendo (*B*) may look similar to the symbols shown, but a crescendo stretches under several notes in a measure, indicating a gradually increasing volume. A staccato mark (*D*) is written as a period underneath a note, showing that this particular note is to be played very short. Choice *C*, an accent mark, is correct. This means that the note under which the accent mark is written should be heavily emphasized (played or sung harder). The answer is *C*.

Answer 10: *Form* refers to the repetition, contrast, and variation of a piece of music. The following shows the repetition of the melody two times, a contrasting section, and a repetition of the original melody for a form of *AABA*. The answer is *B*.

	Rudolph, the Red-nosed Reindeer, Had a very shiny nose,
A	And if you ever saw it, You would even say it glows.
	All of the other reindeer, Used to laugh and call him names,
A	They never let poor Rudolph Join in any reindeer games.
	Then one foggy Christmas Eve, Santa came to say,
B	"Rudolph, with your nose so bright, Won't you guide my sleigh tonight?"
	Then how the reindeer loved him, And they shouted out with glee,
A	"Rudolph, the Red-nosed Reindeer, You'll go down in history."

WEB SITES

Many Websites have been included in this chapter, but there are many more that may help you learn about and teach music. Remember that Websites can change or be discontinued, so if these should not work, try a search with key terms.

http://www.classicsforkids.com/teachers/audio/showview.asp?ID=15 Offers listening, lesson plans, and more for the classics and for children.

http://www.classicsforkids.com/teachers/lessonplans/kodaly/index.asp Same site as the first one, but for more specifically for teachers.

http://www.carnegiehall.org/article/explore_and_learn/art_online_resources_listening_adventures.html Listening adventures and other interesting information from Carnegie Hall that are helpful for children and teachers.

http://www.carnegiehall.org/honor/history/index.aspx Also from Carnegie Hall, this site focuses on the history of many genres of African American music.

http://www.worldmusicalinstruments.com Hear and see instruments of the world.

http://www.dsokids.com/2001/instrumentchart.htm Hear and see instruments of the orchestra.

http://www.baroquemusic.org/ A wealth of information and listening to Baroque music.

http://www.lib.utexas.edu/benson/border/ Music from the Texas border culture.

http://www.pbs.org/theblues/classroom/cd.html#null The PBS Teachers Guide to listening to the blues.

http://dslweb.nwnexus.com/aseaberg A huge resource of music-related Websites for music.

http://ginaotto.com/musicsites.html An excellent resource for teachers and students.

http://www.songsforteaching.com Songs for use across the curriculum.

http://www.childrens-music.org/childrens-music/teachers.htm A general list of music resources.

http://www.classic99.com/terms1.htm Many musical terms and links.

http://en.wikipedia.org/wiki/List_of_music_styles A listing of more than 100 genres of music.

http://dir.yahoo.com/Entertainment/Music/Genres/ A reference for many categories of music.

http://www.dmoz.org/Arts/Music/Styles/ References for many styles of music.

http://finearts.esc20.net/music/music_strategies/mus_strat_crit.html Problem solving in music is offered.

http://kids.niehs.nih.gov/music.htm Many children's sing-along songs are offered.

http://kidsmusictown.com/childrenssongslyrics/educational-learning/socialstudies/oldchisholmtrail.htm An amazing array of different music for children, including finger plays, historic songs, etc.

http://www.pitt.edu/~poole/eledMusic.html A very resourceful site.

The following sites also allow you to listen to music or artists of your choice and, as such, provide many examples of the music discussed in this chapter:

http://www.theradio.com
http://www.pandora.com
http://www.slacker.com
http://www.jango.com
http://www.tropicalglen.com

8 Preparing to Teach Health and Physical Education in Texas

D. Rozena McCabe
Huston–Tillotson University

Diana J. Everett
Texas Association for Health, Physical Education, Recreation, and Dance

Janice L. Nath
University of Houston–Downtown

John M. Ramsey
University of Houston

Mel E. Finkenberg
Stephen F. Austin State University

Domain V of the *Generalist* EC-6 Test Framework addresses "Fine Arts, Health, and Physical Education." This chapter focuses on two of these areas: health and physical education. As is the case with art and music, many schools have a specialist for young children who may teach physical education and health, but other schools must rely on self-contained teachers. Therefore, Texas requires all EC-6 teachers to be tested on these standards and competencies.

Several laws have been passed that address health and physical activity in schools, and educators in colleges and universities have also increased the attention placed on these two areas for teachers as part of the education of the whole child. Texas Education Code (TEC) §28.002 requires that all full-day Pre-K children, students in kindergarten through fifth grades, and sixth graders who are in an elementary setting participate in a minimum of 30 minutes per day (or 135 minutes per week) of moderate to vigorous physical activity. This can be as part of the school's physical education curriculum or through structured activity during the school campus's daily recess. Moderate to vigorous activity involves physical exertion of intensity and duration sufficient to provide positive health benefits to students. Because many Texas school districts do not hire certified physical education teachers, districts often require the classroom *generalist* teacher to organize and teach physical activity lessons for their students. Even in those school districts that have certified physical education teachers, there are many who cannot provide the state required number of minutes in physical education class. Classroom teachers must then provide structured activities to meet the additional minutes of required physical activity during the week.

Studies consistently conclude that children in this country are at risk due to the lack of health and fitness education opportunities provided in schools. The increased heaviness of America can be linked directly to the diminished emphasis on physical education, particularly in the elementary schools, where values can be established early. The U.S. Surgeon General's report on Obesity in 2001 by the U.S. Department of Health and Human Services includes recommendations that address physical activity and proper nutrition. The first recommendation counsels educators to provide daily, quality physical education for all grade levels. The document entitled *Healthy People 2010* provides a framework for the prevention of the most significant threats to the health of individuals. It establishes national goals to reduce these threats and provides 28 focus areas, each of which represents an important public health area. Four of these areas are directly related to physical education and health education: No. 5–Diabetes, No. 12–Heart Disease and Stroke, No. 19–Nutrition and Overweight, and No. 22–Physical Activity and Fitness (U.S. Department of Health and Human Services, 2010).

Physical activity programs are an absolute requisite for healthy youngsters. Yet helping children to become more active adults is not the only health-related area that educators view as important. Educators also believe that emotional development, safety, violence prevention, good communication skills, and other health-related issues can make a difference in a healthy life for children. Perhaps in no other content area does a teacher make such a difference in the long-term lives of children, should the teacher take very seriously the responsibility of addressing the *whole child* in all of these areas.

Consistent with the design of the previous chapters, this chapter is structured with an overview of the various standards and competencies within the health and physical education components of Domain V. These have, in turn, been correlated to the Texas Essential Knowledge and Skills (TEKS) for health and physical education. Sample items with discussion, a lesson plan, a form for writing your own plan, and an observation form are also offered.

Standards are broad statements that present the main idea of the knowledge and skills expected of a beginning educator. Each standard contains a list of specific knowledge and skill statements (the *competencies*) that further explain the focus and requirements of each standard. The standards and their knowledge and skills statements are fundamentally based on the TEKS, which are the statewide expectations for student learning in Texas public and charter schools. In the discussion of the standards and competencies outlined that follow, correlations between standards, the competencies, the TEKS, and the content of the *Generalist* examination will become apparent.

Health Standards

The following list shows the standards for beginning *generalist* EC-6 teachers for teaching health.

Standard I. The health teacher applies knowledge of both the relationship between health and behavior and the factors influencing health and health behavior.

Standard II. The health teacher communicates concepts and purposes of health education.

Standard III. The health teacher plans and implements effective school health instruction and integrates health instruction with other content areas.

Standard IV. The health teacher evaluates the effects of school health instruction.

These educator standards serve as a basis for establishing the following competency and its indicators within the test framework for the *Generalist* EC-6 Texas Examinations of Educator Standards (TExES).

Competency 044

(on health) states that the teacher uses knowledge of the concepts and purposes of health education to plan and implement effective and engaging health instruction. Therefore, the beginning teacher should understand health-related behaviors, ways that personal health decisions and behaviors affect body systems and health, and strategies for reducing health risks and enhancing wellness throughout the life span. This includes responses to early detection and warning signs of illness, to internal injury, and to threats to safety. Teachers should also be knowledgeable of major areas in health instruction, including body systems and development (e.g. structures and functions of various body systems and relationships among body systems), illness and disease (e.g., types of disease, transmission mechanisms, defense systems, disease prevention), nutrition (e.g., types of foods and nutrients, maintenance of a balanced diet), stress (e.g., effects of stress, stress-reduction techniques), and fitness (e.g., components of fitness, methods for improving fitness). New teachers should know and understand stages of human growth and development, including physical and emotional changes that occur during adolescence. Substance use and abuse (including types and characteristics of tobacco, alcohol, and other drugs and of herbal supplements) should be a part of teacher's knowledge base. In addition, they should be able to select and use instructional strategies, materials, and activities related to prevention of violence, safety, accident prevention, and response to emergencies. These teachers can teach about refusal skills and conflict resolution related to unsafe situations (e.g. bullying)—with critical-thinking, goal-setting, problem-solving, and decision-making skills. Beginning teachers should know and understand strategies for coping with unhealthy behaviors in the family (e.g., abuse, alcoholism, neglect) and about the types and symptoms of eating disorders. They should be able use various social and communication skills to build and maintain healthy interpersonal relationships (e.g., tolerance, respect, discussing problems with parents/caregivers, showing empathy). Teachers should have the ability to select and use instructional strategies, materials, and activities to help students build healthy interpersonal relationships (e.g., communication skills) and encourage consideration and respect for self, family, friends, and others (e.g., practicing self-control). Teachers must be able to help students become (1) health-wise consumers; (2) knowledgeable

about the role of health-care professionals; and (3) understanding of the benefits of health maintenance activities by selecting and using appropriate instructional strategies, materials, and activities and by helping students to understand the influence of various factors (e.g., media, technology, peer and other relationships, environmental hazards) on individual, family, and community health. This includes knowledge of sources of health information and ways to use information to make health-related decisions. In sum, teachers should be able to apply knowledge of health content and curriculum based on the Texas Essential Knowledge and Skills (TEKS) and overall knowledge of children in grades EC-6 to plan and implement effective, developmentally appropriate health instruction, including relating the health-education curriculum to other content areas (Texas Education Agency, 2009).

Choosing a Healthy Life

Consider the following question:

Ms. Vasquez is an elementary classroom teacher who is teaching a health unit on nutrition. Which of the following activities is most appropriate for a lesson focused on healthy snacks?

   A. Have students read from short "canned" skits (written by professionals) to other students about healthy snacks.
   B. Have students write a paragraph about what constitutes healthy snacks.
   C. Hold a directed discussion in which children are led to discover the nutritional contents of a variety of their favorite snacks.
   D. Divide the class into collaborative groups and have each group choose a different snack to research, discuss, and present a nutritional report about what they have learned.

Presenting findings through collaborative groups involves each learner in active discussion of what constitutes healthy snacks. This option allows students to be active participants in the determination of nutrition concepts. Although each of the remaining options may meet the instructor's objective, choice *D* is the superior choice due to the active participation and knowledge construction of the learners. Part of a teacher's role in teaching health is to help children with communication skills and to guide them in locating and retrieving factual resources for good health information. They must also learn the vocabulary of health. Projects of this nature help students begin to develop those skills. The answer is *D*.

This practice question relates to the health education component of the TEKS, whereby learners acquire the information and skills necessary to become healthy adults and learn about behavior in which they should and should not participate. To achieve that goal, children need to understand the following: (1) learners should first seek help and guidance in the area of health from their parents; (2) personal behavior can increase or reduce health risks throughout the lifespan; (3) health is influenced by a variety of factors; (4) learners can recognize and utilize health information and products; and (5) personal/interpersonal skills are needed to promote individual, family, and community health.

Let's try another practice question:

Mr. Harris teaches elementary health and physical education. He wishes to teach safety and health skills that relate to the well-being of students, friends, and family. Which of the following instructional units promote self-responsibility as it relates to family and friends?

A. Personal hygiene
B. Exercise and fitness
C. First aid
D. Nutritional needs

The key phrase in this assessment item is "health and safety skills that relate to the well-being of students, friends, and family." Although choices *A, B,* and *D* relate to safety and personal health, they do not specifically correlate with others involved in the application of health and safety principles. Learning the use of basic emergency first aid procedures, as identified in choice *C,* could directly affect the well-being of others, including friends and family, if an emergency should occur. Further, these skills imply and develop decision-making and problem-solving skills that foster healthy interactions and promote learners' interpersonal skills. The correct answer is *C.*

Although many learning experiences related to caring for personal health take place in the home, teachers can also ensure that children are taught, encouraged, and reinforced with activities that maintain a lifestyle of appropriate personal health and safety. A number of inclusive programs offered by the state of Texas and other entities help in this endeavor.

The Texas Education Code §38.013 currently requires all Texas school districts to implement a Texas Education Agency (TEA) approved Coordinated School Health Program (CSHP) for grades kindergarten through eighth grade. The CSHP, entitle Coordinated Approach to Child Health (CATCH) is designed to prevent obesity, cardiovascular disease, and type 2 diabetes in elementary children and is one of the TEA-approved programs. CATCH offers a successful blend of physical education, classroom curriculum, nutrition awareness, student-directed activities, and physical education equipment designed to promote and maintain cardiovascular health in children grades K through eighth grade (http://www.sph.uth.tmc.edu/CATCH). CATCH began as a research study founded by the National Heart, Lung, and Blood Institute. Its purpose was to establish an elementary-based program to reduce the risk factors related to cardiovascular disease. Now expanded to cover grades kindergarten through eighth grade, CATCH remains the largest and most rigorous school-based health promotion study to date. With more than 2,000 school programs, CATCH continues to have an impact on tudents long after they complete the coursework. Data published in *Preventive Medicine* indicate that senior high students who had participated in the CATCH program as third, fourth, and fifth graders continued to make healthier choices in nutrition and physical activity than their peers who had not participated in CATCH (Hoelscher, Feldman, & Johnson, et al., 2004).

CATCH encourages kids to:

- move, run, jump, and dance as they participate in moderate to vigorous physical activities using a variety of equipment
- develop good nutrition habits as they learn to recognize and monitor their fat and salt intake
- declare themselves smoke-free

The four components of CATCH are the classroom curriculum, physical education, the school food service, and the family partnership. Teachers and staff are trained to implement and coordinate these components. These intervention strategies were shown to significantly increase the intensity and duration of physical activity and decrease intake of fat and saturated fat in intervention school lunches. The CATCH school cafeteria is literally a hands-on learning environment. At mealtime, children learn, practice, and utilize healthy eating habits. CATCH classroom and physical education lessons come to life as children experience first-hand the concepts of "GO," "SLOW," and "WHOA" foods. "GO" foods are fruits and vegetables. If fat is added, it becomes a "SLOW" food. If it is fried, it is a "WHOA" food. Basically, as foods have more added fat and sugar, they also becomes "WHOA" foods. CATCH cafeterias display signs in front of foods showing they are a "GO," "SLOW," or "WHOA" food to assist students in making wise nutritional choices.

 # Health-Care Professionals

Maintaining a healthy life also includes having regular medical and dental preventive care. Some children may have their first experience with professional healthcare in school. Even young children must know enough about their bodies to tell the nurse, for example, exactly where it hurts or what symptoms may be present. A teacher should schedule a tour of the clinic facility or nurse's office early in the year, especially for younger children, as it could be a scary experience if the first visit is when the child is sent there ill. Teachers should ask the nurse to visit the class so young children know him or her better and understand the role the nurse plays in their healthcare. Other health-care workers should also be asked to visit (pediatricians, cardiologists, dentists, etc.). Remember to vary the gender and ethnicity of visitors, when possible, to show well-rounded models in health-care careers to children. Many teachers place appropriate real or play medical equipment in a Doctor's Center so that young children can become familiar with these, or for older children, a host of information on health issues and the many health professions available can be a part of a Career Center. In addition, teachers can provide stories that describe examination procedures, use puppets to role-play medical or dental procedures, or practice using a phone to call for help in an emergency. All children should learn about emergencies and how to call for help at school or away from school. The school nurse can also serve as a teacher and a resource for many health issues. The teacher should visit with or coordinate with the nurse about the health topics she/he can discuss with students.

The EC-6 teacher is often the first to see underlying illness or health issues, as she or he spends a considerable amount of time with students during the school day. The teacher must be vigilant as an advocate for any health issues that are noticed, including abuse or neglect (which, by law, requires reporting). The EC-6 teacher must quickly learn the school's policy on the reporting of a student's health issue.

 # Body Systems

According to the TEKS, children should be taught to identify the major systems of the body by the second grade. The major body systems are the respiratory, circulatory, digestive, musculoskeletal, integumentary (skin, nails), and nervous systems. A simple activity to teach this concept is to have the students work in pairs. One student lies on a large piece of butcher paper while the partner traces the outline of the student's body. Each student then has his or her own body tracing to draw various body parts and the body systems.

As children grow older, they must be taught about the basic functions of major body systems. By the fifth grade, a student should be able to describe the structure, function, and interdependence of the major body systems. An example of how the body systems work together is how the respiratory system takes oxygen into the body and is transported by the circulatory system to the musculoskeletal and nervous systems.

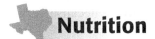 **Nutrition**

Consider the following practice question:

Mrs. Cleary, an elementary school teacher, is concerned about the eating habits of her students. Which of the following dietary guidelines should be stressed to elementary school students?

A. Eat a variety of foods from the basic food groups and avoid added sugar.
B. Eat primarily proteins and avoid carbohydrates.
C. Eat what you like as long as you exercise and take vitamins.
D. Eat only foods low in fat.

The correct choice is *A* (eat a variety of foods from the basic food groups and avoid added sugar). This response supports a balanced diet. It is important to promote positive nutritional habits at the elementary grades because it is difficult to change eating patterns once they have been established. The U.S. Department of Agriculture has many food-related activities at http://www.mypyramid.gov/kids, and the food pyramid can be found at http://www.mypyramid.gov. The answer is *A*.

Poor nutritional status may result in several problems. Although *undernutrition* can be a problem, in the United States the more common malnutrition problem is overnutrition. Texas Education Code §38.101-106 requires that every student in grades 3 through 12 participate in a physical fitness test at least once each year. The instrument currently used to assess a student's fitness level is FITNESSGRAM® (HumanKinetics, 2009). Data from the 2007–2008 school year showed that more than 70 percent of elementary-age students scored in at least one of the unhealthy fitness zones (Texas Education Agency, 2008). Obese children are likely to be at risk of chronic disease later in life and are likely to suffer emotional stress as well, but raising even more concern is that the diagnoses of children with type 2 diabetes (in which obesity is a prime factor) are reaching epidemic proportions (Children with Diabetes, 2005). Healthy eating habits are best begun at an early age. In other words, the best way to maintain ideal weight and eat well throughout life is to learn how to eat and exercise early in life. Teachers should help parents teach their children proper eating habits and exercise habits. Of all the habits of living, the most important to good health are eating properly and exercising regularly.

All foods are made up of various **nutrients** that are building blocks of the body. Six primary categories of nutrients in foods have been identified, three of which provide energy in the form of calories: (1) carbohydrates, (2) proteins, and (3) fats. The remaining categories are necessary for life, even though they do not provide energy/calories. They are (4) vitamins, (5) minerals, and (6) water. The body needs these every day.

Teaching young children about food choices can begin with experimentation. The EC-6 teacher may offer a variety of healthy snacks, even using the opportunity to integrate social studies by use of a cultural or theme food lab ("Today, boys and girls, we are going to visit Hawaii. Let's look on the map to see where Hawaii is and why these wonderful fruits grow there . . . ," as the teacher offers passion fruit juice, fresh chunks of pineapple, mango, and banana, etc.). Cultural lessons can accompany these lessons with information on why, when, and with what foods are eaten in different cultures (forks, knives, and spoons; chopsticks; fingers), and whether the food of a particular culture is a good choice. Because very young children cannot yet classify a number of ideas, we suggest that children be asked to classify food into categories that are easier to sort (such as milk products, eggs, vegetables, breads, meat, fruit, and nuts). Later, they can be introduced to the food pyramid and how to personalize eating plans. This pyramid plays a major role in helping students understand how they can choose a healthy meal by selecting different proportions from different parts of the pyramid (http://www.mypyramid.gov and the CATCH program with "GO," "SLOW," and "WHOA" foods at http://www.sph.uth. tmc.edu/CATCH). The food pyramid can also be used to teach children about various foods within each category and the nutrients in the foods. For example, dairy products contain calcium, which is important to bone growth and density. Additional examples of nutrients include vitamins, carbohydrates, fats, fiber, and cholesterol.

Parents can be used as a resource to reinforce and promote healthy eating. Teachers should always send a list of foods home that will be offered in class for tasting due to the possibilities of food allergies or cultural or religious desires for children not to eat certain items. At school, children should never be forced to eat what is offered in class. However, presenting foods in enticing ways should encourage children to try them. Teachers who reward young children with praise may also encourage others. Rothlein (cited in Brewer, 2001) suggests that only small amounts be offered and the color, texture, and shape should be discussed. The teacher should also be a role model, and he or she should continue food lab lessons, despite children's reluctance. If reluctance is encountered, the teacher should try to determine if another way of serving a food is acceptable (e.g., raw carrots are usually more palatable for children than cooked carrots). The teacher may want to create food lab activities that integrate food preparation with other content (e.g., have young children count out 6 raisins to form a smile on their snack plates). When children are involved in the preparation of foods, they are often more eager to try something new. Older children may participate in food art integration or create edible bouquets.

In the older grades, children should begin to analyze food labels for good health. The U.S. Food and Drug administration offers an excellent site on how to read the nutrition facts on food labels at http://www.fda.gov/Food/LabelingNutrition/ConsumerInformation/ucm078889.htm#twoparts. On the label, one first finds serving size and servings per container, followed by the number of calories per serving. Children should use these two items to ask, "How many servings am I going to eat?" and then multiply that by the calories per serving. The next section describes the percentages of nutrients—with those that have an impact on health (e.g., fats, cholesterol, sodium) listed first. The second section on nutrients lists the daily percentage provided of vitamins, calcium, fiber, iron, and so forth. The former can be used to limit the amount taken in, whereas the latter can be used to gain healthy nutrients. A footnote on daily recommendations is included on each food package with space large enough to print it.

Rackley and Knight (2011) tell us that eating disorders are becoming increasingly prevalent throughout the United States. They note: "According to U.S. estimates from the National Institute of Mental Health (2007), about 1 percent of females and 0.5 percent of males (i.e., 5–10 million people) suffer from eating disorders" (p. 26) such as *bulimia nervosa* (purging), *anorexia nervosa* (self-starvation), and binge eating, with as many as 15 percent of young women adopting unhealthy habits and attitudes toward food. These diseases more often affect those who want to be thin. Tendencies toward these eating disorders can begin in pre-pubescence—often with those who have a low self-concept with regard to their physical appearance (Cole & Cole, 1996) or children with stress. Too often, the media hype of "beauty as thin" conveys unhealthy images to children and young people. Even toys (such as dolls with unrealistic proportions) push these images. It is important for teachers to not only watch for the symptoms of these disorders but also to teach children how dangerous these disorders can be. Symptoms can include unnatural thinness, bad teeth, pale appearance, weakness, brittle skin, or more serious consequences.

Healthy Relationships

Learners are expected to know healthy ways to communicate consideration and respect for self, family, friends, and others. Learners are expected to demonstrate skills in communicating respectfully; describing and practicing techniques of self-control (such as thinking before acting); and expressing needs, wants, and emotions in appropriate ways. Emphasis is placed on teaching children the skills necessary for building and maintaining healthy relationships. Children are expected to learn to identify characteristics needed to be a responsible family member or friend, to list and demonstrate good listening skills, and to demonstrate critical-thinking, decision-making, goal-setting, and problem-solving skills for making health-promoting decisions.

An essential skill for some students may be coping with unhealthy behaviors in the family, including alcoholism, drugs, violence, and others. It is unfortunate to learn, for example, that almost one in every five American children has lived with an alcoholic while growing up (American Academy of Child & Adolescent Psychiatry, 2002), and many of the children of alcoholics will themselves become alcoholics for a number of reasons. The impact on children of various unhealthy family behaviors can be neglect, abuse, difficulty with personal relationships, depression, stress, and low self-esteem. Most often, children try to keep difficulties at home secret, so they do not foster close relationships at school, thus becoming increasingly more isolated and withdrawn. It is important, however, for the teacher to convey to the students that they talk with a trusted adult if they experience these issues and that there are those who want to help. The teacher can identify appropriate professionals or adults with whom the child could talk. The classroom teacher is not trained to counsel the student, but should encourage the student to talk with someone who is. Nonetheless, teachers can provide information on stress reduction and provide an environment that is safe and inclusive of all students. New teachers are reminded, however, that they have a legal obligation to call Child Protective Services (CPS) within 48 hours if they suspect that any child has been abused or neglected. Referral to a nurse, counselor, or an administrator for these two issues does not negate the necessity to report this suspicion to CPS.

Schoolchildren should also be equipped with conflict resolution skills. Despite a teacher's best efforts, conflict is often present in the schools. Conflict resolution represents a range of important skills for children to learn. Students should be made to understand the sources of conflict and instructed on how to effectively and properly manage it. Three primary conflict management techniques include:

- Avoiding the conflict. This means walking away from a fight or not acting in a way that provokes another person.
- Defusing the conflict. Adding humor to the situation or using delaying strategies can help defuse the conflict.
- Negotiation. This management technique means trying to find a way to compromise without inappropriate behavior.

Family members and teachers are especially important role models. The media also offers role models to children through television and video games. Many American children spend more time watching television and on the computer than they do working on schoolwork, so television is seen as a powerful educational medium. It is also apparent that violence on television and in video games can provide violent or aggressive models for children. Teachers should discuss this influence of television (as well as it being a medium for luring children into purchasing both healthy and non-healthy items through advertisements), and they should provide as many other positive role models as possible (appropriate literature, resources in the community, and others) to counter this effect.

The issues of peer pressure, popularity, and high-risk behaviors have an impact even on young children as they watch how others dress, what they say, and how they act. Children need to know that rejection is an unfortunate but inevitable part of life. It can be disappointing, but it should not be devastating. Part of good mental health is resiliency. Children must acquire knowledge and the ability to set limits, communicate effectively, and employ refusal skills. These basic skills are necessary to help students deal with daily pressures. Remember that peer pressure is not always a negative influence. Positive pressure to behave in a health-enhancing fashion can go a long way in helping a child. It is also essential that children understand that parents and other family members are not always opposing forces. Peers do not always lead children astray. Teaching children about what qualities make a good friend (and also how to be that type of friend) and choosing those who would make positive impacts on their lives should also be a part of the EC-6 health curriculum.

Teaching About Illness and Disease

By understanding the difference between sickness and health in persons of all ages, learners are able to explain ways in which germs are transmitted, methods of preventing the spread of germs, and the importance of immunization. In this way, they are able to identify causes of communicable illnesses and disease other than through germs (allergies, heart disease, genetic diseases, etc.) that are non-communicable and explain how the body provides protection in many cases. Children must know the differences for prevention purposes and because when they see grandparents, elderly relatives, or others who are extremely ill with non-communicable diseases, they may become worried that they could "catch" these types of disease, creating stress and worry for the child.

EC-6 children should learn about the three types of *pathogens* (germs that make people sick): bacteria, viruses, and fungi. They should then begin to apply practices to living in more healthy ways and helping to control the spread of pathogens in daily life. The most recommended ways to control germs includes hand washing and skin care, noting that the skin is our body's major protector from germs. The body has many other defenses. Small hairs in the nose can also protect pathogens from entering the body, and coughing expels foreign objects from the lungs. Germs stick in the mucus in the nose and throat to prevent them from going further, and strong acids in the stomach fight germs that may get that far. The eyelids and tears protect the eyes. If germs enter the body, *leucocytes* (or white blood cells) in the body's defense system rush to defend the body by either ingesting the pathogens or producing antibodies to fight them.

Teachers should schedule the time for healthy routines (such as always washing hands before eating and after visits to the restroom). The teacher can also be a role model whenever he or she has an opportunity with *Think-Alouds* ("I have a bit of a cold today, boys and girls, so I am not going to come too close to you to try to keep you from getting it," or "Excuse me a moment . . . I am starting to cough, so I am just going to get a tissue."). Teachers themselves should be very cautious about germs. If a teacher must aid a child in blowing a nose, for example, he or she should always wash his or her hands immediately afterward. Gloves should be available and worn for cleaning up any body fluids as per **universal precautions**, and any materials used in a cleanup should be disposed of safely. Tables where young children work should be cleaned often, as should toys, manipulatives, and technology used by children.

Teaching children about the symptoms of common childhood afflictions can also be a good prevention measure for the class. Head lice, ringworm, pinkeye, and other maladies may become less shared and less of a stigma if children understand how they occur and how they are cured. For example, children must know not to share headgear during times when head lice are prevalent in the school. A teacher may also need to discuss HIV and AIDS. Depending on the age level, children may want to talk about it to help alleviate fears that people can contract AIDS from being around or touching someone with the disease. Certainly, children's fears must be answered by teaching them that one cannot contract HIV/AIDS other than from infected blood, from intravenous needles often associated with drug use, from a mother with HIV to a baby in the womb or through nursing, and from unprotected sex. Teachers are not required to be told if a child has this disease, so it is extremely important for teachers to use universal precautions with any body fluids in helping a child or in any cleanups and for students to know not to touch these fluids.

The EC-6 teacher must always be appropriate in what she or he tells children with regard to age and many types of diseases but should answer children's questions, because learners see and hear much about these and may understand very little. Epidemics of dangerous flu and of others types of illnesses can cause a great deal of concern for children. Teachers can alleviate some fears by empowering children with the knowledge of early warning signs of illness that could include fever, aching, vomiting, headache, and sore throat. Children should be taught to inform an adult at once when they begin to feel ill, and teachers should send children to the nurse immediately if they are notified by a child who has symptoms. Bouts of dangerous flu have recently increased the seriousness of removing children from the classroom at once who may display symptoms. An activity to teach children types of diseases, transmission mechanisms, and disease prevention is to give the children a list of diseases and have them categorize them as communicable and non-communicable. Once the diseases are categorized, have the students discuss strategies for disease prevention. For a communicable disease such as the flu, transmission prevention includes washing hands frequently, blocking one's sneezes from others, avoiding touching others and others' things, and so forth. Children should learn about immunizations for a number of diseases so that they see the value of having society safe from diseases that, in the past, decimated many population areas (and still do in certain areas of the world). They should also learn to be knowledgeable consumers of new treatments and immunizations. Prevention for non-communicable diseases, such as heart disease, is most important and includes exercising regularly and proper nutrition (TAHPERD, 2007).

Consider the following practice question:

Ms. Jackson has noticed that a number of her third-grade students have been coming to school with colds and flu-like symptoms. Which of the following strategies are most useful for helping students understand self-responsibilities as they relate to friends?

A. Students keep a log of their personal health attributes on a daily basis and discuss the logs each Friday.

B. Students work in groups to discuss communicative and non-communicative diseases and how they are transmitted and come up with a plan for a "less germy" classroom.

C. Students interview parents and friends in order to determine their health status.

D. Physicians and other healthcare practitioners are invited to discuss with the students the health hazards they present when they come to school ill.

Whereas maintaining health logs and discussing them with the class is a useful tool for assessing health status (*A*), it does not lend itself to assisting learners in developing self-responsibility. Choice *C* also does not provide the learner the opportunity to promote interpersonal well-being. Choice *D*, although having the potential for providing learners with a cognitive basis regarding health issues, is not structured to provide the learner the opportunity to promote interpersonal well-being. Choice *B* gives students the requisite information needed for preparing them to understand concepts and issues of health, along with self-responsibility and ownership in their classroom. The correct answer is *B*.

Substance Abuse

It is important to remember that individuals make choices about their health behavior. This requires teaching about decision making. For example, a sixth grader who is deliberating about trying tobacco or another harmful substance must be shown choices in order to make good decisions and provided with occasions to practice the skills to avoid drug abuse. Bandura's (cited in Eggen & Kauchak, 2001) social learning theory is conducive to building these skills. For example, Bandura suggests that individuals who are contemplating drug use must (1) understand what methods must be done to avoid it, (2) believe that he or she will be able to use the methods, (3) believe that the method(s) will actually work, and (4) anticipate a benefit after achieving the behavior. Social learning theory tells us that children can learn these concepts, in part from watching others, and with practice, can develop the necessary skills required for good choices and developing healthy habits.

Teachers should teach their students the short-term and long-term effects of substance abuse. The short-term effects of tobacco use can be the foul odor of tobacco on the person or their clothes and the high cost of tobacco products. The long-term effects of tobacco can be yellow teeth, shortness of breath, and the increased risk of cancer or emphysema. The short-term effects of alcohol and drugs can be impaired vision, motor skills, and judgment. The long-term effects of alcohol and drugs can be diseases to a majority of systems and organs, such as the liver, heart, and brain. The use of alcohol and drugs can also result in harm to personal relationships with friends and family. Children must also learn about the legal issues involved in drinking, drugs, and other substances—both to children and to adults later on. Schools almost always suspend or send to alternative programs those children caught with these substances.

Healthy Communication

Students develop many different relationships throughout their elementary school years. For instance, relationships with family members, same-age friends, relatives, and teachers form as children progress through school. Communication skills help them develop healthy relationships.

Although speech develops in most children in predictable developmental sequences, communication, as a skill, does not come naturally to all children. Effective communication includes a range of skills that must be learned. A person's ability to communicate can have a direct effect on self-esteem and the quality of relationships with others. Besides helping a child's self-esteem, good communication skills are important to help a child succeed in the classroom and beyond. Listening and speaking skills have a great deal to do with how well a child will succeed in school and throughout life.

One important area in communications is the ability to recognize facial expressions and emotions. Teachers in the lower grades may use a number of activities to assist with emotional awareness (identifying emotions when given pictures of faces, creating collages to represent a particular emotion, drawing, storytelling, questioning, role playing, and presenting good literature models). A record of what emotions each child is able to easily identify should be maintained. Teachers should also record whether a student can identify the possible causes of emotions. Lack of emotional intelligence has been linked to adult mental health failure in many ways (Goleman, 1995). To help students to develop emotional intelligence, teachers should provide opportunities for students to work together in pairs, small groups, and teams. Practicing roles in cooperative education situations and focusing on a social skill of the day can help children become aware of verbal and nonverbal behaviors (Kagan, 1992).

Tolerance, respect, and empathy for others are skills students must learn, just as any other skill. One activity to teach these skills may begin with the teacher creating a life-size silhouette of a child from green butcher paper. The teacher introduces the silhouette to the class as a new student named "Greenie" and discusses with the class how difficult it is for new students to enter a class where groups of friends have already been formed. Each student is then asked to say one mean thing to Greenie. The teacher might begin with a comment like, "We don't like people who are different from us." After a student says something mean to Greenie, the teacher rips off a piece of Greenie's body and hands it to the student. (It is important to rip off large chunks of paper such that it is obvious where each chunk fits into the whole.) After each student has said something mean, the students must now apologize for what they said and then say something nice to Greenie. With each apology, the student is given a piece of tape to reattach the chunk of paper that was originally ripped off. When Greenie is whole again, discuss with the students how the "scars" of the mean comments are still evident. Hang Greenie on the wall as a reminder of how hurtful words can be to someone (*Education World*, 2009).

Consider the following practice question:

Mr. Washington notices that some of his elementary students are having difficulty communicating effectively, leading to increased classroom arguments. Which of the following skills could he teach to help improve the students' communication skills?

A. Ignoring comments with which you do not agree.
B. Being assertive without being aggressive.
C. Withholding your opinions from the conversation.
D. Using "You" statements instead of "I" statements.

Three of these choices are inappropriate communication skills. Children should be taught that their opinions make important contributions to communication (choices *A* and *C*) and that it is appropriate to share one's opinion. Another good way of doing this involves using "I" statements, not "you" statements. However, children must learn how to express themselves appropriately (*B*). When children first enter school, they are very developmentally self-centered and more concerned about their own needs. They rarely identify with the needs and characteristics of others. As they continue in school, they begin to develop an increasing awareness of others. As they age, children begin to redirect their personal concerns to intellectual concerns and group activities. They begin to expend more energy on friendships and the community around them. In this process, they need greater communication skills. The correct choice is *B*.

Refusal Skills

Refusal skills are an essential part of good decision making. Children need good refusal skills when it is necessary to say "no" to an action or remove themselves from a potentially harmful situation. Any situation that threatens personal safety or health, tempts children to break laws or norms, detracts from personal character, asks students to disobey rules, or results in loss of self-respect calls for strong refusal skills. Teachers should concentrate on lessons that strengthen self-concept, social skills, and prosocial behaviors and offer opportunities for all children to role-play various situations to practice these skills.

Students should be taught that in order to develop good refusal skills, they should:

- Employ assertive (but not aggressive) behavior. This allows others to know that you are in control of your behavior and the situation.
- Use body language that matches your assertive verbal behavior. Body language indicates that you are sincere. Students should make it clear that they do not desire to engage in unsafe situations.
- Avoid potentially harmful/dangerous situations.
- Be a positive role model. Children should act and talk in a manner that commands respect.

Try this practice question:

Mrs. Smith's health class is discussing a model for using communication skills. In practicing refusal skills, Jake responds to pressure to use drugs by stating, "No, thank you." Which of the following is the best assessment of his refusal strategy?

A. Saying "No, thank you" is inappropriate because there is no need to thank people for an invitation to misbehave.

B. It's a good response because you are being polite.

C. It doesn't match his nonverbal communication.

D. It's a good response because it's short and to the point.

You do not have to say "No, thank you." There is no need to be polite when placed in a situation that may be unsafe. Choice *B* is incorrect because it is not an assertive response. We have no information on Jake's nonverbal behavior, so choice *C* is incorrect, and simply having a short answer does not make it the best response. The correct answer is *A*.

Violence

Violence, as the answer to conflict, has become all too common. There is significant concern about the growing rate of violence. Many students attending schools in which violence occurs are unable to focus on meeting rigorous standards, perform at high academic levels, or even complete schooling. Students and teachers who are more concerned about their personal safety than about education cannot concentrate on teaching and learning.

It is the responsibility of educators to help prevent violence of many types. *Violence prevention* means two things: preventing the immediate threat of violence to our children now and reducing our children's risk of facing violence in the future. Teachers should recognize there are behaviors and strategies that can help them safeguard themselves and their students in the classroom. Characteristics of teachers whose classrooms have been identified as relatively violence free include:

- developing positive relationships with students in the classroom and in the community
- taking preventive action by creating classroom environments in which the teacher is clearly in control
- knowing how to diffuse a confrontation
- insisting on backup support when necessary.

Various programs exist that strive to teach children how to manage anger and conflict. These programs typically share the following ideas:

- Conflict is a normal part of human interaction.
- When individual prejudices are explored, students can learn how to appreciate people whose backgrounds are different.
- Disputes need not have winners and losers.
- Children who learn how to assert themselves nonviolently can avoid becoming bullies or victims.
- Children's self-esteem is enhanced when they learn how to build nonviolent, non-hostile relationships with their peers.

Because of heightened security issues in and out of schools, it is imperative that children be taught the difference between just tattling and that of reporting important information on dangerous activities. Many teachers handle tattlers as pariahs or ignore them altogether, perhaps contributing to a behavior of being silent about the harmful behavior of others. Some children see allegiance to their friends as more important than to society as a whole. Teachers must reinforce problem solving with others but also help children understand that sharing the types of information that could be harmful to others (or even themselves) is essential. Reports of weapons brought to school, threats against others, and so forth are essential to the safety of all. Teaching these skills in role play, discussing the differences in tattling versus telling about dangers, and taking children's reports seriously when needed are all ways to increase children's confidence in coming forward when there is a serious concern.

Kortz, Nath, and Parker Braselton (2011) discuss another type of violence for students—that related to technology, noting:

> *Cyberbullying, cyberstalking, text harassment (sending numerous messages that the end user to has to pay for), and sexting (texting explicit messages of a sexual nature) are terms/concepts that were not known 10 years ago in schools throughout America. Now, Winchester (2009) states that 17% of 6- to 11-year-olds and 36% of 12- to 17-year-olds have reported that someone has threatened or embarrassed them through e-mail, instant messages, Websites, chat rooms, or text messages. Not only are threats and disparaging remarks made, but inappropriate pictures of students have been passed through cells and email by their peers. These can be so hurtful, scary, or embarrassing that, in rare cases, suicides have occurred. (p. 363)*

Another form of violence is gang activity. Most people assume that children in elementary schools do not yet have to worry about gang activity, but that is no longer the case. Gangs often attempt to recruit younger members because they believe that law enforcement does not focus on young children or give them stiff penalties should they be caught in gang activities (such as drug running). Younger people are drawn to gangs because they believe that a gang will protect them, that they will be respected or looked up to as a member of a gang, that they will make money, and that they will have someone who cares like a "family" (Gang Reduction through Intervention, Prevention, & Education [GRIPE], n.d.). Most gang prevention programs try to point out the dangers of gangs to students, noting that being a gang member increases the likelihood that they (or family members) could be injured or even killed by rival gangs or law enforcement, that they will likely spend time in jail if they commit crimes to get money, that a real family would never ask them to commit crimes and risk being hurt or incarcerated, and so forth. Teachers must help bust gang myths for students, and, in addition, help provide students with a positive environment that provides for students' needs. GRIPE also tells us that violence is often brought on by a failure in being able to communicate, frustration or isolation, retaliation, peer pressure, the need for attention or respect, low self-esteem, abuse or neglect, and other issues with which a teacher may help. There are other areas that a teacher may not be able to control (witnessing of violence, easy access to weapons, etc.), but if he or she can help in these areas listed, the battle for a safer and happier life for students may be on its way.

Incorporating these principles in the health education curriculum is essential. Research has shown that a coordinated school health program is effective in influencing youth's behaviors and establishing a pattern of healthy behavior in the future (Centers for Disease Control and Prevention [CDC], 2008a).

 Stress

Let's try a practice question:

Joey, a fourth grader, is having trouble coping with stressful situations in school and at home. This unresolved stress has caused him to become angry with his friends for little reason. What is the best thing the teacher could do to help him?

    A. Have him begin an exercise program immediately.
    B. Discover his sleeping habits and see if he needs more sleep.

C. Analyze his diet and make recommendations for a diet that helps reduce stress.

D. Refer Joey to the counselor in the school.

Although it is true that exercise can reduce stress levels (*A*), it is apparent that there could be a number of factors contributing to the child's demeanor. Exercise, although a valuable tool, will not necessarily provide the results anticipated. Although sleeping habits can have an impact on behavior, there is nothing to indicate that the child's stress is a manifestation of lack of sleep, and choice *B* does not provide a comprehensive solution or one that the teacher could control. The same can be said for answer *C*, although too much sugar and caffeine can affect behavior. All of these choices may help with Joey, but we are looking for the best answer over which a teacher has control. Typically, stress and the hostile behavior exhibited by students are a manifestation of several factors. The answer is to seek help from a counselor. Although a teacher can suggest and try other stress-reducing strategies, the role of the counselor in schools is to provide professional help for individual students, offer advice to teachers, and give guidance for parents. Counselors can also explore testing or provide mini-lessons about various emotion-based topics. The correct answer is *D*.

Consider another question:

During a structured physical activity session, members of a fourth-grade class were running relay races. One boy exclaims, "I was so afraid I would drop the baton that I started sweating a lot and my stomach felt bad. I just knew that I was going to let the team down." This statement best reflects the knowledge of what principles and practices needed by teachers?

A. Teachers must be aware that a learner's motivation is best gauged by stress symptoms and measures the learner's level of motivation.

B. Teachers must recognize signs of stress demonstrated by learners, and they should use opportunities like this to teach coping skills that can be used by students.

C. Physical activity lessons should include skills that are stressful during the early learning phases of motor activity.

D. Physical activity lessons should include very stressful situations to match those encountered in the learner's nonschool environment.

One of the unique advantages of structured physical activity is that it provides the opportunity to view students in a variety of mildly stressful situations. Teaching students that stress is a natural outcome of being placed in the competitive situation described is an excellent introduction to teaching students how to cope with stress. As a result, choice *B* is correct. Motivation and stress are not necessarily related to successful achievement of motor skill development, so *A* is incorrect. Providing stress during the early stages of skill development, as in choice *C*, results in frustration on the part of students. Teaching motor skills should result in a balance between mild stress and success. Choice *D* is incorrect, because the goal is to use these situations to teach students coping skills in naturally occurring situations, not to purposefully create stressful environments. The correct answer is *B*.

It is possible to teach children skills in *coping* (the ability to deal with problems successfully) and *decision making* (a process in which a person selects from two or more possible choices) through instruction in physical activity. Specific strategies for teaching children coping skills include:

- admit the problem exists and face it
- define the problem and decide who owns it (Is the problem theirs, or does it belong to others?)
- list alternative solutions to the problem

- predict consequences for oneself and others
- identify and consult sources of help
- experiment with a solution and evaluate the results

Young children can formulate these into the following steps:

RED LIGHT: Stop! Calm down . . . and think before you act.
YELLOW LIGHT: Say the problem and how you feel. Set a positive goal.
　　Think of lots of solutions. Think ahead of the consequences.
GREEN LIGHT: Go ahead and try the best plan (Goleman, 1995).

When making decisions, students should consider each of the following steps:

1. Gather information.
2. Consider the available choices.
3. Analyze the consequences of choices.
4. Make a decision and implement it.
5. Evaluate the decision and begin at step 1 with a new plan if the decision does not yield positive results.

The use of challenge activities such as climbing walls, rope courses, and other physically demanding activities have recently gained impetus because of their value in teaching both coping and decision-making skills. Teachers must remember that young children are still egocentric in development, and children may not yet have the ability to navigate through decisions involving long-term goals. Teachers should help young children begin making simple decisions that deal with short-term goals first. Children who are given opportunities to make choices within a classroom setting and experience the consequences of their decisions learn to make better decisions.

Technology and Health

The technology revolution has had a great impact in various areas of health. Of course, it allows scientists to create new medicines, immunizations, and cures for many diseases and for doctors to communicate and share findings. Within schools, however, it has had dramatic impact on our ability to teach youngsters concepts related to health and fitness. An example is the use of heart rate monitors that permit children to gain a greater understanding of the cardiorespiratory system and the establishment of cardiorespiratory fitness. Another example is the use of video cameras that allow a child's performance to be filmed for immediate self-assessment. Audiovisual aids add another dimension to teaching concepts and are excellent for reinforcing learning. The Internet allows children access to health-related fitness information and to set up interdisciplinary studies across distances to gather health-related data, share active games, and so forth. The Internet also provides teachers with the opportunity to communicate with others and to share their ideas and questions.

As mentioned, technology also brings numerous products to the consumers' attention. Teaching children about being a smart consumer of health products helps them understand that they must read labels, gather more information, and be constantly alert for false advertising. For example, having learners create their own "cure all" or "miracle weight loss" products along with a label and advertisements (which can be filmed and used as assessment) helps children understand that not all products advertised are valid. Teachers must help students become educated consumers.

With all of the positive benefits of technology, it can also bring threats to children's safety—that of predators who attempt to lure children into giving out personal information and, in some cases, trying to establish inappropriate online relationships. Cases where the predator has actually made physical contact with children have been heard often enough in the news that teachers should be sure to instruct children on the dangers of technology in these areas. Kortz, Nath, and Parker Braselton (2011) note:

> [S]tudents should be taught never to give their full names, phone numbers, or addresses, and to report "cyber strangers" to adults if anyone online asks for personal types of information. Also, a teacher should be vigilant about having children sign guestbooks (a space on a Website that allows comments, suggestions on improving the site, and so forth), being sure that they never give more information than their first names and that they always check with the teacher (at school) or the parent (at home) before they do so. Teachers may sometimes want to post pictures or film clips of students or their work to the Web for parents and others, but this is also a safety issue and is not allowed without parental permission. (p. 362)

As mentioned, cases of cyberbullying have lead to considerable stress through technology, and teachers must be vigilant for episodes in which this may be happening to children.

Wise Consumers

The health and beauty industry has grown in amazing proportions recently—as evidenced by the row upon row of these products in grocery stores, department stores, health food shops, and through television and online advertising and sales. Good consumers should learn how to evaluate health and fitness products both for the good that they provide and for the cost value. It is important for consumers not only to get good value for their money but also to purchase products that are safe for them to use.

Elementary and middle-school children have many questions and concerns about personal health matters, including questions about skin care, hair care, dental hygiene, and others. Apart from the formal learning and experiences that take place in a health instructional program, older elementary children often turn to less reliable sources of information, such as popular magazines, product advertisements, radio or television, and peers. These sources may be biased or inaccurate; therefore, standard-based health education is important for children. Learning about the ploys in adverting is an excellent way to help children become wise consumers.

In the past few decades herbal supplements have been a large part of the health industry. In addition to teaching children about proper nutrition, it is important that students are able to distinguish between fact and myth related to the benefits of herbal supplements. Many of these products may be very helpful, but others may do nothing or, worse, be harmful over time. There are "health stores" that sell herbal products, such as aloe vera, black cohosh, ginger root, ginkgo biloba, green tea, and milk thistle. The use of a trained nutritionist or medical professional to speak to the students about herbal supplements is a good way of providing accurate information. As noted earlier, students should also be taught to research on their own about these products, note if their advertising comes from a reliable source, determine that the draw of the product is not coming simply from celebrities who are paid to advertise them, find out if reliable medical groups endorse them, discover any side effects, and so forth. Children should become cognizant of all items that they would ingest or put on their skin or hair for health or beauty purposes. They should be wary of dietary aids, over-the-counter medications, "power" drinks, and so on, and should investigate prior to use.

Safety

Instruction in safety and injury prevention is an important component of an elementary school curriculum. According to a 2008 report from the CDC, the leading cause of death among children is unintentional injuries. Each year, more than 12,000 children between the ages of birth to 19 years die from unintentional injuries, and more than half of these fatalities result from motor vehicle accidents. Other examples include unintentional deaths resulting from garage doors, swimming pools, or accidental poisoning (CDC, 2008b). The more publicized cases show children who have been taken by predators. For this reason, safety instruction cannot be ignored in a school program.

Attitude formation begins early in a child's life and has a major impact on safety behavioral patterns. Although innumerable factors influence attitude formation, the actions of parents and respected adults, including teachers, are a major force, particularly among children in the primary grades. Teachers must always remember that they are some of the most significant models in a child's life because (1) they are with children most of the waking hours of the day, (2) teachers can form strong bonds with students, (3) they are the most visible person in the classroom, and (4) their position is seen publicly as that of a trusted adult. A teacher who models good choices for a safe and healthy life goes a long way in helping children to develop these types of choices. In addition, safety lessons that extend into the home and involve parents are one of the most valuable ways to gain parental involvement and to help keep children and their families safe. For example, several very young children have recently been in the news because they saved a parent or family member after learning at school how to call 911.

For health and safety education to be effective in the elementary school, it is important that the school program be coordinated with health-promotion activities throughout the school and community. Messages delivered in a consistent fashion and from several sources (e.g., teachers, parents, school staff, community leaders, peers) are more effective in changing behaviors.

The teacher's responsibility is to instill in pupils those attitudes that encourage them to act to protect their own safety, that of their families, and that of society. Safety education is not only training in conservation of life and the prevention of accidents but also instruction in how to be a good citizen; that is, to show how one's behavior with regard to health and safety can affect not only their family but the entire country as well (medical costs, possible dependency, increased taxes, etc.). Other responsibilities of the teacher are to guide learners in developing sound values, to direct their thinking and decision making, and to help them regulate their behavior. According to the TEKS in health education, teachers should direct children's understanding of the health information necessary to become safe and healthy adults and to learn about behaviors in which they should and should not participate.

What safety issues are important for a teacher to include in his or her class? Fire, traffic (including bicycles and skateboards), sun, food, water, gun, poison (including use of another person's medications), choking, dangerous objects (knives, sharp scissors, screwdrivers, etc.), and human predator safety are all safety issues of which children should be aware. Several of these issues can scare and worry children, so a teacher must be careful to balance information in a way that is completely age appropriate. Children should also learn about protective equipment that makes their lives safer (e.g., helmets for a number of sports, including bicycles, skateboards, skiing, football, and baseball; kneepads; seatbelts; life preservers; and others). Children should also learn about safe places for sports and play and be able to choose safe places at home (backyards or play areas rather than the street). Instruction, role play, and periodic drills relating to school (fire, lock-downs, and bad weather, as well as with other applicable safety issues) and home should be practiced until they become matter-of-fact. Instead of lining up in the routine way at school during the year, teachers can occasionally say, "Today, when we line up to go the library, we are going to do our fire drill line-up, so listen for my 'three bells,'" or "When we come in from recess today, I want you to practice the lock-down routine," or "When we line up outside our classroom, let me see everybody practice the bad weather position." Children can take responsibly at home, too, to create a safe home fire plan. Outside resources, such as fire departments and police departments, can provide instruction in many of these areas. If outside resources are not available, EC-6 teachers must still provide instruction. "Stop, drop, and roll" (in case of catching one's clothes on fire), exiting an area *before* calling 911, designating a gathering spot in an emergency, and, of course, not playing with fire should be a part of all children's knowledge for school and home. Traffic safety instruction can include areas on the playground and in centers where children pretend to be vehicles or drive small toy vehicles according to traffic rules.

Children should also be taught about strangers through role-play, games, or puppet play. Many videos and police departments deal well with *good touching* versus *bad touching,* and children should learn where to go for help when they are made to feel uncomfortable or unsafe with an adult. Guidelines should be communicated to children and parents to help latchkey children be safer (such as Internet and phone rules of never giving out one's name, parent's name, or address) (Brewer, 2001). Teachers and parents should be careful about labeling children's clothing and materials in large letters (such as notebooks or folders) to prevent a predator from easily seeing this and calling out to a child by his or her name. Teachers should never release children to an adult who has not been cleared through the office that day (even if it is a known relative), and they should take going-home duties most seriously.

The environment can be a factor influencing children's health. Children must be aware of the relationship between the environment and their individual health. In Texas, young children must learn about outdoor safety due to the direct sun and what measures to take to prevent skin cancer later on. Texas teachers should also be cognizant of sunburn and heat stroke when children are engaged in outdoor activities. Weather conditions in Texas can change rapidly and dramatically, so teachers must also help children learn about safety during tornadoes, lightning, flooding, and other dangers. Texas temperatures can also change rapidly, so children should learn that dressing properly can also affect their health and safety (both for warmth and for the extreme heat). Other examples of environmental hazards include air pollution, ozone levels (especially for children with breathing difficulties such as asthma), drinking untreated water, and household toxins. Students can also learn strategies to protect the environment as a way to promote community health; examples include recycling, waste disposal, and safe food packaging.

Consider the following practice question:

An elementary teacher, Mrs. Santos, wishes to promote an understanding of community safety among her children. As the lesson is introduced, several children tell her that some children display unsafe behaviors while riding their bicycles to and from school. For example, they do not wear protective gear and weave in and out of traffic. Mrs. Santos wants her students to understand their roles and responsibilities in helping to ensure community safety while children are riding their bicycles.

Which of the following activities is most appropriate for this purpose?

A. Have students make a list of inappropriate behaviors and the safety problems these behaviors cause.
B. Have the students write a letter to school and city officials, as well as the local police, informing them of the bicycle safety problem and asking for assistance in eliminating the problem.
C. Suggest to the well-behaved students that they avoid streets in which students practicing unsafe bicycle riding behavior is displayed.
D. Start a telephone campaign to report the unsafe bicycle riders to the appropriate officials.

Let's examine the alternatives. Choice *A* is not the correct answer because it does not address the standard targeted in this question; that is, it informs students, but it does not address promoting an understanding of community safety among the students. Choice *B* is the correct choice. By writing a letter to important community members, the learners are demonstrating an understanding of the concepts and issues of community health and safety and applying this understanding to the well-being of people collectively. By selecting this choice, the elementary teacher demonstrates that she understands community health and safety issues and fosters learner understanding of the related responsibilities. Choice *C* is incorrect because these result in a failure to apply the concepts related to community health. Choice *D* affects the community but requires children to use a phone, which is not feasible in schools. Always read the question very carefully to be sure you note nuances such as *community* versus *personal* safety. The correct answer is *B*.

Children make daily choices about their health and, in doing so, establish early patterns of behavior. The child who does not wear a seatbelt is at greater risk of injury. The learner who elects not to wear protective equipment while riding a bicycle, roller boarding, or skateboarding also increases risk. In addition, the learner who refuses to wear eyeglasses exacerbates his or her vision problem. Children who learn to brush and floss their teeth early and maintain regular dental checkups are less likely to develop dental problems later. Children who eat healthy snacks and remain within defined weight limits are less likely to suffer the many health problems associated with obesity. Young people who avoid tobacco products early usually do not take up the habit later. Students learn that their sleep habits can affect their overall academic performance and emotional moods. In fact, recent research has linked sleep apnea to bullying (American Academy of Sleep Medicine, 2007). The common thread interwoven throughout lifestyles and habits is that good health is often a choice, not chance. All these choices can help reduce health-care costs and place the family in a preventive mode rather than a treatment mode. A healthy family is under less emotional and financial stress. Children must understand that in these and many other ways, they are responsible for their health, and there are many ways to teach children personal responsibilities in avoiding hazards, injuries, and health issues later in life. Although many diseases and accidents are unpreventable, teaching children to avoid those that are preventable can place them and society in a better long-term situation. It is essential that they know this responsibility is easily carried out if they make healthful decisions. There is much to teach in the area of health to EC-6 children. Teachers must remember their pedagogy in designing effective lessons in each area by designing clear goals and objectives, creating instruction as close to students' backgrounds and interests as possible, and using various learning styles and modalities for diverse learners.

Physical Education Standards I–X

The following list shows the standards for *generalist* EC-6 beginning teachers for teaching physical education.

Standard I. The physical education teacher demonstrates competency in a variety of movement skills and helps students develop these skills.

Standard II. The physical education teacher understands principles and benefits of a healthy, physically active lifestyle and motivates students to participate in activities that promote this lifestyle.

Standard III. The physical education teacher uses knowledge of individual and group motivation and behavior to create and manage a safe, productive learning environment and promotes students' self-management, self-motivation, and social skills through participation in physical activities.

Standard IV. The physical education teacher uses knowledge of how students learn and develop to provide opportunities that support students' physical, cognitive, social, and emotional development.

Standard V. The physical education teacher provides equitable and appropriate instruction for all students in a diverse society.

Standard VI. The physical education teacher uses effective, developmentally appropriate instructional strategies and communication techniques to prepare physically educated individuals.

Standard VII. The physical education teacher understands and uses formal and informal assessment to promote students' physical, cognitive, social, and emotional development in physical education contexts.

Standard VIII. The physical education teacher is a reflective practitioner who evaluates the effects of his/her actions on others (e.g., students, parents/caregivers, other professionals in the learning environment) and seeks opportunities to grow professionally.

Standard IX. The physical education teacher collaborates with colleagues, parents/caregivers, and community agencies to support students' growth and well-being.

Standard X. The physical education teacher understands the legal issues and responsibilities of physical education teachers in relation to supervision, planning and instruction, matching participants, safety, first aid, and risk management.

Competency 045 (Physical Education) addresses the standards discussed previously, noting that physical education teachers use knowledge of the concepts, principles, skills, and practices of physical education to plan and implement effective and engaging physical education instruction.

The beginning teacher should apply key principles and concepts in physical education and physical activity (e.g., cardiovascular endurance, muscular strength, flexibility, weight control, conditioning, safety, stress management, nutrition) for the promotion of health and fitness. He or she should know and help students understand the benefits of an active lifestyle. This should include applying knowledge of movement principles and concepts to help develop students' motor skills, including understanding key elements of mature movement patterns (e.g., throw, jump, catch) and various manipulative skills (e.g., volley, dribble, punt, strike). The teacher should be able to select and use developmentally appropriate learning experiences that enhance students' locomotor, non-locomotor, body control, manipulative, and rhythmic skills and to modify instruction based on students' individual differences in growth and development. A variety of strategies and tactics designed to improve students' performance, teamwork, and skill combinations in games and sports should be a part of a teacher's repertoire, and he or she should understand appropriate methods, including technological methods, for evaluating, monitoring, and improving fitness levels. In addition, he or she should be able to evaluate movement patterns to help students improve performance of motor skills and to integrate and refine their motor and rhythmic skills. Instructional strategies should be used to promote students' knowledge and application of rules, procedures, etiquette, and fair play in developmentally appropriate games and activities, and the teacher must design, manage, and adapt physical education activities to promote positive interactions and active engagement by all students. Each teacher should understand areas of diverse needs (e.g., physical and emotional challenges, learning disabilities, sensory difficulties, language differences) and their implications for teaching and learning. Finally, the teacher should apply knowledge of physical education content and curriculum based on the Texas Essential Knowledge and Skills (TEKS) and of students in early childhood through grade 6 to plan, implement, and assess effective, developmentally appropriate physical education activities.

Physically Active Lifestyle

These standards and indicators are related to the component of the physical education TEKS that states that learners acquire the knowledge and skills for movement that provide the foundation for enjoyment, continued social development through physical activity, and access to a physically active lifestyle. The goal is for the learner to exhibit a physically active lifestyle and understand the relationship between physical activity and health throughout his or her life. In elementary schools, children learn fundamental movement skills and begin to understand how the muscles, bones, heart, and lungs function in relation to physical activity. Identifying personal fitness goals and beginning to understand how exercise affects different parts of the body are an important part of the instructional process.

Children should learn how to identify components of health-related fitness, such as cardiovascular endurance, muscular strength and endurance, flexibility, and body composition. Children should also be able to identify sources of health fitness information regarding appropriate clothing, safety devices and equipment, and safety precautions in exercise settings. Remember that teachers must be aware of the legally required time for physical activity and provide that time for children if there is no specialized PE teacher. If there is a specialized teacher for PE, but he or she is not able to schedule enough time for the entire requirement, the regular classroom teacher must make up that difference in structured physical activity.

Try this practice question:

Ms. Jones wants to teach her students about the impact of exercise on their heart rate. Which of the following lesson activities is most appropriate for teaching this concept?

A. The students are placed in lines and run relay races.
B. The students keep a journal of the type and amount of physical activity they perform in 1 week.
C. The students take their heart rate before and after they do 2 minutes of moving in place.
D. The students walk for 20 minutes and use a pedometer to record the number of steps they take.

None of the activities described in choices *A, B,* or *D* have the students recording their heart rate. Choice C is correct because the students measure their heart rate prior to and after the physical exercise. It is important for teachers to instruct the proper method of measuring heart rate and provide opportunities for practice. Teachers should also remember that students' heart rates may vary greatly depending on the student's fitness level. Therefore, physical activity should be individualized to each student's capabilities. For example, rather than have all students run a particular distance, the teacher can have all students moving for a specified amount of time. Some students may walk, whereas others may chose to run or jog. Providing a number of stations with a variety of tasks and/or equipment also helps to address individual differences. The important goal is for all students to increase their heart rate with moderate to vigorous physical activity. The answer is *C*.

 Fitness Components

Due to the increasing trend in childhood obesity, Texas now requires each school housing grades kindergarten through eighth grade to implement a TEA-approved Coordinated School Health Program (CSHP) (Texas Education Code §38.013). The excessive numbers of overweight or undernourished children created a need for programs that help children assess their eating habits and plan effective healthy life habits. Lifestyles have changed for American children, creating an increase in **caloric intake** and a decrease in **energy expenditure**. Changes in transportation and activity, easy access to fast foods, controlled temperatures indoors, safety in play out of doors, the popularity of technology, and so forth have left children with more energy than ways in which to use it. As already noted, problems related to stress management and alcohol and drug consumption have also prompted the physical education profession to redefine and emphasize new aspects of physical fitness. This new direction and emphasis toward a positive state of well-being created a need for programs that help children understand how their bodies work, how they can monitor body changes, and how they can design personal fitness programs for improving and maintaining optimal levels of health.

As we have known for some time, health-related physical fitness includes aspects of physiological function that offer protection from diseases resulting from a sedentary lifestyle. Such fitness can be improved or maintained through regular and moderate physical activity. Currently, experts (Pangrazi, Corbin, & Welk, cited in Brewer, 2001) recommend that children be physically active at least 60 minutes every day. The Texas Education Code §28.002 requires all students in grades kindergarten through sixth grade (and prekindergarten, if enrolled for a full day) to participate in a minimum of 30 minutes per day or 135 minutes per week of physical activity. Minutes of physical activity in recess may count only if the activity is structured. If children are simply outside or at recess, it does not meet the requirement.

Cardiovascular fitness offers many health benefits and is often seen as the most important element of fitness. It includes the ability of the heart, the blood vessels, and the respiratory system to deliver oxygen efficiently over an extended period of time. In order to develop cardiovascular fitness, activities must be **aerobic** in nature (i.e., activities that are continuous and rhythmic in nature, requiring that a continuous supply of oxygen be delivered to the muscle cells). Activities that stimulate development in this area are walking, jogging, aerobics, and swimming. Another type of exercise is **anaerobic**, which is strength building in nature. In anaerobic exercises (weightlifting, sprinting, jump roping, interval training, etc.), the activity is high-intensity and cannot last long because the muscles are using more oxygen than is being taken in. This type of exercise is used to strengthen the muscles and can also increase cardiorespiratory fitness.

Body composition is an integral part of health-related fitness and is defined as the proportion of body fat to lean body mass. Attaining physical fitness is made more difficult when an individual's body composition is high in body fat. A standard method for estimating a child's body composition is by calculating the **body mass index (BMI)**, or the ratio of weight to the height squared. Due to the sensitive nature of this measure, teachers are encouraged to consult with the school nurse on guidelines for recording and reporting results. An article by the CDC (2009) provides guidelines on specific safeguards that need to be in place before a school decides to collect students' BMIs.

Another component of health-related fitness is **flexibility**, the range and ease of motion of a joint. The amount of flexibility depends on the structure and nature of the joints involved, the nature of the ligaments surrounding the joint, and the extensibility of the muscles connected to the joint. Through stretching activities, the length of the muscles, tendons, and ligaments can be increased. Flexibility is important to fitness and prevention of injuries. A lack of flexibility can create health problems for individuals. People who are flexible, for example, usually have good posture, better balance and range of movement, and may have less lower-back pain than those who have a limited range of motion. Many physical activities demand a range of motion to generate maximum force, such as serving a tennis ball or kicking a soccer ball.

Muscular strength and endurance are the other components of health-related fitness. **Muscular strength** is the amount of force that a muscle or group of muscles can exert in one contraction. When muscular strength is desired as a training outcome, it is necessary to move near-maximum workloads with minimal repetitions. **Muscular endurance** is the ability of the muscles to continue to function over a long period of time. To develop muscular endurance, a low-resistance, high-repetition workload is suggested. For most people, a balance of the two workloads is probably the most useful. Climbing or pulling exercises and jumping rope are particularly effective for children's strength.

The Texas Education Code §38.101-106 requires that every student in grades 3 through 12 participate in a physical fitness test at least once each year. The instrument currently selected by TEA to assess a student's fitness level is FITNESSGRAM® (Human Kinetics, 2009). In most schools, the certified physical education teacher administers the FITNESSGRAM® test with the assistance of classroom teachers, school nurse, paraprofessional aides, or parents. The students' scores must be reported to the Texas Education Agency in May of each year. FITNESSGRAM® evaluates the student's Healthy Fitness Zones for aerobic capacity, body composition, muscle strength, endurance, and flexibility (Human Kinetics, 2009). The reason for fitness assessment is to provide a baseline and progression of fitness as a learning opportunity for the child to set personal fitness goals. The data collected also provides parents and teachers an overview of the fitness levels of all students by grade level. As an added benefit, empirical research has shown that the more physically fit a student is, especially aerobically, the better they perform academically (Chomitz, Slining, McGowan, et al., 2008; Ratey, 2008; Castelli, Hillman, Buck, et al., 2007; Grissom, 2005).

It is important to distinguish between health-related fitness and skill-related fitness. The focus of **health-related fitness** is to help youngsters understand how much activity is required for good health. Emphasis is placed on the process of activity and participation rather than on the product of high-level performance. **Skill-related fitness**, however, helps improve performance in motor tasks necessary for successful participation in sports and physical activities. The ability to perform well is influenced to a significant degree by predetermined genetic characteristics. If skill-related fitness is taught in elementary school, it should be accompanied with an explanation about why some children and adults perform well in certain sports or on special skills with a minimum of effort whereas others, no matter how much they practice, may not excel in certain areas. This may be due to height, body type, length of specific bones, or other factors, but it should not keep a person from improving in or enjoying a particular physical activity.

Once children are personally convinced that exercise is important for their own well-being and are provided the opportunity to develop a habit of exercise, there is a high probability that physical activity will become a permanent part of their daily lives. Children can also be taught skills and habits such that he or she begins to modify his or her diet and physical activity to complement this positive and healthy way of living (Hoelscher, 2004).

Consider the following practice question:

Mr. Pollack has his students find their heart rates after walking around the gymnasium for 3 minutes. They rest for a few minutes. Children are then to jog for 3 minutes and take their heart rates at the completion of the jog, followed by having them jump rope for 3 minutes and finally by having them sprint for 3 minutes. After each activity, students take their heart rates again. What is the most likely reason for doing this lesson?

A. To identify what types of activities place greater demands on the heart.
B. To complete a variety of cardiovascular activities in one session.
C. To maintain aerobic capacity for 12 minutes.
D. To identify how to measure heart rate effectively during a workout.

It is important for learners to understand that different activities place different demands on the heart (*A*). Having learners see the importance of the effect of different types of activities on the cardiorespiratory system is a valuable tool for understanding the concepts underlying the components of health-related fitness. There is little to be gained by completing a variety of cardiovascular activities in a single session (*B*). Although an activity may be conducted for a significant length of time (*C*), it is the intensity of the activity that determines whether it is aerobic in nature. The walking phase of this activity does not constitute time spent in the *aerobic phase*, which is defined as when the cardiorespiratory system is able to meet the demands of the body's muscles and tissues with an adequate supply of oxygen. Learning how to take one's heart rate (*D*) is an important skill, but it is not the most likely reason for this lesson. The answer is *A*.

Importance of Physical Activity

Physical activity has a positive impact on the growth and development of children. Research supports the value of an active lifestyle for optimum growth and development. As clearly documented in the Surgeon General's report on physical activity and health (U.S. Dept. of Health and Human Services 1996), there is an identifiable correlation between the incidence of health disorders and a sedentary lifestyle. According to a later Surgeon General's report (National Center for Chronic Disease Prevention and Health Promotion, 1999), among the many physical and mental problems caused by lack of exercise (including premature mortality), some of the most common injuries are musculoskeletal resulting from excessive activity when the body is not conditioned. Most hospital personnel can affirm that they are extremely busy on holidays when family members engage in games or other sports for which they have not stayed in shape throughout the rest of the year. Clearly, physical exercise is a lifetime commitment, but lifetime participation in physical activity often depends on early participation and gratification gained from such participation. Developing motor skills at an early age provides the tools needed to be physically active throughout life. A teacher's job is to plan for exciting activities in which all children are physically active and in which they want to participate.

Despite the national interest and research supporting the importance of physical activity, the message has not become a primary focus for local school decision makers. In 2006, a national study showed the extremely low number of schools where students participated in daily physical education: 3.8 percent of elementary schools, 7.9 percent of middle and junior high schools, and 2.1 percent of high schools (Lee, Burgeson, Fulton, et al., 2007). The need for physical activity as an integral part of children's lifestyles and their education is indisputable. Participation in physical activity is more important than the concern to train children to compete in sports or pass fitness tests. Programs that focus on activity give all youngsters the opportunity for success and long-term health. Parents and teachers should advocate for children in support of certified physical education teachers and building a healthy school environment.

Consider the following practice question:

During a fitness unit, students were required to keep a daily journal of activity and food consumed. These journal entries could benefit participants by which of the following?

A. Teaching students the importance of daily exercise for all people.
B. Teaching students how to monitor weight gain/loss by diet.
C. Teaching students the importance of diet and exercise as a lifetime commitment to better health.
D. Teaching students that diet is not a primary consideration in maintaining fitness.

The need for regular physical activity and a focus on proper nutrition is essential (*C*). Choice *A* is not correct, because it does not address the nutritional part of the journal. Monitoring weight gain and loss, as in choice *B*, is not meaningful unless children are taught the significance of weight gain and loss. Muscle weighs approximately 2.5 times the amount that fat weighs. As a result, weight gain does not always indicate a problem. If the ratio of percentage of fat to lean body mass (muscle) decreases, we are more fit. This is an important concept for children to understand, but it does not relate to the lesson activity. Choice *D* is incorrect. Diet is an essential component of fitness. It is critical that students are made aware at an early age of the benefits of a lifelong commitment to the combination of physical activity and nutrition (*C*). The answer is *C*.

Movement

The TEKS guidelines in movement relate to skill development and developmentally appropriate activities. In the early years of elementary school, the emphasis is on applying movement concepts and principles to the learning and development of motor skills. Learners are first taught to demonstrate competency in fundamental movement patterns and proficiency in a few specialized movement forms. As children mature, they are expected to demonstrate appropriate use of levels in dynamic movement situations, such as jumping high for a rebound and bending knees and lowering the center of gravity when guarding an opponent. Skill development should also emphasize smooth combinations of fundamental motor skills, such as changing direction quickly when running. Attention should be given to form, power, accuracy, and follow-through in performing movement skills. Controlled balance on a variety of objects such as balance boards, stilts, scooters, and skates are objectives of this standard, as are simple stunts, such as jumping obstacles with proper landings.

Teaching physical skills is related to the psychomotor domain. The **psychomotor domain** consists of the following levels:

1. **Perception.** Sensory cues are used to focus on how to perform a particular skill. The learner pays attention to, notices, recognizes, senses, perceives, or detects important information about the skill.
2. **Set.** Think of "Ready, set, go!" *Set* means that a learner becomes prepared—not only physically, but mentally and emotionally as well—to do a skill. The learner is ready, prepared, and desires to perform the skill.
3. **Guided response.** This is where a learner tries a skill as the instructor observes and coaches. At this level, the learner tries, performs, and practices the skill.
4. **Mechanism.** The learner practices enough to become proficient, improving the technique and performance of the skill.
5. **Complex or overt response.** The learner now excels in the performance of the skill, having become proficient and able to demonstrate mastery of the skill.
6. **Adaptation.** Now, the learner can modify the skill learned to perform new skills and can adapt and adjust a mastered skill.
7. **Origination.** The learner can create new skills that are based on the original skill, yet are completely original. (Bloom & Kratwohl, 1956, cited in Cruickshank, Jenkins, & Metcalf, 2002)

Try this practice question:

Miss Addis understands the importance of her students developing fundamental movement skills for their success in games and activities. Which of the following represents the appropriate sequence for learning the fundamental skill of kicking?

A. Kick a stationary ball; kick a rolling ball while running; kick a rolling ball from a stationary position.

B. Kick a rolling ball while using a running approach; kick a rolling ball while standing; kick a stationary ball; perform a kicking action without the ball.

C. Perform a kicking leg action without a ball; kicking a stationary ball; kicking a rolling ball while standing; kicking a rolling ball while using a running approach.

D. Kick a rolling ball; kick a rolling ball while running; punting.

Choices *A, B,* and *D* present the development of the kicking skill out of sequence. Presenting more advanced skills in the learning process before basic skills are learned can lead to frustration on the part of the learner. Choice *C* is the only choice that presents the correct sequence, because it starts with the simplest movement without the ball and then progresses to a combination of skills with the ball. The answer is *C*.

- **Fundamental skills** are basic movement skills that help children function in the environment. Related to this experience is the opportunity to learn concepts about stability, force, leverage, and other factors related to efficient movement. These *basic* or *fundamental skills* are divided into three categories: locomotor, non-locomotor, and management skills.
- **Locomotor skills** are used to move the body from one place to another or to project the body upward, as in jumping and hopping. Walking, running, galloping, skipping, and sliding are other examples of locomotor skills.
- **Non-locomotor skills** are performed in place, without appreciable spatial movement. These skills are not as well defined as locomotor skills. Included in this category are bending and stretching, pushing and pulling, raising and lowering, and twisting and turning.
- **Body management skills** are an important component of movement competency. Efficient movement demands integration of a number of physical traits, including agility, balance, flexibility, and coordination. A basic understanding of movement concepts and mechanical principles used in skill performance is necessary for quality movement.
- **Specialized motor skills** include manipulative skills (movements that involve an object, such as kicking, throwing, striking), **rhythmic movement skills** (involving motion that possesses regularity and a predictable pattern, such as marching or dancing), and **tumbling skills** (which help develop body management skills without the need for equipment or apparatus, such as cartwheels, forward rolls, and backward rolls). These types of skills also include **game skills** (which contribute to children's total development by allowing them to experience success and accomplishment (such as tagging, dodging, and fleeing) and **sport skills** (learned in the context of application through skills, drills, and lead-up activities, such as free throws, serving a tennis ball, dribbling a soccer ball, punting [kicking] a football or soccer ball, volleying [the return of a ball before it touches the ground in volleyball or tennis]). In developing specialized skills, progression is attained through planned instruction and drills.

The *development of motor skills* follows an orderly sequence. Between the ages of 2 and 6 years, a child develops the fundamental locomotor and non-locomotor skills of running, jumping, leaping, hopping, skipping, sliding, dodging, stopping, swinging, twisting, bending, turning, and stretching. A child also begins to develop the basic manipulative skills of throwing, catching, and striking. Many of these fundamental motor skills are learned prior to kindergarten and, in most instances, through a process of observation and exploration. Early childhood and kindergarten teachers should help children develop awareness of how various parts of the body move separately and together to create coordinated patterns. For example, Mrs. Adams does this through teaching her kindergarten class "The Duck Song," in which children "flap their wings," put their toes in a make-believe pond to test the water, and "fluff their tail feathers."

For children in first and second grades, the continuing development of these fundamental skills should be through a program that emphasizes exploration of movement rather than refinement of skills. This is primarily important when a child is learning the basic manipulative skills of throwing, catching, and striking. Movement skills can be effectively learned through a variety of informal and creative games.

As children move into third and fourth grades, they begin to refine fundamental motor skills and to develop more complex combinations of locomotor, non-locomotor, and manipulative skill patterns. Increased physical size and strength, coupled with improved perceptual and cognitive development, contribute to a child's ability to perform more coordinated movement patterns with greater speed and accuracy.

Grades 5 and 6 should focus on more specific movement skills required of games, dance, and tumbling. In game activities, children learn the ability to move objects (e.g., balls) through a variety of complex game situations. Similarly, dance and tumbling skills become more fluid and creative as the performer acquires greater skill and understanding of the finer aspects of an individual movement or sequence of movements. **Rhythm** is the ability to repeat an action or movement with regularity to a particular rhythmic pattern. It is an essential ingredient of all movement, whether throwing a ball, dodging a player, or dancing a waltz. Rhythmic activities play an essential role in individual development.

Consider the following practice question:

During a lesson for fourth graders on the fundamental movement skill of kicking, Mr. Iglesias organizes his students into groups of three for an activity. The groups determine the optimum place on the ball to impart force for kicking the ball into the air and which part of the foot to use. The groups experiment with different ideas and develop a solution to be compared with other group's solutions. At the end of the lesson, the solutions are written down, read, demonstrated, and discussed.

This activity is appropriate for developing learners' motor skills because it primarily focuses on:

- **A.** refining the mechanics of the skill of kicking.
- **B.** improving the accuracy of the skill.
- **C.** integration of physical activity with science concepts.
- **D.** cooperation and problem solving.

Choice *A* demonstrates a valuable method for teaching refinement of fundamental movement skills. Too often, children are provided repeated opportunities for perfecting skills with little or no emphasis placed on the understanding of correct mechanics. By emphasizing understanding of correct mechanics, learners are more likely to retain their skills and are able to transfer their knowledge and ability to related activities. The answer is *A*.

Let's try another practice question:

Mrs. Huong has taught her class fundamental manipulative movement skills. Which of the following skills would be included in this instruction?

- **A.** Throwing, kicking
- **B.** Turning, twisting
- **C.** Dancing
- **D.** Jumping, sliding

Although turning and twisting (*B*) and jumping and sliding (*D*) are fundamental skills, they are not classified as being fundamental *manipulative* movement skills. Neither is dancing (*C*). The fundamental manipulative skills of throwing, catching, and striking are the foundation of all major individual and team sport activities. These skills involve controlling or manipulating objects (such as a ball) with the hands or feet. The correct answer is *A*.

 Growth and Development

Although the sequence of motor skill development is predictable, the *rate* at which these sequences appear may be quite variable. Each child is unique in that he or she has an individual timetable for developing. This phenomenon relates to a child's readiness to learn new skills, which refers to conditions that make a particular task appropriate to master. Heredity, gender, nutrition, the home environment, and culture all influence the basic developmental sequence. Physical education programs should provide a foundation of psychological and perceptual–motor readiness while allowing the student to take full advantage of his or her present maturational level.

Three development patterns typify the growth of primary-grade children:

1. Generally, development proceeds from the head to the foot (**cephalocaudal**). Coordination and management of body parts occur in the upper body before they are observed in the lower extremities. This is the reason most students can learn to throw before they learn to kick.
2. Development occurs from midline to extremities (**proximodistal**). Children can control their arms before they can control their hands.
3. Development proceeds from general to specific. Children become competent in **gross motor skills** (large body movement) before they develop refined motor patterns (**fine motor skills**).

Sound knowledge of the developmental aspects of motor behavior provides insight as to which educational techniques and intervention procedures to use in skill development. The process of motor development should constantly remind us of the individuality of the learner. Each individual has a unique timetable for the acquisition and development of movement abilities. The EC-6 teacher should maintain records and provide activities that deal with changes in children's development (recording height and weight). Children's records must always be private and are not to be displayed publicly. Teachers should ensure that their activities do not somehow suggest, for example, "taller is better," but that children understand that their bodies grow and change at different rates.

As girls mature earlier than in years past, even elementary teachers must be ready for the event that signals their sexual maturity and the difficulties that can accompany it as a health issue. Girls are often separated for their talk on menstruation in the fourth grade. However, this onset can be very psychologically difficult should it come earlier, and teachers must be ready. Both males and females can be sexually mature by the time they reach the upper grades of this certification level, so it may be necessary for teachers to conduct health discussions on this topic should there be no specialized teacher. The Texas standards in this area make note that students should become aware of the consequences of sexual activity and the benefits of abstinence as they move into puberty. Young girls must also become aware of the relationship between good menstrual health and reproduction, so the part the sexually transmitted diseases (STDs) can play in development for both girls and boys is important in the upper grades of this certification. Teachers should answer questions forthrightly, but with consideration to age-appropriateness. With the onset of puberty and hormonal changes, children may also develop both the need for the quick release of energy and bouts of fatigue. This, along with rapid bone growth, increases the need for movement at this age. Unfortunately, the opposite often occurs; the older the students, the more they are expected to sit for longer periods. Stress may also occur due to the development of secondary sex characteristics such as breast development of girls, and self-esteem may plummet. It may be necessary to discuss hygiene as "tweens" begin to grow underarm hair and experience acne. Teachers can do much to help their children understand these changes and prevent the development of low self-esteem that is often associated with learners going through this developmental period in their lives. Offering good literature that shows children their age in the same light, for example, is helpful for students to see that growth and change of this nature is normal. Maintaining a safe environment in which hurtful comments are not tolerated is another way of helping students through these stages.

Consider the following practice question:

The students in Mrs. Matthews' third-grade class have shown important variations in terms of their overall physical development and their current skill levels. Which principle should Mrs. Matthews follow in developing a physical education program to meet the students' needs in this class?

    A. Plan units with activities that focus on relatively simple and basic objectives that all learners are able to achieve.

    B. Intersperse units requiring only relatively low skill levels with those that require substantially higher skill levels.

    C. Plan units with activities that give all children opportunities to improve their current skill levels.

    D. Minimize the total number of units planned in order to give all children ample time to develop and refine their skills.

Children should be provided opportunities to enhance existing skills (*C*). More advanced students who are not given the opportunity to continue skill development can become bored and frustrated. The resultant behavior is often a lack of interest in activity or development of behavioral problems. This would be a likely result of choice *A*. Choice *B* may cause frustration in both the skilled participants who do not need exposure to basic activities, as well as the unskilled participants who cannot achieve the higher-level skills. Physical education standards recommend that children be exposed to a variety of activities, with the goal of developing proficiency in many and competence in some. As a result, answer *D* is not in compliance with this standard. The correct answer is *C*.

Assessment and Evaluation

There are many kinds of assessment (both formal and informal) and evaluation, but all should be done to improve instruction and increase learning and skills. Ways to assess student learning and skills include the use of checklists, logs, tests, and scoring rubrics. Informal assessments are often done on the spot when a teacher observes and corrects or reinforces a student's performance.

Scoring rubrics are rating scales that list multiple criteria related to a task or motor skill performance. The criteria are performance levels students are expected to achieve. To employ this method of assessment requires accurate knowledge of different stages of acquiring skills so that a child's pattern of development can be observed and categorized. For instance, a child may receive 1 point for simply attempting to kick a ball, 2 points for making contact, 3 points for some control in the correct direction, and so forth.

Observation checklists are another means of gathering meaningful information about children. In this technique, criteria governing proper technique for the movement pattern are listed, and the child's performance is checked against these points. A teacher may want to keep a list of playground behaviors, recording such behaviors as (1) whether the child plays alone or in a group and for how long and how often, (2) the physical level of play (*active:* vigorous, rough and tumble, games with rules, etc.; or *passive:* talking, walking, sitting, waiting, etc.), (3) play with the same or opposite gender, (4) location of the play, and (5) if the play was adult directed or assisted (Daniels, Beaumont, & Doolin, 2002).

Skills checklists incorporate skills listed across the top of a roster in which individual progress is recorded. The value of using this assessment tool is that it allows the instructor to be alerted to students who are in need of special help. Checklists are usually most effective when skills are listed in the sequence in which they should be learned.

Standardized tests are useful in evaluating measurable outcomes. These types of tests have been administered to large samples of children and the results are useful for comparative purposes. The test results, or at least an interpreted summary, can be included in a child's health record and can be part of a periodic progress report to parents. FITNESSGRAM® (Human Kinetics, 2009) is an example of a standardized test.

Technology can not only help children improve skills but also increases the effectiveness of fitness assessment in the physical education classroom. A *heart-rate monitor* may be worn by the child to measure the number of heart beats per minute and used to help students establish their optimum energy output and healthy activity levels. *Pedometers* are worn on the child's hip and measure the number of steps taken when walking. They are inexpensive and thus more prevalent in physical education classes. Pedometers can be set to the individual student's stride to provide feedback on distance covered, calories consumed, and number of steps taken during exercise. The *bioimpedance analyzer (BIA)* is becoming more familiar to physical educators. It provides an estimate of an individual's total percentage of body fat. Protecting the privacy of students should be of the upmost importance and should be considered before using a BIA. The Texas state requirement for fitness testing of all students in grades 3 through 12 brings another realm of technology to the physical education classroom. FITNESSGRAM® (Human Kinetics, 2009) is the tool chosen by the TEA for assessing the students' fitness levels. All data collected must be entered into the FITNESSGRAM® software. This has required many Texas schools to place computers in the physical educator's classroom or office.

It is important to remember how this fitness information is interpreted and used. Enough information must be collected to make a good judgment or recommendation, and the information on development must be communicated to parents or school health officials with proper concern for the child. If a teacher suspects that a child may have some developmental physical problems, he or she should inform the school nurse or the appropriate school personnel.

Consider the following practice question:

How the curriculum is sequenced is important to the learner's sense of success. Which of the following statements best represents a developmentally appropriate sequence?

A. Relays should be introduced to develop skills.
B. Restriction of activities is best, so the student can become competent in one area before progressing to the next level.
C. Lesson units should begin with skill development and modified versions of sport activities such as lead-up games.
D. Games involving cooperation instead of competition should be emphasized so no student experiences failure.

Teaching games such as relays causes students to focus on competition instead of the development of proper skill technique, so choice *A* can be eliminated. Choice *B* is incorrect because the curriculum should be expansive rather than restrictive to allow children to explore many types of movement. Choice *D* is incorrect because it does not address a developmentally appropriate sequence. It also implies children should not experience defeat. This is incorrect because children must learn to cope with unsuccessful experiences. Choice *C* is the correct answer, because it addresses the appropriate sequence for the development of skills. The answer is *C*.

Positive Interactions and Personal Exploration in Physical Education

The TEKS in Physical Education state that students must acquire the knowledge and skills for movements that provide the foundation for enjoyment, continued social development through physical activity, and access to a physically active lifestyle. In elementary school, children learn fundamental movement skills and begin to understand how the muscles, bones, heart, and lungs function in relation to physical activity. Learners also begin to develop a vocabulary for movement and apply concepts dealing with space and body awareness. Learners are engaged in activities that develop basic levels of strength, endurance, and flexibility. In addition, children learn to work safely in groups, interdependently, and in individual movement settings. Team activities should reinforce working together to help all members achieve a goal and identify strengths that each member brings to a team.

When working as a team or in society, rules are necessary. The best strategy for having children understand and obey rules is having them help establish desired guidelines. When children help make the rules, just as in classroom management, they feel more ownership and thus feel more compelled to comply. Occasionally, the teacher may ask children to play a standard well-known game with rules suspended (other than safety) to help them understand the rationale for following rules and maintaining fair play. Students should learn game strategies, rules, and etiquette procedures for simple games and apply safety practices associated with physical activities. Students should be taught to respond appropriately to starting and stopping signals, demonstrate the ability to play within boundaries during games and activities, follow rules, procedures, and safe practices, work in a group setting in cooperation with others, and share space and equipment with others.

Consider the following practice question:

The primary grades at Angelina Elementary School set goals at the beginning of each school year. One of these goals is students working in a group in cooperation with others. Which of the following activities is most likely to be chosen to meet this goal for the early elementary grades?

A. Playing sports (such as volleyball and basketball) to teach the students how to work together as a team.
B. Moving through space using a variety of locomotor skills.
C. Development of individual sports skills (such as a tennis forehand).
D. Performing parachute activities with music.

Team sports and individual sports (*A* and *C*) are not yet appropriate for early elementary. Moving through space with locomotor skills does not involve cooperation with other students. In choice *D*, students cooperate in manipulating the parachute as a group to perform physical activities to music. The correct answer is *D*.

All people want to be skilled and competent in the area of motor performance. The elementary school years are an excellent time to teach motor skills because children have the time and predisposition to learn. The types and range of skills presented in physical education should be as unlimited as possible. Because children vary in genetic endowment and interest, they should have the opportunity to learn about their personal abilities in a variety of skill types. The school years should be the years of opportunity to explore and experience many different types of physical activity. Thus the curriculum should be expansive rather than restrictive. It should allow learners to better understand their strengths and limitations and to learn what types of activities are available in the real world and what activities they prefer.

 # Designing and Implementing Activities

Developmentally based teaching in physical education has received emphasis in recent years. This type of curriculum focuses on several important factors. First, every child passes through a series of developmental stages. For example, in the process of learning how to throw a ball, every child progresses through an initial and somewhat jerky stage, to a more focused second stage, to a final automatic step in which the movement is performed smoothly and effortlessly. A second important factor is that, although the majority of children follow similar sequences of motor development and arrive at developmental points at approximately the same age level, the rate of motor development varies; hence, the rate of development is not age-dependent. Children pass through each developmental stage according to their own levels of maturity and ability rather than according to an exact chronological age or grade level. Although it is impossible for a classroom teacher to completely individualize a program for each child, it is possible to use organizational techniques and teaching strategies to allow children to develop and learn according to their own levels of interest, ability, and previous experience. Social, emotional, cognitive, and psychomotor development must all be understood to achieve developmentally appropriate programs.

Consideration must be given to students with special needs, such as physical and emotional challenges, learning disabilities, sensory difficulties, and language differences. The ARD/IEP committee makes decisions that determine the amount of physical education services an individual with a disability will receive. Although some school districts hire Adapted Physical Education specialists, teachers should be prepared to modify lesson plans and activities to accommodate students with special needs. Teachers must ensure that all children develop the physical, cognitive, and social skills necessary to enjoy physical activity throughout their lifetime. Some examples for adapting physical activities include using a softer, lighter ball; lowering the net or hoop; using a batting tee instead of pitching; reducing the size of the playing area; or using a balloon instead of a volleyball or badminton birdie.

Consider the following practice question:

When scheduling units and activities in physical education, it is most important for a teacher to follow which of the following to ensure a developmentally appropriate program?

A. Activities of greater interest to learners should be alternated with those of lesser interest in order to maintain learners' motivation.

B. Class activities should coincide with the professional sports in season at that time.

C. Activities that are more familiar to learners should be alternated with those that are less familiar to ensure that learners regularly experience success.

D. Activities should build on learners' previous experience and skills and should progress from simpler to more complex.

In presenting activities that build on previous experience and skills (*D*), the teacher is more assured of the developmentally appropriate nature of the activity. Alternating activities according to interest, as suggested in options *A* and *C,* does not relate to the question of developmental appropriateness. Scheduling activities based on seasonal considerations related to professional sports programs (*B*) does not address developmentally appropriate activities. The best option is *D.*

Physical activity offers many opportunities for integrating subject matter and movement. The TEKS from other academic areas can be taught or reinforced through movement games and activities. Many children are kinesthetic learners who need movement in order to learn more quickly. Examples of integrating subject matter with movement include forming letters with the body, creative movement (becoming a seed and moving through the growing process), large floor games, pantomime and charades, and dance. The history of games or dances of different cultures can also be integrated into a lesson. Studying geographic and climatic factors of various areas to see how they affect athletic performance is a natural integration of subject areas. There are endless creative ways of integrating history, language arts, music, number concepts (mathematics), and science in lessons with physical activities.

In addition to integrating with other subject areas, a quality physical education program teaches fitness and skills so learners may develop and practice an active lifestyle. The ability of students to make responsible decisions concerning their level of wellness depends on a wide range of factors, including (1) an understanding of one's feelings and clarification of personal values, (2) an ability to cope with stress and personal problems, (3) an ability to make decisions, and (4) an understanding of the impact of various lifestyles on health.

 # Professional Development

Professional development is a continuous process of improving professional skills and knowledge to advance the performance of students. The importance of continuing professional development for teachers is paramount to maintaining up-to-date lessons and information for instruction. Teachers are a school's most valuable resource, and they should participate in professional development opportunities whenever possible.

Professional development for teachers of physical education should include the most recent information on management, lesson activities, equipment, student assessment, fitness standards, best practices, and state requirements effecting their profession. Teachers involved in the professional organizations for their discipline discover the content of professional meetings is invaluable, as is the networking with other professionals. Two professional organizations for health and physical educators are the Texas Association for Health, Physical Education, Recreation, and Dance (TAHPERD) at www.tahperd.org and the Texas School Health Association (TSHA) at www.txschoolhealth.org.

SUMMARY

This chapter explores the role of health and physical education within the context of the *Generalist* exam. These disciplines are important, because there is an increase in sedentary lifestyles and poor nutritional habits coupled with a decrease in required health education and physical education requirements in Texas schools. A study from the Harvard School of Public Health (2009) determined that smoking, high blood pressure, and obesity are the top three causes of preventable of death in America.

In fact, the CDC (2008a) determined that obesity has reached epidemic levels. The Surgeon General, in concert with the CDC, maintains that a minimum of 30 minutes a day of moderate to vigorous exercise most days of the week will maintain a healthy lifestyle (U.S. Department of Health, 1996). Healthy students are more physically and mentally ready to learn. Although recess has an important role in unstructured play and developing socialization skills in children, physical activity time is not simply an opportunity to provide students with outside time. Health and physical education are essential components of the learning process, and they should be treated accordingly.

REFERENCES

American Academy of Child & Adolescent Psychiatry. (2002). Children of alcoholics. Retrieved October 21, 2009, from http://www.aacap.org/cs/root/facts_for_families/children_of_alcoholics

American Academy of Sleep Medicine. (2007, June 14). Sleep-related breathing disorder common among aggressive, bullying schoolchildren. *Science Daily.* Retrieved Oct. 22, 2009, from http://www.medicalnewstoday.com/articles/74100.php

Bloom, B. S., & Krathwohl, D. R. (1956). *Taxonomy of educational objectives, Handbook I: The cognitive domain.* New York: David McKay Co., Inc.

Brewer, J. A. (2001). *Introduction to early childhood education: Preschool through primary grades* (4th ed.). Boston: Allyn & Bacon.

Castelli, D. M., Hillman, C. H., Buck, S. M., et al. (2007). Physical fitness and academic achievement in third-and fifth grade students. *Journal of Sport and Exercise Psychology, 29,* 239–252.

Centers for Disease Control and Prevention. (2008a). *State of the CDC, 2008. Partnering for a healthy world.* Atlanta: Author.

Centers for Disease Control and Prevention. (2008b). CDC Childhood Injury Report. Retrieved August 25, 2009, from http://www.cdc.gov/SafeChild/ChildhoodInjuryReport/index.html

Centers for Disease Control and Prevention. (2009). Body mass index measurement in schools. Retrieved October 17, 2009 from http://www.cdc.gov/healthyyouth/obesity/bmi

Children with Diabetes. (2005). Type II diabetes in children. Retrieved Oct. 22, 2009, from http://www.childrenwithdiabetes.com/d_0n_d00.htm#

Chomitz, V. R., Slining, M. M., McGowan, R. J., et al. (2008). Is there a relationship between physical fitness and academic achievement? Positive results from public school children in the northeastern United States. *Journal of School Health, 79*(1), 30–37.

Cole, M., & Cole, S. R. (1996). *The development of children* (3rd ed.). New York: W. H. Freeman & Company.

Daniels, D., Beaumont, L., & Doolin, C. (2002). *Understanding children: An interview and observation guide for educators.* Boston: McGraw-Hill.

Education World. (2009). Those Tear-Me-Apart, Put-Me-Back-Together, Never-Be-the-Same-Again Blues. Retrieved October 16, 2009, from http://www.educationworld.com/a_lesson/03/lp294-03.shtml

Eggen, P., & Kauchak, D. (2001). *Education psychology: Windows on classrooms* (6th ed.). Upper Saddle River, NJ: Merrill Prentice-Hall.

Goleman, D. (1995). *Emotional intelligence.* New York: Bantam Books.

Gang Reduction through Intervention, Prevention, and Education. (n.d.). GRIPE. Retrieved October 21, 2009, from http://www.gripe4rkids.org

Grissom, J. B. (2005). Physical fitness and academic achievement. *Journal of Exercise Physiology, 8*(1), 11–25.

Harvard School of Public Health. (2009). Smoking, high blood pressure and being overweight top three preventable causes of death in the U.S. Retrieved August 30, 2009, from http://www.hsph.harvard.edu/news/press-releases/2009-releases/smoking-high-blood-pressure-overweight-preventable-causes-death-us

Hoelscher, D. M., Feldman, H. A., Johnson, C. C., et al. (2004). School-based health education programs can be maintained over time: Results from the CATCH institutionalization study. *Preventive Medicine. 38,* 594–606.

Human Kinetics, Inc. (2009). FITNESSGRAM®. Champaign, IL: Author.

Lee, S. M., Burgeson, C. R., Fulton, J. E., et al. (2007). Physical education and physical activity: Results from the school health policies and programs study 2006. *Journal of School Health, 77*(8), 435–463.

Kagan, S. (1992). *Cooperative learning.* San Juan Capistrano: Resources for Teachers, Inc.

Kortz, W. J., Nath, J. L., & Parker Braselton, M. (2011). Technology for Texas teachers. In J. L. Nath & M. D. Cohen (Eds.), *Becoming an EC-6 teacher in Texas* (pp. 347–387). Belmont, CA: Cengage.

National Center for Chronic Disease Prevention and Health Promotion. (1999). Physical activity and health: A report of the surgeon general. Retrieved October 21, 2009, from http://www.cdc.gov/nccdphp/sgr/summ.htm

National Institute of Mental Health. (2007). Study tracks prevenlence of eating disorders. Retrieved July 25, 2009, from http://www.nimh.nih.gov/sciencenews/2007/study-tracks-prevalence-ofeating-disorders.shtm

Rackley, R., & Knight, S. (2011). Understanding development in children in grades EC-6. In J. L. Nath & M. D. Cohen (Eds.), *Becoming an EC-6 teacher in Texas* (pp. 1–42). Belmont, CA: Cengage.

Ratey, J. J. (2008). *Spark.* New York: Little, Brown and Company.

Texas Association for Health, Physical Education, Recreation, and Dance. (2007). *Health Education TEKS: A guide for teachers grades K–5.* Austin, Texas.

Texas Education Agency. (2008). Texas youth evaluation project. Austin: Author.

Texas Education Agency. (2009). *TExES: Texas examination of educator standards preparation manual, 191 Generalist EC-6.* Retrieved August 23, 2009, from http://www.texes.ets.org/assets/pdf/testprep_manuals/191_generalist_ec_6.pdf

U.S. Department of Health and Human Services. (1996). *Physical activity and health: A report of the Surgeon General.* Washington, D.C.: Author.

U.S. Department of Health and Human Services. (2010). Healthy People 2010. Retrieved August 29, 2009, at http://www.healthypeople.gov

Winchester, D. (2009). Cyberbullying on the rise. Retrieved March 9, 2009, from http://www.tampabay.com/news/education/k12/article980638.ece

SUGGESTED READINGS AND INTERNET RESOURCES

American Academy of Pediatrics. (1991). *Sports medicine: Health care for young athletes.* Elk Grove Village, IL: Author.

Inspaugh, D. J., & Ezell, G. (2001). *Teaching today's health.* Boston: Allyn & Bacon.

Gabbard, C., Leblanc, E., & Lowy, S. (1987). *Physical education for children.* Englewood Cliffs, NJ: Prentice-Hall.

Gallahue, D. L. (1987). *Developmental physical education for today's elementary school children.* New York: Macmillan.

Gill, E. (2007). A supersize problem. *Education Update, 49*(1). Retrieved May 3, 2010, from http://www.ascd.org/publications/newsletters/education_update/jan07/vol49/num01/A_Supersize_Problem.aspx

Gordon, A., & Brown, K. W. (1996). *Guiding young children in a diverse society.* Boston: Allyn & Bacon.

Graham, G., Holt-Hale, S. A., & Parker, M. (1993). *Children moving.* Mountain View, CA: Mayfield.

Hellison, D. (2003). *Teaching responsibility through physical activity.* Champaign, IL: Human Kinetics.

Landy, J. M., & Burridge, K. R. (1999). *Fundamental motor skills and movement activities for young children.* West Nyack, NY: The Center for Applied Research in Education.

Mosston, M., & Ashworth, S. (1994). *Teaching physical education* (4th ed.). New York: Macmillan.

National Center for Chronic Disease Prevention and Health. (2000). The school health policies and program study (SHPPS). Retrieved May 11, 2007, from http://www.cdc.gov/healthyYouth/shpps/overview/index.htm or http://www.cdc.gov/HealthyYouth/index.htm

Nichols, B. (1986). *Moving and learning—The elementary school physical education experience.* St. Louis: Times Mirror/Mosby.

Pangrazi, R. P. (2001a). *Dynamic physical education for elementary school children* (13th ed.). Boston: Allyn & Bacon.

Pangrazi, R.P. (2001b). *Lesson plans for dynamic physical education for elementary school students* (13th ed.). Boston: Allyn & Bacon.

Pangrazi, R. P., & Hastad, D. N. (1989). *Fitness in the elementary schools* (2nd ed.). Reston, VA: AAHPERD.

PE Central. http://www.pecentral.org

President's Council on Physical Fitness and Sports. (1991). *Get fit! A handbook for youth ages 6–17.* Washington, D.C.: President's Council on Physical Fitness and Sports.

Rink, J. E. (1993). *Teaching physical education for learning* (2nd ed.). St. Louis: Mosby.

Rothlein, L. (1989). Nutrition tips revisited: On a daily basis do we implement what we know? *Young Children, 44,* 30–36.

Schmidt, R. A. (1991). *Motor learning and performance: From principles to practice.* Champaign, IL: Human Kinetics.

Texas Association for Health, Physical Education, Recreation, and Dance. http://www.tahperd.org

Texas Education Agency: http://ritter.tea.state.tx.us/curriculum/hpe

Texas Health Science Technology. http://www.texasshste.com/classroom_resources

U.S. Department of Health and Human Services. (1996). *Physical activity and health: A report of the Surgeon General.* Atlanta: Author.

A HEALTH LESSON PLAN

Title: The Human Heart

Grade Level: Kindergarten

Main Subject Area: Health

Integrated Subjects: Science, Music

Time Frame/Constraints: One period

Overall Goal(s): For children to understand where the heart is located in the body and that it works harder and healthier with exercise.

TEKS OBJECTIVES:

§ 115.2. **Health Education** (b) Knowledge and skills; (1) Health behaviors. The student recognizes that personal health decisions and behaviors affect health throughout life. The student is expected to: (C) identify types of exercise and active play that are good for the body; (4) Health information. The student knows the basic structures and functions of the human body and how they relate to personal health. The student is expected to: (B) name major body parts and their functions;

§ 112.2. **Science** (b) Knowledge and skills; (2) Scientific processes. The student develops abilities necessary to do scientific inquiry in the field and the classroom. The student is expected to: (C) gather information using simple equipment and tools to extend the senses;

(D) construct reasonable explanations using information; and (E) communicate findings about simple investigations;

§ 117.3. **Fine Arts, Kindergarten Music** (b) Knowledge and skills; (1) Perception. The student describes and analyzes musical sound and demonstrates musical artistry; (2) Creative expression/performance. The student performs a varied repertoire of music. The student is expected to: (A) sing or play classroom instruments independently or in a group; and (4) Response/evaluation. The student responds to and evaluates music and musical performance. The student is expected to: (A) identify steady beat in musical performances; and (B) identify higher/lower, louder/softer, faster/slower, and same/different in musical performances.

LESSON OBJECTIVES:

- Students will complete a picture of what they believe a real human heart looks like.
- Students, in a center, will listen to and describe their heartbeats at rest and after physical activity.
- Students, in a center, will construct a stethoscope.
- Students, in a center, will correctly place a magnetic heart on a body form.
- Students will sing "The Heartbeat Song."
- Students will each draw their own bodies with the heart in the correct area of the body.

Readiness Skills or Knowledge Needed: Students should know what a muscle is.

Sponge Activity: Students draw a quick picture of what they think a real human heart looks like.

Environmental Concerns: This lesson is structured as mostly a center activity designed for small groups of two or three children to experience their own normal heartbeat/pulse during rest and during physical activity.

Center Set-up: The center should be set up on a table on the perimeter of the classroom. A free-standing, tri-fold poster board is used to display titles, images, instructions, and safety rules. Instructions supplemented by drawings or digital pictures should be displayed and labeled. The human figure drawing should be mounted where children can easily reach the heart area.

Focus or Set Induction: As a whole class, the teacher tells students, "Everyone clench your fist. This is about the size of your heart. Now clench your fist and unclench it until your hand feels tired. Let's keep doing that as long as you can. This is about what the heart does to pump blood through our bodies. How many times do you think it does that in a lifetime? About 3 billion

times! Do you think it could get tired? That's why it has to stay a very fit muscle!" (If a large transparent container is available, the teacher can also fill it with water and show how clenching one's fist quickly in the water can push water out the top of the fist [or use two hands]).

Rationale(s): Teacher tells students, "Your heart is a muscle that works every minute of the day and night. Everyone make your arm muscle bulge. Feel that muscle? Is it strong? What do people do to make their muscles strong? They go to the gym to lift weights or exercise. Because our heart is also a muscle, we can make it stronger with exercise so that it will be strong for a lifetime. How can you make it stronger, do you think? With exercise—that is correct! Today in the Heart Center you will discover how you know that your heart is getting exercised."

MAKING CONNECTIONS:

1. **Connections to Past or Future Learning:** Have you ever run or exercised so much that you can feel your heart beating very hard in your chest? Has a doctor or nurse ever taken your pulse? How did they do that?
2. **Connections to the Community:** Do people sometimes have trouble with their hearts? Where do they go if that happens? Talk about the local doctors, specialized doctors for hearts, or the hospital in the community.
3. **Connections to Culture:** Ask students if they know a time when we think of the heart in other ways (Valentine's Day). "What is the symbol of Valentine's Day?" "Why do you think we use the heart as a symbol for love?" (The heart can also beat faster with high emotions.)
4. **Connections to Student Interests & Experiences:** "Have you ever been very scared? What happens to your heart then? Do we have sayings about the heart when it beats fast?" ("My heart skipped a beat!" "It made my heart race!" "My heart leaped to my throat!" "My heart is beating out of my chest!")

Materials: (1) Inexpensive stethoscope (available at teacher supply stores); (2) stethoscope model consisting of two small funnels and about 25–30 inches of clear, $3/8$-in. diameter plastic tubing (diameter depends on the funnel tube size); (3) outline of a human figure (about the size of a small child) with a small magnet glued to the back side at the chest location of the heart with several X's marked on the front side of the figure; (4) small laminated human heart image with a small magnet glued to the back; (5) a variety of art supplies, including long sheets of paper; (6) illustrations of tasks; (7) diagram of body with heart shown in correct location; (8) a kitchen timer; and (9) disinfecting wipes for stethoscope ear pieces.

Activities: *Guided Practice:* The teacher will model each of the following activities to be conducted independently by the children in the Health Center: listening to a normal pulse with a stethoscope, listening to a pulse after physical activity, constructing a model stethoscope, and placing a heart image on a human outline.

Activity 1: *Normal Pulse Instructions:* Carefully place the stethoscope ear pieces in your ears. Place the small round end of the stethoscope on your neck just under your ear. Stand or sit quietly and listen. What do you hear? Describe the sound to your group. Repeat by placing the round end of the stethoscope on your wrist near the palm of your hand. What do you hear? Tell your group what you hear. (**Note:** Drawings or photographs about where to place the stethoscope are very useful to help students complete the tasks after modeling.)

Activity 2: *Activity Pulse Instructions:* Set your kitchen timer for two minutes. Walk in place for two minutes or sit down in a chair and get up 10 times in a row or until your timer goes off. Listen to your pulse again. What do you hear? Describe what you hear to your group. How is the pulse after standing and sitting (exercising) different from the normal pulse? Do the same by setting the timer for one minute and running in place.

Activity 3: *Making a Stethoscope:* Use the tube to connect the ends of the small funnels. Place the big, open end of one funnel over your ear. Place the other end on your wrist near your palm. What do you hear? How does this model work? (A diagram for this project should be available.)

Activity 4: Where Is the Heart? Use the small heart image and place it near the X on the human form drawing (where you believe the heart is). Each group member shows the others on their own body. (Students should check the body diagram that is placed in the center to be sure they are correct.)

Independent Practice: Students will complete an art project using the materials of their choice to draw a heart on their body forms. The heart must be located in the correct general area.

Assessment: Participation in each activity (checklist). The heart on the student's drawing of his or her body must be located in the correct area.

What Will Students Do Who Finish Early? Bookmark a Web site where a real heart can be heard. Have children listen. If a computer is not available, tape a real heart beat and have children listen.

Closure: Review major heart concepts: (1) the heart is a muscle; (2) the heart muscle squeezes to pump blood; (3) the heart pumping sound is the pulse; (4) activity increases the pulse rate; (5) the heart is in the human chest; and (6) exercise makes a stronger heart muscle. After all children have rotated through the Heart Center, children in a whole group will sing the "Heart Beat Song" (sung to the tune of "Frère Jacques").

Begin very slowly and speed up with each verse; put hand over heart and pat chest to the beat of the booms in the last verses; also have children do motions (like sleeping), then moving in place.

"The Heart Beat Song"

Hear my heart beat; hear my heart beat. Tick . . . tick . . . tick! Tick . . . tick . . . tick! (or can make ticking sound).

When I'm sleeping soundly, when I'm sleeping soundly, Tick . . . tick . . . tick! Tick . . . tick . . . tick! (or can make ticking sound).

(Sung a little faster).

Hear my heart beat; hear my heart beat. Tick, tick, tick! Tick, tick, tick! (or make ticking sound).

When I'm walking slowly, when I'm walking slowly. Tick, tick, tick! Tick, tick, tick! (or make ticking sound)

(Sung moderately fast)

Hear my heart beat, hear my heart beat. Boom, boom, boom! Boom, boom, boom!

When I'm skipping faster, when I'm skipping faster. Boom, boom, boom! Boom, boom, boom!

(Sung very fast)

Hear my heart beat, hear my heart beat. Boom, boom, boom! Boom, boom, boom!

When I'm running faster, when I'm running faster. Boom, boom, boom! Boom, boom, boom!

Ask children if this song has a steady beat. How is that like a heart beat? Did the song beat go slower and faster? How is that like a heart beat?

Ask students what the heart is (a muscle). Ask children to point to where their own hearts are in their bodies.

Modification for Students with Special Needs: Karla, in a wheelchair, will move her arms rapidly instead of running and standing/sitting.

Reflection: To be addressed after teaching the lesson.

DRAFT YOUR OWN HEALTH OR PHYSICAL EDUCATION LESSON PLAN

Title of Lesson: _____

Grade Level: _____

Main Subject Area: _____

Integrated Subjects : _____

Time Frame/Constraints: _____

Overall Goal(s): _____

TEKS Objectives: _____

_____

_____

Lesson Objectives: _____

_____

_____

Readiness Skills or Knowledge Needed: _____

_____

_____

Sponge Activity: _____

_____

_____

Environmental Concerns: _____

_____

_____

Rationale(s): _____

_____

_____

Focus or Set Induction: _____

_____

_____

Making Connections:

1. Connections to Past or Future Learning: _____

_____

2. Connections to the Community: _____

_____

3. Cultural Connections: _____

_____

4. Connections to Student Interests & Experiences: _____

_____

Materials: _____

_____

_____

Activities: Guided practice: _____

_____

_____

_____

_____

_____

_____

_____

_____

_____

Independent practice: _____

_____

_____

_____

_____

_____

_____

_____

_____

_____

_____

Assessment: _____

_____

_____

What will students do who finish early? _____

_____

_____

Closure: _____

_____

_____

Modification for Students with Special Needs: _____

_____

_____

Reflection: _____

_____

_____

OBSERVING HEALTH OR PHYSICAL EDUCATION EXPERIENCES/ACTIVITIES

During your visit to an EC-6 classroom, use the following form to provide feedback, as well as to reflectively analyze the room, the materials, and the teaching.

The Classroom Environment	Observed	Not Observed	Response
1. Movement is a daily part of the classroom.			If so, describe. If not, what types of movement could easily and logically be added?
2. Safety is discussed when movement is a part of the lesson.			If so, describe. If not, what was or what could have been the result?
3. If games are a part of the lesson, all children are included.			If so, describe. If not, how could each child be included?
4. All movements are developmentally appropriate.			If so, describe. If not, explain why not.
5. Alternative movements are provided for children with special needs (if applicable).			If so, describe. If not, what could be added?
6. Movement is integrated in other content areas.			If so, describe. If not, what could be added?
7. Movement is used as a way to invigorate a class after a long period of study.			If so, describe. If not, describe when and how movement could be useful.
8. If there is no PE specialist, structured PE is provided by the regular classroom teacher (or if there is extra time needed for PE the regular classroom teacher provides it).			If so, what types of activities are provided? If not, what type of activities would be appropriate?
9. A variety of equipment is available for children at different times.			If so, describe. If not, what equipment would be appropriate?
10. Ample space allows children and adults to move around freely during movement activities.			If not, how could the area be rearranged?
11. Movement is appropriately assessed.			If so, describe. If not, what would be appropriate?
12. Health issues are mentioned during the day (cleaning hands, using a tissue, discussing sun safety, etc.).			If so, describe. If not, what could be added?
13. Healthy behaviors are noted by the teacher and rewarded in some manner.			If so, describe. If not, give ideas for what could be added.
14. There is a Health Center of some type in the classroom.			If so, describe. If not, give ideas for what could be added.
15. Health is integrated into other content areas.			If so, describe. If not, give ideas for what could be added.
16. The room is designed to help prevent transmission of illness (area for washing hands or hand wipes provided).			If so, describe. If not, give ideas for what could be changed or added.

The Classroom Environment	Observed	Not Observed	Response
17. The teacher ensures that the room and classroom equipment are sanitized often to prevent the transmission of illness.			If so, describe. If not, how can this be implemented?
18. When children are offered snacks or rewards in the classroom, healthy foods and drinks are used.			If so, describe. If not, what could be offered?
19. Children are encouraged to think at upper levels about health issues.			If observed, describe. If not, describe how this could be encouraged.
20. Health issues are discussed in a respectful way.			If so, describe. If not, suggest how this could change.
21. Health issues are discussed in a developmentally appropriate way.			If so, explain. If not, explain why not.
22. The teacher is a good model of healthy behaviors.			If so, describe. If not, how could this improve?
23. The issue of good mental health is addressed during the day (stress, emotions, peer pressure, etc.).			If so, describe. If not, describe instances where this could easily be addressed.
24. The teacher practices universal precautions with health issues (has gloves for incidents with body fluids, washes hands, etc.).			If so, describe. If not, how should this change?
25. Technology is used with health.			If so, describe. If not, what technological elements could be added?
26. Health is taught as a lesson that follows a structured lesson plan.			If so, describe. If not, how could this be accomplished?
27. Health learning is assessed in an appropriate way.			If so, describe. If not, how could this be accomplished?

TEST YOURSELF ON HEALTH AND PHYSICAL EDUCATION

1. As part of physical development, Mrs. Graham has her second-grade students get with a partner and toss and catch a medium-sized ball. When it is Kayla's turn to receive the ball, she closes her eyes, flinches, and turns her shoulder to the ball. Mrs. Graham should:
   A. allow Kayla to sit out because it is obvious that Kayla is afraid in this game.
   B. call Kayla's parents to set up a conference about Kayla's physical development.
   C. have Kayla's partner move close enough to her that Kayla can catch the ball without flinching.
   D. use a smaller ball and encourage Kayla to watch the ball and catch with her hands alone.

2. Mrs. Rutledge has taught her 3rd grade level students the importance of cardiorespiratory endurance. She regularly takes her students to the school track to practice aerobic activities. She understands the importance of individual differences and developmental levels. Which of the following is the best method for arranging an activity session designed to improve cardiorespiratory endurance?
   A. All students run two laps around the track.
   B. All students run/walk for 20 minutes around the track.
   C. All students run for 5 minutes and then measure their heart rate.
   D. All students participate in a soccer scrimmage.

3. Mr. McNeil wants to incorporate physical activity into his mathematics lesson to teach his second-grade students the difference between two-dimensional and three-dimensional objects. Which of the following activities are best to use?
   A. Have students work in groups of four to use their bodies to create various geometric shapes.
   B. Have students toss round bean bags into cones held by a partner.
   C. Have students stand in a circle and bounce a ball to someone on the opposite side of the circle.
   D. Have students complete a worksheet in which they make a list of items that are square and items that are cubes.

4. Although Mr. Herrera is not the physical education teacher, he sometimes works at recess with his students on the basic movement skills of catching, kicking, and striking. All three of these skills include:
   A. keeping the arms slightly bent at the elbow.
   B. relaxing through the movement.
   C. focusing on the ball to ensure contact.
   D. a weight shift toward the object.

5. Mrs. Li has her children go through a short obstacle course that she designed in her classroom. One part of the course asks them to imagine that they are "walking over a tree branch that is over a stream." This part of the course is a simple line of duct tape on the floor. She is giving children an opportunity to improve their:
   A. agility.
   B. flexibility.
   C. balance.
   D. endurance.

6. The best complex carbohydrate(s), or food(s) that provides energy, is/are:
   A. sugar.
   B. fruits and vegetables.
   C. pasta, wholegrain breads, and grains.
   D. dairy foods.

7. Mr. Getty has his students move through space within the boundaries he established on the playground. The students perform locomotor skills for a period of 3 minutes. When the teacher calls out a new locomotor skill, the students change their movements while moving continuously. This exercise is mostly related to:
   A. balance.
   B. strength.
   C. aerobics.
   D. diastolic/systolic.

8. Ms. Ferguson divides her class into groups of five. She instructs each group to develop a 2–3 minute skit that begins with four students pressuring another student to smoke a cigarette. The students must develop an ending that promotes healthy behavior and perform the skit to the class. The most likely objective of this lesson is to:
   A. explain how to be a good friend.
   B. demonstrate refusal skills.
   C. demonstrate respectful communication.
   D. identify the common diseases and their symptoms of long-term smoking.

9. Mr. Jackson asks his students to look through magazines and newspapers and

cut out an advertisement that relates to health. The students must describe the advertisement to the class and explain if the advertisement is a positive or negative health influence. What is the main objective of this lesson?
A. To explain the influence of peer pressure on individual health decisions
B. To describe the importance of being a positive role model for health
C. To describe how the media can influence knowledge and health behaviors
D. To demonstrate effective listening skills

10. Ms. Richards is presenting a lesson on the interrelatedness of body systems. She explains that the lungs absorb oxygen, which is picked up by the red blood cells. The blood cells are pumped to all parts of the body. Which two body systems is she describing?
A. The circulatory system and respiratory system
B. The respiratory system and digestive system
C. The circulatory system and musculoskeletal system
D. The musculoskeletal system and digestive system

TEST YOURSELF ANSWERS AND RATIONALES FOR HEALTH AND PHYSICAL EDUCATION

Answer 1: Children develop physical skills at individual rates (C). Kayla is in the first stage of learning to catch, exhibited by her protective behavior when she is thrown a ball. In the next stage, Kayla will try to catch the ball using her whole body and then progress to using her hands with her arms. Finally, she will catch with only her hands. Choices A and B show that the teacher is unaware of these stages of development. Choice D makes her skip though the natural progression of development in this skill. The correct answer is C.

Answer 2: Choice B is a better activity than choice A because structuring the activity by time instead of distance allows all students to be successful, regardless of individual differences. Choice C is not correct because 5 minutes of activity is not enough time to improve cardiorespiratory endurance. Choice D is not correct because soccer is not an aerobic activity due to the many stops and starts in the game. The answer is B.

Answer 3: Choice A is correct because it is the only answer in which the students physically explore a variety of two- and three-dimensional shapes. By having students create the shapes with their bodies, the students enhance and reinforce the concept of two- and three-dimensional shapes. Answer D is not correct because it does not involve movement. The answer is A.

Answer 4: The most important element each of these skills has in common is that students must track the ball visually to ensure success. The answer is C.

Answer 5: Agility (A) refers to being able to change one's position easily. Flexibility (B) refers to how much range of motion one has in his/her joints. Endurance (D) refers to how long one's muscles are able to work/contract. In this case, Mrs. Li is asking students to work safely on their equilibrium as they pretend they are balancing along the line. The answer is C.

Answer 6: Although sugars can provide energy, they are called simple carbohydrates and are not the best source. It is pasta, wholegrain breads, and grains such as oats that are the complex carbohydrates and the best choice for fuel food. The answer is C.

Answer 7: Balance (A) is related to maintaining equilibrium and is not related to the purpose of this activity. Strength (B) refers to how much force muscles are able to put forth. Choice D, systolic (contraction) and diastolic (relaxation), refers to measuring of one's blood pressure (as in 140 [systolic] over 90 [diastolic]). Aerobics (C) involve the body in a total active workout to increase the intake of oxygen. The answer is C

Answer 8: Choices A and C are incorrect because children must be taught when they are placed in an unsafe or unhealthy situation by peers, they do not have to be polite or respectful. Choice D is incorrect because the focus of the question is not about the harmful effects of tobacco but about how to resist peer pressure in an unhealthy situation. The correct answer is B.

Answer 9: Students must be able to evaluate if a media message is a positive or negative influence on their health. Answers A, B, and D do not relate to media oriented influences. The correct answer is C.

Answer 10: The lungs are part of the respiratory system and absorb oxygen. The circulatory system of blood vessels, blood cells, and heart muscle pick up the oxygen and transports it to other body structures. The digestive system is involved in the breakdown of food and absorption of nutrients. The musculoskeletal system provides support and movement for the body. The correct answer is A.

9 Preparing to Teach Theatre Arts in Texas

Kathryn L. Jenkins
University of Houston–Downtown

Janice L. Nath
University of Houston–Downtown

Joyce M. Dutcher
University of Houston–Downtown

The *Generalist* examination specifically asks teachers to be knowledgeable about the Fine Arts for music and art. There is, however, an interesting discrepancy between the *Generalist* exam and the Texas curriculum prescribed by the Texas Essential Knowledge and Skills (the TEKS), which all teachers in Texas are required to provide for their students. The Fine Arts TEKS for students (Texas Administrative Code, 2010) present requirements for each grade level in music, art, and the theatre arts, but there are no specific competencies for theatre arts on the *Generalist* examination for teachers. Nevertheless, the TExES competencies clearly state that teachers must be aware of the TEKS for each content area and grade level. Therefore, we have elected to include a chapter on theatre arts based upon this statement about the TEKS and because information in this chapter may also be embedded in both the competencies and questions on the *Generalist* in other content areas. We also decisively believe that the use of theatre arts for children creates positive and enriching learning experiences throughout the curriculum.

If you have already studied for the TExES *Pedagogy and Professional Responsibilities (PPR)*, you undoubtedly remember learning about dramatic **play** and its benefits for young children. This chapter reminds you of those benefits and informs you about other information for the theatre arts TEKS with the hope that you will see the value of providing quality opportunities for children—not only for dramatic play but also by engaging students often in informal and formalized theatre arts activities. This chapter also shows you how to integrate theatre arts into other content areas in ways that make your classroom an exciting place for children to learn. In addition, this chapter provides you with more questions to help you practice for the *Generalist* exam.

What Are Theatre Arts Experiences?

There are two main types of experiences that EC-6 teachers provide within the realm of theatre arts for children—dramatic play and drama activities. **Dramatic play** refers to situations in which the child freely initiates role-play from either the real world or from pretend/make-believe. *Play* is the key word for this concept, and as soon as young children develop the ability to pretend, they are ready to engage in dramatic play (Wortham, 2006). This is particularly important for the early grades, because much of a young childhood teacher's work is spent facilitating, encouraging, and assessing various types of children's developmental play, including dramatic play. *Drama activities* refer to both **structured drama** that requires student participation in set, directed ways (scripted plays, skits, etc.) and other **creative drama experiences** where children are involved in creative activities related to drama. These include such activities as creating improvisational stories or situations, having children write their own plays, or participating in the integrated arts (such as creating costumes, using puppets or masks, designing sets, and setting drama to music).

Dramatic Play

Teachers of younger children clearly understand how important the **process** of dramatic play is for child development. The process of engaging in play can involve children's negotiation of roles, the development of rules, the location or creation of props, and so forth. Teachers have a direct influence on the quality of this developmental area in a number of ways. Knowledgeable teachers provide time and a positive environment for children to engage in the process of dramatic play—both individually and cooperatively. Teachers also encourage specific types of dramatic play for young children by providing certain props in a particular area or **center**. For example, a teacher may "set the stage" in a Home Improvement Center to encourage children to role-play those tasks commonly found in and around their homes. Props such as tools in a tool box, pretend cleaning supplies, gardening equipment, and related dress-up clothes encourage roles in yard work, cleaning, building, repairing, and so forth. Many types of centers have specific purposes for developing content areas through dramatic play. For example, a Grocery Store Center offers mathematical concepts, such as sorting, measuring, and counting, as children role-play customers and sales persons. A Transportation Center, with various land vehicles, airplanes, and boats, offers science and social studies concepts, such as classifying and community job roles; whereas a Pet Center helps children delve into various science concepts, such as living and nonliving things and social development in the areas of caring and responsibility. An enriched indoor (and outdoor) environment is essential for the young child to engage in many types of exploration of roles in play. Centers should also include a number of costumes and other types of props related to the type of center it is. These need not be complete costumes or absolutely realistic props, especially if funds are short. Hats, vests, a lab coat, or other simple items can suggest a wealth of characters (McCaslin, 2006), can spark children to use their imaginations, and can expand children's exploration of various roles—especially those of adults.

Sustaining and extending activity is also important to dramatic play; thus, teachers may observe children's interest and follow up with materials that prolong and enrich a play theme appropriately. For example, Mrs. Kelly notices that Hanna and Miguel, who are in the Home Center, are pretending that their baby brother is hurt. Mrs. Kelly chooses that time to introduce a medical kit with bandages and other home medical props to the center. She also asks those children who are in the Clinic Center to join in helping with Hanna and Miguel's "baby brother." Later, Mrs. Kelly sees children in the Home Improvement Center pretending to plant flowers in their garden. To expand interest in both centers, she makes a note to bring some seeds and plants the following day to "sell" at the Store Center so that children can purchase and plant them in the outside play area. Remember that although the teacher can encourage certain types and ways of dramatic role-taking, it is important for this play be the choice of the child. Although third- through sixth-grade classrooms often design and implement centers with a different approach (tending to be less open play–based and more directed play–based), they may integrate theatre arts into varied centers, such as pretending in the science center to be inventors or working in groups to dramatize science functions (the digestive system, etc.). They may also participate in the Social Studies Center or Language Arts Center by putting together costumes for famous historians or books they read. They may still be encouraged in the similar type of dramatic play as the younger elementary children with skit starters, costume boxes, and open-ended materials that are age appropriate in centers or stations that are theme based or content based.

Drama Activities

Teachers may also provide opportunities in theatre arts through structured or **scripted dramas** or many other types of dramatic activities. These experiences come in varied formats such as unison **movements** to poems, songs, skits, and plays. Miss Chen, for instance, teaches her Pre-K students a choral poem about "Five Little Pumpkins" with motions and voice inflections. Ms. Herrera asks children to use felt board characters to retell a story in her kindergarten class, as children use character voices in the retelling. Mrs. Fenten has her second graders use puppets to problem solve a situation in which two animals are arguing over the same toy. Later, she has them pretend to be butterflies and act out the metamorphosis of the butterfly. Mr. Irving assigned his third-grade class the roles of characters in reenactments of stories to help reinforce children's abilities to develop sequencing skills in more exciting ways. Mrs. Mitchell's fourth-grade class puts on an entire play written for children by professionals (including both singing and dramatic speaking parts) for a Parent–Teacher Organization (PTO) meeting. In their science class, they act out the stages of the human circulatory system. Mr. Simms's fifth-grade social studies class is studying about propaganda. He divides students into groups to write and present an advertisement skit using each type. Finally, in Mrs. McIntosh's sixth grade, students write the screenplay for a short book they are reading and film the results. In many of these types of structured experiences, children must take on specific assigned characters, movements, or situations with varying degrees of freedom on how much they are allowed to improvise or vary from a script. Children may also be involved in a number of other dramatic experiences. For instance, Ms. Claire tells children the *Legend of the Bluebonnet,* and afterward, children write their own short skits that follow the story line. Miss Arwen's class helps build a puppet theatre, and Mrs. Mitchell's class also designs and constructs sets for their fourth-grade play.

Let's try a question:

As a recently hired first-grade teacher, Miss Loya, was asked by several teachers who had been teaching for some years why she integrates theatre arts activities into her lessons. Which statement least supports the incorporation of these activities into other lessons?

A. These activities address various modalities and multiple intelligences.
B. These activities help less exciting lessons become more motivating.
C. These activities promote creativity and critical thinking skills.
D. These integrated activities help in completing the required time set by the state for many of her content areas.

All of these choices are valid to some extent. There are several multiple intelligences and modalities integrated by including various types of theatre arts activities—particularly linguistic, spatial, interpersonal, and bodily kinesthetic (A). Lessons certainly become more exciting for children (and, thus, more motivating) when theatre arts activities are offered (B). Many of the theatre arts activities (particularly dramatic role-play) involve problem solving, creativity, and critical thinking (C). Even choice D is somewhat true, but it is the least substantial reason for supporting the use of theatre arts in a general curriculum. There are many more substantial reasons for doing so. The correct answer is D.

What Are the TEKS in Theatre Arts for Students in EC-6 Classrooms?

The Texas Essential Knowledge and Skills (TEKS) are required to be taught in every Texas classroom, and TEKS have been established by the state in the Theatre Arts for children in grades EC-6. For each grade level, the Theatre Arts TEKS (2009) include four strands: (1) Perception, (2) Creative expression, (3) Historic and cultural heritage, and (4) Critical evaluation.

Within these strands, the TEKS describe specific theatre arts knowledge and skills that teachers must provide for their children during each school year. Each grade level includes and builds on those that were introduced in the previous grades, so a teacher should be familiar with all grade levels of the TEKS. After a brief description of each of these strands and discussion on the focus of each grade level, this chapter elaborates on how these strands can be an integral and exciting part of the curriculum.

Perception (Strand 1)

Sometimes, we do not think about all of the areas that are important in child development—only about our "core" subjects. However, perception is an important base for many of the tasks that we ask of children in all content areas. In helping students develop perception through theatre arts, teachers provide experiences that help children make better sense of themselves, others, and their environment by giving them insight, awareness, sensitivity, and observation skills. It is difficult for children to manage themselves without being able to fully "read" themselves and others. This is important in perception, so beginning in Pre-K, children should have numerous activities to enhance social skills. Dramatic play in Pre-K and K help enhance communication and awareness, along with exploration of space, imitation of sounds, and use of props. In first grade, the **perception** strand requires building on kindergarten experiences. Children should now have activities that increase their confidence through dramatic play. They are ready to participate in more imitation of actions and imitation and creation of both animate and inanimate objects. For example, when teachers say, "Let's pretend to be elephants," they are checking children's perception/understanding of this animal and allowing for expressive movement, imitation of sounds, and the development of spatial skills.

Second graders should be reacting to sensory experiences and be involved in increased spatial awareness through expressive and rhythmic movement. Also at this grade level, children should participate in (1) dramatic play that uses actions, sounds, and dialogue, (2) role-play, (3) imitations, and (4) re-creation of dialogue.

In the third grade, students are reacting to sound, music, images, and the written word with voice and movement added. Children who are in this grade should be responding to sensory and emotional experiences in theatre arts and should be creating their own play spaces as they continue to develop the use of expressive and rhythmic movements. Through classroom **dramatizations**, students should be able to reflect on their environment, portray characters, and demonstrate actions.

Fourth-grade activities for perception should include all of the above. In addition, teachers expand experiences for children in (1) further development of body awareness and spatial perceptions; (2) using interpretive movements, sounds, and dialogue; and (3) imitating and synthesizing life experiences in dramatic play.

In fifth-grade classrooms, the perception strand is expanded to include the emotional aspects and details of theatre. Students are expected to use recall of senses and emotions to more fully develop characters. In addition, they express themselves with responses to sounds, music, images, and movement.

Finally, in sixth grade, they utilize all of the previously mentioned knowledge and skills and apply them by imitating and synthesizing life experiences and making theatre experiences more personal. They also move from portraying environments, characters, and actions to creating them.

Creative Expression/Performance (Strand 2)

Creative expression and performance is an important part of developing children's higher-level thinking, particularly synthesis. In this strand, Pre-K teachers should involve children in spontaneous and expressive dramatics by having them create or re-create stories, moods, or experiences. For example, Elena was telling her teacher about going to her grandparents' house right across the border in Mexico. Her teacher, Ms. Cain, quickly pulled up two chairs to represent a car and asked Elena to drive them both to her grandparents' house. Elena was asked to point out and tell what she "is seeing" along the way. To recall their experiences, young children should have many opportunities to express and interpret their unique feelings through body movements and voice.

As noted, Pre-K and kindergarten students should be encouraged to participate regularly in dramatic play and should be taught how to appropriately use their voices, to move safely in dramatic situations, to assume simple roles, and to interpret characters from real life or stories. One way the kindergarten teacher facilitates students in theatre design, direction, and production is by providing centers (as described earlier) with appropriate props and **manipulatives**. Children should begin to plan dramatic play (both alone and in cooperation with others) and to create their own play spaces, costumes, and simple materials.

First-grade teachers should include experiences for children to dramatize limited action stories, poems, and songs. They should assist children in becoming more sophisticated at adapting their play environment and selecting aspects of the environment for use in dramatic play.

In second grade, children are asked to perform **pantomime** and puppetry, as they dramatize poems, songs, or limited action stories. They are also ready for more advanced role-play from real life or imaginative situations.

In addition to the inclusion of the experiences listed previously, third-grade teachers have their students participate in the performance of a number of different roles in real or imagined situations. Children should also be involved in narrative pantomime, dramatic play, and story dramatization, and when older, they should dramatize literary selections using shadow play, puppetry, pantomime, and imitative dialogue. They are expected to identify and use technical theatre elements like simple lighting, sound, or stage props.

Fourth graders should be extending these skills to include the development, description, and performance of characters (including characters' relationships and surroundings) using personal experiences, heritage, literature, and history. Performances and creative expression should also include dramatization of literary selections and simple student-created stories. These presentations may be in unison, in pairs, or in groups, along with collaborative **improvisation**, or acting without a script as the drama flows along. The teacher must also include issues involved with more advanced use of props, costumes, and **visual elements** as children begin to alter spaces to create suitable environments for play-making in safe ways.

Fifth-grade creative expression and performance experiences allow for more detail in description of characters and surroundings, as they also select their own movements and dialogue to portray developed scenes.

Finally, in sixth grade, students are more in control of their expression, defining many aspects of visual elements and characters. They also begin to alter their spaces, plan collaboratively, and interact cooperatively in brief dramatizations of their own.

Historic and Cultural Heritage (Strand 3)

The historic and **cultural heritage** strand in theatre arts requires that children relate theatre to history, society, and culture to increase understanding and insight. Thus, kindergarten children should be involved in situations in which they reenact real and imaginary scenes or situations from a variety of cultures and stories from their community.

Building on these skills and knowledge, first and second graders should imitate life experiences from historical events in their community. In addition, they should integrate diverse cultural dimensions in reenactments from various historical periods from Texas and America and be able to identify diverse cultural dimensions in dramatic play.

Older elementary children are more deeply involved with culture and history. As students move into third grade, dramatic activities begin to illustrate similarities and differences in life and reflect historical and diverse cultural influences. Fourth- and fifth-grade students should be able to explain theatre as a reflection of life in particular times, places, and cultures. They must also identify the roles of live theatre, film, television, and electronic media in societies. Sixth graders move to demonstrating drama as a reflection of life.

Critical Evaluation (Strand 4)

The last strand for theatre arts is *critical evaluation,* another area that is important in the development of higher-level thinking. Following this strand, teachers must help children respond to and evaluate theatre and theatrical performances. Goals of this strand include promoting children's discriminating judgment and critical thinking and developing their appreciation for the theatre arts (as Texas is cognizant of the need for good evaluative consumers of live theatre, film, television, and other performance-related technologies). The TEKS also convey that students should respond to and critique performances through live theatre, film, television, and other technologies.

Beginning in kindergarten but continuing throughout all grade levels, observation of performances and appropriate audience behavior are highlighted. Young children in the first grade should also begin to demonstrate an awareness of the use of music, creative movement, and visual components in theatre.

By second and third grade, students respond more extensively to dramatic activities by employing creative movement, visual components, and music, and they use simple evaluative processes to do so. For example, Ms. Jamison borrows simple instruments from the music room (cymbals, drums, bells, etc.) and has groups compose a musical background to a recreation of "The Three Little Pigs." After each group's performance, the teacher asks the audience to critique the use of sound in the performance. Children should also be introduced to amateur and professional performances, and they should be comparing many of the vocations found in theatre arts.

Fourth-grade activities employ this strand by including definitions of visual, aural (hearing), oral, and kinesthetic aspects of informal play-making and formal theatre and discussions of these elements found in art, music, and dance. Activities include opportunities to compare and contrast the ways ideas and emotions are depicted (character study) and also of theatre artists and their contributions. Teacher questioning, both before and after performances, should be at the forefront of this strand. In one example, Mrs. Burke reads her children a story that they will re-enact. She then asks children what the main characters' voices should sound like and why, how each should walk, and what expressions should be on their faces. Then she asks a group of children to walk through an *ad lib* of the first part of the story. She follows by having the audience tell why the performance was believable or not. Afterward, she selects another group of performers and repeats the process. Children also increasingly select movement, music, or visual elements to enhance their classroom dramatizations. Fifth and sixth graders should have more experience analyzing and applying varied appropriate audience behaviors.

Remember that the TEKS are always building blocks, so each grade level builds upon the knowledge and skills of the previous grades. The focus should also gradually move from a process to a product orientation in theatre arts as students approach middle school—but always remembering the importance of process as well. Lessons can focus on one or all of the four strands of the TEKS. Each of the four strands allows for creativity and variety on the part of the teacher.

It's time to look at another question:

Mrs. Bertram holds a group discussion and asks her children about their favorite way of listening to a story. She then talks to them about the Pueblo tribe's oral history and storytelling as a way to pass down their Native American traditions. Because this oral tradition was so honored, these Native Americans created two types of dolls for their young children. One was known as the *storyteller doll* (who was always formed with an open mouth), and the other was the *listener doll* (representing the children who were gaining knowledge and heritage from the elderly storyteller). Mrs. Bertram then has children create their own storyteller and listener dolls of clay and puts them in a center where children go to tell, retell, and listen to stories.

In this activity, which of the Theatre Arts TEKS strands has Mrs. Bertram not integrated into her reading/art lesson?

A. Perception and Creative Expression/Performance
B. Creative Expression/Performance and Historic/Cultural Heritage
C. Perception, Creative Expression, and Historic/Cultural Heritage
D. Historic/Cultural Heritage and Critical Evaluation

This integrated reading/art lesson is full of activities that can address the TEKS for theatre arts and other areas such as language arts and art. It is easy to see that the main strand in theatre arts is *Historic and Cultural Heritage,* because of the cultural nature of the activity involving Native American traditions. *Perception* is also addressed appropriately because students increase their awareness, insight of others, and their oral communications skills by telling and retelling stories in the role of Native Americans to others in the center or to their listening dolls. Children are also performing as they tell and retell stories, so the *Creative Expression/Performance* strand is also covered. The only one of these four strands not related to this activity is *Critical Evaluation*—children are not being asked to judge or critique. Remember we are looking for the exception. The correct answer is *D*.

(If you are interested in this activity, you can see an example of these dolls at http://www.penfieldgallery.com/story.shtml).

Why Include Theatre Arts in Daily Activities?

You have already seen in the strands discussed previously some of the key reasons that theatre arts should be an important part of learning. Let's continue to investigate other benefits to children in theatre arts activities.

Theatre arts experiences can help develop children's communication skills along with cognitive and social skills—all within one experience! Skilled teachers provide abundant opportunities during the day for children to use language to invent various themes and roles in dramatic play and to negotiate with each other.

As children observe others in theatre arts activities and dramatic play, they learn by absorbing a wide range of interactions to assorted situations. An increase in understanding in both present and past life experiences takes place as children watch and participate, and they are able to gain and use a wider range of human responses in communicating (both verbally and non-verbally) in various situations in real life. They have a chance to act out their fantasies, fears, and other human emotions in a safe environment.

Play usually begins as an independent activity with very young children and becomes more cooperative and social in nature as they grow older. Teachers should be conscientious of children's experiences as they play alone, with a variety of children, and in applying a variety of skill levels or considering children's varied backgrounds. An unlimited number of positive results come from a teacher's care in structuring cooperative groupings in theatre arts. Students sharpen their skills for socialization as they listen to opinions and ideas of others, lead a group, follow the lead of others, establish roles and rules, communicate, scaffold, and problem solve in play.

Theatre arts is one of the most empowering uses of play for children in the early years; it is during play that children begin to control their own destinies. Thus, theatre arts activities capitalize on a child's intrinsic motivation to have a sense of control of their world and to express their knowledge, their concerns, and their curiosities. As teachers become more competent in encouraging and integrating appropriate theatre arts activities, children become more comfortable and confident in developing their roles, their creativity, and their confidence as role-players. All teachers learn, for example, that puppetry has a unique value, as children shed their own **personas** to "become" others. These experiences often allow children to overcome their apprehension or shyness and become more empowered in expressing themselves.

Theatre arts can also be seen through the lenses of several other domains. For instance, for the **cognitive domain**, students recall, explore, collaborate, analyze, problem solve, and think (and act) creatively. As mentioned, children also reach higher levels of thinking when they discuss and critique performances and compare and evaluate various literary genres. When children act and use their bodies to move during theatre arts, they increase their development of the **physical domain**. Theatre arts activities also contribute directly to children's speech, as they learn to imitate and use their voices to create characters. According to McCaslin (2006), even though written language is highlighted in schools, speech is our most important means of communication. Speaking before an audience (even if that audience is just the class) is advantageous in improving speech. In the affective/social/emotional domains, children develop empathy and understanding of others and learn more about feelings, emotions, and alternative choices in communication. Through **role-playing**, scenery design, prop-making, setting development and/or puppetry, children can also participate in self-analysis, perspective-taking, interpretation of cultures, and character development. Within the *affective domain*, (see page 410) young children also learn about their values, preferences, aesthetics, talents, strengths, and areas of needed practice.

There are even more benefits to including theatre arts—they offer chances to integrate multiple intelligences and modalities, depending on the activity. For example, children use kinesthetic, inter- and intrapersonal, musical, visual, spatial, and other intelligences in many theatre arts activities. Children also grasp the idea of symbols more readily, as they pretend that one object is another, both in play and in drama productions.

Finally, children who are involved in exciting activities, such as theatre arts, are more motivated to be in school. Because theatre arts can be integrated with all other content areas, it can make learning more fun. For example, Mrs. Stanton has her first graders act out the stages of a plant, as they first lie on the floor in the fetal position of a seed, then stretch and break through the soil to catch the light and rain, grow strong and flower as they listen to appropriate music (for example, the opening theme to "2001: A Space Odyssey"). Mr. Casagrande's fourth-grade science class is studying weather patterns, so on the playground, he has children become "air particles." On a hot day, he divides his class into unequal groups—the bigger one becoming a densely packed high pressure cold front and the smaller, more spread out group becoming a low pressure warm front. He has the high pressure group crowd tightly together and asks them to move toward the warmer low pressure area. The smaller low pressure group falls back. Then, the questioning begins. These teachers could simply describe these areas of knowledge, but by instituting a theatre arts activity, they create a memorable and motivating lesson.

As one can readily see, there is a strong case for integrating theatre arts into the classroom on a daily basis for many reasons. Let's continue to look at how skilled teachers go about integrating theatre arts in their classrooms.

First, let us try another question:

Mr. Xu has children pretend that they are first walking on a sticky surface, sliding over ice, then tip-toeing over hot stones. He then has them pretend that the room is filled with smoke, then flowers, and, finally, the smells of a pizza cooking. Finally, he has them pretend the room is freezing cold, wet, and then, blistering hot. What is the least applicable rationale for doing this activity?

A. To encourage students to increase their sensory recall for creative writing
B. To provide a warm-up for some type of theatre arts experience
C. To provide movement for students after an activity that requires them to be in their seats for a long time
D. To prepare students for dramatic play

First, remember that we are looking for the least applicable rationale for this activity. Part of the rationale for using theatre arts is to enhance integration with other activities. This particular activity works very well as a sensory recall for creative writing (A). This type of activity is also suitable for children as a warm-up for a more formal theatre arts activity (*B*). A warm-up can be an important part of having children get into the mood of improvisation or formal acting. This is also a theatre arts activity that can break up a period of sitting too long with some movements (*C*). The rationale that least applies is preparing students for dramatic play (*D*), because dramatic play is spontaneous and should be initiated by children themselves (although dramatic play in certain directions can sometimes be encouraged by the teacher). The correct answer is *D*.

What Is the Teacher's Role in EC-6 Theatre Arts Education?

Instructional Roles

Teachers take on many roles in theatre arts instruction. The *teacher-as-instructor* is charged with teaching students about specific knowledge and terms such as the **elements of theatre arts**: plot or story line, theme, mood, characters, language/dialogue, and spectacle. Instruction also should include the *technical components of theatre:* set, props, lighting, sound, costumes, and makeup. *Technical skills,* such as creating scenery, applying makeup, or props designing, are also important to include in instruction. As children become older, they are taught about the *forms of theatre* (comedy, tragedy, farce, and melodrama). These elements are important for performance but are also critical in helping children with writing their own dramas and critiquing performances.

In addition to organizing opportunities for children to learn and build their skills with the elements listed previously, teachers take on many other roles, one of the most important of which is that of a *facilitator* (or guide). In this role, teachers set up activities and assist along the way, but they also know when to step out of the way to allow students' creativity to emerge.

Planning for theatre arts activities through written lesson plans, creating units of study, and integration of theatre arts into other content areas allow for multiple teacher roles to help children to be more active and engaged in learning. These other roles may include *modeler, motivator, strategist, questioner, creative developer, small group designer, mediator, safeguard,* and *assessor.*

As *modelers,* teachers set the tone for children's comfort levels, confidence, and excitement about creative activities. Teachers are constantly being observed by their students. Children are always listening, analyzing, and reacting to how their teachers introduce new concepts or experiences. If a teacher takes on an excited, active role in theatre arts as a role-player, set designer, puppeteer, or polite audience member, students often follow that lead. A teacher who constantly uses her voice as an "instrument" in reading to children and acting out small snippets whenever possible models the joy that theatre brings to what could be less exciting material. Imagine the image of a teacher reading "The Three Little Pigs" to children in a monotone voice, where "I'll huff and puff and blow your house down" contains no inflection of the theatre. The classroom, instead, should be full of the teacher modeling exciting moments through the use of his or her voice and body language. When it is the children's turn, they have fewer qualms about trying out their own theatre voices and nonverbal actions. Teachers can also model inclusion by planning ahead for *all* children to participate.

The role of a *motivator* through theatre arts is often closely related to that of a modeler. Motivating teachers integrate theatre arts into those areas of the curriculum in which students feel confident and interested; that is, teachers seek connections to children's personal interests by using the TEKS, the local community, and children's developmental levels and background experiences to create purposeful theatre arts activities throughout the year. Teachers utilize exciting literature, cultural and historical backgrounds, familial connections, and all content areas to ensure that students fully understand the role of theatre arts in daily life, as well as to allow for real-life problem solving. During theatre arts, the teacher-as-motivator probes students to think, analyze, question, and defend their choices. A favorite probe of early childhood educators is "What if?" questions to encourage children to develop multiple ideas and solutions in dramatic play ("What if your truck runs out of gas [in the Transportation Center]?" "What if your baby doesn't like the food you are feeding him [in the Home Center]?" "What if your dog [stuffed animal] runs away because you don't have him on a leash?"). Children of all ages need the teacher to support their creativity by using questions or providing activities that focus on the process of learning rather than simply looking for one answer. It is also important for a teacher to maintain balance by avoiding constant intervention to turn an unstructured dramatic play episode into a teaching situation. Children can become disinterested and disempowered when a teacher frequently intercedes in their play to manipulate a situation into an opportunity to teach something. Motivation also includes opportunities for a child to make choices, make mistakes, and to derive meaningful context from his or her own decisions.

As *mediators*, teachers observe and listen to children to ensure that interactions are emotionally safe and appropriate in each theatre arts situation. Teachers should constantly monitor the feedback that children are giving and receiving to be sure that it is acceptable, accurate, and helpful. Teachers should deliver constructive and supportive comments that encourage children to continue their theatre arts activity, but teachers should also be certain to immediately halt any harmful criticism that could discourage a child from participating. When mediating, teachers should use questioning, situational perspective-taking, and past experiences to allow children to make their own decisions and corrections to the greatest possible extent.

Teachers must also be *assessors*. The lesson planning process is always completed by assessing children, informally or formally. Any authentic assessment can be utilized in theatre arts. In addition, teacher-made checklists, rubrics, anecdotal records, and rating scales can be used effectively. Through the integration of technology, teachers can allow students to self-reflect by having them use digital cameras, word-processing programs, electronic journals, and videotaping critiques. As teachers design lessons and activities to address theatre arts, they must consider how they will assess children's participation, behaviors, and skills. Areas such as oral language and social development, spatial abilities, gross- and fine-motor skill development, application of prior learning, cooperation, attitudes, concentration/attention, types of play, and activities chosen by children can be tracked over time (Nath, 2011). In many large Texas cities, magnet schools for the performing arts also exist for children who are gifted and talented in this area. In many cases, it is the teacher who can recognize and recommend children who are interested or are assessed to be exceptional for placement in these special emphasis schools.

During actual performances, the teacher moves from guide or facilitator to *director* and *audience*. As students move into the roles of performers, the teacher is able to show what it means to be a good audience member who is attentive, quiet, responsive at the end, and so forth. This role and the responsibilities of a director are discussed later in the chapter.

The teacher's roles in theatre arts are multidimensional and may include also being a co-player/collaborative participant, along with others. If a teacher wishes to teach in a way that guarantees active, creative students, he or she serves in many roles.

Non-instructional Roles

As an early childhood educator, another role for the teacher of theatre arts involves keeping administrators, teachers, and special interest groups (such as a parent support group or a curriculum advisory group) informed about research, any pertinent issues/policies, curriculum trends, and legislative updates on this area. Because research supports the important role of theatre arts in developing the whole child (cognitively, socially/emotionally, and physically), these activities should be a part of every classroom. Although after-school theatre arts programs can be popular for children who wish to delve more deeply into this area, theatre arts should not be considered by a teacher as an "add-on" to their existing curriculum (whenever time might allow) but should be included as an integral part of every EC-6 instructional program. Therefore, it is the educator's job to keep those who make or influence curricular and instructional decisions aware of needed support. Although finding support can seem discouraging at times, there are many ways to do so.

One effective way to communicate the importance of theatre arts is through students and their work. This may be done by showcasing theatre arts activities as part of an integrated curriculum that promotes creative thinking and problem solving. It can also be achieved through focused student presentations or performances. Setting up field trips for key community performances or asking the district to provide professional dramatic performances at the school shows teachers' concern for fulfilling the theatre arts TEKS. Sometimes support results from merely talking to and having repeated conversations with influential people (the building principal, lead or socially influential teachers, parents) about supporting theatre arts. The most important thing to remember is that support for theatre arts cannot be taken for granted. Teachers should be strong advocates for supporting theatre arts.

Yet another role is that of a *resource provider*. Because theatre arts is rarely funded at the preferred level, it is suggested that teachers do the best job possible with the resources that are accessible or available at a reasonable cost. Teachers can look for costumes and materials in secondhand shops, dollar stores, and garage sales, and they can ask building supply stores to help with construction materials. Individual parents and PTOs with supply drives and fundraisers may be able to provide resources, and teachers can integrate art and mathematics when they need to make props or construct set designs in their classrooms (at age-appropriate levels) by having students create backdrops or simple props when appropriate—in other words, they should be creative! It is through determination that the message is conveyed that theatre arts is essential for children.

When beginning a program, a strategic plan can be designed that includes a budget and a timeline for implementing a more comprehensive program. The plan, along with authentic student work, can be presented to the building administrator before the school's next budget cycle. Funding can come through thoughtful planning and implementation.

Let's try another question:

Mrs. Jewett makes an effort each day to go into each one of her centers, but Ms. Beck enjoys going into the Home Center and the Clinic Center and working with small groups. What does Mrs. Jewett understand that Ms. Beck does not?

   A. The teacher is a role model.
   B. The teacher is a motivator.
   C. The teacher is a constant instructor.
   D. The teacher is a facilitator.

At times, the teacher should fulfill all of these roles. However, Mrs. Jewett understands that she serves as a constant role model in dramatic play activities. As a female teacher, she knows that if she does not go into all of the centers, then girls may see her modeling a "hidden curriculum" that "Girls do not play with machines or blocks or other 'boy' things," and boys may believe that females do not (or should not) go there. The correct answer is *A*.

What Are the Main Aspects of Theatre Arts That Teachers Should Consider?

Considerations in creating experiences in theatre arts include age and developmental appropriateness (including cognitive, social/emotional, and physical areas), material selection, technology, resources, time, space, and safety.

The best environment for theatre arts activities is one that engages all students in active learning. Young children need an unlimited number of opportunities and materials with which to experiment, discover, make choices, collaborate, and connect to their personal experiences with content. Children experience a great deal of empowerment when they are able to choose their own activities and are in control of dramatic play, so offering many choices for this type of play is ideal. There is an optimum balance. Offering too few props and materials does not support high-quality dramatic play experiences; whereas, offering too many materials can create confusion, distraction, and disruption (Driscoll & Nagel, 2005).

Teachers in early childhood classrooms need to learn how to manage time and instructional resources. Fostering an appreciation for theatre arts means structuring time for students with various skills and interests to explore personal paths of self-discovery and self-expression. It also means providing time for children to develop critical and creative thinking skills and for analysis and reflection of production-centered activities. Some researchers (Johnson, Christie, & Yawkey, 1999) suggest that with less than 30 minutes, children do not have time in **sociodramatic** play to establish a storyline, recruit role-players, assign roles, negotiate rules, or choose pretend props or construct new ones. If this process is interrupted numerous times, children stop trying. Teachers must also consider opportunities for start-up, transition, and clean-up time. Time can be addressed effectively by strategically developing dramatic activities as a routine part of content-area instruction rather than an activity left to mornings or recess.

One of the easiest tactics to support creativity has to do, as mentioned, with time allotment and environmental design of theatre arts. Students need more than just time to perform their tasks. Older children should also have the benefit of time to create a good performance. Expert pedagogy in this area dictates that theatre arts should be considered both *process-centered* (children work through a process of creative drama) or *production-centered* (children participate in prewritten scenes, plays, and musicals). During the process of creating, children need thinking time, planning time, exploration time, and analysis and reflection time. Students are more encouraged to express themselves creatively if they know the expectations and have time to go through all of these processes. They are more motivated, their ideas are more developed, and their motivation more inspired when given time for development. As children grow toward the upper grades, their focus should shift more toward product-centered activities, but process-centered activities remain important.

Teachers can also control creativity through offering open-ended or closed materials. **Open-ended (or flexible) materials** are those that encourage a wide range of ways in which to engage in role-play (Johnson, Christie, & Wardle, 2005). For example, a center supplied with water can become a sea for boats, a swimming pool for dolls, or a lab for sink/float activities or for experimental measuring. **Closed materials** can represent only one thing. For example, an airplane can only be an airplane, or a truck only a truck. Both types of materials can be valuable, but teachers must consider what goal they have for students and think carefully about providing the types of materials appropriate for reaching that goal—but, ideally, they provide open-ended materials more often.

Within the environmental framework, teachers must also consider children's development levels and their culture. Children are not likely to engage in dramatic play with toys or props that are too abstract for their reasoning level or that are unknown to them. Very young children (2–3 years) need more realistic props, whereas older children can be creatively involved with low realism props (Johnson, Christie, & Yawkey, 1999). In addition, these researchers remind us

> [T]he activity centers and thematic play materials found in middle-class-oriented schools or childcare centers are less familiar to lower-class children than they are to middle-class children. If young children are not familiar with objects, they tend to explore them initially, only later using them in imaginative play. (pp. 140–141)

Appropriate physical development must be another consideration. When children do not have the skills to manipulate certain props or move in certain ways, they are not inspired to explore and play. However, "children who are more advanced will be motivated by the intricacies of more details in play" (Nath, 2011, p. 113). To set the stage for experiences, it is important that teachers establish a positive, risk-free, encouraging learning environment; thus, dramatic activities should provide diverse and culturally sensitive learning props and experiences for children who are in various cognitive and physical developmental levels. The environment should also accommodate multiple learning styles, and it should create an atmosphere for questioning, creative problem solving, and collaboration.

Teachers are responsible for providing a safe learning environment for their students—both physically and emotionally. Physically, teachers should be certain that theatre arts activities are in spaces that allow for movement, for appropriate volume in voices, for comfort, and for physical safety. Safety cannot be assumed; teachers must actively inspect their sites often for potential hazards. Most dramatic activities require movement and louder voices that require a specified area in order to be safe and beneficial. These areas should be placed away from quiet areas, such as reading centers. Selected areas must be assessed for both potential risks and possible disruptions. Considerations such as the nature of the activity, the number of students involved, furniture, props, media, location with regard to others, equipment, electrical outlets, storage, and the overall room design should not be overlooked when planning and structuring dramatic activities—both those that are teacher directed and those that are initiated by students.

Teachers should also always be aware of hygiene issues, as well those of safety. Costumes and props should always be clean. A teacher must be particularly vigilant when there are outbreaks of communicable illnesses or other infestations that can be spread through sharing of headwear, clothing, and other props. The same is true of other toys, center materials, and games used in dramatic play. All of these should be sanitized often and checked for wear and tear. Teachers should also be watchful for those props and costumes that could cause tripping, fall on top of children, could be unsafe electrically, and so forth.

Safety issues also include the young child's voice. The teacher must engage children in exercises that allow them to project their voices and use their voices in many ways without straining their young vocal chords. Students should have opportunities to practice using different volumes, tones, and inflections. These experiences allow children to learn appropriate and safe use of their voices. Poems can be used for choral speaking that provide safe practice for oral skills and improvement of speech habits. Also see the Chapter 7 (beginning on page 405) in this book for helping children project their singing voices. The exercises and tips in this chapter also help children in speech projection and articulation needed for theatre arts.

Emotional safety is also a concern. It should also be noted that in some cases, students may not feel comfortable right away with performing in front of their peers. Teachers should respect these individual differences in students and address their needs differently. As these children observe others, they are still engaging in participation, just in their own way. Teachers should track those observations and ask these students to share their opinions and impressions one on one. As these students have more experience as observers, teachers should transition them from observers to partners of performances. In these situations, these students can support the performance by participating as audience members or in some secondary roles. Eventually, these children should be transitioned into less significant performance roles in front of smaller audiences until they are feeling more confident and comfortable.

Rules should be made and enforced for certain types of theatre arts activities, particularly centers, and the teacher must be ready to intervene to redirect hurtful physical or emotional behaviors. The purpose of much of the dramatic play during early childhood is to promote friendship, empathy, and perspective-taking among classmates, and the teacher is key to ensuring a psychologically safe classroom. Young children often use dramatic play involving power. One rule should always be in effect: If any type of dramatic activity or play is physically or emotionally harmful to another, it must change or stop. Again, remember that there is a balance—too much teacher interference can undermine the children's problem-solving ability, but teachers must constantly monitor for excessive behaviors and situations that require teacher intervention.

Depending on the developmental stages of children and the activities planned, space requirements vary. Young children often explore dramatic activities through center play. Yet they also need large, open, carpeted spaces to participate in **creative dramatics** that involve coordination and large motor skills. Space should be allotted for both. Young children do well with space reminders (such as colored tape on the floor, or centers divided by trunks, screens, or other furniture that cannot be knocked over). In addition, there should be space for individual, pair, and small-group interactions. Whereas centers provide young children opportunities for creative and dramatic play, their space requirements may vary depending on the curriculum, current interests, and the needs of the children. Spaces that are too small for a group of children can cause them to become more aggressive, but too large of a space does not encourage interaction (Johnson, Christie, & Yawkey, 1999). When a center is not working for dramatic play or other theatre arts activities, the teacher should first check the layout of the room. There should also be sufficient materials and props so children feel invited to work alone or in small groups. Centers also require easy-access storage space for materials that students may unpack and pack, discover, sort, reorganize, or use for cleaning up. Theatre arts activities for older students have additional space requirements. As students begin to collaborate, design, plan, organize, construct, and analyze activities together, they need space and technology that support their efforts. In addition, there must be space available for explorations, performances, and productions.

Many teachers volunteer (or may be required) to put on theatre performances during the year for other grade levels or for parents. Dramatic performances in front of large audiences can be unsettling for some children and are not recommended by some specialists for very young children; however, many children who participate in theatre arts are eager to perform. If a presentation is undertaken, teachers must always meet the emotional and the physical safety needs of all children, and every effort should be made to create enjoyable theatrical experiences. This can be achieved with forethought and preparation. Designing a safe floor plan, for example, can prevent staging that is dangerous for many children moving about at once. Stage areas must be clearly marked with tape (fluorescent, if stage areas are to be darkened at times). Sets, backdrops, and risers should be checked for placement and stability and for ease and safety of movement around them by performers. Any special lighting, sound equipment, or electrical cords should be secured and taped down (if applicable). Choreography and movement should be simply designed to eliminate unnecessary risks, and exits should remain clear. Ample rehearsal time should be scheduled in the actual performance area for children to feel comfortable with their roles and their stage area. Sufficient adult supervision should be in place during rehearsals and during the performance to help manage the cast so that the teacher/director does not become so frustrated with children that he or she resorts to anger and yelling. The idea of performance is to improve children's self-concept through drama, rather than tear it down. All children should be able to have positive memories of school performances rather than those of exasperated, angry teachers. In a performance, *all* members of the group should be able to participate in some way. Teachers should always share the subject matter/content of performances early with parents and ask parental permission for any performance that is outside the child's classroom. Some parents may be concerned for religious, personal, or other pertinent reasons, and their wishes must be respected.

Children should also be instructed in good audience behavior. When children are attending a performance, part of safety is to be a considerate audience when many people are seated close together (particularly in a darkened area). When a class is attending a school or a formal dramatic presentation, teachers are obliged to arrive in plenty of time to seat their classes before the lights dim and the actors begin. However, teachers should be careful not to arrive so early that children become restless prior to the beginning of the performance. Teachers should address the following with students: (1) when they can and cannot leave their seats during a performance, (2) when they should remain silent so that performers do not have to strain their voices and so that others can hear, (3) when and how children should show their appreciation, (4) when and how they should return if an intermission is given, (5) whether food or other objects are allowed in the seating area, and (6) what a *curtain call* means, along with other performance manners. See the question on page 422–3 for more.

Many formal theatre performances for children have packets with excellent activities that teachers can use to orient their children prior to the performance or to engage students in activities afterward. If a packet is not automatically sent, teachers should enquire if one is available. These may include discussion topics, drawing ideas, dances or songs to learn, reenactments for different endings, and so forth. Because reaction to the fine arts is also a personal experience, teachers are cautioned to avoid giving children the feeling that there is a right or wrong answer for many of these activities (McCaslin, 2006). If there are no prepared materials or they are inappropriate for one's class, teachers should still prepare children for the experience by creating **developmentally appropriate** activities so that the performance will be more meaningful.

Let's try the following practice question:

Mrs. Hutchinson was a new teacher in an area of Houston in which the student population was about ⅓ White, ⅓ African American, and ⅓ Asian. Many of the Asian families are recent immigrants. In accordance with her EC-6 teacher preparation, Mrs. Hutchinson immediately set up a Kitchen Center with cooking implements, dishes, silverware, pots and pans, and so on, for her Pre-K class to encourage sociodramatic play. She noticed that many of her White and African American children were using the center very well for role-play, but her Asian children did not seem to be interested. Her best course of action is to:

A. set up a more rigid schedule and monitor children to make sure that each child spends a definite amount of time there.

B. add implements such as chopsticks, a wok, and other kitchen tools often found in Asian kitchens.

C. change the center because students are obviously not motivated by it.

D. go into the center herself and invite the Asian children to role-play with her.

Requiring young children to be in a particular center (*A*) does not necessarily interest them or encourage role-play. A Kitchen Center is, most often, one of the most popular centers to include in a classroom because children have a wealth of experiences that they can bring to role-play. Because it is a place to link the two most important environments of children (school and home), this center should not be removed (*C*). Teachers are encouraged to go into centers and help initiate, encourage, or extend play (*D*), but the *best* way to involve her Asian children is to equip the center with implements that may be found in their homes (*B*). Children are much more likely to initiate role-play when they are using culturally familiar items. Also, when there are less familiar items for children to use, researchers suggest that teachers of culturally different children be especially cognizant to give them plenty of time to become familiar with materials that may not be familiar to them and create partnerships with parents to set up culturally appropriate play centers (Johnson, Christie, & Yawkey, 1999). Before assessing young children who are engaging with new items, these researchers suggest that children be given "a second chance to shine" (p. 145) in performing expressive behaviors. Their findings show that children often show considerable improvement when faced with a more familiar or similar item or situation again. The correct answer is *B*.

Bringing it All Together: How Do Teachers Plan for Activities That Address the Four Strands of the Theatre Arts TEKS?

Teachers can actively engage children in many forms of dramatic expression. Through appropriate materials and well-planned experiences (such as centers, puppetry, art, movement, creative dramatics, music, dramatic play, and a number of other ways), children can develop cognition, language, and socialization. Using the four strands of the theatre arts TEKS as a base, teachers can address the objectives and state requirements through a variety of teaching strategies and activities. The following are a few examples of how teachers can incorporate the four strands of theatre arts into their lessons:

Perception (Strand 1) Poetry, construction, story comprehension, creative writing, music, movement, finger plays, and role-playing

Creative Expression/Performance (Strand 2) Story-telling, creative dramatics and writing, set-making, prop-making, puppetry, music, movement, technical theatre, technology games, role-playing, and costume design

Historic and Cultural Heritage (Strand 3) Re-creating, puppetry (including shadow puppetry), creative dramatics, audience members and role- or persona-taking.

Response/Evaluation (Strand 4) Audience members, choosing music, critiquing renditions, creative movement, visual effects, listening and evaluating, set design, creating scripts and roles

Planning for the four theatre arts strands with a variety of teaching methods works toward a long-term objective of integrating these into many other content areas of the classroom. Using a wheel format (Figure 9.1) helps illustrate flexibility in designing lessons and experiences for young children that can expose them to many aspects of a particular strand (or even several strands) through various actions, tasks, and opportunities. As you can see in the wheel, there are multiple behaviors that can be integrated with the various TEKS from other content areas.

The wheel begins in the center with the four strands of theatre arts as the foundation of a lesson plan or an experience and then expands to show some examples of observable and measurable behaviors (verbs) in the second circle that exemplify each strand. The developmentally appropriate (DAP) experiences

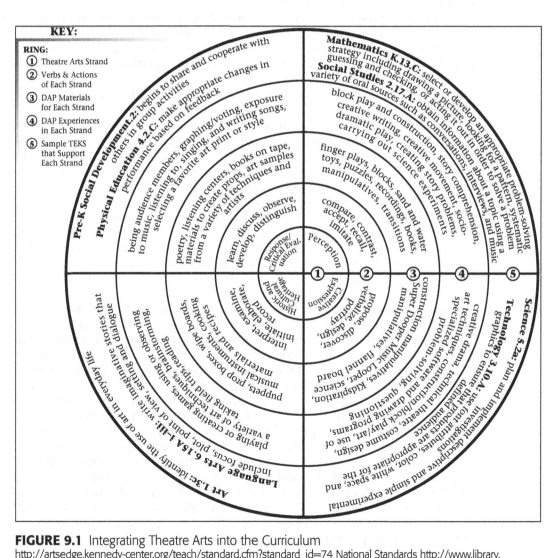

FIGURE 9.1 Integrating Theatre Arts into the Curriculum
http://artsedge.kennedy-center.org/teach/standard.cfm?standard_id=74 National Standards http://www.library.arizona.edu/search/subjects/drama/web.html. Resource page with links to many more resources.

and materials circle (third circle) supports the multidimensional characteristic of each of the strands and illustrates some various ways that teachers can address a strand in a large group, in a small group, or in centers. The outer edge of the wheel is a sampling of TEKS. The outer three circles are a small sample of the ways in which theatre arts can be integrated into the early childhood classroom.

How Can Theatre Arts Be Integrated into Other Content Areas?

Theatre arts has far-reaching influences in other areas of the curriculum—language arts, social studies, music, art, science, mathematics, and even technology. One most often thinks of theatre arts in connection with language arts, but theatre arts can be aligned with almost any subject to enhance instruction and make content more fun, more meaningful, and more concrete. Students engaging in movement, language, word problems, construction, and self-expression can simultaneously strengthen their skills in theatre arts and other content areas in exciting ways.

Through the use of a variety of settings (learning centers, small group lessons, and circle time), theatre arts can be comprehensively addressed throughout the curriculum. For example, while children are solving word problems in mathematics or engaged in scientific experiments, they may assign parts and role-play.

Furthermore, as young children listen to or create original poetry or stories or read literature, they can use imagery, creative dramatics, and role-playing. Goldberg (2001) supports this issue by asking how a child's acting out of a story is different than simply reading it or listening to it. He notes, "When a child acts out a story she has read or heard, she has the opportunity to become the story—to internalize the characters, action, emotions. . . . I suggest that drama can be a fundamental tool that enables children to understand . . . by engaging with it" (p. 67).

Many theatre arts activities (such as choral reading) also have considerable value in practicing oral language skills or second-language learner skills in a "sheltered" manner and are suitable for any grade level (McCaslin, 2006). The natural tie of theatre arts to multicultural elements also helps bring children of many cultures together and helps them with the perspectives of others.

Through technology, children are also able to take on new characters in a game and direct the action themselves. Using a variety of software, students can play with plot designs, character creating, and **storytelling** and retelling. For instance, students may use a simple PowerPoint with clipart characters to design a slide show of an original play. Students may also use Microsoft Publisher to create a mock newsletter for their original skit or characters. Children can videotape their book reports as "newscasters," describing the plot of their books in news terms, or they may role-play weather forecasters in a science class.

Other content-area experiences can rely heavily on theatre arts skills with role-play, imagery, plot and set design, use of props and visual elements, and story creating and telling. During social studies, for example, children learn background knowledge and gain inspiration for their plots, props, and roles to play. Students can create or better understand the behaviors and symbols of certain heritages or cultures through portrayal of roles from different cultures or times. Personas are excellent ways to learn about historical figures. Children, given the knowledge for taking perspective, realize their own connections to certain heritages or cultures or connect their own personal preferences for music, art, or literature with certain groups of people.

Most artistic experiences utilize some form of theatre arts. With music, for example, children can learn to use their creativity to visually express their rhythmical interpretations of certain pieces or match music to enhance a mood in dramatic readings or plays. As students create dance movements artistically, they use imagery, creativity, and evaluation. Students can also refine their artistic skills in making props, designing sets, and improvisation with puppetry. In role-playing and creative dramatics, students analyze and critique their skills, their likes and dislikes, and deepen their knowledge in many areas.

The Texas Professional Development and Appraisal System Alignment (PDAS) is the assessment document on which most teachers in Texas are evaluated. On the document for teachers of fine arts, there is a section for evaluation on teaching the fine arts for the required TAKS test (Texas Assessment of Knowledge and Skills) (scheduled to be replaced by the STAAR tests, or the State of Texas Assessments of Academic Readiness). This document can be accessed at http://www.cedfa.org/growing/PDAS_Elementary.pdf, and it is most helpful in showing exact alignment between other content area TEKS and the theatre arts (and other fine arts as well).

As teachers plan, there is a key approach to teaching theatre arts and that is to incorporate it naturally into other content areas in their lesson plans. Not only is it required, but it is also good for children!

Let's look at another practice question:

Ms. Vasquez wants to introduce some words to her fourth-grade children in a vocabulary lesson. Which activity from the ones described next is the best?

A. She should write the words on the board and pronounce them, have children pronounce them with her, and then have students look them up in their classroom dictionaries and write down the definitions in their personal dictionaries.

B. She should use a puppet to talk through definitions.

C. She should explain the meanings and have students use the words in a short skit that they write and perform.

D. She should have children go to a center in which they can use a variety of materials to write the words.

The first activity (A) is fairly boring for children. The teacher may want students to keep a personal dictionary, but choice A is an activity that should be used only after an introduction. Using a puppet, as in the way it is used in choice B, does not involve children being active learners. Although using a puppet may create some interest, it still uses a telling voice, which does not increase the likelihood of children retaining the meaning. Choice D might be good for a spelling lesson, but it does not help with vocabulary development. Choice C, however, involves children in an activity that requires that they actively **construct** their own vocabulary meaning. This strategy is known as *word plays*. In this experience, the teacher writes down a list of words (the number depends on the grade level), pronounces them, and gives their meaning. Blachowicz and Fisher (2006) describe an example of this type of activity with first graders. After the teacher has told student teams to plan a drama using the words *quack, drip, mother,* and *hole*, she gives specific directions that include having students describe a story, tell what kind of day it is, whom the story is about, what the problem is, and how it works out. Although each team came up with a different story to act out, one team presented the following drama:

Child 1: Once upon a time, there was a little duck who liked to play in the rain.

Child 2: He wanted to go outside on a rainy day, but his *mother* said, "You have to put on your boots."

Child 3: The little duck put on his boots and went outside to jump and play and *quack* all day. *"Quack, quack, quack."*

Child 4: The boots had a *hole* in them, but the little duck didn't know it.

Child 1: It was time to come in, because he heard his *mother* call, *"Quack, quack, quack."*

Child 2: The little duck came in with his boots. He didn't know that they had filled up with water, and they went *drip, drip, drip* all over the house because of the *hole.*

Child 3: When his *mother* saw, she went, *"Q-u-a-c-k!* What is all that *dripping* all over my house? You are in trouble now!"

Child 4: Then she saw the *hole,* and the little duck helped her clean up all the *drips.* The *mother* hugged her little duck.

The correct answer is choice *C.*

SUMMARY

Quite often, theatre arts activities are some of the most popular activities for children, parents, and teachers. Every principal knows that the way to entice parents to come to evening school meetings is for children to perform a musical or a play. Some people may not remember learning certain things in school, but most recall their performances in some type of dramatic activity during their school days. Linquist (1997) calls these *peak experiences* and notes that they are remembered from a particular class or a performance. They are retold again and again by participants through the years ("Remember when Ms. Guthery had the puppet theatre?" or "When I was in school, we did this play in fourth grade and I was a . . . "). Perhaps this is one reason why Texas requires that teachers understand and implement the theatre arts TEKS throughout the early grades.

Skilled teachers incorporate theatre arts in many different ways that contribute much to children's growth and development. It can be a very effective strategy to integrating curriculum in natural ways. Its engaging nature adds creativity and critical thinking to everyday teaching in all content areas. Many developmental areas, the state objectives (TEKS), and life skills can be taught or enhanced through the use of theatre arts in the classroom.

GLOSSARY

Note: There are many terms in the theatre arts that, due to space constraints, could not be identified within the chapter. However, we have included some of these in the glossary to increase your terminology about theatre arts.

Closed materials. Materials that can represent only one thing during play (an airplane can only be an airplane, a truck can be only a truck, etc.).

Cognitive domain. The domain that deals with different types of knowledge: logical–mathematical, social–conventional, scientific understanding, critical-thinking skills, perception; often referred to as the *thinking domain;* related to Bloom's taxonomy (knowledge, comprehension, application, analysis, synthesis, and evaluation).

Collaborator/Co-player role. The teacher becomes an active play partner in sociodramatic play.

Construction. Curricular experiences that focus on creating meaningful representations of objects, events, or group of objects; students construct their own meanings rather than having the teacher tell them what the meaning is.

Creative drama experiences. Children are guided in improvisational stories or situations, writing their own plays, and integrated arts such as creating costumes, puppets, masks, sets, and so forth.

Creative dramatics. Spontaneous play that develops into assignment of roles and the design of a familiar plot to which children have been exposed through stories, poetry, and real life; allows for spontaneous interpretation and unique dialogue.

Creative expression. Children's verbal or nonverbal reaction or response to past experiences or imaginary experiences that can be observed through any variation of the arts, oral communication, or written communication.

Cultural heritage. Usually refers to a child's community, neighborhood, home, or family; ethnicity with regard to shared beliefs and traditions.

Developmentally appropriate. Material selection, lesson planning, activities, and interactions that align with children's developmental levels and focus on play, independence, and choices.

Drama-in-Education (DIE). Children are asked to become part of a dramatic moment (flight to the moon, a major archeological discovery, or other event in any content area) supported by resource materials, so they act and react accordingly in improvisation.

Dramatic play (also pretend play). Symbolic play for children in the age range of 2–7 years old; involves children using props, their imaginations, and role-playing to retell or represent real or make-believe scenarios; in schools, these are often encouraged by centers, such as the water table with plastic manipulatives, Home Living Center, Pizzeria Center, Doctor's Clinic Center, and the Grocery Store Center, or in outside play areas, such as the sandbox with construction vehicles; structured play that expresses inner personal feelings with roles created that depict imaginary or real-life experiences and personal stories.

Dramatization. Presentation of a formally written play or skit with a memorized script; often includes props, backdrops, and costumes with assigned roles.

Elements of theatre arts. Plot, theme, character, language, sound, and spectacle.

Improvisation. Students act as they go along without predetermined actions or a script.

Instructor role. The teacher provides information to children through words or activities designed towards a learning goal; the teacher directs sociodramatic play to teach content (for example the teacher might say, "Oh, no, Miss Baker! I see you only have one doughnut left, and there are two customers here. What can you do? Can you cut it in half? What is that called?"). (This role must be done with care, as it can interrupt sociodramatic play, which teachers do not want to do continuously.)

Language domain. The domain that focuses on listening skills, receptive language, expressive language, reading, writing, listening, and speaking.

Manipulatives. Concrete objects that allow children to problem solve or symbolize parts of a scenario.

Masks/face paint. Materials used in drama to enhance culture or symbolism; to allow an animal or thing to come to life; to classify an emotion or distinguish a particular character; or to hide the actor so he or she is more free and uninhibited when "becoming another."

Mock trial or meeting. A perspective-taking theatre arts activity in which children are assigned roles in terms of a court case (real or imaginary; e.g., the trial of the wolf versus the three little pigs) or a meeting of some type (e.g., city council, school board).

Movement. Physical activities that help to develop fine- and gross-motor skills using locomotor skills, non-locomotor skills, sensory awareness, eye-to-hand coordination, and a combination of any of those varied actions.

Open-ended (flexible) materials. Materials that offer a wide range of ways for children to engage with them during imaginative role-play (Johnson, Christie, & Wardle, 2005); helps with development of symbolism.

Pageant. Mini-skits that, when put together, show a series of events (e.g., the main events of the Texas Revolution, the Pilgrims leaving England and arriving in America).

Pantomime. Acting out ideas or characters with the body only (no words are spoken).

Perception. Opinions, viewpoints, or conceptions; the process by which people attach meaning to experiences.

Persona. A child is assigned an imaginary character, a real person, or a type of person (medieval knight, wagon train guide, etc.) about whom the child must research to become familiar in order to "become" that person/character. Because there is no script, the child is required to ad lib and answer questions as that person or character might do (or would have done), although children can also write their own script as the persona to perform.

Physical domain. The domain that deals with body awareness, fine-motor skills, gross-motor skills, health, safety, movement, and nutrition.

Play. A written work that has a script to be read or memorized and acted out; requires that actors follow the lines and directions written by the playwright.

Play leader. A co-player who tries to enrich or extend a sociodramatic play line.

Plot (structural elements of). Exposition, complication, crisis, climax, resolution.

Pretend play. Play that can include make-believe; pretending with objects, art materials, construction materials, manipulatives, or props;

thematic play, dramatic play, or sociodramatic play; story-telling, reenactment, or a story.

Process. Focusing on the way in which a child solves a problem or creates something instead of looking only at their final product or answer.

Prop boxes. A dramatic play kit in which materials and/or props are stored together. Most often these are on a theme of some type (children 3 years and under usually need more concrete or more realistic props; older children can more easily pretend with more abstract-looking props).

Puppetry/puppets. A teaching tool that can consist of a doll or other prop that has been created to represent a person, an animal, or an object and can be manipulated or transformed through the use of gestures, voices, or other actions.

Reaction story. Children listening to a story or event up to a certain point (not finishing it), then role-playing to show what they think should or will happen afterward.

Readers' Theatre. Children assume roles and read aloud the script of a certain story as they act out with their voices the parts of the story pertaining to their roles; interpretation is the aim, rather than memorization.

Role-playing. A perspective-taking activity that allows children to analyze the thoughts, actions, behaviors, and dialogue of a character or player in a scenario or story; sophisticated role-play can involve the audience and role-takers in reenactments to question: the soundness or preference of decisions (and why), the feelings of all players, and possible improvements.

Scripted dramas. Structured events in which roles are assigned (historical or pretend); unison movements to poems or songs.

Shadow puppetry. A 2,000-year-old technique originating in the Far East and India in which a drama is presented using cut-out forms behind a screen with a backlight to cast shadows of the characters (most often mounted on and manipulated with sticks) and sometimes including set design elements.

Simulations. A dramatic enactment of a particular situation in which students decide roles and make decisions. For example, students may be divided into teams and tasked with simulating the building of the Coast-to-Coast Railroad. They decide roles and decide how their teams will go about the task (e.g., should they build from each coast and meet, or start in the middle and go out?). Then they are given craft sticks and reenact the building, with the team taking the least amount of time declared the winner).

Social domain. The domain that deals with social studies, social skills, and socialization.

Sociodramatic play. A type of dramatic play in which two or more children are involved and in which they communicate about the organization of their play, assign roles for play, and act out those created scenarios.

Storytelling. Children create new endings, new characters, or completely new stories and share them either by dictating to a teacher (can be recorded on audio or video, or may be written down), drawing a picture, or recording them on paper.

Story retelling. Children orally or dramatically share the sequence of events from a story or event.

Strands of Theatre Arts TEKS. (1) perception, (2) creative expression/performance, (3) historical and cultural heritage, and (4) critical evaluation experiences that teachers are required to provide in Texas classrooms.

Structured drama. Activities that require student participation in preset ways, usually with scripted dramas, such as plays and skits, in which roles are assigned or with unison movements to poems, songs, and chants.

Theatre in Education (TIE). A theatre genre that expects children to enter a situation where they are asked to act out decisions or solve problems in order to change attitudes or behaviors, stimulate intellectual curiosity, or motivate further interest in a topic or issue (McCaslin, 2006).

Thematic-fantasy play. After reading a story to children, they are questioned about it, and props are constructed to encourage enactment and reenactment.

Visual elements. Line, texture, color, space.

Visual principles. Repetition, balance, emphasis, contrast, unity.

REFERENCES

Blachowicz, C., & Fisher, P. (2006). *Using vocabulary in all classrooms* (3rd ed.). Upper Saddle River, NJ: Pearson.

Driscoll, A., & Nagel, N. (2005). *Early childhood education birth–8: The world of children, families, & educators*. Boston: Allyn & Bacon.

Goldberg, M. (2001). *Arts and learning* (2nd ed.). New York: Longman.

Grimes Lallier, K., & Marino, N. (1997). *The persona book*. Englewood, CO: Teacher Ideas Press.

Preparing to Teach Theatre Arts in Texas **509**

Johnson, J., Christie, J., & Wardle, F. (2005). *Play, development, and early education*. Boston: Pearson.

Johnson, J., Christie, J., & Yawkey, T. (1999). *Play and early childhood development*. New York: Longman.

Laughlin, M., Black, P., & Loberg, M. (1991). *Social studies readers theatre for children*. Englewood, CO: Teacher Ideas Press.

Linquist, T. (1997). *Ways that work: Putting social studies standards into practice*. Portsmouth, NH: Heinemann.

McCaslin, N. (2006). *Creative drama in the classroom and beyond* (8th ed.). Boston: Pearson/Allyn & Bacon.

Nath, J. L. (2011). Making a difference in student achievement through planning and instruction. In J. Nath & M. Cohen (Eds.), *Becoming an EC-6 teacher in Texas: A course of study for the Pedagogy and Professional Roles (PPR) TExES* (pp. 76–137). Belmont, CA: Cengage.

PDAS: The Professional Development and Appraisal System and fine arts teachers. Revised 2002: Aligned with the Texas Assessment of Knowledge of Skills objectives. Retrieved July 17, 2009, from http://www.cedfa.org/growing/PDAS_Elementary.pdf

Texas Administrative Code. *Chapter 117, Texas Essential Knowledge and Skills for Fine Arts*. Retrieved May 10, 2010, from http://ritter.tea.state.tx.us/rules/tac/chapter117/index.html

Wisniewski, D., & Wisniewski, D. (1997). *Worlds of shadow: Teaching with shadow puppetry*. Englewood, CO: Teacher Ideas Press.

Wortham, S. (2006). *Early childhood curriculum: Developmental bases for learning and teaching* (4th ed.). Upper Saddle River, NJ: Pearson.

A THEATRE ARTS LESSON PLAN

Where the Wild Things Are

Grade Level: Kindergarten

Main Subject Area: Theatre Arts

Integrated Subjects: Language Arts, Music, and Art

Time Frame/Constraints: 2 or 3 days

Overall Goal(s): To guide children's understanding of reality versus fantasy; to assist children with recalling and summarizing the plot; to support children's understanding of emotions through the fine arts; to increase children's creativity in art and movement.

TEKS OBJECTIVES:

§ 117.4. **Theatre Arts** (2) Creative expression/performance. The student interprets characters, using the voice and body expressively, and creates dramatizations. The student is expected to (D) participate in dramatic play;

§ 110.11. **Language Arts** (4) Reading/Beginning Reading/Strategies. Students comprehend a variety of texts. Students are expected to (B) ask and respond to questions about texts read aloud. (8) Reading/Comprehension of Literary Text/Fiction. Students understand, make inferences and draw conclusions about fiction and provide evidence from text to support their understanding. Students are expected to (A) retell a main event from a story read aloud.

§ 117.2. **Art** (b)(2) Creative expression/performance. The student expresses ideas through original artworks, using a variety of media with appropriate skill. The student is expected to (C) develop manipulative skills when drawing, painting, printmaking, and constructing artworks, using a variety of materials;

§ 117.3. **Music** (4) Response/evaluation. The student responds to and evaluates music and musical performance. The student is expected to: (B) identify higher/lower, louder/softer, faster/slower, and same/different in musical performances.

LESSON OBJECTIVES:

Individually: Each student will draw a picture of his or her bedroom.

Large group:

- The whole class will participate in a choral reading poem.
- The whole class, in a circle, will participate orally in an imagination process and make predictions about the book, *Where the Wild Things Are*.
- The whole class will listen to the teacher read *Where the Wild Things Are*.
- The whole class will participate in classifying real versus pretend/make believe/fantasy from the book and from real life on a chart.
- The whole class will participate in pretending to "put on emotions" and use sounds and their bodies to distinguish between emotions.

In Centers:

- Children will make "Wild Thing" puppets.
- Children will correctly select various musical background pieces to match various parts of the story.
- Children will select a correctly retold version of the story from three versions.
- Children will participate in a correct reenactment of the story in the Puppet Center.
- In cooperative groups, children will correctly draw an assigned part of the story. As a small

group they will present their drawing to an audience and summarize the story.

- Students will participate as good audience members.

Readiness or Prior Knowledge Needed: Students should be comfortable in expressing themselves dramatically, comprehend sequencing, be able to use a variety of art materials safely and successfully, and realize that music has meaning.

Sponge Activity: On a piece of paper, children will draw their own bedroom. Ask children to save it for later.

Environmental Concerns: Children need to be in a circle on the carpet. Make sure the area is clear and students are called to the floor as individuals or in small groups. Check each center after rotations to be sure materials/equipment are ready.

Rationale: Teacher: Sometimes we don't feel like ourselves. There are many emotions we experience. Knowing how emotions can affect us can help us to understand our true selves and others better. Sometimes make believe or fantasy can help us describe our feelings to others so they can understand us better. For example, if I tell someone in my family, "I'm 'mad as a hornet,' he or she knows not to bother me just then." Have you ever felt like you were "grouchy as a crab" or "grumpy as an old bear" and wanted to "snap your claws" or "growl at someone" because you weren't feeling good? That is what we will talk about today.

Transition: As students are coming to the gathering area or carpet, the teacher can use the adapted focus song "Wolf Party" as a chant that introduces the lesson. It can be used as a transition to pretend play.

Focus or Set Induction: Have children think about the title of the poem and share what they think might happen at a party for wolves. Have children chant with the teacher as she reads the following poem. Afterwards, discuss how the wolves were feeling at the party. Ask how they expressed their feelings. Ask if children have ever felt like this at a party or another time when they wanted to participate with older children or adults. How did they express themselves?

Adapted from **Wolf Party**[a]

(Original song and lyrics by Nancy Schimmel; music by Candy Forest)

Teacher: I wanna go to a party and howl at the moon

Cause howlin' is really hip.
I wanna learn to howl like the big kids howl,
But all I can do is "yip."

ALL TOGETHER: I wanna go ah-oooo, ah-ooooo . . . !

Teacher: I hear my mommy and my daddy sing
And it sounds so long and cool.
I throw back my head and land flat on my back
And you know I feel like a fool.

ALL TOGETHER: I wanna go ah-oooo, ah-oooo . . . !

Teacher: Well, I went to a party with all of my friends
And we sang 'till the break of day.
I fell on my back, but everyone did
And that made me feel okay.

ALL TOGETHER: Now I can go ah-oooo, ah-oooo . . . !

Teacher: If you want to howl, just take a deep breath,
Close your eyes and throw your head back,
You don't need a moon, don't need to stay on tune.
You can howl like one of the pack.

ALL TOGETHER: Yeah, you can go ah-oooo, ah-oooo . . . !

MAKING CONNECTIONS:

The following are questions the teacher can use to help students make connections.

1. **Connections to Past or Future Learning:** Remember when we talked about our last book and retelling a story so that if we wanted to describe a book we've read to someone else, they could clearly understand what it was about? We are going to use some of those same skills today. Remember that we talked about how we don't tell *every* detail, but we tell about the main parts that happened in order.

2. **Connections to Community:** Do you know anyone in Houston who retells stories as part of his or her job? (Show a short clip of news stories about children from local channels and explain that they are retelling stories/summarizing.)

[a]You can listen to and download "Wolf Party" at http://www.songsforteaching.com/nancyschimmel/wolfparty.htm.

3. **Cultural Connections:** This story for today was written by a man from England (show on globe) who remembered how he felt when he was a child. Do you think that children all over the world have many of the same feelings? Do you think that you have the same kinds of feelings as other children in our school? In our class? What make you think so?

4. **Connections to Student Interests and Experiences:** (After the story is read use these prompts). This book was a make-believe view of how a little boy deals with his emotions. In real life, how do we feel when we want to be a little naughty? How do we feel in real life when we are disciplined? How do we feel when we still know that we are loved?

Materials:

Poem: "Wolf Party"

Book: *Where the Wild Things Are*

Short, taped newscast on a topic that is appropriate for young children

Globe

Clip art or drawings of people or animals that express feelings or are related to emotions (ox suit for frustrated with a burden, bull head for snorting with anger, bouncing bunny for excited, mouse for timid, wasp for mad, etc.)

Drawing paper

Brown paper bags and a variety of art materials (for "Wild Thing" puppets)

Pre-recorded music

Three taped versions of the story

Paper bag with pictures and labels of emotions

"Wild Thing" puppets

Activities: Guided Practice.

1. Ask children to close their eyes and imagine or pretend that they could go any place they wanted. Have them share where that might be (some may share real places and others make-believe places). Ask children if their places are real or make believe. Share yours. Ask children to tell you what it means to imagine and pretend. Ask them from where they think their ideas for imagining and pretending come. Show them the cover of the book, *Where the Wild Things Are,* and ask what they think the book might be about and if they think it will be real or pretend and why. Ask children to close their eyes again and imagine what they think the Wild Things are going to be (big/small, nice/scary) and what kinds of noises they might make, if any. Have

children listen as you read the book and have them silently compare how their own wild things matched those in the book.

2. On a white board, make a T-chart that has one side for "Real" and one side for "Pretend/ Make-Believe." Ask children to classify parts of the story (e.g., trees grew in Max's bedroom, Max got in a boat, Max was wearing a wolf suit, Max's mother was angry, Max's mother brought him dinner). Ask children to classify some real life experiences (cartoon shows, pretend games vs. real events, etc.).

3. Talk about reasons behind Max's actions. Ask: "Why he might be behaving in this way? Why do you think the author said, 'Max put on his wolf suit on'? Do you have "a suit" you put on sometimes? What kind of "suit" do you put on when you are (1) frustrated, (2) mad, (3) silly, (4) excited, (5) sad, and (6) happy? Let's all pretend we are putting on our "frustrated suits," My "frustrated suit" is an ox suit (show picture), and I feel like I'm pulling against a heavy load." Demonstrate facial expressions and sounds in an "ox suit." Ask if any child likes to show his or her actions. Have everyone act out their "frustration suits." Continue with their mad, silly, excited, sad, irritated, and happy "suits" and actions. Have some examples ready (silly monkey suit, irritated crab suit, etc.).

4. **Centers**

Center 1: Art Center: Supply brown lunch sacks and a variety of open-ended materials so that students can create their own "Wild Thing" puppets.

Center 2: Music Center: Record several types of music and have numbered picture cards of the main parts of the story. Have children match each musical selection to parts of the story. Be sure to have a protected tape or CD with voice saying, "Selection 1, 2," etc. Have children tell why they matched each section using music description (soft/loud, fast/slow, high/low). For example, "He was going to his bed, so I thought the music should be soft there."

Center 3: Listening Center: Tape three versions of the story: (1) a version with too many details so the plot gets lost; (2) a version out of order; and (3) the real version. Have children listen and tell each other which was the best version and why.

Center 4: Emotions Center: Have each student pick out an emotion (with a picture) out of a box. Have each student draw himself or herself in that "emotions suit" (as teacher showed earlier).

Center 5: Puppet Center: Have students use puppets to reenact the story.

Independent Practice: In groups of four, have children number off (1–4). Child #1 will draw the scene he/she remembers from the beginning of the story. Child #2 will draw a scene that he or she remembers from the first part of the travels in the story. Child #3 will draw from the second part of the travels, and Child #4 will draw a scene from the ending. Each group will then discuss how they want to show their pictures in order and what they should say. Remind each child about voice projection and being a good audience member. Each group will then present to the class. Ask each group to explain which pictures show something real that Max did and which show something make believe.

Assessment: Centers: (1) Completion: Did each child complete a puppet? (2) Checklist for music: Was each child able to recognize music that matched emotions from the story? Was he or she able to explain the match (fast/slow sounds, etc.)? (3) Reading Comprehension Checklist: Did each child select the correct version of the story and explain why? (4) Satisfactory/ Unsatisfactory: Did each child draw a reasonable emotion suit for the emotion that he or she drew out of the bag? (5) Participation: Did each child participate?

Independent Practice:

Group presentation: Was the story in order and the summary correct? Did each child speak clearly? Did each child participate as a good audience member?

Individual drawing: Did each child complete a drawing? Did the drawing show a good representation of the part of the story assigned?

What Will Students Do Who Finish Early? Ask students to redraw their bedroom when "on an emotional journey," or put pictures that students drew in order so that you can post them on the wall.

Closure: Ask each child to recall their favorite part of the story. Ask children to explain the difference between their bedrooms and Max's bedroom.

Modification for Students with Special Needs: Shon (with hearing difficulties) will need to be seated close to the teacher when the story is read and when groups are presenting. Charlene, who has difficulty holding a pencil, will use large markers or an assistance grip/roll.

Reflection: To be addressed after teaching the lesson.

DRAFT YOUR OWN THEATRE ARTS LESSON PLAN

Title of Lesson: _____

Grade Level: _____

Main Subject Area: _____

Integrated Subjects: _____

Time Frame/Constraints: _____

Overall Goal(s): _____

TEKS Objectives: _____

_____

_____

Lesson Objectives: _____

_____

Readiness Skills or Prior Knowledge Needed: _____

_____

_____

Sponge Activity: _____

_____

_____

Environmental Concerns: _____

_____

_____

Rationale(s): _____

_____

_____

Focus or Set Induction: _____

_____

_____

Making Connections: _____

_____

_____

1. Connections to Past or Future Learning: _____

_____

2. Connections to Community: _____

_____

3. Cultural Connections: _____

_____

4. Connections to Student Interests & Experiences: _____

_____

Materials: _____

_____

_____

Activities: Guided practice: _____

_____

_____

_____

_____

_____

_____

_____

_____

Independent practice: _____

_____

_____

_____

_____

_____

_____

_____

_____

Assessment: _____

_____

What Will Students Do Who Finish Early? _____

_____

Closure: _____

_____

Modification for Students with Special Needs: _____

_____

Reflection: _____

_____

OBSERVING THEATRE ARTS EXPERIENCES/ACTIVITIES

During your visit to an EC-6 classroom, use the following form to provide feedback as well as to reflectively analyze the room, the materials, and the teaching for theatre arts elements. For older children in middle school settings, some of these elements may not necessarily apply. Be sure to note if they are age appropriate for the children you are observing.

The Classroom Environment	Observed	Not Observed	Response
1. Ample space allows students and adults to move around freely.			If not, what could be changed?
2. Dramatic play or prop boxes are accessible to students for a portion of the day.			If so, for how much time? If not, what appropriate props might be made available?
3. Developmentally appropriate free play occurs for a portion of the day.			Is the time sufficient? Explain why or why not.
4. Peer interaction is encouraged through a variety of centers and small group activities.			If so, how? If not, in what ways could the teacher encourage this?
5. Dramatic play materials or props are displayed and stored within student access range in many places throughout the room.			If not, what could be changed?
6. Centers offer opportunities for creative and dramatic or prop play in various content areas.			If so, describe. If not, what changes could be made?
7. Puppets or props are used to stimulate skills on different levels.			If so, what skills do you see being developed? If not, what could be changed?
8. When children initiate dramatic or sociodramatic play in any center or setting, they are encouraged and supported on different levels.			If so, what are the teacher's actions or responses? If not, what opportunities were missed?
9. When children are onlookers, they are helped to become involved in specific activities with a specific role.			If so, by whom (their peers or the teacher)? If not, what could the teacher do?
10. Children can be seen utilizing role-playing, sociodramatic play, audience behavior, or prop-making in several areas of the classroom throughout the day.			If so, give an example of one of these experiences. If not, what could you change to encourage this?
11. Children are allowed to be in control of their learning, their experiences, and their interactions.			If so, what is the effect? If not, how could this change?
12. Alternatives are provided for students who are not comfortable engaging in active participation of theatre arts or in a particular performance.			If so, list the alternatives. If not, what could be added?

The Classroom Environment	Observed	Not Observed	Response
13. Theatre arts is integrated during whole group time in a developmentally appropriate and natural way.			If so, describe. If not, give ideas for what could be added in a developmentally appropriate way.
14. Theatre arts is integrated during circle time or informal group gathering in a developmentally appropriate way.			If so, describe. If not, give ideas for what could be added in a developmentally appropriate way.
15. Theatre arts is integrated during independent small group time in a developmentally appropriate way.			If so, describe. If not, give ideas for what could be added in a developmentally appropriate way.
16. Theatre arts is integrated during teacher-led small group time in a developmentally appropriate way.			If so, describe. If not, give ideas for what could be added in a developmentally appropriate way.
17. Children are comfortable creating roles and actions for play without prompting.			If so, when and how did you see them doing this? If not, why do you think that is?
18. Children are using imaginative play in a variety of times and ways throughout their day.			If observed, describe some of these times. If not, describe how this could be added.
19. Children are using imaginative play in a variety of places in the room.			If observed, describe some examples of where. If not, suggest some areas.
20. The room has at least four or five different centers set up to which children have access at some point.			If so, list them. If not, suggest some that could be developed for a range of ages and abilities.
21. Theatre arts is integrated in a variety of centers.			If so, describe one observation of this and include the center in which you saw it. If not, in which centers could integration take place and how?
22. Children are allowed age-appropriate independence in the centers to elicit creative expression.			If so, describe. If not, how could this change?
23. A wide variety of developmentally appropriate materials are accessible to children in several centers that support theatre arts.			If so, list a few and include in which center they are located. If not, what materials could be added?
24. Many age-appropriate open-ended play materials are accessible (e.g., props, blocks, manipulatives, puppets, vehicles, character clothes, books, audiovisual materials) in many different centers.			If so, list what you observe. If not, list what could be added.
25. Teachers play an active role during center time, asking questions, facilitating play, and encouraging active participation and a variety of responses.			If so, list some of the questions you heard the teacher ask that qualify as higher-order thinking or creative thinking cues. If not, what opportunities were missed?

The Classroom Environment	Observed	Not Observed	Response
26. Students are comfortable and are responsive to the teacher's questions and cues throughout their play and group experiences.			What does the teacher do (or not do) to create a comfort level?
27. The schedule provides a balance of active and sedentary types of play.			If so, list what types of play you see. If not, how could this be changed?
28. A variety of theatre arts activities occur daily.			If so, list what activities you see. If not, list what could be added.
29. During a variety of times throughout the day the teacher engages as an active participant in play.			If so, discuss an example you observed. If not, what could the teacher have changed about his or her role?
30. Children's responses and interpretations are accepted.			If so, describe some of the responses from the teacher. If not, give the reactions of the children.

TEST YOURSELF ON THEATRE ARTS

1. Mrs. Lasner wants to integrate a lesson with mathematics, reading, and theatre arts. What activity from the following allows her to do this in the most effective manner?
   A. Students dramatize a story they have read using shadow puppets they create from basic shapes.
   B. Students act out a story that Mrs. Lasner wrote and read to them about different shapes.
   C. Mrs. Lasner has students go on a walk to see what kinds of shapes they can find in the real world around them and then reenact their walk.
   D. Mrs. Lasner has students rotate through three centers—one where students work with shapes, one where they read a story, and one where they participate in a short dramatic activity.

2. What activity from the following offers Mrs. Glenn's fifth-grade class the best option for higher-level thinking about famous scientists?
   A. Researching on the Internet and writing a research paragraph about a famous scientist
   B. Creating a poster about a famous scientist to celebrate a week of "Famous Scientists"
   C. Participating as a character in a play about several famous scientists
   D. Participating in persona-taking about several famous scientists

3. Ms. Quan conducts the following activity in her fourth-grade social studies class:

   Ms. Quan has children volunteer to take part in a reading. They read *Susanna of the Alamo: A True Story* aloud and write a script using the dialogue from the book (e.g., they might start with Santa Anna's speech to the wives of those killed at the Alamo). The characters (*Santa Anna, Susanna,* and *Sam Houston* plus a *Narrator*) read their scripts to the class, using their voices to convince the audience of their characters' pain, anger, sadness, and other emotions (Laughlin, Black, & Loberg, 1991).

   What type of activity does this describe?
   A. Role-play
   B. Readers' Theatre
   C. Pantomime
   D. Reaction story

4. Mrs. Johnston asked her sixth-grade class during social studies time to get their "city council hats" on because she wanted their help in designing an evacuation plan that

works in case another strong hurricane threatens the Texas coast. Dramatizing a mock meeting has children working at what level of thinking?
   A. Analysis
   B. Evaluation
   C. Comprehension
   D. Application

5. Ms. Espinosa has always been known to incorporate a large variety of theatre arts activities in her classroom, so she has been asked this year to be in charge of her school's theatre arts curriculum. She attributes her success to understanding and applying general skills she learned by reading the state's theatre standards. In planning the school's curriculum, which of the following are the most important factors for Ms. Espinosa to consider?
   A. Age, developmental levels, prior experiences, and interests of students
   B. The lack of resources and expenses incurred
   C. Students' ability to read and memorize their parts
   D. The availability of volunteers who can assist with the productions

6. Providing for centers is one way of incorporating dramatic play activities into the curriculum. Which statement best illustrates an appropriate way of including theatre arts in an early childhood classroom during centers?
   A. Children receive rewards to go to centers for free play once their work has been completed.
   B. Children go to centers to work on assigned group projects.
   C. Individuals or small groups select their centers at structured times for dramatic play around themes, people, or situations.
   D. Individuals are given materials to make puppets that communicate their feelings at any given point in time.

7. Mrs. Ritika furnishes her interdisciplinary young childhood centers for dramatic play with materials that are termed *open-ended materials.* Which of the following is not considered an open-ended type of material?
   A. Sand
   B. Water
   C. Clay
   D. Miniature airplanes

8. Mr. Carpenter's fourth-grade students have just completed reading an age appropriate biography of Stephen F. Austin. Students are now given the option to either retell a favorite story from the biography as if they

were the notable character in the story, or to retell the story from the perspective of another character. Which of the following is not a true statement?

A. Assuming the role of a notable character in order to retell a story in a biography encourages creative expression and reflection in a historical context.

B. Listening and evaluating stories/events from multiple perspectives increase students' sensitivity to emotions and problems others have faced throughout the human experience.

C. Role-playing activities are more appropriately integrated into the curriculum at lower grade levels.

D. Retelling stories from another character's perspective elicits both critical and creative thinking.

9. At recess, Ms. Hart observes her preschoolers imitating animals they saw during a recent visit to the zoo. She decided to let them play a little longer. Which statement best supports her decision to let the play time continue a bit longer?

A. The activity was helping students to express and develop their perceptions about other living creatures.

B. The students were motivated and having fun remembering their experiences.

C. The physical movement allowed them an emotional release of their feelings.

D. She wanted to assess her students during group play.

10. Ms. Beal volunteers once a week in her son's first-grade classroom to read limited action stories to small groups of children. As she reads, the children are encouraged to act out parts of the story line. The most important aspect of this activity is that it:

A. creates an awareness of individual learning styles.

B. accommodates young children's short attention span.

C. provides memory experience by imitating and creating actions and sounds.

D. strengthens parent volunteerism in the school.

TEST YOURSELF ANSWERS AND RATIONALES FOR THEATRE ARTS

Answer 1: Choice *B* is appropriate, but perhaps not the best. The integration of all three topics is present, but children are not involved with much mathematics unless they help construct shapes for the play. Choice *C* is a good activity for mathematics, but the reading component is not there

(only listening), and the drama component is not very valuable. Choice *D* does not involve any true integration between the three content areas—they are all separated. Choice *A*, however, is a very thorough integration. First, children read a story. They then construct shadow puppets using basic shapes (e.g., a chick can be constructed of two circles [the head and body], a square [the neck], three small rectangles [the legs and the beak], and three triangles [the tail and two feet]). They cut out the characters and tape a large flex straw to the form with a toilet tissue roll taped to the bottom of the straw as a handle. To help recall the characters and the sequence of the story, children then reenact the story using the shadow puppets behind a screen with a backlight. Children are actively involved in all three content areas. Shadow puppetry is a very popular activity with children because construction time can be short, there is a low cost for construction, there is less mess, fewer art skills are required, rehearsal is less tiring and time consuming, there is a greater range of visual effects (and children are not as critical as they can be of three-dimensional effects because of their sophistication with special effects of movies and video games) (Wisniewski & Wisniewski, 1997). The correct answer is *A*.

Answer 2: Choice *A* does not really involve higher-level thinking; it is simply reorganizing and repeating what the child has read. Choice *B* is similar, although there is some small amount of synthesis-level creativity in the presentation and more integration of content areas. Choice *C* adds interest, but the student is basically only repeating lines that have already been written, rather than thinking and creating. Choice *D*, however, requires that the student research a famous person and be so familiar with his or her life, actions, inventions, contributions, ideas, personality, the times, and so on, that the student can act like and answer as that famous scientist. This requires a great deal of higher-level thought (Grimes Lallier & Marino, 1997). The answer is *D*.

Answer 3: Choice *A* involves having students take on a particular role and ad lib rather than to read from a script. Choice *C*, pantomime, uses actions and body movement *only* to indicate characters, types of characters, or events. No voice is used. Choice *D*, a *Reaction Story*, or an unfinished story, has children listening to a story or event up to a certain point, then role-playing to show what they think should or did happen. Choice *B*, *Readers' Theatre*, is described in this vignette. The answer is *B*.

Answer 4: Bloom's taxonomy reaches from the lower levels of thinking (knowledge, comprehension, and application) to the higher levels (analysis, synthesis, and evaluation). This activity reaches into Bloom's evaluative level of thinking (*B*). Children, playing the roles of members of a town council, first analyze what did (and did not) work for Houston and New Orleans during the mass evacuations, they create new plans (synthesis), and finally evaluate the new and old plans. The answer is *B*.

Answer 5: Ms. Espinosa's principal knows that theatre arts are a required part of the Texas curriculum (the TEKS); therefore, appointing a faculty member to be in charge of a theatre arts curriculum ensures that they will be taught in her school. Ms. Espinosa knows that, most likely, there will always be a shortage of officially funded resources for this area (*B*), so part of her job is to ask teachers to be creative in obtaining resources for their children. She also knows that children have different levels of reading and memorization abilities (*C*), so part of her position is to ask teachers to find resources to address this so that *all* children in the school can be included. Volunteers are not automatically needed for each dramatic experience (*D*), but it is definitely a plus for larger productions. Therefore, all of these choices are somewhat correct. However, the question asks for the *most* important factors. Choice *A* brings the most important factors to the forefront—children's ages, developmental levels, connections with prior experiences, and interests. These are the areas that all content areas must consider first and foremost when developing any curriculum. The correct answer is *A*.

Answer 6: Choice *A* means that some children, more than likely, will seldom get to go to a center, as some rarely finish their work early. Assignment of a group project (*B*) takes away from the main rationale for dramatic play—that is, child empowerment—because children should control the role taking in dramatic play. Choice *D* does not indicate an integration of activities, but focuses only on psychosocial development (with a concentration on emotions). By providing a structured time, the teacher ensures that all children have opportunities to participate in a number of integrated themes (home, post office, restaurant, etc.) in which a variety of content areas can be touched (*C*). In upper elementary classrooms, a teacher may have children rotate through centers so that all students have a chance to participate in the activities at some point (in addition to having free choice); however, we are looking specifically at a young childhood class in this question. The correct answer is *C*.

Answer 7: *Open-ended materials* refer to those types of materials that offer a wide range of ways to engage in role-play with them (Johnson, Christie, & Wardle, 2005). For example, a center

furnished with sand can become a dumping ground for trucks, a mountain range, a bakery center for mud pies, and so forth. Choices *A*, *B*, and *C* are all open materials, as is most Montessori equipment. Choice *D*, miniature airplanes, can represent only one thing—miniature airplanes—and cannot be used to represent anything else. This is true of other toys, such as trucks, spaceships, jigsaw puzzles (with only one final fit), and other similar materials. Teachers should provide children with both types of materials, but with more opportunities for open-ended materials. Teachers should understand the different functions and values of both types of materials clearly. The answer is *D*.

Answer 8: Choices *A*, *B*, and *D* are all true statements for these activities. Remember that we are looking for a statement that is false. Choice *C* says that theatre arts is not really as effective for older elementary children, and that is certainly not true. Role-playing may be appropriately integrated throughout the EC-6 program. The correct answer is *C*.

Answer 9: One part of the curriculum for young children is to focus on animals. This type of dramatic play always seems to be a motivating way for them to learn, so *B* is true, although not the best support for continuation of play. Choice *C* involves emotional release, which is not really a part of this activity (although, if the question spoke to the physical release of energy, it would have been true). Choice *D* could be an opportunity to gain assessment, as she watches for children's development in this area; however, again it is not the best choice. Choice *A*, imitation, allows children to refine what they have observed at the zoo and to develop a deeper knowledge and perception about animals. Allowing for more time encourages children to reflect more thoroughly and illustrate in more detail what it is that they understand about animals from their experiences at the zoo. This is the best choice for allowing students to continue. The correct answer is *A*.

Answer 10: Choice *A*, a focus on learning styles, is important. Children are getting an additional aspect to their bodily-kinesthetic awareness as they act and move. Choice *B* is also an important feature, because every teacher knows that she or he can hold young children's attention longer when listening is broken up by movement. Choice *D* is important as well, because bringing parents into the school community strengthens children's learning. However, the *most* important reason to have them act out parts is that this use of a dramatic activity can help children recall parts of the story by making it memorable through action. The correct answer is *C*.

10 Teaching English as a Second Language (ESL) in Texas

William J. Kortz, Jr.
University of Houston—Downtown

Janice L. Nath
University of Houston—Downtown

The faces of learners in classrooms throughout Texas (and a good many other states) have changed since the early 1970s, when most students spoke English as their first language. Now, nearly every school in Texas has students for whom English is their second language, and they come to our Texas classrooms with the added burden of not only having to learn the vocabulary and sentence structure of a new language but also the content curriculum required by Texas on the Texas Essential Knowledge and Skills (TEKS). To meet the needs of these learners, many school districts throughout the state require that teachers have certification in English as a Second Language (ESL) prior to being hired or to become certified in ESL as soon as possible after they begin their employment. This chapter discusses how to study for and obtain your ESL supplemental certification.

About Texas ESL Certification

Currently, there are three ways to obtain Texas ESL certification. To teach ESL children at various elementary levels, you can pass the EC-4 *Generalist*/ESL TExES test (104) (which is a combination of content area and supplemental ESL test items) and meet other qualifications to become initially certified. For further information on this test, see http://www.texes.ets.org/assets/pdf/testprep_manuals/104_eslgenec_4_55024_web.pdf. You may also qualify for 4-8 ESL certification by passing test number 120 (http://www.texes.ets.org/assets/pdf/testprep_manuals/120_eslgen4_8.pdf). Because the regular *Generalist* certification levels have changed from EC-4 to EC-6, we suspect that this test will change to EC-6 *Generalist*/ESL (along with the test numbers) in the near future. For those who have already completed an initial teaching certification in Texas, only the EC-12 ESL supplemental certification test (154) is needed (http://www.texes.ets.org/assets/pdf/testprep_manuals/154_esl_supp.pdf). Remember that the state can change its requirements, so be sure to check their Web site (http://www.sbec.state.tx.us) for the most current information.

ESL instruction is built on state and national standards that entail knowledge and classroom applications considered to be best practices for teachers who have students for whom English is not their first language. For these classrooms, there is a growing body of knowledge that teachers should know and skills that they should possess. **Texas ESL standards** for teachers include seven areas to be learned and tested: (1) prerequisite understanding of English language **concepts** and acquisition of English, (2) methodologies, (3) oral communication, (4) literacy skills and assessment, (5) ESL foundations, (6) multicultural and multilingual perceptions, and (7) third-party awareness for a comprehensive overview of ESL instruction. As you study this chapter, you should complete a learning cycle of connecting the standards, domains, and competencies (what a teacher should know and be able to do) to the ESL specialized vocabulary, strategies, methodologies, and various assessments that a teacher will apply in the ESL field. To gain a good grasp of these areas, you will hopefully read each standard, study the competency information that helps to define each one, and complete practice questions located throughout this chapter, at the end of the chapter, and in the State Board for Educator Certification (SBEC; 2007) Preparation Manual 104 that can be downloaded from the Web at http://www.texes.ets.org/prepMaterials.

What Does ESL Certification Mean?

Teaching students who are **English language learners (ELLs)** requires special knowledge and skills in order for them to learn effectively. A teacher who is ESL certified can be expected to have a classroom with only a few ESL students, a classroom of all learners who are ELLs and who may speak only one language (such as Spanish), or a classroom of students who may speak a variety of languages other than English. The teacher may teach these students English language arts in a pull-out situation or teach all subjects in a self-contained room. This ESL certification is not, however, a bilingual certification in which the teacher actually instructs partly in English and partly in the student's **native language** and, thus, must be fluent in that language. An ESL teacher is not expected to speak another language—although it is certainly helpful. All ESL instruction takes place in English, with the use of special knowledge and skills to help learners gain English more quickly.

Teachers should first understand that ESL instruction is good for all students, all ability levels, all ages, all grade levels, and all diverse backgrounds. In fact, because ESL instruction is so heavily grounded in the English language arts and the developmental stages of first language acquisition, all teachers would do well to consider this supplemental certification as a means to improve their overall professional practice for any classroom that they teach.

What Are the Special Knowledge and Skills Needed for Becoming an Effective ESL Teacher?

There are many ways to continue to improve one's ESL teaching skills, and you are urged to seek these out in workshops, online courses, college courses, and similar professional development, even after you pass this test. However, to obtain ESL certification by simply testing, one must gain a full understanding of the importance of what follows in this chapter. Table 10.1 on the next page gives a conceptual overview of each of these components. The descriptors, or *indicators,* follow in each subdivided section of this chapter.

Let's first look at a logical organization pattern of the information for this certification on Table 10.1. Note that the standards can be divided into three important key areas (or *domains*) that ESL teachers must consider: (1) what should happen *before* the classroom (or preparation needed before teaching ESL students), (2) what should happen *in* the classroom (or while teaching ESL students), and (3) what should happen *outside* the classroom (or continuous professional development and community/resource outreach for ESL students and their families).

Table 10.1 divides the standards into three categories (or domains) just discussed in this section and lists the competencies that belong with each. They are listed in domain and competency order rather than order of standards, and notice that there are some standards that overlap. To see how these three domains are weighed on the exam, Table 10.2 divides and describes each domain and its approximate percentage on the ESL supplement exam. Currently, the ESL supplemental has 70 questions, 60 of which are scored and 10 of which are used to test validity for future exams. The test has a similar format to the other TExES, such as the EC-6 Generalist, so if you have not already taken one of these examinations, we urge you to also read Chapter 1 on study and test-taking skills.

Domain I is based on the assumption that an ESL teacher has considerable knowledge of the learner and a clear understanding of how acquisition of one's first language (as well as one's second language) takes place. This is seen as prerequisite knowledge for the ESL teacher before he or she enters the classroom.

Domain II concentrates on planning, implementing, evaluating, and modifying ESL instruction—in other words, all that takes place in the classroom. Students' linguistic ability and conceptual understanding are considered during lesson planning to ensure that students are capable of acquiring new vocabulary and higher levels of **lexical (or academic) application**. Then, the teacher uses **engaging instruction**, applications of appropriate technology, and special methodologies and strategies. Finally, a combination of formal, informal, and authentic assessment is employed, interrelated in daily oral and content-area lessons to measure how much the student has achieved. Much of what is brought to the classroom by way of prerequisite knowledge from Domain I is developed to a higher level in Domain II. This keeps the continuum of professional development constant as the ESL teacher reflects on classroom experiences to continuously improve his or her knowledge and skills.

Domain III includes those areas with which the ESL teacher is affiliated outside of the classroom to make instruction better in the classroom. Such topics include further understanding of the foundations of ESL instruction, the importance of **culture** in any language, and involving families and community in the curriculum as a powerful impetus to instruction and support. As ESL teachers learn more about their students in the classroom, they should place equal emphasis on learning more about the language used in students'

Table 10.1 Standards, Domains, and Competencies in ESL Programs

Domain I	STANDARD I (knows fundamental language concepts, structure, and conventions of English)
Before the Classroom	*Competency 001* The ESL teacher understands fundamental language concepts and knows the structure and conventions of the English language.
	STANDARD III (understands L1 & L2 language acquisition)
	Competency 002 The ESL teacher understands the processes of first-language (L1) and second-language (L2) acquisition and the interrelatedness of L1 and L2 development.
Domain II	STANDARD IV (knows effective ESL methods and instruction)
In the Classroom	*Competency 003* The ESL teacher understands ESL teaching methods and uses this knowledge to plan and implement effective, developmentally appropriate instruction.
	STANDARD III (understands L1 and L2 language acquisition)
	Competency 004 The ESL teacher understands how to promote students' communicative language development in English.
	STANDARD I (knows fundamental concepts, structure, and conventions of English)
	Competency 005 The ESL teacher understands how to promote students' literacy development in English.
	STANDARD V (knows factors that affect ESL learning ESL academic content, language, and culture)
	Competency 006 The ESL teacher understands how to promote students' content-area learning, academic-language development, and achievement across the curriculum.
	STANDARD VI (formal and informal assessment)
	Competency 007 The ESL teacher understands formal and informal assessment procedures and instruments used in ESL programs and uses assessment results to plan and adapt instruction.
Domain III	STANDARD II (knows foundations of ESL and how to create an effective environment for ELLs)
Outside the Classroom	*Competency 008* The ESL teacher understands the foundations of ESL education and types of ESL programs.
	STANDARD V (knows factors that affect ESL learning of academic content, language, and culture)
	Competency 009 The ESL teacher understands factors that affect ESL students' learning and implements strategies for creating an effective multicultural and multilingual learning environment.
	STANDARD VII (advocacy for ELLs; family and community involvement)
	Competency 010 The ESL teacher knows how to serve as an advocate for ESL students and facilitate family and community involvement in their education.

Table 10.2 ESL Supplement Domains[a] and Weights

Domain I	Language Concepts and Language Acquisition	(25 percent of the test)
Domain II	ESL Instruction and Assessment	(45 percent of the test)
Domain III	Foundations, Culture, Family, and Community	(30 percent of the test)

[a]The EC-4 *Generalist* ESL exam adds ELA, mathematics, social studies, science, and fine arts, health, and physical education to the total percentage.

homes and their home culture by going outside the classroom to investigate and collaborate with families, communities, and other quality resources. In concluding the overview to this certification, one can see that what a teacher gains in terms of prerequisite knowledge grows from year to year, due to what he or she does inside and outside the classroom.

Despite the fact that Texas provides many guidelines to learn and apply through these domains and competencies, the teacher must always remember that the expectations for each child must be on an individual basis and grounded on the student's past learning experiences and a multitude of other conditions. Yet, when you look at Table 10.3 on page 528 in the discussion of Domain I, note that the TEKS-based state expectations concerning listening, speaking, reading, and writing have set benchmarks for all ESL learners. Even if a student is unable to achieve at his or her grade level due to the lack of English or deficiencies in his or her **home language** (or a host of other circumstances), he or she is still expected to pass state benchmarks. What is ideal on paper for these state expectations, however, may sometimes not be what is realistic in the classroom for some individual students who come to our schools from a variety of backgrounds—ranging on a continuum from those whose families may be wealthy with great educational advantages in their own countries, to those who are similar in all respects except they lack English, to those who have come from extreme poverty, to those who may have even escaped violence to reach this country. Nonetheless, the teacher and the students are held accountable for their state test scores at a certain point—usually long before either is ready.

We can easily see that the impact an ESL teacher can make is extremely important. Teachers who seek continuous learning grow with the acquired knowledge that each new year's experiences brings them, as does the quality of collaboration with families, colleagues, and community that the teacher seek to establish. The areas of *before*, *inside*, and *outside* the classroom also guide the ESL teacher as a professional (and toward continued professional development) as he or she begins to work with ELLs who are at multiple levels of learning.

DOMAIN I (Language Concepts and Language Acquisition/ Preparation Before Teaching ESL or Before the Classroom)

Standard I (Concepts, Structure, and Conventions of English) and Standard III (L1 and L2 Language Acquisition)

*Note that many of the terms under each standard are found throughout the chapter in bold, italics, or in the glossary at the end of the chapter.

ESL Competency 001: The ESL teacher understands fundamental language concepts and knows the **structure** and conventions of the English language. There are a number of terms and concepts in the following list that relate to this competency.

- Fundamental language concepts
- Language structure
- **Conventions of language**
- **Phonology**
- **Morphology**
- **Syntax**
- Lexical understanding
- **Semantics**
- **Discourse**
- **Pragmatics**

- **Registers of language**
- **Social versus academic language**
- **Modifying instructional materials**
- **Delivery of instruction**
- English language proficiency
- **Interrelatedness of listening, speaking, reading, and writing**
- **Word formation**
- **Grammar**
- **Sentence structure**

Before a teacher ever steps into an ESL classroom, he or she must already understand general *pedagogy,* or the knowledge of teaching. Some of this knowledge includes (but is not limited to) the characteristics of human development, diversity in learning, and the expected knowledge and skills base for students according to the state of Texas (the TEKS). This also includes management and how learning, in general, occurs in terms of acquisition, cognition, and **metacognition**, or thinking about one's own thinking. Hopefully, much of this information was already learned for the *Pedagogy and Professional Responsibilities (PPR)* TExES exam required of all Texas teachers. If not, we recommend reading *Becoming an EC-6 Teacher in Texas* (Nath & Cohen, 2011) or *Becoming a Middle or High School Teacher in Texas* (Nath & Cohen, 2005).

From here, the teacher must also be able to engage the class with effective ESL instruction and create an environment of equity for ESL students. In the course of classroom instruction, the teacher now learns how to help students perfect their oral communication skills while being careful to avoid biases as students are learning their second language. At this point, implementing technology to present and represent information in innovative ways and assessing the effectiveness of instruction through student evaluation become important. Texas suggests that teachers and students use a variety of media (audiotapes, videotapes, DVDs, and CD ROMs). When monitoring and assessments reveal a specific need, the ESL teacher should focus on a student's weak areas and make efforts to improve them immediately (often in collaboration with colleagues who may have the same student for other content areas). What is learned about students' strengths and weaknesses should be shared with families in a manner that they can easily understand and do not find offensive. From working with families, teachers continue to grow in multicultural awareness. In keeping up with these demands, teachers must remain vigilant to improve and **advocate** for all ESL students, knowing that the road for them will be rougher than for those students who do not have to grapple with learning a new language in addition to the state required content and who must find their places in what may be very foreign classrooms and social situations.

Facing the task of learning English requires the prerequisite understanding that **fundamental English language concepts** (basic English rules) are essential for an ELL to become fluent. The **structure** (formal systematic arrangements of a language) and **conventions of English** (generally accepted usage) are acquired in the beginning through oral interactions as an ELL concurrently works toward higher levels of lexical understanding (terms used in academic content, such as mathematics, science, and social studies). To revisit many of these concepts, test takers may want to reread Chapter 2 on the **English Language Arts (ELA)** competencies for the concepts and terms. Table 10.3 shows a comprehensive look at each developmental stage in ELA. All ESL teachers in Texas are expected to know and apply strategies for instruction for each of the ELA competencies.

As an ESL teacher, one should become adept at being able to initiate an individual child's instruction at his or her developmentally appropriate level (Kagan, 1995; Wertsch, 1985), as well as his or her language **proficiency** level. To find that level, the teacher should informally assess the prior knowledge and skills of students through simple **oral discourse** (conversation). Moreover, literacy skills should be built through the **interrelatedness of speaking, listening, reading, and writing.** This delivery depends entirely on where individual students are in their English, in their other academics, and on the dynamics of the classroom. **Social language** versus **academic language** must be intertwined in the curriculum, because true **English language proficiency** does not happen if the learner is not exposed to a rich environment of dialogue that he or she can comprehend, hands-on problem solving, and the chance to frequently reflect on previous verbal and **cognitive processes** (thinking processes). To emphasize the point, the classroom should be alive with conversation in these areas.

When teaching students who are acquiring a second language, it is imperative to understand that language ability level has no set age or grade level. Students learning a new language in the sixth grade may be starting at the same spot as those children who are 2 years old. The key difference is that the sixth grader has usually and more fully learned his or her **first (home) language (L1)** with all the rules of that language and may have the ability to quickly **transfer language skills** from the L1 to the **second language (L2)**. For example, if you know that a pronoun takes the place of a noun in your own language and if there are pronouns in the new language, you understand readily how they function; conversely, if you do not know, you must first learn the general language structure before going on. However, the problem in acquiring a new language for older learners is that making oral mistakes can be embarrassing, which can severely hamper new learning. To their advantage, many young children seem less concerned with errors and continue to practice—with much trial and error, gestures, and so forth.

Try this question:

The following question tests knowledge of English concepts, structure, and conventions. See how you do with your knowledge and application of understanding!

Take note of the following sentence: *Jorge gave his grandmother a kiss.* In this sentence, the word *grandmother* is a/an:

- **A.** indirect object.
- **B.** direct object
- **C.** prepositional phrase.
- **D.** appositive clause.

First, determine what Jorge is giving (or what was it that he directly gave). The direct object (*B*) was a kiss. To whom was it given? He gave the direct object (the kiss) to his grandmother (who is the indirect object or the receiver). Choice *A* is the correct answer.

A *prepositional phrase* (*C*) begins with words such as *across, before, toward, to, from, at, in, up, with,* and so forth and is followed by a noun or a pronoun that creates some type of relationship or direction (*down* the stairs, *on* the counter, *within* her heart). An *appositive clause* (*D*) is a noun or pronoun that usually follows another noun or pronoun to describe or clearly identify the first one in some manner (e.g., Ms. Kelly, *the teacher,* ate lunch in the classroom.).

For a teacher to be able to help ELLs, it is extremely important to understand English grammar and structure first and to try to anticipate the mistakes that ELLs can make. For example, an ESL teacher noticed that all her ELLs missed a mathematics word problem that read: *Jack put three cans on the shelf and then he put three cans on the floor. How many cans did he have altogether?* The ELLs had read the word *can* as a verb rather than a noun and could not decipher what the question was asking. A good ESL teacher could anticipate this problem and help ELLs understand English grammar/structure. Again, be sure to go back to Chapter 2 or other sources if you are uncertain about your English/language arts information. The correct answer is *A.*

In order to best create effective learning for ELLs, the ESL teacher understands that expectations to learn English also involve the eleven vital areas of ELA learning in the following list and in Table 10.3. Thus, the ESL teacher is responsible for two main sets of competencies—(1) the English Language Arts (ELA) (found in Chapter 2) and (2) those ESL competencies presented in this

Table 10.3 EC-4 *Generalist* English Language Arts Competencies for ESL Teachers (ESL EC-4 *Generalist*)

Competency 011 (Oral Language) The teacher understands the importance of oral language, knows the developmental processes of oral language, and provides learners with varied opportunities to develop listening and speaking skills.

Competency 012 (Phonological and Phonemic Awareness) The teacher understands phonological and phonemic awareness and employs a variety of approaches to help children develop phonological and phonemic awareness.

Competency 013 (Alphabetic Principle) The teacher understands the importance of the alphabetic principle for reading English and provides instruction that helps children understand the relationship between printed words and spoken language.

Competency 014 (Literacy Development) The teacher understands that literacy develops over time, progressing from emergent to proficient stages, and uses a variety of approaches to support the development of children's literacy.

Competency 015 (Word Analysis and Decoding) The teacher understands the importance of word analysis and decoding for reading and provides many opportunities for children to improve their word-analysis and decoding abilities.

Competency 016 (Reading Fluency) The teacher understands the importance of fluency for reading comprehension and provides many opportunities for children to improve their reading fluency.

Competency 017 (Reading Comprehension) The teacher understands the importance of reading for understanding, knows the components of comprehension, and teaches children strategies for improving their comprehension.

Competency 018 (Research and Comprehension Skills in the Content Areas) The teacher understands the importance of research and comprehension skills to children's academic success and provides children with instruction that promotes their acquisition and effective use of these skills in the content areas.

Competency 019 (Writing Conventions) The teacher understands the conventions of writing in English and provides instruction that helps children develop proficiency in using writing conventions.

Competency 020 (Development of Written Communication) The teacher understands that writing to communicate is a developmental process and provides instruction that promotes children's competence in written communication.

Competency 021 (Assessment of Developing Literacy) The teacher understands the basic principles of literacy assessment and uses a variety of assessments to guide literacy instruction.

chapter. If the teacher is self-contained, there will be corresponding competencies (and TEKS) for all subjects that he or she teaches, and ESL techniques should then be used across the curriculum. The ELA areas are:

1. Oral language
2. Phonological and phonemic development
3. Understanding the **alphabetic principle**
4. **Literacy development**
5. Word analysis and decoding
6. Reading fluency
7. **Reading comprehension**
8. Research and comprehension skills in the content areas
9. Writing conventions
10. Development of written communication
11. Assessment of developing literacy

As mentioned, one of the most difficult obstacles for many new ESL teachers to overcome is the idea that language proficiency levels may not be age- or grade-level specific. No matter what age the child may be or the grade level in which he or she is placed (Pre-K through grade 12), the English ability or proficiency level of a particular ESL student could be labeled as beginning, intermediate, advanced, and advanced high (in some districts, levels are labeled pre-production, early production, speech emergent, intermediate fluent, and advanced fluent [levels 1–5]). This means that an ESL teacher should become thoroughly aware of the proficiency levels indicators from the early childhood level up through the upper grades (the English Language Proficiency Standards [ELPS], which can be accessed from http://ritter.tea.state.tx.us/rules/tac/chapter074/ch074a.html#74.4). It is the teacher's duty to find and provide developmentally appropriate/on-level lessons for ESL students—no matter what the grade and **language levels**. Further, the student's proficiency level in English may be different in each domain (listening, speaking, reading, and writing). For example, a student may already be a fluent reader in English, but may not yet be a fluent speaker of English. Knowing what happens in each level, as well as knowing the TEKS (especially those for reading and language arts) at each grade level, is the responsibility of an ESL teacher (Wertsch, 1985). Table 10.4 summarizes these ESL TEKS.

Table 10.4 Summary of Pre-K–Grade 6 in ESL Language Arts and Reading

Pre-K

Communication and literacy begin. Interact with responsive adults and peers. Develop listening comprehension, phonological awareness, functions of print, motivation to read, appreciation for literary form, print awareness, and letter knowledge.

Kindergarten

Develop increased oral language. Begin to read and write. Extend vocabulary and conceptual knowledge. Follow directions. Discuss the meanings of words. Express complete thoughts. Listen to children's literature and informational material. Listen attentively, ask, and respond to questions and retell stories. Distinguish fiction from nonfiction. Identify and write the letters of the alphabet. Segment and identify the sounds in spoken words. Write the letters, one's name, and other words. Dictate for others to write.

Grade 1

Develop increased oral language. Become independent readers and writers. Listen attentively and connect experiences and ideas with information and ideas presented in print. Listen and respond to a wide variety of children's literature. Books heard introduce new vocabulary. Recognize features of texts. Develop print with spoken language. Decode words. Read (orally and silently) with fluency and understanding. Demonstrate comprehension. Become adept writers. Use subjects and verbs and write complete sentences. Become more proficient spellers.

Grade 2

Read and write independently. Use spoken language. Understand purposes for speaking and listening. Hold the attention of classmates. Recognize a large number of words and word identification strategies. Read regularly for understanding and fluency in a variety of genres. Read to acquire new information. Summarize what is read and represent ideas. Use references to build word meanings and pronunciation. Revise and edit writing to make ideas more clear and precise. Use appropriate capitalization and punctuation. Use singular and plural nouns and adjust verbs for agreement. Penmanship is legible. Compile notes into outlines.

Grade 3

Read and write more independently. Spend significant time engaged in reading and writing for assigned tasks and projects. Listen critically to spoken messages, contribute to discussions, and plan oral presentations. Read grade-level material fluently and with comprehension. Use root words, prefixes, suffixes, and derivational endings to recognize words. Demonstrate knowledge of synonyms, antonyms, and multi-meaning words. Distinguish fact from opinion. Support ideas and inferences by citing portions of the text discussed. Read in a variety of genres. Write with more complex capitalization and punctuation. Write with contractions and homonyms. Write longer and more elaborate sentences and organize writing into larger units of text. Write several drafts to produce a final product. Master manuscript writing and use cursive writing.

(continued)

Table 10.4 Continued

Grade 4

Read and write for extended periods. Become critical listeners and analyze a speaker's intent. Adapt spoken language to the audience, purpose, and occasion. Read classic and contemporary selections. Read with a growing interest. Expand vocabulary across the curriculum. Read for meaning and paraphrase. Connect, compare, and contrast ideas. Identify and follow varied **text structures**. Produce summaries of texts and more sophisticated analysis of characters, plots, and settings. Use different forms of writing for specific purposes. Writing takes on style and voice. Write in complete sentences. Use adjectives, adverbs, prepositional phrases, and conjunctions. Become proficient spellers. Edit writing based on knowledge of grammar and usage, spelling, punctuation, and other conventions of written language. Produce a polished written composition. Use visual media and compare and contrast visual media to print.

Grade 5

Increase and refine skills in more complex presentations, reading selections, and compositions. Identify persuasive techniques. Read from classic, contemporary, and informational texts. Judge logic and internal consistency. Recognize author organization and analyze characters, plots, and settings. Select and use writing for purposes, such as informing, persuading, or entertaining. Use literary devises, such as suspense, dialogue, and figurative language. Produce error-free composition regularly. Create research reports or projects based on multiple sources supported by visuals.

Grade 6

Take notes during oral presentations (organizing and summarizing spoken messages). Evaluate their own oral presentations. Read widely from classic, contemporary, and informational texts. Understand idioms, multi-meaning words, and analogy. Distinguish between *denotative meaning* (accepted general meaning; dictionary meaning) and *connotative meaning* (associations that a word elicits beyond the dictionary meaning and based on experiences) meanings of words as an aid to understanding historical influences on word meanings. Use study strategies. Recognize literary devices, such as flashback, foreshadowing, and symbolism. Select and use writing for purposes such as informing, persuading, or entertaining. Vary sentence structure. Use complex punctuation (hyphens, semicolons, possessives). Edit and produce error-free writing. Use conventions of written language. Create research reports or projects based on multiple sources supported by visuals. Evaluate purposes/effects of film, print, and technology.

Try this question:

Mrs. Schultz greeted her new third-grade student from Italy who arrived on Monday morning. Mrs. Schultz quickly made time to talk with Elena, who spoke a little English. Mrs. Schultz asked Elena if she had any pets at home, and Elena answered, "I gots two cat." Although Mrs. Schultz continues later with more assessment, this informal oral assessment gives her a good idea on where to begin Elena's instruction. At what level of the TEKS in ESL Language Arts and Reading should she begin?

A. Pre-K–K
B. K–1
C. 1–2
D. 3–4

This question asks us to closely examine Table 10.4. In Grade 2, one finds that students should learn to use singular and plural nouns and adjust verbs for agreement. This is clearly a skill that Elena is lacking. The correct answer is *C.*

Competency 002: The ESL teacher understands the processes of first language (L1) and second language (L2) acquisition and the interrelatedness of L1 and L2 development. Some terms and concepts for this competency are listed below.

- L1 and L2 acquisition
- **Theories**
- **Behaviorist theory**
- Nativist theory

- Cognitive development theory
- Cognitive processes
- Memorization
- **Categorization**
- **Generalization**
- Metacognition
- **Synthesizing**
- **Idiomatic expressions**
- Syntax
- Phonology
- Morphology

Understanding Language Acquisition

There are several ideas about how human beings learn their first language (L1). Some theorists tell us that language is a *human condition;* that is, we are born with an innate ability for it to happen. Because we are internally wired with this ability, as soon as we are exposed to language, this ability kicks in. This is called the **nativist theory**. Others say that language is learned in a **behaviorist** way, so when we are reinforced often by our caregivers or others after making certain sounds, we repeat or correct what we hear. For example, a parent repeatedly says "bye-bye" or "ball" to the toddler, then praises, smiles, and gives further attention to the child when he or she says (or comes close to saying) these words. **Social cognitive** and **social cultural** theorists believe that we learn our first language through continuous social interaction and through the modeling of adults and peers who are more knowledgeable, because these models adjust their language to fit the level of the young child or learner but who then make sure to increase the difficulty as children's language skills develop. This theory explains why many people use baby talk with very young children, but they do not use it as the child grows older.

Those who study language acquisition believe that learning one's first language (L1) progresses through certain stages, beginning at birth. These stages include first listening before being able to speak and progressing into cooing and babbling. Other early stages that perhaps have more relevance to teaching a second language are the use of one word for communication (*Drink!* or *Mine!*). Next comes using two words with pivots (a small group of words to which another is added to create a meaningful sentence of sorts: *bye bye* mommy, *throw* ball, *see* toy, *want* juice, *all* gone) and adding descriptive words but without articles (give big piece; throw red ball). Language learners also progress through a stage where there is **overgeneralization** of the application of a rule for all cases (such as adding *–ed* to make the past tense as in "She *wented* to the store"). These stages are important to know because researchers tell us that second language acquisition (L2) *parallels* these (not including the very early stages). Thus it is vital for the ESL teacher to take on various roles, such as the behaviorist reinforcer, when learners make attempts and to provide specific feedback and modeling that caregivers normally would provide (sometimes referred to as *motherse*). For example, a child might say, "Sue good girl!" and mom gives appropriate feedback by saying, "Yes (smiling), Sue is a very good girl today!" or "No (frowning), Sue is not a good girl today."

In language acquisition, there are also five other important hypotheses concerning how newly arrived English language learners (ELLs) tackle the grueling task of comprehending and speaking a new language (Krashen, 1992). The following section describes each of these five hypotheses:

1. Acquisition-learning hypothesis
2. Natural approach
3. Affective filter hypothesis
4. Comprehensible input hypothesis
5. Monitor hypothesis

Most college graduates have had to learn another language at some point in their schooling, so it is most helpful to remember what helped your learning (or what may have hindered it) and apply those experiences to the following language theories and strategies. It is also helpful to create an empathy needed for understanding the ELL by thinking back on one's own struggle to grasp another language either through a language class or, perhaps, in travelling to a foreign country. Always remember, too, that an ELL is not only besieged with the language but with a new culture—and trying to study content—all at the same time. The more that the teacher can do to assist, the better chance the student has overall in achievement. The ESL teacher must know and apply strategies based on these hypotheses for the purpose of helping students to attain competence in total communication in English.

Let's look more closely at each of these important hypotheses.

The Acquisition-Learning Hypothesis (*Meaning to Structure* with Two Theories Combined)

In the first hypothesis, Krashen (1992) states that there are two distinct types of learning used to understand and communicate in a second language: (1) *acquired knowledge* and (2) *learned knowledge*. Both are connected as the student progresses towards learning English. Language **acquisition** often occurs unconsciously and automatically in various types of interactions with the new language or with native speakers in order to produce an output (either oral or written). For example, if traveling in a foreign country, one might subconsciously acquire the foreign term for *stop* because the word is posted on all stop signs on the roads, and the traveler recognizes the shape and placement of the sign. This same traveler might be able, should a young child run out into a dangerous situation, to say the word *stop* in the foreign language—not really understanding from where the word was acquired. A traveler might also pick up the foreign word for *thank you* after hearing it several times when a salesperson hands over a purchase. Acquired knowledge is also the basis for developing "an ear" for how to say things or why we can sometimes understand what someone has uttered without having studied another language formally.

For Krashen (1992), **learned knowledge** is that which is purposefully gained (or studied) about a language, its structure, and the way it functions. Thus, the sort of formal type of knowledge obtained through grammatical graphing of sentences and other conscious study of language is different from the knowledge of grammar obtained (or acquired) through interpersonal communication. As a beginning **foreign language** learner, for example, one may be able to say a few phrases and conjugate some verbs correctly, but when faced with an actual conversation or having to write quickly, the speaker may become lost. Therefore, knowledge about grammar must also be learned intentionally through some formal work and practiced in listening and in speech consistently. These rules simply must be used in conversation to the point that speech actually sounds correct to the ELL student. This makes the modeling of correctly spoken English (with grammar rules entrenched) extremely important for language learners on a regular basis. When learning grammar rules, an ESL student can often verbalize those rules and state why something is said for one reason or another. However, actually employing those rules while participating in the normal flow of English conversation is difficult, especially in the beginning, and multiple application situations are required. In comparison, structures and concepts of English acquired through communicative experiences become available more automatically. What does all this mean? Acquired language and learned knowledge about English must go hand-in-hand. Meaningful and purposeful communicative experiences in cooperative situations provide some of the best opportunities for learners to link a language rule with its oral application in normal conversation. Although this linking of meaning is a primary process of language acquisition, the study of hard and fast grammar rules usually involves the development of some new, sometimes difficult concepts that may or may not exist as a parallel to the learner's **primary language**. Two examples are (1) that some languages other than English use verb endings only in place of a pronoun and a verb—thus pronouns are not commonly used, and (2) some languages do not have contractions or high-frequency irregular sight words. An ESL teacher must also consider that through age or educational circumstances, a student may not even speak or write his or her first language correctly or understand its mechanics and conventions well. English concepts are, for them, not only difficult, but they need to learn more rules about general language structure that were never needed before. The linking of grammatical terminology to completely new language concepts is part of what Krashen calls *learning*. Conscious efforts made by an ELL to use more advanced grammar at higher levels of lexical understanding (academic English) would also be a part of learned knowledge.

The concepts of *acquisition* and *learning* then become mentally linked (*meaning to structure*) through conversation and from the study of grammar. Therefore, there is always a need for the ELL to read, write, speak, and listen regularly, even at the earliest stages of language development. Acquisition takes place during meaningful communication, but the study of grammar is important to continue language development and for increased understanding and correctness. Studying how sentences are put together in the new language facilitates processing future understanding and allows easier *meaning to structure* connections that are the basis of even deeper acquisition. The two are inevitably intertwined, but for Krashen (1992), emphasizing acquisition experiences is the most important when students are beginning to learn a new language.

The Natural Order Hypothesis

According to the second hypothesis in language acquisition (Krashen & Terrell, 1996), convergent research suggests that language structures tend to be acquired in a predictable, rarely variable order. For example, students of English first use morphemes to communicate without articles such as *the, a,* and so on ("Go lunch now"; Give book"; "Get drink"). The use of plural nouns is also acquired early, whereas possessives (such as *Juan's pencil*) are not. The third person "s" (as in "He talk<u>s</u>") is also acquired later. However, no research reports the exact order of learning and application of the rules of language for each and every student. Moreover, the natural order hypothesis assumes that the order of actual acquisition and the order of learning may be different. For example, students of English who study the rules of verb conjugation (learned early in grammar-translation methodology) may take several years before actually being able to use these correctly in formal and informal conversation. Thus, it appears that, although some grammar rules on language structure are learned early, mastery in the conversational use of other rules happens only after substantial periods of communication in the second language. Still, if ESL teachers know that, in general, some structures are normally acquired before others in language learning, their expectations for students' learning can be applied more easily.

The Affective Filter Hypothesis

The third hypothesis states that language acquisition takes place in low-anxiety, comfortable situations. Students who are asked to stand up and speak to the entire class when they are feeling inadequate and pressured will surely not be able to get past their internal turmoil; hence, emotional mental blocks can prevent the disposition for language learning. Although rote learning can take place under adverse conditions, language acquisition requires that students be able to attend to input and output in a more relaxed environment. This means that students with high-anxiety perceptions about making oral mistakes, poorly motivated students, and those with lower self-esteem often experience problems in acquisition activities. The best programs are those that attempt to remove stress and pressure, for an ESL teacher may already expect frustration, crying, etc. from many new arrivals. Accelerated language programs, for example, seek to override anxiety factors by having students play games, sing songs, and even take on the name and persona of someone else, so that it is not the actual ESL student who might make a mistake—but "another." This program suggests an environment of playfulness in which students acquire much language in social situations, and *Suggestopedia* techniques, first created by Georgi Lozanov for teaching foreign languages, **enhance learning** by centering on the affective domain and includes music, relaxation, and room decoration to heighten the senses and allow acquisition to "simply flow in." ESL teachers should make efforts to use these types of strategies continuously.

Also supported by research is allowing students to wait a short time to participate in English when they do not yet feel ready. This early **silent period** allows beginning ELLs to listen and gain confidence before forcing any output. Although this period may last up to several months before any production in English is made, the learner is taking in a great deal of the language. ESL teachers should consider that this is a natural part of language learning and try to avoid frustration when new ESL students enter their classrooms.

The ESL teacher should be cognizant of the importance of students being interested in the activities in which they participate and in which they feel at ease with their peers. Classroom interactions must be supportive rather than competitive in nature. If the student does not (or cannot) attend to the input, acquisition will not take place. Both a sincere interest in the success of students and a trusting ESL teacher/student relationship are essential.

In order to best create a positive environment for language acquisition, the ESL teacher should understand that learning a new language takes place through multiple oral interactions in the target language (English). Therefore, it is important to have numerous examples of what the intended outcome should sound like modeled by native speakers (e.g., teachers, peers, technology, media). It is only after a student has heard and processed the correct word or phrase in several ways that it shows up in his or her conversation. For this reason, it is of paramount importance that the ESL teacher be a continuous active listener, participant, and reinforcer in normal conversation. Teachable moments in simple conversations with students lend many opportunities for ELLs to quickly relate meaning to structure without damaging their pride. Stopping conversation to impose a language rule can often create confusion or embarrassment, and the teacher must be cognizant of being careful not to crush the self-esteem of the learner in these early exchanges. Think of how you would feel if you were Alberto telling his teacher about learning to ride his new bicycle:

Alberto: I try hard yesterday, teacher.

Ms. Cane: No, Alberto. It's *tried*! *Yesterday* means it was past tense. We almost always add *-ed* to past tense. I *try* today, but I *tried* yesterday! Remember, it's *tried*!

Keeping low-key, natural (rather than more stressful) conversations going—with plenty of examples of how English is to be used at the given moment—is the constant duty of the ESL teacher. Mr. Bennett has a more supportive conversation.

Alberto: I try hard yesterday, teacher.

Mr. Bennett: I know you *tried* hard. If you fell three times, you *tried* very hard. I'm proud of you that you *tried* so hard. Will you *try* again today?

The Input Hypothesis

The fourth hypothesis in Krashen's (1992) language acquisition hypotheses, the Input Hypothesis, attempts to explain that language acquisition can occur within the context of total communication as the student attends to a combination of both spoken language and body language that often accompany oral speech. Spoken language and gestures contain vocabulary, grammatical forms, inferred meaning, and other structures to be acquired. Comprehension takes place when the learner concentrates on the meaning expressed during the *total communication* process (both verbal and nonverbal) and is successful in connecting *meaning to structure*; that is, language acquisition occurs during the course of regular, natural conversation. There is, however, a twist to this theory in teaching. Very similar to Vygotsky's zone of proximal development (Wertsch, 1985), the teacher must determine a zone of conversation that slightly challenges the ELL in English yet remains understandable for the learner, perhaps through the use of extra cues such as pointing, gestures, employing pictures or real objects, using analogy to known vocabulary, and so forth. This is sometimes called *i* + **1**, meaning that the teacher considers the student's ability level to comprehend input (*i*) and adds one level (+1) above that.

The Input Hypothesis for the ESL teacher is one of the most important to use but can be the least understood in ESL instruction. It tells us that ELLs *output* (or what they are able to say) is in direct relation to what they heard and understood. Thus, the Input Hypothesis should concern itself with the interchange of understandable ideas—focusing on the zone of proximal development in which each child can comprehend. Acquisition, according to this theory, is entirely dependent on **comprehensive input** (what the learner can actually understand that is presented to him or her in all levels of discourse). ESL students first understand new words and grammar used in conversation; then the student reproduces those words in other meaningful interactions. The reproduction of this spoken, comprehensible exchange is indispensable for development and continued success in the English language. No amount of explanation and drill can substitute for real communicative experiences; thus, the ESL teacher must continuously provide those experiences within the confines of the daily routine to ensure that she or he is using comprehensive, understandable input for each individual child's level, and that the zone of exchange is slightly challenging for the learner.

The Monitor Hypothesis

Finally, the Monitor Hypothesis blends acquired knowledge and grammatical knowledge in regular conversation—again, with a twist. Language learners use their formal knowledge about the rules of the new language and the way it functions as a monitor to guide correct output before the production—a quick "think about it before you communicate it" brain function with a correction monitor if the thought should come out wrong first. Monitoring speech with grammar rules is usually limited to situations in which there is *time* to think about it. Most learners monitor relatively well when given ample time to think about what they want to say before speaking or answering, but monitoring is very difficult for most second language learners during a normal conversation, because the rapid pace used by native speakers does not lend itself well to giving ample time for this type of thinking. Also, some students are very poor at monitoring in all situations because it is difficult for them to remember the rule or to focus on correctness in a conversational flow at the same time. This is the reason why it is imperative for the ESL teacher to become an active and participatory speaker and listener and to provide immediate feedback when students inaccurately monitor their output. For instance, with the help of the ESL teacher, most students can monitor their errors with little lost time or loss of self-confidence (i.e., a student says, "I go store today," and the ESL teacher uses **circumlocution** for the purpose of letting the student hear how the English should sound by saying, "Oh, you are going to *the* store? What will you buy at *the* store? Is it *the* store at the mall or is it *the* store nearby?" The student replies, "It is the store at the mall." In this exaggerated repetition of the word *the*, the ESL teacher modeled the correct usage enough times that the student could easily self-monitor and continue talking about other matters.

Because monitoring formal knowledge of grammar learned through drill-and-practice is difficult in real-time contexts, it makes more sense to use acquisition-oriented activities in the ESL classroom. Grammar exercises are primarily to be done as written work or homework in order to give adequate time for reflection on and use of those rules. Finally, the Monitor Hypothesis reminds us that the ability to achieve on formal paper-and-pencil exams (where there is more time to think) is not the same as the ability to use language in natural, spontaneous conversation or in rapid fire classroom instruction.

This question tests the ESL teacher's knowledge and application skills related to the competency of language acquisition. See how you do!

Which situation best encourages acquisition of language?

- **A.** Researching a social studies issue on the Internet
- **B.** Academic language proficiency
- **C.** Interpersonal communication
- **D.** Writing a term paper for science

Language acquisition is not really "taught." By providing language interaction in the classroom, language is acquired. It is only after students have perfected understanding through listening and speaking that they can also apply high levels of conceptual skills. For that reason, the ESL teacher knows that higher levels of cognitive application come when ESL students have had plenty of practice in interpersonal communication (or work with the context of speaking and listening in English) (C). The idea of basic communication is what Cummins (1979) referred to as **Basic Interpersonal Communication Skills (BICS)** that students usually develop within *six months to two years*. Researching (A), academic language proficiency (B), and writing papers inundated with lexical terminology (D) are all skills referred to by Cummins as **Cognitive Academic Language Proficiency Skills (CALPS)**. These advanced language skills, needed for academics and higher levels of expression, can take anywhere from 5 to 7 years to learn; therefore, they are not part of a reasonable answer to this question. With that said, it is easy to understand how many students in ESL struggle so intensely to barely pass when the instruction they receive leaps past BICS and heads directly to trying to make sense of higher-order conceptual understanding in CALPS. When teachers move too quickly into teaching at the CALPS level, there may be ELLs who are still trying to acquire simple basic language (BICS) at the same time they are required to use high-level academic terms and thoughts in English.

Language is best *acquired* through common interaction with native speakers and the environment, including culture and experience. The correct answer is C.

DOMAIN II ESL Instruction and Assessment/In the Classroom/ During Teaching

Standard I (Concepts, Structure, & Conventions of English)
Standard III (L1 & L2 Language Acquisition)
Standard IV (ESL Methods and Instruction in the Classroom
Standard V (ESL Academic Content, Language, and Culture)
Standard VI (Formal and Informal Assessment)

Competency 003: The ESL teacher understands ESL teaching methods and uses this knowledge to plan and implement effective, developmentally appropriate instruction. Some important terms and concepts for this competency are listed below.

- Planning instruction
- **Developmentally appropriate instruction**
- **Texas Essential Knowledge and Skills (TEKS)**
- English language arts and reading curriculum
- TEKS (listening, speaking, reading, writing, viewing/representing)

- **Instructional goals**
- Diverse characteristics and needs
- **Content-based ESL** instruction
- Active instruction
- **Critical thinking**
- Communicative competence
- Technology tools
- Classroom management
- Teaching strategies

Planning for effective instruction that is developmentally appropriate and particular to ESL always begins with a firm understanding of expectations for students. Perhaps the best place to find these expectations is in the **Texas Essential Knowledge and Skills (TEKS)** for students. The TEKS, especially the English language arts and reading curriculum as it relates to ESL, are important to address daily, especially in areas such as listening, speaking, reading, writing, and viewing and representing. **Viewing and representing** is an extra language domain that stresses the importance of using various technology and media with ELLs, due to the ease of combining audio, visual, tactile, and graphical organization of content and conceptual overviews. *Viewing* is defined by The University of Texas Center for Reading and Language Arts (UTCRLA) as understanding and interpreting visual communications that are conveyed nonverbally, and *representing* is being able to express understanding through producing some type of visual media (UTCRLA, 2003).

What is important for ESL teachers to remember is that even though the ESL TEKS may be written for the ideal level of student achievement, these aims must often be readjusted to the current student levels in English acquisition and cognitive academic language proficiency levels (CALPS). The ESL teacher must constantly assess students' individual academic levels and plan methodological strategies that match students' current achievement with growth toward future goals in language mastery. The following explains the role of the TEKS in more detail:

- The TEKS are required knowledge for each grade level in all subject areas; therefore, each grade-level listing is prerequisite knowledge for the next higher grade. Looking at the TEKS from a student's previous grade level ensures that the ESL teacher knows what students should know and should be able to do when entering their respective grade levels. Studying the TEKS for the grade level to which a teacher is assigned helps him or her understand what students should know when they exit that grade at the end of that academic year.

- The TEKS are not how to teach content; they are the listed content knowledge and skills required for students at each grade level. The order and emphasis placed on teaching the TEKS is up to the ESL teacher. Methods should be matched to this list of knowledge and skills to provide the most appropriate approach in an effort to ensure student achievement.
- The ESL TEKS are divided into the domains of listening, speaking, reading, writing and viewing and representing, and each of these areas should be included on a daily basis.

ESL Methods

First, the ESL teacher must understand that ESL methodologies are a body of practices and strategies that are especially effective for ELLs. The teacher should learn about those methods that work for learning English, plus those that work well with ESL learning in the content areas (such as sheltered mathematics for ESL, science for ESL, and so on, or for **self-contained ESL**).

- *Linguistic instruction* should include initiating frequent interaction with English-speaking peers (through cooperative groups), as well as materials for language acquisition and cognitive development. One way to accomplish this is to use restructuring groups where students are regrouped often so that they interact with a wide range of peers who may be at different levels in learning English or with those who are native speakers.
- *Sheltered English* (or Specially Designed Academic Instruction in English/SDATE) is an instructional approach used to make academic content instruction in English understandable to ESL students. In the lesson plan, the teacher combines (1) cognitively challenging but understandable instruction in a content area, (2) English language, and (3) a focus on social/affective development. In the sheltered classroom, teachers use physical activities and visual aids in the content areas (e.g., science, social studies, mathematics) in flexible group interactions with considerable **scaffolding** and attention to building on students' prior knowledge.
- *Reciprocal teaching* refers to an instructional activity that takes place in the form of a dialogue between teachers and students using segments of text. The dialogue is structured by the use of four strategies: summarizing, question generating, clarifying, and predicting. The teacher and his or her students take turns assuming the role of teacher in this dialogue.
- *Model reading/big books and pointers* should include the teacher helping beginning ESL learners by modeling the reading process, especially for those who have no literacy experiences or who may have languages with different directionalities for reading (to see that English is read from top to bottom and left to right) and employing *shared reading* (in whole or small groups, the teacher or peers read one story together, and the leader asks many questions and demonstrates explicit ways to read as the entire group reads along together).
- *Audiolingual* (new materials are presented in the form of a dialogue).
- *Brainstorming* (asking students to tell all they know on a topic; this gives the teacher a concrete view on known vocabulary and on what the class knows about a topic).
- *Buddy System Pairing* (combining a beginning speaker with a more capable speaker).

- *Computer-Assisted Instruction (CAI)* (the use of computers in education and training).
- *Computer-Assisted Language (CAL)* (computer technology is used as an aid to the presentation, reinforcement, and assessment of material to be learned; usually includes a substantial interactive element).
- *Communicative Approach* (or the *functional approach*; based on the theory that language is acquired through exposure to meaningful and understandable messages rather than learned through the formal study of grammar and vocabulary).
- *Community Language Learning,* or *participatory approach* (especially for older learners who may fear appearing foolish), where the teacher becomes a "language counselor," and together with the "client," works to understand what is needed, meaningful, and important to the learner in learning the new language; students themselves define their needs for learning English based on the context of their lives in the real world, and the teacher acts as a facilitator.
- *Conferencing* (one-on-one discussion with student to discuss assignments).
- *Cooperative Learning Groups* (heterogeneous groups with varying levels of English who provide support for each other).
- *Counseling Learning (CL)* (facilitation of learning by closely monitoring and guiding student engagement as needed to enhance success).
- *Critical Pedagogy* (teacher leads students to question ideologies and practices considered oppressive; can relate to power issues in speaking particular languages).
- *Critical Thinking* (ELLs are as capable as other students of thinking at higher levels—they just may simply not have enough English to explain; ESL teachers must apply instruction at the linguist level to include critical thinking tasks).
- *Debate* (students gain oral skills through arguing meaningful issues with their peers).
- *Direct Method* (a teaching technique in which the English language is used from the very beginning).
- *English for Special Purposes* (English for science, technological, or other academic or occupational specializations).
- *Grammar Translation* (vocabulary is taught in the form of isolated word lists).
- *Journal Writing or Drawing* (students write or illustrate each day on a topic; drawing is particularly effective for expressing comprehension early on).
- *Language Experience Approach (LEA)* (student dictates as the teacher writes down what was said).
- *Logs on Learning* (having students write down each day what they understood about main concepts).
- *Natural Approach* (pioneered by Krashen, this approach combines acquisition and formal learning as a means of facilitating language development in adults).
- *Notetaking* (teacher gives a note page or outline that is partially filled out or asks students to write down important facts as he/she specifically accentuates these points during a lesson); should match the students abilities.
- *Role-play* (students practice situations that are common in order to feel comfortable in the language; teachers act out appropriate concepts).
- *Semantic Mapping* (a visual strategy for organizing vocabulary around a theme to expand and extend thought; concept mapping).
- *Silent Way* (a method in which the teacher doesn't speak very much but basically uses manipulatives to induce students to learn language structure by having students direct the teacher in certain requests (e.g., the student says, "Take a red pencil" [if there are several red pencils] or "Take the red pencil" [if only one] to teach when to use *a* and *the*).

- *Storytelling* (teachers encourage students to work up a family or traditional tale to perform or tape for others).
- *Story Retelling* (summarizing/sequencing an already heard story).
- *Drawing/Bizarre Images* (when students draw their meaning, it helps them remember more readily; for example, to help remember that *carta* in Spanish is a letter, a learner may draw a picture of a cart with a mailman driving it with a big bag of letters in the back; students who do not feel comfortable retelling a story in English yet can draw it).
- *Suggestopedia* (teachers use visualization, games, play, taking on of a persona, relaxation techniques, music, room decorations, etc.); use all the senses.
- *Total Physical Response (TPR)* (Asher, 2000) (teacher assesses understanding by the learner's physical response to the teacher's directions).
- Using drama.
- Using E-mail/the Internet.
- Using meaningful literature that is age appropriate and is at the appropriate proficiency level.
- Increased, sustained silent reading in English (researchers believe that this helps increase motivation to learn English when students read for pleasure) (Fedyk, 2006).
- Using photographs (students make inferences, draw conclusions, use expression, and increase vocabulary from viewing or making photographs).
- Using songs/music/rhyming chants/choral readings (a memory technique and an opportunity to hear pronunciation).
- Comparing and contrasting; use of synonyms.
- Whole language/integrated or thematic instruction (lessons include content from several areas rather than being divided into specific content areas, such as only social studies or only mathematics; see example lesson plan at the end of this chapter).
- *Writing Response Groups* (gentle critiquing and improvement by students of each other's writing).

Teacher Behaviors and Other Strategies for ESL Learners

Teachers can employ certain behaviors that increase the learners' chances of understanding.

- Use slow, clear speech that is appropriately loud.
- Read aloud to students often at or slightly above their abilities (use a pointer often).
- Paraphrase often.
- Correct mistakes by restating the sentence with correct usage (*circumlocution*) and meaning rather than continuously stating the grammar rule(s).
- Repeat target vocabulary in various contexts (especially from students' real-world experiences).
- Use nonverbal gestures/body language/pantomime to help with understanding.
- Limit slang and idioms.
- Use frequently used words in speaking, reading, and writing (classmates' names, pets, signs, school items, etc.).
- Provide use of hands-on manipulatives or concrete items and point-to models, pictures, diagrams, props, maps, globes, realia, and other visuals; provide films or other technology as demonstrations.
- Check often for understanding.
- Label many parts of the classroom with English words (wall, window, door, desk, bookshelf, etc.).
- Scaffold and build from prior knowledge. Texas states that all instruction in language arts/reading and in any content areas taught must be **linguistically**

accommodated, meaning scaffolding is a part of accommodation for students.

- Pre teach before having students use vocabulary.
- Review before having students reuse vocabulary.
- Use graphic organizers to group terms and concept in meaningful ways for increased memory, vocabulary, and understanding.
- Provide multiple, meaningful, and motivating ways to engage in a concept.
- Provide age-appropriate materials for the interest level of older students (as well as younger students) according to their levels of English.
- Provide experiences for *all* to participate in social interaction.
- Provide a routine schedule and some permanent physical spaces so students feel safer by knowing exactly what to expect through a structured environment; tape a schedule to each ELL's desk.
- Use repeated, simple questions that become routine throughout the day during reading and listening times (Who? What? What's that? Where? When?).
- Use prereading techniques to set exact expectations for the purpose of reading.
- Teach about context clues often.
- Contextualize activities, making them applicable to real-world situations (e.g., measuring items in class with a tape measure, using the computer to develop research skills, using a checklist and a digital camera for field-trip data collection).
- Teach students about various types of research skills and resources (dictionaries, Internet, etc.) so that they can become more independent translators in and outside the classroom.
- Provide other voices (adult, peer, male/female, media) for students to hear.

Technological Tools and Resources

Using and integrating technology can greatly enhance instruction. Following is a list of some technological tools and resources.

- Voice recognition and recording software
- Databases and word processors
- Multimedia presentations using graphics
- Teaching research skills on the Internet in the content areas
- Using taped read-alongs; provide Listening Stations
- Using e-mail to pair students up with e-pals for the purpose of communication in written English
- Presenting electronic portfolios for the purpose of student reflection on previous activities and directing future learning efforts accordingly (highly metacognitive)
- Using appropriate software for different ESL learning levels (beginning, intermediate, advanced, advanced high), which include necessary visual, graphical, and oral components
- Documenting family and community and their events
- Providing programs that give immediate feedback to learners
- Providing student evaluations, modifications, implementation of new curriculum, methodologies, and for special needs

A Discussion of Management and Organization

The best possible management and teaching strategies include purposeful, effective, and engaging lessons that require students to work in a variety of settings with others, particularly cooperative groups. However, there is also a need for some consideration in management issues in the ESL classroom. Rules should be few but inclusive, simple, and easy to understand (e.g., respect others' things, walk safely, listen until it is your turn). They should include student input and consistently be in place so that learners feel there is a safe classroom structure. Consequences must be based on equity. Guiding new ELLs in helping them understand school rules and American norms for classroom behavior should be a priority for the ESL teacher, as students and parents from other parts of the world bring different expectations of classroom behaviors with them. Feeling able to navigate through the day with correct behavioral expectations does a great deal to lower anxiety for a new language learner. Without being able to understand the rules, a student can constantly feel so ill at ease that he or she may break a rule accidentally. One of the authors, for example, remembers driving in a foreign country and being waved down by an angry driver who then proceeded to yell for 10 minutes in the language of that country. At the end of the tirade, the author still had no idea what driving rule or norm had been breached, but remained uncommonly nervous for the remainder of the time without being able to enjoy the rest of the journey. Students must understand in order to comply and to be comfortable.

Schedules should be established and followed as closely as possible. When ESL students can anticipate what happens next, they feel more safe and secure. Teachers who have students in pull-out programs must watch their timing closely with regard to their colleagues and their students. When students do not return to their regular classes on time, the regular class may have already started another lesson, leaving the ELL even more confused and isolated.

Effective management of engaging instruction invokes establishing deadlines to finish class work, cooperative work, and individual projects. Placing a time limit on assignments automatically makes the lesson metacognitive in nature because the ESL student must internalize the quantity, quality, and time limitations to finish tasks. The ESL teacher never waits until the end of deadlines to monitor students' progress. Effective monitoring occurs during various stages of student work; therefore, ESL students who are meeting expectations should be praised effectively, whereas those who are struggling should be helped in an individual manner (both the student and teacher find ways to become successful according to the task criteria).

Understanding students' cultures is also important in management. For example, ESL teachers who demand that their Hispanic or Asian children look them in the eye will not have those children follow that direction. In these cultures, many children do not look fully into an adult's eyes as a learned sign of respect. Guiding, along with some cultural understanding, are keys to good ESL management.

Let's try some questions that depict a sample of the ESL teacher's knowledge and application skill relating to the competency of ESL methodologies:

Why would Mr. Guthrie, an ESL teacher, invoke the **first three-before-me rule** (ask three classmates before asking the teacher) whenever a student asks him about the meaning and pronunciation of a word?

A. It helps engage the student in meaningful and independent problem solving that leads to higher levels of confidence.

B. It models what an adult should do in an inquiry-based approach.

C. It makes the student think at very high levels of reasoning.
D. It encourages the student to invoke a research-based approach for similar problem-solving situations.

In order to best create a positive environment, the ESL teacher understands that learning involves oral acquisition. This means that the ESL teacher should often insist on authentic problem solving in cooperative learning contexts. The "first three-and-then-me" rule asks students to ask three members of their cooperative group for the answer before he or she asks the teacher. This creates the supportive view that others (besides the teacher) can be valued resources and engages them in conversation (*A*). In this scenario, modeling by the teacher (*B*) is important to begin with, but ultimately, it does not create more dialogue. Thinking at high levels of reasoning (*C*) is also important, but simply thinking of the meaning and the pronunciation of a word is not a higher-level thinking activity. Also, encouraging (or cheerleading) students to invoke a research-based approach (*D*) is often a good strategy, but the better answer for confidence is to have students engaged in dialogue. The correct answer is Choice *A*.

Mrs. Clayborn teaches third-grade ESL. She is planning a unit on pets. Which of the following should she do first?

A. Have students go into a Pet Center.
B. Read a short book on pets to them.
C. Have cards with the names and pictures of various pets printed on them and have students use these for flashcards.
D. Have children tell what pets they have and match them with pictures.

Although all of these would be of value, choice *D* encourages dialogue, and teachers should always begin with what children know and their own experiences (or the known to the unknown). Therefore, the answer is *D*.

Competency 004: The ESL teacher understands how to promote students' communicative language development in English. Terms and concepts that are important to this competency are listed next.

- TEKS listening and speaking
- **Linguistic environment**
- Conversational support
- **Rich, comprehensible language environment**
- Communication experiences in English
- Interrelatedness of listening, speaking, reading, and writing for oral language proficiency
- **Transfer from L1 to L2**
- Individual differences
- **Developmental characteristics**
- **Cultural and language background**
- Academic strengths
- **Learning styles**
- Appropriate feedback

Students Acquire Language in a Low-Anxiety Environment with Comprehensible Input

Even after becoming certified in ESL instruction, the ESL teacher may often wonder what to do with newly arrived ELL students. According to the Affective Filter Hypothesis, Krashen (1992) believes that students should not be pushed too hard and made to feel they must speak English immediately. When anxiety levels are high, the affective filter is high; thus we can expect interference with the learning process. As a strong reminder to combat this, the ESL teacher understands that the affective filter should be as low as possible and must be accompanied by the teacher's use of **comprehensible input**; that is, where the new language is based on simple, already familiar terms (i.e., the level at which the child can comprehend or understand what is being said). When students are at ease and using language and when they have conceptual familiarity within their L1, they find it easier to generate English oral communication.

There are a wide variety of techniques for keeping the affective filter level low and the input comprehensible for the child. Some examples are sticking to simple, non-idiomatic language; talking in small groups; using gestures; and avoiding harsh criticism on mistakes. The ESL teacher is most successful when students are interacting in communicative activities that they enjoy about topics that concern them or with which they have had experience. Using the social studies guidelines of teaching what is most familiar to students first (the home, the school, the community, etc.), is a good place to begin. Students must always feel that they can express their ideas in English without fear of continuous direct, interruptive grammatical correction or reprimand. In a study in which researchers (Cohen & Nath, 2009) asked now-adult ELLs to remember their experiences in ESL placements, some referenced their absolute exhaustion each day at concentrating on trying to understand in classes, talking socially with their peers, and in doing homework later. The time factor to simply get through homework for ELLs in the upper grades is something that teachers must consider seriously for students, as many use translation prior to working with the material to learn. Another finding in this study noted that many ELLs remembered three other issues—how lonely it could be, how cruel some students could be when the new arrival did not know the language or the customs, and the difference that a protective, understanding teacher made in their success at learning. The ESL teacher must make sure that students feel as safe as possible. The environment is an important element for learning.

 # Speaking Supports Language Acquisition

As we have seen, much of an ESL teacher's job is to set up informal and formal experiences that encourage students to speak often in their new language. Speaking supports language acquisition in several ways:

- It provides more opportunities for comprehensible input (via conversation), which, in turn, encourages output.

  Example:

  Input: "Hello, how are you?" (*Student is able to comprehend.*) *Output:* "I'm fine."

  or

  Input: "Hello, how is your overall constitution today?" (*No comprehension.*) No output.

- It gives students an avenue for participation in the L2 that contributes to identification with English language and culture. Language and culture are impossible to separate, and, when one learns a second language, the culture of that language must also be considered part of the package.

- It prepares learners for necessary communicative interactions they will begin to have with native speakers outside the classroom. An ultimate duty of the ESL teacher is to provide frequent opportunities for students to interact with native speakers which, in turn, provides them with more comprehensible input/output and contextual, hands-on practice in English.

- It helps create a sense of community as the ESL teacher and students share opinions, perceptions, and life experiences in small groups or whole-class discussions. Students should come together and support peers in problem solving and social communication, while at the same time, build their confidence and pride as they become more successful in acquiring new skills.

Speech Emergence Is Distinguished by Grammatical Errors

When students begin speaking in whole sentences, they make many errors. This is to be expected and never underestimated as a part of language growth (because this is an important part of the process in learning). It is those students who take risks and make mistakes who learn. Those students who may appear to be well-behaved, yet are not making mistakes because they are not using the new language (even after allowing for a silent period) are often the ones who should cause the most concern. One simply cannot learn a language without making mistakes. Indeed, no intense self-monitoring of speech in the early stages of acquisition should be suggested.

Early speech errors that arise during communication activities do not usually become permanent nor do they affect students' future language development. In fact, they lend themselves to opportunities for the ESL teacher to model correct usage, which gives students the ability to self-monitor without loss of time, thought, or self-respect. As in an example, Veronica over-generalizes a plural rule by saying, "The childs went to lunch" (when the correct word is *children*) by applying the plural rule of adding *-s* to the word. What she is doing is a natural progress in language learning, and the astute ESL teacher uses this active listening opportunity of circumlocution to exaggerate the correct oral use of the word. As discussed earlier as an important technique, the teacher might say, "Oh, so the *children* already went to lunch, Veronica? When you saw the *children,* what time was it? Did the *children* have their money or sack lunches with them?" Interference from the structure of the home language can also occur often, causing mistakes in English. For example, in many languages, the modifying adjective follows the noun (i.e., in French, one correctly says *le chat noir,* or "the cat black"), so a French-speaking learner may say in English, "I saw a cat black." During such communication activities, the ESL teacher should pay attention primarily to factual errors. If there are no factual errors, the teacher can expand and re-phrase students' responses in grammatically correct sentences. This allows learners to hear a well-modeled example of communication in English and provides an opportunity to internalize and mimic the correctness of the situation.

The production of speech with few errors depends on a number of factors that cannot always be controlled by the teacher or students. Some forms and structures (e.g., idioms, prepositional phrases, figurative meaning) require an incredibly large number of communicative experiences before acquisition is complete, and no amount of direct correction of speech errors can speed up the process. Again, for this reason, the ESL teacher should not expect students to speak English without errors, especially early in the acquistional process; however, steady improvement in speaking, writing, listening, and so on in English is expected through regular practice. It is not expected that students' errors *fossilize*; that is, become ingrained habits. Fossilization is not a problem in ESL classes; it appears to be more common among second-language learners who live and work in the environment of the new language but who never have the opportunity to interact in a sheltered environment like that of the ESL classroom. It usually takes several years of daily language use with repetitive mistakes for the mistakes to become so ingrained as to be truly fossilized.

Speech Emerges Step-by-Step

There are two very important reasons not to require beginners to speak English immediately—that is, to give students a *silent period:* (1) students' anxiety levels (affective filters) will be lower if they are not pressured, and (2) students' understanding of spoken English develops faster due to the use of comprehensible input. Students who are not pressured at once to produce English feel more comfortable with the language and pronounce it better when they begin to feel more at ease and start to speak in their own time. However, when a student does begin to speak, every opportunity to practice should be provided. A review of Krashen's theories is in order.

The Natural Approach (Krashen & Terrell, 1996) is based on the following tenets:

- Language *acquisition* (an unconscious process developed through using language meaningfully) is different from language *learning* (consciously studying or directly learning rules about a language), and language acquisition is the way to true competence in a second language (acquisition/learning hypothesis).
- Conscious learning operates only as a monitor (or editor) that pre-checks or repairs one's output (monitor hypothesis). For example, a beginning German speaker sees something to buy without a price tag and wants to ask how much it is. Before approaching the clerk, the traveler runs the phrase she wants to use over in her mind: "Wie viel kostet die?" The speaker then quickly self-monitors and corrects *die* to *das* before she actually speaks to the clerk, correctly asking, "Wie Viel kostet das?" instead.
- Some grammatical structures seem to be acquired in a predictable order (Natural Order Hypothesis).
- People acquire language and improve best from messages that are just slightly beyond their current competence (input hypothesis), but learners must be able to comprehend/understand, at the least, the **gist** of what is being said to them or what is written in order to respond.
- The learner's emotional state can act as a filter that impedes or blocks input necessary to acquisition (Affective Filter Hypothesis).

Beginners who are in the Natural Approach are allowed to pass naturally through three stages:

Level 1: Comprehension
Level 2: Early Speech
Level 3: Speech Emergence

In Level 1, students are able to understand/comprehend what is said to them, but they need not respond in the target language (L1). During this pre-speech stage, the ESL teacher asks questions that can be answered with "yes" or "no" or some other single action words. This is the perfect opportunity to employ the **Total Physical Response (TPR)**, a method in which the ESL teacher is the *command giver* and the recently arrived student is the *order taker* (Asher, 2000). Student comprehension is assessed by the student physically performing the requested action/gestures ("Give me the pencil," and the student does so). Exaggerated body language and physical movement is also used to present and represent ideas and concepts similar to charades. In Level 2, students respond with single words or short phrases, and by Level 3, they are able to produce longer utterances. Keep in mind that students continue to pass through these stages as they are introduced to new content areas in subsequent lessons. Words and structures presented may not be fully acquired until much later.

The Goal of the Natural Approach Is Communicative Competence

One way of judging **communicative competence** (or being competent in communicating) is when a student is able to ask a native speaker for directions on how to get from one location to another and can understand the details given by the responding native speaker (Krashen & Terrell, 1996). For this to happen, the ESL student needs enough receptive vocabulary to adequately attend to what the native speaker says with the subject matter. **Receptive vocabulary** is the amount of spoken language one can process aurally (with regard to sound or the ear), or simply understanding the words that are spoken to you. This amount of vocabulary is usually up to four times greater than an individual's ability to speak. Asking for directions is good practice because of the limited output needed for a native speaker to provide a sufficient response (when much more vocabulary than the original question is needed to answer). There are at least four components of proficiency in communicative competence:

1. Discourse competence
2. Sociolinguistic competence
3. Strategic competence
4. Linguistic competence

Discourse competence is the ability to interact with native speakers using various communication strategies, conversation, narration, inquiry for information, directing others, and so forth. **Sociolinguistic competence** is the ability to interact in different social registers using appropriate rules and politeness for that situation. There are five social registers in which people communicate (i.e., formal, consultative, informal, frozen, and intimate registers; Payne, 2005) (see Glossary for more information). New language learners often blunder socially when the incorrect register is used, particularly when language is too informal/casual or intimate for a particular social situation. ELLs are expected to use the correct register increasingly as they grow in English skills and fluency in the informal and formal registers, and they should aim towards **style shifting**, meaning that they can shift to the appropriate register immediately when the social situation shifts. **Strategic competence** is the ability to make use of limited linguistic resources to express ideas and to understand input (what is being said). For example, an American traveler in France went into a shop armed with a map. Not knowing the words for *I'm lost*, the traveler plunked down the map on the counter and asked the salesperson, *"Où est ici?"* ("Where is here?"), after which the shopkeeper pointed out their location on the map. This strategy allowed the traveler to communicate and operate strategically with only limited language and a type of circumlocution. **Linguistic competence** is the ability to use the correct grammatical form and structure to express a given meaning. Linguistic accuracy is important (but comes later on in the acquisition process) and does not weigh as heavily as a needed skill in early production of a second language; it continually improves as the learner matures in English. Even when linguistic proficiency is augmented with reading and writing skills, communicative competence develops from multiple communication experiences, not from just covering the material in a single lesson plan or unit!

Comprehension Comes Before Production

This principle follows the same path as the acquisition process. It is impossible to attach meaning to oral language if the learner has very few opportunities to hear expressions used in context (e.g., an idiom such as "Get over it"). In this example, the listener may think he or she has to jump or climb over something when the phrase is taken literally. If you were learning French, for example, and someone said to you in the middle of an argument, *"Les carottes sont cuites"* ("The carrots are cooked!"), you might look at them as if they were crazy, unless you knew that it was an idiom for, "I've had it!" Classroom activities should be designed to introduce most new vocabulary, idioms, high-frequency irregular words, and grammatical forms and structures in communicative contexts before students are expected to produce these types of word phrases in their own speech. Thus, most ESL instruction should start with input activities before moving on to ask for output (production) activities. In addition, it is important to precede these initial activities with a regular review of new vocabulary and phrases in which new words and grammatical forms and structures are introduced or reviewed for comprehension *before* students are expected to use them correctly. This is especially important for content-area vocabulary that students find later in subject areas like mathematics, science, and social studies.

Group Work Encourages Interaction and Creates Community

As noted, when students begin to be able to communicate orally in English, they should often be encouraged to work in pairs and small groups on cognitive tasks that allow application of their growing language skills. By problem solving and interacting with peers in group work, students find more opportunities to speak in their new language while giving the teacher the opportunity to monitor interactions. At this stage, group work often allows students to enjoy interacting with others on a personal basis, and this helps them feel freer to express themselves in the context of social participation. From observation and listening during these interchanges, the teacher can then target more skills for individuals (such as answering questions and helping individuals with pronunciation, grammar, and concept development). The time students spend working in small groups should increase methodically so that the students themselves become the source of much of the communicative interaction.

See how you do with your knowledge and application of understanding of ESL methodologies:

While speaking with her ESL teacher, Monica remarks, "My mother think I get in trouble at school." In order to help the student understand her verbal mistake, the ESL teacher should:

A. tell her that the third-person present tense is exactly opposite from what it is in her language and, therefore, requires adding an -s to the word *think*.
B. ask, "Why does your mother think that?"
C. say, "Your mother really thinks that? If she thinks that, do you want me to tell her how well you are doing in school?"
D. understand that this is a developmental stage, and this will pass as Monica develops in English.

In order to create the best environment for language acquisition, the ESL teacher understands that a main purpose of ESL is motivating learners to start saying things in English. It is important not to crush the self-esteem of students by interrupting conversations to point out grammatical errors, especially in the beginning (which would happen in choice A). This detracts from listening and speaking in normal conversation. ESL teachers should model correct speech through several oral versions of what the intended outcome should sound like from a native speaker (termed *circumlocution;* choice C). When students have heard and processed the correctly modeled speech multiple times, the correct version begins to appear in their own speech. For this reason, the ESL teacher must be an active listener, participant, and reinforcer in normal conversations! Stopping conversation to impose a language rule (*A*) can often create confusion for the learner, especially if he or she doesn't comprehend enough English to understand the grammar rules when told in English. Asking a question that requires even more language can confuse the ELL (*B*), but keeping the conversation going with plenty of examples of how English is to be used is the duty of the ESL teacher—making the best answer choice *C*. Teachers understand that choice *D*, a developmental stage, is true but simply understanding this does not help Monica with her verbal mistake. The correct answer is *C*.

Competency 005: The ESL teacher understands how to promote students' literacy development in English. Terms and concepts associated with this competency are listed below.

- Prior literary experiences
- TEKS related to the reading and writing strands
- Interrelatedness of listening, speaking, reading, and writing for developing literacy
- English is an alphabetic language
- **Phonological knowledge and skills**
- Phonemic awareness skills
- **Letter-sound associations**
- **Phonograms**
- Sight-word vocabularies
- **Phonetically irregular words**
- **High-frequency words**
- Reading comprehension

- Vocabulary
- Text structures
- Cultural references
- Facilitating reading comprehension
- Transfer literacy and skills from L1 to L2
- Developmental characteristics
- Cultural and language background
- Academic strengths
- Learning styles
- Instructional strategies
- Resources for literacy development
- **Interrupted schooling**
- **Literacy status in the primary language**

Including the Texas Essential Knowledge and Skills (TEKS) in literacy development activities, as mentioned earlier, is a necessary part of ESL teaching. The TEKS **English Language Arts and Reading competencies** at all grade levels are important to know because each student may be at a different development level on this continuum. The idea in literacy is that:

- the English Language Arts TEKS, which are also required learning for ELLs, are divided into listening, speaking, reading, writing, and viewing/representing domains related to the reading and writing strands (http://ritter.tea.state.tx.us/rules/tac/chapter110/index.html; also see Chapter 2 in this book).
- proficiency levels are not necessarily seen as age or grade specific. As we have seen before, students are divided into beginner, intermediate, advanced, and advanced high (usually in the upper grades) levels, and the ESL teacher must quickly be able to assess each student informally (and later formally) in order to individualize appropriate instruction.

An Interrelatedness Review

Because there is an interrelatedness of listening, speaking, reading, and writing, the ESL teacher should select and use the most effective strategies for developing students' literacy in English.

- The ESL student may exhibit *different* proficiency levels within *each* of the **four language components: listening, speaking, reading, and writing.** For instance, he or she may be a star at reading English, but not in writing in English. Because the student is classified as ESL, each child has different skills, shortcomings and strengths, interests, and perceptions about English language learning.
- Listening, speaking, reading, writing, and viewing/representing are functions of language that should be taught concurrently, making the awareness of computer instruction and learning important for both the teacher and student.

 # English Is an Alphabetic Language

An important part of helping ESL students begins with the ESL teacher's understanding that English is an **alphabetic language** (symbols/letters reflect the pronunciation of a sound). Some languages are non-phonetic (Chinese, Japanese, etc.) and use mostly symbols to represent words. The ESL teacher should apply effective strategies for developing students' phonological knowledge and skills and should directly teach the alphabet. Some of important issues are:

- **phonemic awareness skills** (i.e., skills needed to recognize that a spoken word consists of a sequence of individual sounds)
- **sight-word vocabularies** (i.e., phonetically irregular, high-frequency words such as *thought, one, though, been, have*) are those that require other skills instead of decoding skills to read. Such words cannot be pronounced letter by letter, nor do they follow English language rules. Each word has its own rule for pronunciation with no graphophonic clues.

A teacher should measure both accuracy and fluency. Accuracy in reading can be measured by assessing students' oral reading mistakes in using word analysis knowledge for decoding those words they do not know. Most ESL students have primary languages that are even more phonetic than English, making **word analysis skills** (sounding out/phonics) extremely important to teach regularly in the classroom. Determining if a problem is a decoding or a word-analysis issue is imperative in order to plan curriculum and choose the proper methodologies to address these separate English Language Arts (ELA) skills. *Fluency* is also important for a teacher to assess, and this is done often by determining if a student comprehends enough to be able to read with feeling and expression.

 # Reading Comprehension

The ESL teacher also knows factors that affect ESL students' reading comprehension. These may include vocabulary text structures, cultural references, and prior knowledge. A teacher can help by (1) establishing a purpose for reading and listening, (2) retelling and acting out story events, and (3) helping learners to make inferences.

Transfer of Literacy

Cognitive skills transfer from one language to another. Students who are knowledgeable about literacy and subject matter in their first language are able to apply this knowledge and these skills to their second language. Thus, an ESL teacher understands, as mentioned, that learning a second language may not necessarily mean relearning many of the rules of language, literacy, or content knowledge again; the idea is to identify language rules that students may possibly be able to transfer from their L1 to their L2. ESL teachers can use these to help students leap into their new language. Spanish speakers who understand the idea of an adjective, for example, can easily be told that, in English, most adjectives are switched to in front of the noun rather than behind it. They do not have to relearn the role of an adjective—just where it is placed in the new language. Of course, this may take some inquiry on the part of the teacher into the child's home language and its structure, and it also requires that an ESL teacher thoroughly know the rules of English grammar. Also, any knowledge children have about content areas does not go away. If a learner knows mathematics, he or she is still able to calculate, or if historical events and other concepts are there, they are able to transfer this knowledge easily into English.

Individual Differences and Personal Factors

Individual differences (i.e., developmental characteristics, past experiences, cultural/language background, academic strengths, and learning styles) affect ESL students' literacy development. Thus, the ESL teacher should get to know his or her ESL student as quickly as possible. Knowing each individual student can facilitate finding which skills they have already acquired and help the student apply those skills to new learning environments. Language deficits can exist in both the L1 and the L2. Tests in both languages, when possible, can help to determine academic need. Also, individual students show an affinity for different learning styles (cognitive processing) and problem-solving tasks, depending on the academic task. When the ESL teacher is aware of learning styles or modalities (preferences for receiving information such as visual, auditory, tactile, or kinesthetic), he or she can use these for success in new academic problems. Solving problems that require a metacognitive (*reflective*) process are similar across disciplines. Therefore, demonstrating how prior success breeds new success makes an effective connection between students' prior knowledge and their new academic challenges.

Personal factors also affect ESL students' English literacy development, and the ESL teacher must consider effective strategies for addressing these factors. Some are discussed earlier in the chapter. These might include issues in their native country (or in this country), such as interrupted schooling, lack of any schooling, or little experience in literacy development [familiarity with the structure and uses of textbooks and other print, specialized language and vocabulary, etc.]. Personal factors may also include the status of a student's ethnicity, the status of his or her primary language, or students' prior learning experiences. In many instances, the ESL population is highly mobile, creating gaps in learning. Knowing about learning gaps can be of great help to the ESL teacher in terms of diagnosing (then filling) those gaps for increased student achievement.

Three critical areas have been suggested by Peregoy and Boyle (2005) for the teacher to learn about new students: (1) determining the country of origin and the language spoken at home, how long the child has been in the U.S., and any unusual circumstances of immigration (trauma, etc.); (2) discovering as much as possible about prior schooling (including information on literacy in the home language) through any obtainable records or through interviews with caregivers; and (3) obtaining basic information on culture, religion, customs, food preferences/restrictions, and cultural role expectations of adults and children.

This question relates to literacy skills.
See how you do in this area!

Jorge, a fourth-grade ELL, is accustomed to a language that is more phonetic than English. What skill is needed in English (in addition to previous skills for his primary language) as he reads for fluency?

- **A.** Phonemic awareness
- **B.** Word analysis
- **C.** Alphabetic principle
- **D.** Decoding

When a language like English is entrenched with *non-decodable* words (sight words) like *through, thorough, one,* and *have,* learners need extra skills to read fluently. When coming across irregular sight words such as *have,* for example, the student cannot sound out each letter. *Have* would sound differently because the *a* becomes a strong sound such as *hay + v +* the long *e* sound, as in choice *A*. The skill needed to determine how irregular words are to be sounded out when reading for fluency might not even exist in a student's L1, adding difficulty to their reading process. Therefore, the skill of word analysis (*B*) is an extra ability needed for English fluency. When analyzing miscues, or mistakes, in reading fluency, the ESL teacher should clearly distinguish mistakes between decodable words and high-frequency irregular sight words requiring word analysis skills. Literacy also involves making connections between the spoken sounds and symbols or letters in written language, or the alphabetic principle (*C*). However, choice *C* cannot be the answer because the question asks for a skill rather than a principle. The ESL teacher should also clearly know what *phonetic* means and why it is so important for the ESL student; that is, when a language is *phonetic* (generally spelled the way it sounds), it is easy to read out loud with fluency because decoding associating printed letters with the speech sounds the letters make to decipher meaning) (*D*), is the only needed skill. Words like *cat, bat,* and *sat* are sounded out by each letter, but remember that English has many other words where other methods of word analysis skills such as context clues, sight words, and structural analysis (focuses on root words, affixes, etc.) are needed. The correct answer is *B*.

Competency 006: The ESL teacher understands how to promote students' **content-area learning**, academic-language development, and **achievement across the curriculum.** Terms and concepts for Competency 006 are listed here.

- Content-area learning
- Academic-language development
- Achievement across the curriculum
- Effective practices, resources, and materials for content-based instruction
- Critical thinking
- Cognitive-academic language proficiency
- **Preteaching key vocabulary**
- **Applying familiar concepts**
- Cultural backgrounds
- **Hands-on and other experiential learning strategies**
- Using *realia*
- Media
- **Visual supports** to introduce or reinforce concepts
- Developmental characteristics
- Cultural and language background
- Academic strengths
- Learning styles/modalities
- **Cognitive-academic language development**
- Personal factors that affect content-area learning
- Prior learning experiences
- Familiarity with specialized language and vocabulary
- **Familiarity with the structure and uses of textbooks and other print resources**

Applies Knowledge of Effective Practices, Resources, and Materials Across the Curriculum

Remember that an ESL teacher may teach ESL language arts only as a pull out, or may teach all subject areas in a self-contained classroom of ELLs. In addition, he or she should also serve as a resource for teachers of other content areas who have ELLs. Whether or not the ESL teacher has students for all content areas, he or she should always take responsibility for the success of all ELLs by helping regular classroom teachers understand the special needs of ELLs. When students are engaged in content-area reading versus simple narrative reading, the nonfictional, informational type of texts require a different approach. Science, history, mathematics, health, and other subjects all have specialized vocabulary and concepts. All new vocabulary must be pre-taught for students to have any chance of understanding whatever follows in the lesson, and every opportunity should be made by an ESL teacher to provide visuals and models of the new language, vocabulary, and concepts. In the realm of content-area instruction, the ESL teacher knows that language arts are embedded in each of these subject areas. For this reason, the ESL teacher is aware that there are two types of simultaneous lessons taking place: (1) **linguistic** (the ability to comprehend new content terms when listening and to use them in speech) and (2) **conceptual** (academic application of abstract reasoning). While taking advantage of effective practices, resources, and materials, the ESL teacher should be:

- working on the development of students' cognitive-academic language proficiency skills, better known as CALPS (Cummins, 1979)
- engaging students in critical thinking (higher-order thinking as noted through Bloom's taxonomy)
- providing cooperative group work so that the teacher can monitor the level of linguistic challenge for the student in the new content-area vocabulary and conceptual understanding
- listening critically to interpret and evaluate
- using multiple types of strategies for learning and using the multiple intelligences information
- being aware that cognitive learning skills transfer from one language to another, and students who are literate in their first language apply these skills (and other academic proficiencies) to the second language.

Instructional Delivery in the Content Areas

The ESL teacher should always use **instructional delivery** practices or **strategies** that are effective in facilitating ESL students' comprehension in content-area classes by:

- pre-teaching key vocabulary
- applying familiar concepts from students' cultural backgrounds
- applying prior learning experiences to new learning
- using hands-on (contextualized) and other experiential learning strategies (props, models, gestures, etc.)
- using **realia** (real-life examples), media, and other visual supports to introduce and/or reinforce concepts
- using technology to provide enriching experiences

Let's try a question on the teacher's knowledge and application skill as it relates to the competency on content-area instruction:

During a social studies unit, a fourth-grade ESL teacher, Mr. Billingsly, introduces distances in terms of miles and kilometers. In order to understand distances, students measure by walking around the school with the teacher and placing a red flag on the path for 1 kilometer walked and a blue flag for 1 mile walked. Distances are measured by the use of a pedometer, which measures feet, kilometers, and miles. Time is measured by a stopwatch. By the end of 1 mile, the time, number of feet, and the distance of a kilometer and a mile are logged by students and discussed. The teacher's lesson is particularly effective for students' academic language (CALPS) because it best:

A. provides students with innovative approaches to learning.
B. supports content-area learning in a contextual, language-learning environment.
C. encourages students to make language experience connections to prior knowledge.
D. reinforces recognition of traveling distances.

In order to best create an environment for content-area achievement, the ESL teacher understands that academic language (CALPS) in courses such as mathematics, science, and social studies requires both linguistic and conceptual skills. *Linguistic skills* are those used to read, write, speak, and listen to nonfictional or informational vocabulary found in content-area instruction. *Conceptual skills* include the ability to take linguistics skills to a higher level of abstract understanding and eventually to be able to learn without the need for concrete examples (i.e., *abstract reasoning*). For most students, this begins through hands-on and participatory (*cooperative*) problem solving. In this particular lesson, actually walking the given distances helps ESL students build language experience with the vocabulary in the context that they are challenged to learn and later apply. Therefore, the lesson implements the use of a contextual, lexical language-learning environment (*B*). Students develop both linguistic use of the language in the context of the lesson while building conceptual understanding of measurement conversion. This approach not only encourages students to make language connections to concrete activities but also provides language experience for later reflection of distance measurement. Hence, the best answer is what the author calls the *umbrella answer* (an answer under which the rest also fits); that is, choice *B* is best, because it supports achievement by tying language to the concept through active contextualized learning. Choices *A* and *C* may be true, but are more about what the teacher is doing for the students rather than the students engaged in a hands-on (or, in this case, feet-on experience). Choice *D*, even though it is true (the recognition of traveling distances), does not touch on students vocalizing their understanding for monitoring of understanding. The correct answer is *B*.

Competency 007: The ESL teacher understands formal and informal assessment procedures and instruments used in **ESL programs** and uses assessment results to plan and adapt instruction. The terms and concepts listed next are associated with Competency 007.

- Formal assessment
- Informal assessment
- Authentic/alternative assessment
- Using assessment results to plan and adapt instruction (assessment loop)
- Test design, development, and interpretation
- Select, adapt, and develop assessments
- Diagnosis
- Program evaluation

- Standardized tests
- **State-mandated LEP policies**
- LPAC (Language Proficiency Assessment Committee)
- **Identification, placement, and exit of ELLs**
- **State-mandated standards, instruction, and assessment**

- Individual student needs
- Teacher-made tests
- Peer assessment
- Portfolio assessment
- Proficiency level
- Performance assessment

Assessing ESL Students: Best Design, Development, and Interpretation

This competency directs the ESL teacher to know basic concepts, issues, and practices in order to select, adapt, and develop assessments for varied purposes. Some of these purposes may include: program placements, diagnoses, ESL lesson program and lesson design, implementation, evaluation, and modification. ESL teachers should plan for and be aware of ongoing assessment opportunities. These should be informal (oral questioning, observation, etc.) and formal (usually in the form of standardized tests) assessments. To assess how well the teacher has taught, and even more importantly, how well the students have achieved, the following are critical areas to consider:

- **Diagnosis:** centers on finding solutions to a problem or roadblock that hinders a child's advancement in some way. Then, after a treatment has been introduced, it is incumbent on a teacher to determine if this solution worked. An assessment loop includes (1) observing a problem or roadblock in learning; (2) planning for a solution that may include a new curriculum, new strategy, and so on; (3) applying the treatment; (4) evaluating the results to determine the amount of success (or lack thereof); and (5) beginning the cycle again, if needed.
- **Program evaluation:** deciding which program best serves ELLs (e.g., bilingual, ESL, dual language) and being able to make recommendations accordingly; making judgments about particular programs.
- **Proficiency level:** desired proficiency in English for students is to score in the 40th percentile or above on standardized tests or to pass the TAKS (soon to be STAAR). Texas is a data-driven educational system, and evaluation data of student performance determines effectiveness of teaching. One issue in ESL will always be to quickly determine at what level ELLs are in their proficiency so as to match instruction to their individual abilities, remembering that proficiency levels are not necessarily age or grade specific. Students are divided into beginner, intermediate, advanced, and advanced high. The state helps define these levels as follows:

Beginning level. ELLs have very little ability to understand spoken English in very simple conversations, even when the input uses ESL supports, such as slowing speech, using gestures, and so on, and the topic is familiar. Vocabulary in English is a struggle, and the speaker often remains silent when failing to comprehend. Through carefully sequenced listening opportunities, ELLs begin to expand their vocabularies and to evaluate and analyze spoken English for a variety of situations and purposes.

Intermediate level. ELLs produce spoken English with increasing accuracy and fluency to convey appropriate meaning. They can comprehend simple and high-frequency spoken English in both academic and social contexts. These may include simple conversations, discussions, directions, and so on, but normally require ESL techniques for unfamiliar topics.

They may ask the speaker to slow down, repeat, or rephrase because they have the ability to seek clarification when they do not understand.

Advanced level. ELLs (with ESL support) can comprehend grade-level spoken English in both academic and social contexts with more advanced directions, conversations, and discussions. They are able to create, clarify, critique, and evaluate ideas and responses. They may, however, need processing time and ESL techniques for support to comprehend some details and non-modified-for-ELLs information. They may occasionally ask for repetition or rephrasing or for the speaker to slow down.

Advanced high level. ELLs understand with very minimal support and with little need for processing time or ESL support except, perhaps, for when complex academics or when specialized language is used. They are comparable to native speakers in social and most instructional contexts.

Evaluation measures should always be in place prior to instruction as a part of the instructional planning process loop. In good planning for all instruction, teachers should begin with clear goals and solid objectives. This provides a benchmark to gauge differences in student achievement before and after instruction. Well-written objectives for individual learning levels help teachers to set measurable learning advancements for learners. Pre- and post-evaluations show how much growth took place; thus, the teacher can determine the effectiveness of his or her instruction and make a decision to reteach or continue instruction.

Formal, Informal, and Authentic Assessments

The ESL teacher applies knowledge of formal, informal, and authentic or alternative assessments in order to measure in terms of standardized state scores, developmental benchmarks, and actual real world skills for intended outcomes.

We recommend that you access the following Web site that lists current formal assessments for ELL students: http://ritter.tea.state.tx.us/curriculum/biling/bilingualfaq.pdf. In 2009, a Texas ruling noted that ELLs in grades K–12 must be tested in English language proficiency annually in reading, writing, and speaking for reporting purposes under the No Child Left Behind Act (Government Accounting Office of Records, 2006). The Texas English Language Proficiency Assessment System (TELPAS) was designed to chart students' achievement. You can visit the site mentioned previously and the following sites to see a listing of currently approved tests used for placement, such as the Oral Language Proficiency Test [OLPT] and other proficiency tests: (see http://ritter.tea.state.tx.us/taa/stanprog072009a1.pdf and http://ritter.tea.state.tx.us/curriculum/biling/leptests.html).

- **Formal assessment** evaluates student achievement for accountability and is measured after students have ample time to demonstrate mastery of intended objectives. These include standardized tests, TAKS tests (soon to be the STAAR [State of Texas Assessments of Academic Readiness]), and some benchmark testing.
- **Informal assessment** is often done orally or through observations as new material is being covered in order to readjust instruction as the teacher determines that a lesson is too advanced or too easy for students while monitoring the flow of learning. This type of assessment may include mastery checklists, observations, conversations, informal inventories, daily assignments, homework, projects, data collected from others besides the ESL teacher, and so forth.
- **Authentic assessment** (is assessment in real-life situations or those closely simulated to real life). An important aspect of authentic assessment is that the skills mirror real-world tasks as much as possible, such as actually

making a multimedia presentation, keeping a checkbook, delivering a speech in public, following directions for baking a recipe, and so forth. These may not always be items tested on standardized tests, but they are indeed skills for which students apply their academics to real-world situations, and knowledge and skills should transfer to testing.

- **Portfolio assessment.** Portfolios are designed to place students in the assessment loop to help them self-assess. By reflecting on previous learning and choosing artifacts that demonstrate intended learning outcomes, students are given a sense of pride in their accomplishments and, most important, directed toward improvement of learned skills the next time similar tasks are to be completed. This method shows a picture of learning over time.

Standardized Tests

The ESL teacher knows the types of standardized tests commonly used in ESL. **Standardized tests** (formal tests) are termed *standardized* because the results can be *generalized,* meaning that the results of many test takers from several demographic areas on the same test can be grouped together, and assumptions can be made about all of these test-takers' performances, both overall and by individual items on the test. During this type of testing, those who administer the test must follow the same (or standard) rules of test administration (exact reading of instructions, timing, proctoring, etc.) to ensure that the conditions for all test takers are as nearly identical as possible. This type of standardization is seen as *valid* (accurate and fair) and *reliable* (gives consistent results over time) because it gives every test-taker the same chance as others taking the exam. Generally, there are two types of standardized tests:

1. **Norm-referenced tests,** such as ITBS and SAT, are standardized tests because they try to ensure that test-taking conditions are the same for all students (reliability). However, students cannot possibly know all the material for each grade level and subject, so there is not a specific list of criteria *per se.* Scores are *normed* on these tests; that is, a great number of scores are collected and used to find what is "normal" for a particular group (e.g., fourth graders) on this test. These normed scores can then be used to compare those who are similar test takers on how they stand in relationship to others who have taken this test. Groups and individuals can then see whether they compare about the same with others or whether they are above or below the norm. As you may remember, when a large number of people take a standardized fair test, where everyone has an equal chance, scores fall into a bell-shaped curve, with most scores matching the norm, and fewer falling above or below the norm. Students are given *percentile scores.* For instance, a student scoring in the 40th percentile on a norm-referenced English language arts test on their grade level is automatically eligible to exit the bilingual/ESL program because this score indicates that the student performed as well or better than 40 students of out 100 who took the same test. Of course, this student would be monitored for success for the next 2 years by the Language Proficiency Assessment Committee (LPAC), which maintains the responsibility for exiting ELL students.

2. **Criterion-referenced tests** (such as the TAKS/STAAR or the TExES). On a criterion-referenced test, students are expected to know specific *criteria,* or specified knowledge and skills. A criterion-referenced test can be standardized or non-standardized. The Texas Assessment of Knowledge and Skills (TAKS), which is soon to become the STAAR test, is a standardized, criterion-referenced test because it tests specific knowledge and skills listed in the TEKS; the TExES ESL tests specific criteria, or knowledge, of

the competencies found in this book. The test taker receives a *percentage score* (e.g., a 70 percent to pass, 90 percent to demonstrate mastery) for this type of test. Teacher-made tests are informal criterion-related tests when they test for specific knowledge or skills (e.g., a weekly spelling test tells how well students master a word list for that week).

Mean, **median**, and **mode** are used to determine information on tests about students. The *mean* is an average score (all scores are added and the sum is divided by the total number of scores); the *median* is the one score that falls right in the middle of all scores (in a group of tests in which the scores are 80, 90, and 100, the median is 90); and the *mode* is the score from a number of scores that occurs most often (in a group of test scores of 80, 90, 90, and 100, 90 is the mode).

Test bias often occurs for ELLs because tests can contain certain cultural references to which only English speakers and even, perhaps, only Americans (or even Americans from certain areas of the country) can relate. For example, *silos* (grain storage facilities) are a common site in the northern part of the United States but are rarely seen in the South. Thus a test item requiring knowledge of a silo to get the correct answer (e.g., "A silo is a cone (or sometimes a half sphere) on top of a ____ ." [cylinder]) might find students from the North scoring higher but see many from the South lost. When ELLs cannot make a connection to this type of information, they get the item wrong—not because they are less smart, but because the item is tied to a culture or region of which they are not a part. Test makers try to ensure *validity* (or whether a particular test really tests what it says it is testing) by item analysis to search for items like the one just mentioned. The mathematics item in the previous example is not a valid question, because a child may know what a cylinder is but not a silo. ESL teachers must be especially vigilant for test bias both on standardized tests given to ESL students and, especially, on their own teacher-made tests.

 State-Mandated LEP Policies

The ESL teacher, more than likely, will be a regular member of the **Language Proficiency Assessment Committee (LPAC)**, which has the main purposes of recommending English language learners' (ELLs') identification, placement, and exit in bilingual/ESL programs. The following guidelines are in place:

- State guidelines determine the makeup of the committee, functions of the committee, how often the committee meets (must meet at least once per year per student), other tasks of the committee, and administrative forms.
- If there are 20 or more ELLs at one grade level in a district, an ESL program is required.
- All students in an ESL or bilingual program are considered under federal, as well as state, guidelines. As a federally funded program, this is seen as a civil rights issue.
- Each student must have returned a home language survey, and those parents or students who mark that English is not their home language must take a language test within 4 weeks of their enrollment date.
- Any student who is found to have dominance in a **language other than English** should be offered a placement in an ESL program, but the recommended placement is decided by the LPAC.
- All students determined to be eligible for LPAC services must still have parent permission to be enrolled in a bilingual/ESL program. Those students not given parental permission are considered waived and receive no special services. They are expected to meet annual testing requirements in

English, regardless of their student's ability level in English. This can also make a school's accountability test scores very low if students are unable to test well in English. The hope is for the ESL teacher to provide adequate reasoning for the parent to sign permission for student ESL services and then collaborate with families and the community for continued support.

- To exit an ESL program, a student must pass his or her Language Arts (Reading) TAKS (projected to become the STAAR) tests and, in addition, have his or her guardian's signature.
- After exiting, each student is monitored by the LPAC for at least 2 years to ensure that a student can actually succeed in a regular program.

Let's try a policy question:

Mr. Long, a superintendent in a small district in northern Texas, was watching his enrollment numbers of children who would be ELLs in the third grade carefully. How many ELL children must there be before he must hire a third-grade ESL (or bilingual) teacher?

    A. 20
    B. 15
    C. 30
    D. 10

If there are 20 or more ELL children in one grade level, an ESL program is required. The correct answer is *A*.

Instructional Relationships

Just as you have learned about a relationship in other content areas that should result in a reflective cycle between elements of instruction and assessment, so, too, do we find this in teaching ESL. In an effort to make connections to teacher and student standards, competencies, and expectations, the ESL teacher understands the assessment relationships among:

- required instruction of the English Language Proficiency Standards (ELPS)
- required instruction of the state-mandated content standards (Texas Essential Knowledge and Skills [TEKS]), or the requisite knowledge for each grade level and subject area and resulting scores of testing
- special ESL methodologies used in the classroom
- ongoing, continuous student assessment
- assessment of one's own instruction that evaluates planning, instruction, and reteaching or redirecting of instruction when needed
- the immediate need to address any professional development needs (based particularly on student performance on state measures or other assessment measures) or other input.

The ESL teacher must often individualize instruction and assessment in order to address student needs and learning goals. Thinking in terms of measuring everything planned, implemented, evaluated, and redirected should be a continuous goal for ESL teachers. Where gaps in student achievement occur, particularly as revealed by annual state measurements (the TAKS or STAAR), the teacher should plan to come together with fellow colleagues in an effort to plan professional learning activities that provide both linguistic and conceptual improvement for the coming academic year.

See how you do with your knowledge and application of understanding on assessment!

Before beginning a mathematics lesson, Ms. Pruneda, an ESL teacher, has her fifth-grade students discuss their understanding of converting measurements from ounces to pounds and pounds to tons. The best reason for this type of informal assessment is to:

A. assess low-ability students in their participation in the learning.
B. promote a sense of what will be covered as an advanced organizer or focus activity.
C. provide a sense of excitement about the content.
D. determine the appropriate developmental level of instruction at which to begin, according to the prior knowledge of the class.

Even though a good ESL teacher should always be assessing students informally whenever they participate (*A*) and should provide both an advanced organizer or focus of the lesson to come (*B*) as an enticement for students to become involved (*C*), in this case, it is most important for the teacher to start instruction at the correct developmental level. The best answer, therefore, is *D*, and is based on the teacher discovering the prior knowledge of all students in the class. The correct answer is *D*.

DOMAIN III Foundations, Culture, Family, and Community/Outside the Classroom/Continuous Professional Development and Community/Resource Outreach

Standard II (Foundations of ESL)
Standard V (ESL Academic Content, Language, and Culture)
Standard VII (Family and Community Involvement)

Competency 008: The ESL teacher understands the foundations of ESL education and types of ESL programs. Some terms and concepts related to this competency are included here.

- Historical, theoretical, and policy
- Self-contained
- Pull-out
- Newcomer centers

- Dual language
- Immersion
- **Apply research findings**
- Instructional and management

Historical, Theoretical, and Policy Foundations

An ESL teacher should know the historical, theoretical, and policy foundations of ESL education and use this knowledge to plan, implement, and advocate for ESL programs that are truly effective. These areas include the following:

- Historically, immigrants have tried to maintain their home languages and cultures by providing instruction in their native languages, usually by speaking that language at home or by sending their children to after school or Saturday classes in the home language. With the influx of large numbers of immigrants, the Nationality Act of 1906 was passed to make sure that English would be learned, but was later judged to be unconstitutional. In 1968, the Bilingual Education Act provided funds for bilingual/ESL programs. In addition, the **Lau vs. Nichols Act** of 1974 established rules to determine when districts must implement bilingual/ESL programs. Typically, when a district has determined that there are 20 or more students across the district at the same grade level needing bilingual or ESL instruction, the district is bound to act and provide such services.

- Theoretically, **English as a Second Language (ESL)** is an educational approach in which students who have **limited English proficiency (LEP)**, or those now referred to as *English language learners (ELLs)*, are instructed in the use of the English language and in the various content areas in English. Thus, instruction is based on a special curriculum that typically involves little or no use of the native language and is often taught during specific school periods. Frequently, these programs have students "pulled out" of their regular classroom for ESL language arts. For the rest of the school day, students are usually taught in a mainstream classroom, an immersion program, or a bilingual program (U.S. General Accounting Office, 2006). Students may also be taught in a self-contained ESL classroom for all content areas.

- State and national policy tells all districts that they are required to conduct an ESL program and shall conduct continuous diagnosis and periodic assessment in the language of instruction to determine the program's impact and student outcomes in all subject areas. Annual reports of educational performance should reflect the academic progress in either language of the ELL student. Districts should also report to the state the progress of their students annually, and states are required to report proficiencies to No Child Left Behind. Each school year, the principal of each school campus (with the assistance of the campus level committee) must develop, review, and revise the Campus Improvement Plan for the purpose of improving student performance.

Types of ESL Programs

An ESL teacher should know the types of ESL programs (sometimes also termed **English Language Development [ELD] programs**), along with their characteristics, goals, and research findings on effectiveness (Baker, 2001). It is also important to consider the philosophy of each of these types of programs. Some types of programs emphasize **early exit** (or leaving a supporting language program at the earliest possible time to go into regular all-English classrooms). These types of programs are seen as **remedial** or **subtractive**, and usually support the ELL from 1 to 4 years (which is seen by some with the opposite philosophy as "not enough").

Developmental programs that enhance the home language along with the new language, usually recommend **late exit** and continued support in the home language (L1) for as long as possible. Programs termed **maintenance** or **additive bilingual education** also seek to enrich the L1 and the cultural identity of the student as much as possible.

The following lists descriptions of both types of language programs:

- **Self-contained:** students have the same ESL teacher for all subjects (except, perhaps, for special classes such as music, art, or kinesiology [P.E.]).
- **Pull-out:** students are taken out of regular classrooms for ESL instruction for a certain length of time (usually for language arts) but are returned to a regular classroom for most of the day.

- **Newcomer Center:** an entry program for supporting newly arrived immigrants that is short term (usually only up to a year), during which time the home language may be used, at times, for instruction but English and social adjustment is the focus.
- **Immersion:** students are placed in a program in which the L1 (home language) is used rarely and only as needed to clarify English instruction.
- **One-way dual language:** bilingual instruction is provided for students in one classroom who all speak the same language (e.g., Spanish, Vietnamese in Texas) but have different proficiencies in both languages; instruction is provided half in English and half in the home language; content areas for teaching in the L1 and the L2 are normally specified.
- **Dual language:** (*two-way immersion*) native English speakers and students with another language are placed together; half of the day is taught in English and half in the home language of the other students, with the goal of both groups becoming bilingual. This type of **developmental bilingual program** provides two main objectives: pride in the L1 for both groups and peer role models for their L2. Research on this type of program is becoming quite promising.
- **Structured English immersion (SEI):** the teacher maximizes lessons taught in English using ESL techniques with the goal of English proficiency being foremost. Significant time is spent teaching about English, and students are often grouped for lessons targeted to their individual proficiency levels. English teaching methods are treated as synonymous with teaching a foreign language.
- **Submersion:** ELLs are placed in regular classrooms with little or no instructional modifications or special instructions in English language development.

Make Appropriate Instructional and Management Decisions

ESL teachers must take into account all external forces that have a bearing on what it means to implement and maintain an ESL program (i.e., students' needs and achievement so far in both the L1 and the L2, rules governing such programs, and district and campus plans). Because ESL instruction is a federally regulated program and funded through federal money, it is imperative that specific records be kept, rules followed, and deadlines met. This is because students have a *property right*, meaning that they should expect a product for their efforts (such as a diploma on graduation or, in this case, to speak English). Hence, many rules and regulations at the federal, state, and district levels are implemented to ensure that expectations are met. Districts not in compliance with state and federal standards can suffer adverse consequences. The No Child Left Behind Act of 2001 (U.S. Department of Education, 2001) was a federal expectation that implemented measures to ensure that all states addressed accountability expectations. As a result, state and local education agencies became aligned with federal policy for the purpose of student achievement, namely reading on grade level by third grade and continuing to read on grade level for the remainder of a student's academic career. With such strict accountability measures in place and the added component of second language instruction, many districts pay stipends to attract and retain quality ESL teachers or do not hire teachers who do not have ESL certification.

Convergent Research Applied

It is the ethical and legal duty of the ESL teacher to keep abreast of important educational issues and findings about ESL and seize opportunities to collaborate with other professionals, families, and the community to improve instruction. Research is constantly being generated to help ESL teachers better understand what works and what may not work for ELLs. ESL teachers should always apply current knowledge of research findings related to ESL education (including research on instructional and management practices) to assist in planning and implementing effective programs (Baker, 2001). It behooves the ESL teacher to subscribe to professional journals and belong to professional organizations that advocate for ESL instruction. Two of the many organizations to which a teacher may belong are Teachers of English to speakers of Other Languages (TESOL) (www.tesol.org), an international organization for and its Texas affiliate, TEXSOL.

Answer the following question relating to the competency on ESL foundations:

Which of the following programs, according to convergent research, best promotes pride in the primary language while still fostering academic language success in the target language?

A. Transitional bilingual
B. ESL
C. Two-Way Dual Language
D. Submersion

In this question, research firmly supports programs in which pride in the home language (L1) and culture is valued and maintained (**additive bilingualism**). The only program listed here that maintains the L1 after English instruction is choice *C*, two-way dual language. Transitional bilingual programs (*A*) in the state of Texas methodically replace Spanish (or Vietnamese) with English, as more English is acquired. This means that by the end of fifth grade, the student should be ready to enter into an environment of complete English instruction with no more L1 support. ESL instruction (*B*) is completely conducted in English, as well as submersion (*D*), where no program is offered (this can also be referred to as a type of hands-off immersion, or the sink-or-swim approach). However, in choice *C*, a two-way dual language program, monolingual speakers of L1 and monolingual speakers of L2 come together in the same classroom (usually representing equal numbers of students for each language) to learn both languages. Two-way dual language can be called a *serpent model* because it involves switching instruction between the two languages, either by every other day delivery or half a day in the L1 and half a day in English. When the two groups of monolingual speakers come together, they share the same anxiety and pride, depending on whether the current instruction is in their primary language or the target language. This builds pride in the primary language because it is valued and maintained and, at the same time, provides a model and mentor of language support by peers who speak the opposite language. The result is usually two groups of completely bilingual children. The answer is *C*.

Competency 009: The ESL teacher understands factors that affect ESL students' learning and implements strategies for creating an effective **multicultural and multilingual learning environment**. Some terms and concepts for Competency 009 are listed next.

- **Cultural and linguistic diversity**
- Cultural responsiveness
- Developmental characteristics
- Academic strengths and needs

- **Preferred learning styles**
- Personality
- **Sociocultural factors**
- Home environment
- **Attitude**
- Exceptionalities
- Affective, linguistic, and cognitive needs

- **Cultural bias**
- Stereotyping
- Prejudice
- Ethnocentrism
- Diverse cultural and socioeconomic backgrounds
- Awareness of and respect for linguistic and cultural diversity

Cultural and Linguistic Diversity

Cultural and linguistic diversity in the ESL classroom and other factors may affect students' learning of academic **content, language, and culture**. The following should be a focus of an ESL teacher as he or she prepares instruction:

- age, in terms of language acquisition, as mentioned, is neither related to the learner's actual age nor grade-level specific (a new immigrant who is in the sixth grade may be on the same level in English as a kindergartner; however, the teaching materials should be very different for the upper grades instead of the *See Spot Run* variety)
- developmental characteristics (as influenced by students' L1 and L2 experiences and age [the same as one would consider if the child was not an ELL]), although there may be additional experiences involved, such as interrupted schooling, trauma in immigration, and so forth
- academic strengths and needs (due to students' cultural/linguistic background and previous academic experiences)
- preferred learning styles and modalities (e.g., thinking preferences and oral, visual, tactile, and kinesthetic modalities)
- personality (e.g., interpersonal, intrapersonal)
- sociocultural factors (e.g., religion, cultural rites of passage, expectations for genders, values)
- family unit (i.e., single, traditional, nontraditional, extended)
- home environment (e.g., low or high socioeconomic, abuse or neglect, family illiteracy)
- attitude (predisposition to learning may vary due to culture/language)
- exceptionalities (special education, gifted and talented, etc.) (Section 504 is a civil rights law that prohibits discrimination against individuals with disabilities. Section 504 ensures that a child with special needs has equal access to an education. The child may receive accommodations and modifications.) Remember that an ELL could have any of the special needs that other students may have—in addition to ESL needs. The ESL certification is supplemental because an ESL teacher must be knowledgeable enough to address learners with special needs through initial certification.
- **self-fulfilling prophecy**—a teacher's beliefs/expectations create experiences for success when they feel that ESL students (1) can learn English quickly, (2) can compete with native English speakers, and (3) that bilingual learners have advantages over monolingual learners.

Diversity: Multicultural and Multilingual

Creation of an effective multicultural and multilingual learning environment should be a priority for the ESL teacher. It is also incumbent on a teacher to ensure that he or she does not stereotype a culture (Bennett, 1998).

For example, Puerto Ricans are generally considered Hispanic, but their culture is very different from that of Mexicans or Argentineans, just as the Japanese culture is very different from other Asian cultures, such as Korean, Chinese, or Vietnamese. All cultures within an ESL class should be celebrated. Language and culture cannot be separated; therefore the ESL teacher would benefit from learning more about the particular cultures and languages represented in his/her classroom. For instance, if one is in an ESL class where the L1 is Spanish, one would expect to hear such terms as *mariachi* (Mexican musician), *aplácate* (calm down!), *tacos* (tortillas wrapped around a wide variety of meat and other ingredients), and so forth. However, many words of this type may or may not mean the same thing or be similarly understood by Hispanic societies that reside distant from Mexico. As a parallel example, for a Texan, the English word *boot* is footwear, but from the perspective of an English speaker from Britain, a *boot* is also recognized as the trunk of a car. Therefore, a Brit who directs a Texan to find something "in the boot" may have the Texan digging in a closet for footwear. The teacher who is not very fluent or speaks a particular dialect of another language must also attend to translations that he or she attempts in another language. The use of some words may be occasionally offensive or confusing (i.e., *discussion* in Spanish tends to means *to argue*, while in English it means *to talk over,* so if a teacher asks students to have a discussion using this word in Spanish, he or she may be confused as to why students begin to argue).

Cultural Bias

There are a number of factors that contribute to cultural bias (Bennett, 1998). Because ESL students are from an increasing number of cultures, the ESL teacher should reflect on these factors daily to be sure that there is a culturally responsive learning environment in place that indicates a respect and validation for students' home culture (**cultural responsiveness**). **Bias** is defined as unfair preferences for or against a particular group. This is typically seen as creating an unequal balance. The unequal direction in most classrooms involves language used by a teacher that is not familiar or understandable to students. Bias occurs in teaching, testing, and other areas of education in which comprehensible or familiar ideas are not used, leaving many ELL students at an academic disadvantage. The teacher may also select literature or other texts that have bias for or against a particular group. Even the home language a learner speaks can carry power. In the *hidden curriculum* (that which students learn but which is not directly taught), students may "understand" that learners from some cultures and those who speak particular languages (typically Western European) are somehow of higher status than others. Sadly, the teacher him- or herself can project bias for or against particular groups in the demeanor used in the classroom. This can include making comments, calling mostly on certain groups of students, giving certain types of feedback to particular groups, standing close to some and farther from others, and so forth. These actions are, unfortunately, sometimes unconscious, so an ESL teacher must reflect on this constantly and use observers or videotaping to ensure that it is not happening. Cultural bias contains the following elements:

- **stereotyping** (false notions or conceptions of other races, etc.)
- **prejudice** (results in creating unfair actions toward individuals because of a mindset about their particular group or culture)
- **ethnocentrism** (belief one's own group is superior to others)
- **unfamiliar language** used, resulting in a disadvantage to those who do not understand and an advantage to those who do.

Sensitivity and Respect

The ESL teacher must always demonstrate sensitivity to students' diverse cultural and socioeconomic backgrounds and show **respect for language differences**. An ESL teacher quite often represents all Americans to students and their parents, so this is not to be taken lightly. It should be a goal of ESL teachers to learn all there is to know about their students, and they should try to learn some basics of the language of their students, although ESL teachers are not required to be bilingual. Teachers have an opportunity to learn language and culture from their students, if they take advantage of the situation.

The more the ESL teacher knows about his or her students, the better learners respond to intended learning outcomes. As mentioned, even learning a few words (or more) of the child's language is a step, but the teacher should definitely seek information on differences in social values (including differences in personal space, cultural comfort level in touching, patterns of communication with body language, ways of listening and talking, and in childrearing, especially with reference to the adult/child communication norms). One reminder, however, is that each child and family member is an individual and should not be automatically slotted into a stereotype of a particular culture simply because they are a recent arrival from a particular country. The Web is full of sites that give information about almost every country, and there are many suggestions in travel guides (or business travelers' guides) for interactions with the culture and descriptions of social norms of a particular country. Preparing one's class for a newcomer and his/her culture can also ease the way for a new ESL child.

It is not required that teachers take on the beliefs and values of others, but understanding differences always helps in communication and gaining respect with families and their children. For example, in the Thai culture it is distasteful to touch someone on the head, to point one's feet at someone else, or to shove an object at someone with one's feet. Direct eye contact is disrespectful to elders in many Hispanic and Asian cultures, whereas in America, if children do not make eye contact, it is seen as being guilty. Some Americans may find "too much" direct eye contact threatening or even sexual in nature, when this is simply a cultural norm of some groups from the Middle East. In Spain and Brazil, or in some Middle Eastern countries, the sign Americans make to signal OK is considered offensive—even obscene. Personal space can also be a cultural issue. For example, Americans can be seen as cold by cultures with a need for closer personal space, whereas Americans may find "too close" intrusive. Cultural differences may also deal with attention to (or lack of attention to) time, dress, diet, grooming, and other body language. Male versus female roles may be very different in other cultures and may affect the way males interact with female teachers. A savvy ESL teacher who does a bit of research can make students and their families feel more at ease as they are learning about America and its cultural norms. The teacher may also avoid loss of respect from some because of actions that may be offensive to diverse families. Teachers can also avoid mistakes in judging learners' knowledge and behavior versus their culturally different responses.

Strategies for Awareness

There are effective strategies for creating an awareness of and respect for linguistic and cultural diversity among students. Foremost, the teacher always models appropriate behavior. The ESL teacher must be careful to attend to such issues in the context of actual teaching and should demonstrate what linguistic and cultural diversity looks like through modeling by classroom examples. Each child should feel equally welcomed and equally served by the education received in a classroom. As a model for ELLs, the ESL teacher has limited control of the world outside the confines of the classroom, but he or she should be a constant example for students in appropriate dress, conversation, body language, politeness, and overall behavior.

The following question relates to the competency of multicultural and multilingual environments:

A new ESL teacher has been assigned to a classroom that includes students from several different ethnic, cultural, and language backgrounds. In order to best address the needs of the class, which supposition should be used to best guide instruction?

- **A.** Students should be paired with others who have similar backgrounds in order to ensure goals and objectives are understood.
- **B.** Students tend to learn best when they have choices in their own learning and assessments.
- **C.** Students from any one of the various backgrounds can be expected to display a wide range of abilities, shortcomings, and interests.
- **D.** Students from different backgrounds learn best when there is no mention of differences between them.

In order to best understand multicultural and multilingual issues in the classroom, the ESL teacher knows that language and culture cannot be separated. However, within Latin, Asian, and other cultures, there are many linguistic and cultural differences. First, the ESL teacher must be clear on the term *supposition*—it is a belief thought to be true based on incomplete evidence. What the ESL teacher *should* believe about different ethnic, cultural, and language backgrounds should be true or at least measurable in order to include supporting evidence. For this reason, we find that choice A is not measurable, because simply pairing students with similar backgrounds in no way ensures that they will meet goals and objectives of learning. Choice B, giving students a choice in their own learning and assessment, is good motivational theory. However, note that there is a better belief for a multicultural/multilinguist class. In choice D, making no mention of the differences between students is not good for anyone. In fact, celebrating differences should be a focus of multicultural and multilingual awareness, although it is also very beneficial to examine what students have in common as well. This leaves choice C, because it is held to be true. Students from many different backgrounds, cultures, or languages may exhibit traits that can be generalized to their particular culture, but students can also be expected to display a wide variety of abilities, strengths, shortcomings, and interests. Each child is an individual case. The correct answer is C.

Competency 010: The ESL teacher knows how to serve as an advocate for ESL students and facilitate family and community involvement in their education. The terms and concepts listed next relate to this competency.

- Family and community involvement
- **Advocating educational and social equity for ESL students**
- Participating in Language Proficiency Assessment Committee (LPAC) and Admit, Review, and Dismiss (ARD) meetings
- Serving on Site-Based Decision Making (SBDM) committees
- Serving as a resource for other teachers
- Facilitating parent/guardian participation
- Communicating and collaborating effectively with parents/guardians
- Community members and resources positively affect student learning
- Accessing **community resources**

The Teacher as an Advocate for Ells

The ESL teacher advocate should realize that students and their parents who do not speak English cannot often speak up for themselves. When this happens, inequality can often occur. The ESL teacher is always charged to be the voice of ELLs and their parents so that students receive equal opportunities for education. Every ESL teacher should, at least once, go to a country where the language is different, where there are no signs in English, and so forth. Teachers must see how difficult it can be on one's own to order food, to enjoy cultural events, to watch television, to find the restrooms, to use local transportation (because it is difficult to know where to get on or get off), where it is impossible to have a casual conversation with anyone, and so on. It can be a very lonely experience. These experiences should bring home the disadvantages that families and students incur when they move to this country and, indeed, the very need for having an advocate. These difficulties are the reason why English-speaking tours in non-English-speaking areas are so popular. Most people fear putting themselves in a situation where they feel helpless to communicate, so a bilingual guide sees to these details and takes over if there are problems. The tourist can then relax and take in the experience without the anxiety. This is, perhaps, how the ESL teacher should think of parts of his or her role in advocating for ELLs as they are learning English.

ESL teachers must also have considerable knowledge about laws and effective strategies to advocate for educational and social equity for ESL students. In this competency of family and community awareness, it becomes obvious that the ESL teacher must step outside the classroom to stand up for ESL students and their right to learn. This is accomplished by participating in:

- *The Language Proficiency Assessment Committee (LPAC),* which recommends identification, placement, and exit of English language learners (ELL) in bilingual/ESL programs.
- *The Admit, Review, and Dismiss (ARD) Committee,* which determines identification, placement, and exit of special education students and the appropriate **Individual Education Plan (IEP)** for such labeled students. An ELL may also be identified as having special needs.
- The **Site-Based Decision Making Committee (SBDM),** which is charged with planning for better student achievement each year at the building level and which should always include ELL achievement.
- *Becoming a resource* for other classroom teachers by serving as a mentor, sharing research and techniques, taking time to gain joint assessments of students they may have in common, and so forth.

 # Family Involvement

Every teacher hopefully knows the importance of family involvement for his or her children. However, in the education of ESL students, teachers must go a step further in facilitating parent/guardian participation in their children's education and school activities. Although a language difference may make communication difficult, it is not necessary that the parents of ESL students speak English in order to have parental involvement. Many aspects of involvement are fruitful without speaking English. The ESL teacher must communicate with parents because:

- family support has a direct relationship to student achievement.
- families should be encouraged to help their children in academic topics using their home language if they are not fluent in English; having parents/guardians trying to help in non-fluent English for mathematics

or science homework, for example, may confuse students on the academic concepts. Helping in the student's L1 also promotes pride in their native language.

- parents can provide support by visiting the school, seeking to collaborate, attending students' events, working with their children on take-home projects, making sure there is space in the house to do homework and research, establishing routines for doing schoolwork, and seeing that necessary school items are provided so students do not waste time in gathering supplies (e.g., paper, pencils).

 Family Collaboration

The ESL teacher applies skills for effectively communicating and collaborating with the parents/guardians of ESL students in a variety of educational contexts. This means that no matter what it may take, the ESL teacher finds the means to communicate the mission, goals, and routines of effective instruction with the parent. If there is no common language between the parent and the ESL teacher, every effort should be made to find someone in the building or in the community who can translate. Even technology translators are available. Some focus areas should be:

- Collaboration. Asking the family for information about the child, requesting support, and seeking advice can help teachers more quickly understand individual characteristics of students.
- Making the school a welcoming place. For example, one ESL teacher sent a videotape to her ESL students' homes before the first day of school to help parents and children feel comfortable finding the classroom from the point of view of a visitor walking up the walkway to the school, signing in at the secretary's desk, walking to the child's classroom, meeting the ESL teacher at her door, and going into the classroom. Another school provides a *parent room,* where caregivers can meet for socialization, receive free English lessons several mornings a week from other English-speaking parents, help teachers prepare materials, if desired, and so forth.
- Remembering that the entire family is new to this country and that they are often embarrassed, uneasy, or even fearful of communication with teachers; in fact, some families may even believe that the teacher, as a state employee in a government-run system, might report on their immigration status, rather than seeing the school as a helpful entity.
- Having ESL students serve as translators for their families can put them in a difficult spot at times, especially when they could be caught between the most powerful people in their lives. It is never wise to ask the child of a family to serve as the interpreter in these situations, because students may be tempted to translate misinformation to the parents. A teacher candidate recently told about a personal situation where her fourth-grade ESL teacher called to report some misbehaviors, which the student promptly translated into *"excellent behaviors"* for her Korean parents. Her advice is to never (if possible) have students translate information to their parents in which the student has a stake.
- Supplying parents with a developmental look at their child's progress in each area taught is crucial throughout the year.
- Having teachers try their best to encourage parents to come into the schools (establishing social events at which children are performing or where food is served is often profitable; transportation and babysitting can also be problematic, so one school district in Texas runs its buses during Open House and provides some classrooms with volunteer babysitters for very young children, with excellent results).

- Having teachers communicate by many means that parents understand (avoiding jargon, providing plenty of time for translations/understanding to occur, etc.).
- Making sure that the medium used to communicate important information (e-mail, phone conversation, conferencing, etc.) can be used easily by each child's caregiver(s), and if not, teachers provide adequate alternative measures to make sure the information is getting home (e.g., if a Web site is used to inform families and the community of important school events and procedures, teachers ensure ahead of time that all intended parties have access to technology and the necessary language skills to use it), or they provide an alternate and appropriate form of communication; when needed, teachers seek out and arrange translators who can help in all home languages of the students in the classroom.
- Sending take-home literacy or other projects in which parents are able to participate in their children's education.

Community Members and Resources

Community members and other human resources can positively affect student learning in the ESL program. The ESL teacher should access community resources to enhance the education of these students. This means that the ESL teacher must:

- Actively seek successful community member models from the same ethnicity, culture, gender, and so forth. Jumping into abstract ways of conveying the same information never has the same impact as having a real person who "looks like you" sharing his or her skills, perceptions, or advice on how to be successful. Language experience is built by making it easier to process conceptual ideas based on meaningful concrete experiences (e.g., instead of reading about what it takes to be a successful business person, an engineer, or a doctor, have someone who comes from the same socioeconomic and cultural situation come and talk with students). No matter what the discipline, a real person provides an opportunity to answer questions that are of interest to students, as well as providing a model of success that leads students to think, "If that person can overcome his second language adversity and succeed, so can I!"
- Seek community support in school activities (i.e., one-on-one literacy help from the retired community, financial support for equipment from local businesses, discounted rates on field trip activities, and other educational supplies, etc.).
- Be innovative and think outside the box when it comes to asking for outside support and expertise. When students have the opportunity to interact with successful people outside of education, they can begin to internalize the importance of the authentic connection of education to becoming a successful and productive citizen.
- Participate in community events. Teachers show they are interested and care about their ELL students' culture and often gain considerable knowledge about groups when they attend celebrations or other occasions given by diverse groups in their communities.

Let's try a question on family and community awareness for ELLs:

Ms. Zhang is a fourth-grade ESL teacher. She has children who have a variety of home languages but who are working on level with the fourth-grade TEKS. Ms. Zhang is trying to decide how to best provide information on the school Web site so that it can be understood easily by parents. She thought about translating the information to all the languages represented in her diverse class. What strategy would best accomplish this?

   A. Send a flyer home in English (so that she knows which parents have the English skills to translate) to ask for those parents who are able to come to school and work with the teacher on this project.

   B. Call or e-mail students' families with a message translated into their own languages in order to solicit help in this matter.

   C. Have students from each language group translate the information from English to their native languages.

   D. Ask the LPAC specialist in the building to recommend people for this task.

Involving families in the learning environment helps student success, so we might be encouraged to select choice *A*. Unfortunately, that leaves out particular languages in which family members do not have a good **grasp** of English. However, teachers should remember that there are many things caregivers can do to ensure they are active participants in their child's academic life without speaking English well. Each family participates at their own comfort level, provided the teacher opens the doors for a variety of ways to do so. Choices *B* and *D* are also tempting, because we know that family and community involvement in schools is part of these competencies. However, there is a better answer.

By having the students translate Web information into their primary language in an effort to better inform parents, the ESL teacher has captivated the resources of the class community, encouraged students' pride in their primary languages, and inferred to all who may see the Web site that this class celebrates all languages and cultures. In addition, she could ask families to help make sure the translation was correct (if parents are bilingual) to help strengthen students' L1. For this reason, the best answer is *C*.

SUMMARY

Becoming an ESL teacher in Texas is well worth your while. As discussed in the beginning of this chapter, there are few classrooms in the state without students whose first language is not English. In order to serve these students well, a teacher must be knowledgeable about how to meet their needs. This is a moral obligation for their right to an equal opportunity in education and a civil obligation to help them become functioning members of our society who can contribute well to the general prosperity of this nation. In addition, ESL methods help *all* students to better gain concepts and skills in English/language arts and in content areas—whether they are ESL or their primary language is English. Finally, remember that many districts may not hire teachers without this additional supplement or may require it within a certain time to keep one's position. As a part of one's continued professional development, it is hoped that the information within this chapter not only helps you pass this examination but also helps you become a better teacher for *all* students.

GLOSSARY

Academic language development. Development in the language used specifically in content areas; involves student development in semantic and syntactic features, such as vocabulary items, sentence structure, transition markers, and cohesive ties, and/or specialized language functions and tasks that are part of a *content-area classroom* routine, such as defining terms, explaining historical significance, reading expository text, and preparing research reports (Wertsch, 1985).

Academic language. Lexical language or language needed to comprehend and communicate about content-area subjects such as mathematics, science, social studies, and so forth.

Academic English. Includes vocabulary that is used beyond social conversations; the vocabulary needed to communicate effectively and substantively in English in content-area classes and to comprehend various texts in different content-area classes; "the ability to read, write, and engage in substantive conversations about math, science, history, and other school subjects"

(American Educational Research Association, 2004, p. 2); skills related to mastery of academic English include summarizing, analyzing, extracting and interpreting meaning, evaluating evidence, composing, and editing; it relies on a broad knowledge of words, concepts, language structures, and interpretation strategies.

Achievement across the curriculum. ESL teachers must not only help students achieve in learning English but also know and use ESL strategies to help students in the content areas, such as mathematics, science, social studies, the fine arts, and health/P.E.

Acquisition. The subconscious process of learning to comprehend and communicate in a language gained through meaningful interactions in the target language in natural communication (as opposed to book learning, study of grammar, and drill).

Additive bilingualism. A program that stresses enrichment of one's home language and culture while learning a new language and culture.

Advocate. A moral obligation of the ESL teacher to serve as the voice for students and their parents who cannot yet communicate well in English.

Advocating educational and social equity for ESL students. Participating in LPAC and Admission, Review, and Dismissal (ARD) meetings, serving on Site-Based Decision Making (SBDM) committees, involving families, serving as a resource for other teachers, etc., in order to ensure that each ELL has the same chance of success in education as those who are not ELL.

Alphabetic language. English is a written language in which symbols (the alphabet) reflect the pronunciation of the words; Greek, Russian, Thai, Arabic, and Hebrew are also alphabetic languages. If students' first language is not alphabetic, it may possibly make the transfer to English more difficult.

Alphabetic principle. Making connections with the fact that symbols stand for *sounds* in a written language.

Apply familiar concepts. Using prior knowledge from students' cultural backgrounds and prior experiences to connect new learning; using hands-on and other experiential learning strategies; using realia, media, and other visual supports to introduce or reinforce concepts.

Apply research findings. ESL teachers must stay current in the latest research on ESL learners.

Assessment to plan and adjust instruction. Continuously asking "How is [student's name] progressing?" (through informal and formal means), then changing techniques to address both the needs of the class and of individuals if and when needed.

Attitude. When working with ELLs, it is important to emphasize positive, meaningful, motivating activities that promote students' positive mindsets and interests in learning English; a positive attitude has been shown to affect learning.

Authentic assessment. A form of assessment in which students are asked to perform real-world tasks (or as near to real world as the classroom allows) rather than pen-and-paper drills.

Basic Interpersonal Communication Skills (BICS). Students can usually develop the basic ability to communicate socially in a new language within 6 months to 2 years.

Behaviorist theory. A belief that humans learn language through reinforcement.

Biliteracy. The ability to read proficiently in two languages.

Cognitive Academic Language Proficiency Skills (CALPS). Proficiency in academic language development needed for content areas with specialized, lexical terminology; usually takes 5–7 years to develop.

Categorization. The basic cognitive process of arranging information into classes or categories (e.g., classification, sorting).

Circumlocution. Correcting an ELL's statement by restating the student's mistake several times in correct English within a conversation rather than drawing direct attention to it or providing a rule.

Code-switching. Switching back and forth between two languages in one sentence or within one conversation when proficiency exists in two languages (e.g., "That is *bueno!*").

Cognitive processes. Memorization, categorization, generalization, metacognition; are involved in synthesizing and internalizing language rules for second-language acquisition.

Communicative competence. Having the skills to speak and comprehend when spoken to in order to communicate in a language.

Community resources. Positive community role models and resources can positively enhance student learning in the ESL program.

Comprehensible instruction. The goal of ESL instruction, in which teachers employ instructional strategies that help scaffold language learning so that students can understand their lessons.

Comprehensive input. Teachers must be sure that the language they are using to address students (input) can be understood by ELLs, especially in academic subjects.

Concept. A general idea derived or inferred from specific instances or occurrences; something formed in the mind; a thought or notion; ELLs must often gain academic concepts at the same time they are grappling with learning English.

Content, language, and culture. Factors that may affect students' learning of academic content, language, and culture (e.g., age, developmental characteristics, academic strengths and needs, preferred learning styles, personality, sociocultural factors, home environment, attitude, exceptionalities).

Content-area learning. Learning in mathematics, science, social studies, music, and so on that requires both linguistic and conceptual skills, particularly with the academic or lexical vocabulary (CALPS).

Content-based ESL. A teacher uses special ESL techniques in teaching mathematics, science, the fine arts, and so on to help the student in these areas and also in second language development; integrating content and second language instruction.

Conventions of language. General agreement on or acceptable practices of the use of language, including grammar, spelling, punctuation, language usage, capitalization, legibility, sentence structure, and paragraphing; language practice or procedure widely observed in a group, especially to facilitate social interaction; a custom (for example, the usage of *y'all* for *you* or *all of you* in the South).

Critical thinking. The intellectual process of actively and skillfully conceptualizing, applying, analyzing, synthesizing, or evaluating information gathered from (or generated by) observation, experience, reflection, reasoning, or communication.

Cultural bias. Stereotyping, prejudice, or ethnocentrism that causes one group to look down on another group or to see their own group as superior; also, assessments that are unfair because they contain items based on cultural references unknown to those who are outside the culture and could not be answered correctly without that knowledge.

Cultural and language background. Language and culture work together in language development and cannot be separated; furthermore, the importance of understanding individuals' cultures and language backgrounds is paramount for promoting language development.

Cultural and linguistic diversity. ESL teachers can expect to have students from many diverse backgrounds; teachers should gain knowledge in each individual's cultural and linguistic background rather than stereotype an umbrella culture (e.g., not all Hispanics come from the same country, area, or culture; Hispanics come from Europe, the Caribbean, and Asia, as well as North, Central, and South America with cultural and language differences [and dialects] that are not necessarily the same as that of Mexico).

Cultural responsiveness. Teachers provide an environment that respects and validates students' home cultures.

Culture. Socially transmitted behavior patterns, arts, beliefs, institutions, and all other products of human work and thought; these patterns, traits, and products are considered the expression of a particular period, class, community, or population.

Delivery of instruction. Ways of providing instruction that can be found in several different areas: learner support and various resources, instructional design and delivery, assessment and evaluation of student learning, use of technology, teacher use of student feedback, addressing learning styles, and so on.

Developmental bilingual education. Programs such as dual language or other bilingual programs that seek to develop the home language, as well as the L2 (English, in this case).

Developmental characteristics. Social, emotional, academic, and behavioral features that are interrelated parts of language development.

Developmentally appropriate instruction. Refers to Vygotsky and the *zone of proximal development,* or the place current learning and potential learning can be targeted for growth under adult guidance or in collaboration with more capable peers (Slavin, 2009). For ESL purposes, a teacher should slightly challenge the student with input.

Diagnosis. The critical analysis of the language development of ESL students to determine possible barriers to progress.

Discourse. Verbal expression in speech or in writing; conversation.

Discourse competence. The ability to competently interact with native speakers using various communication strategies, social registers, conversation, narration, inquiry for information, directing others, and so forth.

Dual language. Teaching two languages equally; a language approach where half English-speaking and half non-English-speaking students are taught together to instill a mutual respect for both; students are taught half of the time in the L1 (home language) of half of the students and half of the time in the L1 of the other half so that both become bilingual.

Early exit. Having students leave a supporting language program at the earliest possible time to go into a regular all-English classroom.

Engaging instruction. Motivating instruction that increases the involvement of students and seeks for them to take ownership of their learning and do meaningful and effective work.

English language arts and reading competencies (ELA). The basis of ESL instruction; all ESL teachers must also attend to both these and to the ESL competencies.

English language learners (ELLs). Students who are placed in ESL or bilingual classrooms; formerly, the label was Limited English Proficient (LEP).

English language proficiency. Proficiency in English for ESL students is typically determined on passing a standardized English language test. A score of 70 percent for criterion-referenced tests or 40th percentile for norm-reference tests are adequate levels to be labeled *proficient*. Students are tested on their ability to comprehend English in order to be exited from an ESL program; students are monitored for the following 2 years after exiting an ESL program to ensure academic success in the regular English classroom.

English Speakers of Other Languages (ESOL). The designated term for ELL high school students who are new arrivals.

Enhanced learning. Provides improved, advanced, or sophisticated features to the learning process (computer software is one such medium that enhances instruction and learning with cutting-edge functionalities that include interactions, immediate feedback, guided practice, self-direction in learning, etc.).

ESL programs. Types of ESL programs designed for English language learners that include pull-out, self-contained, Newcomer Centers, dual language, and immersion.

ESL standards for Texas teachers. (1) Pre-requisite understanding of English language concepts and acquisition of English; (2) methodologies; (3) oral communication; (4) literacy skills and assessment; (5) ESL foundations; (6) multicultural and multilingual perceptions; and (7) third-party awareness for a comprehensive overview of ESL instruction.

ESL teaching strategies. Groups of activities specially designed to produce outcomes that create an effective environment leading to positive ELL student achievement.

Ethnocentrism. A belief in the superiority of one's own ethnic group.

Facilitate learning. To increase the likelihood, strength, or effectiveness of learning.

Familiarity with the structure and uses of textbooks and other print resources. ESL teachers understand that students from other countries may not know how to address print resources, such as magazines, newspapers, and Web-based articles (e.g., students may not understand the concept of reading by scanning left to right and top to bottom in English).

Foreign language. A language other than the speaker's home language (English is a foreign language to those whose home language is different).

Foreign Language in the Elementary School (FLES) Program. Programs that begin to teach a second language very early on to English speakers to allow students to become functionally proficient and to learn about a foreign country (or countries) and its culture.

Foreign Language Exploratory (FLEX) Program. A program to introduce a foreign language and foreign culture to younger English speakers (rather than to obtain proficiency) with the aim of motivating them to continue to study later on and to help understand the structure of English better.

Formal assessment. A structured measure of learner achievement over a period of time, usually meaning the use of tests and exams (which are often standardized, such as the TAKS or STAAR tests).

Foundations of ESL education. The ESL teacher knows the historical, theoretical, and policy background of ESL.

Fundamental language rules. The fundamental rules of a language's structure at initial stages of language development.

Generalization. A language principle, statement, or idea having general application.

Gist. ELLs who understand just enough to gain the general idea or basic information.

Grammar. The branch of linguistics that deals with syntax, morphology, and semantics.

Grasp. A term used to describe students who are functional in English but not completely in full command yet (http://ritter.tea.state.tx.us/student.assessment/admin/rpte/Glossary_of_TELPAS_Training_Terms.pdf).

Hands-on and other experiential learning strategies. Using manipulatives and other concrete objects (realia, props, models, pictures, etc.) in the context of building conceptual understanding.

High-frequency vocabulary. Words that allow the learner to initially function in the classroom (pencil, paper, take out your book, sit down, etc.) and that are used frequently in all areas (colors, names/titles of people [family members, teachers, etc.])

High-frequency words. Words that appear many more times than most other words in spoken or written language (*very*, *about*, *then*, *and*, etc.).

Home language. The language that is predominate in the home of the student; one's native language; one's first language.

i + 1. The teacher assesses the learner's language level and adds one level up to encourage challenging learning, as in Vygotsky's zone of proximal development.

Identification, placement, and exit. The major role of the Language Proficiency Assessment Committee (LPAC) for individual students that is based on student achievement and standardized tests scores.

Idiomatic expressions. Expressions that are sentences or phrases that do not exactly or literally mean what they say, so that even if one knows the meaning of every word used, they can rarely be understood due to cultural and linguistic differences (e.g., "Does the cat have your tongue?").

Immersion. A classroom placement where using the home language (L1) for ELLs is rarely (if ever) employed, and then only to clarify English.

Informal assessment. Ongoing appraisal by casual observation, discussion, or by other nonstandardized procedures.

Instructional goals. Clear statements of what teachers want learners to accomplish.

Instructional and program management practices. All ESL program decisions should be data driven.

Instructional strategies for ESL. Specific activities (what the teacher and students do) that should be based on accepted ESL methodologies or ESL theories designed to expand the potential of students for fluency in the L2.

Integrate technology tools. Combining technology (e.g., hardware, software, peripherals, use of the Internet) with content areas and reading/language arts to enhance instruction in ESL.

Internalized language. Vocabulary and other language concepts that have been permanently fixed through meaningful use versus newly learned English that is not yet part of memory.

Interpretation of results. Understanding formal, informal, and authentic assessment procedures and instruments (both in English proficiency and academic achievement); used in ESL programs to place students and to plan and adapt instruction as needed.

Interrelatedness of listening, speaking, reading, and writing. ESL teachers should instruct in all of these areas in concert to increase mastery in English (because what students learn in one area helps them learn in other areas).

Interrupted schooling. ELLs may have not had the opportunity to attend school regularly, which becomes a personal factor that can have an effect on ESL students' English literacy development and growth in content knowledge.

Language. Involves communication of thoughts and feelings through a system of arbitrary signals such as sounds, gestures, or written symbols; such a system includes rules for combining these components and is used by a nation, people, or other distinct community.

Language levels. Texas labels ELLs as beginning level, intermediate level, advanced, or advanced high, but some school districts distinguish levels as in pre-production, early production, speech emergent, intermediate fluent, and advanced fluent.

Language minority. Refers to a student whose family predominately speaks another language, whether the student actually speaks English well or not.

Language Proficiency Assessment Committee (LPAC). Maintains responsibility for identification, placement, and exiting of ELLs from an ESL or bilingual program; monitors ELLs for success for 2 years after exiting.

Languages Other Than English (LOTE). A coordinating division of TEA that handles foreign language instruction and, in particular, the TEKS that govern any instruction in these languages.

Late exit. Having students stay in a developmental type of language program for as long as possible where support is provided in the L1, as well as the L2.

Lau vs. Nichols. Established that a school district must provide an ESL or bilingual program if there are 20 or more ELLs in a grade level to give ESL students an equal opportunity in education.

Learned knowledge (versus acquisition). The conscious, intentional study of a language, its structure, and the way it functions through formal work.

Learning styles. Preferences for thinking and learning in specific ways that facilitate ESL students' communicative, literacy, and cognitive-academic development.

Letter-sound associations. The understanding that a written letter stands for a certain sound(s); phonics.

Lexical understanding. Vocabulary belonging to a particular subject (as in mathematics, science, or social studies) that one must understand in order to navigate through that particular content area.

Limited English Proficiency (LEP). A term that has been commonly replaced by the Office of Civil Rights with ELL (English language learner), considered to be less negative in its connotation.

Linguistic competence. The ability to use the correct grammatical form and structure to express a given meaning.

Linguistic environment. A supportive, positive oral/speaking environment with considerable conversational opportunities that is important for ESL development.

Linguistically accommodated. Texas states that ESL instruction that is delivered in the L2 (English) must be communicated, sequenced, and scaffolded commensurate with the ELL's proficiency in English.

Literacy development. Usually occurs in stages starting with oral language development and continues to high levels of oral and written language applications; therefore, the continuum of eleven ELA EC-6 competencies (see Table 10.3) is written in this order.

Literacy status in the primary language. The level of a student in his or her native language has an effect on the level to be achieved in the L2; the better one knows his or her home language (L1), the easier it is to learn the L2.

Maintenance bilingual education. Programs in which the aims are to help students keep/maintain their L1 skills as they are learning English.

Mean. Average of a number of scores.

Median. A score that falls in the middle of a range of scores.

Metacognition. Awareness and understanding of one's own thinking and cognitive processes; thinking about one's thinking.

Methods (of instruction). Methodologies that are identifiable techniques that can be widely used in ESL instruction; examples include total physical response (Asher, 2000), grammar translation, computer-assisted instruction, and so forth.

Mode. The most frequent score in a number of scores.

Modifying instructional materials. The teacher uses assessment and appropriate data to determine what are the most appropriate materials for achieving instructional goals and changes them based on continuously gathered feedback.

Morphology. The branch of linguists that studies the structure and form of words in a language, including inflection, derivation, the formation of compounds, affixes, etc. Morphemes are the smallest segment of sound that carries meaning, such as *un-true*, where *un* is a suffix and *true* is the smallest "free" segment of sound that carries meaning; words are the interface among phonology, syntax, and semantics.

Multicultural and multilingual learning environment. An effective, supportive, and respective environment (Bennett, 1998) that addresses the affective, linguistic, and cognitive needs of students from many countries (who may speak a variety of languages) and facilitates students' learning and language acquisition.

Native language. The home, L1, or primary language.

Nativist theory. Belief that humans are born with the innate ability for speaking language, and when exposed to language, this ability engages automatically; an innate propensity for language acquisition.

Newcomer Centers. A bilingual or ESL program that makes use of facilities to separate first-year ELLs from the general population and takes advantage of ESL methodologies to better enhance academic success for this population of students. Newcomer Centers serve these students through a program of intensive language development and academic and cultural orientation for a limited period of time (usually from 6 to 18 months) before placing them in the regular school language support and academic programs.

One-way dual language. Bilingual instruction is provided in one classroom for students who all speak the same language but with varying levels of proficiency in the L1 and the L2 and in which instruction should be provided half in English and half in the other language (in Texas, this is most often Spanish); certain content areas are usually specified as being taught in each language.

Oral discourse. Conversation.

Overgeneralization. A language learner applies a rule to all circumstances (e.g., adding *-ed* to the past as in "I *goed* to the store" or "He *stoled* my pencil").

Personal factors. Factors that can affect learning a new language that can include prior learning experiences (e.g., familiarity with specialized language and vocabulary, familiarity with the structure and uses of textbooks and other print resources), backgrounds (including status, socioeconomics), and special needs.

Phonemic awareness. Skills for the ability to hear, identify, and manipulate individual sounds (or *phonemes*) in spoken words; teachers should teach phonics skills because they are a good predictor of overall reading success, spelling, and comprehension; teaching the *alphabetic principle* (sound-to-symbol awareness) is effective in promoting phonemic awareness.

Phonetically irregular words. Words that are not pronounced like the rules that should govern them state.

Phonograms. The correspondence of a symbol to its sound, or the letter and combination of letters in a phonetic alphabet that represent a sound in speech; for example, *s* represents the /s/ sound in *Sam*, or *oy* that represents the /oi/ sound in *toy*.

Phonological knowledge and skills. Include phonemic awareness skills, knowledge of English letter–sound associations, and knowledge of common English phonograms.

Phonology. The study of speech sounds in language or a language with reference to their distribution and patterning and to tacit rules governing pronunciation.

Pragmatics. Language messages often consist of interpretation not based on the exact words (although not idioms). For example, if a boy asked a girl who was not interested in him on a date, she might reply in the negative by saying, "You've got to be kidding me, right?" Or if someone asked, "Where is the rest of that homemade pie?" and the reply was, "Well, John was here, . . ." which could be interpreted that John ate it (Payne, 2005).

Preferred learning styles. Learners have thinking and modality preferences for input (visual, auditory, tactile, or kinesthetic) that teachers should tap into to enhance individual success.

Prejudice. The act or state of holding judgments or convictions about a particular group of people that normally results in unfair treatment (either for or against) particular groups.

Pre-teaching key vocabulary. Before a content-area lesson begins, teaching the vocabulary necessary to understand the particular lesson helps in building linguistic and conceptual understanding with required informational, nonfictional vocabulary.

Primary language. A person's home or native language; the L1.

Prior literacy experience. Some ESL students may or may not have had formal or informal experiences with literacy due to interrupted schooling, poverty, and so on.

Proficiency. The level of ability to use the L2; the ESL teacher understands the difference between the lack of language proficiency and academic achievement and knows that ESL students who do not acquire the new language with the academic concepts will suffer academically.

Program evaluation. The systematic collection of information about the activities, characteristics, and outcomes of an ESL program to make judgments, improve effectiveness, or develop informed decisions about future development.

Pull-out. An ESL model in which students leave the regular classroom for a period of time during the school day to work with a special ESL teacher alone or in a small group (usually for language arts in English).

Reading comprehension. Factors that affect ESL students' reading comprehension, including vocabulary, text structures, and cultural references.

Realia. Real things such as objects, photos, posters, books, souvenirs, postcards; types of real materials that the teacher can introduce to make instruction more concrete.

Receptive vocabulary. The amount of spoken language one can aurally process, which is usually up to four times greater than an individual's ability to speak.

Registers of language. Ways of communicating in particular social situations. Sociolinguistic competence has been divided into five levels: (1) the casual register (language used with family and friends that is not always correct English); (2) the consultative register (correctly spoken English); (3) the formal register (very correct English used in academic situations and business); (4) the frozen register (words do not change and most people know them well, such as the "Pledge of Allegiance" and religious passages, such as the Lord's Prayer); and (5) the intimate register (language that is used between lovers or with wanted and unwanted sexual connotations); ESL students can blunder by using conversation in the wrong register or by not being able to style shift, so ESL teachers must also address this aspect (Payne, 2005).

Respect for language differences. The teacher demonstrates sensitivity to ELLs in showing students that they can achieve; simply because students currently do not have sufficient English skills, they are not necessarily below-average learners.

Rich, comprehensible language environment. The ESL teacher understands the role of a linguistic environment and conversational support in second-language development and uses multiple opportunities and activities for communication in English.

Scaffolding. An adult or capable peer supporting a learner until he or she can become more independent.

Self-contained ESL. (1) A number of ELLs are taught with regular English-speaking students for the entire day, and the teacher uses ESL techniques with the entire class, or (2) students are placed in an ESL classroom which contains *all* ESL students for all content areas, perhaps with the exception of fine arts and P.E.

Self-fulfilling prophecy. A teacher's *belief* in a student's (or students') potential success or failure will influence the end result.

Semantics. The study of meanings of words, expressions, and sentences.

Sentence structure. The grammatical arrangement of words in sentences and the patterns and conventions of written and spoken English.

Sheltered instruction. Content areas (usually in the upper grades) are taught in English but using techniques where teachers adjust the lesson in many ways with ESL techniques (such as speaking more slowly; using context clues, concrete items, and models; relating instruction to past experiences; and so forth).

Sight-word vocabularies. Phonetically irregular words, high-frequency words (*and, then, could, know,* etc.) usually memorized for rapid reading.

SIOP (Sheltered Instruction Observation Protocol). Teachers who are using sheltered instruction in the content areas can use this tool to help plan and deliver ESL lessons and also help teachers be accountable for the instructional needs of their ELLs.

Site-Based Decision Making (SBDM) Committee. Schools in Texas each have a committee established to make decisions with an impact on the achievement of learners at their particular schools; ESL teachers should serve on this committee to advocate and ensure the rights of ELL students.

Social cognitive and social cultural theories. Belief that language is learned through social interactions and through models who adjust their levels for children as they grow older.

Social versus academic language. Vernacular or commonly spoken English (BICS) used in informal conversations versus lexical or academic English (CALPS).

Sociocultural factors. Includes values, religion, rites of passage, expectations for genders, and so forth.

Sociolinguistic competence. The ability to interact in different social registers using appropriate rules and politeness for that situation.

Standardized tests. Tests such as the TAKS or STAAR that are uniformly developed, administered, and scored so that students are on an equal footing in terms of the conditions of testing, item biases, and so forth.

State-mandated Limited English Proficient (LEP) policies. Includes the role of the Language Proficiency Assessment Committee (LPAC) and procedures for implementing LPAC recommendations for ELL identification, placement, and exit; establishes mandatory requirements of schools to offer an ESL program under certain conditions (i.e., 20 or more ELL students registered per grade level).

State-mandated standards, instruction, and assessment. The ESL teacher understands he or she must plan instruction according to Texas standards (the TEKS), implement instruction according to research-based methods and strategies, and assess student achievement (through the TAKS or STAAR) in order to improve student achievement.

Stereotyping. Holding beliefs about a group of people that often places them in categories that can often lessen their chances of interaction and diminish their potential; believing that individuals hold certain identified characteristics simply because they belong to a particular group.

Strategic competence. The ability to make use of limited linguistic resources to express one's ideas and comprehend input.

Structure. Formal systematic arrangements of a language.

Style shifting. Ability to shift into the correct register to match the social context.

Subtractive bilingualism. Taking away the use of the native language and cultural aspects and moving to "English only" as soon as possible.

Syntax. The grammatical arrangement of words in sentences.

Synthesizing. Integrating analyses of data to discover facts or develop knowledge concepts or interpretations.

TEKS in English Language Arts. Texas Essential Knowledge and Skills for ELA: Listening, speaking, reading, writing, and viewing/representing.

Test bias. Test construction that can skew the test scores toward or against a particular group(s) of test takers; this can often work for American students and against ELLs (e.g., a mathematics question may require one to know terms and scoring of American football to answer the question, so an ELL may fail the question, even if he or she knows the mathematics).

Texas Essential Knowledge and Skills (TEKS). Teachers are required by the state of Texas to teach the Texas curriculum for each grade level in content areas and in English Language Arts; ESL also has TEKS for each grade level and subject area.

Text structures. Incorporating cause and effect, comparing and contrasting, sequencing, main idea, and so on to apply effective strategies for facilitating ESL students' reading comprehension in English.

Theories. Beliefs derived from many supporting studies; models based on currently accepted hypotheses.

Total Physical Response (TPR). A method used for assessing understanding; the ESL teacher gives a command and ELL performs the command correctly (Asher, 2000); concepts or vocabulary can be acted out (similar to charades).

Transfer from L1 to L2. Students use concepts learned about their first language (L1) to help them learn their second language (L2); language transfer theory supports the idea that literacy skills and concepts learned in the first language enhance and transfer to the second.

Transitional bilingual education. Part of instruction is given in the native language until students can keep up in English.

Viewing and representing. An extra domain that stresses the importance of using technology with ELLs, both in terms of them being able to understand and interpret technological messages and to produce communication through technology due to the ease of combining audio, visual, tactile, and graphical organization of content and conceptual overviews.

Visual supports. Pictures, models, video, graphics, realia, body language, and so on makes content-area concepts easier to understand.

Word analysis skills. Students can sound out words that they cannot automatically recognize by sight through phonics strategies that relate to the *alphabetic principle* (a letter stands for a sound).

Word formation. The basic part of any word is the root; a prefix at the beginning of a root word or a suffix at the end can be added to change the meaning.

REFERENCES

American Educational Research Association. (2004). *Research points. English language learners: Boosting academic achievement.* Retrieved May 1, 2010, from http://www.aera.net/uploadedFiles/Journals_and_Publications/Research_Points/RP_Winter04.pdf

Asher, J. J. (2000). *Learning a language through actions* (6th ed.). Los Gatos, CA: Sky Oaks Productions.

Baker, C. (2001). *Foundations of bilingual education and bilingualism* (3rd ed.). Bristol, PA: Multilingual Matters Ltd.

Bennett, C. I. (1998). *Comprehensive multicultural education: Theory and practice* (4th ed.). Boston: Allyn & Bacon.

Cohen, M., & Nath, J. L. (2009, August). *Helping teachers help English language learners.* Paper presented at the annual summer conference of the Association of Teacher Educators, Reno, NV.

Cummins, J. (1979). Cognitive/academic language proficiency, linguistic interdependence, the optimum age question and some other matters. *Working Papers on Bilingualism, 19,* 121–129.

Fedyk, C. (2006). Reading and L2 acquisition: *International TEYL Journal.* Retrieved November 12, 2009, from http://www.teyl.org/article5.html

Government Accounting Office of Records. (2006). *No Child Left Behind Act: Assistance from education could help states better measure progress of students with limited English proficiency.* Retrieved January 5, 2007, from http://www.gpoaccess.gov/gaoreports/index.htm

Kagan, S. (1995). We can talk: Cooperative learning in the elementary ESL classroom. Retrieved November 3, 2009, from http://www.cal.org/resources/digest/kagan001.html

Krashen, S.D. (1992). *Fundamentals of language education.* Torrance, CA: Laredo Press.

Krashen, S. D., & Terrell, T. D. (1996). *The natural approach: Language acquisition in the classroom* (revised ed.). Englewood Cliffs, NJ: Prentice Hall.

Nath, J. L., & Cohen, M. D. (Eds.) (2011). *Becoming an EC-6 teacher in Texas: A course of study for the Pedagogy and Professional Responsibilities (PPR) TExES.* Belmont, CA: Wadsworth/Cengage.

Nath, J. L., & Cohen, M. D. (Eds.) (2005). *Becoming a middle or high school teacher in Texas: A course of study for the Pedagogy and Professional Responsibilities (PPR) TExES.* Belmont, CA: Thomson/Wadsworth.

Payne, R. K. (2005). *A framework for understanding poverty* (4th ed.). Highlands, TX: aha! Process Inc.

Peregoy, S., & Boyle, O. (2005). *Reading, writing, and learning in ESL: A resource book for K–12 teachers* (4th ed.). Boston: Pearson/Allyn & Bacon.

Slavin, R. (2009). *Educational Psychology: Theory and Practice* (9th ed.). Upper Saddle River, NJ: Pearson.

Texas Education Agency. (2009). *Texas Essential Knowledge and Skills (TEKS).* Retrieved on April 29, 2010, from http://www.tea.state.tx.us/index3.aspx?id=3264&menu_id=793

University of Texas Center for Reading and Language Arts. (2003). *Teaching the viewing and representing Texas Essential Knowledge and Skills in the English language arts curriculum: Professional development guide.* Retrieved November 8, 2009, from http://www.texasreading.org/downloads/secondary/guides/2003VR_bw.pdf

U.S. Department of Education. (2001). *No Child Left Behind Act of 2001.* Retrieved November 6, 2009, from http://www.ed.gov/policy/elsec/leg/esea02/index.html

Wertsch, J. V. (1985). *Vygotsky and the social formation of mind.* Cambridge, MA: Harvard University Press.

RESOURCES

Center for Applied Linguistics: http://www.cal.org.

Center for Research on Education, Diversity & Excellence: http://www.crede.ucsc.edu.

National Clearinghouse for English Language Acquisition: http://www.ncela.gwu.edu/.

Bilingual Research Journal: http://brj.asu.edu/search.html

IDRA (Intercultural Development Research Association) Newsletter: http://www.idra.org/Newslttr/Newslttr.htm

National Association for Bilingual Education (NABE) Journal of Research and Practice: http://www.uc.edu/njrp

TEA LEER MAS: http://ritter.tea.state.tx.us/curriculum/biling/tearesources.html

AN ESL LESSON PLAN

Title of Lesson: Pets

Grade Level: K–5 (Beginning ESL Level)

Main Subject Area: ESL

Subjects Integrated: Language Arts, Math, Science, Social Studies

Time Frame/Constraints: Depends on grade level

Overall Daily Goal: Constantly build on acquisition (listening and speaking), cognition (hands-on), and metacognition (reflection) of all instruction, linguistic and conceptual.

TEKS OBJECTIVES:

§ 128K-12 Reading/inquiry/research. The student generates questions and conducts research about topics . . . from a variety of sources, and (C) draws conclusions from information gathered.

LESSON OBJECTIVES:

- Students will view a multimedia or PowerPoint presentation on pets (viewing).
- Students will listen to the teacher telling about his or her pet experience(s) (listening).
- Students will participate orally in a K-W-L chart and tell about their own pet experiences (speaking), pointing out their own types of pets on flashcards.
- Students, in groups, will research an assigned pet on the Web (reading/viewing).
- Students, in groups, will complete a poster on an assigned pet (listening/speaking/writing).
- Students will write sentences on their favorite pets (number will be assigned on an individual basis, according to English level) (writing).
- Students will sing simple, repetitive pet songs (learned earlier) during transitions.

Readiness Skills or Prior Knowledge Needed: Beginning Web searching experience; knowledge of following verbs: *have, eat, need, like, want, cost, care.*

Environmental Concerns: Be sure to place students in heterogeneous groups with regard to English levels so that there is a stronger English speaker in each group. If a child has just lost a pet or had to leave a pet behind, it could be emotional for him or her.

Sponge Activity: Students review visual images on a looped multimedia or PowerPoint slide showing of many types of pets (dogs, cats, fish, gerbils, turtles, snakes, birds, etc.) with names of the pets beneath each picture.

Focus: The teacher will tell about her experience with pets. Students complete the first two parts of a K-W-L chart (what they *know*, *want* to learn, and what they *learned*) about pets. (When students share their understanding and past experiences in a whole-class forum about such items, the ESL teacher is informed as to what level of understanding is pervasive.)

Connections to Past or Future Leaning: K-W-L chart.

Connections to Community: Ask students where they can obtain pets in their community and where they can get supplies to care for pets. What are the most popular pets in their community? Where in their community do they take a pet if it gets ill or is injured?

Cultural Connections: Are there pets that are more popular in some cultures than in others? Are pets more respected in some cultures (e.g., in ancient Egypt cats were seen as gods)? In British culture, if you cross the path of a black cat, it is seen as good luck, but in American culture, it is seen as bad luck.

Connections with Student Interests and Experiences: Tell if you have a pet(s) at home. If not, what pet would you most like to have? Why? Do you care for the pet?

Rationale: Many families would like to keep pets, but they are not sure how much it will cost or how to care for them. Knowing this information in advance may help decide whether or not to obtain a certain type of animal for a pet.

Materials: PowerPoint presentation of pets; bookmarked Web sites for the level of English needed; list of pet foods and other needed supplies and their costs; poster boards; art paper for illustrations.

Activities:

Guided Practice: Students will view looped PowerPoint slideshow and review vocabulary words for each pet. The teacher will ask students to complete the "K" and "W" in a K-W-L chart on pets. The teacher will show other vocabulary with pictures related to pet supplies (bowl for fish/turtle, litter, leash, etc.). Groups will be assigned a pet and will look on specially bookmarked Web sites at the price of obtaining their assigned pet and to obtain information about their pet's care. Groups will examine a list of food prices from a local pet store to care for their pet and determine how much it might cost to keep their assigned pet per week. Groups will design and complete a poster on their assigned pet, giving basic information on their pet, its needs, and cost per week. They will have a choice of presenting it to the class or putting it up on the wall so others can see. In a whole class setting, students will complete the "L" of the K-W-L chart.

Independent Practice: Students will write complete sentences in English on what pet they would like the most and why (individually assigned based upon individual ability).

What Will Students Do Who Finish Early? Students will illustrate their own pets or their favorite type of pet.

Assessment: Each group will design and complete a poster showing three areas: their pet, its basic needs, and how much it costs to keep it each week. All students will have a walk-about to view the posters. Each child will receive an individual paper assignment to write a specific number of sentences in English (according to individual levels), explaining why he or she would most like to have a specific pet. The teacher will assess on an individual basis, according to level.

Closure: The teacher will play "20 Questions" with students ("I'm thinking of a pet . . . "). Students must ask the teacher questions to guess the pet about which the teacher is thinking.

Possible Transitions: Circle back to computers (in groups) back to group tables. Use simple (pre-learned) pet songs when transitioning.

Modifications: Number of sentences assigned will be according to level of individual student.

Reflection: Add after teaching.

DRAFT YOUR OWN ESL LESSON PLAN

Title of Lesson: _____

Grade Level: _____

Main Subject Area: _____

Integrated Subjects: _____

Time Frame/Constraints: _____

Overall Goal(s): _____

TEKS Objectives: _____

_____

_____

Lesson Objective(s): _____

_____

_____

Sponge Activity: _____

_____

_____

Readiness Skills or Prior Knowledge Needed: _____

_____

Environmental Concerns: _____

_____

_____

Rationale(s): _____

_____

_____

Focus or Set Induction: _____

_____

_____

Making Connections: _____

_____

_____

1. Connections to Past or Future Learning: _____

_____

2. Connections to Community: _____

_____

3. Cultural Connections: _____

_____

4. Connections to Student Interest(s) & Experience(s): _____

_____

Materials: _____

_____

_____

Activities: Guided practice: _____

_____

_____

_____

_____

_____

_____

_____

_____

_____

Independent practice: _____

_____

_____

_____

_____

_____

_____

_____

_____

_____

_____

_____

_____

Assessment: _____

_____

Possible Transitions: _____

What Will Students Do Who Finish Early? _____

_____

Closure: _____

_____

Modification for Students with Special Needs: _____

_____

Reflection: _____

_____

OBSERVATION OF ESL EXPERIENCES/ACTIVITIES

During your visit to an ESL classroom, use the following form to provide feedback, as well as to reflectively analyze the room, the materials, the students, and the teaching.

The Classroom Environment	Observed	Not Observed	Response
1. Teacher adapts to learner's language level on an individual basis.			If so, how? If not, what could be changed?
2. Teacher adapts content-area language to the appropriate level (comprehensible but slightly challenging input).			If so, how? If not, what could be changed?
3. Teacher links content to past learning.			If so, how? If not, how could this have been accomplished?
4. Teacher makes use of the growing capacity of computers or other technology for audio, visual, and tactile advantages in modern applications.			If so, how? If not, how could this have been accomplished?
5. Teacher makes connections to students' backgrounds/community.			If so, how? If not, how could this have been accomplished?
6. Teacher uses various multiple intelligences and modalities.			If so, how? If not, how could this have been accomplished?
7. Teacher makes use of body language and gestures to aid comprehension.			If so, how? If not, how could this have been accomplished?
8. Teacher makes use of concrete items (realia), pictures, gestures, and so on to aid comprehension.			If so, how? If not, what could be added?
9. Teacher makes use of specific ESL strategies and methodologies to aid comprehension.			If so, describe. If not, what could the teacher add?
10. Teacher models tasks to aid in comprehension.			If so, how? If not, what effect did this have on a completed project?
11. Teacher checks for understanding often to ensure comprehensible input.			If so, how? If not, how could this have been accomplished?
12. Teacher integrates other content areas or uses thematic units.			If so, describe. If not, what could be added?
13. Teacher provides an effective guided practice.			If so, describe. If not, what were the results?
14. Teacher provides an authentic (real-world) connection (rationale) or tasks for learning.			If so, how? If not, how could this have been accomplished?
15. Teacher uses authentic assessment for skills (e.g., multimedia presentations, speeches, constructing projects, writing real letters).			If so, how? If not, how could this have been accomplished?

The Classroom Environment	Observed	Not Observed	Response
16. Teacher facilitates (as well as teaches) the lessons.			If so, how? If not, describe other roles the teacher may have used. Tell if they were effective.
17. Teacher provides various seating configurations (whole group, cooperative groups, partners, and independent).			If so, describe. If not, what configurations would have been more appropriate?
18. Teacher uses a variety of assessment instruments in written work.			If so, describe. If not, give ideas for what could have been added in a developmentally appropriate way.
19. Teacher uses various ongoing assessment instruments in oral work.			If so, describe. If not, give ideas for what could be added in a developmentally appropriate way.
20. Teacher provides materials that are developmentally, as well as linguistically, appropriate.			If so, describe. If not, give ideas for what could be added.
21. Teacher effectively pre-teaches all important content terminology before lessons begin (provides visuals, graphs, models, etc.).			If so, describe. If not, give ideas for what could be added.
22. Teacher clearly defines the stage of the lesson (i.e., acquisition [new learning], cognition [cooperative learning], and metacognition [reflective learning]).			If so, describe. If not, give ideas for what could be added.
23. Teacher provides students with expectations for the product, process, quantity, quality, and time limit of the intended learning.			If so, describe. If not, give ideas for what could be added.
24. Teacher demonstrates collaboration of family and community somehow in the teaching process.			If so, how? If not, how could this be accomplished?
25. Teacher introduces objectives that are clearly measurable and understood by students to direct their own learning.			If so, describe. If not, give ideas for what could be added.
26. Teacher clearly demonstrates expertise in English, so as to serve as a good model.			If so, describe. If not, explain.
27. The environment is positive and relaxed for students.			If so, describe. If not, what could be improved and how?
28. Students make use of the interrelation of reading, writing, speaking, and listening as they are engaged in their own learning.			If so, describe. If not, what could be improved and how?
29. Students vocalize key terms often.			If so, describe. If not, when could this element be added?

The Classroom Environment	Observed	Not Observed	Response
30. Students are self-assessing and continually reflecting on the product, process, quantity, quality, and time limits involved in their learning.			If observed, describe some examples of where. If not, suggest some areas.
31. Students understand rules, and management provides safety and security for ESL students.			If observed, describe some examples. If not, suggest some areas for improvement.
32. Students are involved with technology in some manner (e.g., word processors, databases, audio/video files, interactive computer programs, Internet investigations, computer reference materials, multimedia presentations).			If so, list those that are currently set up to which students have access. If not, describe how technology could improve this classroom.
33. If the program is a pull-out, students transition easily to their regular classroom.			If so, describe. If not, discuss what changes could be made to help.
34. Student uses content-area language orally with appropriate linguistic use of the lexical (academic) terms.			If so, how? If not, what could be changed?
35. All students participate orally.			If so, how? If not, how could this be accomplished?
36. The teacher projects a caring and respectful attitude with each child.			If so, how? If not, how could this be accomplished?
37. Students use strategies to solve problems.			If so, how? If not, what could be added?
38. Students are engaged in contextual (hands-on) activities to enhance understanding of abstract concepts.			If so, how? If not, how could this have been accomplished?
39. Students work cooperatively and share leadership and support roles.			If so, how? If not, how could this have been accomplished?
40. Students understand the concept involved in the lesson.			If so, tell how you would know. If not, how could this have been accomplished?
41. Students make use of organizers, rubrics, timers, journals, and other support materials.			If so, how? If not, how what could be added?

TEST YOURSELF ON ESL

1. Mrs. Bradford's lesson for today focuses on *phonology*. On what will students be working?
   A. Pragmatic language
   B. Graphemes
   C. Target sound
   D. Syntax

2. Helene said to her father, "Dad, I gotted this toy out of the closet." The language error committed by the child is common for children of her age. In which area of language development is she having trouble?
   A. Overextension
   B. Hyperbole
   C. Overgeneralization
   D. Assimilation

3. Trang, a mid-level ESL student, would have the most problems with which of the following statements?
   A. She got to school on time.
   B. She got against the wall to be safe.
   C. She got under the umbrella when it started to rain.
   D. She got over not making the cheerleading team.

4. What two language theories usually go together in order to promote beginning ESL students in speaking English?
   A. Affective filter–comprehensible input
   B. Self-monitor–affective filter
   C. Acquisition and learning theories
   D. Comprehensible input–self-monitor

5. Mr. Kuan pairs up Sunil, a new student from India, with Meera, also from India, who has been in the United States for more than 2 years. Which of the following is the most important reason for Mr. Kuan's actions?
   A. It ensures that there is someone who can translate important information to the new student when the need arises.
   B. It takes advantage of the affective filter theory and acclimates the new student to the class with little wasted time.
   C. It ensures that the ESL teacher will not have behavioral problems with a student who is bored when he cannot comprehend.
   D. Students paired together who are from the same language and culture base tend to learn more quickly.

6. Mrs. Sarenson, a beginning ESL teacher, is taking advantage of the district Web site to keep parents informed of class activities, homework assignments, school events, and so forth. What is the most important thing she should keep in mind in using this type of medium?
   A. To use an attractive, colorful, and hyper-linked format so it is easy to find.
   B. To give written instructions that are simple and easy to understand.
   C. To supply the information to caregivers in other ways, in case they do not have access to the Internet.
   D. To send home flyers for parents that give explicit instructions on how to use computers in the school, public library, or other computers connected to the Internet so they are able to access information in various locations.

7. Mr. Verde, the ESL teacher, regularly leads a class discussion in English with beginning-level students about things he knows that students understand in their primary languages. He is sure this will help students acquire new English vocabulary because:
   A. students who do not perform well in English have a model for dialoguing.
   B. this process encourages students to set a purpose in their interactions.
   C. students should make direct connections between their prior knowledge and the ability to translate terms mentally.
   D. activating prior knowledge, regardless of the language in which it was learned, facilitates acquisition of new vocabulary and subsequent conceptual understanding.

8. When planning content-area curriculum, the ESL teacher should first:
   A. determine if students are too linguistically challenged by the unit's language goals and objectives.
   B. plan the assessment that will be used at the end of the unit.
   C. develop a rubric that ensures that students follow the goals and objectives of the unit.
   D. use grading scales that allow each level of learner to achieve at his or her own pace.

9. Ms. Zheng reads a passage to her third-grade intermediate-level students and comes across an expression the students do not understand: *out of the blue* (meaning "all of sudden" or "out of nowhere").

The teacher quickly realizes the need to teach language like this on a regular basis. These type of phrases are called:

A. a nonstandard regionalism of English.
B. idioms.
C. dialectic phrases.
D. lexical references.

10. Languages such as Spanish, German, Italian, Vietnamese, and French are alphabetic. Some students from these diverse backgrounds have varying levels of difficulty when reading English because:

A. prior knowledge of the alphabet from a student's first language does not transfer to English.
B. phonetic differences with English tend to create confusion with figurative meaning.
C. phonemic awareness in the first language is unique to that language only.
D. the phonetic irregularities of English can make understanding difficult, especially when decoding or reading aloud.

11. What are the two most important areas an ESL teacher must consider when planning new lessons and curriculum in mathematics, science, and social studies?

A. Language acquisition and learning theories in the instruction
B. Linguistic and conceptual challenges of the instruction
C. Authentic and formal assessment of the instruction
D. Formative and summative evaluations of the instruction

12. ESL learning in the content areas begins with:

A. encouraging students to make sure they identify areas that they did not understand well and ask for help in those areas.
B. calling on the more advanced students so lower-level students benefit from the dialogue.
C. speaking clearly and using language that is not biased in nature.
D. previewing unfamiliar terminology, representing and presenting new concepts in a variety of ways, and providing multiple opportunities to reflect on cognitive learning.

13. In addition to formal assessment in the ESL classroom, Mr. Rosenthall also uses authentic assessment, the purpose of which is to:

A. provide a measure that is more reliable than other measures.
B. provide the benchmark by which all students are compared for grading.
C. provide a rubric for students in order to determine what the expectations are.
D. provide for measuring actual skills from the real world.

14. The Texas Assessment of Knowledge and Skills (TAKS) examinations are released to the public each year after all districts complete testing. These exams can be located online for current and previous even-numbered years at the Texas Education Agency Web site (2009). Each item on the answer keys for the TAKS includes the objective measured and Texas Essential Knowledge and Skills (TEKS) expectation for the student. It is assumed that the new test (the STAAR) will maintain the same format. The intent of showing both the objective and the student expectation for each item on the answer key is to:

A. make parents aware of school performance.
B. help school personnel better analyze test results and plan professional development and possible individual intervention.
C. justify the validity and reliability of formal state testing.
D. single out schools and districts not performing at acceptable levels so the state can plan adequate interventions.

15. Which Supreme Court decision supported the contention that non-English-speaking students do not have equal access to education when instruction is delivered in English only?

A. The Bilingual Education Act, Title VII of 1968
B. The Nationality Act of 1906
C. The *Lau vs. Nichols* Decision of 1974
D. The National Defense and Education Act of 1958

16. According to the rules of the Language Proficiency Assessment Committee (LPAC), how often should this committee follow up on students who have exited the program? LPAC committees must monitor the progress of exited LEP students for:

A. 2 academic years.
B. 1 academic year.
C. every semester.
D. until the student graduates from high school.

17. An elementary third-grade ESL teacher, Mrs. Strahan, has been told by her

grade-level team that they will be celebrating *Cinco de Mayo,* Mexico's Independence Day. However, after some research, she finds out that the information that they plan to use is not exactly true, and the true Mexican Independence Day is in September. *Cinco de Mayo,* she finds, represents only one important battle that Mexico won against a European force. However, from what she understands, this is a very large event that the school celebrates each year. She has already planned for students to bring in photos, food, clothes, and other relics related to *Cinco de Mayo.* What should she do first in light of her new cultural awareness?
A. Cancel class participation this year because the information is wrong.
B. Promote cultural awareness and respect by going along with it this year because she is new to the team.
C. Bring this issue to the grade-level team immediately and try to work toward consensus on a reasonable adjustment in light of the new information.
D. Tell her students about what she has learned and have them tell their parents in case any of them would be offended by this error.

18. During an informal conversation, a third-grade ESL student from the Caribbean tells his ESL teacher that he is embarrassed to invite his parents to the student award celebration because his parents did not go to school. He is afraid that his parents will not be accepted by others. The student's comment about his parents shows that:
A. he does not respect his parents.
B. he is experiencing culture shock.
C. he still needs more time to acculturate to the ways of this area of the United States.
D. he is experiencing cultural and social conflict.

19. Maria, a fourth-grade ESL student, tells her teacher, Ms. Newhauser, that she has to miss school again the following day. Concerned about the child missing school so often, the teacher asks if there is anything she should know or do for Maria. On further explanation, the student reports she is going with her parents to get the lights turned on for their new apartment and that Maria has to translate for them (just like when she translated for them to purchase some larger items like their washer/dryer and helped translate during their doctor's

appointments). Worried that this may cause undue stress on the student and cause her to miss too much class time, the ESL teacher should:
A. inform the parents by phone call or personal visit that their daughter is expected to be in school, and if absent, the school does not receive funding from the state according to average daily attendance.
B. explain to the mother that it is not appropriate for the parents to put such a burden on a fourth-grade student and that in addition to the stress, it will cause the student to get behind and possibly fail.
C. arrange for the student to make up the work and send supplemental instructions for the work to the parents to ensure the student does not get too far behind.
D. obtain the parents' permission to call ahead to the light company (or whatever the situation is) to determine if there are people there who can translate for them and ask if they can make a reservation for these services.

20. Some parents of ESL students have made it clear they do not want to cause any problems with the school by interfering with what the teacher is doing in class. Many of them are under the assumption that the school is a state institution, and parent collaboration is not allowed or encouraged because they may have nothing to offer. What would be the first thing the teacher should do to change this assumption?
A. Communicate clearly that when parents (whether they speak English or not) are involved in the education of their children, children tend to succeed academically.
B. Promise that all concerns will be dealt with according to parent wishes.
C. Explain that their helping in school can only help improve English skills.
D. Plan various school events designed to help parents be more involved in the academic affairs of their children.

21. Mr. Gladstone greeted his new student, Bon-hwa, when Ms. Carlton brought him into the teacher's regular fourth-grade classroom in October. "I have a new fourth grader for you for this year, Todd," she said, "and he doesn't speak any English yet." "What!" said Mr. Gladstone, "Why aren't you

taking him to Susan's ESL class?" Ms. Carlton replied:
- A. "Her room is full. There isn't any more space right now. We'll place him later."
- B. "His parents would not sign for special language services."
- C. "We have four weeks to get him tested, so he will be with you for those four weeks."
- D. "We don't have an ESL class in Korean, Todd."

22. Mrs. Vadelia was asking the rest of her LPAC if they had to meet for Roberto this year. "He passed his Language Arts/Reading test and his parents signed off when I had him last year at the end of third grade," she noted. Which response is correct:
- A. "No, we don't have to meet. He's good to go."
- B. "Yes, because you signed him off too early."
- C. "Yes, we have to meet about him through his fifth-grade year."
- D. "Yes, we have to meet about him through his sixth grade year."

TEST YOURSELF ANSWERS AND RATIONALES FOR ESL

Answer 1: *Phonology* is target sound or patterning of speech sounds in a language (C). Choice A, *pragmatics,* represents the ability to understand meaning when the actual words do not translate exactly (e.g., "Dude!" in some parts of the country means, "Hey, how are you?"). *Graphemes* (B) are simply letters of a language (which represent letter sounds [as in *ph, th,* or *sh*] that represent a phoneme). Syntax (D) represents the order or grammatical formation of sentences. The correct answer is C.

Answer 2: *Overgeneralization* (C) is the normal developmental process in learning English of extending the application of a rule of language to every case. Here, she adds *–ed* to an irregular verb to make the past tense. *Overextension* (A) is the overuse of a label/word in the early development of spoken language that children employ to denote meaning (e.g., a child learns what a cat is and uses *cat* for all four-legged animals). *Hyperbole* (B) is an intentional or obvious exaggeration (e.g., "I'm so hungry that I could eat a horse!"). *Assimilation* (D), in second language theory, is when a student replaces his or her native language with English and may also give up one's home values and culture. The correct answer is C.

Answer 3: *Getting over* something is using English figuratively, not literally. Such idioms are very difficult for ESL students to understand. Choices A, B, and C are all *literal*—that is, they mean exactly what they say. The correct answer is D.

Answer 4: A *low affective filter* (low level of nervousness) and *comprehensible input* (understanding speech) (A) are two things needed simultaneously in order for beginning English language learners to begin conversing in the target language. Self-monitoring (B) is only possible after early literacy speech is apparent and output of speech begins to follow a more grammatically correct format. Acquisition and learning theories (C) distinguish subconscious and conscious learning, respectively. Comprehensible input–self-monitor theories (D) are two theories mentioned at very different stages of language development. The correct answer is A.

Answer 5: When beginning-level ESL students arrive at a new school and begin with a new teacher, it is most important to pair them up with someone who can speak their language (when possible) and who knows the rules and routines. The student can more readily engage in classroom activities and lessons without concern. All the answers have some merit, but we are looking for the best one. Choice A ensures that there is someone who can translate important information to the new student when the need arises, but the continued act of translating makes it unnecessary for the new student to attend to English as much. When students figure out the routine of the class, they should be separated from students who speak the same language, when possible, to take advantage of attending to more English. Considering that a teacher may have behavioral problems with a student who is bored when he or she cannot comprehend can certainly be a factor, but it is not the most important issue for a newly arrived student (C). Getting ESL students into a routine of engagement and purposeful learning quickly is paramount. The belief that students paired together who are from the same language and culture base tend to learn more quickly (D) is a common misconception. In order to learn English, it is better (after the initial arrival) to pair students with others who do not share the same language in order to investigate and problem solve with the target language of English in common. The answer is B.

Answer 6: Even though using technology is the goal of many schools these days, the ESL teacher cannot forget that many parents, particularly those who may have just arrived, still require more traditional methods to disseminate important information (*C*). They simply may not have access to the Internet or may not know how to use it. To use an attractive, colorful, and hyperlinked format so it is easy to find (*A*) does not get the job done with parents and guardians. Presenting written instructions that are simple and easy to understand (*B*) may be desirable, but they are useless if they are not read because the parents do not have access to the Internet. Sending home flyers for parents that give explicit instructions on how to use computers in the school, public library, or other computers connected to the Internet so they will be able to access information in various locations (*D*) may be condescending and could cause alienation problems. It is also very possible that some parents could not get to these places. The correct answer is *C*.

Answer 7: Activating prior knowledge, both factual and conceptual, is helpful when ESL students understand content, but not the English words. All students in all languages have many things in common that they understand (e.g., riding in a car, eating supper, going shopping, working, sleeping, having animals). The only thing they lack is the vocabulary to talk about these things. The best answer is *D*.

Answer 8: All of these options have merit for ESL instruction. However, if students are linguistically challenged in their ability to speak content-area or *lexical* (academic) words in mathematics, science, and social studies (e.g., *quadratic equation, scientific method, apartheid*), they will have difficulty understanding the concepts (when they are not understood in either the L1 or L2). First, an ESL teacher must determine linguistic abilities and plan to pre-teach vocabulary. The best answer is *A*.

Answer 9: Idioms (*B*) are one of the most difficult areas of English for ESL students to understand because they have no literal meaning, making them truly confusing when translated. Examples include, *starting from scratch*, which is an equestrian term of lining up horses for a race on a straight line scratched in the dirt (in the days before starting gates), or "I would kill for a hamburger right now," meaning the speaker really does not intend to kill anyone but really wants to have this particular food. A *regionalism* of English (*A*) is a speech form, expression, custom, or other feature peculiar to, or characteristic of, a particular area. A *dialect* (*C*) is considered a language with a common root to another language (as in Hawaiian Pidgin

English), but it may not be understood well by majority language speakers. *Lexicon* (*D*) refers to the vocabulary of a particular language, field, class, or subject—a language within a language. The correct answer is *B*.

Answer 10: Phonetic irregularities (*D*), exhibited by words such as *thought, have, mother, the,* and *been,* are words that are not *decodable* (or able to be read graphophonically) and they do not follow regular English rules. They also may not have representative sounds in other languages. This part of English acquisition and learning requires the ESL teacher to teach word analysis skills and physically model how to produce such sounds. Prior knowledge of the alphabet from a student's first language (*A*) transfers to English. The fact that phonetic differences with English tends to create confusion with figurative meaning cannot be substantiated (*B*). It is not an easily measurable variable for such advanced understanding of English. Phonemic awareness in the first language being unique to that language only (*C*) is not completely true. Because all the languages mentioned are alphabetic, many of the target sounds are the same. The correct answer is *D*.

Answer 11: Content-area instruction has two major components, *linguistic* (language) skills and *conceptual* (cognitive) skills (*B*). The ESL teacher knows that in order to master mathematics, science, social studies, and so on, the ELL must acquire new content vocabulary, use that vocabulary in cognitive activities with peers while speaking and problem solving, and frequently reflect on what has been learned and what can be improved in future attempts to learn similar vocabulary and concepts. Language acquisition and learning theories (*A*) are much more global than a new lesson. Authentic and formal assessments of the instruction (*C*) are done after linguistics and conceptual understanding take place. Formative and summative evaluations of instruction (*D*) are steps the ESL teacher takes during and after lessons, although the teacher should plan for measuring how much students learn during the planning process. The answer is *B*.

Answer 12: Content-area understanding starts with previewing unfamiliar terminology and making sure that when the new lexical language shows up in reading, the ESL student is not confused about pronunciation or the concept (*D*). In addition, teachers should represent and present new concepts in a variety of ways, including maps, charts, graphic organizers, pictures, and images (all of which can be done in conjunction with technology). Finally, teachers should provide multiple opportunities to reflect on cognitive learning. Too often, ESL students, even adults, are too shy or timid to ask for help (B). Calling on the more advanced students so lower-level students benefit from the dialogue is not inclusive and also singles out those that are not advanced (B). This can be demoralizing for the less advanced students. Even if you raise the level of your voice and speak clearly, this does not help (C). A teacher simply must pre-teach all vocabulary and use visuals, etc., when possible, in the content areas. The correct answer is D.

Answer 13: Authentic measures of intended learning usually refer to assessing by other than paper and pencil. For example, in order to assess public speaking ability, the student should give a speech, or in order to use multimedia effectively, the student should manipulate a computer and the required software. These types of skills are authentic to real-world applications and are necessary to accompany purely cognitive skills. The correct answer is D.

Answer 14: Instruction must be informed by data obtained through assessment. Assessment may be informal, formal, or authentic. Released TAKS tests (and it is assumed that released STAAR tests will follow soon) are a good way to obtain more formal data on students at the beginning of the school year, which informs both the student and the teacher of achievement on attained knowledge and skills and, afterward, the year spent with the teacher, to determine growth. The data can also be used to inform professional development needs in instruction. Although in reality the state tests are used for other, less-positive purposes, Choice B represents action and improvement; the others do not. The best answer is B.

Answer 15: In the famous *Lau vs. Nichols Decision* of 1974 (C), it was found that one of the major purposes of bilingual education was to keep the student on grade level by providing content instruction in the L1 while acquiring English. Simply providing instruction in English is not equal access to education if the student does not know English and loses out on content instruction. Choice A, the Bilingual Education Act, Title VII of 1968, gave money to bilingual education, but it did not provide much direction as to how to plan and implement good programs. Choice B, the Nationality Act of 1906, found to be unconstitutional, gave immigrants a certain amount of time to learn English or else. Choice D, the National Defense and Education Act of 1958, was the first federal legislation that

promoted foreign language curriculum. The correct answer is C.

Answer 16: Students who exit ESL programs and who pass the proper standardized tests (indicating that they can operate effectively in a regular English-speaking program) must still continue to be monitored by the LPAC for continued success for a period of 2 years. The correct answer is A.

Answer 17: Any curricular concerns in a grade level or department must be brought to the team and a proper solution must be found. In the event that all team members do not agree on the best solution, competent professionals should work toward consensus in the best interest of students. This particular issue is not difficult to correct with the proper understanding, while avoiding the cancellation of an important tradition in the school (A). The fact that it has become mislabeled does not negate the fact that it is an important celebration in many parts of Texas. The answer is C.

Answer 18: Some students in ESL classes can lean toward English as being superior to their home language for many reasons and can also begin to see their families in a negative light. Cultural and social conflict can occur if there is a perception that their first language is not important or that they should be ashamed of it or their home culture in some way. The ESL teacher should realize that it is important to foster pride in students' L1 and find many opportunities to celebrate the differences in language and cultural backgrounds. The correct answer is D.

Answer 19: A family's needs often come before their concern for school policies (A). Choice B is true, but it is very harsh when translations are truly needed for important matters. It is in the best interest of the student to be in school without interruptions and without having to make up work. The ESL teacher knows there are many avenues to get help in a number of languages other than English. District offices may have access to information on translators who can help, and translation technology is available. Collaborating can frequently keep both parents and teachers informed about the needs of students and the family. Being so direct (A) may cause the ESL teacher more problems than remedies in further communication with this family, and the same is true with choices B and C. The correct answer is D.

Answer 20: Whether parents do or do not know English or are reluctant to participate in school affairs, they can be instrumental in the academic success of their children if they simply become involved in the efforts of their children in regards to academics. There are many ways to be supportive without much contact with the school itself. However, they should always be encouraged to attend and participate in school events, and teachers should work toward events that invite parents into school (Literacy Night, Math Night, etc.). Promising that all concerns will be dealt with according to parent wishes (B) is simply not feasible or reasonable. Explaining that helping in school can only help improve English skills (C) can be condescending and threatening. Many parents are already overwhelmed by the idea of communicating in English (D). Planning various school events designed to help parents be more proficient in the academic affairs of their children (D) is a very good idea; however, it is not necessary to come to school in order to support their children. Parents can provide a home environment and routines that support the academic efforts of the school. Parents coming to school are an added bonus, but many parents may not be able to take advantage of this avenue because of work or family obligations. The best answer is A.

Answer 21: The principal tells Mr. Gladstone that the student will be with him for the rest of the year. Therefore, we can eliminate choices A and C (even though C is true—a school has 4 weeks from time of enrollment to test a child). An ESL class is never conducted in another language (only bilingual classes), so choice D is a misleading statement (and incorrect). However, if parents do not sign for their children to receive ESL or bilingual services, the child cannot receive them automatically from the school, and he or she will be placed in a regular classroom. Bon-hwa will, unfortunately, be expected to meet all the district and state objectives in English. The correct answer is B.

Answer 22: The Language Proficiency Assessment Committee (LPAC) must meet at least once a year for the 2 years following a child's exit from an ESL or bilingual program to ensure that the child is still being successful in a regular classroom; therefore, choice A is incorrect. Choice D indicates 3 years of meetings. The teacher cannot simply sign him off, so choice B is incorrect. The correct answer is C, 2 years.

Index